P9-DGJ-365

Fourth Edition

ELEMENTARY STATISTICS IN CRIMINAL JUSTICE RESEARCH

James Alan Fox
Northeastern University

Jack Levin
Northeastern University

David R. Forde
University of North Florida

Boston   Columbus   Indianapolis   New York   San Francisco   Upper Saddle River
Amsterdam   Cape Town   Dubai   London   Madrid   Milan   Munich   Paris   Montréal   Toronto
Delhi   Mexico City   São Paulo   Sydney   Hong Kong   Seoul   Singapore   Taipei   Tokyo

Editorial Director: Vernon R. Anthony
Editor, Digital Projects: Nichole Caldwell
Senior Acquisitions Editor: Gary Bauer
Assistant Editor: Tiffany Bitzel
Editorial Assistant: Lynda Cramer
Director of Marketing: David Gesell
Marketing Manager: Mary Salzman
Senior Marketing Coordinator: Alicia Wozniak
Marketing Assistant: Les Roberts
Production Manager: Susan Hannahs
Senior Art Director: Jane Conte
Cover Designer: Bruce Kenselaar
Cover Image: Dreaming Andy/Fotolia
Media Project Manager: Karen Bretz
Full-Service Project Management: Moganambigai/Integra Software Services Pvt. Ltd.
Composition: Integra Software Services, Ltd.
Printer/Binder: LSC Communications
Cover Printer: LSC Communications
Text Font: 10/12, Minion Pro-Regular

Credits and acknowledgments borrowed from other sources and reproduced, with permission, in this textbook appear on the appropriate page within text.

Microsoft® and Windows® are registered trademarks of the Microsoft Corporation in the U.S.A. and other countries. Screen shots and icons reprinted with permission from the Microsoft Corporation. This book is not sponsored or endorsed by or affiliated with the Microsoft Corporation.

Copyright © 2014, 2009, 2002 by Pearson, Inc. All rights reserved. Manufactured in the United States of America. This publication is protected by Copyright, and permission should be obtained from the publisher prior to any prohibited reproduction, storage in a retrieval system, or transmission in any form or by any means, electronic, mechanical, photocopying, recording, or likewise. To obtain permission(s) to use material from this work, please submit a written request to Pearson, Inc., Permissions Department, One Lake Street, Upper Saddle River, New Jersey 07458, or you may fax your request to 201-236-3290.

Many of the designations by manufacturers and sellers to distinguish their products are claimed as trademarks. Where those designations appear in this book, and the publisher was aware of a trademark claim, the designations have been printed in initial caps or all caps.

Library of Congress Cataloging-in-Publication Data
Fox, James Alan.
    Elementary statistics in criminal justice research / James Alan Fox, Jack Levin, David R. Forde.—4th ed.
        p. cm.
    Includes index.
    ISBN-13: 978-0-13-298730-1 (alk. paper)
    ISBN-10: 0-13-298730-9 (alk. paper)
    1. Social sciences—Statistical methods.   2. Criminal justice, Administration of.   3. Criminal statistics.
    I. Levin, Jack, 1941–   II. Forde, David R. (David Robert), 1959–   III. Title.
    HA35.F69 2014
    519.5024'364—dc23
                                                                                        2012045165

ISBN 10:   0-13-298730-9
ISBN 13: 978-0-13-298730-1

We dedicate this book to our loving families.

KD 09 09 2022 2117

CONTENTS

PREFACE

NEW TO THIS EDITION:

- New discussion of Meta-Analysis in Chapter 1
- New introduction to the concept and calculation of Coefficient of Variation in Chapter 4
- New introduction to the One Sample Test of Means in Chapter 7
- New introduction to the concept and calculation of Effect Size in Chapter 7
- New discussion of the Mann-Whitney *U* Test and Kruskal-Wallis Test in Chapter 9
- New introduction to Logistic Regression in Chapter 11
- New discussion of Elaboration in Chapter 12
- Expanded discussions of Non-Sampling Error, Standard Error, Partial Correlation, and Multicollinearity
- Updated Examples and Exercises throughout the text
- Supplementary Computer Exercises that utilize a subset of the 2010 General Social Survey

The fourth edition of *Elementary Statistics in Criminal Justice Research* provides an introduction to statistics for students in criminal justice and criminology. This book is not intended to be a comprehensive reference work on statistical methods. On the contrary, our first and foremost objective is to be understandable to a broad range of students, particularly those who may not have a strong background in mathematics.

Through several editions, *Elementary Statistics in Criminal Justice Research* has undergone refinements and improvements in response to instructor and student feedback. For this revision, we have added several new techniques, including meta-analysis (Chapter 1), coefficient of variation (Chapter 4), one sample test of means and effect size (Chapter 7), Mann-Whitney *U* test and Kruskal-Wallis test (Chapter 9), logistic regression (Chapter 11), and elaboration (Chapter 12). We have expanded the discussion of several topics, including non-sampling error, standard error, partial correlation, and multicollinearity. We have updated examples and exercises throughout the text. Finally, the supplementary computer exercises in this edition utilize a subset of the 2010 General Social Survey available for download from www.pearsonhighered. com/careers. For those instructors who do not teach with computer software, however, this feature can be easily excluded.

This edition continues to contain a number of pedagogical features. Most notably, detailed step-by-step illustrations of statistical procedures continue to be located at important points throughout the text. We have again attempted to provide clear and logical explanations for the rationale and use of statistical methods in criminal justice research. And, as in the earlier editions, we have included a number of end-of-chapter questions and problems. Students sometimes get lost in the trees of statistics, without seeing the forest. To counter this tendency, we have ended each part of the text with a section entitled "Looking at the Larger Picture," which carries the student through the entire research process based on hypothetical data.

Following a detailed overview in Chapter 1, the text is divided into five parts. Part One (Chapters 2 through 4) introduces the student to the most common methods for describing and comparing data. Part Two (Chapters 5 and 6) serves a transitional purpose. Beginning with a discussion of the basic concepts of probability, Part Two leads the student from the topic of the normal curve as an important descriptive device to the use of the normal curve as a basis for generalizing from samples to populations. Continuing with this decision-making focus, Part Three (Chapters 7 through 9) contains several well-known tests of significance. Part Four (Chapters 10 through 12) includes procedures for obtaining correlation coefficients and an introduction to regression analysis. Finally, Part Five consists of an important chapter (Chapter 13) in which students learn, through examples, the conditions for applying statistical procedures to various types of research problems.

The text provides students with background material for the study of statistics. An Introduction to using *SPSS*, StatCrunch™, a set of statistical tables, a review of basic mathematics, and a list of formulas are located in appendixes at the end of the book. Students will also find a glossary of terms and answers to the end-of-chapter problems at the end of the book.

INSTRUCTOR RESOURCES

Instructor Supplements include an Instructors Manual, a solutions manual containing step-by-step calculations for the end-of-chapter problems, the General Social Survey data set, a companion statistics calculator (ABCalc), Powerpoint slides featuring step-by-step solutions to problems, and a test generator.

To access supplementary materials online, instructors need to request an instructor access code. Go to www.pearsonhighered.com/irc, where you can register for an instructor access code. Within 48 hours of registering you will receive a confirming e-mail including an instructor access code. Once you have received your code, locate your text in the online catalog and click on the Instructor Resources button on the left side of the catalog product page. Select a supplement and a log in page will appear. Once you have logged in, you can access instructor material for all Pearson textbooks.

ACKNOWLEDGEMENTS

We are grateful to the many reviewers of this and previous editions of the text who have given us countless insightful and helpful suggestions. We also want to thank instructors who generously shared with us any errors they located in our problems and illustrations. We acknowledge the outstanding work of Chad Posick who assisted us in updating and improving problem sets, and Adam Stearn who constructed several of the book's supplementary materials. In addition, we benefitted tremendously from the skillful editorial assistance of Jenna Savage. We also thank the National Opinion Research Council (NORC) for permission to use the 2010 General Social Survey. Finally, we note the important role of our personal computers, without "whose" assistance this book would not have been possible.

James Alan Fox
Jack Levin
David R. Forde

Why the Criminal Justice Researcher Uses Statistics

A little of the social scientist can be found in all of us. Almost daily, we make educated guesses concerning the future events in our lives in order to plan for new situations or experiences. As these situations occur, we are sometimes able to confirm or support our ideas; other times, however, we are not so lucky and must face the sometimes unpleasant consequences.

To take some familiar examples: We might invest in the stock market, vote for a political candidate who promises to solve domestic problems, play the horses, take medicine to reduce the discomfort of a cold, throw dice in a gambling casino, try to anticipate the questions on a midterm, or accept a blind date on the word of a friend.

Sometimes we win; sometimes we lose. Thus, we might make a sound investment in the stock market, but be sorry about our voting decision; win money at the craps table, but discover we have taken the wrong medicine for our illness; do well on a midterm, but have a miserable blind date; and so on. It is unfortunately true that not all of our everyday predictions will be supported by experience.

THE NATURE OF CRIMINAL JUSTICE RESEARCH

Similar to our everyday approach to the world, social and behavioral scientists attempt to explain and predict human behavior. They also take "educated guesses" about the nature of crime and justice, although in a far more precise and structured manner. In the process, social scientists examine characteristics of human behavior called **variables**—characteristics that differ or vary from one individual to another (e.g., age, social class, and attitude) or from one point in time to another (e.g., unemployment, crime rate, and population).

Not all human characteristics vary. It is a fact of life, for example, that the gender of the person who gave birth to you is female. Therefore, in any group of individuals, gender of the mother is the *constant* "female." A biologist would spend considerable time discussing why only females give birth and the conditions under which birth is possible, but a social scientist would consider the mother's gender a given, one that is not worthy of study because it never varies. It could not be used to explain differences in the mental health of children because all of their mothers are females. In contrast, mother's age, race, and mental health are variables: In any group of individuals, they will differ from person to person and can be the key to a greater understanding of the development of the child. A researcher, therefore, might study

VARIABLE

Any characteristic that varies from one individual/ group to another or from one point in time to another. Hypotheses usually contain an independent variable (cause) and a dependent variable (effect).

differences in the mental health of children depending on the age, race, and mental health of their mothers.

In addition to specifying variables, the researcher must also determine the **unit of observation** for the research. Usually, social and behavioral scientists collect data on individual persons. For example, a researcher might conduct interviews to determine if the elderly are victimized by crime more often than younger respondents. In this case, an individual respondent is the unit to be observed by the researcher.

However, researchers sometimes focus on *aggregates*—that is, on the way in which measures vary across entire collections of people. For example, a criminologist might study the relationship between the average age of the population and the crime rate in various metropolitan areas. In this study, the units of observation are metropolitan areas rather than individuals.

Whether focusing on individuals or aggregates, the ideas that social scientists have concerning the nature of social reality are called **hypotheses**. These hypotheses are frequently expressed in a statement of the relationship between two or more variables: at minimum, an *independent variable* (or presumed cause) and a *dependent variable* (or presumed effect). For example, a researcher might hypothesize that socially isolated children watch more television (TV) than children who are well integrated into their peer groups, and he or she might conduct a survey in which both socially isolated and well-integrated children are asked questions regarding the time they spend watching TV (social isolation would be the independent variable; TV-viewing behavior would be the dependent variable). Or a researcher might hypothesize that the one-parent family structure generates greater delinquency than the two-parent family structure and might proceed to interview samples of delinquents and nondelinquents to determine whether one or both parents were present in their family backgrounds (family structure would be the independent variable; delinquency would be the dependent variable).

Thus, not unlike their counterparts in the physical sciences, researchers in criminal justice and criminology often conduct research to increase their understanding of the problems and issues in their field. Research takes many forms and can be used to investigate a wide range of problems. Among the most useful research methods employed by researchers for testing their hypotheses are the experiment, the quasi-experiment, and the survey.

The Experiment

Unlike everyday observation (or, for that matter, any other research approach), the *experiment* is distinguished by the degree of *control* a researcher is able to apply to the research situation. In an experiment, researchers actually manipulate one or more of the independent variables to which their subjects are exposed. The manipulation occurs when an experimenter assigns the independent variable to one group of people (called an *experimental group*) but withholds it from another group of people (called a *control group*). Ideally, all other initial differences between the experimental and control groups are eliminated by assigning subjects on a random basis to the experimental and control conditions.

For example, a researcher who hypothesizes that drug abuse treatment prior to release from prison reduces subsequent criminal behavior might randomly assign a number of subjects to the experimental and control groups by flipping a coin (heads they're in the experimental group and receive drug treatment; tails they're in the control group and receive no drug treatment). This random assignment tends to ensure that the groups do not differ initially in any significant way. The experimental groups members might receive 6 months of intensive treatment to address their substance abuse issues, while the control group members reside in the same prison and are handled no differently *except* that they do not receive the drug treatment. The researchers would then follow the progress of both groups for 2 years after their release, examining state and federal records for indications that the released inmates were convicted for crimes committed during this period. If the conviction rate of the experimental group was lower than that of the control group, the difference would be attributable to the drug treatment program since the only

UNIT OF OBSERVATION

The element that is being studied or observed. Individuals are most often the unit of observation, but sometimes collections or aggregates—such as families, census tracts, or states—are the unit of observation.

HYPOTHESIS

An idea about the nature of social reality that is testable through systematic research.

known difference between the two groups was the program. The conclusion would be that drug abuse treatment prior to release from prison reduces subsequent criminal involvement.

Levin and Thomas conducted an experiment designed to test the effect of the racial identity of the police on perceptions of police brutality.[1] The investigators produced three videotapes, each simulating a black male suspect being arrested by two police officers. The three arrest situations were as close to identical as possible, with one exception. The two criminologists varied the racial identity of the two arresting officers—two whites, one black and the other white, or two blacks—by giving each one a full face mask to wear, consisting of either light- or dark-colored panty hose, depending on whether the actor played the role of a black or white officer. One version of the tape then was viewed by each randomly assigned subject, 28 white and 33 black college students, who were then asked to estimate the degree of violence and illegality (i.e., brutality) employed by the arresting officers they had seen. Results showed that subjects' perceptions of both violence and illegality were influenced by the officers' racial identity: Both black and white students were significantly more likely to see violent and illegal behavior when both the arresting police officers were white.

In 2011, Levin and Genovesi[2] sought to investigate aspects of films about serial murder that contribute to their widespread public appeal. In a regular classroom setting, the researchers randomly distributed to 232 male and female students various versions of a review of a motion picture purporting to feature a serial killer's biography. The following independent variables were experimentally manipulated: killer's body count (half of the subjects read that 3 victims were murdered; half read that 30 victims were murdered), torture (one-third read that the killer's torture was sexual, one-third read that the killer's torture was physical, and one-third read that the killer shot his victims absent any torture), and victims' gender (one-half read that the victims were female; one-half read that the victims were male). The dependent variable was measured by asking all students, on a four-point rating scale, to indicate "How badly do you want to see this movie when it is released to the public?" Greater attraction to cinematic versions of serial murder was indicated by a greater desire to view the film.

Results suggest that female students were significantly more attracted to the serial killer film than were their male counterparts, but no significant differences were found for either body count or victims' gender. Moreover, torture—whether sexual or physical—was significantly more appealing than killing alone, especially for male subjects. Findings provide little support for the hypothesis that females are more fascinated than males by cinematic portrayals of serial murder. The appeal of media-depicted torture may, in part, be a result of treating the sadistic and cruel punishment of victims as "forbidden fruit."

The Quasi-Experiment

For ethical reasons, experiments are rarely employed by researchers in the field of criminal justice. Given the important variables studied by criminologists, systematically withholding or administering an experimental treatment—for example, a drug rehabilitation or educational program, the death penalty, antigang policy, or the like—might very well increase the risk of harm, perhaps even death, for vulnerable groups such as defendants, inmates, or criminal justice professionals.

As a result, researchers in criminal justice are much more likely to employ a *quasi-experimental* (quasi = semi or almost) research design that doesn't approach the effectiveness of the true experiment with respect to systematically manipulating the independent variables. In a quasi-experiment, there is no control group. But there may be a *comparison group* whose

---

[1]Jack Levin and Alexander R. Thomas, "Experimentally Manipulating Race: Perceptions of Police Brutality in an Arrest," *Justice Quarterly* 14, 3 (September 1997): 577–586.

[2]Jack Levin and Maya Genovesi, "Fascination with Serial Murder Movies," a paper presented at the annual meeting of American Society of Criminology (November 2011), Washington DC.

members are matched in important respects to those of the experimental group. The hope, of course, is that the experimental and comparison groups will differ only in terms of the independent variable under investigation—for example, gun laws, death penalty, opportunities for rehabilitation. But it is all but impossible in a quasi-experimental design to ensure that all important characteristics of the two groups will be held constant.

Take, for example, a study of Megan's Law, which was enacted after the 1994 rape and murder of 7-year-old Megan Kanka by a repeat sex offender in Hamilton Township, New Jersey. This law requires states across the country to register high-risk sex offenders who have been released from prison and then to disclose their whereabouts to community members. In 2008, Duwe and Donnay[3] published the results of a study to determine whether community notification actually reduces sex offender recidivism.

For ethical and legal reasons, it was not possible for the researchers to randomly assign sex offenders to either an experimental or a control group. Using a retrospective quasi-experimental design, however, the criminologists compared the recidivism rates of 155 high-risk sex offenders released from Minnesota prisons (the *notification group*) with two comparison groups: 125 sex offenders who had been released prior to the imposition of Megan's Law and therefore were not subject to community notification (the *prenotification group*) and 155 lower-risk sex offenders who were released at the same time as the high-risk notification group but whose location was not disclosed to community members (the *nonnotification group*). In other words, the released sex offenders whose locations in the community were made public were compared with sex offenders who were not required to register or to have their locations disclosed. The recidivism rates—arrest, conviction, and incarceration for a new offense—were tracked for offenders in all three groups for an average of 8 years.

Results obtained by Duwe and Donnay provide evidence that Minnesota's version of community notification significantly reduces sexual recidivism as measured by arrest, conviction, and incarceration for a new offense. Because their design was only quasi-experimental, however, the researchers were not able to control for possible differences in community-based treatment and in historical factors between time periods under investigation. Moreover, previous research has demonstrated that community notification imposes numerous adversities on the lives of released sex offenders. Many have reported being harassed, being fired, and losing their homes. Some have been rejected from shelters, only to be forced into living under a bridge or on the streets where their behavior is totally uncontrolled.

Another quasi-experiment was employed to test the impact of animal abuse on human violence and other forms of antisocial behavior. Arluke and his colleagues[4] compared each of 153 animal abusers with someone *on the same street* matched by sex and age who had not abused animals. Selecting members of the comparison group (those who had not exhibited cruelty toward animals) by their residential address reduced the socioeconomic differences between abusers and non-abusers. Neighborhoods, by definition, tend to be homogenous in terms of socioeconomic status and related characteristics; residents on the same city or suburban blocks rarely differ substantially by income or property levels, and many observers have commented on the racial and ethnic segregation of America's neighborhoods. Acts of animal cruelty as well as criminal histories were obtained through official reports at the state level.

Results of the study by Arluke and his associates indicated that individuals who perpetrate acts of cruelty toward animals are also prone to be antisocial generally. The abusers were significantly more likely than members of the comparison group to have committed acts of human violence, property offenses, and drug crimes.

---

[3]Grant Duwe and William Donnay, "The Impact of Megan's Law on Sex Offender Recidivism: The Minnesota Experience," *Criminology* 46, 2 (2008): 411–446.

[4]Arnold Arluke et al. "The Relationship of Animal Abuse to Violence and Other Forms of Antisocial Behavior," *Journal of Interpersonal Violence* 14, 9 (September 1999): 963–975.

The Survey

As we have seen, experimenters actually have a direct hand in creating the effect that they seek to achieve. By contrast, *survey* research is *retrospective*—the effects of independent variables on dependent variables are recorded *after*—and sometimes long after—they have occurred. Survey researchers typically seek to reconstruct these influences and consequences by means of verbal reports from their respondents in self-administered questionnaires, face-to-face interviews, telephone interviews, or online surveys.

Surveys lack the tight controls of experiments: Variables are not manipulated and subjects are not assigned to groups at random. As a consequence, it is much more difficult to establish cause and effect. Suppose, for instance, in a survey measuring fear of crime, that a researcher finds that respondents who had been victims of crime tend to be more fearful of walking alone in their neighborhoods than those who had not been victimized. Because the variable *victimization* was not manipulated, we cannot make the logical conclusion that victimization *causes* increased fear. An alternative explanation that the condition of their neighborhoods (poverty, for example) produces both fear among residents and crime in the streets is just as plausible.

At the same time, surveys have advantages precisely because they do not involve an experimental manipulation. As compared with experiments, survey research can investigate a much larger number of important independent variables in relation to any dependent variable. Because they are not confined to a laboratory setting in which an independent variable can be manipulated, surveys can also be more *representative*—their results can be generalized to a broader range of people.

For example, a survey researcher who hypothesizes that frustration increases aggression might locate a number of severely aggressive individuals and interview them to identify the frustrating events in their lives, such as isolation, physical disabilities, poor grades in school, and poverty. Obviously, survey researchers cannot manipulate the variables by introducing these frustrating life events themselves, but they can attempt to discover and record them after they have occurred. To study the relationship between frustration and aggression, Stuart Palmer[5] interviewed the mothers of 51 convicted murderers. He found many more frustrating circumstances in the early lives of these killers than in the lives of their brothers who had not committed murder. Specifically, the research showed that the murderers as children had been subjected to more serious illnesses, operations; accidents, beatings, physical defects, frightening experiences, and disapproval from their peers than had the comparison group.

The Gallup polling organization employs a survey approach. To determine what Americans believe about trends in the rate of crime, Gallup researchers conducted telephone interviews in 2011 with a random sample of 1,005 adults living in all 50 states and the District of Columbia.[6] Gallup asked: "Is there more crime in the U.S. than there was a year ago, or less?" Despite a sharp decrease in the rate of serious crime since the mid-1990s, Gallup determined that the majority of Americans continue to believe that the nation's crime problem has worsened. Following a long-standing pattern, some 68% of respondents in 2011 believed that there was more crime in the United States than there had been a year earlier. These results were compared with estimates of trends in the crime rate obtained in surveys of Americans every year from 1989 on. Not surprisingly, during the late 1980s and early 1990s, when the rate of serious crime had soared to unprecedented heights, 84% to 89% of all Americans correctly responded that the crime rate had risen from year to year. Apparently, however, the actual level of serious crime has little if any bearing on people's perceptions of it. Americans tend to see (or fear) an increase in crime, regardless of whether the crime rate goes up or down.

[5]Stuart H. Palmer, *The Psychology of Murder* (New York: Crowell, 1960).
[6]Lydia Saad, "Most Americans Believe That Crime in U.S. Is Worsening," *Gallup News* (October 31, 2011), 1.

Meta-Analysis

An especially important use of the existing literature for conducting research can be found in the approach known as *meta-analysis*. Rather than collect new data or depend on a few unrepresentative studies to draw a conclusion, the investigator combines the results obtained in a number of previous studies that have addressed the same hypothesis and subjects all of them collectively to a single statistical test. In conducting a meta-analysis, the researcher may, with the aid of a well-supported finding, be able to end a debate in the literature or confirm the validity of an important idea. The meta-analysis process essentially consists of a literature search in which the conclusions reached by previous investigators are ignored. Instead, the researcher reexamines the data collected previously and then calculates an estimate of what is called the *effect size*—a measure of the extent to which a relationship exists in the population (see Chapter 7).

In 2008, Merrell, Gueldner, Ross, and Isava conducted a meta-analysis of 16 studies in which the effectiveness of various school-based bullying interventions had been tested during a 25-year period from 1980 through 2004.[7] Employing either an experimental or a quasi-experimental design, the 16 studies included a total of 15,386 student participants from six countries in Europe and North America, including the United States. The dependent variables included a number of teacher and/or student reports as well as school records as to educational, social, and behavioral outcomes associated with the interventions.

Overall, the researchers' meta-analysis yielded some evidence in support of the effectiveness of school bullying intervention programs. These initiatives tended to improve students' social competence, self-esteem, and peer acceptance as well as teachers' knowledge of effective strategies and their feelings of efficacy in terms of intervention skills. Unfortunately, about 60% of these intervention effects were not strong enough to be considered of much practical benefit. Only slightly more than one-third of the outcome variables yielded an effect large enough to be deemed beneficial with respect to reducing the negative impact of bullying. Apparently, there is still much to be learned about constructing effective anti-bullying intervention programs.

Other Methods

As an alternative to experiments, quasi-experiments, surveys, and meta-analyses, *content analysis* is a method whereby a researcher objectively seeks to describe the content of previously produced messages. He or she may study the content of books, magazines, newspapers, films, radio broadcasts, photographs, cartoons, letters, verbal dyadic interaction, political propaganda, or music.

A 2012 content analysis conducted by Callister, Coyne, Robinson, Davies, Near, Valkenburg, and Gillespie examined substance use—alcohol, tobacco, or illegal drugs—portrayed among the adult and teen-age characters appearing in the 90 top-grossing teen-oriented films from the 1980s, 1990s, and 2000s.[8] Films included in the sample centered on issues of interest to teenagers and featured a teenager as the central character. All movies were coded by one of two coders after being trained and tested for their reliability in applying coding procedures. A total of 609 characters—36% adults and 64% teenagers—were coded from all of the films in the sample.

Results obtained by Callister and his colleagues indicated that substance users in teen-oriented films were portrayed in a positive light as being more attractive than their nonuser counterparts. Moreover, for about 95% of all characters, the use of substances—whether alcohol, tobacco, or drugs—was free of any consequences, risky or otherwise. Reflecting real-world trends in American society since the 1980s, the trend as depicted in teen-oriented movies was surprisingly toward a reduced prevalence of smoking, drinking, and taking illegal drugs over the

---

[7]K. W. Merrell et al. "How Effective Are School Bullying Intervention Programs? A Meta-Analysis of Intervention Research," *School Psychology Quarterly* 23, 1 (2008): 26–42.

[8]Mark Callister et al., "A Content Analysis of the Prevalence and Portrayal of Sexual Activity in Adolescent Literature," *The Journal of Sex Research* 5, 19 (October 31, 2012): 477–486. Available at www.highbeam.com

decades. To the extent that teenagers imitate media portrayals of attractive models, this finding may prove to be of importance in the future.

Another widely used method is *participant observation*, whereby a researcher actively participates in the daily life of the people being studied, either openly in the role of researcher or covertly in an undercover role, observing events, interaction, and conversation as they happen, and questioning people over some period of time.

In 2005, for example, Janese Free explored the influence of alternative schooling on at-risk youth.[9] As a participant observer, Free spent approximately 750 hours over the course of a year at an alternative school in New England volunteering as a classroom aide. The alternative school was a middle school for at-risk students who had been removed from conventional programs due to drug use, violence, truancy, or failing out of school.

Free was a semi-covert participant observer, meaning the teachers knew she was there to collect data for her research but the students did not. In her role as classroom aide, she participated in the students' daily activities (including classroom time, recess, gym, lunch duty, etc.) and in her role as researcher, she observed and recorded the students' behaviors and interactions in each of these settings. In an attempt to gather the most accurate data possible, Free recorded her observations in private (bathrooms, teacher's lounge, and her car) on small pieces of paper carried in her pocket so the students would not be aware they were being observed. These field notes were later transcribed into documents and then analyzed by coding the data and looking for common themes.

One of the participant observer's guiding research questions was "How does attending an alternative school influence its students' development, both academically and behaviorally?" Free identified six major influential factors (or "themes") influencing students' development: (1) alternative educational practices; (2) dedication of the teachers and staff; (3) school culture and environment; (4) student home lives; (5) student behaviors, violence, and arrests; and (6) school disciplinary responses. Of these major influences, Free argued that alternative education practices and the dedication of teachers and staff were "enhancers" to student development, whereas the school culture and environment, student home lives, student behaviors, violence, arrests, and school disciplinary factors were "inhibitors" to student development and progress.

MAJOR DATA SOURCES IN CRIMINOLOGY AND CRIMINAL JUSTICE

Surveys

While all of the previously described methods are used, most of the data in criminology and criminal justice is produced by surveys. The largest and most prominent of these is the National Crime Victimization Survey (NCVS) conducted since 1973 by the U.S. Department of Justice, Bureau of Justice Statistics. For this survey, a nationwide representative sample of approximately 40,000 households is selected, and interviews of all household members at least 12 years old are conducted by U.S. Census Bureau personnel. Households stay in the sample for 3 years, are interviewed every 6 months, and new households are rotated in and out of the sample on an ongoing basis.

The NCVS provides information on crimes committed against individuals and households, regardless of whether the crimes were reported to police or anyone else. The survey produces information about victim and household characteristics (such as age, sex, race, and education of each resident, and total household income), offender characteristics (such as victims' perceptions of offender sex, race, age, possible intoxication, and their relationship with the offender), and characteristics of the crimes (such as type, when and where they occurred, use of weapons, and impact on victims). Crime victims also are asked about their efforts to

[9]Janese Free, "Best Practices in Alternative Education," presented at the National Alternatives to Dropout and Expulsion Conference (February 2005), Orlando, FL.

protect themselves from crime, and their experiences with the criminal justice system. Among the products of the NCVS are estimates of crime rates that are not dependent on the criminal justice system records, changes in crime rates over time, the level of underreporting of crime to the police, and lifetime likelihood of victimization.

While the NCVS is the largest continuous survey project in criminal justice, there are many others. For example, the National Youth Survey, conducted by the Institute of Behavioral Science, in 1977, for example, began its study of a national sample of 1,725 people aged 11–17 years, and surveyed these same individuals again in 1984, 1987, 1990, and 1993. The respondents in this study provided information about their own criminal and delinquent behavior such as their use of illegal drugs and commission of crimes such as larceny, assault, auto theft, sexual assault, and burglary.

In addition to studying crime victimization and self-reported criminal involvement, surveys are often used to study attitudes and opinions about crime and the criminal justice system, as well as to examine theories about the causes of crime. For example, several polling organizations including Gallup and Pew frequently conduct surveys of the public on issues of crime and justice. Numerous surveys examine criminological theories, including studies testing Michael R. Gottfredson and Travis Hirschi's general theory of crime, Robert Agnew's general strain theory, Edwin H. Sutherland's differential association theory, and other studies examining how the threat of punishment deters people from committing crimes.

Police Reports

Another major source of crime information is the reported Uniform Crime Reports (UCR). Since 1929, police agencies have sent information about homicide, rape, robbery, aggravated assault, burglary, larceny-theft, motor vehicle theft, and arson to the UCR. The information is compiled by the FBI and is used to count crime and to track trends over time. In addition to the number of crimes reported to police, the report contains information about crimes cleared by arrest and characteristics of arrested persons.

The data presented in the annual UCR publication *Crime in the United States* are summary measures, meaning that only total counts of crimes reported, arrests, and so on are presented for each police agency. This makes the UCR data unsuitable for studying individual crimes, offenders, or victims. To address this, the U.S. Department of Justice also provides data that use individual crime incidents (not cities or counties) as the units of analysis. The Supplemental Homicide Reports (SHR) were begun in 1961 and, for each individual homicide, contain detailed information such as the relationship between victims and offenders, location, use of weapons, and characteristics of the victims and offenders. Like the UCR, the SHR are based on police records of crimes reported to them. This incident-based data, as opposed to the summary data of the UCR, allow the description and analysis of individual events, and the comparison of features of different events. For example, it is possible to compare whether male and female victims tend to be killed with different weapons or if they have different relationships to their assailants.

The National Incident-Based Reporting System (NIBRS) was planned in the mid-1980s as a replacement for the UCR and is similar to the SHR but extends to all of the crimes covered in the UCR and dozens more. Owing to the vastly greater volume of data required for NIBRS compared to the UCR, the transition to NIBRS is ongoing.

WHY TEST HYPOTHESES?

Social science is often referred to, quite unfairly, as the study of the obvious. However, it is desirable, if not necessary, to test hypotheses about the nature of crime and justice, even those that seem logical and self-evident. Our everyday commonsense observations are generally based on narrow, often biased preconceptions and personal experiences. These can lead us to accept without criticism invalid assumptions about the characteristics of crime and criminal behavior.

To demonstrate how we can be so easily misled by our preconceptions and stereotypes, consider what we "know" about mass murderers. How many of the following characteristics seem obvious to you? How many would not be worth studying because they are so obvious?

1. Mass murderers are almost always insane. (After all, a sane person would never shoot 32 people at Virginia Tech as Seung-Hai Cho did in April 2007.)
2. Mass murderers are usually loners. (The neighbors always seem to say, "He was quiet, he stayed pretty much to himself, we never really knew him.")
3. Mass murderers look different from the rest of us. (One generally imagines a glassy-eyed lunatic, as in the horror movies.)
4. Mass murderers are usually strangers to their victims, who are unlucky enough to be in the wrong place at the wrong time. (Cases like the mass murder at an Aurora, Colorado, cinema in 2012 typically come to mind.)

That these conceptions about mass murderers seem so clear-cut and indisputable might explain why it took until 1985 for anyone to look systematically at the profile of the mass murderer. Compiling detailed information about 42 mass killers, we found that every one of these notions was incorrect. In fact, mass murderers are rarely insane—they know exactly what they are doing and are not driven to kill by voices of demons. Mass murderers are usually not loners—they have friends and often wives and children who do not anticipate their actions. Mass murderers do not look any different—they are "extraordinarily ordinary." Finally, random shootings in a public place are the exceptions—most mass murders occur within families or among acquaintances. Therefore, as illustrated by the example of mass murderers, it is foolish to draw conclusions on the basis of common sense alone.

THE STAGES OF CRIMINAL JUSTICE RESEARCH

Systematically testing our ideas about the nature of crime and justice often demands carefully planned and executed research in which the following occur:

1. The problem to be studied is reduced to a testable hypothesis (e.g., "one-parent families generate more delinquency than two-parent families").
2. An appropriate set of instruments is developed (e.g., a questionnaire or an interview schedule).
3. The data are collected (i.e., the researcher might go into the field and conduct a poll or a survey).
4. The data are analyzed for their bearing on the initial hypotheses (e.g., comparing rates of delinquency among youth raised in single-parent and two-parent homes).
5. Results of the analysis are interpreted and communicated to an audience (e.g., by means of a lecture, journal article, or press release).

As we shall see in subsequent chapters, the material presented in this book is most closely tied to the data analysis stage of research, in which the data collected or gathered by the researcher are analyzed for their bearing on the initial hypotheses. It is in this stage of research that the raw data are tabulated, calculated, counted, summarized, rearranged, compared, or, in a word, *organized,* so that the accuracy or validity of the hypotheses can be tested.

USING SERIES OF NUMBERS TO DO CRIMINAL JUSTICE RESEARCH

Anyone who has conducted research knows that problems in data analysis must be confronted in the planning stages of a research project, because they have a bearing on the nature of decisions at all other stages. Such problems often affect aspects of the research design and even the types of instruments employed in collecting the data. For this reason, we constantly seek techniques or methods for enhancing the quality of data analysis.

Most researchers would agree on the importance of **measurement** in analyzing data. When some characteristic is measured, researchers are able to assign to it a series of numbers according to a set of rules.

MEASUREMENT

The use of a series of numbers in the data-analysis stage of research.

Criminologists, criminal justice researchers, and other social scientists have developed measures of a wide range of phenomena including fear of crime, approval of capital punishment, criminal justice program quality, posttraumatic stress, offense type, perceived likelihood of committing crime, race, recidivism risk, crime seriousness, education level, hostility, impulsivity, socioeconomic status, substance abuse treatment need, and victim blame.

Numbers have at least three important functions for researchers, depending on the particular *level of measurement* that they employ. Specifically, series of numbers can be used to

1. *classify* or *categorize* at the nominal level of measurement,
2. *rank* or *order* at the ordinal level of measurement, and
3. assign a *score* at the interval level of measurement.

The Nominal Level

NOMINAL LEVEL OF MEASUREMENT

The process of placing cases into categories and counting their frequency of occurrence.

The **nominal level of measurement** involves naming or labeling, that is, placing cases into categories and counting their frequency of occurrence. To illustrate, we might use a nominal-level measure to indicate whether each respondent is prejudiced or tolerant toward Latinos. As shown in Table 1.1, we might question the 10 probation officers and determine that 5 can be regarded as (1) prejudiced and 5 can be considered as (2) accepting.

Other nominal-level measures in criminology and criminal justice research are crime type (e.g., property, violent, drug, sex), offense history (past criminal record versus no record), race (e.g., Asian, Caucasian, African American, Latino), status as high school graduate (did or did not graduate), gang memberships (is or is not a member), sex (male versus female), personality type (authoritarian, passive–aggressive, extrovert), and guilt (innocent or guilty of committing a crime).

When dealing with nominal data, we must keep in mind that *every case must be placed in one, and only one, category*. This requirement indicates that the categories must be nonoverlapping or **mutually exclusive**. Thus, a respondent's race classified as white cannot also be classified as black; any respondent labeled male cannot also be labeled female. The requirement also indicates that the categories must be **exhaustive**—there must be a place for every case that arises. For illustrative purposes, imagine a study in which all respondents are interviewed and categorized by race as either black or white. Where would we categorize a Chinese respondent if he or she were to appear? In this case, it might be necessary to expand the original category system to include Asians or, assuming that most respondents will be white or black, to include an "other" category in which such exceptions can be placed.

MUTUALLY EXCLUSIVE OUTCOMES

Two outcomes or events are mutually exclusive if the occurrence of one rules out the possibility that the other will occur.

EXHAUSTIVE OUTCOMES

A set of outcomes that cover all possibilities.

The reader should note that nominal data are not graded, ranked, or scaled for qualities such as better or worse, higher or lower, more or less. Clearly, then, a nominal measure of sex does not signify whether males are superior or inferior to females. Nominal data are merely labeled, sometimes by name (male versus female or prejudiced versus tolerant), other times by number (1 versus 2), but always for the purpose of grouping the cases into separate categories to indicate sameness or differentness with respect to a given quality or characteristic. Thus, even when a number is used to label a category (e.g., 1 = white, 2 = black, 3 = other), a quantity is not implied.

TABLE 1.1	Attitudes of 10 Probation Officers toward Latinos: Nominal Data	
Attitude toward Latinos		**Frequency**
1 = Prejudiced		5
2 = Accepting		5
Total		10

TABLE 1.2	Attitudes of 10 Probation Officers toward Latinos: Ordinal Data
Officer	**Rank**
Joyce	1 = most prejudiced
Paul	2 = second
Cathy	3 = third
Mike	4 = fourth
Judy	5 = fifth
Joe	6 = sixth
Kelly	7 = seventh
Ernie	8 = eighth
Linda	9 = ninth
Ben	10 = least prejudiced

The Ordinal Level

When the researcher goes beyond the nominal level of measurement and seeks to order his or her cases in terms of the degree to which they have any given characteristic, he or she is working at the **ordinal level of measurement**. The nature of the relationship among ordinal categories depends on that characteristic the researcher seeks to measure. To take a familiar example, one might classify individuals with respect to socioeconomic status as lower class, middle class, or upper class. Or, rather than categorize the probation officers as *either* prejudiced *or* accepting, the researcher might rank them according to their degree of prejudice against Latinos, as indicated in Table 1.2.

The ordinal level of measurement yields information about the ordering of categories but does not indicate the *magnitude of differences* between numbers. For instance, the researcher who employs an ordinal-level measure to study prejudice toward Latinos *does not know how much more prejudiced one respondent is than another*. In the example given earlier, it is not possible to determine how much more prejudiced Joyce is than Paul or how much less prejudiced Ben is than Linda or Ernie. This is because the intervals between the points or ranks on an ordinal scale are not known or meaningful. Therefore, it is not possible to assign *scores* to cases located at points along the scale.

ORDINAL LEVEL OF MEASUREMENT

The process of ordering or ranking cases in terms of the degree to which they have any given characteristic.

The Interval (and Ratio) Level

By contrast to the ordinal level, the **interval and ratio levels of measurement** indicate not only the ordering of categories but also the exact distance between them. Interval and ratio measures employ constant units of measurement (e.g., dollars or cents, degrees Fahrenheit or Celsius, yards or feet, minutes or seconds) that yield equal intervals between points on the scale.

Some variables in their natural form are interval/ratio level—for example, how many pounds you weigh, how many siblings you have, or how long it takes a student to complete an exam. In criminal justice, naturally formed interval/ratio measures might include the length of a prison sentence or a defendant's number of prior convictions.

Other variables are interval/ratio because of how we scale them. Typically, an interval/ratio measure that we construct generates a set of scores that can be compared with one another. By this method, an interval/ratio measure of prejudice against Latinos—such as a set of responses to a series of questions about Latinos that is scored from 0 to 100 (100 is extreme prejudice)—might yield the data shown in Table 1.3 about the 10 probation officers.

As presented in Table 1.3, we are able to order the probation officers in terms of their prejudices and, in addition, indicate the distances separating one from another. For instance, it is possible to say that Ben is the least prejudiced probation officer, because he received the lowest score. We can also say that Ben is only slightly less prejudiced than Linda or Ernie but much

INTERVAL/ RATIO LEVEL OF MEASUREMENT

The process of assigning a score to cases so that the magnitude of differences between them is known and meaningful.

TABLE 1.3	Attitudes of 10 Probation Officers toward Latinos: Interval Data
Officer	**Score[a]**
Joyce	98
Paul	96
Cathy	95
Mike	94
Judy	68
Joe	21
Kelly	20
Ernie	15
Linda	11
Ben	6

[a] Higher scores indicate greater prejudice against Latinos.

less prejudiced than Joyce, Paul, Cathy, or Mike, all of whom received extremely high scores. Depending on the purpose for which the study is designed, it is important to determine such information, but this information is not available at the ordinal level of measurement.

Consider another example. A diagnosis of the psychological condition *psychopathy* is most commonly based on the checklist created by Robert Hare to measure the degree to which an individual, over the course of a lifetime, controls others and satisfies his or her selfish desires through manipulating, charming, and intimidating other people. This checklist is currently used by criminologists worldwide.

One version of the Psychopathy Checklist consists of a 20-item rating scale, each item representing a symptom or characteristic of psychopathy—for example, superficial charm, lack of empathy, juvenile delinquency, impulsivity, lack of remorse, and pathological lying. For any given individual, each item in the checklist is rated on a 3-point scale (0, item does not apply; 1, item applies somewhat; and 2, item applies completely). All of the items are then summed to generate a total score per individual, from 0 (20 × 0 points) to 40 (20 × 2 points), indicating the degree to which he or she possesses psychopathic qualities.

As depicted in Table 1.4, we are able to order a group of eight violent inmates in terms of their degree of psychopathy and, in addition, determine the exact distances separating one from another. This requires making the assumption that the Psychopathy Checklist uses a constant unit of measurement (one psychopathy point).

Thus, we can say that inmate A is the most psychopathic in the group because he or she received the highest score on the checklist. We can also say that inmate A is only slightly more psychopathic than inmate B but much more psychopathic than inmates G and H, both of whom

TABLE 1.4	Psychopathy Scores of Eight Violent Inmates: Interval Data
Inmate	**Psychopathy Score**
A	40
B	39
C	37
D	36
E	32
F	28
G	5
H	3

received extremely low scores. Additionally, we can say that inmate E falls exactly halfway between inmates D and F with respect to degree of psychopathy.

The *ratio* level is the same as the interval level but in addition presumes the existence of an absolute or true zero point. In contrast, an interval level variable may have an artificial zero value or even none at all.

For example, age meets the condition for the ratio level, because a zero represents birth, or the complete absence of age. In contrast, the Fahrenheit scale of temperature possesses an artificial zero point, because "zero degrees" does not represent the total absence of heat, even though it does not feel particularly warm. Similarly, the IQ scale has no zero point at all—that is, there is no such thing as a zero IQ—and therefore qualifies only as an interval scale.

Similarly, a score of zero on the Psychopathy Checklist would probably indicate a total absence of any psychopathic tendencies and therefore potentially represents a ratio scale. In reality, however, just as in the case of IQ, there are few, if any, individuals totally lacking in any of the checklist items—for example, it is hard to imagine anyone who isn't somewhat manipulative or impulsive or who always accepts total responsibility for his or her behavior under all circumstances. For the purpose of comparing individuals on the Psychopathy Checklist, many investigators have instead employed an arbitrary cutoff point of 30 to separate high and low scorers on the checklist. That is, any score of 30 or above is considered high; any score below 30 is treated as low.

When it comes right down to classifying the variable, it makes little difference whether a variable is interval or ratio level. There are many important statistical techniques that assume a standard distance between scale points (i.e., an interval scale), but there are very few that require valid ratios between scale points (i.e., a ratio scale). Thus, throughout the remainder of the book, we shall indicate whether a technique requires the nominal level, the ordinal level, or the interval/ratio level.

Treating Ordinal Data as Interval

As we have seen, levels of measurement vary in terms of their degree of sophistication or refinement, from simple classification (nominal), to ranking (ordinal), to scoring (interval). At this point, the distinction between the nominal and ordinal levels should be quite clear. It would be difficult to confuse the level of measurement attained by the variable "color of hair" (blond, redhead, brunette, and black), which is nominal, with that of the variable "condition of hair" (dry, normal, oily), which is ordinal.

The distinction between ordinal and interval, however, is not always clear-cut. Oftentimes, variables that in the strictest sense are ordinal may be treated as if they were interval, when the ordered categories are fairly evenly spaced. For example, the following two variables (*rank of police department staff* and *attitude toward the police*) are both ordinal.

Scale Value	Police Staff Rank	Attitude toward Police
1	Police Chief	Strongly favorable
2	Captain	Somewhat favorable
3	Detective	Neutral
4	Patrol Sergeant	Somewhat unfavorable
5	Patrol Officer	Strongly unfavorable

The *rank-of-police-staff* variable could hardly be mistaken for interval. At this particular police department, the difference between detective (3) and patrol sergeant (4) is minimal in terms of prestige, salary, or qualifications, whereas the difference between (1) police chief and (2) captain is substantial in terms of salary as well as status and required qualifications. By contrast, the *attitude-toward-police* variable has scale values that are roughly evenly spaced. The difference between (4) *somewhat unfavorable* and (5) *strongly unfavorable* appears to be virtually the same as the difference between (4) *somewhat unfavorable* and (3) *neutral*. In fact, this is true of most attitude scales ranging from *strongly agree* to *strongly disagree, strongly favorable* to *strongly unfavorable, strongly approve* to *strongly disapprove*, and the like.

Rather than split hairs, many researchers make a practical decision. Whenever possible, they choose to treat ordinal variables as interval, but only when it is reasonable to assume that the scale has roughly equal intervals. Thus, they would treat the *attitude-toward-police* variable as if it were interval, but they would never treat the *rank-of-police* variable as anything other than ordinal. As you will see later in the text, treating ordinal variables that have nearly evenly spaced values as if they were interval allows researchers to use more powerful statistical procedures.

Further Measurement Issues

Whether a variable is measured at the nominal, ordinal, or interval/ratio level is sometimes a natural feature of the characteristic itself and is not at all influenced by the decisions that the criminal justice researcher makes in defining and collecting data. Relationship between offender and victim (e.g., family member, friend, acquaintance, and stranger), race (e.g., black, white, Asian), and region of residence (e.g., Northeast, Mid-Atlantic, South, Midwest, Mountain, and West) are unquestionably nominal-level variables. A researcher, however, can still expand the meaning of basic characteristics like these in an attempt to increase the precision and power of his or her data. Victim–offender relationship, for example, can be redefined in terms of intimacy (e.g., from close family member to stranger) to elevate the level of measurement to ordinal status. Similarly, for the purpose of measuring geographic proximity to Southern culture, an ordinal-level "Southerness scale" might be developed to distinguish Mississippi and Alabama at one extreme, Kentucky and Tennessee next, followed by Maryland and Delaware, and then Connecticut and Vermont at the other extreme. Although it may be someone stretching the point, a researcher could also develop an interval-level Southerness scale, using the number of miles a state's center lies above or below the Mason–Dixon line.

Often, there are situations in which variables must be downgraded in their level of measurement, even though this might reduce their precision. To increase the response rate, for example, a telephone interviewer might decide to redefine age, an interval-level variable, into ordinal categories such as toddler, child, teenager, young adult, middle-aged, and senior.

Another important measurement distinction that researchers confront is between discrete and continuous variables. Discrete data take on only certain specific values. For example, arrests can be expressed only in whole numbers from 1 on up (there is no such thing as 3.47 arrests; it is either 1, 2, 3, or so on); number of arrests therefore represents a discrete interval-level measure. Moreover, nominal variables (such as New England states: Massachusetts, Connecticut, Rhode Island, Vermont, Maine, and New Hampshire; Gender: female and male; Sentence: prison, probation, execution) by virtue of their categorical nature are always discrete.

Continuous variables, on the other hand, present an infinite range of possible values, although the manner in which we measure them may appear to be discrete. Body weight, for example, can take on any number of values, including 143.4154 pounds. Some bathroom scales may measure this weight to the nearest whole pound (143 pounds), and others may measure weight to the nearest half pound (143.5), and some even to the nearest tenth of a pound (143.4) Underlying whatever measuring device we use, however, is a natural continuum. Similarly, age represents a gradual process that begins at birth and ends with death. Age is therefore a continuous variable that theoretically could be measured in nanoseconds from birth on. Yet it is customary to use whole numbers (years for adults, weeks for infants) in recording this variable. As shown earlier, it is also common practice to arbitrarily divide the continuum of age into categories such as toddler, child, teenager, young adult, middle-aged, and senior.

FUNCTIONS OF STATISTICS

It is when researchers use numbers—they *quantify* their data at the nominal, ordinal, or interval level of measurement—that they are likely to employ statistics as a tool of (1) *description* or (2) *decision making*. Let us now take a closer look at these important functions of statistics.

Description

To arrive at conclusions or to obtain results, a researcher often studies hundreds, thousands, or even larger numbers of persons or groups. As an extreme case, the United States Bureau of the Census conducts a complete enumeration of the U.S. population, in which millions of individuals are contacted. Despite the aid of numerous sophisticated procedures, it is always a formidable task to describe and summarize the mass of data generated from large-scale research projects in research.

Even relatively small samples can be daunting. Take, for example, the data listed in Table 1.5 representing the number of years spent on death row by 71 inmates executed in Florida between 1979 and 2011. Thus, the shortest period of time incarcerated was 2 years; the longest period of time was 30 years. Looking through Table 1.5, do you see any patterns in these data? Can you easily summarize the years served on death row by these inmates in a few words? In a few sentences? Would you be able to draw conclusions about whether they remained on death row for a lengthy period of time on the whole? The answer is, "Probably not."

Using even the most basic principles of descriptive statistics, however, we can characterize the distribution of the years served by these death row inmates with a good deal of clarity and precision, so that overall tendencies or group characteristics are quickly observed and easily communicated to almost anyone. First, the number of years served can be rearranged in consecutive order (either from shortest to longest or from longest to shortest) and grouped into a much smaller set of categories. As shown in Table 1.6, this grouped frequency distribution (discussed in detail in Chapter 2) presents the years served within broader categories along with the number or frequency (*f*) of inmates whose time served fell into these categories. It can easily be seen, for example, that 21 out of 71 executed inmates spent between 6 and 10 years on death row and 28 spent between 11 and 15 years there, but only 2 inmates spent between 26 and 30 years on death row prior to execution.

TABLE 1.5 Years on Death Row for 71 Inmates Executed in Florida between 1979 and 2011

5	13	4
10	9	13
7	12	17
7	13	14
10	11	11
7	11	22
7	13	26
10	2	13
10	15	9
7	15	18
9	14	3
11	14	4
7	14	23
9	14	20
11	14	13
9	14	21
9	16	15
14	12	14
8	12	23
9	16	25
10	21	24
14	14	30
6	22	17
6	16	

TABLE 1.6	Years on Death Row for 71 Inmates Executed in Florida between 1979 and 2011: Grouped Frequency Distribution	
Years on death row		**f**
1–5		5
6–10		21
11–15		28
16–20		7
21–25		8
26–30		2
Total		71

Another useful procedure (explained in Chapter 2) is to rearrange the years spent on death row graphically. As shown in Figure 1.1, the categories of years incarcerated on death row (from 1–5 years to 26–30 years) are placed along one axis of a graph (i.e., the horizontal baseline) and their frequencies along another axis (i.e., the vertical axis). This arrangement results in a rather easily visualized graphic representation (e.g., the histogram), in which we can see that most executed inmates spent between 11 and 15 years on death row, whereas relatively few remained there for fewer than 6 years or longer than 25 years.

As discussed in Chapter 3, a particularly convenient and useful statistical method—one with which you are already more or less familiar—is to ask: "What is the average length of time on death row, in years, served by the 71 executed inmates?" The arithmetic average (or mean), which can be obtained by adding the entire list of years on death row and dividing this sum by the total number of inmates, gives us a clearer picture of the overall group tendency. The average in this example turns out to be 12.9 years, a rather lengthy period of time to be kept on death row prior to execution (perhaps while the appeals process is being exhausted).

Consider this analogy to the objectives of descriptive statistics. Suppose a friend calls and wants to set you up on a blind date with someone who is "a perfect match." You would probably have a few questions before deciding whether or not to agree to meet this "perfect" stranger. Knowing such things as the person's age might be critical to your decision, while other attributes such as hair length and eye color would probably be less informative.

In certain respects, confronting a large array of data, such as those in Table 1.5, is like confronting the prospect of a blind date. Statisticians attempt to describe a set of "blind data" not only using frequency distributions (as in Table 1.6) but also with a variety of summary measures. Statistics such as the minimum and maximum values in the data set are mildly informative, while quantities such as the arithmetic mean or middle-most score are extremely telling about the distribution of data.

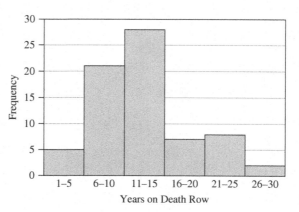

FIGURE 1.1 Years on Death Row for 71 Inmates Executed in Florida between 1979 and 2011.

Returning to the possible fix-up, your friend might be able to e-mail a photograph of the potential date. This would be helpful, of course, but only to the extent that the photo is of high quality—taken with good lighting and free of distortion. Similarly, a chart like Figure 1.1 depicting a distribution helps researchers make sense of the data, but only if the graphic is accurately drawn and distortion free.

Thus, with the help of statistical devices such as grouped frequency distributions, graphs, and the arithmetic average, it is possible to detect and describe patterns or tendencies in distributions of scores (e.g., in the years on death row in Table 1.5) that might otherwise have gone unnoticed by the casual observer. In the present context, then, statistics may be defined as *a set of techniques for the reduction of quantitative data (i.e., a series of numbers) to a small number of more convenient and easily communicated descriptive terms.*

Decision Making

To test hypotheses, it is frequently necessary to go beyond mere description. It is often also necessary to make inferences, that is, to make decisions based on data collected on only a small portion or sample of the larger group we have in mind to study. Factors such as cost and time often preclude taking a complete enumeration or poll of the entire group; researchers call this larger group from which the sample was drawn a **population or universe**.

Returning once more to the fix-up analogy, there is one other aspect in which the blind date and blind data comparison holds. One, two, or just a few dates will rarely be enough to determine if this is someone with whom you'd want to spend the rest of your life. Only with sufficient exposure to this person can you gain a sense of his or her true nature, beyond the superficial aspects of personal appearance. In statistics, we use a **sample** of data to understand the characteristics of the population from which it was drawn. A small sample is hardly reliable, whereas a large sample allows us to generalize to the population. Many points of data, like many dates with a potential life partner, allow us to make decisions with a high degree of confidence.

As we shall see in Chapter 6, every time researchers test hypotheses on a sample, they must decide whether it is indeed accurate to generalize the findings to the entire population from which it was drawn. Error inevitably results from sampling, even sampling that has been properly conceived and executed. This is the problem of generalizing or *drawing inferences* from the sample to the population.[10]

Statistics can be useful for purposes of generalizing findings, with a high degree of confidence, from small samples to larger populations. To understand better this decision-making purpose of statistics and the concept of generalizing from samples to populations, let us examine the results of a hypothetical study that was conducted to test the following hypothesis:

Hypothesis: Male college students are more likely than female college students to have tried marijuana.

The researchers in this study decided to test their hypothesis at an urban university in which some 20,000 students (10,000 males and 10,000 females) were enrolled. Due to cost and time factors, they were not able to interview every student on campus but did obtain from the

POPULATION (UNIVERSE)

Any set of individuals who share at least one characteristic.

SAMPLE

A smaller number of individuals taken from some population (for the purpose of generalizing to the entire population from which it was taken).

---

[10]The concept of *sampling error* is discussed in greater detail in Chapter 6. However, to understand the inevitability of sampling error when sampling from a larger group, you may now wish to conduct the following experiment. Refer to Table 1.5, which contains the years on death row of 71 executed inmates. At random, for example by closing your eyes and pointing, select a sample of five scores from the entire list. Find the average by adding the five scores and then dividing by 5, the total number of scores in your sample. It has already been mentioned that the average for all 71 convicts was 12.9 years. To what extent does your sample average differ from the entire group average of 12.9? Try this demonstration on several more samples of five scores randomly selected from the larger group. With great consistency, you should find that your sample average will almost always differ at least slightly from that obtained from the entire group of 71 scores. This is what we mean by *sampling error.*

TABLE 1.7 Marijuana Use by Gender of Respondent: Case I

Marijuana Use	Gender of Respondent	
	Male	*Female*
Number who have tried it	35	15
Number who have not tried it	65	85
Total	100	100

registrar's office a complete listing of university students. From this list, every one-hundredth student (one-half of them male, one-half of them female) was selected for the sample and subsequently interviewed by members of the research staff. The interviewers asked each of the 200 members of the sample whether he or she had ever tried marijuana and then recorded the student's gender as either male or female. After all interviews had been completed and returned to the staff office, the responses on the marijuana question were tabulated by gender and are presented in Table 1.7.

Notice that results obtained from this sample of 200 students as presented in Table 1.7 are in the hypothesized direction: 35 out of 100 males reported having tried marijuana, whereas only 15 out of 100 females reported having tried marijuana. Clearly, in this small sample, males were more likely than females to have tried marijuana. For our purposes, however, the more important question is whether these gender differences in marijuana use are large enough to generalize them confidently to the much larger university population of 20,000 students. Do these results represent true population differences? Or have we obtained chance differences between males and females strictly due to sampling error—the error that occurs every time we take a small group from a larger group?

To illuminate the problem of generalizing results from samples to larger populations, imagine that the researchers had, instead, obtained the results shown in Table 1.8. Notice that these results are still in the predicted direction: 30 males as opposed to only 20 females have tried marijuana. But, are we still willing to generalize these results to the larger university population? Is it not likely that a difference of this magnitude (10 more males than females) would have happened simply by chance? Or can we confidently say that such relatively small differences reflect a real difference between males and females at that particular university?

Let us carry out the illustration a step further. Suppose that the researchers had obtained the data shown in Table 1.9. Differences between males and females shown in the table could not be much smaller and still be in the hypothesized direction: 26 males in contrast to 24 females tried marijuana—only 2 more males than females. How many of us would be willing to call *this* finding a true population difference between males and females rather than a product of chance or sampling error?

Where do we draw the line? At what point does a sample difference become large enough so that we are willing to treat it as significant or real? With the aid of statistics, we can readily, and with a high degree of confidence, make such decisions about the relationship between samples and populations. To illustrate, had we used one of the statistical tests of significance

TABLE 1.8 Marijuana Use by Gender of Respondent: Case II

Marijuana Use	Gender of Respondent	
	Male	*Female*
Number who have tried it	30	20
Number who have not tried it	70	80
Total	100	100

TABLE 1.9	Marijuana Use by Gender of Respondent: Case III	
	Gender of Respondent	
Marijuana Use	*Male*	*Female*
Number who have tried it	26	24
Number who have not tried it	74	76
Total	100	100

discussed later in this text (e.g., chi-square—see Chapter 9), we would already have known that *only those results* reported in Table 1.7 can be generalized to the population of 20,000 university students—that 35 out of 100 males but only 15 out of 100 females have tried marijuana is a finding substantial enough to be applied to the entire population with a high degree of confidence and is therefore referred to as a **statistically significant difference**. Our statistical test tells us there are only 5 chances out of 100 that we are wrong! By contrast, application of the same statistical criterion shows the results reported in Tables 1.8 and 1.9 are *statistically nonsignificant,* quite possibly being the product of sampling error rather than real gender differences in the use of marijuana.

In the present context, then, statistics is *a set of decision-making techniques that aid researchers in drawing inferences from samples to populations and, hence, in testing hypotheses regarding the nature of social reality.*

STATISTICALLY SIGNIFICANT DIFFERENCE

A sample difference that reflects a real population difference and not just sampling error.

An Important Note about Rounding

If you are like most students, the issue of rounding can be confusing. It is always a pleasure, of course, when an answer comes out to be a whole number because rounding is not needed. For those other times, however, when you confront a number such as 34.233333 or 7.126534, determining just how many digits to use in rounding becomes problematic.

For occasions when you need to round, the following rule can be applied: *Round a final answer to two more decimal digits than contained in the original scores.* If the original scores are all whole numbers (e.g., 3, 6, 9, and 12), then round your final answer to two decimal places (e.g., 4.45). If the original scores contain one decimal place (e.g., 3.3, 6.0, 9.5, and 12.8), then round your answer to three decimal places (e.g., 4.456). Note that a discussion of *how* to round is given in Appendix B, "A Review of Some Fundamentals of Mathematics."

Many of the problems in this book require a number of intermediate steps before arriving at the final answer. When using a calculator, it is usually not necessary to round off calculations done along the way, that is, for intermediate steps. Your calculator will often carry many more digits than you will eventually need. As a general rule for intermediate steps, therefore, do not round until it is time to determine your final answer.

Rules of thumb, of course, must be used with some degree of good judgment. As an extreme example, you wouldn't want to round to only two decimal places in calculating the trajectory or thrust needed to send a missile to the moon; even a slight imprecision might lead to disaster. In doing problems for your statistics class, on the other hand, the precision of your answer is less important than learning the method itself. There may be times when your answer will differ slightly from that of your classmate or that contained in this book. For example, you may obtain the answer 5.55, whereas your classmate may get 5.56, yet you both may be correct. The difference is trivial and could easily have resulted from using two calculators with different memory capacities or from doing calculations in a different sequence.

In this text, we have generally followed this rule of thumb. In some illustrations, however, we rounded intermediate steps for the sake of clarity—but only to an extent that would not invalidate the final answer.

Summary

In the first chapter, we linked our everyday predictions about the course of future events with the experiences of criminal justice researchers who use statistics as an aid to test their hypotheses about the nature of crime and justice. Almost daily, everyone takes educated guesses about future events in their lives. Unlike haphazard and biased everyday observations, however, researchers seek to collect *systematic* evidence in support of their ideas. For this purpose, and depending on their particular research objective, they might decide to conduct a survey, an experiment, a quasi-experiment, a meta-analysis, participant observation, or a content analysis. Depending on the particular level of measurement, a series of numbers are often employed by researchers to categorize (nominal level), rank (ordinal level), or score (interval/ratio level) their data. Finally, researchers are able to take advantage of two major functions of statistics in the data-analysis stage of criminal justice research: description (i.e., reducing quantitative data to a smaller number of more convenient descriptive terms) and decision making (i.e., drawing inferences from samples to populations).

Questions and Problems

1. Someone who ranks a list of crimes from "least severe" to "most severe" is operating at the _____ level of measurement.
   a. nominal
   b. ordinal
   c. interval/ratio
   d. all of the above

2. A scale designed to measure the degree of empathy for crime victims is scored from 1 to 10. This scale is probably working at the _____ level of measurement.
   a. nominal
   b. ordinal
   c. interval/ratio
   d. all of the above

3. The race of police officers in a major southwestern city includes members from Asian (1), black (2), Hispanic (3), white (4), and other groups. This classification is working at the _____ level of measurement.
   a. nominal
   b. ordinal
   c. interval/ratio
   d. all of the above

4. A criminologist wants to understand what contributes to fear of crime. She collects data on age, gender, and fear of crime from individuals who lived in New Orleans during Hurricane Katrina. The dependent variable in this study is _____.
   a. age
   b. fear of crime
   c. gender
   d. Hurricane Katrina

5. Every time researchers want to test a hypothesis, they must decide if
   a. their sampling strategy allows them to generalize to the entire population.
   b. they have enough resources (time and money) to obtain an adequate sample.
   c. the results accurately reflect the population or if they are due to sampling error.
   d. all of the above

6. A criminologist undertakes a variety of studies to investigate various aspects of violence. For each of the following research situations, identify the research strategy (experiment, quasi-experiment, survey, content analysis, or participant observation) and the independent and dependent variables:
   a. Female offenders have historically been perceived as less of a problem than male offenders. A researcher wonders, though, whether women in her city are becoming more violent in their offenses. The researcher collects 100 arrest reports involving women from the past year and 100 arrest reports from 25 years ago. She records and compares the types of criminal offenses, the language used to describe the level of violence (if any), and the level of resistance to arrest.
   b. Does violence in video games produce violent behavior among high school students? To find out, researchers distributed handheld video games that could be played during homeroom to students in 10 participating high schools. Five schools were randomly assigned to receive a violent video game and five schools were randomly assigned to receive a nonviolent video game. The researchers then compared the number of violent incidents within the schools in the two groups over a 4-month period.
   c. Are panhandlers more violent at night? To find out, the researcher spends his weekends in a downtown location near bars and restaurants in a location that city leaders have described as a "problem" area. He dresses as a tourist in a loose-fitting shirt and becomes one of the crowd. At the same time, he observes and compares the number of panhandling incidents, counts loud confrontations, and compares daytime versus night time.
   d. Is income level related to attitudes toward stiffer sentences for gun crimes? To find out, the researcher calls by telephone a random sample of adults. Included in the telephone

interviews are items asking people to report their household income and to rate on a 10-point scale their approval of stiffer sentences for persons who commit felonies using guns.

   e. Are Hollywood films becoming more violent? To find out, the researcher takes a random sample of 50 films from each period, 1989–1991, 1999–2001, and 2009–2011, and studies the number of violent incidents in each.

7. Identify the level of measurement—nominal, ordinal, or interval/ratio—represented in each of the following questionnaire items used in a study of traffic stops:

   a. Gender (choose one)
      1. Male
      2. Female

   b. Race/ethnicity (choose one)
      1. African American
      2. Asian
      3. Hispanic
      4. White
      5. Other (Not Apparent)

   c. Approximate age (choose one)
      1. Under 15
      2. 15–24
      3. 25–34
      4. 35–44
      5. 45–59
      6. 60–69
      7. 70 and older

   d. Reason for initiating stop (choose one)
      1. Moving traffic violation
      2. Vehicle equipment violation
      3. Criminal activity

   e. Speeding
      1. Yes
      2. No

   f. Speed limit in zone _____ (miles per hour)

   g. Speed of vehicle _____ (miles per hour)

   h. Number of miles per hour above speed limit (choose one)
      1. Under 5
      2. 5–9
      3. 10–19
      4. 20 or above

   i. Result of stop (choose one)
      1. Verbal warning
      2. Written warning
      3. Citation issued
      4. Arrest made

   j. Whom was action taken against? (choose all that apply)
      1. Driver
      2. Passenger(s)

8. For the following items, indicate the level of measurement—nominal, ordinal, interval/ratio:

   a. How many neighbors do you know well enough to ask them to watch your home when you are gone? Would you say

None	1
A few	2
Many	3
Most of them	4

   b. In general, how satisfied are you with your neighborhood as a place to live? Are you

Very satisfied	1
Somewhat satisfied	2
Somewhat dissatisfied	3
Very dissatisfied	4

   c. Do you or anyone else in the household own any guns?

| Yes | 1 |
| No | 2 |

   d. Have you ever used marijuana?

| Yes | 1 |
| No | 2 |

   e. How many times have you used marijuana?

Never	0
1–2 times	1
3–6 times	2
7–10 times	3
More than 10 times	4

   f. How often do you play the Lottery? Would you say

Never	1
A few times a year	2
Monthly	3
Weekly	4
Daily	5

   g. How many speeding tickets have you had in your lifetime? Number _____

   h. Police patrols can be used as a way to catch speeders. How much would you agree or disagree that there should be MORE traffic enforcement against speeding? Would you

Strongly agree	1
Agree	2
Neither agree nor disagree	3
Disagree	4
Strongly disagree	5

   i. Questions 8d and 8e both provide a measure of marijuana use. Why would a researcher choose to use the level of measurement in "d" versus "e"? Which level of measurement would you prefer to use for a study of marijuana use among college students? Why?

   j. Add categories to question 8g so that the level of measurement is nominal with just two categories. What cutoff do you use if your goal is to measure speeders versus nonspeeders? Explain your choice.

9. The Federal Bureau of Investigation (FBI) reports crime in the United States as the number of crimes per 100,000 population.

   a. In 2010, the violent crime rate in the United States was 403.6. What is the level of measurement for the violent crime rate?

   b. The FBI reports the violent crime rate in large cities with populations of 100,000 or more. Suppose you were to find the 10 cities with the highest violent crime rates. What is the level of measurement for these 10 cities if you list them from highest to lowest in a top-10 list?

   c. Find a table that is of interest to you in the online version of the Uniform Crime Reports (available at www.fbi.gov). Which table did you choose? What is the level of measurement?

10. A research team was hired to determine whether a rehabilitation program reduces the likelihood that prisoners will re-offend after they are released. Four hundred inmates were declared eligible for the program, and half were randomly assigned to it while the others were kept in prison without participating in any rehabilitation programs. All of the inmates were studied for 2 years after their release to see whether they were arrested again. A comparison of arrest rates was made between the rehabilitation program and the conventional prison groups.
   a. Which research strategy was used here?
   b. What was the independent variable?
   c. What was the level of measurement for the independent variable?
   d. What was the dependent variable?
   e. What was the level of measurement for the dependent variable?

Computer Exercises

1. Identify the level of measurement—nominal, ordinal, interval/ratio—for each of the following variables from the General Social Survey:
   a. DEGREE
   b. EDUC
   c. PAEDUC
   d. CLASS
2. Identify the level of measurement—nominal, ordinal, interval/ratio—for each of the following variables from the General Social Survey:
   a. COURTS
   b. POLVIEWS
   c. SEX
   d. MARITAL
3. Identify the level of measurement—nominal, ordinal, interval/ratio—for each of the following variables from the General Social Survey:
   a. JOBSAT
   b. INCOME06
   c. INCOM16
   d. PRESTG80
4. The method of research used originally to conduct the General Social Survey is known as
   a. the experiment.
   b. the survey.
   c. content analysis.
   d. participant observation.
5. The information about levels of measurement for variables in the GSS can be identified using
   a. the codebook.
   b. a frequency distribution.
   c. the GSS website.
   d. all of the above can be used.
   e. none of the above can be used.

LOOKING AT THE LARGER PICTURE
A Student Survey

Each chapter of this textbook examines particular topics at close range. At the same time, it is important, as they say, to "see the forest through the trees." Thus, at the close of each major part of the text, we shall apply the most useful statistical procedures to the same set of data drawn from a hypothetical survey. This continuing journey should demonstrate the process by which the researcher travels from having abstract ideas to confirming or rejecting hypotheses about human behavior. Keep in mind both here and in later parts of the book that "Looking at the Larger Picture" is not an exercise for you to carry out, but a summary illustration of how research is done in practice.

For many reasons, surveys have long been the most common data-collection strategy employed by social researchers. Through the careful design of a survey instrument—a questionnaire filled out by survey respondents or an interview schedule administered over the telephone or in person—a researcher can elicit responses tailored to his or her particular interests. The adage "straight from the horse's mouth" is as true for informing social researchers and pollsters as it is for handicapping the Kentucky Derby.

A rather simple yet realistic survey instrument designed to study smoking and drinking among high school students follows. The ultimate purpose is to understand not just the extent to which these students smoke cigarettes and drink alcohol, but the factors that explain why some students smoke or drink while others do not. Later in this book, we will apply statistical procedures to make sense of the survey results. But for now, it is useful to anticipate the kind of information that we can expect to analyze.

Suppose that this brief survey will be filled out by a group of 250 students, grades 9 through 12, in a hypothetical (but typical) urban high school. In this chapter, we introduced levels of measurement. Note that many of the variables in this survey are nominal—whether the respondent smokes or has consumed alcohol within the past month, as well as respondent characteristics such as race and sex. Other variables are measured at the ordinal level, specifically the extent of respondent's peer group involvement, his or her participation in sports/exercise, as well as academic performance. Finally, still other variables are measured at the interval level, in particular, daily consumption of cigarettes as well as age and grade in school.

To experience firsthand the way that data are collected, you may decide to distribute this survey or something similar on your own. But just like on those television cooking shows, for our purposes here, we will provide at the end of each part of the text, "precooked" statistical results to illustrate the power of these techniques in understanding behavior. As always, it is important not to get caught up in details, but to see the larger picture.

Student Survey

Please answer the following questions as honestly as possible. Do not place your name on the form so that your responses will remain completely private and anonymous.

1. What grade in school are you currently in? _____
2. How would you classify your academic performance? Are you
   an excellent, mostly "A's" student _____
   a good, mostly "B's" student _____
   an average, mostly "C's" student _____
   a below average, mostly "D's" student _____
3. Within the past month, have you smoked any cigarettes?
   Yes _____
   No _____
4. If you are a smoker, how many cigarettes do you tend to smoke on an average day?
   _____ per day
5. Within the past month, have you had any beer, wine, or hard liquor?
   Yes _____
   No _____
6. If you have had beer, wine, or hard liquor in the past month, on how many separate occasions?
   _____ times
7. In terms of your circle of friends, which of the following would best describe you?
   _____ I have lots of close friends
   _____ I have a few close friends
   _____ I have one close friend
   _____ I do not really have any close friends
8. Does either of your parents smoke?
   Yes _____
   No _____
9. To what extent do you participate in athletics or exercise?
   _____ Very frequently
   _____ Often
   _____ Seldom
   _____ Never
10. What is your current age? _____ years old
11. Are you: _____ Male _____ Female
12. How would you identify your race/ethnicity?
    White _____
    Black _____
    Latino _____
    Asian _____
    Other _____

Organizing the Data

Collecting data entails a serious effort on the part of criminologists and criminal justice researchers who seek to increase their knowledge of crime and criminal justice issues. To interview or otherwise elicit information from judges, drug addicts, gang members, police, lawyers, middle-class Americans, or other respondents requires a degree of foresight, careful planning, and control, if not actual time spent in the field.

Data collection, however, is only the beginning as far as statistical analysis is concerned. Data collection yields the raw materials that criminal justice researchers use to analyze data, obtain results, and test hypotheses about the nature of crime and justice issues.

FREQUENCY DISTRIBUTIONS OF NOMINAL DATA

The cabinetmaker transforms raw wood into furniture; the chef converts raw food into the more palatable versions served at the dinner table. Similarly, the criminal justice researcher—aided by "recipes" called *formulas* and *statistical techniques*—attempts to transform raw data into a meaningful and organized set of measures that can be used to test hypotheses.

What can researchers do to organize the jumble of raw numbers that they collect from their subjects? How do they go about transforming this mass of raw data into an easy-to-understand summary form? The first step is to construct a **frequency distribution** in the form of a table.

FREQUENCY DISTRIBUTION

A table containing the categories, score values, or class intervals and their frequency of occurrence.

Suppose a researcher who studies victimization is interested in how people think they would respond if they were faced with different crime situations. In one experiment, the researcher presents 50 adult men with written descriptions of a hypothetical scenario where a person is walking toward his car and finds that a man has broken the window and is attempting to steal the car. The respondents are asked to imagine themselves in the role of the hypothetical car owner and to indicate how they would react in such a situation.

A frequency distribution of nominal data reporting the responses of the 50 men is presented in Table 2.1. Notice first that the table is headed by a number and a title that gives the reader an idea of the nature of the data presented—responses of men to hypothetical auto theft. This is a standard arrangement; every table must be clearly titled and, when presented in a series, labeled by number as well.

Frequency distributions of nominal data consist of two columns. As in Table 2.1, the first column indicates which characteristic is being presented (response of person) and contains the categories of analysis (physically confront thief, verbally confront thief, shout for help and call the police). An adjacent column (headed *frequency*, or *f*) indicates the number of men in each category (10, 25, 5, and 10, respectively) as well as the total number of men (50), which can be indicated

TABLE 2.1	Response of Men to Hypothetical Auto Theft
Response	*f*
Physically confront thief	10
Verbally confront thief	25
Shout for help	5
Call the police	10
	N = 50

by either $N = 50$ or by including the word "Total" below the categories. A quick glance at the frequency distribution in Table 2.1 clearly reveals that more men believe that they would respond by either verbally or physically confronting the thief than by seeking help from the police or anyone else.

COMPARING DISTRIBUTIONS

Suppose next that the same researcher wishes to compare the responses of men and women to the hypothetical auto theft. Making comparisons between frequency distributions is a procedure often used to clarify results and add information. The particular comparison a researcher makes is determined by the question he or she seeks to answer.

In this example, the researcher decides to investigate gender differences. Are men more likely than women to seek help? To provide an answer, the researcher might present the same scenarios and questions to a group of 50 women and then compare the results. Let us imagine that the data shown in Table 2.2 are obtained. As shown in the table, 15 out of 50 men but only 35 of the 50 women said they would either shout for help or call the police.

PROPORTIONS AND PERCENTAGES

When a researcher studies distributions of equal size, the frequency data can be used to make comparisons between the groups. Thus, the numbers of men and women who would seek help can be directly compared because there are exactly 50 people of each gender in the study. In research, however, it is relatively rare to have distributions with exactly the same number of cases.

For more general use, we need a method of standardizing frequency distributions for size—a way to compare groups despite differences in total frequencies. Two of the most popular and useful methods of standardizing for size and comparing distributions are the proportion and the percentage.

The **proportion** compares the number of cases in a given category with the total size of the distribution. We can convert any frequency into a proportion P by dividing the number of cases in any given category f by the total number of cases in the distribution N:

PROPORTION

A method for standardizing for size that compares the number of cases in any given category with the total number of cases in the distribution.

$$P = \frac{f}{N}$$

TABLE 2.2	Response to Hypothetical Auto Theft by Gender	
	Gender	
Response	*Male*	*Female*
Physically confront thief	10	3
Verbally confront thief	25	12
Shout for help	5	10
Call the police	10	25
Total	50	50

TABLE 2.3	Gender of Students Majoring in Criminal Justice at Colleges A and B			
	Criminal Justice Major			
Gender of	**College A**		**College B**	
Student	*f*	%	*f*	%
Male	879	65	119	65
Female	473	35	64	35
Total	1352	100	183	100

Therefore, 35 out of 50 women who said they would seek help can be expressed as the following proportion:

$$P = \frac{35}{50} = .70$$

PERCENTAGE

A method of standardizing for size that indicates the frequency of occurrence of a category per 100 cases.

Despite the usefulness of the proportion, many people prefer to indicate the relative size of a series of numbers in terms of the **percentage**, the frequency of occurrence of a category per 100 cases. To calculate a percentage, we simply multiply any given proportion by 100. By formula,

$$\% = (100)\frac{f}{N}$$

Therefore, 35 out of 50 women who responded that they would seek help can be expressed as the proportion $p = \frac{35}{50} = .70$, or as a percentage $\% = (100)\left(\frac{35}{50}\right) = 70\%$. Thus, 70% of the women in the sample said they would either shout for help or call the police.

To illustrate the utility of percentages in making comparisons between large and unequal-sized distributions, let's examine the gender of criminal justice majors at two colleges where the criminal justice programs are of very different size. Suppose, for example, that College A has 1,352 criminal justice majors, while College B has only 183.

Table 2.3 indicates both the frequencies and the percentages for criminal justice majors at colleges A and B. Notice how difficult it is to quickly determine the gender differences among criminal justice majors from the frequency data alone. By contrast, the percentages clearly reveal that females were equally represented among criminal justice majors at Colleges A and B. Specifically, 35% of the criminal justice majors at College A are females, and 35% of the criminal justice majors at College B are females as well.

RATES

RATE

A kind of ratio that indicates a comparison between the number of actual cases and the number of potential cases.

Criminologists and criminal justice researchers often analyze populations regarding **rates** of crime, recidivism, incarceration, victimization, arrest, and conviction. Rates standardize for size by comparing the number of *actual* cases against the number of *potential* cases. For instance, to determine the recidivism rate (the rate at which offenders released from custody re-offend) for a given offender population, we might show the number of arrested persons in a population of people recently released from prison. Similarly, to ascertain the victimization rate, we might compare the number of crimes against the number of potential victims during a particular period (such as 1 year).

Rates are often given in terms of a base having 1,000 potential cases. Thus, victimization rates are sometimes presented as the number of crimes per 1,000 citizens who are potential victims. For example, the U.S. Department of Justice presents the rape and sexual assault rate as the number of such crimes per 1,000 females ages 12 and older. If 30 rapes occurred among 4,000 females ages 12 or older,

$$\text{Rape and sexual assault rate} = (1,000)\frac{f\text{ actual cases}}{f\text{ potential cases}} = (1,000)\left(\frac{30}{4,000}\right) = 7.5$$

It turns out there would be 7.5 rapes for every 1,000 females ages 12 or older.

There is nothing particularly special about calculating rates per potential case or per 1,000 potential cases. In fact, expressing rates per capita (i.e., per person), per 1,000, or even per million simply comes down to the decision of what would be the most convenient basis. For example, expenditures for prisons are usually expressed per inmate (as determined by average daily population of inmates in a particular prison, because prison populations can change from day to day due to factors such as transfers, releases, new commitments, and deaths). To calculate this rate, we divide the total expenditure in dollars by the average daily prison inmate population:

$$\text{Per capita (inmate) expenditure} = \frac{\text{prison expenditure}}{\text{average number of inmates}}$$

In contrast to the previous per capita rate, homicide rates are measured as the number of murders per 100,000 residents:

$$\text{Homicide rate} = (100,000)\left(\frac{\text{number of homicides}}{\text{population}}\right)$$

Suppose, for example, that a city has 121 homicides and a population of 586,500. Its homicide rate (HR) would then be

$$\begin{aligned} \text{HR} &= (100,000)\left(\frac{121}{586,500}\right) \\ &= (100,000)(0.000206) \\ &= 20.6 \end{aligned}$$

Thus, there are 20.6 homicides for every 100,000 residents.

It is important to note that we could have defined the rate as homicides per capita without multiplying the fraction (homicides over population) by the 100,000 scale factor. However, the rate of 0.000206 that would result, although correct, is very awkward because of its small size. So we magnify the rate to a more readable and digestible form by multiplying by 100,000 (moving the decimal point five places to the right), which then converts the per capita rate of 0.000206 to a per 100,000 rate of 20.6.

So far, we have discussed rates that make comparisons between different populations. For instance, we might seek to compare victimization rates between men and women, between middle-class and lower-class males, or among religious groups or entire nations. Another kind of rate, *rate of change*, can be used to compare the same population at two points in time. In computing rate of change, we compare the actual change between time period 1 and time period 2 with the level at time period 1 serving as a base. Thus, a state prison population that increases from 20,000 to 30,000 between 1990 and 2010 would experience the following rate of change:

$$(100)\left(\frac{\text{time }2f - \text{time }1f}{\text{time }1f}\right) = (100)\left(\frac{30,000 - 20,000}{20,000}\right) = 50\%$$

In other words, there was a population increase of 50% over the period 1990–2010.

Notice that a rate of change can be *negative* to indicate a decrease in size over any given period. For instance, if a population changes from 15,000 to 12,000 over a period of time, the rate of change would be

$$(100)\left(\frac{12,000 - 15,000}{15,000}\right) = -20\%$$

It should be noted that a very small number of cases (*f*) at time 1 can seriously mislead a researcher who employs rate of change to document increases and decreases over time. For example, an increase in homicides from six in 2011 to nine in 2012 would yield a rate of change equal to 50%, indicating an "alarming" 50% rise in the murders committed from 1 year to the next. Looking instead at the changing number (*f*) of homicides (only three more), it is clear that there is no cause for panic. The percentage change of 50% may be large, but the increase in the number of homicides is extremely small.

SIMPLE FREQUENCY DISTRIBUTIONS OF ORDINAL AND INTERVAL DATA

Any variable, regardless of measurement, can be displayed in a *simple frequency distribution,* a basic tally with frequencies and percentages of the values in the distribution. Because nominal data are labeled rather than graded or scaled, the categories of nominal-level distributions do not have to be listed in any particular order. Thus, the data on career preferences of criminal justice majors shown in Table 2.4 are presented in three different, yet equally acceptable arrangements. In contrast, the categories or score values in ordinal or interval distributions represent the degree to which a particular characteristic is present. The listing of such categories or score values in simple frequency distributions must reflect that order.

For this reason, ordinal and interval categories are always arranged in order, either from highest to lowest value or from lowest to highest value. For instance, we might list the categories of social class from upper to lower or post the results of a criminology midterm examination in consecutive order from the highest grade to the lowest grade. Disturbing the order of ordinal and interval categories reduces the readability of the researcher's findings. This effect can be seen in Table 2.5, where both the "incorrect" and "correct" versions of a distribution of attitudes among judges toward televised criminal trials have been presented. Which version do you find easier to follow?

TABLE 2.4   Distribution of Career Preferences Shown Three Ways

Career Preference	f	Career Preference	f	Career Preference	f
Law enforcement	45	Corrections	15	Social work	15
Law	25	Law	25	Corrections	15
Corrections	15	Law enforcement	45	Law enforcement	45
Social work	15	Social work	15	Law	25
Total	100	Total	100	Total	100

TABLE 2.5   A Frequency Distribution of Attitudes among Judges toward Televised Criminal Trials: Incorrect and Correct Presentations

Attitude toward Televised Trials	f	Attitude toward Televised Trials	f
Slightly favorable	9	Strongly favorable	10
Somewhat unfavorable	7	Somewhat favorable	21
Strongly favorable	10	Slightly favorable	9
Slightly unfavorable	6	Slightly unfavorable	6
Strongly unfavorable	12	Somewhat unfavorable	7
Somewhat favorable	21	Strongly unfavorable	12
Total	65	Total	65
INCORRECT		CORRECT	

GROUPED FREQUENCY DISTRIBUTIONS OF INTERVAL DATA

Interval-level values are sometimes spread over a wide range (highest to lowest values), making the resultant simple frequency distribution difficult to read. When such instances occur, few cases may fall at each score value, and the group pattern becomes blurred. Going back to an example from Chapter 1, the years on death row served by 71 Florida inmates prior to their execution are presented in Table 2.6 as a simple frequency distribution containing values from 2 to 30.

Presented in a simple frequency distribution, the data are a bit difficult to summarize and interpret because of the large number of different values. To clarify our presentation further, we might construct a **grouped frequency distribution** by condensing the separate scores into a number of smaller categories or groups, each containing more than one value. Each category or group in a grouped distribution is known as a **class interval**, the size of which is determined by the number of values it contains. As shown in Table 2.7, by grouping the data, we now have only six class intervals, each having a size of five. Thus, the lowest class interval (1–5) contains the five values 1, 2, 3, 4, and 5. Similarly, the interval 6–10 is of size five and contains the values 6, 7, 8, 9, and 10.

The grouped frequency distribution in Table 2.7 also contains a column labeled f (for frequency) that indicates the number of cases in each of the categories. Thus, for example, the class interval 6–10 spans five values (6, 7, 8, 9 and 10) and includes the years on death row for 21 inmates who spent between 6 and 10 years imprisoned on death row before being executed.

The more meaningful column, particularly if comparisons to other distributions are to be made (e.g., if we were comparing years on death row between two states or among inmates of

GROUPED FREQUENCY DISTRIBUTION

A table that indicates the frequency of occurrence of cases located within a series of class intervals.

CLASS INTERVAL

A category in a group distribution containing more than one score value.

TABLE 2.6	Simple Frequency Distribution of Years on Death Row for 71 Executed Inmates
Years	***f***
2	1
3	1
4	2
5	1
6	2
7	6
8	1
9	7
10	5
11	5
12	3
13	6
14	11
15	3
16	3
17	2
18	1
20	1
21	2
22	2
23	2
24	1
25	1
26	1
30	1
Total	71

TABLE 2.7	Grouped Frequency Distribution of Years on Death Row for 71 Executed Inmates	
Years on death row	**f**	**%**
1–5	5	7.0
6–10	21	29.6
11–15	28	39.4
16–20	7	9.9
21–25	8	11.3
26–30	2	2.8
Total	71	100.0

PERCENTAGE DISTRIBUTION

The relative frequency of occurrence of a set of scores or class intervals out of 100%.

different races) is the percentage column (%). This column is often called the **percentage distribution**. It represents the percentage of the cases that falls within a particular class interval, found by dividing the frequency of that interval (*f*) by the total number of cases (*N*), and then multiplying by 100. The percentage distribution sums to 100%.

The Midpoint

MIDPOINT

The middle-most score value in a class interval.

Another characteristic of any class interval is its **midpoint** (*m*), which we define as the middle-most score value in the class interval. A quick-and-simple method of finding a midpoint is to look for the point at which any given interval can be divided into two equal parts. From Table 2.7, for example, 3 is the midpoint of the interval 1–5, and 8 is the midpoint of the interval 6–10. The midpoint can also be computed from the lowest and highest score values in any interval. To illustrate, the midpoint of the interval 11–15 is

$$m = \frac{\text{lowest score value} + \text{highest score value}}{2}$$

$$= \frac{11 + 15}{2} = \frac{26}{2} = 13$$

In a sense, the midpoint can be regarded as the spokesperson for all score values in a class interval. It is a single number that can be used to represent the entire class interval.

Guidelines for Constructing Class Intervals

Constructing class intervals is just a special way of categorizing data. As discussed earlier, categories, and thus class intervals, must be mutually exclusive (nonoverlapping) and exhaustive (a place for every case).

Beginning students generally find it difficult to construct class intervals on their own. Indeed, it is a skill that develops only with practice. However, there are some general guidelines that make the task easier. Note that these are only guidelines, which, under certain circumstances, can be violated.

To present interval data in a grouped frequency distribution, the criminal justice researcher must consider the number of categories he or she wishes to employ. Texts generally advise using as few as 3 or 4 intervals to as many as 20 intervals. In this regard, it would be wise to remember that grouped frequency distributions are employed to reveal or emphasize a group pattern. Either too many or too few class intervals may blur that pattern and thereby work against the researcher who seeks to add clarity to the analysis. In addition, reducing the individual score values to an unnecessarily small number of intervals may sacrifice too much precision—precision that was originally attained by knowing the identity of individual scores in the distribution. In sum, then, the researcher generally makes a decision as to the number of intervals based on the set of data and personal objectives, factors that may vary considerably from one research situation to another.

After deciding on the number of class intervals, a researcher must then begin constructing the intervals themselves. Two basic guidelines help make this task easier and should be followed whenever possible. First, it is preferable to make the size of class intervals a whole number rather than a decimal. This tends to simplify calculations in which size is involved. Second, it is conventional to make the lowest score in a class interval some multiple of its size. Customarily, for example, exam scores are categorized as 90–99, 80–89, and so on, so that the lowest scores (e.g, 80 and 90) are multiples of 10.

CUMULATIVE DISTRIBUTIONS

It is sometimes desirable to present frequencies in a cumulative fashion, especially when locating the position of one case relative to overall group performance. **Cumulative frequencies** (cf) are defined as the total number of cases having any given score *or a score that is lower*. Thus, the cumulative frequency cf for any category (or class interval) is obtained by adding the frequency in that category to the total frequency for all categories below it.

CUMULATIVE FREQUENCY

The total number of cases having any given score or a score that is lower.

In the case of the police officer entrance exam scores in Table 2.8, we see that the frequency f associated with the class interval 50–54 is 8. This is also the cumulative frequency for this interval, because no applicant scored below 50. The frequency in the next class interval 55–59 is 10, and the cumulative frequency for this interval is $8 + 10 = 18$. Thus, we learn that 10 applicants received entrance exam scores between 55 and 59, but that 18 applicants earned scores of 59 *or lower*. We might continue this procedure, obtaining cumulative frequencies for all class intervals, until we arrive at the topmost entry 95–99, whose cumulative frequency (142) is equal to the total number of cases, because no applicant scored above 99.

In addition to cumulative frequency, we can also construct a distribution that indicates **cumulative percentage** ($c\%$), the percentage of cases that fall in any particular category or have a score that is lower. To calculate the cumulative percentage, we modify the formula for percentage (%) introduced earlier in this chapter as follows:

CUMULATIVE PERCENTAGE

The percentage of cases having any score or a score that is lower.

$$c\% = (100)\frac{cf}{N}$$

where cf = cumulative frequency in any category

        N = total number of cases in the distribution

TABLE 2.8	Cumulative Frequency (cf) Distribution of Police Officer Entrance Exam Scores for 142 Applicants		
Class Interval	*f*	**%**	*cf*
95–99	6	4.23	142
90–94	4	2.82	136
85–89	8	5.63	132
80–84	14	9.86	124
75–79	24	16.90	110
70–74	34	23.94	86
65–69	24	16.90	52
60–64	10	7.04	28
55–59	10	7.04	18
50–54	8	5.63	8
Total	142	100	

Note: The percentages as they appear add to 99.99%. We write the sum as 100% instead, because we know that 0.01% was lost in rounding.

Applying the foregoing formula to the data in Table 2.8, we find that the percentage of applicants who scored 54 or lower was

$$c\% = (100)\left(\frac{8}{142}\right)$$
$$= (100)(0.0563)$$
$$= 5.63$$

The percentage who scored 59 or lower was

$$c\% = (100)\left(\frac{18}{142}\right)$$
$$= (100)(0.1267)$$
$$= 12.67$$

Moving up to the class interval 75–79, we see that the percentage who scored 79 or lower was

$$c\% = (100)\left(\frac{110}{142}\right)$$
$$= (100)(0.7745)$$
$$= 77.45$$

If the cutoff point for passing the police officer entrance exam was a score of 80, then we know that more than 77% of all applicants failed to make the grade because they scored 79 or lower.

A cumulative percentage distribution based on the data in Table 2.8 is shown in Table 2.9. Note that the $c\%$ can also be obtained by summing the percentage (%) distribution. There may be tiny differences in the results obtained by the two approaches merely because of small differences in rounding.

Dealing with Decimal Data

Not all data come in the form of whole numbers. This should not disturb us in the least, however, because the procedures we have learned and will learn in later chapters apply to decimals as well as whole numbers. So that we get used to decimal data from the start, let's consider constructing a frequency distribution of the state data on murder and nonnegligent manslaughter shown in Table 2.10 (rates are shown in crimes per 100,000 population). From the raw scores, we do not

TABLE 2.9	Cumulative Percentage (c%) Distribution of Police Officer Entrance Exam Scores for 142 Applicants			
Class Interval	**f**	**%**	**cf**	**c%**
95–99	6	4.23	142	100.00
90–94	4	2.82	136	95.76
85–89	8	5.63	132	92.94
80–84	14	9.86	124	87.31
75–79	24	16.90	110	77.45
70–74	34	23.94	86	60.55
65–69	24	16.90	52	36.61
60–64	10	7.04	28	19.71
55–59	10	7.04	18	12.67
50–54	8	5.63	8	5.63
Total	142	100		

Note: The percentages as they appear add to 99.99%. We write the sum as 100% instead, because we know that 0.01% was lost in rounding.

TABLE 2.10	State Homicide Rates—2010		
State	**Rate**	**State**	**Rate**
Alabama	5.7	Montana	2.6
Alaska	4.4	Nebraska	3.0
Arizona	6.4	Nevada	5.9
Arkansas	4.7	New Hampshire	1.0
California	4.9	New Jersey	4.2
Colorado	2.4	New Mexico	6.9
Connecticut	3.6	New York	4.5
Delaware	5.3	North Carolina	5.0
Florida	5.2	North Dakota	1.5
Georgia	5.8	Ohio	4.1
Hawaii	1.8	Oklahoma	5.2
Idaho	1.3	Oregon	2.4
Illinois	5.5	Pennsylvania	5.2
Indiana	4.5	Rhode Island	2.8
Iowa	1.3	South Carolina	6.1
Kansas	3.5	South Dakota	2.8
Kentucky	4.3	Tennessee	5.6
Louisiana	11.2	Texas	5.0
Maine	1.8	Utah	1.9
Maryland	7.4	Vermont	1.1
Massachusetts	3.2	Virginia	4.6
Michigan	5.7	Washington	2.3
Minnesota	1.8	West Virginia	3.3
Mississippi	7.0	Wisconsin	2.7
Missouri	7.0	Wyoming	1.4

get a very clear picture of nationwide patterns of murder. We are drawn to the extremes: The numbers range from a high of 11.2 in Louisiana to a low of 1.0 in New Hampshire. Little else emerges until we construct a grouped frequency distribution.

Because there are only 50 cases, we would not want too many categories. An excessive number of class intervals would spread the cases too thinly. Determining the actual limits of the class intervals is the most difficult part of all. Satisfactory results come with a great deal of trial and error as well as practice. There is no "right" setup of class intervals, but those in Table 2.11 might be a place to start.

Once we have the skeleton for the frequency distribution (its class intervals and the frequencies), the rest is fairly straightforward. Percentages, cumulative frequencies, and cumulative percentages are obtained in the usual way. For other calculations such as midpoints, however,

TABLE 2.11	Frequency Distribution of State Homicide Rates—2010 (Six Categories)
Class Interval	**f**
10.0–11.9	1
8.0–9.9	0
6.0–7.9	6
4.0–5.9	21
2.0–3.9	12
0.0–1.9	10
Total	50

TABLE 2.12	Frequency Distribution of State Homicide Rates—2010 (Four Categories)
Class Interval	**f**
6.0 and over	7
4.0–5.9	21
2.0–3.9	12
0.0–1.9	10
Total	50

bear in mind that these data are expressed with one decimal digit. As a consequence, this digit is important in determining the interval size or the range of score values spanned by a class interval. For example, the size of the 4.0–5.9 interval is 2.0, because it contains the score values 4.0 through 5.9 inclusive. There are actually 20 score values between 5.0 and 6.9 (5.0, 5.1, 5.2, etc.), each one-tenth apart, so the size is $(20)(1/10) = 2.0$.

Flexible Class Intervals

Although we did not make a point of it earlier, you may have noticed that all the frequency distributions used so far have had class intervals of equal size. There are occasions, however, in which this practice is not at all desirable. The distribution of state homicide data is one such case. It seems unnecessary to have a separate class interval for just two observations. We can, however, combine or collapse the two upper categories into a top class with an open upper boundary, that is, 6.0 and over. This slightly modified distribution is shown in Table 2.12.

Grouped frequency distributions can have open-ended top or bottom class intervals. The other major departure from the simple distributions provided earlier is the use of class intervals of varying size. For example, Table 2.13 presents a distribution of census data on household income for 2010, which is typical of distributions constructed with income data. Note that the class interval containing the lowest incomes have a size of $15,000 and then the next two class intervals have size $10,000. In contrast, the size of the class intervals is stretched to $50,000 for higher-income levels. What would have been the result had a fixed class interval size of $10,000 been maintained throughout the distribution? The $150,000–$199,999 class interval, for example, would have become subdivided into five categories: $150,000–$159,999, $160,000–$169,999, and so on. The effect would be to make unnecessarily fine distinctions among the families with higher income and to produce a needlessly lengthy frequency distribution. That is, in terms of standard of living, there is a big difference between the $15,000–$24,999 and the

TABLE 2.13	Household Income in the United States—2010	
Income Category	**Families (in 1,000s)**	**%**
Under $15,000	16,243	13.7
$15,000–$24,999	14,228	12.0
$25,000–$34,999	12,923	10.9
$35,000–$49,999	16,480	13.9
$50,000–$74,000	20,986	17.7
$75,000–$99,999	13,516	11.4
$100,000–$149,999	14,346	12.1
$150,000–$199,999	5,335	4.5
$200,000 and over	4,624	3.9
Total	118,682	100.0

$25,000–$34,999 class interval. In contrast, the difference between a $170,000–$179,999 category and a $180,000–$189,999 category would be relatively unimportant.

These new twists in frequency distributions should not cause you much difficulty in adapting what you have already learned in this chapter. Fortunately, the computations of cumulative distributions and the like do not change for frequency distributions with class intervals of unequal size or with unbounded top or bottom class intervals.

Cross-Tabulations

Frequency distributions such as those discussed so far are seen everywhere. Census Bureau publications consistently employ frequency distributions to describe characteristics of the U.S. population; presentation of the raw data—all the millions of observations—would be impossible.

We even see frequency distributions in daily newspapers; journalists, like criminal justice researchers, find tables a very convenient form of presentation. Most newspaper readers are capable of understanding basic percentages (even though they may forget how to compute them). A basic table of frequencies and percentages for some variable is usually sufficient for the level of depth and detail typically found in a newspaper. Researchers, however, want to do more than just describe the distribution of some variable; they seek to explain why some individuals fall at one end of the distribution while others are at the opposite extreme.

To accomplish this objective, we need to explore tables more deeply by expanding them into two and even more dimensions. In particular, a **cross-tabulation** (or cross-tab for short) is a table that presents the distribution—frequencies and percentages—of one variable (usually the dependent variable) across the categories of one or more additional variables (usually the independent variable or variables).

CROSS-TABULATION

A frequency and percentage table of two or more variables taken together.

Let's suppose we are interested in examining sex differences in the victim–offender relationships in homicide cases. First, we should look at the overall distribution of the victim–offender relationship for the 14,747 homicide victims in the United States in 2010, as shown in Table 2.14. The intimate category includes spouses and ex-spouses as well as boyfriends and girlfriends; the family category includes all family relationships other than spouse; acquaintance includes friends (other than boyfriends/girlfriends), neighbors, coworkers, and other perpetrators known but not related to the victim; and the stranger category includes all cases in which the victim and perpetrator have no prior association.

The simple frequency distribution shows that altogether more than one-quarter of murder victims were killed by someone close to them—13.4% by intimate partners and 13.0% by other family members. Nearly half (48.7%) were killed by acquaintances, and exactly one-quarter (25.0%) were killed by strangers. Constructing a simple frequency distribution is just the beginning of the analytic journey, however. We want to learn, for example, which victims are killed by strangers as opposed to relatives—in general, which variables influence victim–offender relationships in murder cases.

We can employ a cross-tabulation to look at differences between male and female victims in terms of their relationships to their killers. That is, we can construct a frequency distribution of two variables taken simultaneously. The cross-tabulation given in Table 2.15 shows, for

TABLE 2.14	Frequency Distribution of Victim–Offender Relationship in U.S. Homicides—2010	
Relationship	***f***	**%**
Intimate	1,969	13.4
Family	1,915	13.0
Acquaintance	7,180	48.7
Stranger	3,683	25.0
Total	14,747	100.0

TABLE 2.15	Cross-Tabulation of Victim–Offender Relationship by Victim Sex in U.S. Homicides—2010		
	Victim sex		
Relationship	*Male*	*Female*	**Total**
Intimate	496	1,473	1,969
Family	1,309	606	1,915
Acquaintance	6,273	907	7,180
Stranger	3,334	349	3,683
Total	11,412	3,335	14,747

example, that 496 men and 1,473 women were killed by their intimate partners. Also, 1,309 males and 606 females were slain by family members (other than spouses). Next, we see that 6,273 males but only 907 females were killed by friends or acquaintances. Finally, the most disparate results involve murders by strangers, where 3,334 men but as few as 349 women were murdered by someone they did not know.

The foundation for cross-tabulations was presented earlier in the chapter when the gender distributions of engineering majors across two colleges were compared. Cross tabulations can be thought of as a series of frequency distributions (in this case two of them) attached together to make one table. In this example, we have essentially a frequency distribution of victim–offender relationship among male victims juxtaposed with a comparable frequency distribution of victim–offender relationship for female victims.

As with one variable frequency distributions, percentages give the results in a cross tabulation fuller meaning than frequencies alone. If we retain the same procedure as before, that is dividing each frequency (*f*) by the sample size (*N*),

$$\% = (100)\frac{f}{N}$$

we obtain the percentage results for the two variables jointly, shown in Table 2.16. For example, the percentage of homicides involving a female murdered by her intimate partner is obtained

TABLE 2.16	Cross-Tabulation of Victim–Offender Relationship by Victim Sex (with Total Percents) in U.S. Homicides—2010		
	Victim sex		
Relationship	*Male*	*Female*	**Total**
Intimate	496	1,473	1,969
	3.4%	10.0%	13.4% ← Row marginal (row totals)
Family	1,309	606	1,915
	8.9%	4.1%	13.0%
Acquaintance	6,273	907	7,180
	42.5%	6.2%	48.7%
Stranger	3,334	349	3,683
	22.6%	2.4%	25.0%
Total	11,412	3,335	14,747 ← Total sample size
	77.4%	22.6%	100.0%

Column marginal (column totals)

from dividing the number of women killed by their husband, ex-husband, or boyfriend by the total number of murders overall,

$$(100)\frac{1{,}473}{14{,}747} = 10.0\%$$

Thus, relatively few homicides involve women killed by their intimate partners. By contrast, nearly half of the homicides involve men killed by acquaintances, specifically,

$$(100)\frac{6{,}273}{14{,}747} = 42.5\%$$

These calculations pertain to percentages of two variables jointly—for example, female victims and intimate-partner relationship as well as male victims and acquaintance relationship. The frequency distribution of each variable separately can be found along the margins of the cross-tabulation. These are called **marginal distributions**. That is, the right margin of the table provides a frequency and percentage distribution for victim–offender relationship identical to what we had in Table 2.15. Because the victim–offender relationship variable is placed along the rows of the cross-tabulation, the frequencies and percentages for this variable form the row totals. Likewise, the marginal distribution for sex is found in the bottom margin of the cross-tabulation. These frequencies and percentages for male and female murderers are the column totals, because sex is the variable heading the columns.

The percentages in Table 2.16 are called **total percents** (total %) because they are obtained by dividing each frequency by the total number of cases:

$$\boxed{total\% = (100)\frac{f}{N_{total}}}$$

For instance, 3.4% of the incidents involved a male killed by his intimate partner and 6.2% involved a female killed by a friend or acquaintance.

There is, however, something rather unsettling or ambiguous about these total percents. For example, the small percentage of cases involving males killed by their intimate partners (3.7%) could reflect a low representation of males among victims, a low percentage of intimates among murder victims generally, or a low tendency for male victims to be targeted by their intimate partners.

Other approaches to calculating percentages might resolve this ambiguity and might give a clearer picture of the connection between victim–offender relationship and sex of victim. One alternative would be to divide the number of males killed by their intimate partners by the total number of intimate partner murders, the number of males killed at the hands of family members by the total number of family murders, and so on, and then perform comparable calculations for female victims. In other words, we divide the frequencies in each row by the number of cases in that row (see Table 2.17). These are called **row percents:**

$$\boxed{row\% = (100)\frac{f}{N_{row}}}$$

For example, the percentage of females among intimate-partner victims is 74.8%, nearly three-quarters of such cases. This is obtained by dividing the number of females killed by intimate-partners as follows:

$$(100)\frac{1{,}473}{1{,}969} = 74.8\%$$

As shown in Table 2.17, females represent about a third of those killed by other family members—31.6% to be exact. By contrast, females are rarely targeted in stranger murders, representing only 9.5% of the victims of these crimes. Finally, we also see in the column margin that nearly 8 out of 10, that is, 77.4%, of all murder victims are male, and 22.6% are female.

MARGINAL DISTRIBUTION

In a cross-tabulation, the set of frequencies and percentages found in the margin that represents the distribution of one of the variables in the table.

TOTAL PERCENT

In a cross-tabulation, the result of dividing a cell frequency by the total number of cases in the sample. Total percents sum to 100% for the entire cross-tabulation.

ROW PERCENT

In a cross-tabulation, the result of dividing a cell frequency by the number of cases in the row. Row percents sum to 100% for each row of a cross-tabulation.

TABLE 2.17	Cross-Tabulation of Victim–Offender Relationship by Victim Sex (with Row Percents) in U.S. Homicides—2010		
	Victim sex		
Relationship	*Male*	*Female*	**Total**
Intimate	496	1,473	1,969
	25.2%	74.8%	100.0%
Family	1,309	606	1,915
	68.4%	31.6%	100.0%
Acquaintance	6,273	907	7,180
	87.4%	12.6%	100.0%
Stranger	3,334	349	3,683
	90.5%	9.5%	100.0%
Total	11,412	3,335	14,747
	77.4%	22.6%	100.0%

Row percents give the distribution of the column variable for each value of the row variable. Row percents represent the victim sex distribution within each type of victim–offender relationship. Also, row percents sum to 100% across the rows, including the column marginals in the bottom of the cross-tabulation. Conversely, one could calculate percentages in the opposite direction—along the columns rather than the rows. **Column percents** (column %) are obtained by dividing each frequency by the number of cases in that column:

COLUMN PERCENT

In a cross-tabulation, the result of dividing a cell frequency by the number of cases in the column. Column percents sum to 100% for each column of a cross-tabulation.

$$column\% = (100)\frac{f}{N_{column}}$$

The percentage of male victims who were killed by intimate partners is obtained, for example, by dividing the number of males killed by intimates by the number of male victims overall:

$$(100)\frac{496}{11,412} = 4.3\%$$

Therefore, a rather small percentage of the male victims (4.3%) were murdered by their intimate partners.

The column percents are presented in Table 2.18. By contrast to the small percentage of male victims targeted by an intimate partner (4.3%), as many as 44.2% of female victims were killed by their intimate partners. Thus, female murder victims were about 10 times more likely than male victims to have been killed by an intimate partner. A difference not quite so pronounced, female victims were almost twice as likely as male victims to have been killed by a family member: 18.2% for female victims and 11.5% for male victims. These tendencies reverse dramatically in acquaintance and stranger killings. While 55.0% of male victims were slain by friends or acquaintances, 27.2% of female victims were slain by friends or acquaintances. In addition, 29.2% of male victims were killed by strangers, but only 10.5% of female victims were killed by someone they did not know. Finally, the percentages sum to 100% down each column, as well as in the right-hand margin. Thus, the column percents represent the victim–offender relationship distribution for males and females separately.

CHOOSING AMONG TOTAL, ROW, AND COLUMN PERCENT We now have three sets of percentages—total, row, and column percents. You might wonder which is correct. In a mathematical sense, all are correct; that is, these were calculated in the correct way. But in terms of substantive meaning, certain percentages may be misleading or even useless. First, as we noted previously, the total percents are sometimes ambiguous in their meaning, as in our cross-tabulation of victim–offender relationship by victim sex.

| **TABLE 2.18** | Cross-Tabulation of Victim–Offender Relationship by Victim Sex (with Column Percents) in U.S. Homicides—2010 |

	Victim sex		
Relationship	*Male*	*Female*	**Total**
Intimate	496	1,473	1,969
	4.3%	44.2%	13.4%
Family	1,309	606	1,915
	11.5%	18.2%	13.0%
Acquaintance	6,273	907	7,180
	55.0%	27.2%	48.7%
Stranger	3,334	349	3,683
	29.2%	10.5%	25.0%
Total	11,412	3,335	14,747
	100.0%	100.0%	100.0%

The choice between row and column percents essentially comes down to which is more relevant to the purpose of the analysis. If we want to know the sex-of-victim breakdown of various types of homicide (intimate-partner homicide, family murder, acquaintance homicide, or stranger killings), we would compare row percents. We would conclude that while men predominate among murder victims, they do so especially as the victim–offender relationship grows distant. On the other hand, if we want to compare male and female victims, we would focus on the column percents. We would conclude that both males and females are often killed by friends/acquaintances. Beyond that, females have a greater tendency to be targeted by intimates or family members, while men tend to be killed by strangers more than intimates or family members.

Fortunately, there is a rule of thumb to guide our choice between row and column percents: *If the independent variable is on the rows, use row percents; if the independent variable is on the column, use column percents.* In our example, we would likely be more interested in the effect of sex of victim on victim–offender relationship and therefore focus on column percents (since sex of victim, the independent variable, is given on the columns). Another way of stating this rule may be more meaningful: If we wish to compare rows in a cross-tabulation, we need to use row percents; column percents are required for comparing columns. Again, in our example, we want to compare the males to the females in terms of victim–offender relationship. Sex is the column variable, and the column percents provide distributions of victim–offender relationship for males and females separately. Thus, these column percents should be used for making the comparison between males and females.

In certain cases, it may not be easy to tell which is the independent variable. For example, in the cross-tabulation of husbands' and wives' illegal drug use history (Table 2.19), neither variable can clearly be said to be the result of the other. (Note: The figures in each cell of the table represent frequency, row percent, column percent, and total percent, respectively.) To some extent, the drug use of husband and wife may affect each other reciprocally, and in many cases, it may have occurred long before the couple ever met. Similarly, involvement in drug use may have been part of the attraction. With the data in Table 2.19, we could compute the percentage of husbands and wives who have both used illegal drugs (70 out of 100, row% = 70.0%), or we could compute the percentage of wives who have used drugs and who are married to husbands who have also used drugs (70 out of 110, column% = 63.6%). Both would be meaningful depending on the researcher's particular interest. However, for cases like this in which there is no one variable that can be singled out as the cause of the other, total percents (which implicate neither one as being the independent variable) are frequently used. For Table 2.19, in 36.8% of the marriages, both partners have used illegal drugs at some point in their lives (70 out of 190).

TABLE 2.19	Cross-Tabulation of Husband's Illegal Drug Use by Wife's Illegal Drug Use: Frequency and Row, Column, and Total Percentages		
Frequency Row % Column % Total %	**Wife Has Ever Used Illegal Drugs**		
	Yes	*No*	**Total**
Husband Has Ever Used Illegal Drugs			
Yes	70 70.0% 63.6% 36.8%	30 30.0% 37.5% 15.8%	100 52.6%
No	40 44.4% 36.4% 21.1%	50 55.6% 62.5% 26.3%	90 47.4%
Total	110 57.9%	80 42.1%	190 100.0%

GRAPHIC PRESENTATIONS

Columns of numbers have been known to evoke fear, anxiety, boredom, apathy, and misunderstanding. Although some people seem to tune out statistical information presented in tabular form, they may pay close attention to the same data presented in graphic or picture form. As a result, many commercial researchers and popular authors prefer to use graphs as opposed to tables. For similar reasons, criminal justice researchers often use visual aids such as pie charts, bar graphs, histograms frequency polygons, line charts, and maps in an effort to increase the readability of their findings.

Pie Charts

PIE CHART

A circular graph whose pieces add up to 100%.

The **pie chart**, a circular graph whose pieces add up to 100%, is one of the simplest methods of graphical presentation. Pie charts are particularly useful for showing the differences in

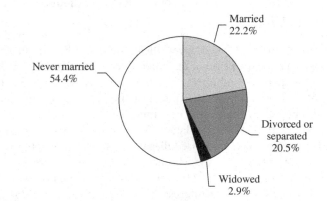

FIGURE 2.1   Pie Chart of Marital Status of Prisoners Sentenced to Death—2005.   *Source:* U.S. Department of Justice, Bureau of Justice Statistics, *Capital Punishment—2005.* Bulletin NCJ 215083 Washington, DC.

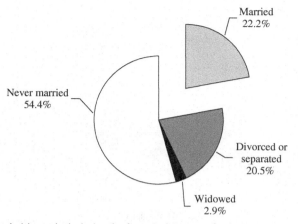

FIGURE 2.2 Pie Chart (with exploded piece) of Marital Status of Prisoners Sentenced to Death—2005. *Source:* U.S. Department of Justice, Bureau of Justice Statistics, *Capital Punishment—2005*. Bulletin NCJ 215083. Washington, DC.

frequencies or percentages among categories of a nominal-level variable. To illustrate, Figure 2.1 presents the distribution of marital status of prisoners under sentences of death in the United States as of the last day of 2005. Notice that 54.4% were single (never married), 22.2% were married, 20.5% were divorced or separated, and 2.9% were widowed.

In many instances, a researcher may want to direct attention to one particular category in a pie chart. In this case, a researcher may wish to highlight the married group. To highlight this aspect of the pie chart, we can "explode" (move slightly outward) the section of the pie that is most noteworthy, as in Figure 2.2.

Bar Graphs and Histograms

The pie chart provides a quick and easy illustration of data that can be divided into a few categories only. (In fact, some computer graphics software packages limit the number of possible pie sections.) By comparison, the **bar graph** and **histogram** can accommodate any number of categories at any level of measurement and, therefore, are far more widely used in criminal justice research.

Figure 2.3 illustrates a bar graph of the percentage distribution of victim–offender relationship for U.S. homicides in 2010, presented in Table 2.14. The bar graph is constructed following

BAR GRAPH AND HISTOGRAM

Graphic methods in which rectangular bars indicate the frequencies for the range of score values or categories.

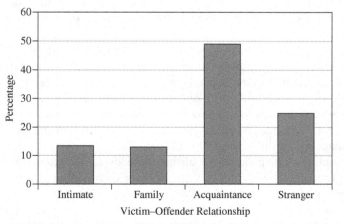

FIGURE 2.3 Bar Graph of Victim–Offender Relationship in 2010 Homicides.

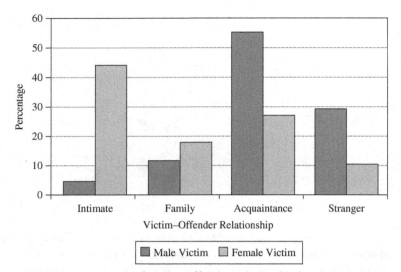

FIGURE 2.4 Bar Graph of Victim–Offender Relationship by Victim Sex in 2010 Homicides.

a standard arrangement: A horizontal base line (or *x*-axis) along which the score values or categories (in this case, the categories of victim–offender relationship) are displayed, and a vertical line (*y*-axis) along the left side of the figure that provides the percentages (or frequencies) for each score value or category. (For grouped data, either the midpoints of the class intervals or the interval ranges themselves are arranged along the base line.) As we see in Figure 2.3, the taller the bar, the greater the percentage for that category.

In addition to portraying a frequency or percentage distribution of some variable, bar graphs can display the effect of one variable on another. For example, Figure 2.4 shows the distribution of victim–offender relationship for U.S homicides in 2010 broken down by sex of the victim, using the percentages from Table 2.18. From the chart, the sex differences in victim–offender relationship become crystal clear.

The applications of bar graphs in criminal justice are virtually limitless. Not only can one- and two-variable distributions be displayed, but so can various tabulations of rates. For example, we might display the rate of gun homicide for various cities by using a bar graph with the heights of the bars reflecting the respective rates of gun homicide per 100,000 population. Graphic designers can sometimes get quite imaginative by replacing rectangular bars of varying heights with a series of firearm symbols whereby each gun represents a specified number of victims. If the purpose is to make an impression, such features often do so in a dramatic way.

The terms *bar graph* and *histogram* are often used interchangeably, although there is a simple but important difference between the two graphical techniques. Bar graphs are typically used to display the frequency or percentage distribution of a discrete variable, especially at the nominal level. Because of the lack of continuity from category to category, a bar graph includes space between the bars to emphasize differentness rather than continuity along a scale. Histograms, by contrast, are used to display continuous measures; the bars of the histogram are joined to emphasize continuity of the points along a scale.

These examples will help clarify the distinction between bar graphs and histograms. The bar graph in Figure 2.5 has space between the bars for each college major (science, business, humanities, social science, engineering, health, and undecided) because the appearance of continuity would be completely misleading. By contrast, as shown in Figure 2.6, the variable grade point average represents a real continuum and therefore a histogram with no separation between categories would be appropriate.

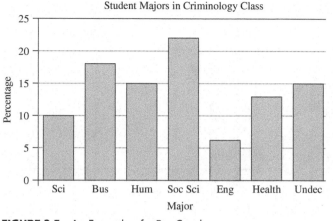

FIGURE 2.5 An Example of a Bar Graph.

Frequency Polygons

Another commonly employed graphic method is the frequency polygon. Although the frequency polygon can accommodate a wide variety of categories, it tends to stress continuity along a scale rather than differentness; therefore, it is particularly useful for depicting ordinal and interval data. This is because frequencies (or percentages) are indicated by a series of points placed over the score values or midpoints of each class interval. Adjacent points are connected with a straight line, which is dropped to the baseline at either end. The height of each point or dot indicates frequency of occurrence.

Recall the distribution of examination scores for a group of 142 police recruits presented in Table 2.8. Figure 2.7 provides a **frequency polygon** for this distribution. Note that the frequencies of the class intervals are plotted above their midpoints; the points are connected by straight lines, which are dropped to the horizontal baseline at both ends, forming a polygon. To graph cumulative frequencies (or cumulative percentages), it is possible to construct a cumulative frequency polygon.

The Shape of a Frequency Distribution

Frequency polygons can help us visualize the variety of shapes and forms taken by frequency distributions. Some distributions are *symmetrical*—folding the curve at the center creates two identical halves. Therefore, such distributions contain the same number of extreme score values

FREQUENCY POLYGON

A graphic method in which frequencies are indicated by a series of points placed over the score values or midpoints of each class interval and connected with a straight line that is dropped to the baseline at either end.

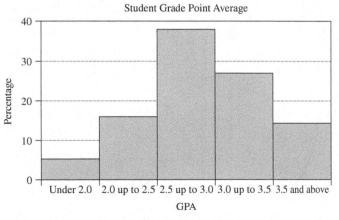

FIGURE 2.6 An Example of a Histogram.

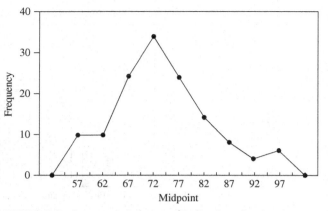

FIGURE 2.7   Frequency Polygon of Police Examination Scores.

in both directions, high and low. Other distributions are said to be *skewed* and have more extreme cases in one direction than the other.

There is considerable variation among symmetrical distributions. For instance, they can differ markedly in terms of peakedness or **kurtosis**. Some symmetrical distributions, as in Figure 2.8(a), are quite peaked or tall, called **leptokurtic**; others, as in Figure 2.8(b), are rather flat, called **platykurtic**; still others are neither very peaked nor very flat, called **mesokurtic**. One kind of mesokurtic symmetrical distribution, as shown in Figure 2.8(c), the **normal curve**, has special significance for criminal justice research and will be discussed in some detail in Chapter 5.

There is a variety of skewed or asymmetrical distributions. When skewness exists so that scores pile up in one direction, the distribution will have a pronounced "tail." The position of this tail indicates where the relatively few extreme scores are located and determines the *direction* of **skewness**.

The distribution in Figure 2.9(a) is **negatively skewed** (skewed to the left), because it has a much longer tail on the left than the right. This distribution shows that most cases had high scores, but only a few had low scores. If this were the distribution of grades on a final examination, we could say that most students did quite well and a few did poorly.

Next, look at the distribution given in Figure 2.9(b), whose tail is situated to the right. Because skewness is indicated by the direction of the elongated tail, we can say that the distribution is **positively skewed** (skewed to the right). The final examination grades for the students in this hypothetical classroom would be quite low, except for a few who did well.

Finally, let us examine the distribution given in Figure 2.9(c), which contains two identical tails. In such a case, there are same number of extreme scores in both directions. The distribution is not at all skewed but is perfectly symmetrical. If this were the distribution of grades on the final examination, we would have a large number of more or less average students and few students receiving very high or very low grades.

KURTOSIS

The peakedness of a distribution.

LEPTOKURTIC

Characteristic of a distribution that is quite peaked or tall.

PLATYKURTIC

Characteristic of a distribution that is rather flat.

MESOKURTIC

Characteristic of a distribution that is neither very peaked nor very flat.

NORMAL CURVE

A smooth, symmetrical distribution that is bell-shaped and unimodal.

SKEWNESS

Departure from symmetry.

NEGATIVELY SKEWED DISTRIBUTION

A distribution in which more respondents receive high than low scores, resulting in a longer tail on the left than on the right.

POSITIVELY SKEWED DISTRIBUTION

A distribution in which more respondents receive low rather than high scores, resulting in a longer tail on the right than on the left.

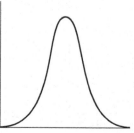
(a) Leptokurtic

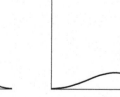
(b) Platykurtic

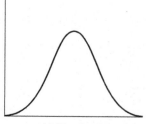
(c) Mesokurtic

FIGURE 2.8   Some Variation in Kurtosis among Symmetrical Distributions.

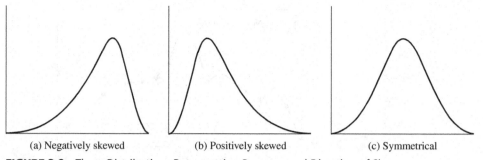

FIGURE 2.9   Three Distributions Representing Presence and Direction of Skewness.

Line Chart

The frequency (or percentage) polygon is actually a special type of **line chart**. We previously saw that bar graphs could be used to display frequencies and percentages from a distribution of scores as well as volumes and rates across groups, areas, or time. Line charts can similarly be modified to display volumes and rates between groups or across time, although this method uses a line chart. In other words, frequency polygons show the frequency distribution of a set of scores on a single variable, whereas line charts display changes in a variable or variables between groups or over time.

In a line chart, the amount or rate of some variable is plotted and then these points are connected by line segments. Figure 2.10, for example, shows the U.S. homicide rate (the number of homicides reported to the police per 100,000 residents) from 1950 to 2010. In the graph, we can clearly see a sharp and sudden upturn in the rate of homicides in the mid-1960s, an upward trend that continued until 1980, a downturn until the mid-1980s, a resurgence in the late 1980s, and another downturn in the 1990s before a leveling off since 2000. It is incumbent on the researcher, of course, to attempt an explanation for these trends. Among those reasons advanced in the literature were an increase in racial violence, a rise in drug use and the emergence of crack cocaine, changes in sentencing, changes in police practices, changes in the size of the adolescent population, and increased access to firearms.

Line charts are especially useful for depicting patterns over time for comparative subgroups. For example, Figure 2.11 shows the time-of-day patterns for violent offenses committed by juveniles, separately for school days and non-school days (weekends and vacations combined) for the year 2005. On school days, we observe a sudden peak in offending just after the school bell rings. In fact, nearly half the violent offenses committed by teenagers on school days occur from 2 p.m. to 8 p.m. when many are poorly supervised. By contrast, on days when school is out (weekends or vacation), violent offending by teens tends to increase in volume gradually throughout the late afternoon and evening.

LINE CHART

A graph of the differences between groups or trends across time on some variable(s).

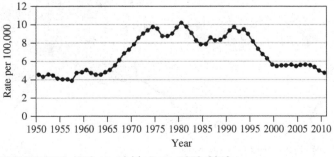

FIGURE 2.10   U.S. Homicide Rate, 1950–2010.

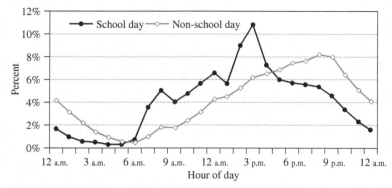

FIGURE 2.11   Time and School-Day Patterns for Violent Juvenile Offenders, 2005.

Maps

At one time, researchers relied almost exclusively on pie charts, bar graphs, frequency polygons, and line charts. In recent years, however, as graphics software for the computer has matured, researchers have begun to employ other forms of graphic presentation. One type in particular—the map—has become quite popular in conjunction with the greater use of data collected and published by the government (e.g., census data) as well as data coded by address or location. The map offers an unparalleled method for exploring geographical patterns in data.

For example, a three-category frequency distribution of homicide rates is displayed in Figure 2.12. Each state is shaded according to its category membership in the frequency distribution. The tendency for rates of homicide to be greater as one moves south is immediately apparent. Using mapping techniques, moreover, researchers can delve down to a more precise level of geography. In recent years, crime analysts have capitalized on local crime maps to observe and track so-called hot spots where crime tends to flourish.

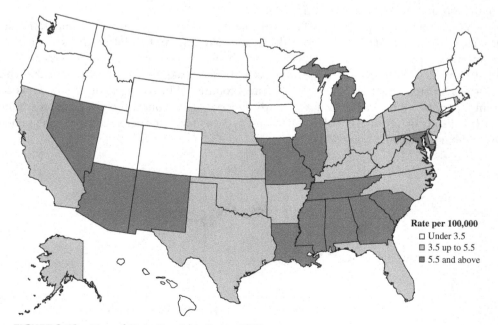

FIGURE 2.12   Map of State Homicide Rates, 2010.

Summary

In this chapter, we introduced some of the basic techniques used by the criminal justice researcher to organize the jumble of raw numbers that he or she collects from respondents. The first step when working with nominal data is usually to construct a frequency distribution in the form of a table that presents the number of respondents in all of the categories of a nominal-level variable or compares different groups on the categories of the same variable. Comparisons between groups or periods can also be made by means of proportions, percentages, and rates. For the purpose of presenting ordinal or interval data, there are simple, grouped, and cumulative frequency (and percentage) distributions. Frequency and percentage distributions can be extended to include two or more dimensions. In a cross-tabulation, the table presents the distribution of frequencies or percentages of one variable (usually, the dependent variable) over the categories of one or more additional variables (usually, the independent variable). There are three possible ways to determine percentages for cross-tabulations: row percents, column percents, and total percents. The choice between row and column percents depends on the placement of the independent variable within the cross-tabulation. Total percents are occasionally used instead, but only when neither the row nor the column variable can be identified as independent. Graphic presentations are often employed to enhance the readability and appeal of research findings. Pie charts have limited utility, being most appropriate for providing a simple illustration of data that can be divided into only a few categories. Bar graphs and histograms are more widely used, because they can accommodate any number of categories. Stressing continuity along a scale, frequency polygons are especially useful for depicting ordinal and interval data. Among their many applications, line charts are particularly useful for tracing trends over time. Finally, maps provide a method for displaying the geographical patterns in a set of data.

Questions and Problems

1. A _____ is the most basic technique for the organization of raw numbers.
   a. cross-tabulation
   b. frequency distribution
   c. midpoint
   d. rate

2. A cross-tabulation would be useful for comparing the amount of attention—a little, a moderate amount, or a great deal— that a particular attorney gives to _____.
   a. two different clients
   b. 30 wealthy clients and 30 poor clients
   c. 30 clients
   d. poor clients

3. The direction of skewness is determined by the relative position of the _____.
   a. peak of the distribution
   b. midpoint of the distribution
   c. tail of the distribution
   d. column percentages

4. Rates of change can be inaccurate if you are working with a _____.
   a. large divisor
   b. small divisor
   c. large numerator
   d. small numerator

5. A frequency distribution of the number of defendants sentenced to death in each of the 50 states during the year would be depicted best in the form of a _____.
   a. pie chart
   b. bar graph
   c. frequency polygon
   d. line chart

6. A frequency distribution of the percentages of male and female patrol officers in a police department would be depicted best in the form of a _____.
   a. pie chart
   b. bar graph
   c. frequency polygon
   d. line chart

7. To show changes in the rate of homicide from 1980 to the present, by year, a researcher would probably use a _____.
   a. pie chart
   b. bar graph
   c. line chart
   d. histogram

8. From the following table representing attitudes toward capital punishment for persons convicted of murder for men and women in the United States in 2010, find (a) the percentage of men who are in favor of capital punishment, (b) the percentage of women who are in favor of it, (c) the proportion of men who oppose capital punishment, and (d) the proportion of women who oppose it.

Attitude toward Capital Punishment	Gender	
	Men	Women
Favor	239	243
Oppose	102	169
Total	341	412

9. For the following table representing attitudes toward the legalization of marijuana of Americans in 1970 and 2010, find (a) the percentage of Americans in 1970 in favor of legalization of marijuana, (b) the percentage of Americans in 2010 in favor of it, (c) the proportion of Americans in 1970 against legalization of marijuana, and (d) the proportion of Americans in 2010 who oppose it.

Attitude toward Legalization of Marijuana	Year	
	1970	*2010*
Favor	65	245
Oppose	456	408
Total	521	653

10. If 162 homicides occur in a city with a population of 652,412 persons, what is the homicide rate (per 100,000 population)?
11. If 351 date rapes occur on a campus with 4,200 women, what is the date rape rate (per 1,000 females)?
12. What is the rate of change for the number of prisoners on death row in the United States that decreased from 3,254 in 2005 to 3,158 in 2010?
13. The National Crime Victimization Survey indicates that the number of aggravated assaults in 2009 was 823,340 and in 2010 the number was 725,180. What is the rate of change from 2009 to 2010?
14. Nonmetropolitan cities in New Hampshire had a total of 1 homicide in 2009 and 4 homicides in 2010. What is the rate of change? Is this change cause for alarm? Why or why not?
15. Twenty offenders were asked at what age they committed their first offense. The ages were 12, 12, 13, 13, 13, 14, 14, 14, 15, 15, 15, 15, 15, 16, 16, 16, 16, 17, 17, and 18. Present these data in a simple frequency distribution including a percentage distribution.
16. A police department has tracked the speeding tickets given by an officer over the past week. The data include how many miles over the speed limit each driver was traveling for each stop resulting in a ticket. Place the values into a grouped frequency distribution with 4 class intervals such that the starting value is 0 and the ending value is 40. Using the following data, find (a) the size of the class interval, (b) the midpoint of each interval, and (c) the percentage of each class interval. Miles per hour above the speed limit: 8, 8, 7, 12, 11, 12, 14, 22, 25, 12, 11, 14, 14, 11, 11, 10, 11, 12, 14, 14, 22, 33, 37, 39.
17. The following is a cross-tabulation of gender and victimization among a sample of 600 males and 600 females.

	Gender		
Victimization	*Male*	*Female*	*Total*
Yes	125	78	203
No	475	522	997
Total	600	600	1200

a. What is the dependent variable? What is the independent variable?
b. Compute column percents for each cell.
c. Which gender is victimized more frequently?
d. What can be concluded about gender and victimization risk?

18. The following is a cross-tabulation of the number of youths in a juvenile detention center who were predicted by a risk assessment tool to recidivate or desist after release.

	Prediction		
Actual	*Recidivate*	*Desist*	*Total*
Recidivated	66	11	77
Desisted	17	71	88
Total	83	82	165

a. What is the dependent variable? What is the independent variable?
b. Compute row percents for each cell.
c. What percentage of the sample overall did the risk assessment tool predict correctly?
d. What can be concluded about the ability of the risk assessment tool to accurately predict recidivism?

19. Use a pie chart to depict the following:

Murder, Type of Firearm in 2010

Type of Firearm	
Handgun	6,009
Rifle	358
Shotgun	373
Unknown/Other	2,035
Total	8,775

20. Depict the following data in a bar graph:

State Executions in 2011

State	Executions
Alabama	6
Arizona	4
Delaware	1
Florida	2
Georgia	4
Idaho	1
Mississippi	2
Missouri	1
Ohio	5
Oklahoma	2
South Carolina	1
Texas	13
Virginia	1

21. Display the following homicide totals as a histogram:

Homicide Victims by Age Group for 2010

Age	Homicides
20–24	2,256
25–29	1,964
30–34	1,541
35–39	1,072
40–44	882
45–49	838
50–54	686
55–59	473
60–64	325
65–69	189
70–74	137
75 and older	259

22. Create a grouped frequency distribution with four categories using the following hate crime data. Then, using your grouped frequency distribution and a blank map of the United States, display the data on the number of hate crimes reported in 2010.

Reported Hate Crimes by State, 2010

State	Total Number of Incidents Reported	State	Total Number of Incidents Reported
Alabama	19	Nebraska	61
Alaska	7	Nevada	68
Arizona	236	New Hampshire	31
Arkansas	63	New Jersey	543
California	1,092	New Mexico	24
Colorado	154	New York	699
Connecticut	147	North Carolina	94
Delaware	20	North Dakota	8
Florida	136	Ohio	247
Georgia	17	Oklahoma	49
Idaho	28	Oregon	134
Illinois	94	Pennsylvania	57
Indiana	94	Rhode Island	20
Iowa	17	South Carolina	109
Kansas	58	South Dakota	51
Kentucky	173	Tennessee	147
Louisiana	13	Texas	174
Maine	61	Utah	63
Maryland	80	Vermont	17
Massachusetts	316	Virginia	175
Michigan	304	Washington	232
Minnesota	127	West Virginia	33
Mississippi	11	Wisconsin	93
Missouri	142	Wyoming	2
Montana	31		

Computer Exercises

1. From the General Social Survey data, find the valid percentage of Americans in 2010 who favor gun permits (GUNLAW). Find the percentage of people who said that they read a newspaper every day (NEWS). Choose another variable and comment on some aspect of it. Hint: To obtain nationally representative estimates, the data set must be analyzed with the weight "on." Weight cases by selecting DATA, then WEIGHT CASES, and select WTSSALL. The frequencies procedure in *SPSS* can be located by clicking on ANALYZE, then DESCRIPTIVE STATISTICS, and finally FREQUENCIES.

2. Use the General Social Survey data to find the valid percentage of Americans who said that the federal government is spending too much as it works to deal with drug addiction (NATDRUG). Find the cumulative percentage of people who say that their family income in 2010 was below $50,000 (INCOME06). Why do you think that family income for a survey in 2010 was reported in 2006 dollars? Choose another variable and comment on some aspect of it. Hint: To obtain nationally representative estimates, the data set must be analyzed with the weight "on." Weight cases by selecting DATA, then WEIGHT CASES and select WTSSALL. The frequencies procedure in *SPSS* can be located by clicking on ANALYZE, then DESCRIPTIVE STATISTICS, and finally FREQUENCIES.

3. Use the General Social Survey to make a pie chart about respondents' fear of crime while walking in their own neighborhood at night (FEAR). Be sure to provide a title and source and show percentages on the pie chart.

4. From the General Social Survey, generate a bar graph for the number of nights per month that Americans visit with friends (SOCFRND). Be sure to provide a title and source and show percentages on the bar graph.

5. The Federal Bureau of Investigation collects information about crime and publishes it in *Crime in the United States* on an annual basis. Use *SPSS* to produce a line chart for the violent crime rate in the United States from 1987 to 2010 based on the following table of data values:

Violent Crime Rate in the U.S., 2007–2010

Year	Violent Crime Rate
1987	612.5
1988	640.6
1989	666.9
1990	729.6
1991	758.2
1992	757.7
1993	747.1
1994	713.6
1995	684.5
1996	636.6
1997	611.0
1998	567.6
1999	523.0
2000	506.5
2001	504.5
2002	494.4
2003	475.8
2004	463.2
2005	469.0
2006	479.3
2007	471.8
2008	458.6
2009	431.9
2010	403.6

Measures of Central Tendency

Researchers in criminology and criminal justice have used the term *average* to ask such questions as: What is the *average* age at first arrest for drug offenses? What is the *average* caseload for public defenders? What is the *average* prison sentence for convicted sex offenders? How many robberies are committed by the *average* prisoner convicted of robbery? What are the *average* monthly shoplifting losses for small retail businesses? On *average*, how many automobile accidents happen as the direct result of drug or alcohol abuse?

A useful way to describe a group as a whole is to find a single number that represents what is average or typical of that set of data. Such a value is known as a measure of **central tendency**, because it is generally located toward the middle or center of a distribution where most of the data tend to be concentrated.

What the layperson means by the term *average* is often vague and even confusing. The criminal justice researcher's conception is much more precise; it is expressed numerically as one of several different kinds of measures of average or central tendency that may take on quite different numerical values in the same set of data. Only the three best-known measures of central tendency are discussed here: the mode, the median, and the mean.

CENTRAL TENDENCY

What is average or typical of a set of data; a value generally located toward the middle or center of a distribution.

THE MODE

The **mode** (Mo) is the most frequent, most typical, or most common value in a distribution. For example, there are more Protestants in the United States than people of any other religion, and so we refer to this religion as the mode. Similarly, if at a given university, engineering is the most popular major, this too would represent the mode. The mode is the only measure of central tendency available for nominal-level variables, such as religion and college major. It can, however, be used to describe the most common score in any distribution, regardless of the level of measurement.

To find the mode, find the score or category that occurs most often in a distribution. The mode can be easily found by inspection, rather than by computation. For instance, in the set of scores ①, 2, 3, ①, ①, 6, 5, 4, ①, 4, 4, 3, the mode is 1, because it is the number that occurs more than any other score in the set (it occurs four times). Make no mistake: The mode is *not* the frequency of the most frequent score ($f = 4$), but the value of the most frequent score (Mo = 1).

Some frequency distributions contain two or more modes. In the following set of data, for example, the scores 2 and 6 *both* occur most often: 6, 6, 7, 2, 6, 1, 2, 3, 2, 4. Graphically, such

MODE

The most frequent, typical, or common value in a distribution; a measure of central tendency.

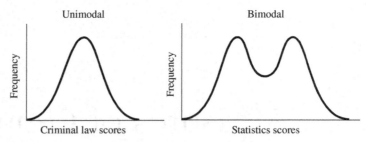

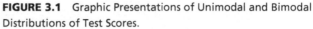

FIGURE 3.1   Graphic Presentations of Unimodal and Bimodal Distributions of Test Scores.

BIMODAL DISTRIBUTION

A frequency distribution containing two (or more) modes.

UNIMODAL DISTRIBUTION

A frequency distribution containing a single mode.

MEDIAN

The middle-most point in a frequency distribution; a measure of central tendency.

distributions have two points of maximum frequency, suggestive of the humps on a camel's back. These distributions are referred to as being **bimodal** in contrast to the more common **unimodal** variety, which has only a single hump or point of maximum frequency.

Figure 3.1, for example, shows the test scores on a criminal law and a criminal justice statistics final exam. The criminal law scores are unimodal, that is, the performance levels cluster around a single mode. The statistics scores, however, are bimodal, that is, the performance levels cluster around two modes. In the statistics course, apparently, there are many students who caught on, and another distinct group who did not.

THE MEDIAN

When ordinal or interval data are arranged in order of size, it becomes possible to locate the **median** (Mdn), the *middle-most* point in a distribution. Therefore, the median is regarded as the measure of central tendency that cuts the distribution into two equal parts, just as the median strip of a highway cuts it in two.

The position of the median value can be located by inspection or by the formula

$$\text{Position of median} = \frac{N + 1}{2}$$

If we have an odd number of cases, then the median will be the case that falls exactly in the middle of the distribution. Thus, 16 is the median value for the scores 11, 12, 13, ⑯, 17, 20, 25; this is the case that divides the distribution of numbers, so that there are three scores on either side of it. According to the formula $(7 + 1)/2 = 4$, we see that the median 16 is the fourth score in the distribution counting from either end.

If the number of cases is even, the median is always that *point* above which 50% of the cases fall and below which 50% of the cases fall. For an even number of cases, there will be two middle cases. To illustrate, the numbers 16 and 17 represent the middle cases for the following data: 11, 12, 13, ⑯, ⑰, 20, 25, 26. By the formula $(8 + 1)/2 = 4.5$, the median will fall midway between the fourth and fifth cases; the middle-most point in this distribution turns out to be 16.5, because it lies halfway between 16 and 17, the fourth and fifth scores in the set. Likewise, the median is 9 in the data 2, 5, ⑧, ⑩, 11, 12, again because it is located exactly midway between the two middle cases $(6 + 1)/2 = 3.5$.

Another circumstance must be explained and illustrated—we may be asked to find the median from data containing several middle scores having identical numerical values. The solution is simple—that numerical value becomes the median. Therefore, in the data 11, 12, 13, ⑯, ⑯, ⑯, 25, 26, 27, the median case is 16, although it occurs more than once.

Finally, if the data are not in order from low to high (or high to low), you should put them in order before trying to locate the median. Thus, in the data 3, 2, 7, the median is 3, the middle score after arranging the numbers 2, ③, 7.

TABLE 3.1	Calculating the Mean	
Offender	**X(IQ)**	
Jake	112	$\overline{X} = \dfrac{\Sigma X}{N}$
Sam	82	
Wayne	86	$= \dfrac{780}{8}$
Antwoine	118	
James	92	$= 97.5$
Luis	102	
Moe	91	
Tyrone	97	
	$\Sigma X = 780$	

THE MEAN

By far the most commonly used measure of central tendency, the arithmetic **mean** ($\overline{X}$) is obtained by adding up a set of scores and dividing by the number of scores. Therefore, we define the mean more formally as *the sum of a set of scores divided by the total number of scores in the set.* By formula,

$$\overline{X} = \frac{\Sigma X}{N}$$

MEAN

The sum of a set of scores divided by the total number of scores in the set; a measure of central tendency.

where $\overline{X}$ = mean (read as X bar)

  Σ = sum (expressed as the Greek capital letter sigma)[1]

  X = raw score in a set of scores

  N = total number of scores in a set

Suppose we have the IQ scores for a group of eight offenders, as displayed in Table 3.1. The formula for the mean has us sum the IQ scores and then divide by the number of cases. According to the formula, $\Sigma X = 780$ is divided by $N = 8$, which yields $\overline{X} = 97.5$ as the mean IQ for the group of offenders.

Unlike the mode, the mean is not always the score that occurs most often. Unlike the median, it is not necessarily the middle-most point in a distribution. Then, what does the *mean* mean? How can it be interpreted?

As we shall see, the mean can be regarded as the "center of gravity" of a distribution. It is similar to the notion of a seesaw or a fulcrum and lever (see Figure 3.2). Four blocks of weight are placed on the lever. The block marked 11 is 7 units (inches, feet, or whatever) to the right of the fulcrum. It balances with the blocks marked 1, 2, and 2, which are 3, 2, and 2 units to the left of the fulcrum, respectively. In a distribution of data, the mean acts as a fulcrum: It is the point in a distribution around which the scores above it balance with those below it.

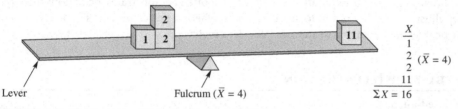

Lever   Fulcrum ($\overline{X} = 4$)

$$
\begin{array}{c}
\dfrac{X}{1} \\
2 \quad (\overline{X} = 4) \\
2 \\
\dfrac{11}{\Sigma X = 16}
\end{array}
$$

FIGURE 3.2   The Lever and Fulcrum Analogy to the Mean.

[1]The Greek capital letter sigma (Σ), called the summation sign, will be encountered many times throughout the text. It simply indicates that we must *sum* or add up what follows. In the present example, ΣX indicates adding up the raw scores. See Appendix B for a discussion of the summation sign.

TABLE 3.2	Deviations of a Set of Raw Scores from $\overline{X}$
X	**X − $\overline{X}$**
9	+3 ⎫
8	+2 ⎬ +5
6	0 $\overline{X} = 6$
5	−1 ⎫
2	−4 ⎬ −5

DEVIATION

The distance and direction of any raw score from the mean.

To understand this characteristic of the mean, we must first understand the concept of **deviation**. The deviation indicates the distance and direction of any raw score from the mean, just as we noted that a particular block is 7 units to the right of the fulcrum.

To find the deviation for a particular raw score, we simply subtract the mean from that score:

$$\text{Deviation} = X - \overline{X}$$

where X = any raw score in the distribution

$\overline{X}$ = mean of the distribution

For the set of raw scores 9, 8, 6, 5, and 2 in Table 3.2, $\overline{X} = 6$. The raw score 9 lies exactly three raw score units above the mean of 6 (or $X - \overline{X} = 9 - 6 = +3$). Similarly, the raw score 2 lies four raw score units below the mean (or $X - \overline{X} = 2 - 6 = -4$). Thus, the greater the deviation$(X - \overline{X})$, the greater is the distance of that raw score from the mean of the distribution.

Considering the mean as a point of balance in the distribution, we can now say that the sum of the deviations that fall above the mean is equal in absolute value (ignoring the minus signs) to the sum of the deviations that fall below the mean. Let us return to the set of scores 9, 8, 6, 5, 2 in which $\overline{X} = 6$. If the mean for this distribution is the "center of gravity," then disregarding minus signs and adding together the positive deviations (deviations of raw scores 8 and 9) should equal adding together the negative deviations (deviations of raw scores 5 and 2). As shown in Table 3.2, this turns out to be the case because the sum of deviations below $\overline{X}(-5)$ equals the sum of deviations above $\overline{X}(+5)$.

TAKING ONE STEP AT A TIME

When you open a cookbook to find a method for making a chocolate cake, the recipe can at first appear overwhelming. But when you approach the cake "formula" step by step, you often find that it was easier than it looked. In a similar way, some of the statistical "recipes" that you will encounter later in this book can also look overwhelming, or at least very complicated. Our advice is to confront formulas step by step, that is, to perform a series of small mathematical tasks to achieve the eventual solution. Throughout this book, we will often demonstrate calculations through step-by-step illustrations. Try not to focus so much on whether there are four, six, or seven steps, but on the progression from one to another. Now let's review the steps to calculate the mode, median, and mean.

STEP-BY-STEP ILLUSTRATION

Mode, Median, and Mean

Suppose that a criminal justice researcher surveys a population of drug abusers to find out the average number of times they use illegal drugs each month. She collects the following responses from her first seven respondents:

5   10   25   15   18   2   5

Step 1 Arrange the scores from highest to lowest.

$$
\begin{array}{c}
25 \\
18 \\
15 \\
10 \\
5 \\
5 \\
2
\end{array}
$$

Step 2 Determine the mode by finding the most frequent score.

$$\text{Mo} = 5$$

Step 3 Determine the median by finding the middle-most score. Because there are seven scores (an odd number), the fourth from either end is the median.

$$\text{Mdn} = 10$$

Step 4 Determine the sum of the scores.

$$
\begin{array}{r}
25 \\
18 \\
15 \\
10 \\
5 \\
5 \\
\underline{2} \\
\Sigma X = 80
\end{array}
$$

Step 5 Determine the mean by dividing the sum by the number of scores.

$$\overline{X} = \frac{\Sigma X}{N} = \frac{80}{7} = 11.43$$

Thus, the mode, median, and mean provide very different pictures of the average monthly drug use. The mode suggests relatively infrequent drug use, while the median and mean indicate much more frequent use.

Obtaining the Mode, Median, and Mean from a Simple Frequency Distribution

In the last chapter, we saw how a set of raw scores could be rearranged in the form of a simple frequency distribution—that is, a table of the frequency of occurrence of each score value. It is important to note that a simple frequency distribution does not change the data in any way; it only displays them in a different format. Therefore, the mode, median, and mean obtained from a simple frequency distribution also do not change, but they are calculated a bit differently. Let's consider the following raw scores representing the age at first incarceration in a sample of 25 prison inmates:

18 18 19 19 19 19 20 20 20 21 21 22 22 23 23 24 25 26 26 26 27 27 29 30 31

There are more inmates first incarcerated at age 19 than at any other age; thus, Mo = 19. The middle-most score (the 13th from either end) is 22; thus, Mdn = 22. Finally, the scores sum to 575; thus,

$$\overline{X} = \frac{575}{25} = 23$$

These data can be rearranged as a simple frequency distribution as follows:

	X	f
	18	2
Mo →	19	4
	20	3
	21	2
	22	2
	23	2
	24	1
	25	1
	26	3
	27	2
	28	0
	29	1
	30	1
	31	1

In the case of a simple frequency distribution in which the score values and frequencies are presented in separate columns, the mode is the score value that appears most often in the frequency column of the table. Therefore, Mo = 19 in the simple frequency distribution. This agrees, of course, with the mode obtained from the raw scores. To find the median for this simple frequency distribution, we start by identifying the position of the median. There are 25 age at first incarceration scores (as opposed to 14 score values, 18 through 31). With $N = 25$,

$$\text{Position of median} = \frac{N + 1}{2} = \frac{26}{2} = 13$$

The median turns out to be the 13th score in this frequency distribution. To help locate the 13th score, we construct a cumulative frequency distribution, accumulating the frequencies from lowest value to the highest value (regardless of whether the distribution is arranged from low to high or high to low). The cumulative frequencies are shown in the third column of the following table (for a small number of scores, this can be done in your head):

	X	f	cf
	18	2	2
	19	4	6
	20	3	9
	21	2	11
Mdn →	22	2	13
	23	2	15
	24	1	16
	25	1	17
	26	3	20
	27	2	22
	28	0	22
	29	1	23
	30	1	24
	31	1	25

Beginning with the lowest score value (18), we add frequencies until we reach a score value that represents the 13th score in the distribution. This is accomplished by searching for the smallest score value having a cumulative frequency that is at least 13.

In this distribution of age at first incarceration, the cumulative frequency for the score value 18 is 2, meaning that the two youngest were incarcerated at age 18. The cumulative frequency for the score value 19 is 6, indicating that 6 inmates were first incarcerated by age 19. Continuing, we eventually see that the score value of 22 has a cumulative frequency of at least 13. Here, 13 respondents were incarcerated by age 22. Thus, the median, the 13th score, is 22, which agrees with the result obtained from raw scores. Note, finally, that the median is not the middle-most score value (there are 14 different values, and 22 is not middle-most in the column).

To obtain the mean, we first need to calculate the sum of the scores. In a simple frequency distribution, this can be done efficiently by noting that there are, for example, two scores of 18, four scores of 19, and so on. Thus, rather than adding 18 twice and 19 four times, we can first multiply 18 by 2 and 19 by 4 before adding. That is, we can multiply the score values by their respective frequencies and then add the products in order to obtain the sum of scores. Next, just as in the raw-score formula, we divide the sum by the number of scores to determine the mean. Thus, a more practical and less time-consuming way to compute the mean from a simple frequency distribution is provided by the following formula:

$$\overline{X} = \frac{\sum fX}{N}$$

where $\overline{X}$ = the mean
X = a score value in the distribution
f = the frequency of occurrence of X
N = the number of scores

In the following table, the third column (headed fX) contains the products of the score values multiplied by their frequencies of occurrence. Summing the fX column, we obtain $\sum X = 575$.

X	f	fX
18	2	36
19	4	76
20	3	60
21	2	42
22	2	44
23	2	46
24	1	24
25	1	25
26	3	78
27	2	54
28	0	0
29	1	29
30	1	30
31	1	31
	$N = 25$	$\sum fX = 575$

Thus,

$$\overline{X} = \frac{\sum fX}{N}$$
$$= \frac{575}{25}$$
$$= 23$$

This result also agrees with the mean previously obtained from the raw scores themselves.

COMPARING THE MODE, MEDIAN, AND MEAN

The time comes when the criminal justice researcher chooses a measure of central tendency for a particular research situation. Will he or she employ the mode, the median, or the mean? The decision involves several factors, including the following:

1. Level of measurement
2. Shape or form of the distribution of data
3. Research objective

Level of Measurement

Because the mode requires only a frequency count, it can be applied to any set of data at the nominal, ordinal, or interval level of measurement. For instance, we might determine that the modal category in a nominal-level measure of religious affiliation (Protestant, Catholic, or Jewish) is Protestant, because the largest number of our respondents identify themselves as such. Similarly, we might learn that the largest number of students attending a particular university have a 2.5 grade point average (Mo = 2.5).

The median requires an ordering of categories from highest to lowest or lowest to highest. For this reason, it can only be obtained from ordinal or interval data, *not* from nominal data. To illustrate, we might find that the median annual income is $47,000 among police officers in a small town. The result gives us a meaningful way to examine the central tendency in our data. By contrast, it would make little sense if we were to compute the median for religious affiliation or criminal offense type (e.g., burglary, arson, murder), when ranking or scaling cannot be carried out.

The use of the mean is exclusively restricted to interval data. Applying it to ordinal or nominal data yields a meaningless result, generally not at all indicative of central tendency. What sense would it make to compute the mean for a distribution of religious affiliation or gender? Although less obvious, it is equally inappropriate to calculate a mean for data that can be ranked but not scored.

Shape of the Distribution

The shape, or form, of a distribution is another factor that can influence the researcher's choice of a measure of central tendency. In a perfectly symmetrical unimodal distribution, the mode, median, and mean will be identical, because the point of maximum frequency (Mo) is also the middle-most score (Mdn), as well as the "center of gravity" ($\overline{X}$). As shown in Figure 3.3, the measures of central tendency will coincide at the most central point, the "peak" of the symmetrical distribution.

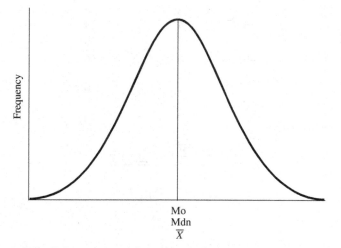

FIGURE 3.3 A Unimodal, Symmetrical Distribution Showing that the Mode, Median, and Mean Have Identical Values.

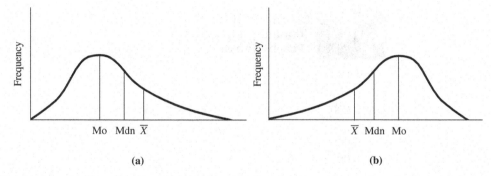

FIGURE 3.4 The Relative Positions of Measures of Central Tendency in (a) a Positively Skewed Distribution and (b) a Negatively Skewed Distribution.

When criminal justice researchers work with a symmetrical distribution, their choice of measure of central tendency is chiefly based on their particular research objectives and the level at which their data are measured. When they work with a skewed distribution, however, this decision is very much influenced by the shape, or form, of their data.

As shown in Figure 3.4, the mode, median, and mean do not coincide in skewed distributions, *although their relative positions* tend to remain unchanged—moving away from the "peak" and toward the "tail," the order is typically from mode to median to mean. The mode is at the peak of the curve, because this is the point where the most frequent scores occur. The mean, by contrast, is found closest to the tail, where the relatively few extreme scores are located. For this reason, the mean score in the positively skewed distribution in Figure 3.4(a) lies toward the high-score values; the mean in the negatively skewed distribution in Figure 3.4(b) falls close to the low-score values.

The mean is very much influenced by extreme scores in either direction, whereas the median is modified little, if at all, by changes in extreme values. This is because the mean considers all of the scores in any distribution, whereas the median (by definition) is concerned only with the numerical value of the score that falls at the middle-most position in a distribution. As illustrated, changing an extreme score value from 10 in distribution A to 95 in distribution B does not at all modify the median value (Mdn $=$ 7.5), whereas the mean shifts from 7.63 to 18.25.

$$\text{Distribution A:}\quad 5\ 6\ 6\ 7\ 8\ 9\ 10\ 10\quad \text{Mdn} = 7.5\quad \overline{X} = 7.63$$
$$\text{Distribution B:}\quad 5\ 6\ 6\ 7\ 8\ 9\ 10\ 95\quad \text{Mdn} = 7.5\quad \overline{X} = 18.25$$

In a skewed distribution, the median usually falls somewhere between the mean and the mode. It is this characteristic that makes the median the most desirable measure of central tendency for describing a skewed distribution of scores. To illustrate this advantage of the median, let us turn to Table 3.3 and examine the average annual salary among legal secretaries working in a public interest law firm. If we were public relations practitioners hired by the firm to give it a favorable public image, we would probably want to calculate the mean to show that the average employee makes $50,000 and is relatively well paid. On the other hand, if we were union representatives seeking to upgrade salary levels, we would probably want to employ the mode to demonstrate that the most common salary is only $30,000. Finally, if we were criminal justice researchers seeking to report accurately the average salary among the legal secretaries in the firm, we would wisely employ the median ($40,000), because it falls between the other measures of central tendency and, therefore, gives a more balanced picture of the salary structure. The most acceptable method would be to report all three measures of central tendency and permit the audience to interpret the results. It is unfortunately true that few researchers—let alone public relations practitioners or union representatives—report more than a single measure of central tendency. Even more unfortunate is that some reports of research fail to specify exactly which

TABLE 3.3	Measures of Central Tendency in a Skewed Distribution of Annual Salaries
Salary	
$120,000	
$60,000	$\overline{X}$ = $50,000
$40,000	Mdn = $40,000
$40,000	Mo = $30,000
$30,000	
$30,000	
$30,000	

measure of central tendency—the mode, median, or mean—was used to calculate the average amount or position in a group of scores. As shown in Table 3.3, a reasonable interpretation of findings may be impossible without such information.

It was noted earlier that some frequency distributions can be characterized as being bimodal, because they contain two points of maximum frequency. To describe bimodal distributions properly, it is generally useful to identify *both* modes; important aspects of such distributions can be obscured using either the median or the mean.

Consider the situation of a criminologist who conducted personal interviews with 20 randomly selected registered voters to determine their support for trying juvenile felony defendants as adults. Each respondent was asked, "On a scale from 1 to 10 (1 = definitely should not, 10 = definitely should), rate how strongly you believe that juveniles accused of felony offenses should be tried as adults."

$$1 \quad 2 \quad 2 \quad 2 \quad \underbrace{3 \quad 3 \quad 3 \quad 3}_{\text{Mode}} \quad 4 \quad 4 \quad 5 \quad 6 \quad 6 \quad \underbrace{7 \quad 7 \quad 7 \quad 7}_{\text{Mode}} \quad 8 \quad 8 \quad 9$$

As shown, there is a wide range of responses to this question, from believing that juveniles definitely should not be tried as adults to definitely should. Most people fell somewhere between the two extremes. Using either the mean ($\overline{X}$ = 4.85) or median (Mdn = 4.5), we might conclude that the average respondent felt neither in favor of nor opposed to trying juveniles as adults. Some might interpret these results as indicating that the average person is undecided. Knowing that the distribution is bimodal, however, we can see that there were actually two concentrations of responses—one indicating moderate rejection of trying juveniles as adults (Mo = 3) and the other indicating moderate acceptance (Mo = 7).

Research Objective

Until this point, we have discussed the choice of a measure of central tendency in terms of the level of measurement and the shape of a distribution of scores. We now ask: What does the researcher expect to do with this measure of central tendency? If he or she seeks a fast, simple, yet crude descriptive measure or is working with a bimodal distribution, the researcher generally will employ the mode. In most situations encountered by the researcher, however, the mode is useful only as a preliminary indicator of central tendency, which can be quickly obtained from briefly scanning the data. If he or she seeks a precise measure of central tendency, the decision is usually between the median and the mean.

To describe a skewed distribution, the researcher generally chooses the median, since it tends to give a balanced picture of extreme scores. (The mean, in contrast, tends to be distorted by very extreme scores.) In addition, the median is sometimes used as a point in the distribution where the scores can be divided into two categories containing the same number of respondents. For instance, we might divide respondents at the median into two categories according to their family size preferences—those who like a small family versus those who like a large family.

For a precise measure of distributions that are at least roughly symmetrical, the mean tends to be preferred over the median since the mean can be easily used in more advanced statistical analyses, such as those introduced in subsequent chapters of the text. Moreover, the mean is more stable than the median, in that it varies less across different samples drawn from any given population. This advantage of the mean—although perhaps not yet understood or appreciated by the student—will become more apparent in subsequent discussions of the decision-making function of statistics.

Summary

In this chapter, we introduced the three best-known measures of central tendency—indicators of what is average or typical of a set of data. The mode is the category or score that occurs most often; the median is the middle-most point in a distribution; and the mean is the sum of a set of scores divided by the total number of scores in a set. Which of these three measures of central tendency is appropriate to employ in any research project can be determined with reference to three criteria: level of measurement, shape or form of distribution, and research objective. The mode can be used with nominal, ordinal, or interval data; is especially useful for displaying a bimodal distribution; and provides a fast, simple, but rough measure of central tendency.

The median can be used with ordinal or interval data, is most appropriate for displaying a highly skewed distribution, and provides a precise measure of central tendency. Moreover, the median can sometimes be used for more advanced statistical operations or for splitting distributions into two categories (e.g., high versus low). The mean can be employed only with interval data, is most appropriate for displaying a unimodal symmetrical distribution, and provides a precise measure of central tendency. In addition, the mean can often be used for more advanced statistical operations including the decision-making tests we discuss in subsequent chapters of the text.

Questions and Problems

1. *Measures of central tendency* are given this label because they tend to _____.
   a. fall toward the center of a distribution, where most scores are located
   b. be central to our understanding of statistics
   c. indicate how far scores deviate from the center of a distribution
   d. all of the above
2. Which measure of central tendency represents the maximum frequency in a distribution?
   a. mode
   b. median
   c. mean
   d. multiplier
3. Which measure of central tendency is calculated as the arithmetic average of a distribution?
   a. mode
   b. median
   c. mean
   d. multiplier

4. Which measure of central tendency cuts the distribution in half when the scores are arranged from low to high?
   a. mode
   b. median
   c. mean
   d. multiplier
5. A distribution of the number of delinquent acts is highly skewed. Which measure of central tendency would you recommend for the purpose of characterizing delinquent acts?
   a. mode
   b. median
   c. mean
   d. multiplier
6. A recent homicide in a Southern town involved a woman who killed her preacher husband. As jury selection began, her lawyer polled people in the community and found that attitudes toward domestic violence as a defense for this homicide had two points of maximum frequency, indicating that many people strongly oppose it and many people strongly support it. Which measure of central tendency are you likely

to use for the purpose of characterizing public attitudes in this Southern town toward domestic violence as a defense?
a. mode
b. median
c. mean
d. multiplier

7. You have a unimodal symmetrical distribution of scores for people's attitudes toward more punitive sentences for first-time drug offenders. Which measure of central tendency are you likely to use for the purpose of characterizing these scores?
a. mode
b. median
c. mean
d. multiplier

8. The following is a list of seven Massachusetts state prisons and their security levels (prerelease is the lowest level; maximum is the highest).

Prison	Security level
Cedar Junction	Maximum
Old Colony	Medium
Lancaster	Prerelease
Shirley	Medium
Shirley	Minimum
Park Drive	Prerelease
Concert	Minimum

a. Find the modal security level.
b. Find the median security level.
c. Explain why it is inappropriate to calculate a mean security level.

9. The following is a list of 10 people who were arrested for drug offenses and are participating in a diversion program so that they do not have to go to prison:

Person	Offense	Sex	Assigned Drug Testing	Months in Program
Gilliand, J.	Drugs	Male	Daily	1
Baker, L.	Drugs	Female	Biweekly	1
Hall, E.	Drugs	Male	None	2
Scroggins, L.	DUI	Male	Daily	3
Wilson, A.	Drugs	Male	Daily	5
Harwood, R.	Drugs	Female	Weekly	4
Beams, K.	DUI	Female	Weekly	2
Olive, B.	Drugs	Female	Daily	2
Skelton, R.	Drugs	Male	Daily	5
Jones, S.	Drugs	Male	Biweekly	1

Calculate the most appropriate measure of central tendency for each of the variables (offense, sex, assigned to drug testing, and months in the program).

10. A group of college students on an urban campus were asked how often in the past 6 months they had used the campus safety patrol to escort them to their car at night. They responded:

0, 1, 0, 0, 1, 3, 0, 1, 0, 10

Calculate (a) the median and (b) the mean for these scores.

11. A group of five convicts was given the following prison sentences (in years):

3, 5, 3, 4, 45

a. Find the mode.
b. Find the median.
c. Find the mean.
d. Which measure provides the most accurate indication of central tendency for these prison sentences?

12. Truancy is a problem in many urban school systems. A researcher gathers information from a random sample of students in a middle school. The raw data on unexcused absences, whereby a child missed school without a legitimate reason (e.g., sickness), are as follows:

0, 0, 1, 1, 0, 0, 1, 2, 0, 19, 0, 0, 1, 1, 10, 2, 0, 0, 1, 2

Find the mode, median, and mean.

13. The scores on a fear of crime survey for 21 college students are shown below (higher scores indicate greater fear of crime on a 1–7 scale):

1, 2, 2, 2, 3, 3, 3, 3, 3, 3, 4, 4, 4, 5, 5, 5, 6, 6, 6, 7, 7

Find the mode, median, and mean.

14. A focus group of 10 registered voters was chosen to evaluate the performance of a Senate candidate during a debate about preventing terrorism.

Rater	Knowledge Rating	Delivery Rating
1	7	5
2	8	8
3	9	8
4	3	2
5	3	5
6	5	4
7	9	8
8	2	3
9	6	7
10	3	2

a. Calculate the mode, the median, and the mean for the knowledge rating.
b. Calculate mode, the median, and the mean for the delivery rating.
c. On which characteristic was the candidate rated more favorably?

15. A criminologist conducts a survey of residents concerning their sense of safety in their walking alone in their neighborhood. She uses a seven-point scale from 1 = very unsafe to 7 = very safe. Find the mode, median, and mean perception

of safety based on the following simple frequency distribution of responses:

Perception of safety	f
1	28
2	34
3	42
4	56
5	46
6	24
7	20

16. A state board of education collects data from each high school on the number of serious violent incidents occurring during the school year. Find the mode, median, and mean number of violent incidents per school using the following simple frequency distribution:

Number of incidents	f
0	54
1	62
2	32
3	24
4	18
5	10

Computer Exercises

1. From the General Social Survey, find out the average number of hours per day that people have to relax. Find the mode, median, and mean for hours per day that people have to relax (HRSRELAX). Hint: Open the STATISTICS option within the FREQUENCIES procedure to obtain the mode, median and mean for selected variables. Verify that the data set is weighted by WTSSALL by checking DATA and WEIGHT CASES.

2. How often during the past year did people in the United States pray? Use the General Social Survey to find the median, and mode for peoples' reports about praying during the past year (PRAY). Should you calculate a mean for this variable? Why or why not?

3. How much money does an American family make in constant dollars (The constant refers to "Year 2000" dollars)? Income is estimated using information from the General Social Survey and then converting it into constant dollars in year 2000 (CONINC). What is the level of measurement for this variable? Which measures of central tendency are appropriate for this kind of variable?

4. What is the highest year of school completed by fathers in the United States? Using the General Social Survey, analyze fathers' education (PAEDUC). What is the level of measurement for this variable? Which measures of central tendency are appropriate for this kind of variable?

5. Using the General Social Survey, find the mode, median, and mean for the number of siblings in the United States (SIBS).

4

Measures of Variability

In Chapter 3, we saw that the mode, median, and mean could be used to summarize in a single number what is average or typical of a distribution. When employed alone, however, any measure of central tendency yields only an incomplete picture of a set of data and, therefore, can mislead or distort as well as clarify.

To illustrate this possibility, consider that Honolulu, Hawaii, and Phoenix, Arizona, have almost the same mean daily temperature of 75°F. Can we, therefore, assume that the temperature is basically alike in both localities? Or is it not possible that one city is better suited for year-round swimming and for other outdoor activities?

As shown in Figure 4.1, Honolulu's temperature varies only slightly throughout the year, usually ranging between 70°F and 80°F. By contrast, the temperature in Phoenix can differ seasonally from a low of about 40°F in January to a high of more than 100°F in July and August. Needless to say, Phoenix's swimming pools are not overcrowded year-round.

Consider another example. Suppose that Judge A and Judge B both average (mean) 24 months in the prison sentences that they hand down to defendants convicted of assault. One could easily be misled by this statistic into thinking that the two judges agree in their philosophies about proper sentencing. Suppose we learn further that Judge A, believing in complete equality in sentencing, gives all defendants convicted of assault 24 months, whereas Judge B gives anywhere from 6 months to 6 years, depending on her assessment of both the defendant's demeanor in court and the nature of the prior criminal record. If you were an attorney maneuvering to have your client's case heard by a particular judge, which judge would you choose?

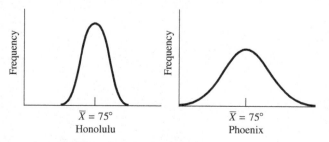

FIGURE 4.1 Differences in Variability: The Distribution of Temperature in Honolulu and Phoenix (Approximate Figures).

It can be seen that we need, besides a measure of central tendency, an index of how the scores are scattered around the center of the distribution. In a word, we need a measure of what is commonly referred to as **variability** (also known as *spread, width,* or *dispersion*). Returning to an earlier example, we might say that the distribution of temperature in Phoenix has greater variability than the distribution of temperature in Honolulu. In the same way, we can say that the distribution of sentences given by Judge A has less variability than the distribution of sentences given by Judge B. This chapter discusses only the best known measures of variability: the range, the variance, and the standard deviation.

VARIABILITY

The manner in which the scores are scattered around the center of the distribution. Also known as dispersion or spread.

THE RANGE

To get a quick but rough measure of variability, we might find what is known as the **range** (R), the difference between the highest and lowest scores in a distribution. For instance, if Honolulu's hottest temperature of the year was 89°F and its coldest temperature of the year was 65°F, then the range of temperature in Honolulu would be 24°F ($89 - 65 = 24$). If Phoenix's hottest day was 106°F and its coldest day 41°F, the range of temperature in Phoenix would be 65°F ($106 - 41 = 65$). By formula,

RANGE

The difference between the highest and lowest scores in a distribution. A measure of variability.

$$R = H - L$$

where R = range

H = highest score in a distribution

L = lowest score in a distribution

The advantage of the range—its quick-and-easy computation—is also its most important disadvantage. That is, the range is totally dependent on only two score values: the largest and smallest cases in a given set of data. As a result, the range usually gives merely a crude index of the variability of a distribution.

In a particular week, for example, probation officer A received eight new offenders ages 18, 18, 19, 19, 20, 20, 22, and 23. Probation officer B also received eight new offenders, ages 18, 18, 19, 19, 20, 20, 22, and 43. Officer A comments that his offenders range in age from 18 to 23. Officer B responds that he has a much older caseload, ranging in age from 18 to 43. With the exception of one offender, however, the two groups are identical in age distribution. The range is clearly affected by just one case and can provide a misleading or distorted picture of the variability within the whole group. Any measure that is so strongly affected by just one score may not give a precise indication of variability and, for most purposes, should be considered only a preliminary or rough index.

THE VARIANCE AND THE STANDARD DEVIATION

In the previous chapter, the concept of deviation was defined as the distance of any given raw score from its mean. To find a deviation, we were told to subtract the mean from any raw score $(X - \overline{X})$. If we now wish to obtain a measure of variability that takes into account every score in a distribution (rather than only two score values), we might be tempted to add together all the deviations. However, the sum of actual deviations, $\Sigma(X - \overline{X})$, is always zero. Plus and minus deviations cancel themselves out and therefore cannot be used to describe or compare the variability of distributions.

To overcome this problem, we might square the actual deviations from the mean and add them together $\Sigma(X - \overline{X})^2$. As illustrated in Table 4.1, using data on the length of probation (in months) for six first-time offenders, this procedure would get rid of minus signs, since squared numbers are always positive.

TABLE 4.1	Squaring Deviations in Lengths of Probation ($\overline{X} = 5$)	
X	**X − $\overline{X}$**	**(X − $\overline{X}$)²**
9	+4	16
8	+3	9
6	+1	1
4	−1	1
2	−3	9
1	−4	16
	0	$\Sigma(X - \overline{X})^2 = 52$

Having added the squared deviations from the mean, we might divide this sum by N to control for the number of scores involved. This is the mean of the squared deviations, but it is better known as the **variance**. Symbolized by s^2, the variance is

VARIANCE

The mean of the squared deviations from the mean of a distribution. A measure of variability in a distribution.

$$s^2 = \frac{\Sigma(X - \overline{X})^2}{N}$$

where s^2 = variance

$\Sigma(X - \overline{X})^2$ = sum of the squared deviations from the mean

N = total number of scores

Continuing with the illustration in Table 4.1, we see that the variance is

$$s^2 = \frac{\Sigma(X - \overline{X})^2}{N}$$
$$= \frac{52}{6}$$
$$= 8.67$$

One further problem arises, however. As a direct result of having squared the deviations, the unit of measurement is altered, making the variance rather difficult to interpret. The variance is 8.67, but 8.67 of what? The variance is expressed as the square of whatever unit expresses our data. In this case, we would have squared months!

To put the measure of variability into the right perspective, that is, to return to our original unit of measurement, we take the square root of the variance. This gives us the **standard deviation**, an interval/ratio level a measure of variability that we obtain by summing the squared deviations from the mean, dividing by N, and then taking the square root. Symbolized by s, the standard deviation is

STANDARD DEVIATION

The square root of the mean of the squared deviations from the mean of a distribution. A measure of variability that reflects the typical deviation from the mean.

$$s = \sqrt{\frac{\Sigma(X - \overline{X})^2}{N}}$$

where s = standard deviation

$\Sigma(X - \overline{X})^2$ = sum of the squared deviations from the mean

N = the total number of scores

STEP-BY-STEP ILLUSTRATION

Standard Deviation

With reference to the length of probation data, the following steps are carried out to calculate the standard deviation:

Step 1 Find the mean for the distribution.

X
9
8
6
4
2
1
$\Sigma X = 30$

$$\overline{X} = \frac{\Sigma X}{N}$$

$$= \frac{30}{6}$$

$$= 5$$

Step 2 Substract the mean from each raw score to get the deviation.

X	$X - \overline{X}$
9	+4
8	+3
6	+1
4	−1
2	−3
1	−4

Step 3 Square each deviation before adding together the squared deviations.

X	$X - \overline{X}$	$(X - \overline{X})^2$
9	+4	16
8	+3	9
6	+1	1
4	−1	1
2	−3	9
1	−4	16
		$\Sigma(X - \overline{X})^2 = 52$

Step 4 Divide by N and take the square root of the result.

$$s = \sqrt{\frac{\Sigma(X - \overline{X})^2}{N}}$$

$$= \sqrt{\frac{52}{6}}$$

$$= \sqrt{8.67}$$

$$= 2.94$$

We can now say that the standard deviation is 2.94 months for the six offenders. On average, that is, the scores in this distribution deviate from the mean by nearly 3 months. For example, the 2 in this distribution is below the mean, but only by an average amount.

While there are other ways to avoid having the positive and negative deviations from the mean cancel each other out (e.g., taking absolute values), squaring the deviations before summing them has some rather desirable advantages. Most immediately, it causes the measure of variability to be sensitive to the impact of extremes. When we square the deviations, for example, five scores that deviate by one unit from the mean do not compare with one score that deviates by five units. Thus, extremes are given appropriately greater emphasis in the calculation of variance and standard deviation.

Another advantage of squaring the deviations relates to the "center of gravity" characteristic of the mean against which the scores are compared. To take a basic example, the scores 1, 2, and 6 shown in the table that follows have a mean of 3 and a median of 2. If calculating how far each score deviates from the measure of central tendency, it is actually the median that comes closer to the scores in terms of overall distance, whereas the mean comes closer in terms of the squared distances. Because we generally prefer the mean as a measure of central tendency (except where there is severe skewness), we should also prefer a measure of variability that best fits the mean—that is, one based on the squared deviations from the mean.

Score	Distance from Median	Distance from Mean	Squared Distance from Median	Squared Distance from Mean
1	1	2	1	4
2	0	1	0	1
6	4	3	16	9
Sum	5	6	17	14

Note: Distances from median/mean ignore direction or sign.

THE RAW-SCORE FORMULA FOR VARIANCE AND STANDARD DEVIATION

Until now, we have used the deviation to obtain the variance and standard deviation. There is an easier method for computing these statistics, especially with the help of a calculator. This method works directly with the raw scores. The raw-score formulas for variance and standard deviation are, respectively,

$$s^2 = \frac{\Sigma X^2}{N} - \overline{X}^2$$

and

$$s = \sqrt{\frac{\Sigma X^2}{N} - \overline{X}^2}$$

where ΣX^2 = sum of the squared raw scores (*Important:* Each raw score is *first* squared and then these squared raw scores are summed.)

N = total number of scores

$\overline{X}^2$ = mean squared

STEP-BY-STEP ILLUSTRATION

Variance and Standard Deviation Using Raw Scores

The step-by-step procedure for computing s^2 and s by the raw-score method can be illustrated by returning to the months on probation data: 9, 8, 6, 4, 2, and 1.

Step 1 Square each raw score and then add the squared scores together.

X	X^2
9	81
8	64
6	36
4	16
2	4
1	1
	$\Sigma X^2 = 202$

Step 2 Obtain the mean and square it.

X
9
8
6
4
2
1
$\Sigma X = 30$

$$\overline{X} = \frac{\Sigma X}{N} = \frac{30}{6} = 5$$

$$\overline{X}^2 = 25$$

Step 3 Insert the results from Steps 1 and 2 into the formulas.

$$s^2 = \frac{\Sigma X^2}{N} - \overline{X}^2 \qquad s = \sqrt{\frac{\Sigma X^2}{N} - \overline{X}^2}$$

$$= \frac{202}{6} - 25 \qquad = \sqrt{\frac{202}{6} - 25}$$

$$= 33.67 - 25 \qquad = \sqrt{8.67}$$

$$= 8.67 \qquad = 2.94$$

As Step 3 shows, applying the raw-score formulas to the length of probation data yields exactly the same results as the original method, which worked with deviations.

As a final note, there are actually two approaches to calculating the variance and standard deviation depending on whether the sum of squared deviations is divided by N or $N - 1$. As later discussed in Chapter 6, we suggest using N in the divisor when our objective is simply to describe the variability of a set of scores and using $N - 1$ in the divisor when our purpose is to generalize beyond the particular set of scores. Some statistical software makes the same distinction, but SPSS employs $N - 1$ for all of its calculations, regardless of objective. You should bear this in mind if and when you use a software package. Of course, for large samples, the difference is minimal. For example, when calculating the variance of exam scores for 143 police recruits, the variance is nearly the same whether dividing by $N = 143$ or $N - 1 = 142$. Until we reach the topic of samples versus populations beginning with Chapter 6, however, we will continue to place N in the denominator for calculating both the variance and the standard deviation.

Obtaining the Variance and Standard Deviation from a Simple Frequency Distribution

In the last chapter, we saw how measures of central tendency could be calculated from a set of scores rearranged in the form of a simple frequency distribution. The variance and standard deviation can be obtained in a similar fashion.

Let's return to the following raw scores representing the age at first incarceration in a sample of 25 prison inmates:

18 18 19 19 19 19 20 20 20 21 21 22 22 23 23 24 25 26 26 26 27 27 29 30 31

Calculated from these raw scores, the mean $\overline{X} = 23$ years old. In terms of variability around the mean, the variance $s^2 = 14.56$ and the standard deviation $s = 3.82$, almost 4 years of age.

As in the last chapter, these data can be rearranged as a simple frequency distribution as follows:

X	f
18	2
19	4
20	3
21	2
22	2
23	2
24	1
25	1
26	3
27	2
28	0
29	1
30	1
31	1

To obtain the variance and standard deviation from a simple frequency distribution, we apply the following formulas:

$$s^2 = \frac{\sum fX^2}{N} - \overline{X}^2$$

and

$$s = \sqrt{\frac{\sum fX^2}{N} - \overline{X}^2}$$

where $s^2 =$ the variance

$s =$ the standard deviation

$X =$ a score value in the distribution

$f =$ the frequency of occurrence of X

$N =$ the number of scores

$\overline{X} =$ the mean

STEP-BY-STEP ILLUSTRATION

Variance and Standard Deviation of a Simple Frequency Distribution

To obtain the variance and standard deviation, we must first calculate the mean using the steps outlined in the previous chapter.

Step 1   Multiply each score value (X) by its frequency (f) to obtain the fX products, and then sum the fX column.

X	f	fX
18	2	36
19	4	76
20	3	60
21	2	42
22	2	44
23	2	46
24	1	24
25	1	25
26	3	78
27	2	54
28	0	0
29	1	29
30	1	30
31	1	31
	$N = 25$	$\sum fX = 575$

Step 2   Square each score value (X^2) and multiply by its frequency (f) to obtain the fX^2 products, and then sum the fX^2 column.

X	f	fX	fX²
18	2	36	648
19	4	76	1,444
20	3	60	1,200
21	2	42	882
22	2	44	968
23	2	46	1,058
24	1	24	576
25	1	25	625
26	3	78	2,028
27	2	54	1,458
28	0	0	0
29	1	29	841
30	1	30	900
31	1	31	961
	$N = 25$	$\sum fX = 575$	$\sum fX^2 = 13,589$

Step 3   Obtain the mean and square it.

$$\overline{X} = \frac{fX}{N} = \frac{575}{25} = 23$$

$$\overline{X}^2 = (23)^2 = 529$$

Step 4   Calculate the variance using the results from the previous steps.

$$s^2 = \frac{\sum fX^2}{N} - \overline{X}^2$$

$$= \frac{13,589}{25} - 529$$

$$= 543.56 - 529$$

$$= 14.56$$

Step 5 Calculate the standard deviation (the square root of the variance).

$$s = \sqrt{\frac{\sum fX^2}{N} - \overline{X}^2}$$

$$= \sqrt{\frac{13,589}{25} - 529}$$

$$= \sqrt{543.56 - 529}$$

$$= \sqrt{14.56}$$

$$= 3.82$$

Finally, note that the variance and standard deviation calculated from the simple frequency distribution are identical to the values obtained from the raw scores.

Coefficient of Variation

A researcher sometimes seeks to compare variability for two or more characteristics that have been measured in different units. For example, a researcher might study the variability of hourly wages as well as the variability of hours worked per week among correctional officers in a particular state penitentiary. In which characteristic—wages per hour ($\overline{X}$ = 22) or hours worked per week ($\overline{X}$ = 35 hours)—is there greater spread or width?

The first step might be to calculate the standard deviation for wages (s = 10.50) and for hours worked (s = 10 hours). The problem is that it is meaningless to use the standard deviation to compare directly the spread or width of scores for characteristics measured in two entirely different units—wages and hours worked. It would be like trying to measure the variability of weight measured in pounds versus kilograms. The value of the standard deviation will differ depending on the unit of measurement.

COEFFICIENT OF VARIATION (CV)

A measure of variability that expresses the standard deviation as a percentage of the sample mean.

By contrast, the **coefficient of variation** (**CV**) is based on the size of the standard deviation, but its value is independent of the unit of measurement employed by the researcher. The coefficient of variation expresses the standard deviation as a percentage of the mean.

Thus,

$$\boxed{CV = 100\left(\frac{s}{\overline{X}}\right)}$$

For hourly wages:

$$CV = 100\left(\frac{10.5}{22}\right)$$

$$= 100(.4773)$$

$$= 47.73\%$$

For hours worked per week:

$$CV = 100\left(\frac{10}{35}\right)$$

$$= 100(.2857)$$

$$= 28.57\%$$

The result obtained for the comparison of coefficients of variation indicates greater variability for hourly wages (the standard deviation is almost 48% of the average wage) than for hours worked (the standard deviation is almost 29% of the average). Apparently, the wages earned by the correctional officers in this particular state prison are scattered further away from the mean than the number of hours they worked per week.

THE MEANING OF THE STANDARD DEVIATION

We noted earlier that the standard deviation is more easily interpreted than the variance because it is in the correct unit of measurement. Even so, the series of steps required to compute the standard deviation can leave the reader with an uneasy feeling as to the meaning of his or her result. For example, suppose we learn that $s = 4$ in a particular distribution of scores. What is indicated by this number? Exactly what can we say now about that distribution that we could not have said before?

Chapter 5 will seek to clarify the full meaning of the standard deviation. For now, we note briefly that the standard deviation represents the average variability in a distribution, because it measures the average of deviations from the mean. The procedures of squaring and taking the square root also enter the picture, but chiefly to eliminate minus signs and return to the more convenient unit of measurement, the raw-score unit.

We note also that the greater the variability around the mean of a distribution, the larger the standard deviation. Thus, $s = 4.5$ indicates greater variability than $s = 2.5$. For instance, the distribution of daily temperatures in Phoenix, Arizona, has a larger standard deviation than does the distribution of temperatures for the same period in Honolulu, Hawaii.

Let's also reconsider the case of prison sentencing, which we encountered earlier, to see the importance of variance and standard deviation for understanding and interpreting distributions. Table 4.2 displays the sentences given to two sets of six defendants in robbery trials by the respective judges. Note first the advantage of the standard deviation over the variance. Even though they are equal in their abilities to measure variability or dispersion, the standard deviation has a more tangible interpretation. In this case, the standard deviation is expressed in terms of months—something that has meaning to us. The variance, however, is stated in terms of months squared, which renders the variance more difficult to understand.

Returning to a comparison of the two judges, we see that Judge A has a larger mean yet a smaller variance and standard deviation than Judge B. One might say, at least on the basis of these data alone, that Judge A is harsher but fairer, and Judge B is more lenient but inconsistent. For an attorney, your best bet might be Judge A. Even though you can expect a longer sentence (because of the higher mean), you may not want to risk the severe sentences that Judge B has been known to give.

Now let's add another piece to the puzzle. The highly variable sentences of Judge B are not so unreasonable as they may seem. The long sentences were given to offenders with long

TABLE 4.2	Sentences in Months for Robbery by Two Judges
Judge A	**Judge B**
34	26
30	43
31	22
33	35
36	20
34	34
$\bar{X} = 33.0$	$\bar{X} = 30.0$
$s^2 = 4.0$	$s^2 = 65.0$
$s = 2.0$	$s = 8.1$

criminal records and the short sentences to first- and second-time offenders. (We will consider techniques for measuring the sources of variability in later chapters.) As an attorney, your preference for a judge would depend, therefore, on the criminal history of your client. If he had a history of minor offenses or no criminal history at all, you would prefer Judge B, because you would expect a shorter sentence from her than from Judge A, who now seems rather inflexible. On the other hand, if representing a repeat offender, you would prefer Judge A, because she seems to focus less on the background of the offender than on the current charge.

Thus, the standard deviation is a useful device for measuring the degree of variability in a distribution or for comparing the variability in different distributions. It is also employed, and quite frequently, for calibrating the relative standing of individual scores within a distribution. The standard deviation in this sense is a standard against which we assess the placement of one score (such as your examination score) within the whole distribution (such as the examination scores of the entire class).

To understand this meaning of the standard deviation, consider first an analogy to the placement of a plant in a room. If we wish to discuss the distance of a plant from a living room wall, we might think in terms of feet as a unit of measurement of distance (e.g., "The plant in the living room is located a distance of 5 ft from this wall"). But how do we measure the width of a baseline of a frequency polygon that contains the scores of a group of respondents arranged from low to high (in ascending order)? As a related matter, how do we come up with a method to find the distance between any raw score and its mean—a standardized method that permits comparisons between raw scores in the same distribution as well as between different distributions? If we were talking about plants, we might find that one plant is 5 ft from the living room wall, and another plant is 10 ft from the kitchen wall. In the concept of feet, we have a standard unit of measurement and, therefore, we can make such comparisons in a meaningful way. But how about comparing raw scores? For instance, can we always compare 85 on an English exam with an 80 in German? Which grade is really better? A little thought will show that it depends on how the other students in each class performed.

One method for giving a rough indicator of the width of a baseline is the range, because it gives the distance between the highest and lowest scores along the baseline. But the range cannot be effectively used to locate a score relative to its mean, because—aside from its other weaknesses—the range covers the entire width of the baseline. By contrast, the size of the standard deviation is smaller than that of the range and usually covers far less than the entire width of the baseline.

Just as we "lay off" a carpet in feet or yards, so we might lay off the baseline in units of standard deviation. For instance, we might add the standard deviation to the value of the mean to find which raw score is located exactly one standard deviation from the mean. As shown in Figure 4.2, therefore, if $\overline{X} = 80$ and $s = 5$, then the raw score 85 lies exactly one standard

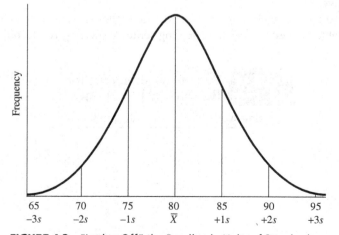

| 65 | 70 | 75 | 80 | 85 | 90 | 95 |
| $-3s$ | $-2s$ | $-1s$ | $\overline{X}$ | $+1s$ | $+2s$ | $+3s$ |

FIGURE 4.2 "Laying Off" the Baseline in Units of Standard Deviation When the Standard Deviation(s) Is 5 and the Mean ($\overline{X}$) Is 80.

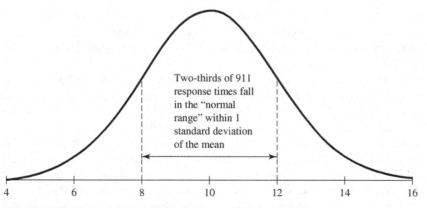

Two-thirds of 911 response times fall in the "normal range" within 1 standard deviation of the mean

FIGURE 4.3 Distribution of Police Response Times to 911 Calls.

deviation *above* the mean (80 + 5 = 85), a distance of +1s. This direction is *plus* because all deviations above the mean are positive; all deviations below the mean are *minus*, or negative.

We continue laying off the baseline by adding the value of the standard deviation to the raw score 85. This procedure gives us the raw score 90, which lies exactly two standard deviations above the mean (85 + 5 = 90). Likewise, we add the standard deviation to the raw score 90 and obtain 95, which represents the raw score falling exactly three standard deviations from the mean: We subtract 5 from 80, 5 from 75, and 5 from 70 to obtain −1s, −2s, and −3s.

The process of laying off the baseline in units of standard deviation is in many respects similar to measuring the distance between a plant and the wall in units of feet. The analogy, however, breaks down in at least one important respect: Although feet and yards are of constant size (1 foot always equals 12 inches; 1 yard always equals 3 feet), the value of the standard deviation varies from distribution to distribution. Otherwise, we could not use the standard deviation as previously illustrated to compare the variability of distributions (e.g., the judges in Table 4.2). For this reason, we must calculate the size of the standard deviation for any distribution with which we happen to be working.

As we will see in detail in the next chapter, the standard deviation has a very important meaning for interpreting scores in what we call the normal distribution. Actually, unless a distribution is highly skewed, approximately two-thirds of its scores fall within one standard deviation above and below the mean. Sometimes, this range is called the *normal range* because it contains cases that are considered close to the norm.

Consider, for example, the time it takes, in minutes, for a police officer to respond to a 911 call, where a life-threatening crime—an armed robbery, an assault, a shooting—is in progress. The police officer whose response time falls precisely at the mean is, in a strict sense, average; but officers whose response times are close to the mean in either direction, more specifically within one standard deviation of the mean, also are regarded as being within normal range. Thus, if for a particular police jurisdiction, the mean response time is 10 min with a standard deviation of 2 min then the normal range may be defined as between 8 and 12 min, and approximately two-thirds of the police responses to a 911 emergency call lie within the normal range (see Figure 4.3). We will return to this concept of the standard deviation in Chapter 5.

COMPARING MEASURES OF VARIABILITY

The range is regarded generally as a preliminary or rough index of the variability of a distribution. It is quick and simple to obtain but not very reliable, and it can be applied to interval or ordinal data.

The range does serve a useful purpose in connection with computations of the standard deviation. As illustrated in Figure 4.2, six standard deviations cover almost the entire distance from the highest to lowest score in a distribution (−3s to +3s). This fact alone gives us a convenient method for estimating (but not computing) the standard deviation. Generally, the size of the standard deviation is approximately one-sixth of the size of the range. For instance, if the range is 36, then the standard deviation might be expected to fall close to 6; if the range is 6, the standard deviation will likely be close to 1.

This rule can take on considerable importance for the reader who wishes to find out whether her or his result is anywhere in the vicinity of being correct. To take an extreme case, if $R = 10$ and our calculated $s = 12$, we have made some sort of an error, because the standard deviation cannot be larger than the range. A note of caution: The one-sixth rule applies when we have a large number of scores. For a small number of cases, there will generally be a smaller number of standard deviations to cover the range of a distribution.

Although the range is calculated from only two score values, both the variance and the standard deviation take into account every score value in a distribution. Also, the variance and the standard deviation are used for obtaining certain other statistical measures, especially in the context of statistical decision making. We shall be exploring this characteristic in detail in subsequent chapters.

Summary

In Chapter 3, we discussed measures of how scores cluster around the center of a distribution. Notwithstanding the immense value of the mode, median, and mean, there is much more to learn about a distribution than just central tendency. In this chapter, we introduced three measures of variability—the range, variance, and standard deviation—for indicating how the scores are scattered around the center of a distribution. Just as was true of indicators of central tendency, each measure of variability has its particular weaknesses and strengths. The range is a quick but very rough indicator of variability, which can be easily determined by taking the difference between the highest and the lowest scores in a distribution. A more precise measure of the spread of scores can be found in the variance, the mean of the squared deviations from the mean. The variance and its square root, known as the standard deviation, are two reliable, interval-level measures of variability that can be employed for more advanced descriptive and decision-making operations. In addition to its ability to compare the variability in different distributions, for example, the standard deviation is useful for calibrating the relative standing of individual scores within a distribution. We actually lay off the baseline of a distribution in units of standard deviation to determine how far any particular score falls from the mean. The full meaning of the standard deviation will be explored in subsequent discussions of generalizing from a sample to a population.

Questions and Problems

1. Measures of how scores scatter around the center of a distribution include the _____.
   a. variance
   b. standard deviation
   c. range
   d. all of the above
2. The greater the variability around the mean of a distribution the larger the_____.
   a. mean
   b. standard deviation
   c. normal distribution
   d. all of the above
3. The variance and standard deviation assume _____.
   a. nominal data
   b. ordinal data

   c. interval/ratio data
   d. a normal distribution
4. How many standard deviations tend to fall on either side of the mean in a distribution?
   a. 1
   b. 2
   c. 3
   d. 4
5. To bring consistency to the process and to enhance the quality of police officers, many agencies have adopted Police Officer Standards and Training (POST) requirements for in-service training and education. A police manager wanted to see whether officers in two precincts were making progress toward their 10-unit goal. He compared the scores of five officers from each precinct.

Precinct A	Precinct B
4	6
9	5
3	7
8	5
9	6

Considering both concepts of central tendency and variability, find (a) which precinct tended to complete more units and (b) which precinct tended to be more consistent in the number of hours completed.

6. The following are the actual number of weeks in jail for six persons who were convicted of a second offense for driving under the influence (DUI) of alcohol.

$$1 \quad 1 \quad 2 \quad 2 \quad 2 \quad 4$$

   a. Calculate the range of weeks.
   b. Calculate the variance.
   c. Calculate the standard deviation using the raw score formula.

7. A large metropolitan police department develops a test for potential officers. A researcher looking at the results of these tests found that over a 10-year period, the standardized test has a mean of 74 and a standard deviation of 11. Using the idea of laying off the baseline, find the test scores that are located one standard deviation above and one standard deviation below the mean.

8. The following are the weeks in drug rehabilitation programs for six parolees:

$$1 \quad 3 \quad 3 \quad 4 \quad 3 \quad 5$$

   a. Calculate the range.
   b. Calculate the variance.
   c. Calculate the standard deviation.

9. The number of prior arrests for a group of individuals at their parole hearings are 0, 2, 2, 3, 4, 5, and 12. Compute the (a) range, (b) variance, and (c) standard deviation.

10. Correctional officers were surveyed about their satisfaction with their job (high numbers indicate greater satisfaction on a 1–7 scale).

$$4 \quad 7 \quad 4 \quad 5 \quad 7 \quad 4 \quad 5$$

Find the (a) range, (b) variance, and (c) standard deviation.

11. A researcher examines court dispositions on sentencing where two judges make sentencing recommendations for very similar convictions. Ten cases were identified, and sentence length in years follows:

Case Number										
Judge	1	2	3	4	5	6	7	8	9	10
Allison	2	2	2	5	6	7	9	10	12	25
Dixon	5	5	6	6	7	9	10	10	10	12

Compare the variability in court dispositions of these two judges by calculating the (a) range, (b) variance, and (c) standard deviation. Which judge has greater variability of sentences?

12. A criminologist conducts a survey of residents concerning their sense of safety in walking alone in their neighborhood. She uses a seven-point scale where 1 = very unsafe and 7 = very safe. Find the variance and standard deviation for perceptions of safety based on the following simple frequency distribution of responses:

Perception of safety	f
1	28
2	34
3	42
4	56
5	46
6	24
7	20

13. A state board of education collects data from each high school on the number of serious violent incidents occurring during the school year. Find the variance and standard deviation for the number of violent incidents per school using the following simple frequency distribution:

Number of incidents	f
0	54
1	62
2	32
3	24
4	18
5	10

Computer Exercises

1. Using information from the General Social Survey, examine the dispersion of the number of days of poor mental health in the past 30 days (MNTLHLTH). Hint: Open the STATISTICS option within the FREQUENCIES procedure and check the range and standard deviation for selected variables. Remember to weight cases by WTSSALL. For your information, *SPSS* uses N-1 rather than N when it calculates variance and standard deviation. This slight difference in computation will be explained in more detail in the text for Chapter 6.

2. In the previous chapter, you were asked to find the mode, median and mean for hours per day that Americans have to relax. Now, find the range, standard deviation and variance for hours per day that Americans have to relax (HRSRELAX).

3. From the General Social Survey, which measures of central tendency and variability are most appropriate for attitudes toward spanking to discipline children (SPANKING)? Use a computer to obtain this information.

4. Which measures of central tendency and variability are most appropriate for an analysis of respondent's income (RINCOM06)? Analyze the General Social Survey to calculate this information.

5. Analyze a variable of your choice where you find the most appropriate measures of central tendency and variability.

LOOKING AT THE LARGER PICTURE
Describing Data

At the close of Chapter 1, we presented a hypothetical survey of 250 students, grades 9 through 12, in a typical urban high school. The survey questionnaire asked about the use of cigarettes and alcohol, as well as about a variety of other variables. Before we can attempt to understand the factors underlying smoking and drinking, it is necessary to describe the variables in our survey—the extent of smoking and drinking as well as some of the academic, social, and background characteristics. Let's examine, in particular, frequency distributions and bar charts of the primary variables of interest—smoking and drinking.

The extent of smoking was assessed with two questions—whether the respondent smoked during the past month, and, if so, how many cigarettes on a typical day. Suppose that 95 of the 250 respondents reported that they had not smoked; among those who did smoke, the responses were wide ranging, from many who reported one, two, or three cigarettes per day to a few who reported smoking as many as two packs or more per day. Because the number of cigarettes smoked per day has so many possible values, from zero for the nonsmokers on up, it is convenient to use a grouped frequency distribution to present these data.

Daily Cigarette Consumption

Number	f	%
0	95	38.0
1–9	45	18.0
10–19	58	23.2
20–29	33	13.2
30–39	15	6.0
40+	4	1.6
Total	250	100.0

As shown in Figure 4.4. 38% of the students could be considered nonsmokers, not having smoked at all during the past month. Eighteen percent could be considered light smokers, consuming less than half a pack per day; another 23.2% could be called moderate smokers, between half a pack and under a pack per day. The remaining 20.8% (combining the last three categories) could be labeled heavy smokers, having at least a pack per day.

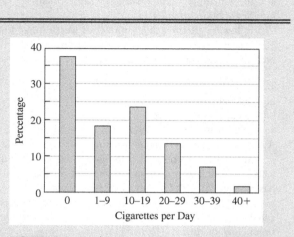

FIGURE 4.4 Smoking among High School Students.

Alcohol use (occasions using alcohol during the month) can be shown in a simple frequency distribution, with values ranging from 0 through 5. Barely more than half the respondents drank on no more than one occasion (20.8% reporting no drinking and 30.8% reporting drinking on one occasion; see Figure 4.5). At the other extreme, only about 5% reported drinking on four or more occasions during the month (or at least once per week).

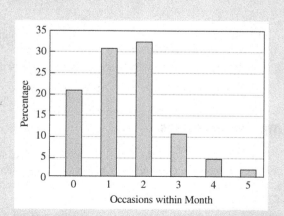

FIGURE 4.5 Drinking among High School Students.

Alcohol Consumption during Month

Occasions	f	%
0	52	20.8
1	77	30.8
2	82	32.8
3	26	10.4
4	9	3.6
5	4	1.6
Total	250	100.0

The distributions of smoking and drinking can be displayed in the form of a bar graph. The smoking distribution peaks at zero, representing a relatively large group of nonsmokers. As a result, the distribution is extremely skewed to the right. Unlike the situation with smoking, there does not appear to be such a clearly defined group of nondrinkers to dominate the distribution. Although not perfectly so, the drinking variable is, therefore, more symmetrical in shape than the smoking distribution. In future analyses, we will look at whether or not a respondent smokes separately from how many cigarettes the smokers consume daily. In other words, we will examine two distinct measures of smoking: smokers versus nonsmokers and the extent of smoking among those who do use cigarettes. By contrast, the analysis of drinking will include all respondents, even those who did not drink during the month.

We can further describe these variables in terms of their central tendency and variability (see table below). Looking just at the 155 smokers, we see that the mean is 16.9 cigarettes per day, slightly above the mode and median. There is still some slight skewness—a few really heavy smokers at the high end. For the drinking variable, the mean is 1.58 occasions per month, with a median at 1 (once in the month) and mode at 2 (twice in the month).

The standard deviations for daily smoking (for smokers) and drinking occasions are quite dissimilar, reflecting very different kinds of distributions. Because of the wider variability in smoking (from just a few cigarettes to more than 40 cigarettes) compared to drinking (from a low of 0 occasions to a high of 5), the standard deviation for cigarette consumption is many times greater than that for alcohol. We can also say that roughly two-thirds of the smokers are within one standard deviation of the mean (16.9 ± 10.4, indicating that about two-thirds smoke between 7 and 27 cigarettes daily). For drinking, about two-thirds are included in the range 1.58 ± 1.16. In the next part of the text, we will say a lot more about intervals like these.

We might also attempt to describe differences in smoking and drinking between male and female students. As shown in Figure 4.6, a much higher percentage of the males (47.3%) than the females (28.5%) are nonsmokers, and a higher percentage of the females could be considered heavy smokers. For drinking, the sex differences are reversed. A larger percentage of the females had not had alcohol during the month (26.8% versus 14.2%), whereas the males tended more toward moderate or frequent drinking (see Figure 4.7). In the third part of the text, we will return to this issue and try to determine if these sex differences are sizable enough to be truly meaningful or indicative of male/female differences among urban high school students in general.

Finally, it is useful to examine descriptive statistics for some of the background variables as well. Because age is measured at the interval level, we not only can create a simply frequency distribution but also can calculate all three measures of central tendency. There are more 15-year-olds in

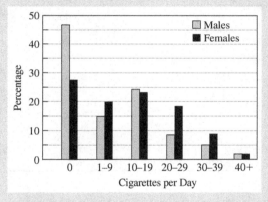

FIGURE 4.6 Smoking among Students by Gender.

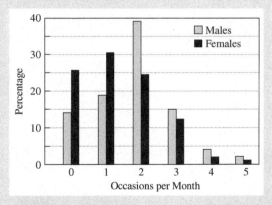

FIGURE 4.7 Drinking among Students by Gender.

Central Tendency and Variability Measures

Variable	N	Mean	Mdn	Mo	s^2	s
Smoking (smokers only)	155	16.99	15	15	108.5	10.4
Drinking occasions	250	1.58	1	2	1.35	1.16

the survey than any other age (Mo = 15), but both the median and mean are a bit higher. For sports/exercise participation, both the mode and median are "Sometimes," whereas the mean should not be calculated since this variable is at the ordinal level. The variable "race" is measured at the nominal level; we can see that the mode is "white," but there can be no median or mean. Last, parental smoking is nominal, with most students not having a parent who smokes.

At this juncture, there is little more that we can do to analyze these and other background characteristics. In the final two parts of the book, however, we shall examine differences in smoking and drinking by race, as well as such things as age and athleticism in their relationship with the smoking and drinking measures.

Descriptive Measures for Background Characteristics

Variable	Group	%	Mean	Median	Mode
Age	19	2.4			
	18	15.6			
	17	20.0			
	16	26.0	16.1	16	16
	15	21.2			
	14	14.8			
Sports/exercise participation	Very frequent	17.2			
	Sometimes	34.8	—	Sometimes	Sometimes
	Seldom	32.4			
	Never	15.6			
Race	White	62.4			
	Black	17.6			
	Latino	12.8	—	—	White
	Asian	4.0			
	Other	3.2			
	Yes	26.0			
Parental smoking	No	74.0	—	—	No

Probability and the Normal Curve

In Part One, we focused on ways to describe variables. In particular, we began to explore variables by concentrating on their distributions through categorizing data and graphing frequencies. This permitted us to see patterns and trends, and to see the most frequent and extreme occurrences. We further summarized these distributions by computing measures of central tendency and variability.

Until now, our interpretations and conclusions about variables have come solely from what we observed. We collected information about a variable and then described what we obtained using a variety of statistical measures, such as percentages and means. From this point on, our approach will be somewhat different. We will first suggest certain theories, propositions, or hypotheses about variables, which will then be tested using the data we observe.

The cornerstone of decision making—the process of testing hypotheses through analysis of data—is probability. Probability is a difficult concept to grasp, yet we use it quite frequently. We ask such questions as: "How likely is it that I will get an A on this exam?" "How likely is it that this marriage will last?" "If I draw a card, what is the chance that it will be smaller than a 5?" or "What is the chance that the home team will win the series?" In everyday conversation, we answer these questions with vague responses such as "probably," "pretty good chance," or "unlikely." With probability, we offer far more precise answers, such as "There is an 80% chance, or probability, of rain."

In mathematical terms, probability (P) varies from 0 to 1, although sometimes a percentage rather than a decimal is used to express the level of probability. For example, a .50 probability (or 5 chances out of 10) is sometimes called a 50% chance. Although percentages may be used more in everyday language, the decimal form is more appropriate for statistical use.

A zero probability implies that something is impossible; probabilities near zero, such as .05 or .10, imply very unlikely occurrences. At the other extreme, a probability of 1.0 constitutes certainty, and high probabilities such as .90, .95, or .99 signify very probable or likely outcomes.

Some probabilities are easy to calculate: Most people know that the probability of getting heads on a coin flip is .50. However, more complex situations involve the application of various basic rules of probability. Just as we had to learn basic arithmetic operations, so we must learn a few basic operations that will permit us to calculate more complex and interesting probabilities.

RULES OF PROBABILITY

PROBABILITY

The relative frequency of occurrence of an event or outcome. The number of times any given event could occur out of 100, converted to a decimal value between 0 and 1.

The term **probability** refers to the relative likelihood of occurrence of any given outcome or event—that is, the probability associated with an event is the number of times that event can occur relative to the total number of times any event can occur:

$$Probability = \frac{Number\ of\ times\ the\ outcome\ or\ event\ can\ occur}{Total\ number\ of\ times\ any\ outcome\ or\ event\ can\ occur}$$

For example, suppose a particular jury consists of five men and seven women. Furthermore, suppose that the court clerk selects the jury foreperson by randomly drawing an index card from a pile of 12, each card with the name of a juror printed on it. Denoting $P(\text{F})$ as the probability that the foreperson will be female.

$$P(\text{F}) = \frac{Number\ of\ female\ jurors}{Total\ number\ of\ jurors} = \frac{7}{12} = .58$$

CONVERSE RULE

The probability of an event not occurring equals one minus the probability that it will occur.

The probability of an event not occurring, known as the **converse rule** of probability, is 1 minus the probability of that event occurring. Thus, the probability that the foreperson of the jury is not female, denoted $P(\overline{\text{F}})$ where the bar over the F symbolizes "not," or the converse, is

$$P(\overline{\text{F}}) = 1 - P(\text{F}) = 1 - .58 = .42$$

For another example, suppose that a particular city police department is able to clear (or solve) 60% of its homicides. Thus, the probability of homicide clearance is $P(\text{C}) = .60$ (or simply .6). For any particular homicide, say the first one of the year, the probability that it will not be cleared is $P(\overline{\text{C}}) = .4$.

ADDITION RULE

The probability of obtaining any one of several outcomes equals the sum of their separate probabilities.

An important characteristic of probability is found in the **addition rule**, which states that the probability of obtaining any one of several different and distinct outcomes equals the sum of their separate probabilities. That is, the probability that either event A or event B occurs is

$$P(\text{A or B}) = P(\text{A}) + P(\text{B})$$

For example, suppose that a defendant in a first-degree murder trial has a .52 probability of being convicted as charged, a .26 probability of being convicted of a lesser charge, and a .22 chance of being found not guilty. The chance of a conviction on any charge is the probability of a conviction on the first-degree murder charge plus the probability of a conviction on a lesser charge, or $.52 + .26 = .78$. Note also that this answer agrees with the converse rule by which the probability of being found guilty of any charge (the converse of not guilty) is $1 - .22 = .78$.

The addition rule always assumes that the outcomes being considered are mutually exclusive—that is, no two outcomes can occur simultaneously. More precisely, the occurrence of any particular outcome (say, conviction on the first-degree murder charge) excludes the possibility of any other outcome, and vice versa.

Assuming mutually exclusive outcomes, we can say that the probability associated with all possible outcomes of an event always equals 1. Here, adding the probabilities for the three possible verdicts that the jury may return, we find:

$$P(\text{Guilty as charged}) + P(\text{Guilty lesser charge}) + P(\text{Not guilty}) = .52 + .26 + .22 = 1$$

MULTIPLICATION RULE

The probability of obtaining a combination of independent outcomes equals the product of their separate probabilities.

This indicates that some outcome must occur: if not a conviction on the charge of murder in the first degree, then either conviction on a lesser crime or an acquittal.

Another important characteristic of probability becomes evident in the **multiplication rule**, which focuses on the possibility of obtaining two or more outcomes in combination. The multiplication rule states that the probability of obtaining a combination of independent outcomes equals the product of their separate probabilities. Thus, the probability that both event A and event B occur is

$$P(\text{A and B}) = P(\text{A}) \times P(\text{B})$$

The assumption of independent outcomes means that the occurrence of one outcome does not change the likelihood of the other. Rather than considering the probability of outcome 1 or outcome 2 occurring as in the addition rule, the multiplication rule concerns the probability that both outcome 1 and outcome 2 will occur.

Returning to the city police department with a 60% clearance rate, the probability that any two particular homicides during the year are both cleared is

$$
\begin{aligned}
P(\text{Homicides A and B are both cleared}) &= P(\text{A is cleared}) \times P(\text{B is cleared}) \\
&= (.6)(.6) \\
&= .36
\end{aligned}
$$

Extending it just a bit further, the probability that any three particular homicides are all solved is the product of the three respective probabilities:

$$
\begin{aligned}
P(\text{Homicides A, B, and C are all cleared}) &= P(\text{A is cleared}) \times P(\text{B is cleared}) \\
&\quad \times P(\text{C is cleared}) \\
&= (.6)(.6)(.6) \\
&= .216
\end{aligned}
$$

For this calculation to be valid, we must assume that the three homicides considered are independent of one another. If the three homicides were part of a string of killings believed to have been committed by an unidentified serial killer, then neither the independence assumption nor the calculation itself would be valid.

Finally, the multiplication rule applies more broadly than just to repetitions of similar events such as solving homicides. Rather, the multiplication rule allows us to calculate the joint probability of any number of outcomes so long as they are independent. Suppose that a prosecutor is working on two cases, a robbery trial and a kidnapping trial. From previous experience, she believes that she has a .80 chance of getting a conviction on the robbery and a .70 chance of a conviction on the kidnapping. Thus, the probability that she will get convictions on both cases is $.7 \times .8 = .56$ (slightly better than half).

PROBABILITY DISTRIBUTIONS

In Part One, we encountered distributions of data in which frequencies and percentages associated with particular values were determined. For example, Table 2.8 shows the frequency distribution of examination scores of 142 police department applicants. The possible values of the scores are represented by the categories, and the frequencies and percentages represent the relative occurrences of the scores among the group.

A *probability distribution* is directly analogous to a frequency distribution, except that it is based on theory (probability theory) rather than on what is observed in the real world (empirical data). In a probability distribution, we specify the possible values of a variable and calculate the probabilities associated with each value. The probabilities represent the likelihood of each value, directly analogous to the percentages in a frequency distribution.

Suppose we were again to flip two coins, and let X represent the number of heads we obtain. The variable X has three possible values, 0, 1, and 2, according to whether we obtain zero, one, or two heads. Zero heads ($X = 0$) has a probability of

$$
\begin{aligned}
P(0 \text{ heads}) &= P(\text{tails on flip 1})P(\text{tails on flip 2}) \\
&= (.50)(.50) = .25
\end{aligned}
$$

We multiply the probability of getting tails on the coins because the flips of the two coins are independent.

Similarly, for two heads ($X = 2$),

$$P(2 \text{ heads}) = P(\text{heads on flip 1})P(\text{heads on flip 2})$$
$$= (.50)(.50) = .25$$

Determining the probability of heads on one of two flips ($X = 1$) requires an additional consideration. There are two ways to obtain one flip of heads: (1) heads on flip 1 and tails on flip 2 (HT) or (2) tails on flip 1 and heads on flip 2 (TH). Because these two possible outcomes are mutually exclusive (they cannot both occur), we may add their respective probabilities. That is,

$$P(1 \text{ heads}) = P(\text{HT or TH})$$
$$= P(\text{HT}) + P(\text{TH})$$

As before, the individual coin flips are independent. Thus, we can multiply the probability of a head times the probability of a tail to get the probability of first a head then a tail, $P(\text{HT})$; we can also multiply the probability of a tail times the probability of a head to obtain the probability of first a tail and then a head, $P(\text{TH})$. That is,

$$P(\text{HT}) + P(\text{TH}) = P(\text{H})P(\text{T}) + P(\text{T})P(\text{H})$$
$$= (.50)(.50) + (.50)(.50)$$
$$= .25 + .25$$
$$= .50$$

The complete probability distribution for variable X is summarized in Table 5.1. Note that the probabilities sum to 1.00. The distribution can be plotted much the way we did with frequency distributions in Chapter 2. A bar graph of a probability distribution places the values of the variable along the horizontal baseline, and the probabilities along the vertical axis (see Figure 5.1). We see that the distribution is symmetric, as one would expect of coins that favor neither of their sides.

We can construct a probability distribution for the number of clearances among a group of homicides in a manner similar to the simple case of two coins, except that the shape will not be symmetric because clearance and non-clearance are not equally likely as are the two sides of a coin. Determining the probability distribution for the number of clearances among three homicides is manageable. Beyond three, the logic is unchanged, but the steps become rather exhausting. There are alternative methods for handling larger problems, but they are outside the scope of this introductory taste of probability.

Shown below are all the possible combinations of clearance and non-clearance, denoted by C and N, respectively, for the group of three homicide cases, where P(C) = .6 and P(N) = .4. Because of the multiplication rule for independent outcomes, the probability of any one of the sequences of Cs and Ns can be expressed as the product of their respective probabilities. Finally, the eight possible combinations of outcomes are mutually exclusive. That is, whatever combination does occur for a particular group of three homicides rules out the other seven alternative combinations. As a consequence of the combinations being mutually exclusive, the

TABLE 5.1 Probability Distribution for Number of Heads in Two Flips	
X	**Probability (P)**
0	.25
1	.50
2	.25
Total	1.00

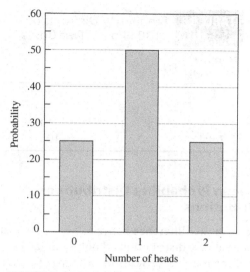

FIGURE 5.1 Probability Distribution of Two Coins.

probabilities for the alternative combinations can be added, and the probabilities of all eight possible combinations sum to 1.

Combination	Outcomes	Probability
A	NNN	P(NNN) = P(N)P(N)P(N) = (.4)(.4)(.4) = .064
B	CNN	P(CNN) = P(C)P(N)P(N) = (.6)(.4)(.4) = .096
C	NCN	P(NCN) = P(N)P(C)P(N) = (.4)(.6)(.4) = .096
D	NNC	P(NNC) = P(N)P(N)P(C) = (.4)(.4)(.6) = .096
E	CCN	P(CCN) = P(C)P(C)P(N) = (.6)(.6)(.4) = .144
F	CNC	P(CNC) = P(C)P(N)P(C) = (.6)(.4)(.6) = .144
G	NCC	P(NCC) = P(N)P(C)P(C) = (.4)(.6)(.6) = .144
H	CCC	P(CCC) = P(C)P(C)P(C) = (.6)(.6)(.6) = .216
Total		1

Given these probabilities, we can form the theoretical probability distribution in Table 5.2 for X, the number of cleared homicides among a group of three cases. Of course, X has four possible values, ranging from 0 (none cleared) to 3 (all cleared). In forming the probability distribution, we can add the three ways (combinations B through D) that one case out of three can be solved, as well as adding the probabilities for the three ways (combinations E through G) that two out of three homicides can be cleared.

TABLE 5.2	Probability Distribution of the Number of Clearances for Three Homicides
X	**P(X)**
0	.064
1	.288
2	.432
3	.216
	1

TABLE 5.3	Frequency Distribution of 10 Flips of Two Coins	
Number of Heads	***f***	**%**
0	3	30.0
1	6	60.0
2	1	10.0
Total	10	100.0

The Difference between Probability Distributions and Frequency Distributions

It is important to be clear on the difference between frequency distributions, like those we saw in Chapter 2, and probability distributions. Look again at Figure 5.1, which shows the probability distribution of the number of heads in two flips of a coin. This is a perfectly symmetrical distribution, with the probability of two heads equal to .25, identical to the probability of no heads. Furthermore, it shows that the probability of one head out of two is .50. This distribution is based on probability theory. It describes what *should* happen when we flip two coins.

Now let's observe some data. Flip two coins and record the number of heads. Repeat this nine more times. How many times did you get zero heads, one head, and two heads? Our own results of a sample of 10 flips of a pair of coins are shown in Table 5.3.

This is a frequency distribution, not a probability distribution. It is based on actual observations of flipping two coins 10 times. Although the percentages (30%, 60%, and 10%) may seem like probabilities, they are not. The percentage distribution does not equal the probability distribution given earlier in Table 5.1. A probability distribution is theoretical or ideal: It portrays what the percentages should be in a perfect world. Unfortunately, we did not get a perfect outcome—there were more zero-head outcomes than two-head outcomes, for instance. The problem is that just about anything can happen in only 10 pairs of flips. In fact, we could have obtained even more skewed results than these.

Imagine if we were to repeat our flips of two coins many more times. The results of our flipping the two coins 1,000 times are shown in the frequency distribution in Table 5.4.

This frequency distribution (with $N = 1,000$) looks a lot better. Why is that? Was our luck just better this time than when we flipped the coins 10 times? In a sense, it is a matter of luck, but not completely. As we said previously, with only 10 sets of flips almost anything can happen—you could even get a streak of zero heads. But when we run our experiment for 1,000 pairs of flips, things even out over the long run. There will have been streaks of zero heads, but so too will there have been streaks of one head and two heads. As we approach an infinite number of flips of the two coins, the laws of probability become apparent. Our luck, if you want to call it that, evens out.

TABLE 5.4	Frequency Distribution of 1,000 Flips of Two Coins	
Number of Heads	***f***	**%**
0	253	25.3
1	499	49.9
2	248	24.8
Total	1,000	100.0

A probability distribution is essentially a frequency distribution for an infinite number of flips. Thus, we may never observe this distribution of infinite flips, but we know it looks like Figure 5.1.

Mean and Standard Deviation of a Probability Distribution

Returning to the frequency distribution in Table 5.3 for 10 flips of two coins, let's compute the mean number of heads:

$$\overline{X} = \frac{\Sigma fX}{N}$$

$$= \frac{3(0) + 6(1) + 1(2)}{10}$$

$$= .8$$

This is low. The probability distribution of the two coin flips shown in Figure 5.1 clearly suggests that the average should be 1.00. That is, for the flip of two coins, in the long run, you should expect to average one head. Note, however, that $N = 1,000$ frequency distribution seems to be more in line with this expectation. For Table 5.4,

$$\overline{X} = \frac{\Sigma fX}{N}$$

$$= \frac{253(0) + 499(1) + 248(2)}{1,000}$$

$$= .995$$

Again, our "luck" averages out in the long run.

As you might suspect, a probability distribution has a mean. Because the mean of a probability distribution is the value we expect to average in the long run, it is sometimes called an *expected value*. For our case of the number of heads in two coin flips, the mean is 1. We use the Greek letter μ (mu) for the mean of a probability distribution (here $\mu = 1$) to distinguish it from $\overline{X}$, the mean of a frequency distribution. $\overline{X}$ is something we calculate from a set of observed data and their frequencies. On the other hand, the mean of a probability distribution (μ) is a quantity that comes from our theory of what the distribution should look like.

A probability distribution also has a standard deviation, symbolized by σ (sigma), the Greek letter equivalent of s. Up to this point, we have used s to signify standard deviation generally. But, from here on, s will represent the standard deviation of a set of observed data obtained from research, and σ will represent the standard deviation of a theoretical distribution that is not observed directly. Similarly, s^2 will denote the variance of a set of observed data, and σ^2 will be the variance of a theoretical distribution. We will encounter μ, σ, and σ^2 often in chapters to come, and it is important to keep in mind the difference between $\overline{X}$, s, and s^2 (summary measures of observed data) on the one hand and μ, σ, and σ^2 (characteristics of theoretical distributions) on the other.

The mean, variance, and standard deviation of a probability distribution are calculated from the possible values of X and their associated probabilities $P(X)$.

$$\mu = \Sigma XP(X)$$

$$\sigma^2 = \Sigma(X - \mu)^2 P(X)$$

$$\sigma = \sqrt{\Sigma(X - \mu)^2 P(X)}$$

where the summation extends over the possible values of X. Using these formulas, for example, we can determine that the probability distribution for the number of cleared homicides (X) among a group of three cases (given in Table 5.2) has the following mean, variance, and standard deviation:

$$
\begin{aligned}
\mu &= \Sigma X P(X) \\
&= 0(.064) + 1(.288) + 2(.432) + 3(.216) \\
&= 0 + .288 + .864 + .648 \\
&= 1.8
\end{aligned}
$$

$$
\begin{aligned}
\sigma^2 &= \Sigma(X - \mu)^2 P(X) \\
&= (0 - 1.8)^2(.064) + (1 - 1.8)^2(.288) + (2 - 1.8)^2(.432) + (3 - 1.8)^2(.216) \\
&= (-1.8)^2(.064) + (-.8)^2(.288) + (.2)^2(.432) + (1.2)^2(.216) \\
&= 3.24(.064) + .64(.288) + .04(.432) + 1.44(.216) \\
&= .207 + .184 + .017 + .311 \\
&= .72
\end{aligned}
$$

$$
\begin{aligned}
\sigma &= \sqrt{\Sigma(X - \mu)^2 P(X)} \\
&= \sqrt{.72} \\
&= .8485
\end{aligned}
$$

Thus, although for any group of three homicides, the police could solve $X = 0, 1, 2,$ or 3 of them, in the long run, we would expect an average of 1.8 clearances for every three homicide cases and a standard deviation of about .85.

THE NORMAL CURVE AS A PROBABILITY DISTRIBUTION

Previously, we saw that frequency distributions can take a variety of shapes or forms. Some are perfectly symmetrical or free of skewness, others are skewed either negatively or positively, still others have more than one hump, and so on. This is true as well for probability distributions.

Within this great diversity, there is one probability distribution with which many students are already familiar, if only from being graded on "the curve." This distribution, commonly known as the **normal curve**, is a theoretical or ideal model that was obtained from a mathematical equation, rather than from actually conducting research and gathering data. However, the usefulness of the normal curve for the researcher can be seen in its applications to actual research situations.

NORMAL CURVE

A smooth, symmetrical distribution that is bell-shaped and unimodal.

As we will see, for example, the normal curve can be used for describing distributions of scores, interpreting the standard deviation, and making statements of probability. In subsequent chapters, we will see that the normal curve is an essential ingredient of statistical decision making, whereby the researcher generalizes her or his results from samples to populations. Before proceeding to a discussion of techniques of decision making, it is first necessary to gain an understanding of the properties of the normal curve.

CHARACTERISTICS OF THE NORMAL CURVE

How can the normal curve be characterized? What are the properties that distinguish it from other distributions? As indicated in Figure 5.2, the normal curve is a type of smooth, symmetrical curve whose shape reminds many individuals of a bell and is thus widely known as the bell-shaped curve. Perhaps the most outstanding feature of the normal curve is its *symmetry*: If we were to fold the curve at its highest point at the center, we would create halves, each the mirror image of the other.

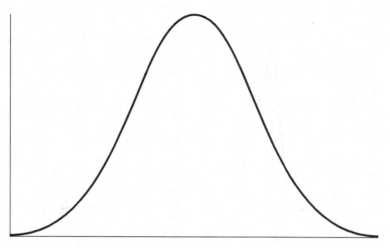

FIGURE 5.2 The Shape of the Normal Curve.

In addition, the normal curve is unimodal, having only one peak or point of maximum likelihood—that point in the middle of the curve at which the mean, median, and mode coincide (the student may recall that the mean, median, and mode occur at different points in a skewed distribution—see Chapter 3). From the rounded central peak of the normal distribution, the curve falls off gradually at both tails, extending indefinitely in either direction and getting closer and closer to the baseline without actually reaching it.

THE MODEL AND THE REALITY OF THE NORMAL CURVE

Because it is a probability distribution, the normal curve is a theoretical ideal. We might then ask: To what extent do distributions of actual data (i.e., the data collected by researchers in the course of doing research) closely resemble or approximate the form of the normal curve? For illustrative purposes, let us imagine that all social, psychological, and physical phenomena are normally distributed. What would this hypothetical world be like?

So far as physical human characteristics are concerned, most adults would fall within the 5 to 6 ft range of height, with far fewer being either very short (less than 5 ft) or very tall (more than 6 ft). As shown in Figure 5.3, IQ would be equally predictable—the greatest proportion of IQ scores would fall between 85 and 115. We would see a gradual falling off of scores at either end with few "geniuses" who score higher than 145 and equally few who score lower than 55. Likewise, relatively few individuals would be regarded as political extremists, either of the right or of the left, whereas most would be considered politically moderate or middle-of-the-roaders.

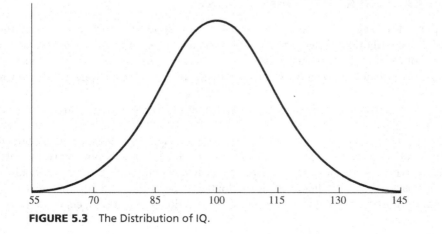

FIGURE 5.3 The Distribution of IQ.

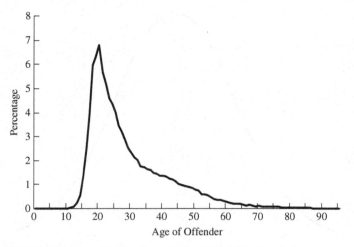

FIGURE 5.4   Age Distribution of Homicide Offenders in the United States.

Finally, even the pattern of wear resulting from the flow of traffic in doorways would resemble the normal distribution: Most wear would take place in the center of the doorway, whereas gradually decreasing amounts of wear would occur at either side.

Some readers have, by this time, noticed that the hypothetical world of the normal curve does not differ radically from the real world. Characteristics such as height, IQ, political orientation, and wear in doorways do, in fact, seem to approximate the theoretical normal distribution. Because so many phenomena have this characteristic—because it occurs so frequently in nature (and for other reasons that will soon become apparent)—researchers in many fields have made extensive use of the normal curve by applying it to the data that they collect and analyze.

But it should also be noted that some variables in criminal justice, as in other fields of study, simply do not conform to the theoretical notion of the normal distribution. Many distributions are skewed, others have more than one peak, and some are symmetrical but not bell-shaped. As a concrete example, consider the age distribution of homicide offenders in the United States shown in Figure 5.4. The "age curve," as it is often called, is severely skewed to the right. The distribution peaks at its mode of age 20, whereas the median is 25 and the mean is as high as 29.

When we have good reason to expect radical departures from normality, as with the age curve shown in Figure 5.4, the normal curve cannot be used as a model of the data. Thus, the normal curve cannot be applied at will to all the distributions encountered by criminal justice researchers but must be used with a good deal of discretion.

THE AREA UNDER THE NORMAL CURVE

It is important to keep in mind that the normal curve is an ideal or theoretical distribution (i.e., a probability distribution). Therefore, we denote its mean by μ and its standard deviation by σ. The mean of the normal distribution is at its exact center (see Figure 5.5). The standard deviation (σ) is the distance between the mean (μ) and the point on the baseline just below where the reversed S-shaped portion of the curve shifts direction.

To employ the normal distribution in solving problems, we must acquaint ourselves with the **area under the normal curve**: *the area that lies between the curve and the baseline containing 100% or all of the cases in any given normal distribution.* Figure 5.5 illustrates this characteristic.

AREA UNDER THE NORMAL CURVE

That area which lies between the curve and the baseline containing 100% or all of the cases in any given normal distribution.

We could enclose a portion of this total area by drawing lines from any two points on the baseline up to the curve. For instance, using the mean as a point of departure, we could draw one line at the mean (μ) and another line at the point that is 1σ (1 standard deviation distance) above the mean. As illustrated in Figure 5.6, this enclosed portion of the normal curve includes 34.13% of the total frequency.

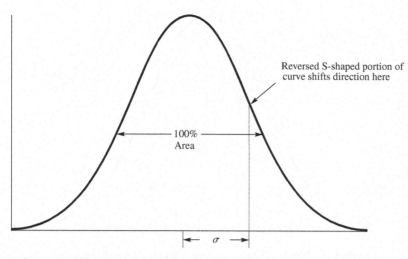

FIGURE 5.5   The Total Area under the Normal Curve.

In the same way, we can say that 47.72% of the cases under the normal curve lie between the mean and 2σ above the mean and that 49.87% lie between the mean and 3σ above the mean (see Figure 5.7).

As we shall see, *a constant proportion of the total area under the normal curve will lie between the mean and any given distance from the mean as measured in sigma (σ) units.* This is true regardless of the mean and standard deviation of the particular distribution and applies universally to all data that are normally distributed. Thus, the area under the normal curve between the mean and the point 1σ above the mean *always* turns out to include 34.13% of the total cases, whether we are discussing the distribution of height, intelligence, political orientation, or the pattern of wear in a doorway. The basic requirement, in each case, is that we are working with a *normal* distribution of scores.

The symmetrical nature of the normal curve leads us to make another important point: *Any given sigma distance above the mean contains the identical proportion of cases as the same sigma distance below the mean.* Thus, if 34.13% of the total area lies between the mean and 1σ *above* the mean, then 34.13% of the total area also lies between the mean and 1σ *below* the mean; if 47.72% lies between the mean and 2σ *above* the mean, then 47.72% lies between the mean and 2σ *below* the mean; if 49.87% lies between the mean and 3σ *above* the mean, then 49.87% also lies between the mean and

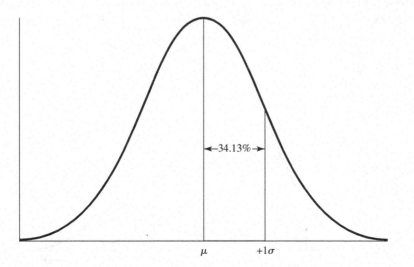

FIGURE 5.6   The Percentage of Total Area under the Normal Curve between μ and the Point 1σ above μ.

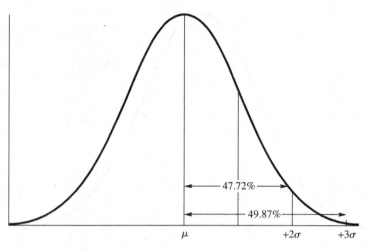

FIGURE 5.7 The Percentage of Total Area under the Normal Curve between μ and the Points That Are 2σ and 3σ from μ.

3σ *below* the mean. In other words, as illustrated in Figure 5.8, 68.26% of the total area of the normal curve (34.13% + 34.13%) falls between -1σ and $+1\sigma$ from the mean; 95.44% of the area (47.72% + 47.72%) falls between -2σ and $+2\sigma$ from the mean; and 99.74%, or almost all, of the cases (49.87% + 49.87%) falls between -3σ and $+3\sigma$ from the mean. It can be said, then, that six standard deviations include practically all of the cases (more than 99%) under any normal distribution.

Clarifying the Standard Deviation

An important function of the normal curve is to help interpret and clarify the meaning of the standard deviation. To understand how this function is carried out, let us examine what some researchers tell us about gender differences in IQ. Despite the claims of male chauvinists, there is evidence that both males and females have mean IQ scores of approximately 100. Let us also say these IQ scores differ markedly in terms of variability around the mean. In particular, let us suppose hypothetically that male IQs have greater *heterogeneity* than female IQs; that is, the distribution of male IQs contains a much larger percentage of extreme scores representing very bright as well as very dull individuals, whereas the distribution of female IQs has a larger percentage of scores located closer to the average, the point of maximum frequency at the center.

Because the standard deviation is a measure of variation, these gender differences in variability should be reflected in the sigma value of each distribution of IQ scores. Thus, we might find

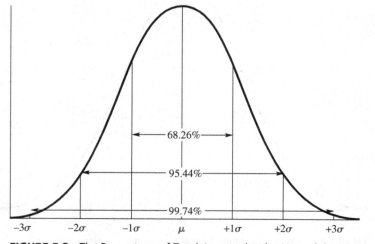

FIGURE 5.8 The Percentage of Total Area under the Normal Curve between -1σ and $+1\sigma$, -2σ and $+2\sigma$, and -3σ and $+3\sigma$.

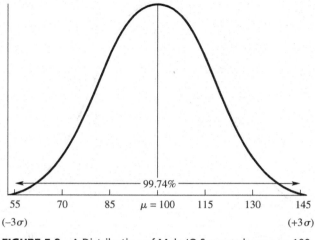

FIGURE 5.9 A Distribution of Male IQ Scores where $\mu = 100$ and $\sigma = 15$.

that the standard deviation is 15 for male IQs, but only 10 for female IQs. Knowing the standard deviation of each set of IQ scores and assuming that each set is normally distributed, we could then estimate and compare the percentage of males and females having any given range of IQ scores.

For instance, measuring the baseline of the distribution of male IQ in standard deviation units, we would know that 68.26% of male IQ scores fall between -1σ and $+1\sigma$ from the mean. Because the standard deviation is always given in raw-score units and $\sigma = 15$, we would also know that these are points on the distribution at which IQ scores of 115 and 85 are located ($\mu - \sigma = 100 - 15 = 85$ and $\mu + \sigma = 100 + 15 = 115$). Thus, 68.26% of the males would have IQ scores that fall between 85 and 115.

Moving away from the mean and further out from these points, we would find, as illustrated in Figure 5.9, that 99.74%, or practically all, of the males have IQ scores between 55 and 145 (between -3σ and $+3\sigma$).

In the same manner, looking next at the distribution of female IQ scores as depicted in Figure 5.10, we see that 99.74% of these cases would fall between scores of 70 and 130 (between -3σ and $+3\sigma$). In contrast to males, then, the distribution of female IQ scores could be regarded as being relatively homogeneous, having a smaller range of extreme scores in either direction. This difference is reflected in the comparative size of each standard deviation and in the range of IQ scores falling between -3σ and $+3\sigma$ from the mean.

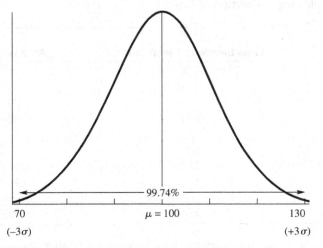

FIGURE 5.10 A Distribution of Female IQ Scores where $\mu = 100$ and $\sigma = 10$.

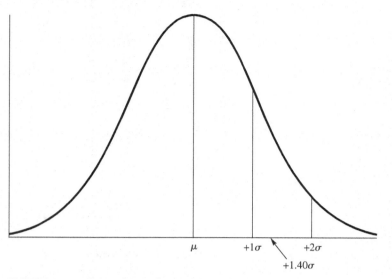

FIGURE 5.11 The Position of a Raw Score that Lies 1.40σ above μ.

Using Table A

In discussing the normal distribution, we have so far treated only those distances from the mean that are exact multiples of the standard deviation. That is, they were precisely one, two, or three standard deviations either above or below the mean. The question now arises: What must we do to determine the percentage of cases for distances lying between any two score values? For instance, suppose that we wish to determine the percentage of total area that falls between the mean and, say, a raw score located 1.40σ above the mean. As illustrated in Figure 5.11, a raw score 1.40σ above the mean is obviously greater than 1σ but less than 2σ from the mean. Thus, we know this distance from the mean would include more than 34.13% but less than 47.72% of the total area under the normal curve.

To determine the exact percentage within this interval, we must employ Table A in Appendix C. This shows the percentage under the normal curve (1) between the mean and various sigma distances from the mean (in column b) and (2) at or beyond various scores toward either tail of the distribution (in column c). These sigma distances (from 0.00 to 4.00) are labeled z in the left-hand column (column a) of Table A and have been given to two decimal places.

Notice that the symmetry of the normal curve makes it possible to give percentages for only one side of the mean, that is, only one-half of the curve (50%). Values in Table A represent either side. The following is a portion of Table A:

(a) z	(b) Area between Mean and z	(c) Area beyond z
.00	.00	50.00
.01	.40	49.60
.02	.80	49.20
.03	1.20	48.80
.04	1.60	48.40
.05	1.99	48.01
.06	2.39	47.61
.07	2.79	47.21
.08	3.19	46.81
.09	3.59	46.41

When learning to use and understand Table A, we might first attempt to locate the percentage of cases between a sigma distance of 1.00 and the mean (the reason being that we already know that 34.13% of the total area falls between these points on the baseline). Looking at column b of Table A (in Appendix C), we see it indeed indicates that exactly 34.13% of the total frequency falls between the mean and a sigma distance (z) of 1.00. Likewise, we see that the area between the mean and the sigma distance 2.00 includes exactly 47.72% of the total area under the curve.

But what about finding the percentage of cases between the mean and a sigma distance of 1.40? This was the problem in Figure 5.11, which necessitated the use of the table in the first place. The entry in column b corresponding to a sigma distance of 1.40 includes 41.92% of the total area under the curve. Finally, how do we determine the percentage of cases at or beyond 1.40 standard deviations from the mean? Without a table to help us, we might locate the percentage in this area under the normal curve by simply subtracting our earlier answer from 50%, because this is the total area lying on either side of the mean. However, this has already been done in column c of Table A, where we see that exactly 8.08% (50 − 41.92 = 8.08) of the cases fall at or above the score that is 1.40 standard deviations from the mean.

STANDARD SCORES AND THE NORMAL CURVE

We are now prepared to find the percentage of the total area under the normal curve associated with any given sigma distance from the mean. However, at least one more important question remains to be answered: How do we determine the sigma distance of any given raw score? That is, how do we translate our raw score—the score that we originally collected from our respondents—into units of standard deviation? If we wished to translate feet into yards, we would simply divide the number of feet by 3, because there are 3 ft in a yard. Likewise, if we were translating minutes into hours, we would divide the number of minutes by 60, because there are 60 min in every hour. In precisely the same manner, we can translate any given raw score into sigma units by dividing the distance of the raw score from the mean by the standard deviation. To illustrate, let us imagine a raw score of 6 from a distribution in which μ is 3 and σ is 2. Taking the difference between the raw score and the mean and obtaining a deviation (6 − 3), we see that a raw score of 6 is 3 raw-score units above the mean. Dividing this raw-score distance by $\sigma = 2$, we see that this raw score is 1.5 (one and one-half) standard deviations above the mean. In other words, the sigma distance of a raw score of 6 *in this particular distribution* is 1.5 standard deviations above the mean. We should note that regardless of the measurement situation, there are always 3 ft in a yard and 60 min in an hour. The constancy that marks these other standard measures is not shared by the standard deviation. It changes from one distribution to another. For this reason, we must know the standard deviation of a distribution by calculating it, estimating it, or being given it by someone else before we are able to translate any particular raw score into units of standard deviation.

The process that we have just illustrated—that of finding sigma distance from the mean—yields a value called a **z score** or **standard score**, which indicates the *direction and degree that any given raw score deviates from the mean of a distribution on a scale of sigma units* (notice that the left-hand column of Table A in Appendix C is labeled z). Thus, a z score of +1.4 indicates that the raw score lies 1.4σ (or almost $1\frac{1}{2}\sigma$) *above* the mean, whereas a z score of −2.1 means that the raw score falls slightly more than 2σ *below* the mean (see Figure 5.12).

We obtain a z score by finding the deviation $(X - \mu)$, which gives the distance of the raw score from the mean, and then dividing this raw-score deviation by the standard deviation.

Computed by formula,

$$z = \frac{X - \mu}{\sigma}$$

where μ = mean of a distribution
σ = standard deviation of a distribution
z = standard score

Z SCORE (STANDARD SCORE)

A value that indicates the direction and degree that any given raw score deviates from the mean of a distribution on a scale of standard deviation units.

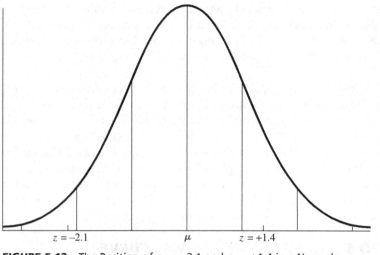

FIGURE 5.12   The Position of $z = -2.1$ and $z = +1.4$ in a Normal Distribution.

As an example, suppose we are studying the response times for emergency calls into a city's 911 phone system. Suppose also that the distribution of response time (the time between police dispatch and arrival at the scene) is normal with a mean of 5.6 min and a standard deviation of 1.8 min. Given the normality assumption, we can translate any raw score from this distribution, such as 8.0 min, into a standard score in the following manner:

$$z = \frac{8.0 - 5.6}{1.8}$$

$$= \frac{2.4}{1.8}$$

$$= +1.33$$

Thus, a response time of 8.0 min is 1.33 standard deviations above the mean response time of 5.6 min (see Figure 5.13).

We can also work with values that fall below the mean. Positioned to the left of the center point, these below-average values translate into negative z scores. Suppose we were interested in

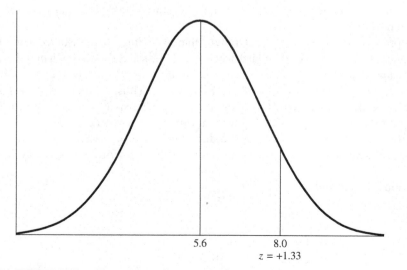

FIGURE 5.13   The Position of $z = +1.33$ for the Raw Score of 8.0.

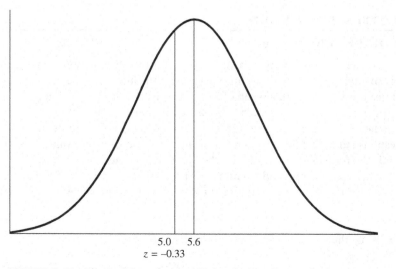

5.0   5.6
z = −0.33

FIGURE 5.14   The Position of $z = -.33$ for the Raw Score of 5.0.

calculating the standard score corresponding to a 5-min response time, again within a normal distribution having a mean $\mu = 5.6$ and a standard deviation $\sigma = 1.8$.

$$z = \frac{5.0 - 5.6}{1.8}$$

$$= \frac{-0.6}{1.8}$$

$$= -.33$$

Thus, as shown in Figure 5.14, the raw score of 5 in this distribution of scores falls 0.33 standard deviations below the mean.

Finding Probability under the Normal Curve

The normal curve can be used in conjunction with z scores and Table A to determine the probability of obtaining any raw score in a distribution. In the present context, the normal curve is a distribution in which it is possible to determine probabilities associated with various points along its baseline. As noted earlier, the normal curve is a probability distribution in which the total area under the curve equals 100%; it contains a central area surrounding the mean, where scores occur most frequently, and smaller areas toward either end, where there is a gradual flattening out and thus a smaller proportion of extremely high and low scores. In probability terms, then, we can say that probability decreases as we travel along the baseline away from the mean in either direction. Thus, to say that 68.26% of the total frequency under the normal curve falls between -1σ and $+1\sigma$ from the mean is to say that the probability is approximately 68 in 100 that any given raw score will fall within this interval. Similarly, to say that 95.44% of the total area under the normal curve falls between -2σ and $+2\sigma$ from the mean is also to say that the probability is approximately 95 in 100 that any raw score will fall within this interval, and so on.

This is precisely the same concept of probability or relative frequency that we saw in operation when flipping pairs of coins. Note, however, that the probabilities associated with areas under the normal curve are always given relative to 100%, which is the entire area under the curve (e.g., 68 in 100, 95 in 100, 99 in 100).

STEP-BY-STEP ILLUSTRATION

Probability Under the Normal Curve

To apply the concept of probability in relation to the normal distribution, let us return to an earlier example involving response times for emergency calls into a 911 system. The distribution of response times was normal with a mean of 5.6 min and a standard deviation of 1.8 min.

By applying the z-score formula, we learned earlier that an 8.0-min response time was 1.33σ above the mean of 5.6 min, that is, $z = +1.33$. Let us now determine the probability of obtaining a response time that lies between the mean of 5.6 and the score value of 8.0 min. In other words, what is the probability of randomly choosing, in just one attempt, a call into 911 having a response time between 5.6 min and 8.0 min? The problem is graphically illustrated in Figure 5.15 (we are solving for the shaded area under the curve) and can be solved in two steps using the z-score formula and Table A in Appendix C.

Step 1 Translate the raw score (8.0 min) into a z score.

$$z = \frac{X - \mu}{\sigma}$$

$$= \frac{8.0 - 5.6}{1.8}$$

$$= \frac{2.4}{1.8}$$

$$= +1.33$$

Thus, a raw score of 8.0 min is located $+1.33\sigma$ above the mean.

Step 2 Using Table A, find the percentage of total area under the curve falling between the z score ($z = 1.33$) and the mean.

In column b of Table A, we find that 40.82% of response times are between 5.6 min and 8.0 min. Thus, $P = .4082$ is the probability that we would obtain a response time that lies between 5.6 min and 8.0 min.

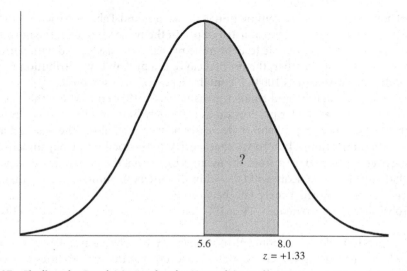

FIGURE 5.15 Finding the Total Area under the Normal Curve between $\mu = 5.6$ and $z = +1.33$.

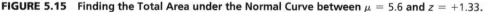

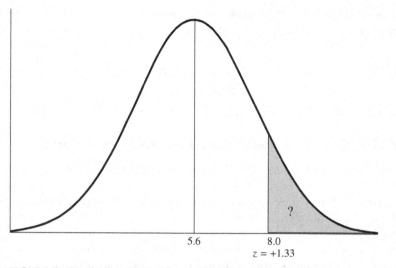

FIGURE 5.16 Finding the Total Area under the Normal Curve beyond $z = +1.33$.

In the previous example, we were asked to determine the probability associated with the distance between the mean and a particular sigma distance from it. Many times, however, we may wish to find the percentage of area that lies at or beyond a particular raw score toward either tail of the distribution or to find the probability of obtaining these scores. For instance, in the present case, we might wish to learn the probability of obtaining a response time of 8.0 or greater.

This problem can be illustrated graphically, as shown in Figure 5.16 (we are solving for the shaded area under the curve). In this case, we would follow steps 1 and 2, obtaining the z score and then finding the percentage under the normal curve between the mean and $z = +1.33$ (from Table A). In the present case, however, we must go a step beyond and subtract the percentage obtained in Table A (column b) from 50%—that percentage of the total area lying on either side of the mean. Fortunately, column c of Table A has already done this for us.

Therefore, subtracting 40.82% from 50% or simply looking in column c of Table A, we learn that slightly more than 9% (9.18%) of response times fall at or beyond 8.0 min. In probability terms, $P = .0918$; Thus, we can say there are only slightly more than 9 chances in 100 that we select at random a call for service having a response time of 8.0 min or longer.

It was earlier noted that because the normal curve is symmetrical, any given sigma distance above the mean contains the identical proportion of cases as the same sigma distance below the mean. For this reason, our procedure in finding probabilities associated with points below the mean is identical to that followed in the previous examples.

For instance, the percentage of total area between $z = -1.33$ and the mean is identical to the percentage between $z = +1.33$ and the mean. Therefore, we know that $P = .4082$ of selecting at random a 911 call having a response time between 3.2 min and the mean of 5.6 min. Likewise, the percentage of total area at or beyond $z = -1.33$ (3.2 min or less) equals that at or beyond $z = +1.33$ (8.0 min or more). Thus, we know $P = .0918$ that we select at random a call for service with a response time of 3.2 min or less.

We can also use Table A to find the probability of obtaining more than a single portion of the area under the normal curve. For instance, we have already determined that $P = .09$ for response times of 3.2 or less as well as response times of 8.0 or more. To find the probability of obtaining a response time of either 3.2 or less or 8.0 or more, we simply add their separate probabilities as follows:

$$P = .0918 + .0918$$
$$= .1836$$

Similarly, we can find the probability of obtaining a response time that falls between 3.2 min and 8.0 min by adding the probabilities associated with z scores of 1.33 on either side of the mean. Therefore,

$$P = .4082 + .4082$$
$$= .8164$$

Notice that $.8164 + .1836$ equals 1.00, representing all possible outcomes under the normal curve.

Finding Scores from Probability Based on the Normal Curve

In the previous section, we used knowledge about the mean and standard deviation of a normally distributed variable (such as 911 response times) to determine particular areas under the normal curve. The portions of area were used in turn to calculate various percentages or probabilities about the distribution, such as determining the percentage calls of 911 having response times of at least 8.0 min.

The process of using Table A to translate z scores into portions of the total area can be reversed to calculate score values from particular portions of area or percentages. We know without having to consult Table A that 50% of the response times are at or above 5.6 min. Because of symmetry of shape, the median response time that divides the distribution in half is the same as the mean. But what if we wanted to know the response time that defines the top 25% of the distribution, the shaded portion in Figure 5.17?

The threshold for the top 25% can be determined by consulting Table A for a particular portion of area (such as the highest 25% tail) to determine the z-score values and then translating that z score into its raw score (response time) equivalent. Specifically, we scan through column c to locate the area beyond (in this case, above) z that is closest to 25%. Apparently, 25.14% falls beyond a z score of .67. We can then use a modified form of the usual z-score formula to solve for X given a particular value of z.

$$\boxed{X = \mu + z\sigma}$$

To find the top 25% threshold with $\mu = 5.6$ and $\sigma = 1.8$, and as we found from Table A, $z = .67$,

$$X = 5.6 + .67(1.8)$$
$$= 5.6 + 1.2$$
$$= 6.8$$

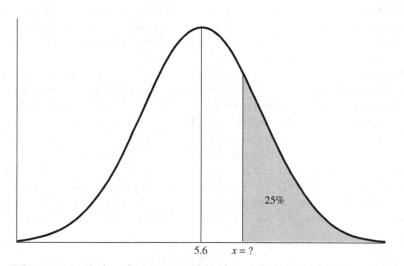

FIGURE 5.17 Finding the Response Time above Which 25% of the Cases Fall.

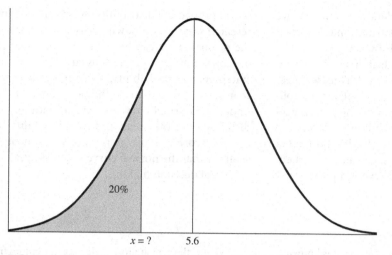

FIGURE 5.18 Finding the Response Time below Which 20% of the Cases Fall.

Thus, on the basis of the normal shape of the response time distribution with a mean of 5.6 min and a standard deviation of 1.8 min, we can determine that 25% of response times are 6.8 min or longer.

Step-by-Step Illustration

Finding Scores From Probability Based on the Normal Curve

Continuing with the response time distribution having a mean of 5.6 min and a standard deviation of 1.8 min, let us determine the cutoff for the quickest 20%.

Step 1 Locate in Table A the z score that cuts off the area closest to 20% below it (see Figure 5.18). Scanning column c of Table A for an area closest to 20%, we see that .84 cuts off 20.05% of the total area. But note that because the point of interest is below the mean, we use a z score of $-.84$.

Step 2 Convert the z value into its raw score equivalent:

$$
\begin{aligned}
X &= \mu + z\sigma \\
&= 5.4 - .84(1.8) \\
&= 5.4 - 1.5 \\
&= 3.9
\end{aligned}
$$

Thus, we can say that about 20% of the calls to 911 are handled within 3.9 min. Conversely, 80% of the calls have a response time of 3.9 min or longer.

Summary

In this chapter, we introduced the concept of probability—the relative likelihood of occurrence of any given outcome or event—as the foundation for decision making in statistics. Indicated by the number of times an event can occur relative to the total number of times any event can occur, probabilities range from 0 (an impossible event) to 1 (a certainty). Probabilities can be summed as in the addition rule, so as to establish the likelihood of obtaining any one of several different outcomes; they can also be multiplied as in the multiplication rule, to determine the likelihood of obtaining a combination of independent outcomes. As we saw in earlier chapters, a frequency distribution is based on actual observations in the real world. By contrast, a probability distribution is theoretical or ideal; it specifies what the percentages should be in a perfect world. Thus, we specify the possible values of a variable and calculate the probabilities associated with each. Analogous to the percentages in a frequency distribution, the probabilities we obtain in a probability distribution represent the likelihood (rather than the frequency of occurrence) of each value. The theoretical model known as the normal curve is a particularly

useful probability distribution for its applications to actual research situations. Known for its symmetrical "bell shape," the normal curve can be used for describing distributions of scores, interpreting the standard deviation, and making statements of probability. In conjunction with standard scores, we can determine the percentage of the total area under the normal curve associated with any given sigma distance from the mean and the probability of obtaining any raw score in a distribution. In subsequent chapters, we shall see that the normal curve is an essential ingredient of statistical decision making.

Questions and Problems

1. The relative likelihood of occurrence of an event is known as that event's _____.
   a. area under the curve
   b. probability
   c. standard deviation
   d. all of the above
2. Five youths are in detention at juvenile court. One of these youths committed a violent offense. What is the probability of selecting at random this youth from this group?
   a. 1
   b. 2
   c. .2
   d. 4
   e. cannot be determined from information provided
3. A statement that the probability of catching the robber is $P = 1.67$ must be false because probability varies from _____.
   a. zero to infinity
   b. zero to 1.0
   c. zero to 100
   d. -3.0 to $+3.0$
4. A _____ indicates how far an individual score falls from the mean of a distribution.
   a. standard deviation
   b. z score
   c. percentage
   d. probability
5. The following students are enrolled in a course in forensics. They are listed along with their year in school and their major.

Student	Year	Major
1	Sophomore	Biology
2	Junior	Criminal justice
3	Junior	Criminal justice
4	Senior	Criminal justice
5	Junior	English
6	Senior	Biology
7	Junior	Criminal justice
8	Sophomore	Criminal justice
9	Junior	Criminal justice
10	Senior	Psychology

What is the probability of selecting at random from this class _____?
   a. a sophomore
   b. a student majoring in criminal justice
   c. a junior or a senior
   d. not a psychology major
6. Under any normal distribution of scores, what percentage of the total area falls _____?
   a. between the mean (μ) and a score that lies one standard deviation (1σ) above the mean
   b. between the mean (μ) and a score that lies one standard deviation (-1σ) below the mean
   c. between the mean (μ) and a score that lies two standard deviations (2σ) above the mean
   d. between a score that lies two standard deviations (-2σ) below the mean and a score that lies two standard deviations (2σ) above the mean
7. Police departments use exams as part of their promotion process whereby officers have to score higher than 80% of those taking the exam to be considered for promotion. (This is a z score of 0.83 or above.) Two officers write their exams. Officer #1 receives a grade of 76. Officer #2 receives a grade of 52. Note that the mean $\mu = 62$ and the standard deviation $\sigma = 11$.
   a. Calculate the z score for officer #1. Was this score high enough to be considered for promotion?
   b. Do the same calculations and summary for officer #2.
8. A police detective was interested in studying the amount of time spent interrogating criminal suspects. Collecting data from police reports on all of the interrogations she and her colleagues performed over the past 2 years, she found that the lengths of time were normally distributed with a mean length of 106 min and a standard deviation of 8 min. Find the
   a. percentage of interrogations that last 2 h or more.
   b. probability that a particular interrogation lasted 2 h or more.
9. Among the correctional officers in a particular state, the mean number of sick days per year is $\mu = 5.3$ with a standard deviation $\sigma = 2.4$. Assuming absences among correctional officers are normally distributed, determine the probability that
   a. a particular officer missed 8 or more days.
   b. a particular officer missed between 3.5 and 4 days.

10. Anger management (AM) scores are normally distributed with a mean $\mu = 250$ and a standard deviation $\sigma = 35$. On the basis of this distribution, determine the
    a. percentage of AM scores between 250 and 285.
    b. probability of selecting a person at random having an AM score between 250 and 285.
    c. percentage of AM scores between 215 and 285.
    d. probability of selecting a person at random having an AM score between 215 and 250.
    e. probability of selecting a person with an AM score below 220.

11. Examination of court records in a particular state shows that the mean prison sentence length for first-offense drug dealers is 26 months with a standard deviation $\sigma = 2$ months. The records also reveal that sentence lengths are approximately normally distributed.
    a. What percentage of first-time offenders convicted for drug dealing receive 23 or fewer months?
    b. A defense attorney was concerned that his client's sentence was particularly harsh at 30 months. What is the probability of receiving a sentence length of 30 months or more?

    c. Another defense attorney is pleased that his client received a sentence of 18 months. How likely is it that a person would receive a sentence of 18 or fewer months?

12. Traffic safety for police officers can be a dangerous business. A recent study in a Southern city shows that officers averaged $\mu = 2.2$ accidents and a standard deviation of $\sigma = 1.5$ over a 2-year period.
    a. What percentage of police officers had one or fewer accidents?
    b. What is the probability of selecting a police officer at random who had two or more accidents?

13. Individuals sentenced to death spend a certain amount of time on death row. The amount of time spent on death row is normally distributed with a few people spending a relatively short or long amount of time on death row with the majority spending about the same amount of time on death row. The mean time spent on death row in 2010 was 178 months with a standard deviation of 30 months.
    a. What is the z score of a person on death row for at least 184 months?
    b. Find the number of months on death row below which 75% of the inmates fall.

Computer Exercises

1. Education is an important issue. Using the General Social Survey, find the mean and standard deviation for the highest year of school completed (EDUC).
    a. Using this mean and standard deviation, what percentage of Americans are expected to complete 16 or more years of education (16 or above)?
    b. What percentage of Americans are expected to report 10 or fewer years as their highest year of school completed?
    c. What is the probability of selecting at random a person in America who completes more than 12 years of school (13 or more)?

2. Using the frequencies procedure (ANALYZE, DESCRIPTIVE STATISTICS, FREQUENCIES), request a histogram of television viewing data from the General Social Survey (TVHOURS) with the normal curve overlay (from the Charts button), as well as the mean and standard deviation (from the Statistics button).
    a. Comment on the closeness of the actual distribution to the normal curve.

    b. Based on the normal distribution (using the z score and Table A), what is the probability that a person watches 3 or more hours of television per day?
    c. Compare the probability from the normal distribution to the actual proportion of reports of 3 or more hours of television viewing per day.

3. Using the frequencies procedure (ANALYZE, DESCRIPTIVE STATISTICS, FREQUENCIES), request a histogram of total family income (INCOME06) from the General Social Survey with the normal curve overlay (from the Charts button), as well as the mean and standard deviation (from the Statistics button).
    a. Comment on the closeness of the actual distribution to the normal curve.
    b. Based on the normal distribution (using the z score and Table A), what is the probability that a family has an income of $75,000 to $89,000 (21 on the scale)?
    c. Compare the probability from the normal distribution that you just calculated in part b to the proportion of the actual scores of persons who have a family income of $75,000 or more (21 to 25 on the scale).

6

Samples and Populations

Criminologists and criminal justice researchers generally seek to draw conclusions about large numbers of individuals. For instance, they might be interested in the 310 million inhabitants of the United States, 1,000 members of a particular police union, the 10,000 African Americans who are living in a southern town, or the 45,000 individuals under probation supervision for drunk driving in a particular state.

Until this point, we have been pretending that the researcher investigates the entire group that he or she tries to understand. Known as a **population** or **universe**, this group consists of a set of individuals who share at least one characteristic, whether common citizenship, membership in a police union, ethnicity, or the like. Thus, we might speak about the population of the United States, the population of police union members, the population of African Americans residing in a particular town, or the population of people with drunk-driving convictions.

Because criminal justice researchers operate with limited time, energy, and financial resources, they rarely study each and every member of a given population. Instead, researchers study only a **sample**—a smaller number of individuals from the population. Through the sampling process, researchers seek to generalize from a sample (a small group) to the entire population from which it was taken (a larger group).

In recent years, for example, sampling techniques have allowed political pollsters to make fairly accurate predictions of election results based on samples of only a few hundred registered voters. For this reason, candidates for major political offices routinely monitor the effectiveness of their campaign strategy by examining sample surveys of voter opinion.

Sampling is an integral part of everyday life. How else would we gain much information about other people than by sampling those around us? For example, we might casually discuss political issues with other students to find out where students generally stand with respect to their political opinions; we might attempt to determine how our classmates are studying for a particular examination by contacting only a few members of the class beforehand; we might even invest in the stock market after finding that a small sample of our associates have made money through investments.

ERRORS IN THE CONDUCT OF RESEARCH

In carrying out even the most effective research design, error can play a role. In fact, it can be seen as a likely presence whenever a study is conducted. We can, however, anticipate and reduce error to the point where it does not obliterate the value of the findings.

The data-collection process is replete with possible errors. If large numbers of potential respondents refuse to cooperate, then their absence from a study can be an important source of bias. Those

POPULATION (UNIVERSE)

Any set of individuals who share at least one characteristic.

SAMPLE

A smaller number of individuals taken from some population (for the purpose of generalizing to the entire population from which it was taken).

who participate might differ in significant ways from those who refuse. In opinion surveys, those who refuse might not have made up their minds regarding an issue, resulting in a sample of respondents whose views are more extreme than those in the larger population. Investigating public opinion regarding the death penalty, a large refusal rate might lead a researcher to exaggerate the proportion of the population holding extremely favorable and unfavorable attitudes toward executions. The refusal to cooperate can be particularly problematic for interviewing inmates who may regard the researcher as an authority figure who cannot be trusted. The net result may be to scare potential respondents into an unwillingness to participate.

The procedures employed by researchers might also fail to contact a segment of the population. For example, lack of adequate training or supervising of interviewers can result in the underrepresentation of individuals who are hard to reach; for example, they might live in third-floor walk-ups, might be homeless and live on the streets, or might be away from their residences for prolonged periods of time. In a survey of a particular community, interviewers who go door to door might be reluctant to collect data from respondents in high-crime or impoverished neighborhoods. In a telephone survey, the use of a telephone directory might exclude the growing number of individuals who have a cell phone but no landline. Relying on e-mail addresses might be an efficient approach for studying users of the Internet but would not be representative of technology-shy members of a population who probably differ sharply from their high-tech counterparts in terms of socioeconomic status and age.

Even when respondents are contacted by researchers and are willing to answer questions, they might not be totally honest or candid. Errors can occur among respondents who refuse to answer certain sensitive questions or give deceptive answers. Hoping for a reprieve or a new trial, for example, some inmates may have a vested interest in portraying themselves as innocent or remorseful. As a result, an interviewer might be forced to frame questions so as to be answered in general terms or in the third person.

Of course, it is not only inmates who are concerned about how they come across to researchers. What respondents in the general population tell researchers may be affected by a tendency to give a socially desirable response, that is, to report what they believe makes them look good, even if it is untruthful. Or, they might want to please the researcher by giving an answer that they believe the researcher would like to hear. In surveys of American adults, respondents might not want to reveal their age or their income. As a result, researchers may ask only for their year of birth rather than directly asking for their age. Moreover, they might place the most sensitive items (e.g., income categories) at the end of an interview, just to make sure of securing as much information as possible before asking the more difficult questions. Still, those respondents who are especially concerned about their own aging might indicate a birth date that makes them out to be younger than they really are. Or, they might be willing to indicate their income, but falsely place themselves in a category that suggests they make more money than is the case. If they are asked about their participation in illegal or unethical behavior (e.g., cheating or the use of illicit drugs), they might give a false report to an interviewer or on a questionnaire.

Even more likely, respondents may have forgotten the specific circumstances of events that have happened in the past. Individuals who are asked to recall their activities over a period of time (e.g., number of visits to a doctor, tutoring sessions, classroom absences during the past year) may be willing to share this information but unwittingly provide inaccurate data based simply on faulty memory. The National Crime Victimization Survey asks a nationally representative sample of some 75,000 individuals to recall characteristics of their victimization by sexual assault, robbery, assault, theft, burglary, and motor vehicle theft, during the 6-month period prior to the interview. Some victims have simply forgotten the details of the crimes committed against them.

Moreover, it is also possible that items on a questionnaire have been constructed with ambiguous wording, so that respondents misunderstand the questions they are supposed to answer. This error can be easily reduced, if not eliminated, by pretesting the questionnaire or interview schedule for willingness and ability to give credible responses on a small group of individuals prior to its administration to members of the sample.

Finally, much error originates in the use of incorrect procedures for collecting or processing data. Especially when they work with large amounts of data, researchers can make mistakes when they input numbers, analyze results, and construct tables and graphs displaying their results. The use of computer software has greatly reduced the prevalence of procedural mistakes, but they continue to be a possible source of error that may lead to reaching confusing and misleading conclusions.

SAMPLING METHODS

The criminal justice researcher's methods of sampling are usually more thoughtful and scientific than the methods of everyday life. He or she is primarily concerned with whether sample members are representative enough of the entire population to permit making accurate generalizations about that population. Under optimal conditions, the researcher would collect data using a **random sampling** method, whereby each and every member of the population is given an equal chance of being selected for the sample. But optimal conditions do not always prevail, and a researcher might have to settle for a sampling method that is less than random.

There are times when a researcher might simply include the most convenient cases in a sample. For example, an instructor might ask all students in the class to take part in an experiment or fill out a questionnaire. Or, a researcher might sample characteristics in the proportions they occupy in the population. For example, if 42% of a population is known to consist of females, then the interviewers in a study would be given a quota, so that 42% of their respondents would be expected to be females.

By contrast, the equal probability characteristic of random sampling indicates that every member of the population must be identified before the random sample is drawn (so that each has an equal probability of being selected for the sample), a requirement usually fulfilled by obtaining a list that includes every population member. A little thought will suggest that getting such a complete list of the population members is not always an easy task, especially if one is studying a large and diverse population. To take a relatively easy example, where could we get a *complete* list of students currently enrolled in a large university? Those researchers who have tried will attest to its difficulty. For a more laborious assignment, try finding a list of every resident in a large city. How can we be certain of identifying everyone, even those residents who do not wish to be identified?

A **simple random sample**, the most basic sampling approach, can be obtained by a process not unlike that of the now familiar technique of putting everyone's name on separate slips of paper and, while blindfolded, drawing only a few names from a hat. This procedure ideally gives every population member an equal chance for sample selection since one, and only one, slip per person is included. For several reasons (including the fact that the researcher would need an extremely large hat), the criminal justice researcher attempting to take a random sample usually does not draw names from a hat. Instead, she or he uses a *table of random numbers* such as Table B in Appendix C. A portion of a table of random numbers is shown here:

Column Number

Row	1	2	3	4	5	6	7	8	9	10	11	12	13	14	15	16	17	18	19	20
1	0	6	9	0	6	2	8	5	3	6	9	6	4	3	3	2	8	1	2	0
2	4	9	6	8	5	5	3	0	7	8	9	2	9	2	2	1	0	1	1	0
3	9	4	6	2	2	3	8	6	7	8	4	0	1	1	1	7	0	3	7	0
4	9	5	0	4	6	2	2	4	6	4	0	9	6	7	4	8	0	0	7	4
5	2	0	3	2	7	6	6	2	3	9	7	5	1	4	8	8	7	9	7	5

A table of random numbers is constructed so as to generate a series of numbers having no particular pattern or order. As a result, the process of using a table of random numbers yields a representative sample similar to that produced by putting slips of paper in a hat and drawing names while blindfolded.

To draw a random sample by means of a table of random numbers, the researcher first obtains a list of the population and assigns a unique identifying number to each member. For instance, if she

---

RANDOM SAMPLING

A sampling method whereby each and every population member has an equal chance of being drawn into the sample.

SIMPLE RANDOM SAMPLING

A random sampling method whereby a table of random numbers is employed to select a sample that is representative of the larger population.

is conducting research on the 500 students enrolled in Introduction to Criminal Justice, she might secure a list of students from the instructor and give each student a number from 001 to 500. Having prepared the list, she proceeds to draw the members of her sample from a table of random numbers. Let us say the researcher seeks to draw a sample of 50 students to represent the 500 members of a class population. She might enter the random numbers table at any number (with eyes closed, for example) and move in any direction, taking appropriate numbers until she has selected the 50 sample members. Looking at the earlier portion of the random numbers table, we might arbitrarily start at the intersection of column 1 and row 5, moving from left to right to take every number that comes up between 001 and 500. The first numbers to appear at column 1 and row 5 are 2, 0, and 3. Therefore, student number 203 is the first population member chosen for the sample. Continuing from left to right, we see that 2, 7, and 6 come up next, so that student number 276 is selected. This process is continued until all 50 sample members have been taken. A note to the student: In using the table of random numbers, always disregard numbers that come up a second time or are higher than needed.

All random sample methods are actually variations of the simple random sampling procedure just illustrated. For instance, with **systematic sampling**, a table of random numbers is not required, because a list of population members is sampled by fixed intervals—every *n*th member is included. To illustrate, in drawing a sample from the population of the tenants in a particular housing project, we might arrange a list of tenants, then beginning at a random starting point, take every 10th name on the list, and come up with a sample of 1,000 tenants.

Another variation on simple random sampling, the **stratified sample**, involves dividing the population into more homogeneous subgroups or *strata* from which simple random samples are then taken. Suppose, for example, we wish to study the acceptance of capital punishment among the population of a certain city. Because attitudes toward the death penalty vary by religion and socioeconomic status, we might stratify our population on these variables, thereby forming more homogeneous subgroups with respect to acceptance of capital punishment. More specifically, we could identify Catholics, Protestants, Muslims, and Jews as well as upper-class, middle-class, and lower-class members of the population. Having identified our strata, we would then proceed to take a simple random sample from each subgroup or stratum (e.g., from lower-class Protestants, from middle-class Catholics), until we have sampled the entire population. That is, each stratum is treated for sampling purposes as a complete population, and simple random sampling is applied. Thus, each member of a stratum is given an identifying number, listed, and sampled by means of a table of random numbers. As a final step, the selected members of each subgroup are combined to produce a sample of the entire population.

Before leaving the topic of sampling methods, let us examine the nature of an especially popular form of random sampling known as the *cluster* or **multistage sampling** method. Such samplings are frequently employed to minimize the costs of large surveys that require interviewers to travel to many scattered localities over a wide area.

Employing the cluster method, at least two levels of sampling are put into operation: first, the **primary sampling unit** or cluster, which is a well-delineated area that includes characteristics found in the entire population (e.g., a city, census tract, or city block); second, the sample members within each cluster. The cluster procedure can be applied, for example, to nationwide surveys by treating counties as the primary sampling units initially selected. We would first list all counties and then sample them on a random basis (e.g., with a table of random numbers). Then, we would interview a simple random sample of respondents from each of the chosen counties. In this way, interviewers need not cover each and every county in the United States, but only a much smaller number of such areas that have been randomly selected for inclusion.

SYSTEMATIC SAMPLING

A random sampling method whereby every *n*th member of a population is included in the sample.

STRATIFIED SAMPLING

A random sampling method whereby the population is first divided into homogenous subgroups from which simple random samples are then drawn.

MULTISTAGE SAMPLING

A random sampling method whereby sample members are selected on a random basis from a number of well-delineated areas known as clusters (or primary sampling units).

PRIMARY SAMPLING UNIT (CLUSTER)

In multistage sampling, a well-delineated area considered to include characteristics found in the entire population.

SAMPLING ERROR

Throughout the remainder of the text, we will be careful to distinguish between the characteristics of the samples we study and populations to which we hope to generalize. To make this distinction in our statistical procedures, we can therefore no longer use the same symbols to

TABLE 6.1	A Population and Three Random Samples of Final Examination Grades					
	Population			**Sample A**	**Sample B**	**Sample C**
70	80	93		96	40	72
86	85	90		99	86	96
56	52	67		56	56	49
40	78	57		52	67	56
89	49	48		303	249	273
99	72	30				
96	94	$\Sigma X = 1431$		$\overline{X} = 75.75$	$\overline{X} = 62.25$	$\overline{X} = 68.25$
	$\mu = 71.55$					

signify the mean and the standard deviation of both sample and population. Instead, we must employ different symbols, depending on whether we are referring to sample or population characteristics. We will always symbolize the mean of a *sample* as $\overline{X}$ and the mean of a *population* as μ. The standard deviation of a *sample* will be symbolized as *s* and the standard deviation of its *population* as σ. Because population distributions are rarely ever observed in full, just as with probability distributions, it is little wonder we use the symbols μ and σ for both the population and the probability distributions.

The criminal justice researcher typically tries to obtain a sample that is representative of the larger population in which he or she has an interest. Because random samples give every population member the same chance for sample selection, they are in the long run more representative of population characteristics than nonrandom methods. As discussed briefly in Chapter 1, however, by chance alone, we can *always* expect some difference between a sample, random or otherwise, and the population from which it is drawn. A sample mean ($\overline{X}$) will almost never be exactly the same as the population mean (μ); a sample standard deviation (*s*) will hardly ever be exactly the same as the population standard deviation (σ). This difference, known as **sampling error**, results regardless of how well the sampling plan has been designed and carried out, under the researcher's best intentions, when no cheating occurs and no mistakes have been made.

Even though the term *sampling error* may seem strange, you are probably more familiar with the concept than you realize. Recall that election polls, for example, typically generalize from a relatively small sample to the entire population of voters. When reporting the results, pollsters generally provide a **margin of error**, a measure of the extent to which the sample mean can vary from the population mean due to sampling error. You might read that the Gallup or Pew organization predicts that candidate X will receive 56% of the vote, with a $\pm 4\%$ margin of error. In other words, the pollsters feel confident that somewhere between 52% (56% − 4%) and 60% (56% + 4%) of the vote will go candidate X's way. *Why can't they simply say that the vote will be precisely 56%?* The reason for the pollsters' uncertainty about the exact vote is the effect of sampling error. By the time you finish this chapter, you will not only understand this effect but also be able to calculate the margin of error involved when you generalize from a sample to a population.

Table 6.1 illustrates the operation of sampling error. The table contains the population of 20 final examination grades and three samples A, B, and C drawn at random from this population (each taken with the aid of a table of random numbers). As expected, there are differences among the sample means, and none of them equals the population mean ($\mu = 71.55$).

SAMPLING ERROR

The inevitable difference between a random sample and its population based on chance alone.

MARGIN OF ERROR

The extent of imprecision expected when estimating the population mean or proportion, obtained by multiplying the standard error times the table value of *z* or *t*.

SAMPLING DISTRIBUTION OF MEANS

Given the presence of sampling error, the student may wonder how it is possible *ever* to generalize from a sample to a larger population. To come up with a reasonable answer, let us consider the work of a hypothetical criminologist studying public interest in televised

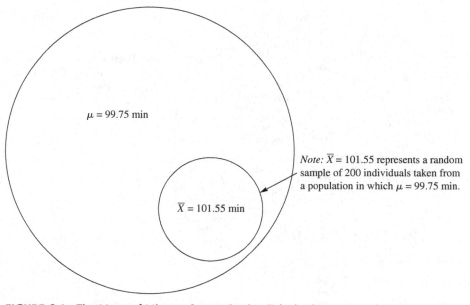

$\mu = 99.75$ min

Note: $\overline{X} = 101.55$ represents a random sample of 200 individuals taken from a population in which $\mu = 99.75$ min.

$\overline{X} = 101.55$ min

FIGURE 6.1 The Mean of Minutes Spent Viewing Televised News Broadcasts about Campus Massacre for a Random Sample Selected from the Hypothetical Population.

coverage of high-profile crimes. He decided to examine the extent of the public's viewing of one evening's network and cable news coverage of a massacre on the campus of one of the nation's premiere universities. Rather than attempt to study the millions of U.S. residents whose households have TV sets, he selected 200 such individuals at random from the entire population. The criminologist interviewed each of the 200 individuals, asking them how many minutes they watched television news coverage of the tragic event between the hours of 7 P.M. and 11 P.M. on the evening the massacre occurred. He found that in his sample of 200 randomly selected individuals, the minutes of viewing coverage of the mass murder during this 4-hr period ranged from 0 to 240 min, with a mean of 101.5 min (see Figure 6.1).

It turns out that this hypothetical criminologist is mildly eccentric. He has a notable fondness—or rather compulsion—for drawing samples from populations. So intense is his enthusiasm for sampling that he continues to draw many additional 200-person samples and to calculate the average (mean) time spent viewing television coverage of the massacre for the people in each of these samples. Our eccentric criminologist continues this procedure until he has drawn 100 samples containing 200 people *each*. In the process of drawing 100 random samples, he actually studies 20,000 people ($200 \times 100 = 20,000$).

Let us assume, as shown in Figure 6.1, that among the entire population of Americans, the average (mean) viewing of televised coverage of the campus massacre is 99.75 min. Also, as illustrated in Figure 6.2, let us suppose that the samples taken by our eccentric researcher yield means that range between 92 and 109 min. In line with our previous discussion, this could easily happen simply on the basis of sampling error.

Frequency distributions of *raw scores* can be obtained from both samples and populations. Similarly, we can construct a **sampling distribution of means**, a frequency distribution of a large number of random sample *means* that have been drawn from the same population. Table 6.2 presents the 100 sample means collected by our eccentric criminologist in the form of a sampling distribution. As when working with a distribution of raw scores, the means in Table 6.2 have been arranged in consecutive order from high to low and their frequency of occurrence indicated in an adjacent column.

SAMPLING DISTRIBUTION OF MEANS

A frequency distribution of a large number of random sample means that have been drawn from the same population.

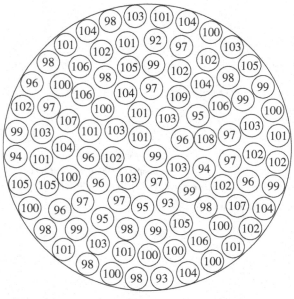

Note: Each $\bar{X}$ represents a sample of 200 individuals. The 100 $\bar{X}$s average to 100.4.

FIGURE 6.2 The Mean of Minutes Spent Viewing Televised News Broadcasts about Campus Massacre for 100 Random Samples Selected from a Hypothetical Population in which $\mu = 99.75$ min.

TABLE 6.2	Observed Sampling Distribution of Means (Televised News Viewing Time) for 100 Samples
Mean	***f***
109	1
108	1
107	2
106	4
105	5
104	7
103	9
102	9
101	11
100	11
99	9
98	9
97	8
96	6
95	3
94	2
93	2
92	1
	$N = \overline{100}$

Note: Mean of 100 sample means = 100.4

Characteristics of a Sampling Distribution of Means

Until now we have not directly come to grips with the problem of generalizing from samples to populations. The theoretical model known as the *sampling distribution of means* (approximated by the 100 sample means obtained by our eccentric researcher) has certain properties, which give the model an important role in the sampling process. Before moving on to the procedure for making generalizations from samples to populations, we must first examine the characteristics of a sampling distribution of means:

1. *The sampling distribution of means approximates a normal curve.* This is true of all sampling distributions of means regardless of the shape of the distribution of raw scores in the population from which the means are drawn, as long as the sample size is reasonably large (more than 30). If the raw data are normally distributed to begin with, then the distribution of sample means is normal regardless of sample size.
2. *The mean of a sampling distribution of means (the mean of means) is equal to the true population mean.* If we take a large number of random sample means from the same population and find the mean of all sample means, we will have the value of the true population mean. Therefore, the mean of the sampling distribution of means is the same as the mean of the population from which it was drawn. They can be regarded as interchangeable values.
3. *The standard deviation of a sampling distribution of means is smaller than the standard deviation of the population.* The sample mean is more stable than the scores that comprise it.

This last characteristic of a sampling distribution of means is at the core of our ability to make reliable inferences from samples to populations. As a concrete example from everyday life, consider how you might compensate for a digital bathroom scale that tends to give you different readings of your weight, even when you immediately step back on it. Obviously, your actual weight doesn't change, but the scale says otherwise. More likely, the scale is very sensitive to where your feet are placed or how your body is postured. The best approach to determine your weight, therefore, might be to weigh yourself four times and take the mean. Remember, the mean weight will be more reliable than any of the individual readings that go into it.

Let's now return to the eccentric criminologist who conducts research on the public's interest in televised coverage of high-profile crimes. As illustrated in Figure 6.3, the variability of a sampling distribution is always smaller than the variability in either the entire population or any one sample. Figure 6.3(a) shows the population distribution of viewing time with a mean (μ) of 99.75 (ordinarily, we would not have this information). The distribution is skewed to the right: More people spend less than the mean of 99.75 min viewing news coverage of the mass murder on this particular evening, but a few in the right tail of the distribution seemed unable to tear themselves away for even a moment. Figure 6.3(b) shows the distribution of viewing time within one particular sample of 200 individuals. Note that it is similar in shape and somewhat close in mean ($\overline{X} = 102$) to the population distribution. Figure 6.3(c) shows the sampling distribution of means (the means from our eccentric researcher's 100 samples). It appears fairly normal rather than skewed, has a mean ($\overline{X} = 100.4$) almost equal to the population mean μ, and has far less variability than either the population distribution in Figure 6.3(a) or the sample distribution in Figure 6.3(b), which can be seen by comparing the baseline values. Had the eccentric criminologist continued forever to take samples of 200 individuals, a graph of the means of these samples would look like a normal curve, as in Figure 6.3(d). This is the true sampling distribution.

Let's think about the diminished variability of a sampling distribution in another way. In the population, there are some individuals who spent a little time watching the coverage of the campus massacre, for less than 30 min, for example. How likely would it be to get a sample of 200 households with a mean of less than 30 min? Given that $\mu = 99.75$, it would be virtually impossible. We would have to obtain by random draw a huge number of tele-phobics and very few tele-holics. The laws of chance make it highly unlikely that this would occur. In other words, means will almost always be less extreme than the scores that comprise them, which is why there's less variability in a distribution of means than there is in a distribution of raw scores.

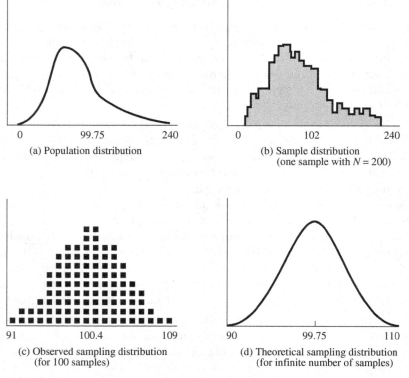

FIGURE 6.3 Population, Sample, and Sampling Distributions.

The Sampling Distribution of Means as a Normal Curve

As indicated in Chapter 5, if we define probability in terms of the likelihood of occurrence, then the normal curve can be regarded as a probability distribution (we can say that probability decreases as we travel along the baseline away from the mean in either direction).

In Chapter 5, we used the normal curve to determine the probabilities associated with a range of values, such as a range of 911 response times from a distribution with a given mean μ and standard deviation σ. In the present context, we are no longer interested in obtaining probabilities associated with a distribution of *raw scores*. Instead, we find ourselves working with a distribution of *sample means*, which have been drawn from the total population of scores, and we wish to make probability statements about those sample means.

As illustrated in Figure 6.4, because the sampling distribution of means takes the form of the normal curve, we can say that probability decreases as we move further away from the mean of means (true population mean). This makes sense because the sampling distribution is a product of chance differences among sample means (sampling error). For this reason, we would expect by chance and chance alone that most sample means will fall close to the value of the true population mean, and relatively few sample means will fall far from it.

It is critical that we distinguish clearly between the standard deviation of raw scores in the population (σ) and the standard deviation of the sampling distribution of sample means. For this reason, we denote the standard deviation of the sampling distribution by $\sigma_{\overline{X}}$. The use of the Greek letter σ reminds us that the sampling distribution is an unobserved or theoretical probability distribution, and the subscript $\overline{X}$ signifies that this is the standard deviation among all possible sample means.

Figure 6.4 indicates that about 68% of the sample means in a sampling distribution fall between $-1\sigma_{\overline{X}}$ and $+1\sigma_{\overline{X}}$ from the mean of means (true population mean). In probability terms, we can say that $P = .68$ of any given sample mean falling within this interval. In the same way, we can say the probability is about .95 (95 chances out of 100) that any sample mean falls between $-2\sigma_{\overline{X}}$ and $+2\sigma_{\overline{X}}$ from the mean of means, and so on.

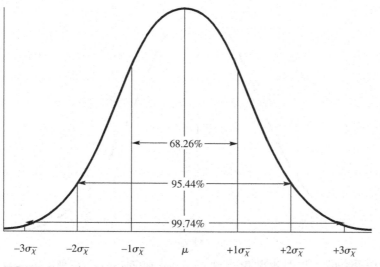

FIGURE 6.4 The Sampling Distribution of Means as a Probability Distribution.

Because the sampling distribution takes the form of the normal curve, we are also able to use z scores and Table A to get the probability of obtaining any sample mean, not just those that are exact multiples of the standard deviation. Given a mean of means (μ) and standard deviation of the sampling distribution $\sigma_{\bar{X}}$, the process is identical to that used in the previous chapter for a distribution of raw scores. Only the names have been changed.

Imagine, for example, that a certain university claims its recent graduates earn an average (μ) annual income of $40,000. We have reason to question the legitimacy of this claim and decide to test it out on a random sample of 100 new alumni. In the process, we get a sample mean of only $38,500. We now ask: How probable is it that we would get a sample mean of $38,500 or less if the true population mean is actually $40,000? Has the university told the truth? Or is this only an attempt to propagandize to the public to increase enrollments or endowments? Figure 6.5 illustrates the area for which we seek a solution. Because the sample size is fairly large ($N = 100$), the sampling distribution of means is approximately normal, even if the distribution of incomes of the individual alumni is not.

To locate a sample mean in the sampling distribution in terms of the number of standard deviations it falls from the center, we obtain the z score:

$$z = \frac{\bar{X} - \mu}{\sigma_{\bar{X}}}$$

where $\bar{X}$ = sample mean in the distribution

μ = mean of means (equal to the university's claim as to the true population mean)

$\sigma_{\bar{X}}$ = standard deviation of the sampling distribution of means

Suppose we know hypothetically that the standard deviation of the sampling distribution is $700. Following the standard procedure, we translate the sample mean $38,500 into a z score as follows:

$$z = \frac{38,500 - 40,000}{700} = -2.14$$

The result of the previous procedure is to tell us that a sample mean of $38,500 lies exactly 2.14 standard deviations below the claimed true population mean of $40,000. Going to column b of Table A in Appendix C, we see that 48.38% of the sample means fall between $38,500 and $40,000. Column c of Table A gives us the percentage of the distribution that represents sample means of $38,500 or less, if the true population mean is $40,000. This figure is 1.62%. Therefore, the probability is .02 rounded off (2 chances out of 100) of getting a sample mean of $38,500 or less, when

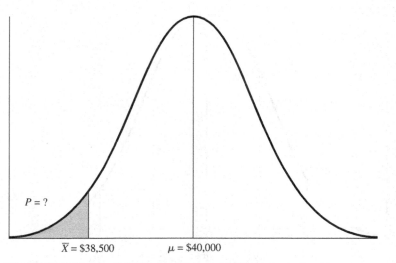

$\overline{X} = \$38,500$ $\mu = \$40,000$

FIGURE 6.5   The Probability Associated with Obtaining a Sample Mean of $38,500 or Less if the True Population Mean Is $40,000 and the Standard Deviation Is $700.

the true population mean is $40,000. With such a small probability of drawing this sample mean at random from a population with a mean of $40,000, we can say with some confidence that the true population mean is *not* actually $40,000. It is doubtful whether the university's report of alumni annual income represents anything but bad propaganda.

STANDARD ERROR OF THE MEAN

Until now, we have pretended that the criminal justice researcher actually has first-hand information about the sampling distribution of means. We have acted as though he or she, like the eccentric researcher, really has collected data on a large number of sample means, which were randomly drawn from some population. If so, it would be a simple enough task to make generalizations about the population, because the mean of means takes on a value that is equal to the true population mean.

In actual practice, the criminal justice researcher rarely collects data on more than one or two samples, from which he or she still expects to generalize to an entire population. Drawing a sampling distribution of means requires the same effort as it might take to study each and every population member. As a result, the researcher does not have actual knowledge as to the mean of means or the standard deviation of the sampling distribution. However, the standard deviation of a theoretical sampling distribution (the distribution that would exist in theory if the means of all possible samples were obtained) can be derived. This quantity—known as the **standard error of the mean**$(\sigma_{\overline{X}})$—is obtained by dividing the population standard deviation by the square root of the sample size. That is,

STANDARD ERROR OF THE MEAN

An estimate of the standard deviation of the sampling distribution of means based on the standard deviation of the population.

$$\sigma_{\overline{X}} = \frac{\sigma}{\sqrt{N}}$$

To illustrate, the IQ test is standardized to have a population mean (μ) of 100 and a population standard deviation (σ) of 15. If one were to take a sample size of 10, the sample mean would be subject to a standard error of

$$\sigma_{\overline{X}} = \frac{15}{\sqrt{10}}$$

$$= \frac{15}{3.1623}$$

$$= 4.74$$

Thus, the population of IQ scores has a standard deviation $\sigma = 15$, whereas the sampling distribution of the sample mean for $N = 10$ has a standard error (theoretical standard deviation) $\sigma_{\overline{X}} = 4.74$.

As previously noted, the criminal justice researcher who investigates only one or two samples cannot know the mean of means, the value of which equals the true population mean. He or she only has the obtained sample mean, which differs from the true population mean as the result of sampling error. But have we not come full circle to our original position? How is it possible to estimate the true population mean from a single sample mean, especially in light of such inevitable differences between samples and populations?

If you're like most students, the distinction between standard deviation and standard error can be especially confusing given the daunting number of symbols using σ and s. A standard deviation characterizes the dispersion of a set of scores around their mean (a population of scores around the population mean or a sample of scores around a sample mean). By contrast, a standard error reflects the variability of a sample-based summary statistic, such as $\overline{X}$, used to estimate a population parameter, such as μ, from the true value of that parameter. This variability arises from the fact that the statistic is calculated from a sample rather than the entire population. Thus, σ is the variability of a population of scores around μ; s is the variability of a sample of scores around $\overline{X}$, and $\sigma_{\overline{X}}$ reflects the extent to which $\overline{X}$ might diverge from μ.

In the example of the compulsive researcher who amassed an infinite collection of sample means, we focused on the variability of the collection of $\overline{X}$'s from μ. Technically, this would be the standard deviation of $\overline{X}$. But in practice, where we have only one sample mean, we focus on the standard *error* of that sample mean in terms of the potential divergence of the sample mean from the population mean.

The process is illustrated in Figure 6.6, in which a criminal justice researcher wishes to know the average age (μ) of the population distribution of crime victims in some large community. On the top right is the age distribution from a random sample of N victims having a mean of 35.8.

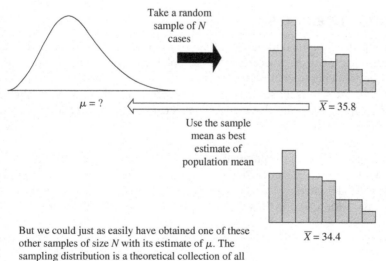

But we could just as easily have obtained one of these other samples of size N with its estimate of μ. The sampling distribution is a theoretical collection of all possible sample means that reflects the effects of random sampling error. The standard error measures the inherent fallibility in estimating μ.

FIGURE 6.6 Estimating the Population Mean.

This sample mean provides the best estimate of the average age in the victim population, but as suggested, this particular sample mean value is but one of any number of possible outcomes depending on which population members were selected.

The standard error reflects the fallibility of estimating a population parameter such as μ with a sample statistic such as $\overline{X}$. The smaller the standard error, the more reliable $\overline{X}$ is as an estimate of μ. As we can see in its formula, the magnitude of $\sigma_{\overline{X}}$ depends on two factors: the variability of the scores within the population and the sample size. The more homogenous the population and the larger the sample, the more reliably we can estimate the population mean from sample data.

Consider a pizza-tasting analogy that might help in understanding these factors. Suppose that you were to take a few random bites out of a pizza in order to rate its quality and tastiness. Obviously, four randomly placed bites from the pizza give you a better sense than do two bites, and six bites are better than four. But it would also matter if the pizza were a simple cheese pizza as opposed to "the works." In a cheese pizza, there is very little variation from bite to bite, just the amount of sauce and cheese at various places in the pizza. Thus, the taste of bites would vary very little. By contrast, the bites in "the works" pizza would vary quite a bit, depending on the presence or absence of pepperoni, onions, and so on in each bite.

Back to criminal justice research situations. If one were to attempt to estimate the mean age of a population of crime victims, the precision of that estimate, as measured by the standard error $\sigma_{\overline{X}}$, improves with large sample sizes. The inherent variability in the population matters as well. The mean age of a sample of 100 college students would tend to be closer to the population mean than would the mean age of a sample of 100 residents of a town because of the relative similarity among the ages in the population of college students.

Having discussed the nature of the sampling distribution of means, we are now prepared to estimate the value of a population mean. With the aid of the standard error of the mean, we can find *the range of mean values within which our true population mean is likely to fall. We can also estimate the probability that our population mean actually falls within that range of mean values.* This is the concept of the *confidence interval.*

CONFIDENCE INTERVALS

*CONFIDENCE
INTERVAL*
_____

The range of mean values
(proportions) within which
the true population mean
(proportion) is likely to fall.

To explore the procedure for finding a **confidence interval**, let us continue with the case of IQ scores. Suppose that the dean of a certain law school wants to estimate the mean IQ of her student body without having to go through the time and expense of administering tests to all 1,000 students. Instead, she selects 25 students at random and gives them the test. She finds that the mean for her sample is 105. She also realizes that because this value of $\overline{X}$ comes from a sample rather than the entire population of students, she cannot be sure that $\overline{X}$ is actually reflective of the student population. As we have already seen, after all, sampling error is the inevitable product of only taking a portion of the population.

We do know, however, that 68.26% of all random sample means in the sampling distribution of means will fall between -1 standard error and $+1$ standard error from the true population mean. In our case (with IQ scores for which $\sigma = 15$), we have a standard error of

$$\sigma_{\overline{X}} = \frac{\sigma}{\sqrt{N}}$$
$$= \frac{15}{\sqrt{25}}$$
$$= \frac{15}{5}$$
$$= 3$$

Therefore, using 105 as an *estimate* of the mean for all students (an estimate of the true population mean), we can establish a range within which there are 68 chances out of 100 (rounded off)

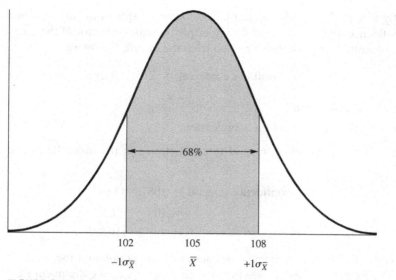

FIGURE 6.7 A 68% Confidence Interval for True Population Mean
with $\overline{X} = 105$ and $\sigma_{\overline{X}} = 3$.

that the true population mean will fall. Known as the *68% confidence interval,* this range of mean
IQs is graphically illustrated in Figure 6.7.

The 68% confidence interval can be obtained in the following manner:

$$68\%\,\text{confidence interval} = \overline{X} \pm \sigma_{\overline{X}}$$

where $\overline{X}$ = sample mean

$\sigma_{\overline{X}}$ = standard error of the sample mean

By applying this formula to the problem at hand,

$$68\%\,\text{confidence interval} = 105 \pm 3$$
$$= 102 \text{ to } 108$$

The dean can therefore conclude with 68% confidence that the mean IQ for the entire school
(μ) is 105, give or take 3. In other words, there are 68 chances out of $100 (P = .68)$ that the true
population mean lies within the range $102-108$. This estimate is made despite sampling error, but
with a ± 3 margin of error and at a specified probability level (68%), known as the *level of confidence.*

Confidence intervals can technically be constructed for any level of probability. Criminal
justice researchers are not confident enough to estimate a population mean knowing there are
only 68 chances out of 100 of being correct (68 out of every 100 sample means fall within the
interval between 102 and 108). As a result, it has become a matter of convention to use a *wider,*
less precise confidence interval having a *better probability* of making an accurate or true estimate
of the population mean. Such a standard is found in the **95% confidence interval**, whereby the
population mean is estimated, knowing there are 95 chances out of 100 of being right; there are
5 chances out of 100 of being wrong (95 out of every 100 sample means fall within the interval).
Even when using the 95% confidence interval, however, it must always be kept firmly in mind
that the researcher's sample mean could be one of those five sample means that fall outside of the
established interval. In statistical decision making, one never knows for certain.

How do we go about finding the 95% confidence interval? We already know that 95.44%
of the sample means in a sampling distribution lies between $-2\sigma_{\overline{X}}$ and $+2\sigma_{\overline{X}}$ from the mean of
means. Going to Table A, we can make the statement that 1.96 standard errors in both directions

**95% CONFIDENCE
INTERVAL**

The range of mean values
(proportions) within which
there are 95 chances out of
100 that the true population
mean (proportion) will fall.

cover exactly 95% of the sample means (47.50% on either side of the mean of means). To find the 95% confidence interval, we must first multiply the standard error of the mean by 1.96 (the interval is 1.96 units of $\sigma_{\overline{X}}$ in either direction from the mean). Therefore,

$$95\% \text{ confidence interval} = \overline{X} \pm 1.96\sigma_{\overline{X}}$$

where $\overline{X}$ = sample mean

$\sigma_{\overline{X}}$ = standard error of the sample mean

If we apply the 95% confidence interval to our estimate of the mean IQ of a student body, we see

$$95\% \text{ confidence interval} = 105 \pm (1.96)(3)$$
$$= 105 \pm 5.88$$
$$= 99.12 - 110.88$$

Therefore, the dean can be 95% confident that the population mean lies in the interval 99.12–110.88. Note that if asked whether her students are above the norm in IQ (the norm is 100), she could not quite conclude that to be the case with 95% confidence. This is because the true population mean of 100 is within the 95% realm of possibilities based on these results. However, given the 68% confidence interval (102–108), the dean could assert with 68% confidence that students at her school average above the norm in IQ.

An even more stringent confidence interval is the **99% confidence interval**. From Table A in Appendix C, we see that the z score 2.58 represents 49.50% of the area on either side of the curve. Doubling this amount yields 99% of the area under the curve; 99% of the sample means fall into that interval. In probability terms, 99 out of every 100 sample means fall between $-2.58\sigma_{\overline{X}}$ and $+2.58\sigma_{\overline{X}}$ from the mean. Conversely, only 1 out of every 100 means falls outside of the interval. By formula,

$$99\% \text{ confidence interval} = \overline{X} \pm 2.58\sigma_{\overline{X}}$$

where $\overline{X}$ = sample mean

$\sigma_{\overline{X}}$ = standard error of the sample mean

With regard to estimating the mean IQ for the population of students,

$$99\% \text{ confidence interval} = 105 \pm (2.58)(3)$$
$$= 105 \pm 7.74$$
$$= 97.26 - 112.74$$

Consequently, based on the sample of 25 students, the dean can infer with 99% confidence that the mean IQ for the entire school is between 97.26 and 112.74.

Note that the 99% confidence interval consists of a wider band (97.26 to 112.74) than does the 95% confidence interval (99.12 to 110.88). The 99% interval encompasses more of the total area under the normal curve and therefore a larger number of sample means. This wider band of mean scores gives us greater confidence that we have accurately estimated the true population mean. Only a single sample mean in every 100 lies outside of the interval. On the other hand, by increasing our level of confidence from 95% to 99%, we have also sacrificed a degree of precision in pinpointing the population mean. Holding sample size constant, the researcher must choose between greater precision or greater confidence that he or she is correct.

The precision of an estimate is determined by the *margin of error*, obtained by multiplying the standard error by the z score representing a desired level of confidence. Again, this is the extent to which the sample mean is expected to vary from the population mean due to sampling error alone.

99% CONFIDENCE INTERVAL

The range of mean values (proportions) within which there are 99 chances out of 100 that the true population mean (proportion) will fall.

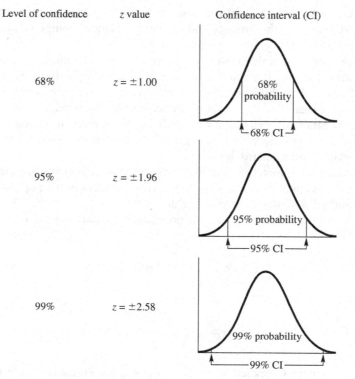

Level of confidence	z value	Confidence interval (CI)
68%	z = ±1.00	68% probability 68% CI
95%	z = ±1.96	95% probability 95% CI
99%	z = ±2.58	99% probability 99% CI

FIGURE 6.8 Levels of Confidence.

Figure 6.8 compares confidence intervals for the 68%, the 95%, and the 99% levels of confidence. The greater the level of confidence that the interval includes the true population mean, the larger the z score, the larger the margin of error, and the wider the confidence interval.

THE *t* DISTRIBUTION

Thus far, we have only dealt with situations in which the standard error of the mean was known or could be calculated from the population standard deviation by the formula

$$\sigma_{\bar{X}} = \frac{\sigma}{\sqrt{N}}$$

If you think about it realistically, it makes little sense that we would know the standard deviation of our variable in the population (σ) but not know and need to estimate the population mean (μ). Indeed, there are very few cases when the population standard deviation (and thus the standard error of the mean $\sigma_{\bar{X}}$) is known. In certain areas of education and psychology, the standard deviations for standardized scales such as the SAT and IQ scores are determined by design of the test. Usually, however, we need to estimate not only the population mean from a sample but also the standard error from the same sample.

To obtain an *estimate* of the standard error of the mean, one might be tempted simply to substitute the sample standard deviation (*s*) for the population standard deviation (σ) in the previous standard error formula. This, however, would have the tendency to underestimate the size of the true standard error ever so slightly. This problem arises because the sample standard deviation tends to be a bit smaller than the population standard deviation.

Recall from Chapter 3 that the mean is the point of balance within a distribution of scores; the mean is the point in a distribution around which the scores above it perfectly balance with those below it, as in the lever and fulcrum analogy in Figure 3.2. As a result, the sum of squared deviations (and, therefore, the variance and standard deviation) computed around the mean is smaller than from any other point of comparison.

Thus, for a given sample drawn from a population, the sample variance and standard deviation (s^2 and s) are smaller when computed from the sample mean than they would be if one actually knew and used the population mean (μ) in place of the sample mean. In a sense, the sample mean is custom tailored to the sample, whereas the population mean is off the rack; it fits the sample data fairly well but not perfectly like the sample mean does. Thus, the sample variance and the standard deviation are slightly biased estimates (tend to be too small) of the population variance and standard deviation.

It is necessary, therefore, to let out the seam a bit, that is, to inflate the sample variance and standard deviation slightly to produce more accurate estimates of the population variance and population standard deviation. To do so, we divide by $N - 1$ rather than N. That is, unbiased estimates of the population variance and the population standard deviation are given by

$$\hat{\sigma}^2 = \frac{\Sigma(X - \overline{X})^2}{N - 1}$$

and

$$\hat{\sigma} = \sqrt{\frac{\Sigma(X - \overline{X})^2}{N - 1}}$$

The caret over the Greek letter σ indicates that it is an unbiased sample estimate of this population value.[1] Note that in large samples, this correction is trivial (s^2 and s are almost equivalent to $\hat{\sigma}^2$ and $\hat{\sigma}$). This should be the case because in large samples, the sample mean tends to be a very reliable (close) estimate of the population mean.

The distinction between the sample variance and the standard deviation using the sample size N as the denominator versus the sample estimate of the population variance and standard deviation using $N - 1$ as the denominator may be small computationally but is important theoretically. That is, it makes little difference in terms of the final numerical result whether we divide by N or $N - 1$, especially if the sample size N is fairly large. Still, there are two very different purposes for calculating the variance and standard deviation: (1) to describe the extent of variability within a sample of cases or respondents and (2) to make an inference or generalize about the extent of variability within the larger population of cases from which a sample was drawn. It is likely that an example would be helpful right about now.

Suppose that an elementary school teacher is piloting a new language-based math curriculum that teaches math skills through word problems and logical reasoning rather than through rote memorization of math facts. Just before the end of the school year, she administers a math test to her class of 25 pupils to determine the extent to which they have learned the material using the novel teaching strategy. Her interest lies not only in the average performance of the class (mean score) but also in whether the new approach tends to be easy for some pupils but difficult for others (standard deviation). In fact, she suspects that the curriculum may be a good one, but not for all kinds of learners. She calculates the sample variance (and standard deviation) using the N denominator because her sole interest is in her particular class of pupils. She has no desire to generalize to pupils elsewhere.

---

[1]Alternatively, $\hat{\sigma}^2$ and $\hat{\sigma}$ can by calculated from s^2 and s by multiplying by a bias correction factor. $N/(N - 1)$. Specifically,

$$\hat{\sigma}^2 - s^2 \frac{N}{N - 1} \quad \text{and} \quad \hat{\sigma} = s\sqrt{\frac{N}{N - 1}}$$

As it turns out, this same class of students had been identified by the curriculum design company as a "test case." Because it would not be feasible to assemble a truly random selection of fourth graders from around the country into the same classroom, this particular class was viewed as "fairly representative" of fourth graders. The designers' interest extends well beyond the walls of this particular classroom, of course. Their interest is in using this sample of 25 fourth graders to estimate the central tendency and variability in the overall population (i.e., to generalize to all fourth graders were they to have had this curriculum). The sample mean test score for the class could be used to generalize to the population mean, but the sample variance and standard deviation would have to be adjusted slightly. Specifically, using $N - 1$ in the denominator provides an unbiased or fair estimate of the variability that would exist in the entire population of fourth graders.

At this point, we have only passing interest in estimating the population standard deviation. Our primary interest here is in estimating the standard error of the mean based on a sample of N scores. The same correction procedure applies, nevertheless. That is, an unbiased estimate of the standard error of the mean is given by replacing σ with s and N with $N - 1$,

$$s_{\overline{X}} = \frac{s}{\sqrt{N - 1}}$$

where s is the sample standard deviation, as obtained in Chapter 4, from a distribution of raw scores or from a frequency distribution. Technically, the unbiased estimate of the standard error should be symbolized by $\hat{\sigma}_{\overline{X}}$ rather than $s_{\overline{X}}$. However, for the sake of simplicity, $s_{\overline{X}}$ can be used without any confusion as the unbiased estimate of the standard error.

One more problem arises when we estimate the standard error of the mean. The sampling distribution of means is no longer quite normal if we do not know the population standard deviation. That is, the ratio

$$\frac{\overline{X} - \mu}{s_{\overline{X}}}$$

with an estimated standard error in the denominator, does not quite follow the z or normal distribution. The fact that we estimate the standard error from sample data adds an extra amount of uncertainty in the distribution of sample means, beyond that which arises due to sampling variability alone. In particular, the sampling distribution of means when we estimate the standard error is a bit wider (more dispersed) than a normal distribution, because of this added source of variability (i.e., the uncertainty in estimating the standard error of the mean). The ratio

follows what is known as the t distribution, and thus it is called the **t ratio**. There is actually a whole family of t distributions (see Figure 6.9). A concept known as **degrees of freedom** (which we will encounter often in later chapters) is used to determine which of the t distributions applies in a particular instance. The degrees of freedom indicate how close the t distribution comes to approximating the normal curve.[2] When estimating a population mean, the degrees of freedom are one less than the sample size; that is,

$$df = N - 1$$

t RATIO

A statistical technique that indicates the direction and degree that a sample mean difference falls from zero on a scale of standard error units.

DEGREES OF FREEDOM

In small-sample comparisons, a statistical compensation for the failure of the sampling distribution of differences to assume the shape of the normal curve.

[2]Another way to look at the concept of degrees of freedom is a bit more subtle. Degrees of freedom are the number of observations that are free rather than fixed. When calculating the sample variance for use in determining the estimate of the standard error ($\sigma_{\overline{X}}$), we really do not have N free observations. Because the sample mean is an element in calculating the sample standard deviation, this must be considered a fixed quantity. Then once we have all but the last observation ($N - 1$ of them), the last observation is predetermined. For example, for the set of data 2, 3, and 7, we take as given that the mean is 4 when we calculate the sample standard deviation. If someone told you that the mean of three cases was 4 and that two of the cases were 2 and 3, you would then know that the last case had to be 7. This is because for the mean of three observation to be 4, $\Sigma X = 12$.

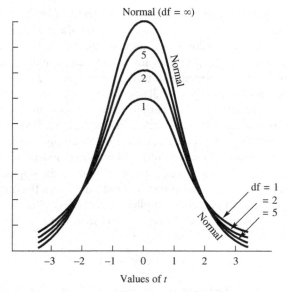

FIGURE 6.9   The Family of t Distributions.

The larger the sample size, the greater the degrees of freedom, and the closer the *t* distribution gets to the normal distribution. This makes good sense, because the extent of uncertainty that causes us to use a *t* ratio rather than a *z* score diminishes as the sample size gets larger. In other words, the quality or reliability of our estimate of the standard error of the mean increases as our sample size increases, and so the *t* ratio approaches a *z* score. Recall that the only difference between the *t* ratio and the *z* score is that the former uses an estimate of the standard error based on sample data. We repeat for the sake of emphasis that as the sample size and thus the degrees of freedom increase, the *t* distribution becomes a better approximation of the normal or *z* distribution.

When dealing with the *t* distribution, we use Table C rather than Table A. Unlike Table A, for which we had to search out values of *z* corresponding to 95% and 99% areas under the curve, Table C is calibrated for special areas. More precisely, Table C is calibrated for various levels of the Greek letter α (alpha). The alpha value represents the area in the tails of the *t* distribution. Thus, the alpha value is *one minus the level of confidence.* That is,

$$\alpha = 1 - \text{level of confidence}$$

For example, for a 95% level of confidence, $\alpha = .05$. For a 99% level of confidence, $\alpha = .01$.

We enter Table C with two pieces of information: (1) the degrees of freedom (which, for estimating a sample mean, is $N - 1$) and (2) the alpha value, the area in the tails of the distribution. For example, if we wanted to construct a 95% confidence interval with a sample size of 20, we would have 19 degrees of freedom ($df = 20 - 1 = 19$), $\alpha = .05$ area combined in the two tails, and, as a result, a *t* value from Table C of 2.093.

What would we do, however, for larger samples for which the degrees of freedom may not appear in Table C? For instance, a sample size of 50 produces 49 *df*. The *t* value for 49 *df* and $\alpha = .05$ is somewhere between 2.021 (for 40 *df*) and 2.000 (for 60 *df*). Given that these two values of *t* are so close, it makes little practical difference what we decide on for a compromise value. However, to be on the safe side, it is recommended that one go with the more modest degrees of freedom (40) and thus the larger value of *t* (2.021).

The reason *t* is not tabulated for all degrees of freedom higher than 30 is that they become so close that it would be like splitting hairs. Note that the values of *t* get smaller and tend to converge as the degrees of freedom increase. For example, the *t* values for $\alpha = .05$

begin at 12.706 for 1 *df*, decrease quickly to just under 3.0 for 4 *df*, gradually approach a value of 2.000 for 60 *df*, and finally approach a limit of 1.960 for infinity degrees of freedom (i.e., an infinitely large sample). This limit of 1.960 is also the .05 value for *z* we found earlier from Table A. Again, we see that the *t* distribution approaches the *z* or normal distribution as the sample size increases.

Thus, for cases in which the standard error of the mean is estimated, we can construct confidence intervals using an appropriate table value of *t* as follows:

$$\text{Confidence interval} = \overline{X} \pm t s_{\overline{X}}$$

STEP-BY-STEP ILLUSTRATION

Confidence Interval Using *t*

With a step-by-step example, let's see how the use of the *t* distribution translates into constructing confidence intervals. Suppose that a criminal justice researcher wanted to examine the number of security cameras in the stores of a large shopping mall. He selected a random sample of 10 stores and counted the number of security cameras in each store:

1   5   2   3   4   1   2   2   4   3

Step 1 Find the mean of the sample. Using this sample, we can now estimate the population mean number of security cameras with 95% confidence.

$$
\begin{array}{c}
\textbf{\textit{X}} \\
\hline
1 \\
5 \\
2 \\
3 \\
4 \\
1 \\
2 \\
2 \\
4 \\
\underline{3} \\
\Sigma X = 27
\end{array}
$$

$$\overline{X} = \frac{\Sigma X}{N} = \frac{27}{10} = 2.7$$

Step 2 Obtain the standard deviation of the sample (we will use the formula for raw scores).

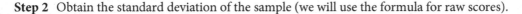

X	**X²**
1	1
5	25
2	4
3	9
4	16
1	1
2	4
2	4
4	16
3	9
	ΣX² = 89

$$s = \sqrt{\frac{\Sigma X^2}{N} - \overline{X}^2}$$

$$= \sqrt{\frac{89}{10} - (2.7)^2}$$

$$= \sqrt{8.9 - 7.29}$$

$$= \sqrt{1.61}$$

$$= 1.2689$$

Step 3 Obtain the estimated standard error of the mean.

$$s_{\overline{X}} = \frac{s}{\sqrt{N-1}}$$

$$= \frac{1.2689}{\sqrt{10-1}}$$

$$= \frac{1.2689}{3}$$

$$= .423$$

Step 4 Determine the value of t from Table C.

$$df = N - 1 = 10 - 1 = 9$$

$$\alpha = .05$$

Thus,

$$t = 2.262$$

Step 5 Obtain the margin of error by multiplying the estimated standard error of the mean by 2.262.

$$\text{Margin of error} = ts_{\overline{X}}$$

$$= (2.262)(.423)$$

$$= .96$$

Step 6 Add and subtract this product from the sample mean to find the interval within which we are 95% confident the population mean falls:

$$95\% \text{ confidence interval} = \overline{X} \pm ts_{\overline{X}}$$

$$= 2.7 \pm .96$$

$$= 1.74 - 3.66$$

Thus, we can be 95% certain that the mean number of security cameras per store is between 1.74 and 3.66.

In order to construct a 99% confidence interval, Steps 1 through 3 would remain the same. Next, with $df = 9$ and $\alpha = .01$ (i.e., $1 - .99 = .01$), from Table C, we find $t = 3.250$. The 99% confidence interval is then

$$99\% \text{ confidence interval} = \overline{X} \pm ts_{\overline{X}}$$

$$= 2.7 \pm (3.250)(.423)$$

$$= 2.7 \pm 1.37$$

$$= 1.33 - 4.07$$

Thus, we can be 99% confident that the population mean (mean number of security cameras per store) is between 1.34 and 4.06. This interval is somewhat wider than the 95% interval (1.75−3.65), but for this trade-off, we gain greater confidence in our estimate.

Admittedly, the confidence intervals, for both the 95% and the 99% levels, do not produce a particularly precise estimate of the population mean. The reason is simple: A sample size of only 10 is not large enough to produce a small standard error. That is, results from such a limited sample are heavily subject to sampling variability.

In estimating the population mean number of security cameras in retail stores, we had to assume that the population is normally distributed so that the sampling distribution of $\overline{X}$ would in turn be normal. Besides the matter of imprecision noted earlier, the sample size is too small to ensure a normal sampling distribution. When sample sizes are reasonably large, say more than 30, we need not worry about the shape of the population distribution in order to use a z distribution (when σ is known) or the t distribution (when, as is more commonly the case, σ is not known and must be estimated from the sample).

STEP-BY-STEP ILLUSTRATION:

Confidence Interval Using t (large sample case)

Suppose a researcher is interested in estimating the average number of convictions among inmates in the state prison population. He obtains the following conviction data (arranged in the form of a simple frequency distribution) from a random sample of 120 inmates and wants to estimate the population mean number of convictions with a 95% confidence interval:

X	f
1	21
2	32
3	22
4	17
5	13
6	8
7	4
8	3
	$N = 120$

The sample distribution is fairly skewed to the right: There is a small percentage of inmates with many convictions and a large percentage with fewer. We would expect, based on this evidence, that the population distribution would be skewed right as well. However, by virtue of the large sample size, the sampling distribution of $\overline{X}$ will be normal in shape. Since we still need to estimate the standard deviation (as well as the mean), the t distribution can be used to derive confidence intervals for μ.

Step 1 Calculate the mean of the sample.

X	f	fX
1	21	21
2	32	64
3	22	66
4	17	68
5	13	65
6	8	48
7	4	28
8	3	24
	120	384

$$\overline{X} = \frac{\Sigma fX}{N}$$

$$= \frac{384}{120}$$

$$= 3.2$$

Step 2 Calculate the standard deviation of the sample.

X	f	fX	fX²
1	21	21	21
2	32	64	128
3	22	66	198
4	17	68	272
5	13	65	325
6	8	48	288
7	4	28	196
8	3	24	192
	120	384	1620

$$s = \sqrt{\frac{\sum fX^2}{N} - \bar{X}^2}$$

$$= \sqrt{\frac{1620}{120} - (3.2)^2}$$

$$= \sqrt{13.5 - 10.24}$$

$$= \sqrt{3.26}$$

$$= 1.806$$

Step 3 Calculate the estimated standard error of the mean.

$$s_{\bar{X}} = \frac{s}{\sqrt{N-1}}$$

$$= \frac{1.806}{\sqrt{119}}$$

$$= \frac{1.806}{10.909}$$

$$= 0.166$$

Step 4 Determine the value of t from Table C.

$$df = N - 1 = 120 - 1 = 119$$

$$\alpha = .05$$

Thus

$$t = 2.00$$

Note: Because 119 *df* is not included in Table C, we should use the t value corresponding to the next lowest available (here *df* = 60).

Step 5 Obtain the margin of error by multiplying the standard error of the mean by the t value.

$$\text{Margin of error} = ts_{\bar{X}}$$

$$= (2.00)(0.166)$$

$$= 0.312$$

Step 6 Add/subtract the margin of error to/from the sample mean.

$$95\% \, CI = \bar{X} \pm ts_{\bar{X}}$$

$$= 3.2 \pm .31$$

$$= 2.89 \text{ to } 3.51$$

Thus, we can be 95% certain that the mean number of convictions for the entire population of state prison inmates is between 2.89 and 3.51.

To construct a 99% confidence interval, steps 1–3 would remain the same. Next, we would use the tabled t value for $\alpha = .01$ (and 60 degrees of freedom since the actual df of 119 is not provided). The 99% confidence interval is then:

$$99\%\,\text{CI} = \overline{X} \pm ts_{\overline{X}}$$
$$= 3.2 \pm (2.660)(0.166)$$
$$= 3.2 \pm .44$$
$$= 2.76-3.66$$

Thus, we can be 99% certain that the mean number of convictions for the entire population of state prison inmates is between 2.76 and 3.66. The interval is wider than before because we are using a higher degree of confidence. The only way to have increased confidence *and* a smaller confidence interval would be to draw a larger sample.

ESTIMATING PROPORTIONS

Thus far, we have focused on procedures for estimating population means. The researcher often seeks to come up with an estimate of a population *proportion* strictly on the basis of a proportion obtained in a random sample. A familiar circumstance is the pollster whose data suggest that a certain proportion of the vote will go to a particular political issue or candidate for office. When a pollster reports that 45% of the vote will be in favor of a certain candidate, he does so with the realization that he is less than 100% certain. In general, he is 95% or 99% confident that his estimated proportion falls within the range of proportions (e.g., between 40% and 50%).

We estimate proportions by the procedure that we have just used to estimate means. All statistics—including means and proportions—have their sampling distributions, and the sampling distribution of a proportion is normal. Just as we found earlier the standard error of the mean, we can now find the **standard error of the proportion**. By formula,

$$s_P = \sqrt{\frac{P(1-P)}{N}}$$

STANDARD ERROR OF THE PROPORTION

An estimate of the standard deviation of the sampling distribution of proportions based on the proportion obtained in a single random sample.

where s_P = standard error of the proportion (an estimate of the standard deviation of the sampling distribution of proportions)

P = sample proportion

N = total number in the sample

For illustrative purposes, let us say 45% of a random sample of 100 college students report they are in favor of the legalization of all drugs. The standard error of the proportion would be

$$s_P = \sqrt{\frac{(.45)(.55)}{100}}$$
$$= \sqrt{\frac{.2475}{100}}$$
$$= \sqrt{.0025}$$
$$= .05$$

The t distribution was used previously for constructing confidence intervals for the population mean when *both* the population mean (μ) and the population standard deviation (s) were unknown and had to be estimated. When dealing with proportions, however, only *one* quantity is unknown: We estimate the population proportion (π, the Greek letter *pi*) by the sample proportion P. Consequently, we use the z distribution for constructing confidence intervals for the population proportion (π) (with $z = 1.96$ for a 95% confidence interval and $z = 2.58$ for a 99% confidence interval) rather than the t distribution.

To find the 95% confidence interval for the population proportion, we multiply the standard error of the proportion by 1.96 and add and subtract this product to and from the sample proportion:

$$95\% \text{ confidence interval} = P \pm 1.96 s_P$$

where
$$P = \text{sample proportion}$$
$$s_P = \text{standard error of the proportion}$$

If we seek to estimate the proportion of college students in favor of the legalization of drugs,

$$95\% \text{ confidence interval} = .45 \pm (1.96)(.05)$$
$$= .45 \pm .098$$
$$= .352 - .548$$

Thus, we are 95% confident that the true population proportion is neither smaller than .352 nor larger than .548. More specifically, somewhere between 35% and 55% of this population of college students are in favor of the legalization of all drugs. There is a 5% chance we are wrong; 5 times out of 100 such confidence intervals will not contain the true population proportion.

STEP-BY-STEP ILLUSTRATION

Confidence Interval for Proportions

Suppose that a criminologist wishes to estimate the recidivism rate of inmates released from prison in a particular state. In particular, he wants to determine the percentage of ex-inmates who are arrested for a new felony within 3 years of their release from prison. Given the impracticality of following up on all releasees, he randomly selects 550 to investigate and determines that 341 members of the sample had recidivated within 3 years of release. Let us now derive the standard error, margin of error, and 95% confidence interval for the proportion of all inmates released from state prison who recidivate.

Step 1 Estimate the sample proportion.

$$P = \frac{f}{N} = \frac{341}{550} = .62$$

Step 2 Obtain the standard error of the proportion.

$$s_P = \sqrt{\frac{P(1-P)}{N}}$$

$$= \sqrt{\frac{.62(1-.62)}{550}}$$

$$= \sqrt{\frac{.2356}{550}}$$

$$= \sqrt{.000428}$$

$$= .0207$$

Step 3 Multiply the standard error of the proportion by 1.96 to obtain the margin of error.

$$\text{Margin of error} = 1.96 s_p$$
$$= 1.96(.0207)$$
$$= .0406$$

Step 4 Add and subtract the margin of error to find the confidence interval.

$$95\% \text{ confidence interval} = P \pm 1.96 s_p$$
$$= .62 \pm .0407$$
$$= .5793 - .6607$$

Thus, with a sample size of 550 and 95% level of confidence, the estimated recidivism rate of .62 (or 62%) has a margin of error of $\pm.0407$ (or $\pm4.07\%$). The researcher can then conclude, with 95% confidence, that the population recidivism rate is roughly between 58% and 66%. Were he to desire a more precise estimate (i.e., a narrower confidence interval), he would need to increase the sample size or else settle for a lower level of confidence.

Summary

Researchers rarely work directly with each and every member of a population. Instead, they study a smaller number of cases known as a sample. In this chapter, we explored the key concepts and procedures related to generalizing from a sample to the entire group (i.e., population) that a researcher in criminal justice attempts to understand. If every population member is given an equal chance of being drawn into the sample, a random sampling method is being applied; otherwise, a nonrandom type is employed. It was suggested that sampling error—the inevitable difference between a sample and a population based on chance—can be expected to occur despite a well-designed and well-executed random sampling plan. As a result of sampling error, it is possible to characterize a sampling distribution of means, a theoretical distribution in the shape of a normal curve whose mean (the mean of means) equals the true population mean. With the aid of the standard error of the mean, it is possible to estimate the standard deviation of the sampling distribution of means. Armed with this information, we can construct confidence intervals for means (or proportions) within which we have confidence (95% or 99%) that the true population mean (or proportion) actually falls. In this way, it is possible to generalize from a sample to a population. In this chapter, we also introduced the t distribution for the many circumstances in which the population standard deviation is unknown and must be estimated from sample data. The t distribution will play a major role in hypothesis tests presented in the following chapter.

Questions and Problems

1. Alpha represents the area _____.
   a. in the center of the distribution
   b. in the tails of the distribution
   c. higher than the mean of the distribution
   d. lower than the mean of the distribution
2. Confidence intervals are used to _____.
   a. provide an exact score for our estimate of the mean
   b. provide a lower and upper limit on our estimate of the population mean
   c. find the sampling confidence
   d. none of the above
3. Researchers in criminal justice most often use the _____ level of confidence.
   a. 68%
   b. 90%
   c. 95%
   d. 99%
4. The margin of error in a 99% confidence interval is _____ the margin of error in a 95% confidence interval.
   a. larger than
   b. the same as
   c. smaller than
   d. random and unrelated to

5. The confidence interval for proportions can be used when the level of measurement is _____.
   a. nominal
   b. ordinal
   c. interval/ratio
   d. all of the above

6. The confidence interval for means is used when the level of measurement is _____.
   a. nominal
   b. ordinal
   c. interval/ratio
   d. all of the above

7. The inevitable difference between the mean of a random sample and the mean of a population is known as _____.
   a. confidence interval
   b. probability
   c. random sample
   d. sampling error

8. A survey of college students asks the participants how many times they smoked marijuana in the past year. Ten students reported that they smoked marijuana the following number of times: 1, 5, 0, 3, 2, 10, 15, 2, 0, 25. If a researcher wants to generalize to the population of college students with (a) 95% confidence and (b) 99% confidence, what is the margin of error the researcher must use in developing his or her confidence interval?

9. With the sample mean in problem 8, find (a) the 95% confidence interval and (b) the 99% confidence interval.

10. A policing researcher is interested in citizen encounters with the police and offers a survey to people who have had an encounter with a police officer in the past week. The researcher estimates the percentage of all citizens who report a positive interaction with the police by surveying a random sample of 50 citizens. At the end of the survey period, 34 people responded that they had a positive encounter with the officer and 16 responded that they had a negative encounter with the officer. Find (a) the 95% confidence interval and (b) the 99% confidence interval for the proportion of respondents who had a positive encounter with the police officer.

11. Domestic violence in the United States is a serious problem. Once arrested, offenders are very likely to re-offend. Domestic violence counseling programs define success when an offender completes a counseling program and goes 6 or more months (180 days) without re-offending. Determine the 95% confidence interval on days to re-offend for men who repeat domestic violence based on the following sample:

    17 17 14 31 33 35 45 65 20 58

12. The 2010 National Crime Victimization Survey indicates that 25.8 households per 1,000 were the victims of home burglary. These data are obtained from a survey of about 40,000 households. Estimate the 95% confidence interval for the proportion of households experiencing burglary in 2010.

13. A researcher is interested in the number of delinquent friends that juvenile offenders have in a juvenile detention center. The detention center is large and it is not possible to survey everyone. The researcher surveys 15 juveniles and their number of delinquent friends are as follows: 4, 6, 3, 6, 9, 11, 7, 12, 10, 9, 7, 10, 6, 11, 14. Estimate a 95% confidence interval for the number of delinquent friends of detained juveniles in the facility.

14. A researcher is interested in the mean number of arrests for recently released inmates of a prison in the Midwest. The frequency of arrests for 10 recently released inmates is as follows: 12, 13, 10, 8, 9, 11, 15, 12, 10, 8. Estimate a 99% confidence interval for the number of individuals who were arrested after their release.

15. A criminologist conducts a survey of residents concerning their sense of safety when walking alone in their neighborhood. She uses a 7-point scale from 1 = very unsafe to 7 = very safe. Using the following simple frequency distribution of sample responses, find (a) the 95% confidence interval and (b) the 99% confidence interval for estimating the mean level of fear in the population.

Perception of safety	f
1	28
2	34
3	42
4	56
5	46
6	24
7	20

16. A recent survey of 1,000 teens indicated that 1 in 5 teenagers has been bullied using some form of social media (e.g., Facebook, Twitter). This is accurate within 3.0 percentage points 19 times out of 20.
   a. What kind of confidence interval is reported (means or proportions)?
   b. What is the level of confidence?
   c. What is the margin of error?

17. A national newspaper says that three out of four parents are in favor of home drug testing of their children. The report says that it is from a survey of 2,011 people and is accurate within 2.5 percentage points 19 times in 20.
   a. What kind of confidence interval is it (means or proportions)?
   b. What is the level of confidence?
   c. How much is the margin of error?
   d. Rewrite the information as an equation.

Computer Exercises

1. Using the General Social Survey, calculate 95% and 99% confidence intervals for the population mean for the number of hours per week that they spend on e-mails. (EMAILHR). *Hint:* ANALYZE, COMPARE MEANS, ONE-SAMPLE T-TEST, and set options to desired percentages.
2. Using the General Social Survey, calculate a 95% confidence interval for the population mean for individual income (RINCOM06) of Americans in 2006 dollars.
3. Using the General Social Survey, calculate a 95% confidence interval for the percentage of Americans in favor of allowing a police officer to hit a citizen if that citizen was hitting the police officer with his or her fists (POLATTAK).
4. Using the General Social Survey, calculate a 95% confidence interval for the percentage of Americans in favor of requiring gun permits (GUNLAW).
5. Choose a variable from the General Social Survey to calculate a 95% confidence interval. Remember it has to be an interval-level variable or a dichotomous (two-category) variable.

LOOKING AT THE LARGER PICTURE
Generalizing from Samples to Populations

At the end of Part Two, we described characteristics of the survey of high school students regarding cigarette and alcohol use. We determined that 62% of the respondents smoked, and that among smokers, the average daily consumption was 16.9 cigarettes. In terms of alcohol, the mean number of occasions on which respondents had had a drink in the past months averaged 1.58.

Confidence Intervals

Variable	Statistic	
If a smoker		
	N	250
	%	62.0%
	SE	3.1%
	95% CI	55.9%–68.1%
Daily cigarettes		
	N	155
	Mean	16.9
	SE	0.84
	95% CI	15.3–18.6
Occasions drinking		
	N	250
	Mean	1.58
	SE	0.17
	95% CI	1.44–1.73

Recognizing that these survey respondents are but a sample drawn from a larger population, we can now estimate the population proportions and means along with confidence intervals for this larger population. But what exactly is the population or universe that this sample can represent? In the strictest sense, the population is technically the entire high school student body. But since it may be safe to assume that this high school is fairly typical of urban public high schools around the country, we might also be able to generalize the findings to urban public high school students nationwide. By contrast, it would be hard to assume that the students selected at this typical urban high school could be representative of all high school students, even those in suburban and rural areas or private and sectarian schools. Thus, all we can reasonably hope for is that the sample drawn here (250 students from a typical urban high school) can be used to make inferences about urban public high school students in general.

As shown, 62% of the students within the entire sample smoked. From this, we can calculate the standard error of the proportion as 3.1% and then generate a 95% confidence interval for the population proportion who smoke. We find that we can be 95% certain that the population proportion (π) is between 55.9% and 68.1%, indicating that somewhere between 56% and 68% of all urban public high school students smoke. Moving next to daily smoking habits for the smokers alone, we can use the sample mean (16.9) to estimate with 95% confidence the population mean (μ). The standard error of the mean is 0.84, producing a 95% confidence interval between 15.3 and 18.6, indicating that the average smoker in urban public high schools consumes between 15 and almost 19 cigarettes daily. Finally, for drinking, the mean is 1.58 and the standard error is .07, yielding a 95% confidence interval that extends from 1.44 to 1.73 occasions, a fairly narrow band. Thus, the average student drinks on less than two occasions per month.

At the end of Part Two, we also looked at differences in the distribution of daily smoking for male and female students. Just as we did overall, we can construct confidence intervals separately for each sex. As shown in the following table, the confidence interval for percentage of males who smoke (44.1%–60.1%) is entirely below the corresponding confidence interval for the percentage of females who smoke (63.5%–79.5%). Although we will encounter a formal way to test these differences in Part Three, it does seem that we can identify with some confidence a large sex difference in the percentage who smoke. In terms of the extent of smoking for male and female smokers, we are 95% confident that the population mean for males is between 13.5 and 18.3 cigarettes daily, and we are also 95% confident that the population mean for females is between 15.4 and 20.0 cigarettes daily. Since these two confidence intervals overlap (i.e., the population mean for both males and females could quite conceivably be about 17), we cannot feel so sure about a real sex difference in the populations. We will take on this question again in Part Three.

Confidence Intervals by Sex

Variable	Statistic	Group	
		Males	*Females*
If a smoker			
	N	127	123
	%	52.8%	71.5%
	SE	4.4%	4.1%
	95% CI	44.1%–60.1%	63.5%–79.5%
Daily smoking			
	N	67	88
	Mean	15.9	17.7
	SE	1.24	1.14
	95% CI	13.5–18.3	15.4–20.0

7

Testing Differences between Means

In Chapter 6, we saw that a population mean or proportion can be estimated from the information we gain from a single sample. For instance, we might estimate the mean level of anomie in a certain city, the proportion of businesses that hire private security, or the mean attitude toward community registration of convicted sex offenders.

Although the descriptive, fact-gathering approach of estimating means and proportions has obvious importance, it *does not* constitute the primary decision-making goal or activity of research. Quite to the contrary, most criminal justice researchers are preoccupied with the task of *testing hypotheses* about a population mean or proportion and especially about how they differ between two or more groups.

Suppose, for example, that a local restaurant announces a contest designed to enhance its lunchtime business. According to the promotion, 20% of the computer-generated meal checks, selected at random, will have a red star printed on them, signifying that lunch is "on the house." You have eaten at the restaurant four times since the promotion was started, and still no free lunch. Should you begin to question the authenticity of the restaurant's promotion? How about if you go 0 for 8, or 0 for 16; is it time to complain, or should you pass it off as your bad luck?

We know that 80% of all customers lose on their first meal (no red star). On their second visit, 80% of the first-time losers again lose ($80\% \times 80\% = 64\%$). Going one step further, $80\% \times 80\% \times 80\% = 51.2\%$ or about half of all customers lose three times in a row. In probability terms, $P = .512$ of being a three-time loser. The chance of losing eight times in a row is $P = (.8)^8 = .168$—less likely, but still hardly justification for a complaint to the Better Business Bureau. But 16 losses is very improbable, $P = (.8)^{16} = .028$, assuming that the restaurant's claim that a random 20% of the meals are free is indeed valid.

Indeed, 16 losses is so improbable that you should question whether the assumption that 20% of checks have a lucky red star is true. Of course, there is that small probability (.028) that you are "cursed," but the social scientist (not believing in curses) would conclude instead that the assumption that 20% of the checks have red stars should be rejected.

This is the logic (though not quite the mechanics) of hypothesis testing. We establish a hypothesis about populations, collect sample data, and see how likely the sample results are, given our hypothesis about the populations. If the sample results are reasonably plausible under the hypothesis about the populations, we retain the hypothesis and attribute any departure from our expected results to pure chance based on sampling error. On the other hand, if the sample results are highly unlikely (e.g., less than 5 chances in 100), we attribute the departure from our expected outcome to an incorrect hypothesis, which we then reject.

TESTING THE DIFFERENCE BETWEEN SAMPLE AND POPULATION MEANS

In the previous chapter, we used information from a random sample—specifically N, $\overline{X}$, and s—to estimate the mean of the population from which it was drawn. The sample mean $\overline{X}$ provided our best estimate for μ, while the standard error ($s_{\overline{X}}$), which is estimated from the sample standard deviation (s) and the sample size (N), enabled us to specify a range within which we are confident that μ indeed falls. We also suggested that a confidence interval could sometimes be used to test the plausibility of some particular value of μ that was believed to be true.

There is a more direct way that we can use a sample—specifically, its mean ($\overline{X}$) and the standard error of that mean ($s_{\overline{X}}$)—to test some hypothesis about μ. Consider a police chief of a small department who has claimed that the average response time to calls for service is 5 min. He bases this on anecdotal evidence—his general sense of response times—not on the basis of some scientific analysis of actual calls for service.

We wish to test the hypothesis that μ is indeed 5.0 min by drawing a random sample of 50 calls for which response times are determined. Suppose that we obtain a sample mean $\overline{X} = 5.49$ and a sample standard deviation $s = 1.47$. From this, we can estimate the standard error of the sample mean:

$$s_{\overline{X}} = \frac{s}{\sqrt{N-1}}$$

$$= \frac{1.47}{\sqrt{50-1}}$$

$$= \frac{1.47}{7}$$

$$= .21$$

Thus, even though our sample mean is as high as 5.49, nearly half a minute more than the chief's claim, we understand that this can occur just as the result of sampling. The standard error gauges how much this comes into play.

Rather than using a t value to calculate the margin of error to construct a confidence interval, as in the last chapter, we can calculate a t ratio that compares the sample mean to the hypothesized population mean based on units of the standard error. Recall that in Chapter 5, we converted the distance of a raw score from the mean into standard deviation units to obtain a z score. Now, we use a t ratio to convert the difference between sample mean $\overline{X}$ and the hypothesized population mean μ into units of standard error. The t ratio for testing the difference between a sample mean and a presumed population mean is given by the formula:

$$\boxed{t = \frac{\overline{X} - \mu}{s_{\overline{X}}}}$$

We can then calculate the t ratio as follows:

$$t = \frac{5.49 - 5.0}{.21}$$

$$= \frac{.49}{.21}$$

$$= 2.33$$

Thus, the mean obtained from a sample of 50 calls into 911 is 0.49 min above, or 2.33 standard error units above, the chief's claim. Table C, which we used before to construct confidence intervals, can now be used to assess whether the sample results, specifically the difference between the sample mean of 5.49 min and the chief's hypothesis of 5.0 min, can be attributed to chance or instead casts doubt on the chief's claim. With $\alpha = .05$ and $df = N - 1 = 49$, we locate a table value of t (for 40 df, since 49 is not available) of 2.021. This means that a t ratio larger than 2.021 (in either the positive or negative direction) is less than 5% likely to occur by sampling variability alone. As a result, we can conclude that the chief is understating the mean response time for the entire population of calls into 911. Note that had we used the same sample data to construct a confidence interval, we would have learned in a less direct way that the chief's speculation was well outside the range of likely values for μ.

TESTING THE DIFFERENCE BETWEEN TWO SAMPLE MEANS

We hope this illustration shows the link between constructing confidence intervals and testing basic hypotheses about a sample mean. As it happens, the so-called one sample test used previously is not especially applicable to criminal justice because rarely do researchers have in mind a particular value of μ against which to compare a sample mean. It is much more common to compare the means of two samples (e.g., the mean response times for samples of weekday and weekend calls) to test whether or not it is plausible that they both have the same population mean.

When testing differences between samples, criminal justice researchers ask such questions as the following: Do political conservatives approve of longer prison sentences for violent criminals than do political liberals? Do female prosecutors have higher conviction rates than male prosecutors? Do offenders who have completed drug rehabilitation programs have lower recidivism rates than offenders who have not had any drug rehabilitation programming? Do urban police have higher death rates than rural police? Note that each research question involves making a comparison between two groups: conservatives versus liberals, male versus female lawyers, offenders who have versus have not completed a drug rehabilitation program, urban versus rural police.

Take a more concrete example. Suppose that a researcher interested in crime victim recovery wanted to evaluate crime victim counseling services provided by the courts in his city. He selects 10 crime victims and randomly assigns 5 to the "treatment" group where they receive the counseling services provided by the court, and 5 victims to the "control" group where they do not receive counseling.

Suppose further that following the time in which the treatment group receives counseling, all 10 of the victims are administered the same questionnaire assessing their levels of anxiety. The sample mean score for the five subjects in the control group was 82, and the sample mean for the treatment group was 77 (higher scores indicate higher anxiety). Is the victim counseling provided by the court effective in reducing anxiety? Perhaps. Perhaps not. It is impossible to draw any firm conclusions until we know more about the data.

Let us say just for a moment that the sets of anxiety scores for the two groups of crime victims were as follows:

Control	Treatment
82	78
83	77
82	76
80	78
83	76
Mean = 82	Mean = 77

In the control group, the anxiety scores are consistently in the low 80s, so we would have a good deal of confidence that the population mean would be close to the sample mean of 82. Similarly, we would say with confidence that the population mean for the treatment group is likely near the sample mean of 77. Given the homogeneity of the scores and thus the sample means, we could probably conclude that the difference between sample means is more than just a result of pure chance or sampling error. In fact, the counseling received by the individuals in the treatment group does appear to reduce anxiety.

Now suppose instead that the following sets of scores produced the two sample means 82 and 77. It is clear that in both groups there is wide variability or spread among the anxiety scores. As a result, both sample means are relatively unstable estimates of their respective population means. Given the heterogeneity of the sample scores and the unreliability of the sample means, we therefore could not conclude that the difference between sample means is anything more than a result of pure chance or sampling error. In fact, there is not enough evidence to conclude that the victim counseling services affect anxiety.

Control	Treatment
90	70
98	90
63	91
74	56
85	78
Mean = 82	Mean = 77

THE NULL HYPOTHESIS: NO DIFFERENCE BETWEEN MEANS

NULL HYPOTHESIS

The hypothesis of equal population means. Any observed difference between samples is seen as a chance occurrence resulting from sampling error.

It has become conventional in statistical analysis to set out testing the **null hypothesis**—the hypothesis that says two samples have been drawn from equivalent populations. According to the null hypothesis, any observed difference between samples is regarded as a chance occurrence resulting from sampling error alone. Therefore, an obtained difference between two sample means does not represent a true difference between their population means.

In the present context, the null hypothesis can be symbolized as

$$\mu_1 = \mu_2$$

where μ_1 = mean of the first population
μ_2 = mean of the second population

Let us examine null hypotheses for the research questions posed earlier:

1. Conservatives are no more or less likely than liberals to approve of longer prison sentences.
2. Male and female prosecutors have the same conviction rate.
3. Drug rehabilitation program graduates have the same recidivism rates as offenders who do not go through such programs.
4. Urban and rural police have the same death rates.

It should be noted that the null hypothesis does not deny the possibility of obtaining differences between *sample* means. On the contrary, it seeks to explain such differences between sample means by attributing them to the operation of sampling error. In accordance with the null hypothesis, for example, if we find that a *sample* of female probation officers earn less money ($\overline{X}$ = \$32,000) than a *sample* of male probation officers ($\overline{X}$ = \$33,000), we do not, on that basis, conclude that the population of female probation officers earns less money than the population of male probation officers. Instead, we treat our obtained sample difference (\$33,000 − \$32,000 = \$1,000) as a product of sampling error—the difference that inevitably results from the process of sampling from a given population. As we shall see later, this aspect of the null hypothesis provides an important link with sampling theory.

To conclude that sampling error is responsible for our obtained difference between sample means is to *retain* the null hypothesis. The use of the term *retain* does not imply that we have proven the population means are equal ($\mu_1 = \mu_2$) or even that we believe it. Technically, we are merely unable to reject the null hypothesis due to lack of sufficient contradictory evidence. For the sake of simplicity, the phrase *retain the null hypothesis* will be used throughout the text when we are unable to reject it.

THE RESEARCH HYPOTHESIS: A DIFFERENCE BETWEEN MEANS

The null hypothesis is generally (although not necessarily) set up with the hope of rejecting it. This makes sense, for most criminal justice researchers seek to establish differences between groups. That is, they are often more interested in finding differences than in determining that differences do not exist. Differences between groups—whether expected on theoretical or empirical grounds—often provide the rationale for research.

If we reject the null hypothesis, if we find our hypothesis of no difference between means probably does not hold, we automatically accept the **research hypothesis** that a true population difference does exist. This is often the hoped-for result in criminal justice research. The research hypothesis says that the two samples have been taken from populations having different means. It says that the obtained difference between sample means is too large to be accounted for by sampling error alone.

The research hypothesis for mean differences is symbolized by

$$\mu_1 \neq \mu_2$$

where μ_1 = mean of the first population
        μ_2 = mean of the second population

Note: $\neq$ is read *does not equal*.

RESEARCH HYPOTHESIS

The hypothesis that regards any observed difference between samples as reflecting a true population difference and not just sampling error.

The following research hypotheses can be specified for the research questions posed earlier:

1. Conservatives differ from liberals in approval of longer prison sentences.
2. Male and female prosecutors do not have the same conviction rates.
3. Drug rehabilitation program graduates do not have the same recidivism rates as offenders who do not go through such programs.
4. Urban and rural police have different death rates.

SAMPLING DISTRIBUTION OF DIFFERENCES BETWEEN MEANS

In the preceding chapter, we saw that the 100 means from the 100 samples drawn by our eccentric criminologist could be plotted in the form of a sampling distribution of means. In a similar way, let us now imagine that the same criminologist studies not one but two samples at a time to make comparisons between them.

Suppose, for example, that our eccentric criminologist is interested in people's attitudes toward criminal justice punishment. Specifically, he wants to assess whether people are lenient in their attitudes toward punishing convicted offenders, and to examine whether there is a relationship between gender and leniency.

To test for gender differences, he first constructs a multi-item scale, which includes several questions about approval of capital punishment, mandatory sentences (including "three-strikes" legislation), trying juveniles as adults, the use of parole, and opinions about appropriate prison sentence lengths for various crimes. His leniency scale ranges from a minimum of 1 (not at all lenient) to a maximum of 100 (extremely lenient). Next, he selects a random sample of 30 females and a random sample of 30 males from the student directory and administers his questionnaire

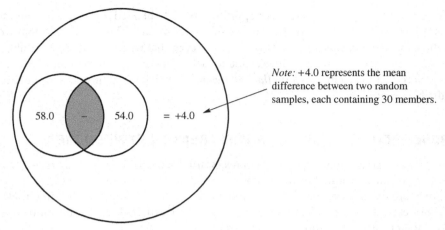

Note: +4.0 represents the mean difference between two random samples, each containing 30 members.

FIGURE 7.1   The Mean Difference in Leniency between a Sample of Females and a Sample of Males Taken from a Hypothetical Population.

to all 60 students. As graphically illustrated in Figure 7.1 our eccentric researcher finds his sample of females is more lenient ($\overline{X} = 58.0$) than his sample of males ($\overline{X} = 54.0$).

Before our eccentric researcher concludes that women are actually more lenient than men, he might ask: In light of sampling error, can we expect a difference between 58.0 and 54.0 ($58.0 - 54.0 = +4.0$) strictly on the basis of chance and chance alone? Based solely on the luck of the draw, could the female sample have been comprised of more lenient people than the male sample? Must we retain the null hypothesis of no population difference, or is the obtained sample difference +4.0 large enough to indicate a true population difference between females and males with respect to their criminal justice punishment attitudes?

In Chapter 2, we were introduced to frequency distributions of raw scores from a given population. In Chapter 6, we saw it was possible to construct a sampling distribution of mean scores, as a frequency distribution of all possible sample means. In addressing ourselves to the question at hand, we must now take the notion of frequency distribution a step further and examine the nature of a **sampling distribution of differences between means**, that is, a frequency distribution of a large number of *differences* between sample means that have been randomly drawn from a given population.

To illustrate the sampling distribution of differences between means, let us return to the compulsive activities of our eccentric researcher whose passion for drawing random samples has once again led him to continue the sampling process beyond its ordinary limits. Rather than draw a single sample of 30 females and a single sample of 30 males, he studies 70 *pairs* of such samples (70 pairs of samples, *each* containing 30 females and 30 males), feeling fortunate that he teaches at a large school.

For each pair of samples, the eccentric researcher administers the same scale of leniency. He then calculates a mean for each female sample and a mean for each male sample. Thus, he has a female mean and a male mean for each of his 70 pairs of samples.

Next, he derives a difference-between-means score by subtracting the mean score for males from the mean score for females for each pair of samples. For example, his first comparison produced a difference between means of +4.0. His second pair of means might be 57.0 for the female sample and 56.0 for the male sample, yielding a difference-between-means score of +1.0. Likewise, the third pair of samples may have produced a mean of 60.0 for the females and a mean of 64.0 for the males, and the difference between means would be −4.0. Obviously, the larger the difference score, the more the two samples of respondents differ with respect to leniency. Note that we always subtract the second sample mean from the first sample mean (in the present case, we subtract the mean score for the male sample from the mean score for the female sample). The 70 difference-between-means scores derived by our eccentric researcher have been illustrated in Figure 7.2.

SAMPLING DISTRIBUTION OF DIFFERENCES BETWEEN MEANS

A frequency distribution of a large number of differences between random sample means that have been drawn from a given population.

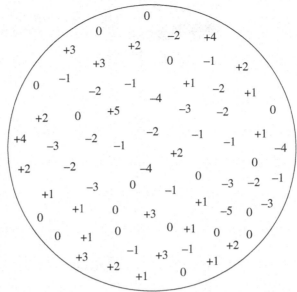

Note: Each score represents the difference between a sample of 30 females and a sample of 30 males.

FIGURE 7.2   Seventy Mean Difference Scores Representing Differences in Leniency between Samples of Females and Males Taken at Random from a Hypothetical Population.

Let us suppose that we know that the populations of females and males do not differ at all with respect to leniency in criminal justice punishment attitudes. Let us say for the sake of argument that $\mu = 57.0$ in both the female and male populations. If we assume the null hypothesis is correct, and that females and males are identical in this respect, we can use the 70 mean differences obtained by our eccentric researcher to illustrate the sampling distribution of differences between means. This is true because the sampling distribution of differences between means makes the assumption that all sample pairs differ only by virtue of sampling error and not as a function of true population differences.

The 70 scores representing differences between means shown in Figure 7.2 have been rearranged in Table 7.1 as a sampling distribution of differences between means. Like the scores in other types of frequency distributions, these have been arranged in consecutive order from high to low, and frequency of occurrence is indicated in an adjacent column.

To depict the key properties of a sampling distribution of differences between means, the frequency distribution from Table 7.1 has been graphically presented in Figure 7.3. As illustrated therein, we see that the *sampling distribution of differences between means approximates a normal curve whose mean (mean of differences between means) is zero.*[1] This makes sense because the positive and negative differences between means in the distribution tend to cancel out one another (for every negative value, there tends to be a positive value of equal distance from the mean).

As a normal curve, most of the differences between sample means in this distribution fall close to zero—its middle-most point: There are relatively few differences between means having extreme values in either direction from the mean of these differences. This is to be expected, because the entire distribution of differences between means is a product of sampling error rather than actual population differences between females and males. In other words, if the actual mean difference between the populations of females and males is zero, we also expect the mean of the sampling distribution of differences between sample means to be zero.

[1]This assumes we have drawn large random samples from a given population of raw scores.

TABLE 7.1	Sampling Distribution of Differences for 70 Pairs of Random Samples	
Mean Difference[a]		*f*
+5		1
+4		2
+3		5
+2		7
+1		10
0		18
−1		10
−2		8
−3		5
−4		3
−5		1
		$N = 70$

[a]These difference scores include fractional values (e.g., −5 includes the values −5.0 through −5.9).

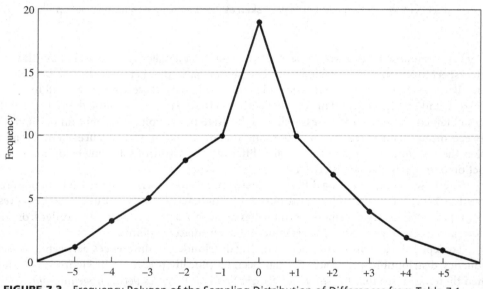

FIGURE 7.3 Frequency Polygon of the Sampling Distribution of Differences from Table 7.1.

TESTING HYPOTHESES WITH THE DISTRIBUTION OF DIFFERENCES BETWEEN MEANS

In earlier chapters, we learned to make probability statements regarding the occurrence of both raw scores and sample means. In the present case, we seek to make statements of probability about the difference scores in the sampling distribution of differences between means. As pointed out earlier, this sampling distribution takes the form of the normal curve and, therefore, can be regarded as a probability distribution. We can say that probability decreases as we move further and further from the mean of differences (zero). More specifically, as illustrated in Figure 7.4, we see that 68.26% of the mean differences fall between $+1\sigma_{\overline{X}_1 - \overline{X}_2}$ and $-1\sigma_{\overline{X}_1 - \overline{X}_2}$ from zero. The notation $\sigma_{\overline{X}_1 - \overline{X}_2}$ represents the standard deviation of the differences between $\overline{X}_1$ and $\overline{X}_2$. In probability terms, this indicates $P = .68$ that any difference between sample

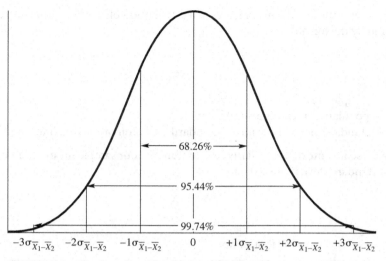

FIGURE 7.4 The Sampling Distribution of Differences between Means as a Probability Distribution.

means falls within this interval. Similarly, we can say the probability is roughly .95 (95 chances in 100) that any sample mean difference falls between $-2\sigma_{\overline{X}_1-\overline{X}_2}$ and $+2\sigma_{\overline{X}_1-\overline{X}_2}$ from a mean difference of zero, and so on.

The sampling distribution of differences provides a sound basis for testing hypotheses about the difference between two sample means. Unlike the eccentric researcher who compulsively takes pairs of samples, one after another, most normal researchers would study only one pair of samples to make inferences on the basis of just one difference between means.

Suppose, for instance, that a normal criminologist wanted to test the eccentric criminologist's hypothesis, or at least a variation of it, in a realistic way. She is interested in the relationship between gender and criminal justice attitudes and decides to examine gender differences in leniency or punitiveness of attitudes regarding criminal justice punishment among criminal justice professionals.

She randomly selects 30 female and 30 male probation officers and administers the eccentric researcher's leniency scale to all 60 officers. She obtains mean leniency scores of 45 for the female probation officers and 40 for the male probation officers. The researcher's reasoning then goes like this: If the obtained difference between means of $5(45 - 40 = 5)$ lies so far from a difference of zero that it has only a small probability of occurrence in the sampling distribution of differences between means, we reject the null hypothesis—the hypothesis that says the obtained difference between means is a result of sampling error. If, on the other hand, our sample mean difference falls so close to zero that its *probability* of occurrence by chance is large, we must retain the null hypothesis and treat our obtained difference between means merely as a result of sampling error.

Therefore, we seek to determine how far our obtained difference between means (in this case, 5) lies from a mean difference of zero. In so doing, we must first translate our obtained difference into units of standard deviation.

Recall that we translate *raw scores* into units of standard deviation by the formula

$$z = \frac{X - \mu}{\sigma}$$

where X = raw score
μ = mean of the distribution of raw scores
σ = standard deviation of the distribution of raw scores

Likewise, we translate the *mean scores* in a distribution of sample means into units of standard deviation by the formula

$$z = \frac{\overline{X} - \mu}{\sigma_{\overline{X}}}$$

where $\overline{X}$ = sample mean

μ = population mean (mean of means)

$\sigma_{\overline{X}}$ = standard error of the mean (standard deviation of the distribution of means)

In the present context, we similarly seek to translate our sample mean difference $(\overline{X}_1 - \overline{X}_2)$ into units of standard deviation by the formula

$$z = \frac{(\overline{X}_1 - \overline{X}_2) - 0}{\sigma_{\overline{X}_1 - \overline{X}_2}}$$

where $\overline{X}_1$ = mean of the first sample

$\overline{X}_2$ = mean of the second sample

0 = zero, the value of the mean of the sampling distribution of differences between means (we assume that $\mu_1 - \mu_2 = 0$)

$\sigma_{\overline{X}_1 - \overline{X}_2}$ = standard deviation of the sampling distribution of differences between means

Because the value of the mean of the distribution of differences between means is assumed to be zero, we can drop it from the z-score formula without altering our result. Therefore,

$$\boxed{z = \frac{\overline{X}_1 - \overline{X}_2}{\sigma_{\overline{X}_1 - \overline{X}_2}}}$$

With regard to leniency between the female and male probation officer samples, we must translate our obtained difference between means into its z-score equivalent. If the standard deviation of the sampling distribution of differences between means $\sigma_{\overline{X}_1 - \overline{X}_2}$ is 2 (more on how to get this number later), we obtain the following z score:

$$z = \frac{45 - 40}{2}$$
$$= \frac{5}{2}$$
$$= +2.5$$

Thus, a difference of 5 between the means for the two samples falls 2.5 standard deviations from a mean difference of zero in the distribution of differences between means.

What is the probability that a difference of 5 or more between sample means can happen strictly on the basis of sampling error? Going to column c of Table A in Appendix C, we learn that $z = 2.5$ cuts off 0.62% of the area in each tail, or 1.24% in total (see Figure 7.5). We consider both tails because the difference between the male and female sample means could be in either direction. Rounding off, $P = .01$ that the mean difference of 5 (or greater than 5) between samples can happen strictly on the basis of sampling error. That is, a mean difference of 5 or more occurs by sampling error (and therefore appears in the sampling distribution) *only once* in every 100 mean differences. Knowing this, would we not consider rejecting the null hypothesis and accepting the research hypothesis that a population difference actually exists between male and female probation officers with respect to the leniency of their attitudes regarding criminal justice punishment? One chance out of 100 represents pretty good odds.

Given that situation, most of us would choose to reject the null hypothesis, even though we might be wrong in doing so (don't forget that 1 chance out of 100 still remains). However, the decision is not always so clear-cut. Suppose, for example, we learn our difference between

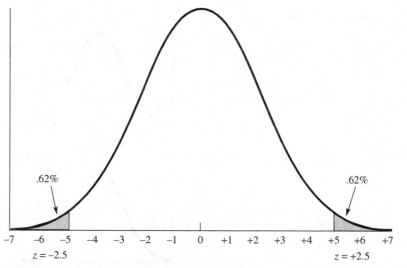

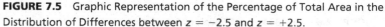

FIGURE 7.5 Graphic Representation of the Percentage of Total Area in the Distribution of Differences between $z = -2.5$ and $z = +2.5$.

means happens by sampling error 10 ($P = .10$), 15 ($P = .15$), or 20 ($P = .20$) times out of 100. Do we still reject the null hypothesis? Or do we play it safe and attribute our obtained difference to sampling error?

We need a consistent cutoff point for deciding whether a difference between two sample means is so large that it can no longer be attributed to sampling error. In other words, we need a method for determining when our results show a **statistically significant difference**.

LEVELS OF SIGNIFICANCE

To establish whether our obtained sample difference is statistically significant—the result of a real population difference and not just sampling error—it is customary to set up a **level of significance**, which we denote by the Greek letter α (alpha). The alpha value is the level of probability at which the null hypothesis can be rejected with confidence, and the research hypothesis can be accepted with confidence. Accordingly, we decide to reject the null hypothesis if the probability is very small (e.g., less than 5 chances out of 100) that the sample difference is a product of sampling error. Conventionally, we symbolize this small probability by $P < .05$.

It is a matter of convention to use the $\alpha = .05$ **level of significance**. That is, we are willing to reject the null hypothesis if an obtained sample difference occurs by chance less then 5 times out of 100. The .05 significance level has been graphically depicted in Figure 7.6. As shown, the .05 level of significance is found in the small areas of the tails of the distribution of mean differences. These are the areas under the curve that represent a distance of ± 1.96 standard deviations from a mean difference of zero. In this case (with an $\alpha = .05$ level of significance), the z scores 1.96 are called *critical values*; if we obtain a z score that exceeds 1.96 (i.e., $z > 1.96$ or $z < -1.96$), it is called statistically significant. The shaded regions in Figure 7.6 are called the **critical** or **rejection regions**, because a z score within these areas leads us to reject the null hypothesis (the top portion of the figure shows the critical regions for a .05 level of significance).

To understand better why this particular point in the sampling distribution represents the .05 level of significance, we might turn to column c of Table A in Appendix C to determine the percentage of total frequency associated with 1.96 standard deviations from the mean. We see that 1.96 standard deviations in *either* direction represent 2.5% of the differences in sample means. Combined, only 5% fall beyond this point (2.5% + 2.5% = 5%)—in other words, 95% of these differences fall between $-1.96\sigma_{\bar{X}_1 - \bar{X}_2}$ and $+1.96\sigma_{\bar{X}_1 - \bar{X}_2}$ from a mean difference of zero; only 5% fall at or beyond this point (2.5% + 2.5% = 5%).

STATISTICALLY SIGNIFICANT DIFFERENCE

A sample difference that reflects a real population difference and not just sampling error.

LEVEL OF SIGNIFICANCE

A level of probability at which the null hypothesis can be rejected and the research hypothesis can be accepted.

FIVE PERCENT LEVEL (.05) OF SIGNIFICANCE

A level of probability at which the null hypothesis is rejected if an obtained sample difference occurs by chance only 5 times or less out of 100.

CRITICAL REGION (REJECTION REGION)

The area in the tail(s) of a sampling distribution that dictates that the null hypothesis be rejected.

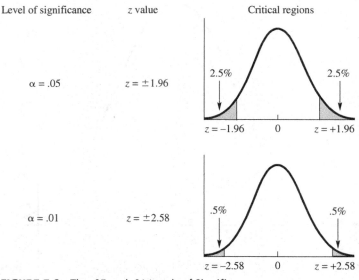

FIGURE 7.6 The .05 and .01 Levels of Significance.

ONE PERCENT (.01) LEVEL OF SIGNIFICANCE

A level of probability at which the null hypothesis is rejected if an obtained sample difference occurs by chance only 1 time or less out of 100.

TYPE I ERROR

The error of rejecting the null hypothesis when it is true.

Significance levels can be set up for any degree of probability. For instance, a more stringent level is the **.01 level of significance**, whereby the null hypothesis is rejected if there is less than 1 chance out of 100 that the obtained sample difference could occur by sampling error. The .01 level of significance is represented by the area that lies 2.58 standard deviations in both directions from a mean difference of zero (see the bottom portion of Figure 7.6).

Levels of significance do not give us an *absolute* statement as to the correctness of the null hypothesis. Whenever we decide to reject the null hypothesis at a certain level of significance, we open ourselves to the chance of making the wrong decision. Rejecting the null hypothesis when we should have retained it is known as **Type I error** (see Figure 7.7). A Type I error can only arise when we reject the null hypothesis, and its probability varies according to the level of significance we choose. For example, if we reject the null hypothesis at the .05 level of significance and conclude that there are gender differences in criminal justice punishment attitudes, then there are 5 chances out of 100 we are wrong. In other words, $P = .05$ that we have committed Type I error, and that gender actually has no effect at all. Likewise, if we choose the $\alpha = .01$ level of significance, there is only 1 chance out of 100 ($P = .01$) of making the wrong decision regarding the difference between genders. Obviously, the more stringent our level of significance (the further

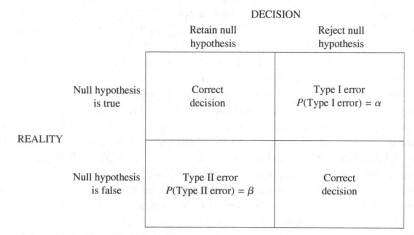

FIGURE 7.7 Type I and Type II Errors.

out in the tail it lies), the less likely we are to make Type I error. To take an extreme example, setting up a .001 significance level means that Type I error occurs only 1 time in every 1,000. The probability of Type I error is symbolized by α (alpha).

The further out in the tail of the curve our critical value falls, however, the greater the risk of making another kind of error known as **Type II error**. This is the error of retaining the null hypothesis when we should have rejected it. Type II error indicates that our research hypothesis may still be correct, despite the decision to retain the null hypothesis. One method for reducing the risk of committing Type II error is to increase the size of the samples, so that a true population difference is more likely to be represented. The probability of Type II error is denoted by β (beta).

We can never be certain that we have not made a wrong decision with respect to the null hypothesis, for we examine only differences between sample means, not between means of the complete population. As long as we do not have knowledge of true population means, we take the risk of making either a Type I or a Type II error, depending on our decision. This is the risk of statistical decision making that the criminal justice researcher must be willing to take.

ALPHA

The probability of committing a Type I error.

TYPE II ERROR

The error of retaining the null hypothesis when it is false.

Choosing a Level of Significance

We have seen that the probabilities of Type I error and Type II error are inversely related: The greater the likelihood of one error is, the smaller the likelihood of the other. In practice, a researcher does not have actual control of the likelihood of Type II error (β) directly. That is, she or he cannot set the probability of a Type II error to whatever level is desired. On the other hand, the chance of a Type I error is a quantity directly controlled by the researcher, because it is precisely the level of significance (α) he or she chooses for the hypothesis test. Of course, the larger the chosen level of significance (say, .05 or even .10), the larger the chance of Type I error and the smaller the chance of Type II error. The smaller the chosen significance level (say, .01 or even .001), the smaller the chance of Type I error, but the greater the likelihood of Type II error.

We predetermine our level of significance for a hypothesis test on the basis of which type of error (Type I or Type II) is more costly or damaging and therefore riskier. If in a particular instance it would be far worse to reject a true null hypothesis (Type I error) than to retain a false null hypothesis (Type II error), we should opt for a small level of significance (e.g., $\alpha = .01$ or .001) to minimize the risk of Type I error, even at the expense of increasing the chance of Type II error. If, however, it is believed that Type II error would be worse, we would set a larger significance level ($\alpha = .05$ or .10) to produce a lower chance of Type II error, that is, a lower β value.

Suppose, for example, a researcher were doing research on gender differences in SAT performance for which she administered an SAT to a sample of males and a sample of females. Before deciding upon a level of significance, she should pause and ask: Which is worse—claiming that there is a true gender difference on the basis of results distorted by excessive sampling error (Type I error) or not claiming a difference when there is in fact one between the population of males and the population of females (Type II error)? In this instance, a Type I error would probably be far more damaging—could even be used as a basis for discriminating unfairly against women—and so she should select a small α value (say, .01).

Let's consider a reverse situation—one in which Type II error is far more worrisome. Suppose a researcher is testing the effects of marijuana smoking on SAT performance, and he compares a sample of smokers with a sample of nonsmokers. If there was even a modest indication that marijuana smoking affected one's performance, this information should be disseminated. We would not want a researcher to retain the null hypothesis of no population difference between smokers and nonsmokers in spite of an observed difference in sample means just because the difference was not quite significant. This Type II error could have a serious impact on public health and safety. A Type I error, by which the researcher was misled to believe marijuana smoking altered performance when the sample difference was only due to chance, would certainly not be as problematic. Given this situation, the researcher would be advised to select a large α level (like .10) to avoid the risk of a serious Type II error. That is, he should be less stringent in rejecting the null hypothesis.

What Is the Difference between *P* and α?

The difference between P and α can be a bit confusing. To avoid confusion, let's compare the two quantities directly. Put simply, P is the exact probability that the null hypothesis is true in light of the sample data; the α value is the threshold below which is considered so small that we decide to reject the null hypothesis. That is, we reject the null hypothesis if the P value is less than the α value and otherwise retain it.

In testing hypotheses, a researcher decides ahead of time on the α value. This choice is made on the basis of weighing the implications of Type I and Type II errors or is simply made by custom—that is, $\alpha = .05$. The α value refers to the size of the tail regions under the curve (of z, for example) that will lead us to reject the null hypothesis. That is, α is the area to the right of the tabled critical value of $+z$ and to the left of the tabled value of $-z$. With $\alpha = .05$, these regions are to the right of $z = +1.96$ and to the left of -1.96 (see Figure 7.8). (With the t distribution, the critical values depend also on the degrees of freedom.) Thus, α represents the chance of Type I error that we are willing to tolerate.

In contrast, P is the actual probability that the null hypothesis is true. If this probability is small enough (i.e., if the null hypothesis is very unlikely), we tend to reject the null hypothesis. Unlike the α value, which is determined by the researcher in advance, the P value is determined by the data themselves—specifically by the computed value of the test statistic, such as the z score—and is not set by the researcher. The P value is the area to the right of the calculated $+z$ on the positive side plus the area to the left of the calculated $-z$ on the negative side. Thus, if after data collection, a z score of 2.12 is obtained, we learn from column c of Table A that $P = .034$ (.017 in each tail). If this were the result, we would conclude that $P < .05$, and so we would reject the null hypothesis (see Figure 7.8).

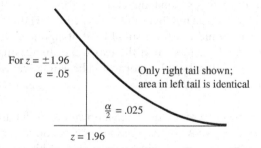

For $z = \pm1.96$
$\alpha = .05$

Only right tail shown;
area in left tail is identical

$\frac{\alpha}{2} = .025$

$z = 1.96$

Critical value of $z = \pm1.96$ cuts off an $\alpha = .05$ rejection area

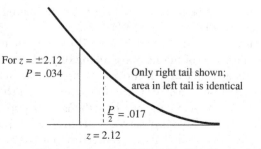

For $z = \pm2.12$
$P = .034$

Only right tail shown;
area in left tail is identical

$\frac{P}{2} = .017$

$z = 2.12$

Obtained value of $z = 2.12$ yields $P < .05$ and rejects null hypothesis

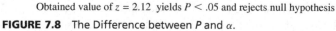

FIGURE 7.8 The Difference between P and α.

In practice, one does not regularly look up the actual value of P, as we just did from Table A. One only needs to look at whether the calculated z value exceeds the critical value for the chosen α level. Note that the quickest way to determine the critical value for z is to look at the bottom row of the t table. That is, with infinity degrees of freedom, t is equal to z.

If the calculated z exceeds the critical value, we simply say that $P < .05$ (if .05 were the significance level preselected) and that the results are statistically significant at the .05 level. If the calculated z does not exceed the critical value, we would say the result (or difference) was not significant. In other words, one does not need to determine the actual value of P to make a decision on the hypothesis. With most statistical software currently available, however, the exact P values are automatically calculated from elaborate formulas. Therefore, in the future, we may see more people giving the actual P value rather than just saying $P < .05$.

STANDARD ERROR OF THE DIFFERENCE BETWEEN MEANS

We rarely have firsthand knowledge of the standard deviation of the distribution of mean differences. And just as in the case of the sampling distribution of means (Chapter 6), it would be a major effort if we were actually to draw a large number of sample pairs to calculate it. Yet this standard deviation plays an important role in the method for testing hypotheses about mean differences and, therefore, cannot be ignored.[2]

Fortunately, we do have a simple method whereby the standard deviation of the distribution of differences can be estimated on the basis of just two samples that we actually draw. The sample estimate of the standard deviation of the sampling distribution of differences between means, referred to as the **standard error of the difference between means** and symbolized by $s_{\bar{X}_1 - \bar{X}_2}$, is

STANDARD ERROR OF THE DIFFERENCE BETWEEN MEANS

An estimate of the standard deviation of the sampling distribution of differences between means based on the variances and sizes of two random samples.

$$s_{\bar{X}_1 - \bar{X}_2} = \sqrt{\left(\frac{N_1 s_1^2 + N_2 s_2^2}{N_1 + N_2 - 2} \right) \left(\frac{N_1 + N_2}{N_1 N_2} \right)}$$

where s_1^2 and s_2^2 are the variances of the two samples first introduced in Chapter 4:

$$s_1^2 = \frac{\sum X_1^2}{N_1} - \bar{X}_1^2$$

$$s_2^2 = \frac{\sum X_2^2}{N_2} - \bar{X}_2^2$$

The formula for $s_{\bar{X}_1 - \bar{X}_2}$ combines information from the two samples. Thus, the variance for each sample in addition to the respective sample sizes goes into our estimate of how different $\bar{X}_1$ and $\bar{X}_2$ can be due to sampling error alone. A large difference between $\bar{X}_1$ and $\bar{X}_2$ can result if (1) one mean is very small, (2) one mean is very large, or (3) one mean is moderately small while the other is moderately large. The likelihood of any of these conditions occurring is dictated by the variances and sample sizes present in the respective samples.

---

[2]In the last chapter, it was pointed out that the true population standard deviation (σ) and standard error ($\sigma_{\bar{X}}$) are rarely known. Also in the two-sample cases, the true standard error of the difference is generally unknown. However, for the rare situation in which the standard errors of both sample means are known, the true standard error of the difference between means is

$$\sigma_{\bar{X}_1 - \bar{X}_2} = \sqrt{\sigma_{\bar{X}_1}^2 + \sigma_{\bar{X}_2}^2} = \sqrt{\frac{\sigma_1^2}{N_1} + \frac{\sigma_2^2}{N_2}}$$

TESTING THE DIFFERENCE BETWEEN MEANS

Suppose that we obtained the following data for a sample of 25 liberals and 35 conservatives on the leniency scale:

Liberals	Conservatives
$N_1 = 25$	$N_2 = 35$
$\overline{X}_1 = 60$	$\overline{X}_2 = 49$
$s_1 = 12$	$s_2 = 14$

From this information, we can calculate the estimate of the standard error of the difference between means:

$$s_{\overline{X}_1 - \overline{X}_2} = \sqrt{\left(\frac{N_1 s_1^2 + N_2 s_2^2}{N_1 + N_2 - 2}\right)\left(\frac{N_1 + N_2}{N_1 N_2}\right)}$$

$$= \sqrt{\left[\frac{(25)(12)^2 + (35)(14)^2}{25 + 35 - 2}\right]\left(\frac{25 + 35}{(25)(35)}\right)}$$

$$= \sqrt{\left(\frac{3.600 + 6.860}{58}\right)\left(\frac{60}{875}\right)}$$

$$= \sqrt{(180.3448)(.0686)}$$

$$= \sqrt{12.3717}$$

$$= 3.52$$

The standard error of the difference between means (our estimate of the standard deviation of the theoretical sampling distribution of differences between means) turns out to be 3.52. If we were testing the difference in leniency between liberals (mean of 60) and conservatives (mean of 49), we could use our standard error result to translate the difference between sample means into a t ratio:

$$t = \frac{\overline{X}_1 - \overline{X}_2}{s_{\overline{X}_1 - \overline{X}_2}}$$

Here,

$$t = \frac{60 - 49}{3.52}$$

$$= \frac{11}{3.52}$$

$$= 3.13$$

We use t rather than z because we do not know the true population standard deviations for liberals and conservatives. Because we are estimating both σ_1 and σ_2 from s_1 and s_2, respectively, we compensate by using the wider t distribution, with degrees of freedom $N_1 + N_2 - 2$. For each population standard deviation that we estimate, we lose one degree of freedom from the total number of cases. Here, we have 60 cases from which we subtract 2 to obtain the 58 degrees of freedom.

Turning to Table C in Appendix C, we use the critical value for 40 degrees of freedom, the next lowest to 58, which is not given explicitly. Our calculated t value of 3.13 exceeds all the standard critical points, except that for the .001 level. Therefore, we could reject the null hypothesis at the .10, .05, or .01 level, whichever we had established for the α value at the start of our study. Had a .001 α value been established for whatever reason (there would seem little justification for choosing such a stringent test in this instance), we would have to accept the null hypothesis despite the large t value. Our chance of a Type II error would run quite high as a consequence.

STEP-BY-STEP ILLUSTRATION

Test of Difference between Means

To provide a step-by-step illustration of the foregoing procedure for testing a difference between two sample means, let us say we wanted to test the null hypothesis at the $\alpha = .05$ significance level that male and female residents of a particular city have, on average, the same level of confidence in the local police department ($\mu_1 = \mu_2$). Our research hypothesis is that male and female residents differ with respect to their confidence in the police ($\mu_1 \neq \mu_2$). To test this hypothesis, a random sample of 35 males and 35 females is asked a series of questions about the local police department, which is used to form a "confidence in police" scale, ranging from 1 (for no confidence at all) to 10 (for absolutely complete confidence). The scale scores (along with their squared values) are as follows:

Males ($N_1 = 35$)		Females ($N_2 = 35$)	
X_1	X_1^2	X_2	X_2^2
8	64	4	16
7	49	3	9
6	36	1	1
10	100	7	49
2	4	6	36
1	1	9	81
4	16	10	100
3	9	4	16
5	25	3	9
6	36	6	36
7	49	4	16
5	25	3	9
9	81	6	36
8	64	8	64
10	100	6	36
6	36	5	25
6	36	7	49
7	49	3	9
4	16	4	16
5	25	6	36
9	81	9	81
10	100	8	64
2	4	4	16
4	16	5	25
3	9	8	64
5	25	2	4
4	16	7	49
8	64	1	1
7	49	5	25
4	16	6	36
9	81	4	16
8	64	8	64
9	81	7	49
10	100	6	36
6	36	4	16
$\Sigma X_1 = 217$	$\Sigma X_1^2 = 1{,}563$	$\Sigma X_2 = 189$	$\Sigma X_2^2 = 1{,}195$

Step 1 Find the mean for each sample.

$$\overline{X}_1 = \frac{\sum X_1}{N_1} \qquad \overline{X}_2 = \frac{\sum X_2}{N_2}$$

$$= \frac{217}{35} \qquad = \frac{189}{35}$$

$$= 6.2 \qquad = 5.4$$

Step 2 Find the variance for each sample.

$$s_1^2 = \frac{\sum X_1^2}{N_1} - \overline{X}_1^2 \qquad s_2^2 = \frac{\sum X_2^2}{N_2} - \overline{X}_2^2$$

$$= \frac{1,563}{35} - (6.2)^2 \qquad = \frac{1,195}{35} - (5.4)^2$$

$$= 44.66 - 38.44 \qquad = 34.14 - 29.16$$

$$= 6.22 \qquad = 4.98$$

Step 3 Find the standard error of the difference between means.

$$s_{\overline{X}_1 - \overline{X}_2} = \sqrt{\left(\frac{N_1 s_1^2 + N_2 s_2^2}{N_1 + N_2 - 2}\right)\left(\frac{N_1 + N_2}{N_1 N_2}\right)}$$

$$= \sqrt{\left[\frac{35(6.22) + 35(4.98)}{35 + 35 - 2}\right]\left(\frac{35 + 35}{35 \times 35}\right)}$$

$$= \sqrt{\left(\frac{217.6 + 174.4}{68}\right)\left(\frac{70}{1,225}\right)}$$

$$= \sqrt{\left(\frac{392}{68}\right)\left(\frac{70}{1,225}\right)}$$

$$= \sqrt{(5.7647)(.0571)}$$

$$= \sqrt{.3294}$$

$$= .574$$

Step 4 Compute the *t* ratio by dividing the difference between means by the standard error of the difference between means.

$$t = \frac{\overline{X}_1 - \overline{X}_2}{s_{\overline{X}_1 - \overline{X}_2}}$$

$$= \frac{6.2 - 5.4}{.574}$$

$$= 1.394$$

Step 5 Determine the critical value for *t*.

$$df = N_1 - N_2 - 2 = 68$$

Because the exact value for degrees of freedom ($df = 68$) is not provided in the table, we use the next lowest value ($df = 60$) to find

$$\alpha = .05$$

$$\text{table } t = 2.000$$

The calculated t (1.394) does not exceed the table t (2.000) in either a positive or negative direction, and so we retain the null hypothesis of no difference in population means. That is, the observed difference in mean level of confidence in the police between samples of males and females could easily have occurred as a result of sampling error.

Thus, even though the sample means are indeed different (6.2 for the males and 5.4 for the females), they were not sufficiently different to conclude that the populations of male and female residents differ in mean level of confidence in the local police. Of course, we could be committing a Type II error (retaining a false null hypothesis), in that there could in fact be a difference between population means. However, neither are these sample results disparate enough ($\overline{X}_1 - \overline{X}_2$ is not large enough) nor are the sample sizes N_1 and N_2 large enough to allow us to infer that the sample difference would hold in the population.

COMPARING DEPENDENT SAMPLES

So far, we have discussed making comparisons between two *independently* drawn samples (e.g., males versus females, blacks versus whites, or liberals versus conservatives). Before leaving this topic, we must now introduce a variation of the two-mean comparison referred to as a *before-after* or *panel* design: the case of a *single* sample measured at two different points in time (time 1 versus time 2). For example, a researcher may seek to measure hostility in a single sample of children both before and after they watch a certain television program. In the same way, we might want to measure differences in attitudes toward capital punishment before and after a highly publicized murder trial.

Keep in mind the important distinction between studying the same sample on two different occasions versus sampling from the same population on two different occasions. The t test of difference between means for the same sample measured twice generally assumes that the same people are examined repeatedly—in other words, each respondent is compared to himself or herself at another point in time.

For example, a polling organization might interview a sample of 1,000 adults, 1 week before and 1 week after a trial to measure changes in attitudes over time. Because the same sample is measured twice, the t test of difference between means for the same sample measured twice is appropriate.

Suppose, instead, that this polling organization administered the same survey instrument to one sample of 1,000 adults before the trial and to a different sample of 1,000 adults after the trial. Even though the research looks at changes in attitudes over time, the two samples would have been chosen independently—that is, the selection of respondents after the trial would not have depended in any way on who was selected before the trial. Although the same population would have been sampled twice, the particular people interviewed would be different, and thus the t test of difference between means for independent groups would apply.

STEP-BY-STEP ILLUSTRATION

Test of Difference between Means for Same Sample Measured Twice

The calculation of the standard error for the dependent samples case differs from that for independent samples. To provide a step-by-step illustration of a before-after comparison, let us suppose that we wish to evaluate the effectiveness of a treatment program for men who are convicted of battering their wives or girlfriends. Specifically, corrections officials are interested in examining the effectiveness of a 2-month anger management program in reducing levels of hostility toward women. In this case, then, μ_1 is the mean score of hostility toward women at time 1 (*before* the treatment program), and μ_2 is the mean score on the hostility scale at time 2 (*after* the program). Therefore

Null hypothesis: ($\mu_1 = \mu_2$)   *The degree of hostility does not differ before and after the program.*

Research hypothesis: ($\mu_1 \neq \mu_2$)   *The degree of hostility differs before and after the program.*

To examine the program's impact, a random sample of six of the men selected for the program is administered a questionnaire (the Hostility Toward Women Scale) before the men participate in the program, and again 1 month after they have completed the program. The research team obtained the following Hostility Toward Women Scale scores from the pre- and post-program administrations of the questionnaire:

Program Participant	Before Program X_1	After Program X_2	Difference $D = X_1 - X_2$	(Difference)^2 D^2
Jeffrey	2	1	1	1
Bill	1	2	−1	1
George	3	1	2	4
Leon	3	1	2	4
Mitchell	1	2	−1	1
Myron	4	1	3	9
	$\Sigma X_1 = 14$	$\Sigma X_2 = 8$		$\Sigma D^2 = 20$

As the table shows, making a before-after comparison focuses our attention on the *difference* between time 1 and time 2, as reflected in the formula to obtain the standard deviation (for the distribution of before-after difference scores):

$$s_D = \sqrt{\frac{\Sigma D^2}{N} - (\overline{X}_1 - \overline{X}_2)^2}$$

where s_D = standard deviation of the distribution of before-after difference scores
D = after raw score subtracted from before raw score
N = number of cases or respondents in sample

Finally, the standard error of the mean difference is given by

$$s_{\overline{D}} = \frac{s_D}{\sqrt{N - 1}}$$

Step 1 Find the mean for each point in time.

$$\overline{X}_1 = \frac{\Sigma X_1}{N} \qquad \overline{X}_2 = \frac{\Sigma X_2}{N}$$

$$= \frac{14}{6} \qquad\qquad = \frac{8}{6}$$

$$= 2.33 \qquad\qquad = 1.33$$

Step 2 Find the standard deviation for the difference between time 1 and time 2.

$$s_D = \sqrt{\frac{\Sigma D^2}{N} - (\overline{X}_1 - \overline{X}_2)^2}$$

$$= \sqrt{\frac{20}{6} - (2.33 - 1.33)^2}$$

$$= \sqrt{\frac{20}{6} - (1.00)^2}$$

$$= \sqrt{3.33 - 1.00}$$

$$= \sqrt{2.33}$$

$$= 1.53$$

Step 3 Find the standard error of the mean difference.

$$s_{\overline{D}} = \frac{s_D}{\sqrt{N-1}}$$

$$= \frac{1.53}{\sqrt{6-1}}$$

$$= \frac{1.53}{2.24}$$

$$= .68$$

Step 4 Calculate the t ratio.

$$t = \frac{\overline{X}_1 - \overline{X}_2}{s_{\overline{D}}}$$

$$= \frac{2.33 - 1.33}{.68}$$

$$= 1.47$$

Step 5 Calculate the degrees of freedom noting that N is the number of subjects and not scores.

$$df = N - 1$$

$$= 6 - 1$$

$$= 5$$

Step 6 Compare the obtained t ratio to the appropriate value from Table C.

$$\text{Obtained } t = 1.47$$

$$\text{Table } t = 2.571$$

$$df = 5$$

$$\alpha = .05$$

To reject the null hypothesis of no before-after difference in mean degree of hostility toward women, the t ratio would need to be greater than 2.571. Because the obtained t is only 1.47, we must retain the null hypothesis of no difference.

Testing differences in means for the same sample measured twice is just one of several applications of the t test for dependent samples. Any time that one group is sampled based on the cases in another group, this special t test should be used. For example, comparing the development of identical twins raised apart; comparing the attitudes of women and their husbands to public spending on after-school programs; and comparing the impact of custodial and noncustodial treatment programs for delinquents in groups matched by age, race, gender, and crime type all offer the opportunity to measure and test the average difference between scores among pairs of subjects. In fact, using groups that are matched or paired in some way can offer increased control and power over drawing two samples completely independent of each other (as in the t test for independent samples).

STEP-BY-STEP ILLUSTRATION

Test of Difference between Means for Matched Samples

Criminologists often compare the homicide rates in states with capital punishment and the states without it. Of course, states differ from one another in countless ways that may impact the homicide rate other than whether or not a death penalty statute is on the books. One approach that has been used to overcome the extraneous impact of the other variables is to match death penalty and non–death penalty states in terms of geographic similarity.

Shown in the following table are 2010 homicide rates per 100,000 population for seven pairs of states, differing in whether or not capital punishment is on the books at the time but similar in terms of geography and other critical demographic and socioeconomic variables. In addition, the differences and squared differences in homicide rates between the seven pairs are calculated.

Death Penalty		No Death Penalty			
State	**HR**	**State**	**HR**	**D**	**D²**
Nebraska	3.0	Iowa	1.3	1.7	2.89
Indiana	4.5	Michigan	5.7	−1.2	1.44
South Dakota	2.8	North Dakota	1.5	1.3	1.69
Connecticut	3.6	Rhode Island	2.8	0.8	0.64
New Hampshire	1.0	Vermont	1.1	−0.1	0.01
Kentucky	4.3	West Virginia	3.3	1.0	1.00
Minnesota	1.8	Wisconsin	2.7	−0.9	0.81
	$\Sigma X_1 = 21.0$		$\Sigma X_2 = 18.4$	$\Sigma D = 2.6$	$\Sigma D^2 = 8.48$

Based on these data, we can test the equality of mean homicide rates for the two groups of paired states, using the following hypotheses:

Null hypothesis ($\mu_1 = \mu_2$)   *There is no difference in mean homicide rate between death penalty and non-death penalty states.*

Research hypothesis ($\mu_1 \neq \mu_2$)   *There is a difference in mean homicide rate between death penalty and non-death penalty states.*

Step 1 Find the mean for both groups. Note that N refers to the number of matched pairs of scores.

$$\overline{X}_1 = \frac{\Sigma X_1}{N} \quad \overline{X}_2 = \frac{\Sigma X_2}{N}$$

$$= \frac{21.0}{7} \qquad = \frac{18.4}{7}$$

$$= 3.0 \qquad = 2.63$$

Step 2 Find the standard deviation of the differences between each pair of cases.

$$s_D = \sqrt{\frac{\Sigma D^2}{N} - (\overline{X}_1 - \overline{X}_2)^2}$$

$$= \sqrt{\frac{8.48}{7} - (3.0 - 2.63)^2}$$

$$= \sqrt{\frac{8.48}{7} - (.37)^2}$$

$$= \sqrt{1.2114 - .1380}$$

$$= \sqrt{1.0735}$$

$$= 1.0361$$

Step 3 Find the standard error of the mean difference.

$$s_{\overline{D}} = \frac{s_D}{\sqrt{N - 1}}$$

$$= \frac{1.0361}{\sqrt{7 - 1}}$$

$$= \frac{1.0361}{\sqrt{6}}$$

$$= \frac{1.0361}{2.4495}$$

$$= .4230$$

Step 4 Calculate the t ratio.

$$t = \frac{\overline{X}_1 - \overline{X}_2}{s_{\overline{D}}}$$

$$= \frac{3.0 - 2.63}{.4230}$$

$$= \frac{.37}{.4230}$$

$$= .878$$

Step 5 Find the degrees of freedom.

$$df = N - 1$$

$$= 7 - 1$$

$$= 6$$

Step 6 Compare the obtained t ratio with the appropriate value from Table C.

$$df = 6$$

$$\alpha = .05$$

$$\text{Table } t = 2.447$$

$$\text{Obtained } t = .878$$

To reject the null hypothesis of no difference in mean homicide rate between death penalty and non-death penalty states, the t ratio would need to be at least 2.447. Because our obtained t ratio of .878 is less than the table critical value, we must retain the hypothesis of no difference.

TWO-SAMPLE TEST OF PROPORTIONS

In the previous chapter, we learned how to construct confidence intervals for means and for proportions using the notion of the standard error of the mean and of the proportion. In this chapter, we shifted attention to the difference between samples and employed a standard error of the difference between means. It would seem logical also to consider the sampling distribution of the difference between proportions.

The important role of testing the difference between proportions goes far beyond simply a desire to have our presentation symmetrical and complete. So many important measures used in criminology and criminal justice are cast in terms of proportions. We are often interested in knowing if two groups (e.g., males/females, whites/blacks, northerners/southerners) differ in the percentage who favor some criminal justice policy, who have some characteristic or attribute, or who succeed on some test.

Fortunately, the logic of testing the difference between two proportions is the same as for testing the difference between means. The only change is in the symbols and formulas used for calculating sample proportions and the standard error of the difference. As before, our statistic in this case (z) is once again representing the difference between sample proportions divided by the standard error of the difference.

Rather than the z formula we used for testing the difference between means (with known σ_1 and σ_2), we use

$$z = \frac{P_1 - P_2}{s_{P_1 - P_2}}$$

where P_1 and P_2 are the respective sample proportions. The standard error of the difference in proportions is given by

$$s_{P_1 - P_2} = \sqrt{P^*(1 - P^*)\left(\frac{N_1 + N_2}{N_1 N_2}\right)}$$

where P^* is the combined sample proportion,

$$P^* = \frac{N_1 P_1 + N_2 P_2}{N_1 + N_2}$$

STEP-BY-STEP ILLUSTRATION

Test of Difference between Proportions

We will describe the necessary steps for this test by illustration. A criminal justice researcher is interested in the characteristics of people who drive under the influence of alcohol. In particular, she is interested in whether men admit to drunk driving more or less often than women do. She takes a sample of 200 males and 200 females older than 21 and asks them to fill out a questionnaire. Early in the questionnaire, respondents are asked whether they have ever consumed alcohol. Respondents saying they have not are eliminated from the samples but are not replaced by someone else. Consequently, the final sample sizes for the analysis are fewer than 200 each. The following hypotheses address the population proportions of men who say they have driven a car while under the influence of alcohol (π_1), and the proportion of women who say they have done so (π_2):

Null hypothesis: ($\pi_1 = \pi_2$)   *The proportion of men and women who say they have driven under the influence of alcohol is equal.*

Research hypothesis: ($\pi_1 \neq \pi_2$)   *The proportion of men and women who say they have driven under the influence of alcohol is not equal.*

The researcher obtains the following data:

	Male	**Female**	**Total**
Sample size (*N*)	180	150	330
Driven under the influence (*f*)	81	48	129
Proportion who have driven under the influence (*P*)	0.45	0.32	0.39

Step 1 Compute the two sample proportions and the combined sample proportion.

$$P_1 = \frac{f_1}{N_1} = \frac{81}{180} = .45$$

$$P_2 = \frac{f_2}{N_2} = \frac{48}{150} = .32$$

$$P* = \frac{N_1 P_1 + N_2 P_2}{N_1 + N_2}$$

$$= \frac{(180)(.45) + (150)(.32)}{180 + 150}$$

$$= \frac{81 + 48}{180 + 150}$$

$$= \frac{129}{330}$$

$$= .39$$

Step 2 Compute the standard error of the difference.

$$s_{P_1 - P_2} = \sqrt{P*(1 - P*)\left(\frac{N_1 + N_2}{N_1 N_2}\right)}$$

$$= \sqrt{(.39)(1 - .39)\left[\frac{180 + 150}{(180)(150)}\right]}$$

$$= \sqrt{(.39)(.61)\left(\frac{330}{27,000}\right)}$$

$$= \sqrt{\frac{78.507}{27,000}}$$

$$= \sqrt{.002908}$$

$$= .0539$$

Step 3 Translate the difference between proportions into units of the standard error of the difference.

$$z = \frac{P_1 - P_2}{s_{P_1 - P_2}}$$

$$= \frac{.45 - .32}{.0539}$$

$$= 2.41$$

Step 4 Compare the obtained z value with the critical value in Table A (or from the bottom row of Table C).

For $\alpha = .05$, the critical value of $z = 1.96$. Because the obtained $z = 2.41$, we reject the null hypothesis. Because the difference between sample proportions was statistically significant, the criminal justice researcher was able to conclude that, according to self-reports, men and women drive under the influence of alcohol at different rates.

ONE-TAILED TESTS

The tests of significance covered thus far are known as **two-tailed tests:** We can reject the null hypothesis at both tails of the sampling distribution. A very large t ratio in *either* the positive or negative direction leads to rejecting the null hypothesis. A **one-tailed test**, in contrast, rejects the null hypothesis at only one tail of the sampling distribution.

Many statistics texts, particularly older editions, stress both one- and two-tailed tests. The one-tailed test has been deemphasized in recent years because statistical software packages (e.g., *SPSS*) routinely produce two-tailed significance tests as part of their standard output.

TWO-TAILED TEST

A test that is used when the null hypothesis is rejected for large differences in either direction.

ONE-TAILED TEST

A test in which the null hypothesis is rejected for large differences in only one direction.

Still, there are some occasions in which a one-tailed test is appropriate. We will briefly discuss the differences between one- and two-tailed tests for those instances. It should be emphasized, however, that the only changes are in the way the hypotheses are stated and the place where the *t* table is entered; fortunately, none of the formulas presented thus far change in any way.

Suppose that in a neighborhood with very high rates of juvenile crime, community leaders have created new crime prevention programs for youth that focus on providing remedial academic programs for first-year high school students. The community leaders' hope is that improved skill levels will reduce high school dropout rates, which in turn are expected to reduce crime rates.

A team of criminal justice researchers is enlisted to help evaluate the program. One part of their evaluation is an examination of the program's effectiveness in improving math skills. The researchers decide to use a before-after design in which nine youngsters targeted for remediation are administered a math test and then are given a similar test 6 months later following participation in the remedial math program. The approach discussed earlier (two-tailed test) would have us set up our hypotheses as follows:

Null hypothesis: $(\mu_1 = \mu_2)$ *Math ability does not differ before and after remediation.*

Research hypothesis: $(\mu_1 \neq \mu_2)$ *Math ability differs before and after remediation.*

The research hypothesis covers two possible results—that the students do far better (the mean score on the posttest is higher than on the pretest) or that they do far worse (the posttest mean is lower than the pretest mean). However, in evaluating whether the remedial program is worthwhile (i.e., produces a significant improvement in math skills), the researcher would not be excited by a significant reduction in performance.

A one-tailed test is appropriate when a researcher is only concerned with a change (for a sample tested twice) or difference (between two independent samples) in one prespecified direction, or when a researcher anticipates the *direction* of the change or difference. For example, an attempt to show that black defendants receive harsher sentences (mean sentence) than whites would indicate the need for a one-tailed test. If, however, a researcher is just looking for differences in sentencing by race, whether it is blacks or whites who get harsher sentences, he or she would instead use a two-tailed test.

In our example of remedial education, the following hypotheses for a one-tailed test would be appropriate:

Null hypothesis: $(\mu_1 \geq \mu_2)$ *Math ability does not improve after remediation.*

Research hypothesis: $(\mu_1 < \mu_2)$ *Math ability improves after remediation.*

Note carefully the difference in these hypotheses from those stated earlier. The null hypothesis includes the entire sampling distribution to the right of the critical value; the research hypothesis only includes a change in one direction. This translates into a critical region on the distribution of *t* with only one tail. Moreover, the tail is larger than with a two-tailed test, because the entire area (e.g., $\alpha = .05$) is loaded into one tail rather than divided into the two sides. As a consequence, the table value of *t* that permits the rejection of the null hypothesis is somewhat lower and easier to achieve. However, any *t* value in the opposite direction—no matter how extreme—would not allow rejection of the null hypothesis.

The differences between two-tailed and one-tailed tests are summarized in Figure 7.9. As a general rule, to construct a one-tailed test from two-tailed probabilities, simply use a table value with twice the alpha (α) of the two-tailed test. Thus, for example, the critical value for a two-tailed test with $\alpha = .10$ is identical to that for a one-tailed test with $\alpha = .05$. For convenience, however, a separate table of one-tailed critical values for *t* is given in Table C.

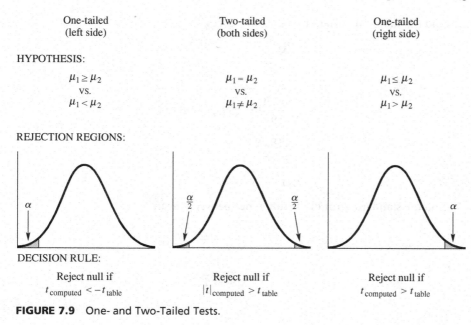

One-tailed (left side)	Two-tailed (both sides)	One-tailed (right side)

HYPOTHESIS:

$$\mu_1 \geq \mu_2$$
$$\text{vs.}$$
$$\mu_1 < \mu_2$$

$$\mu_1 = \mu_2$$
$$\text{vs.}$$
$$\mu_1 \neq \mu_2$$

$$\mu_1 \leq \mu_2$$
$$\text{vs.}$$
$$\mu_1 > \mu_2$$

REJECTION REGIONS:

DECISION RULE:

Reject null if
$$t_{\text{computed}} < -t_{\text{table}}$$

Reject null if
$$|t|_{\text{computed}} > t_{\text{table}}$$

Reject null if
$$t_{\text{computed}} > t_{\text{table}}$$

FIGURE 7.9 One- and Two-Tailed Tests.

STEP-BY-STEP ILLUSTRATION

One-Tailed Test of Means for Dependent Samples

Note as we carry out our example that the mechanics for calculating t are unchanged when we employ a one-tailed rejection region. Suppose the before and after math scores for a sample of nine remedial students are as follows:

Student	Before X_1	After X_2	Difference $D = X_1 - X_2$	(Difference)^2 D^2
1	58	66	−8	64
2	63	68	−5	25
3	66	72	−6	36
4	70	76	−6	36
5	63	78	−15	225
6	51	56	−5	25
7	44	69	−25	625
8	58	55	3	9
9	50	55	−5	25
	$\Sigma X_1 = 523$	$\Sigma X_2 = 595$		$\Sigma D^2 = 1{,}070$

We can compute the t value exactly as we did in the previous section.

Step 1 Find the mean for both the before and the after tests.

$$\overline{X}_1 = \frac{\Sigma X_1}{N} \qquad \overline{X}_2 = \frac{\Sigma X_2}{N}$$

$$= \frac{523}{9} \qquad = \frac{595}{9}$$

$$= 58.11 \qquad = 66.11$$

Step 2 Find the standard deviation of the differences.

$$s_D = \sqrt{\frac{\sum D^2}{N} - (\overline{X}_1 - \overline{X}_2)^2}$$

$$= \sqrt{\frac{1,070}{9} - (58.11 - 66.11)^2}$$

$$= \sqrt{118.89 - 64}$$

$$= \sqrt{54.89}$$

$$= 7.41$$

Step 3 Find the standard error of the difference between means.

$$s_{\overline{D}} = \frac{s_D}{\sqrt{N-1}}$$

$$= \frac{7.41}{\sqrt{9-1}}$$

$$= \frac{7.41}{2.83}$$

$$= 2.62$$

Step 4 Translate the sample mean difference into units of the standard error of the difference.

$$t = \frac{\overline{X}_1 - \overline{X}_2}{s_{\overline{D}}}$$

$$= \frac{58.11 - 66.11}{2.62}$$

$$= \frac{-8.00}{2.62}$$

$$= -3.05$$

Step 5 Find the degrees of freedom.

$$df = N - 1$$

$$= 9 - 1$$

$$= 8$$

Step 6 Compare the obtained t ratio with the critical value from Table C.

$$\text{Obtained } t = -3.05$$

$$\text{Table } t = -1.86$$

$$\alpha = .05$$

Because we hypothesized that the posttest mean should be higher than the pretest mean, t should be negative. Therefore, we use the negative critical value. The obtained t (-3.05) is more extreme in the negative direction than the critical value (-1.86), so we reject the null hypothesis. Thus, the remedial math program has produced a statistically significant improvement in math ability.

All the tests of sample differences that we have presented in this chapter can be modified into one-tailed tests. If the researcher who tested for differences in proportions of males and females who have driven while under the influence of alcohol had anticipated that the proportion for males would be larger, a one-tailed test could have been employed.

By the same token, the t test of difference in mean leniency between males and females discussed earlier could have been structured as a one-tailed test, if the researcher's theory suggested, for example, that men would be more lenient on the average. Changing to a one-tailed test affects only the hypotheses and the critical value of t, but not any of the calculations. The null hypothesis would instead be that men (group 1) are no more lenient than women (group 2), or symbolically ($\mu_1 \leq \mu_2$), and the research hypothesis would be that men are more lenient ($\mu_1 > \mu_2$). With a .05 level of significance and again using 60 degrees of freedom in lieu of the actual 68, we obtain now from Table C a critical value $t = 1.67$. Locating the entire .05 rejection region into one tail lessens somewhat the size of t needed for significance (from 2.00 to 1.67), but still the calculated t ratio ($t = +0.71$, the same as before) is not nearly significant.

STEP-BY-STEP ILLUSTRATION

Independent Groups, One-Tailed Test

A professor who teaches a course in criminal law required for all first-year law school students wants to determine whether students who had graduated from private universities were better prepared than those who had graduated from public universities. The professor decides to test her hypothesis using her class of 72 students.

During the first week of class, the professor gives a test covering knowledge of basic criminal law; she also asks students to indicate whether they had graduated from public or private universities. The professor learns that there are 22 private university graduates and 50 public university graduates in her class. She then calculates descriptive statistics separately for the two groups of test scores:

Private Universities	Public Universities
$N_1 = 22$	$N_2 = 50$
$\overline{X}_1 = 85$	$\overline{X}_2 = 82$
$s_1 = 6$	$s_2 = 8$

Because she anticipated that the graduates of private universities would score better on the test, the professor set up her hypotheses as follows:

Null hypothesis: ($\mu_1 \leq \mu_2$) *Criminal law knowledge is not greater among private university graduates than among public university graduates.*

Research hypothesis: ($\mu_1 > \mu_2$) *Criminal law knowledge is greater among private university graduates than among public university graduates.*

Step 1 Obtain the sample means (these are given as 85 and 82, respectively).

$$\overline{X}_1 = \frac{\sum X_1}{N_1} = 85$$

$$\overline{X}_2 = \frac{\sum X_2}{N_2} = 82$$

Step 2 Obtain sample standard deviations (these are given as 6 and 8, respectively).

$$s_1 = \sqrt{\frac{\sum X_1^2}{N_1} - \overline{X}_1^2} = 6$$

$$s_2 = \sqrt{\frac{\sum X_2^2}{N_2} - \overline{X}_2^2} = 8$$

Step 3 Calculate the standard error of the difference between means.

$$s_{\overline{X}_1 - \overline{X}_2} = \sqrt{\left(\frac{N_1 s_1^2 + N_2 s_2^2}{N_1 + N_2 - 2}\right)\left(\frac{N_1 + N_2}{N_1 N_2}\right)}$$

$$= \sqrt{\left[\frac{(22)(6)^2 + (50)(8)^2}{22 + 50 - 2}\right]\left[\frac{22 + 50}{(22)(50)}\right]}$$

$$= \sqrt{\left[\frac{(22)(36) + (50)(64)}{70}\right]\left(\frac{72}{1.100}\right)}$$

$$= \sqrt{\left(\frac{3.992}{70}\right)\left(\frac{72}{1.100}\right)}$$

$$= \sqrt{3.7328}$$

$$= 1.93$$

Step 4 Translate the sample mean difference into units of the standard error of the difference.

$$t = \frac{\overline{X}_1 - \overline{X}_2}{s_{\overline{X}_1 - \overline{X}_2}}$$

$$= \frac{85 - 82}{1.93}$$

$$= \frac{3}{1.93}$$

$$= 1.55$$

Step 5 Determine the degrees of freedom.

$$df = N_1 + N_2 - 2$$

$$= 22 + 50 - 2$$

$$= 70$$

Step 6 Compare the obtained t ratio with the appropriate t ratio in Table C.

$$\text{Obtained } t = 1.55$$

$$\text{Table } t = 1.671$$

$$df = 70$$

$$\alpha = .05$$

Because the calculated t (1.55) does not exceed the table value (1.671), the professor cannot reject the null hypothesis. Therefore, although the difference between sample means was consistent with the professor's expectations (85 versus 82), the difference was not larger than she could have observed by chance alone. Furthermore, using a one-tailed test with the entire 5% critical region on one side of the sampling distribution made it easier to find a significant difference by lowering the critical value. Still, the results obtained by the professor were not statistically significant.

EFFECT SIZE

Finding a statistically significant difference between means informs us that it is a real difference, but it does not provide evidence as to the extent to which this result occurs in the population. A difference might be significant because the effect is large, but it is also influenced by sample size. If found in a large enough sample of respondents, even a very small mean difference might be determined to be statistically significant.

To go beyond a test of significance, we also need a measure of the extent to which the group difference exists in the population. Known as **effect size** (ES), the magnitude of the difference obtained by the researcher can be calculated by means of **Cohen's *d*,** whereby a difference between two sample means is divided by a measure of the combined (or pooled) variability. The larger the obtained value of *d*, the greater is the effect size that can be generalized to the population. More specifically,

EFFECT SIZE

A measure of the size of the difference between two populations means.

COHEN'S d

An estimate of effect size based on sample means and standard deviations.

$$d = \frac{\overline{X}_1 - \overline{X}_2}{s_{pooled}}$$

where $\overline{X}_1$ = mean of the first sample

$\overline{X}_2$ = mean of the second sample

and s_{pooled} is the combined sample standard deviations

$$s_{pooled} = \sqrt{\frac{s_1^2 + s_2^2}{2}}$$

STEP-BY-STEP ILLUSTRATION

Cohen's *d*

Suppose that a researcher sought to determine whether gender influences the extent to which men and women enjoy reading true-crime books. She asked a sample of 1,000 respondents—530 women and 470 men—to indicate how much they enjoyed true crime on a scale from 1 (very little) to 7 (very much). Results indicated that women differed significantly from men in their enjoyment of true-crime books. Specifically, for women, $\overline{X}_1 = 4.00$ and $s_1 = 1.83$, while for men, $\overline{X}_2 = 3.71$ and $s_2 = 1.71$, yielding a significant *t* ratio of 2.12 ($p < .05$). Based on the researcher's findings, we can therefore feel safe concluding that women *tend* to enjoy reading true-crime books more than their male counterparts do, but we do not know the extent of that tendency.

Step 1 Determine the pooled standard deviation (s_{pooled}).

The two sample standard deviations can be combined by calculating the square root of the average of the squared standard deviations—that is, by adding the two squared standard deviations, dividing them by 2, and obtaining the square root. Thus, in the study of male/female differences in the enjoyment of true crime,

$$s_{pooled} = \sqrt{\frac{s_1^2 + s_2^2}{2}}$$

$$= \sqrt{\frac{1.83^2 + 1.71^2}{2}}$$

$$= \sqrt{\frac{3.35 + 2.92}{2}}$$

$$= \sqrt{\frac{5.27}{2}}$$

$$= 1.77$$

Step 2 Find Cohen's *d*.

$$d = \frac{\overline{X}_1 - \overline{X}_2}{s_{pooled}}$$

$$= \frac{4.00 - 3.71}{1.77}$$

$$= \frac{.29}{1.77}$$

$$= .16$$

Step 3 Interpret the degree of overlap between the scores in the two groups.

An effect size can be treated like a *z* score in a normal distribution. For example, in the study of gender differences in enjoyment of true-crime books, *d* = .16, indicating that the score of the average female falls .16 (about one-sixth) of a standard deviation above the average male. From column a in Table A, we find that 6.36% of scores fall between the mean and *z* = .16. Therefore, the mean female enjoyment score exceeds the enjoyment mean enjoyment score for males by 50% + 6.36% = 56.36%.

Thus, just like a *z* score, the further away from the mean in standard deviation units, the larger is the difference between groups. The larger the value of Cohen's *d*, the larger is the effect size. An effect size of *d* = 0.0 suggests that only half (50% + 0%) of the scores of one group fall below the score of the average member of the other group, indicating that the population difference is nonexistent. By contrast, an effect size of 1.0 indicates that 84% (50% + 34%) of the scores of the first group fall below the average score in the second group. Moreover, a very large effect size, *d* = 3.0 indicates that 99.87% (50% + 49.87%) of the scores of one group lie below the mean score in the other group. If the study of gender differences in the enjoyment of true crime had yielded *d* = 3.0 (three standard deviations from the mean), we would have concluded that almost all of the male readers expressed less enjoyment than the average score of their female counterparts. Instead, our gender difference was found to be significant or real, but the effect size turned out to be very small. Expressed as *d* = .16, there was much overlap between the enjoyment of male and female readers of true crime.

For most researchers in criminal justice, three levels of the strength of effect size are regarded as meaningful—weak (.20–.49), moderate (.50–.79), and strong (.80 and higher). Thus, applying this widely used criterion, .16 falls below *d* = .20, the smallest effect size that is considered to have any practical or substantive meaning.

REQUIREMENTS FOR TESTING THE DIFFERENCE BETWEEN MEANS

As we shall see throughout the remainder of this text, every statistical test should be used only if the criminal justice researcher has at least considered certain requirements, conditions, or assumptions. Employing a test inappropriately may confuse an issue and mislead the investigator. As a result, the following requirements should be kept firmly in mind when considering the appropriateness of the *z* score or *t* ratio as a test of significance:

1. *A comparison between two means.* The *z* score and *t* ratio are employed to make comparisons between two means from independent samples or from a single sample measured twice (repeated measures).
2. *Interval data.* The assumption is that we have scores at the interval level of measurement. Therefore, we cannot use the *z* score or *t* ratio for ranked data or data that can be categorized only at the nominal level of measurement (see Chapter 1).
3. *Random sampling.* We should have drawn our samples on a random basis from a population of scores.

4. *A normal distribution.* The *t* ratio for small samples requires that the sample characteristic we have measured be normally distributed in the underlying population (the *t* ratio for large samples is not much affected by failure to meet this assumption). Often, we cannot be certain that normality exists. Having no reason to believe otherwise, many researchers pragmatically assume their sample characteristic to be normally distributed. However, if the researcher has reason to suspect that normality cannot be assumed, and the sample size is not large, he or she is best advised that the *t* ratio may be an inappropriate test.

5. *Equal variances.* The *t* ratio for independent samples assumes that the population variances are equal. The sample variances, of course, may differ as a result of sampling. A moderate difference between the sample variances does not invalidate the results of the *t* ratio. But when this difference in sample variances is extreme (e.g., when one sample variance is 10 times larger than the other), the *t* ratio presented here may not be appropriate. An adjusted formula for unequal variances does exist but is beyond the scope of this text.

Summary

In Chapter 6, we saw how a population mean or proportion can be estimated from the information we obtain from a single sample. In this chapter, we turned our attention to the task of testing hypotheses about differences *between* sample means or proportions. Studying one sample at a time, we previously focused on characteristics of the sampling distribution of means. As demonstrated in this chapter, there is also a probability distribution for comparing mean differences. As a result of sampling error, the sampling distribution of differences between means consists of a large number of differences between means, randomly selected, that approximate a normal curve whose mean (mean of differences between means) is zero. With the aid of this sampling distribution and the standard error of the difference between means (our estimate of the standard deviation of the sampling distribution based on the two samples we actually draw), we were able to make a probability statement about the occurrence of a difference between means. We asked: What is the probability that the sample mean difference we obtain in our study could have happened strictly on the basis of sampling error? If the difference falls close to the center of the sampling distribution (i.e., close to a mean difference of zero), we retain the null hypothesis. Our result is treated as merely a product of sampling error. If, however, our mean difference is so large that it falls a considerable distance from the sampling distribution's mean of zero, we instead reject the null hypothesis and accept the idea that we have found a true population difference. Our mean difference is too large to be explained by sampling error. But at what point do we retain or reject the null hypothesis? To establish whether our obtained sample difference reflects a real population difference (i.e., constitutes a statistically significant difference), we need a consistent cutoff point for deciding when to retain or reject the null hypothesis. For this purpose, it is conventional to use the .05 level of significance (or the stricter .01 level of significance). That is, we are willing to reject the null hypothesis if our obtained sample difference occurs by chance less than 5 times out of 100 (1 time out of 100 at the .01 level). We determine the exact probability that the null hypothesis is true by calculating degrees of freedom and a significance test known as the *t* ratio. We then compare our obtained *t* ratio against the *t* ratios at varying degrees of freedom given in Table C. Using the same logic, there is also a test of significance for differences between proportions. In either case, the researchers must choose between a one- and two-tailed test of significance, depending on whether the direction of the difference can be anticipated in advance.

Questions and Problems

1. Rejecting the null hypothesis using a t test assumes which of the following?
   a. There is no difference between sample means.
   b. There is no difference between population means.
   c. The difference between means is significant.
   d. The difference between means is too small to be a sampling error.

2. At $P = .05$, a mean difference in a sampling distribution occurs _____.
   a. by sampling error 5 times in every 100 mean differences
   b. by sampling error more than 95 times in every 100 mean differences
   c. very frequently by sampling error
   d. never by sampling error

3. The further out in the tail of a distribution that our critical value falls, the greater the risk of making a _____.
   a. Type I error.
   b. Type II error.
   c. Type I and Type II error.
   d. Type III error.

4. The size of the tail (area under the curve) that will lead us to reject the null hypothesis is called _____.
   a. the alpha level
   b. the confidence interval
   c. P
   d. standard error of the difference

5. In a statistical sense, rejecting the null hypothesis and saying that a difference in means is "significant" means that the difference is _____.
   a. small
   b. important
   c. large
   d. real

6. Research consistently shows that lack of self-control, a strong correlate of antisocial behavior, is greater in males than in females. A researcher randomly surveys 10 boys and 10 girls from a middle school and wants to find out whether boys do, in fact, report lower levels of self-control. Using the scores reported by the respondent below (on a scale from 0 to 20), test the null hypothesis that boys and girl have the same mean level of self-control.

Boys	Girls
10	18
13	14
8	15
15	10
7	14
12	8
13	16
10	8
9	11
17	15

7. A corrections researcher was interested in race differences in the amount set for bail for whites and nonwhites. She recorded the dollar amounts of bail for a sample of 9 white and 9 nonwhite defendants. The data are shown below:

Whites	Nonwhites
$1,000.00	$500.00
$ 300.00	$250.00
$1,500.00	$250.00
$ 200.00	$200.00
$ 500.00	$500.00
$ 150.00	$250.00
$1,000.00	$100.00
$ 500.00	$150.00
$1,200.00	$250.00

   a. Test the null hypothesis of no race difference in the amount of bail.
   b. Based on the result, should there be concern about the presence of racial disparity in bail setting?

8. A criminologist was interested in whether there was any disparity in sentencing based on the race of the defendant. She selected at random 19 drug convictions for cocaine distribution and compared the prison terms given to the 10 whites and 9 blacks sampled. The sentence lengths (in years) are shown below for the white and black offenders.

White	Black
3	4
5	8
2	7
7	7
4	5
5	9
5	7
4	4
3	5
2	

   a. Using these data and $\alpha = .05$, test the null hypothesis that whites and blacks convicted of distribution of cocaine do not differ with respect to sentence length.
   b. Using these same data and $\alpha = .01$, what is the result? Explain why the result is the same? Or different?

9. In a field experiment on the effects of community crime prevention efforts on fear of crime, residents of one large condominium complex were encouraged to participate in a variety of efforts: Monthly condo association meetings were held to discuss effective crime prevention strategies, signs were posted stating that the complex was part of a neighborhood crime watch, and parking lot lighting was improved. In a physically identical complex several blocks away, none of these measures was taken. After 6 months, five condo owners in each complex were randomly chosen and were given a

fear-of-crime questionnaire. Crime occurring in both complexes was then tracked and found to be identical, so differences in fear of crime could not be attributed to differences in actual crime. Using the following data, test the null hypothesis that the community crime prevention program had no impact on residents' feelings of safety from crime. Higher scores indicate feelings of greater safety.

Program	Control
15	8
17	7
14	9
11	12
13	14
18	11
15	10
12	17
15	9
18	13

10. A researcher believes that the alcohol intoxication even half the legal limit—that is, .04 blood alcohol instead of .08—might severely impair driving ability. To test this, he subjects 10 volunteers to a driving simulation test first while sober and then after drinking amounts sufficient to raise their blood alcohol level to .04. The researcher measures performance as the number of simulated obstacles with which the driver collides. Thus, the higher the number, the poorer the driving. The obtained results are as follows:

Before Drinking	After Drinking
1	4
2	2
0	1
0	2
2	5
1	3
4	3
0	2
1	4
2	3

Test the null hypothesis that there is no difference in driving ability before and after alcohol consumption to the .04 blood alcohol level (use the .05 significance level).

11. A well-evaluated cognitive behavioral program is administered to youth on juvenile probation to teach them how to reduce levels of aggression. Researchers are interested only in whether or not the youth improved (i.e., if their aggression was reduced) and have good reason to believe that the individual's aggression will decrease because research has found it to be effective. Therefore, use a one-tailed t test to identify whether or not levels of aggression (higher numbers reflect greater aggressiveness) were reduced after the cognitive behavioral program. Before and after results are presented below:

Before	After
18	15
15	13
14	14
16	14
10	7
17	14
14	11
15	14
10	11
9	8
16	12
13	13
9	7
16	15
12	14

Test the null hypothesis that the cognitive-behavioral program has no effect on level of aggression.

12. One of the goals of restorative justice programs for juveniles is to improve the self-esteem of offenders so that they can reintegrate into the community and respect the victim of crime. Juveniles were given a self-esteem questionnaire during the first and last weeks of their stay in a restorative justice program. Test for the significance of the differences in the before-after scores on the self-esteem scale (higher numbers reflect higher self-esteem) of a random sample of restorative justice program graduates.

Offender	Self-Esteem	
	Before	*After*
A	18	39
B	15	30
C	10	21
D	12	10
E	9	20
F	11	15
G	17	19
H	15	25
I	14	19
J	19	22
K	13	20
L	10	15
M	11	30
N	10	19
O	14	34

13. There is much current debate about the importance of early childhood interventions for learning success, education, and keeping children out of crime. A researcher looks to see whether attending a preschool program is related to the propensity for committing violence by age 18. Comparing samples with 250 children in each group, she finds that 7% of children who attended preschool and 15% of children who did not attend it had committed a violent crime by age

18 years. Using $\alpha = .05$, test the significance of the difference in sample proportions.

14. A pollster interviews by telephone a national sample of adults age 18 and older about their attitudes toward capital punishment. Test the significance of the difference between proportions of men and women who support the death penalty. *Hint:* Find the proportions of men and women who favor capital punishment first.

	Men	Women
Favor	502	572
Oppose	105	209
Total	607	781

15. A regional polling organization conducts a telephone survey of adults in a Southern city. He asks people a variety of questions about criminal victimization, including a question about aggravated assault where they may have been attacked by a person with a weapon, threatened with force, grabbed, punched, and so forth. The results of the study show that 5.8% of males ($N = 1{,}344$) and 2.3% of females ($N = 1{,}526$) report that they were the victim of an aggravated assault during the past year. Test the significance of the difference in sample proportions.

Computer Exercises

1. Using the General Social Survey, determine whether there is a difference in the number of hours spent on e-mails (EMAILHR) comparing men and women (SEX). *Hint:* ANALYZE, COMPARE MEANS, INDEPENDENT SAMPLES *T* TEST, and set SEX as the grouping variable with "Male" as "1" and "Female" as "2." Which *t* test is used? Why? What is the result of the comparison?

2. Using the General Social Survey, determine whether there is a difference in the number of hours spent on e-mails (EMAILHR) comparing people younger than age 65 to people older than age 65 (AGE). *Hint:* ANALYZE, COMPARE MEANS, INDEPENDENT SAMPLES *T* TEST, and set AGE as the grouping variable with 65 used as the "cut-point." Which *t* test is used? Why? What is the result of the comparison?

3. Is there a gender difference in individual income? Using the General Social Survey, find out whether respondent income (RINCOM06) differs by sex (SEX).

4. Use the General Social Survey to find out whether there is a statistically significant difference in self-reports of poor mental health during the past 30 days comparing males to females (MNTLHLTH and SEX).

5. Use the General Social Survey to find out whether there is a statistically significant difference in self-reports of poor physical health during the past 30 days comparing males to females (PHYSHLTH and SEX).

6. Analyze the General Social Survey to find out whether there is a statistically significant difference in attitudes toward extramarital sex comparing males to females (XMARSEX and SEX).

7. Use the General Social Survey to find out whether there is a statistically significant difference in self-reports of job satisfaction comparing males to females (SATJOB and SEX).

8. Analyze the General Social Survey to find out if there is a statistically significant difference in self-reports in the number of hours worked last week comparing males to females (HRS1 and SEX).

9. The Center for the Study of Violence wanted to determine whether a conflict-resolution program in a particular high school alters aggressive behavior among its students. For 10 students, aggression was measured both before and after they participated in the conflict-resolution course. The scores were the following (higher scores indicating greater aggressiveness):

Before Participating	After Participating
10	8
3	3
4	1
8	5
8	7
9	8
5	1
7	5
1	1
7	6

a. Test the null hypothesis that aggression does not differ as a result of the participation in the conflict resolution program. *Hint:* First, using *SPSS*, enter the data into a new data set. Second, select ANALYZE, COMPARE MEANS, PAIRED-SAMPLES *T* TEST, and then chose variables.

b. What do your results indicate?

10. Use *SPSS* to analyze the information shown below on time spent interviewing witnesses and sex of the officer (where 1 = Male and 2 = Female). Test the null hypothesis that there are no gender differences in time spent:

Time	Sex
8	1
15	1
9	1
6	1
4	1
15	2
19	2
11	2
13	2
12	2

Analysis of Variance

Blacks versus whites, males versus females, and liberals versus conservatives represent the kind of two-sample comparisons that occupied our attention in the previous chapter. Yet reality cannot always be conveniently sliced into two groups; respondents do not always divide themselves in so simple a fashion.

As a result, the criminal justice researcher often seeks to make comparisons among three, four, five, or more samples or groups. To illustrate, he or she may study the influence of racial identity (black, white, or Asian) on job discrimination, degree of economic deprivation (severe, moderate, or mild) on juvenile delinquency, or subjective social class (upper, middle, working, or lower) on support for drug legalization.

The student may wonder whether we use a *series* of *t* ratios to make comparisons among three or more sample means. Suppose, for example, we want to test the influence of social class on support for drug legalization. Why can we not pair-compare all possible combinations of social class and obtain a *t* ratio for each comparison? Using this method, four samples generate six paired combinations for which six *t* ratios must be calculated:

1. Upper class versus middle class
2. Upper class versus working class
3. Upper class versus lower class
4. Middle class versus working class
5. Middle class versus lower class
6. Working class versus lower class

Not only does the procedure of calculating a series of *t* ratios involve a good deal of work, but it has a statistical limitation as well. This is because it increases the probability of making a Type I error—the error of rejecting the null hypothesis when it should be retained. Recall that the criminal justice researcher is generally willing to accept a 5% risk of making a Type I error (the .05 level of significance). He or she therefore expects that *by chance alone*, 5 out of every 100 sample mean differences will be large enough to be considered as significant. The more statistical tests we conduct, however, the more likely we are to get statistically significant findings by sampling error (rather than by a true population difference) and hence to commit a Type I error. When we run a large number of such tests, the interpretation of our result becomes problematic. To take an extreme example: How would we interpret a significant *t* ratio out of 1,000 such comparisons made in a particular study? We know that at least a few large mean differences can be expected to occur simply on the basis of sampling error.

For a more typical example, suppose a researcher wished to survey and compare voters in eight regions of the country (New England, Middle Atlantic, South Atlantic, Midwest, South,

Southwest, Mountain, and Pacific) on their feelings about new federal crime legislation. Comparing the regional samples would require 28 separate t ratios (New England vs. Middle Atlantic, New England vs. South Atlantic, Middle Atlantic vs. South Atlantic, and so on). Out of 28 separate tests of difference between sample means, each with a .05 level of significance, 5% or about 1 (1.4 to be exact) would be expected to be significant due to chance or sampling error alone.

Suppose that from his 28 different t ratios, the researcher obtains two t ratios (New England vs. South and Middle Atlantic vs. Mountain) that are significant. How should the researcher interpret these two significant differences? Should he go out on a limb and treat both as indicative of real population differences? Should he play it safe by maintaining that both could be the result of sampling error and go back to collect more data? Should he, based on the expectation that one t ratio will come out significant by chance, decide that only one of the two significant t ratios is valid? If so, in which of the two significant t ratios should he have faith? The larger one? The one that seems more plausible? Unfortunately, none of these solutions is particularly sound. The problem is that as the number of separate tests mounts, the likelihood of rejecting a true null hypothesis (Type I error) grows accordingly. Thus, although for each t ratio the probability of a Type I error may be .05, overall the probability of rejecting any true null hypothesis is far greater than .05.

To overcome this problem and clarify the interpretation of our result, we need a statistical test that holds Type I error at a constant level by making a *single* overall decision as to whether a significant difference is present among the three, eight, or however many sample means we seek to compare. Such a test is known as the *analysis of variance*.

THE LOGIC OF ANALYSIS OF VARIANCE

ANALYSIS OF VARIANCE

A statistical test that makes a single overall decision as to whether a significant difference is present among three or more sample means.

To conduct an **analysis of variance**, also called ANOVA for short, we treat the total *variation* in a set of scores as being divisible into two components: the distance or deviation of raw scores from their group mean, known as *variation within groups*, and the distance or deviation of group means from one another, referred to as *variation between groups*.

To examine variation within groups, the approval-of-drug-legalization scores of members of four social classes—lower, working, middle, and upper—have been graphically represented in Figure 8.1, where X_1, X_2, X_3, and X_4, are any raw scores in their respective groups, and $\overline{X}_1$, $\overline{X}_2$, $\overline{X}_3$, and $\overline{X}_4$, are the group means. In symbolic terms, we see that variation within groups refers to the distance between X_1 and $\overline{X}_1$, between X_2 and $\overline{X}_2$, between X_3 and $\overline{X}_3$, and between X_4 and $\overline{X}_4$.

We can also visualize variation between groups. With the aid of Figure 8.2, we see that degree of support for drug legalization varies by social class: The upper-class group has ($\overline{X}_4$) greater support than the middle-class group ($\overline{X}_3$), which, in turn, has greater support than the working-class group ($\overline{X}_2$), which, in its turn, has greater support than the lower-class group ($\overline{X}_1$).

The distinction between variation *within* groups and variation *between* groups is not peculiar to the analysis of variance. Although not named as such, we encountered a similar distinction in the form of the t ratio, wherein a difference *between* $\overline{X}_1$ and $\overline{X}_2$ was compared against the standard error of the difference ($s_{\overline{X}_1 - \overline{X}_2}$), a combined estimate of differences *within* each group. Therefore,

$$t = \frac{\overline{X}_1 - \overline{X}_2}{s_{\overline{X}_1 - \overline{X}_2}} \quad \begin{array}{l} \leftarrow \text{variation between groups} \\ \leftarrow \text{variation within groups} \end{array}$$

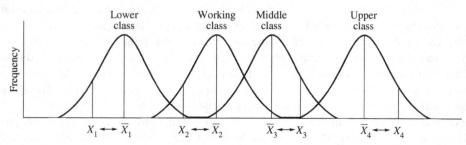

FIGURE 8.1 Graphic Representation of Variation within Four Groups of Social Class.

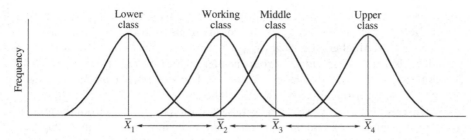

FIGURE 8.2 Graphic Representation of Variation between Four Groups of Social Class.

In a similar way, the analysis of variance yields an **F ratio**, whose numerator represents variation between the groups being compared, and whose denominator contains an estimate of variation within these groups. As we shall see, the F ratio indicates the size of the difference between groups *relative* to the size of the variation within each group. As was true of the t ratio, the larger the F ratio (the larger the variation between groups relative to the variation within groups), the greater the probability of rejecting the null hypothesis and accepting the research hypothesis.

THE SUM OF SQUARES

At the heart of the analysis of variance is the concept of **sum of squares**, which represents the initial step for measuring total variation as well as variation between and within groups. It may come as a pleasant surprise to learn that only the label "sum of squares" is new to us. The concept itself was introduced in Chapter 4 as an important step in the procedure for obtaining the variance. In that context, we learned to find the sum of squares by squaring the deviations from the mean of a distribution and adding these squared deviations together $\Sigma(X-\overline{X})^2$. This procedure eliminated minus signs, while still providing a sound mathematical basis for the variance and standard deviation.

When applied to a situation in which groups are being compared, there is more than one type of sum of squares, although each type represents *the sum of squared deviations from a mean*. Corresponding to the distinction between total variation and its two components, we have the *total* sum of squares (SS_{total}), *between-groups* sum of squares ($SS_{between}$), and *within-groups* sum of squares (SS_{within}).

Consider the hypothetical results shown in Figure 8.3. Note that only part of the data is shown to help us focus on the concepts of total, within-groups, and between-groups sums of squares.

F RATIO

The result of an analysis of variance, a statistical technique that indicates the size of the between-groups mean square relative to the size of the within-groups mean square.

SUM OF SQUARES

The sum of squared deviations from a mean.

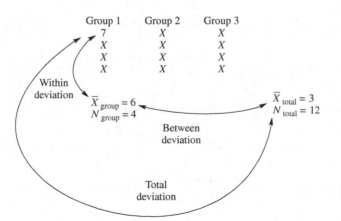

FIGURE 8.3 Analysis of Variance.

The respondent with a 7 scored substantially higher than the total mean ($\overline{X}_{total} = 3$). His deviation from the total mean is $(X - \overline{X}_{total}) = 4$. Part of this elevated score represents, however, the fact that his group scored higher on average ($\overline{X}_{group} = 6$) than the overall or total mean ($\overline{X}_{total} = 3$). That is, the deviation of this respondent's group mean from the total mean is $(\overline{X}_{group} - \overline{X}_{total}) = 3$. After accounting for the group difference, this respondent's score remains higher than his own group mean. Within the group, his deviation from the group mean is $(X - \overline{X}_{group}) = 1$.

As we shall see very shortly, we can take these deviations—of scores from the total mean, of scores from their group means, and of group means from the total mean—square them, and then sum them to obtain SS_{total}, SS_{within}, and $SS_{between}$.

A Research Illustration

Let's consider a research situation in which each type of sum of squares might be calculated. Suppose a criminologist is interested in examining the extent to which the race/ethnicity of a violent juvenile offender influences public support for trying the offender as an adult. The researcher creates four versions of a hypothetical case description of an armed robbery committed by a 15-year-old male. The four versions differ only in terms of the race/ethnicity of the alleged perpetrator, alternatively described as white, black, Latino, or not-indicated (serving as a control group). He randomly assigns 20 subjects to one of the four conditions or groups, asking each subject to indicate, based on the facts as given in the case description, how appropriate it would be to try the offender as an adult on a scale of 1 for not at all appropriate to 10 for absolutely appropriate.

The criminologist sets up his hypotheses as follows:

Null hypothesis: *Public support for trying the offender as an*
$(\mu_1 = \mu_2 = \mu_3 = \mu_4)$ *adult does not differ by race/ethnicity.*

Research hypothesis: *Public support for trying the offender as an adult does*
$(some\, \mu_i \neq \mu_j)$ *differ by race/ethnicity.*

TOTAL SUM OF SQUARES

The sum of the squared deviations of every raw score from the total mean of the study.

The **total sum of squares** is defined as the sum of the squared deviation of every raw score from the total mean. By formula,

$$SS_{total} = \Sigma(X - \overline{X}_{total})^2$$

where X = any raw score
        $\overline{X}_{total}$ = total mean for all groups combined

Using this formula, we subtract the total mean ($\overline{X}_{total}$) from each raw score (X), square the deviations that result, and then add. Applying this formula to the data in Table 8.1, we obtain the following results:

$$
\begin{aligned}
SS_{total} = \ & (1 - 5)^2 + (4 - 5)^2 + (2 - 5)^2 + (6 - 5)^2 + (2 - 5)^2 \\
& + (4 - 5)^2 + (7 - 5)^2 + (9 - 5)^2 + (6 - 5)^2 + (9 - 5)^2 \\
& + (3 - 5)^2 + (9 - 5)^2 + (5 - 5)^2 + (4 - 5)^2 + (9 - 5)^2 \\
& + (1 - 5)^2 + (5 - 5)^2 + (3 - 5)^2 + (5 - 5)^2 + (6 - 5)^2 \\
= \ & (-4)^2 + (-1)^2 + (-3)^2 + (1)^2 + (-3)^2 \\
& + (-1)^2 + (-2)^2 + (-4)^2 + (-1)^2 + (-4)^2 \\
& + (-2)^2 + (4)^2 + (0)^2 + (-1)^2 + (-4)^2 \\
& + (-4)^2 + (0)^2 + (-2)^2 + (0)^2 + (-1)^2 \\
= \ & 16 + 1 + 9 + 1 + 9 \\
& + 1 + 4 + 16 + 1 + 16 \\
& + 4 + 16 + 0 + 1 + 16 \\
& + 16 + 0 + 4 + 0 + 1 \\
= \ & 132
\end{aligned}
$$

| TABLE 8.1 | Support for Adult Prosecution by Race/Ethnicity of Juvenile Arrestee | | | | | |

White			Black		
X_1	$X_1 - \overline{X}_1$	$(X_1 - \overline{X}_1)^2$	X_2	$X_2 - \overline{X}_2$	$(X_2 - \overline{X}_2)^2$
1	−2	4	4	−8	9
4	1	1	7	0	0
2	−1	1	9	2	4
6	3	9	6	−1	1
2	−1	1	9	2	4
$\Sigma X_1 = 15$	$\overline{X}_1 = \frac{15}{5} = 3$	$\Sigma(X_1 - \overline{X}_1)^2 = 16$	$\Sigma X_2 = 35$	$\overline{X}_2 = \frac{35}{5} = 7$	$\Sigma(X_2 - \overline{X}_2)^2 = 18$

Latino			Not Indicated		
X_3	$X_3 - \overline{X}_3$	$(X_3 - \overline{X}_3)^2$	X_4	$X_4 - \overline{X}_4$	$(X_4 - \overline{X}_4)^2$
3	−3	9	1	−3	9
9	3	9	5	1	1
5	−1	1	3	−1	1
4	−2	4	5	1	1
9	3	9	6	2	4
$\Sigma X_3 = 30$	$\overline{X}_3 = \frac{30}{5} = 6$	$\Sigma(X_3 - \overline{X}_3)^2 = 32$	$\Sigma X_4 = 20$	$\overline{X}_4 = \frac{20}{5} = 4$	$\Sigma(X_4 - \overline{X}_4)^2 = 16$

$$\overline{X}_{total} = \frac{100}{20} = 5$$

The **within-groups sum of squares** is the sum of the squared deviations of every raw score from its group mean. By formula,

$$SS_{within} = \Sigma(X - \overline{X}_{group})^2$$

WITHIN-GROUPS SUM OF SQUARES

The sum of the squared deviations of every raw score from its sample group mean.

where

X = any raw score

$\overline{X}_{group}$ = mean of the group containing the raw score

Using this formula, we subtract the group mean ($\overline{X}_{group}$) from each raw score (X), square the deviations that result, and then add. Applying this formula to the data in Table 8.1, we obtain the following results:

$$\begin{aligned}
SS_{within} &= (1-3)^2 + (4-3)^2 + (2-3)^2 + (6-3)^2 + (2-3)^2 \\
&+ (4-7)^2 + (7-7)^2 + (9-7)^2 + (6-7)^2 + (9-7)^2 \\
&+ (3-6)^2 + (9-6)^2 + (5-6)^2 + (4-6)^2 + (9-6)^2 \\
&+ (1-4)^2 + (5-4)^2 + (3-4)^2 + (5-4)^2 + (6-4)^2 \\
&= (-2)^2 + (1)^2 + (-1)^2 + (3)^2 + (-1)^2 \\
&+ (-3)^2 + (0)^2 + (2)^2 + (-1)^2 + (2)^2 \\
&+ (-3)^2 + (3)^2 + (-1)^2 + (-2)^2 + (3)^2 \\
&+ (-3)^2 + (1)^2 + (-1)^2 + (-1)^2 + (2)^2 \\
&= 4 + 1 + 1 + 9 + 1 \\
&+ 9 + 0 + 4 + 1 + 4 \\
&+ 9 + 9 + 1 + 4 + 9 \\
&+ 9 + 1 + 1 + 1 + 4 \\
&= 82
\end{aligned}$$

Notice that the within-group sum of squares could have been obtained simply by combining the sum of squares within each group. That is, with four groups,

$$SS_{within} = \sum(X_1 - \overline{X}_1)^2 + \sum(X_2 - \overline{X}_2)^2 + \sum(X_3 - \overline{X}_3)^2 + \sum(X_4 - \overline{X}_4)^2$$

From Table 8.1, we have

$$SS_{within} = 16 + 18 + 32 + 16 = 82$$

BETWEEN-GROUPS SUM OF SQUARES

The sum of the squared deviations of every sample mean from the total mean.

The **between-groups sum of squares** represents the sum of squared deviations of every group mean from the total mean. Accordingly, we must determine the difference between each group mean and the total mean ($\overline{X}_{group} - \overline{X}_{total}$), square this deviation, multiply by the number of scores in that group, and add these quantities. Summing across groups, we obtain the following definitional formula for the between-groups sum of squares:

$$SS_{between} = \sum N_{group}(\overline{X}_{group} - \overline{X}_{total})^2$$

where N_{group} = number of scores in any group
$\overline{X}_{group}$ = mean of any group
$\overline{X}_{total}$ = mean of all groups combined

Applying the formula to the data in Table 8.1, we obtain the following results.

$$
\begin{aligned}
SS_{between} &= 5(3-5)^2 + 5(7-5)^2 + 5(6-5)^2 + 5(4-5)^2 \\
&= 5(-2)^2 + 5(2)^2 + 5(1)^2 + 5(-1)^2 \\
&= 5(4) + 5(4) + 5(1) + 5(1) \\
&= 20 + 20 + 5 + 5 \\
&= 50
\end{aligned}
$$

Thus, the sums of squares are

$$
\begin{aligned}
SS_{total} &= 132 \\
SS_{within} &= 82 \\
SS_{between} &= 50
\end{aligned}
$$

Notice that the total sum of squares is equal to the within-groups and between-groups sums of squares added together. This relationship among the three sums of squares can be used as a check on your work.

Computing Sums of Squares

The definitional formulas for total, within-groups, and between-groups sums of squares are based on the manipulation of deviation scores, a time-consuming and difficult process. Fortunately, we may instead employ the following much simpler computational formulas to obtain results that are identical (except for rounding errors) to the lengthier definitional formulas:

$$
\begin{aligned}
SS_{total} &= \sum X_{total}^2 - N_{total}\overline{X}_{total}^2 \\
SS_{within} &= \sum X_{total}^2 - \sum N_{group}\overline{X}_{group}^2 \\
SS_{between} &= \sum N_{group}\overline{X}_{group}^2 - N_{total}\overline{X}_{total}^2
\end{aligned}
$$

where $\sum X_{total}^2$ = all the scores squared and then summed
$\overline{X}_{total}$ = total mean of all groups combined
N_{total} = total number of scores in all groups combined
$\overline{X}_{group}$ = mean of any group
N_{group} = number of scores in any group

TABLE 8.2   Computations for Data on Support for Adult Prosecution

White		Black	
X_1	X_1^2	X_2	X_2^2
1	1	4	16
4	16	7	49
2	4	9	81
6	36	6	36
2	4	9	81
$\Sigma X_1 = 15$	$\Sigma X_1^2 = 61$	$\Sigma X_2 = 35$	$\Sigma X_2^2 = 263$
$\overline{X}_1 = \dfrac{15}{5} = 3$		$\overline{X}_2 = \dfrac{35}{5} = 7$	

Latino		Not Indicated	
X_3	X_3^2	X_4	X_4^2
3	9	1	1
9	81	5	25
5	25	3	9
4	16	5	25
9	81	6	36
$\Sigma X_3 = 30$	$\Sigma X_3^2 = 212$	$\Sigma X_4 = 20$	$\Sigma X_4^2 = 96$
$\overline{X}_3 = \dfrac{30}{5} = 6$		$\overline{X}_4 = \dfrac{20}{5} = 4$	
$N_{total} = 20$	$\overline{X}_{total} = 5$	$\Sigma X_{total} = 100$	$\Sigma X_{total}^2 = 632$

The raw scores in Table 8.1 have been set up in Table 8.2 for illustrating the use of the computational sum of squares formulas. Note that before applying the formulas, we must first obtain the sum of scores(ΣX_{total}), sum of squared scores(ΣX_{total}^2), number of scores (N_{total}), and mean for all groups combined:

$$\Sigma X_{total} = \Sigma X_1 + \Sigma X_2 + \Sigma X_3 + \Sigma X_4$$
$$= 15 + 35 + 30 + 20$$
$$= 100$$
$$\Sigma X_{total}^2 = \Sigma X_1^2 + \Sigma X_2^2 + \Sigma X_3^2 + \Sigma X_4^2$$
$$= 61 + 263 + 212 + 96$$
$$= 632$$
$$N_{total} = N_1 + N_2 + N_3 + N_4$$
$$= 5 + 5 + 5 + 5$$
$$= 20$$
$$\overline{X}_{total} = \frac{\Sigma X_{total}}{N_{total}}$$
$$= \frac{100}{20}$$
$$= 5$$

Next, we move on to calculating the following sums of squares:

$$SS_{total} = \Sigma X_{total}^2 - N_{total}\overline{X}_{total}^2$$
$$= 632 - (20)(5)^2$$
$$= 632 - (20)(25)$$
$$= 632 - 500$$
$$= 132$$

$$SS_{within} = \Sigma X_{total}^2 - \Sigma N_{group} \overline{X}_{group}^2$$
$$= 632 - [(5)(3)^2 + (5)(7)^2 + (5)(6)^2 + (5)(4)^2]$$
$$= 632 - [(5)(9) + (5)(49) + (5)(36) + (5)(16)]$$
$$= 632 - (45 + 245 + 180 + 80)$$
$$= 632 - 550$$
$$= 82$$

$$SS_{between} = \Sigma N_{group} \overline{X}_{group}^2 - N_{total} \overline{X}_{total}^2$$
$$= 550 - 500$$
$$= 50$$

These results agree with the values obtained using the definitional formulas. For most problems and applications, however, the computational formulas are more efficient for performing calculations.

MEAN SQUARE

As we might expect from a measure of variation, the value of the sums of squares tends to become larger as variation increases. For example, $SS = 10.9$ probably designates greater variation than $SS = 1.3$. However, the sum of squares also gets larger with increasing sample size, so that $N = 200$ will yield a larger SS than $N = 20$. As a result, the sum of squares cannot be regarded as an entirely "pure" measure of variation, unless, of course, we can find a way to control the number of scores involved.

Fortunately, such a method exists in a measure of variation known as the **mean square** (or *variance*), which we obtain by dividing $SS_{between}$ and SS_{within} by the appropriate degrees of freedom. Recall that in Chapter 4, we similarly divided $\Sigma(X - \overline{X})^2$ by N to obtain the variance. Therefore,

MEAN SQUARE

A measure of variation used in an *F* test obtained by dividing the between-group sum of squares or within-group sum of squares (in analysis of variance) or the regression sum of squares or error sum of squares (in regression analysis) by the appropriate degrees of freedom.

$$MS_{between} = \frac{SS_{between}}{df_{between}}$$

where $MS_{between}$ = between-groups mean square
         $SS_{between}$ = between-groups sum of squares
         $df_{between}$ = between-groups degrees of freedom

and

$$MS_{within} = \frac{SS_{within}}{df_{within}}$$

where MS_{within} = within-groups mean square
         SS_{within} = within-groups sum of squares
         df_{within} = within-groups degrees of freedom

But we must still obtain the appropriate degrees of freedom. For between-groups mean square,

$$df_{between} = k - 1$$

where k = number of groups

To find degrees of freedom for within-groups mean square,

$$df_{within} = N_{total} - k$$

where N_{total} = total number of scores in all groups combined
   k = number of groups

Illustrating with the data from Table 8.2, for which there are four groups and a total of 20 scores in all those groups, we calculate our degrees of freedom as follows:

$$df_{between} = 4 - 1$$
$$= 3$$

and

$$df_{within} = 20 - 4$$
$$= 16$$

We are now prepared to obtain the following mean squares:

$$MS_{between} = \frac{50}{3}$$
$$= 16.67$$

and

$$MS_{within} = \frac{82}{16}$$
$$= 5.13$$

THE *F* RATIO

As previously noted, the analysis of variance yields an *F* ratio in which variation between groups and variation within groups are compared. We are now ready to specify the degree of each type of variation as measured by mean squares. Therefore, the *F* ratio can be regarded as indicating the size of the between-groups mean square relative to the size of the within-groups mean square, or

$$\boxed{F = \frac{MS_{between}}{MS_{within}}}$$

For the current problem

$$F = \frac{16.67}{5.13}$$
$$= 3.25$$

Having obtained an *F* ratio, we must now determine whether it is large enough to reject the null hypothesis and accept the research hypothesis. Does public support for trying the offender as an adult differ by race/ethnicity? The larger our calculated *F* ratio (the larger the $MS_{between}$ and the smaller the MS_{within}), the more likely we will obtain a statistically significant result.

But exactly how do we recognize a significant *F* ratio? Recall that in Chapter 7, our obtained *t* ratio was compared against a table *t* ratio for the .05 level of significance with the appropriate degrees of freedom. Similarly, we must now interpret our calculated *F* ratio with the aid of Table D in Appendix C. Table D contains a list of critical *F* ratios—*F* ratios that we must obtain to reject the null hypothesis at the .05 and .01 levels of significance. As was the case with the *t* ratio, the exact *F* value that we must obtain depends on its associated degrees of freedom.

TABLE 8.3	Analysis of Variance Summary Table for the Data in Table 8.2			
Source of Variation	**SS**	**df**	**MS**	**F**
Between groups	50	3	16.67	3.25
Within groups	82	16	5.13	
Total	132	19		

Therefore, we enter Table D looking for the two *df* values, between-groups degrees of freedom and within-groups degrees of freedom. Degrees of freedom associated with the numerator ($df_{between}$) have been listed across the top of the page, and degrees of freedom associated with the denominator (df_{within}) have been placed down the left side of the table. The body of Table D presents critical *F* ratios at the .05 and .01 significance levels.

For the data in Table 8.2, we have found $df_{between} = 3$ and $df_{within} = 16$. Thus, we move to the column marked $df = 3$ in Table D and continue down the page from that point until we arrive at the row marked $df = 16$. By this procedure, we find that a significant *F* ratio at the $\alpha = .05$ level must exceed 3.24, and at the $\alpha = .01$ level it must exceed 5.29. Our calculated *F* ratio is 3.25. As a result, we reject the null hypothesis at the .05 level of significance and accept the research hypothesis: Race/ethnicity appears to affect public support for trying the offender as an adult.

The results of our analysis of variance can be presented in a summary table such as the one shown in Table 8.3. It has become standard procedure to summarize an analysis of variance in this manner. The total sum of squares ($SS_{total} = 132$) is decomposed into two parts: the between-groups sum of squares ($SS_{between} = 50$) and the within-groups sum of squares ($SS_{within} = 82$). Each source of sum of squares is converted to mean square by dividing by the respective degrees of freedom. Finally, the *F* ratio (mean square *between* divided by mean square *within*) is calculated, which can be compared to the table critical value to determine significance.

To review some of the concepts presented thus far, consider Figure 8.4, which shows two contrasting situations. Both Case 1 and Case 2 consist of three samples (A, B, and C) with sample

Case 1 data

Sample A	Sample B	Sample C
2	6	10
3	7	11
4	8	12
Mean 3	7	11

Analysis-of-variance summary table

Source of variation	SS	df	MS	F
Between groups	96	2	48	48
Within groups	6	6	1	
Total	102	8		

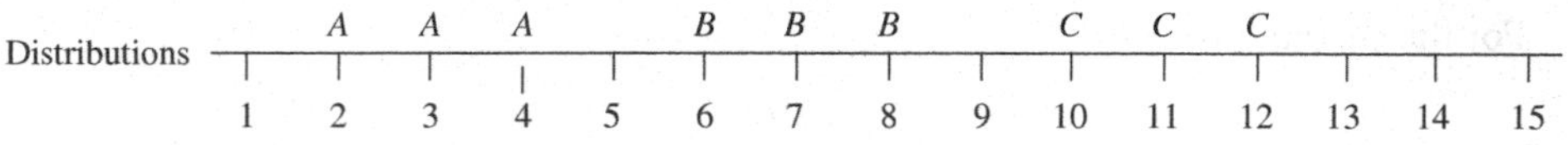

Case 2 data

Sample A	Sample B	Sample C
1	3	7
3	5	12
5	13	14
Mean 3	7	11

Analysis-of-variance summary table

Source of variation	SS	df	MS	F
Between groups	96	2	48	3.2
Within groups	90	6	15	
Total	186	8		

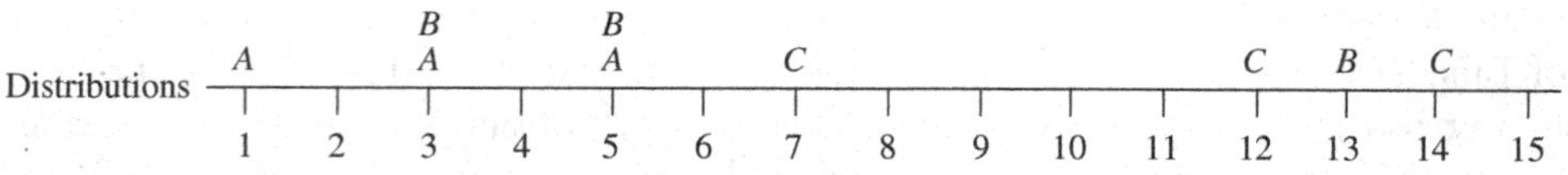

FIGURE 8.4 Two Examples of Analysis of Variance.

means $\overline{X}_A = 3$, $\overline{X}_B = 7$, and $\overline{X}_C = 11$, and with $N = 3$ in each sample. Because the means are the same in both data sets, the between-groups sums of squares are identical ($SS_{between} = 96$).

In Case 1, the three samples are clearly different. It would seem then that we should be able to infer that the population means are different. Relative to between-groups variation (the differences between the sample means), the within-groups variation is rather small. Indeed, there is as much as a 48-to-1 ratio of between-groups mean square to within-groups mean square. Thus, $F = 48$ and is significant. Although the sample means and between-groups sum of squares are the same for Case 2, there is far more dispersion within groups, causing the samples to overlap quite a bit. The samples hardly appear as distinct as in Case 1, and so it would seem unlikely that we could generalize the differences between the sample means to differences between population means. The within-groups mean square is 15. The ratio of between to within mean square is then only 48-to-15, yielding a nonsignificant F ratio of 3.2.

STEP-BY-STEP ILLUSTRATION

Analysis of Variance

To provide a step-by-step illustration of an analysis of variance, suppose that a security specialist wishes to examine whether students attending high schools in urban, suburban, and rural settings differ in terms of their sense of safety while at school. The hypotheses are as follows:

Null hypothesis: ($\mu_1 = \mu_2 = \mu_3$)	*Students in urban, suburban, and rural high schools do not differ in terms of feelings of safety.*
Research hypothesis: (*some* $\mu_i \neq \mu_j$)	*Students in urban, suburban, and rural high schools differ in terms of feelings of safety.*

To investigate and test the hypotheses, the researcher selects at random five students from urban, suburban, and rural high schools, administering a fear of school crime inventory, with the measure of fear ranging from 0 for fearless to 10 for extremely fearful. Her data (the fear scores and their squared values) are shown in the table that follows.

Urban School Students ($N_1 = 5$)		Suburban School Students ($N_2 = 5$)		Rural School Students ($N_3 = 5$)	
X_1	X_1^2	X_2	X_2^2	X_3	X_3^2
6	36	2	4	3	9
7	49	5	25	2	4
8	64	4	16	4	16
6	36	3	9	4	16
4	16	5	25	3	9
$\Sigma X_1 = 31$	$\Sigma X_1^2 = 201$	$\Sigma X_2 = 19$	$\Sigma X_2^2 = 79$	$\Sigma X_3 = 16$	$\Sigma X_3^2 = 54$

Step 1 Find the mean for each sample.

$$\overline{X}_1 = \frac{\Sigma X_1}{N_1}$$
$$= \frac{31}{5}$$
$$= 6.2$$

$$\overline{X}_2 = \frac{\Sigma X_2}{N_2}$$
$$= \frac{19}{5}$$
$$= 3.8$$

$$\bar{X}_3 = \frac{\Sigma X_3}{N_3}$$

$$= \frac{16}{5}$$

$$= 3.2$$

Notice that differences do exist, the tendency being for students in urban schools to report greater levels of fearfulness.

Step 2 Find the sum of scores, sum of squared scores, number of subjects, and mean for all groups combined.

$$\Sigma X_{\text{total}} = \Sigma X_1 + \Sigma X_2 + \Sigma X_3$$

$$= 31 + 19 + 16$$

$$= 66$$

$$\Sigma X_{\text{total}}^2 = \Sigma X_1{}^2 + \Sigma X_2{}^2 + \Sigma X_3{}^2$$

$$= 201 + 79 + 54$$

$$= 334$$

$$N_{\text{total}} = N_1 + N_2 + N_3$$

$$= 5 + 5 + 5$$

$$= 15$$

$$\bar{X}_{\text{total}} = \frac{\Sigma X_{\text{total}}}{N_{\text{total}}}$$

$$= \frac{66}{15}$$

$$= 4.4$$

Step 3 Find the total sum of squares.

$$SS_{\text{total}} = \Sigma X_{\text{total}}^2 - N_{\text{total}}\bar{X}_{\text{total}}^2$$

$$= 334 - (15)(4.4)^2$$

$$= 334 - (15)(19.36)$$

$$= 334 - 290.4$$

$$= 43.6$$

Step 4 Find the within-groups sum of squares.

$$SS_{\text{within}} = \Sigma X_{\text{total}}^2 - \Sigma N_{\text{group}}\bar{X}_{\text{group}}^2$$

$$= 334 - [(5)(6.2)^2 + (5)(3.8)^2 + (5)(3.2)^2]$$

$$= 334 - [(5)(38.44) + (5)(14.44) + (5)(10.24)]$$

$$= 334 - (192.2 + 72.2 + 51.2)$$

$$= 334 - 315.6$$

$$= 18.4$$

Step 5 Find the between-groups sum of squares.

$$SS_{\text{between}} = \Sigma N_{\text{group}}\bar{X}_{\text{group}}^2 - N_{\text{total}}\bar{X}_{\text{total}}^2$$

$$= [(5)(6.2)^2 - (5)(3.8)^2 + (5)(3.2)^2] - (15)(4.4)^2$$

$$= [(5)(38.44) + (5)(14.44) + (5)(10.24)] - (15)(19.36)$$

$$= (192.2 + 72.2 + 51.2) - 290.4$$

$$= 315.6 - 290.4$$

$$= 25.2$$

Step 6 Find the between-groups degrees of freedom.

$$df_{between} = k - 1$$
$$= 3 - 1$$
$$= 2$$

Step 7 Find the within-groups degrees of freedom.

$$df_{within} = N_{total} - k$$
$$= 15 - 3$$
$$= 12$$

Step 8 Find the within-groups mean square (df within is 12, not 2).

$$MS_{within} = \frac{SS_{within}}{df_{within}}$$
$$= \frac{18.4}{12}$$
$$= 1.53$$

Step 9 Find the between-groups mean square.

$$MS_{between} = \frac{SS_{between}}{df_{between}}$$
$$= \frac{25.2}{2}$$
$$= 12.6$$

Step 10 Obtain the F ratio.

$$F = \frac{MS_{between}}{MS_{within}}$$
$$= \frac{12.6}{1.53}$$
$$= 8.24$$

Step 11 Compare the obtained F ratio with the appropriate value found in Table D.

$$\text{Obtained } F \text{ ratio} = 8.24$$
$$\text{Table } F \text{ ratio} = 3.88$$
$$df = 2 \text{ and } 12$$
$$\alpha = .05$$

As shown in Step 11, to reject the null hypothesis at the .05 significance level with 2 and 12 degrees of freedom, our calculated F ratio must exceed 3.88. Because we have obtained an F ratio of 8.24, we can reject the null hypothesis and accept the research hypothesis. Specifically, we conclude that high school students in urban, suburban, and rural locations differ in terms of levels of fear.

A MULTIPLE COMPARISON OF MEANS

A significant F ratio informs us of an overall difference among the groups being studied. If we were investigating a difference between only two sample means, no additional analysis would be needed to interpret our result: In such a case, either the obtained difference is statistically significant or it is not. However, when we find a significant F for the differences among three or more means, it may be important to determine exactly where the significant differences lie. For example, in the foregoing illustration, the school safety researcher uncovered statistically significant differences in levels of fear among urban, suburban, and rural high school students.

Consider the possibilities raised by this significant F ratio: Urban students might differ significantly from suburban students; suburban students might differ significantly from rural students; and urban students might differ significantly from rural students. As explained earlier in this chapter, obtaining a t ratio for each comparison—$\overline{X}_1$ versus $\overline{X}_2$, $\overline{X}_2$ versus $\overline{X}_3$, and $\overline{X}_1$ versus $\overline{X}_3$— would entail a good deal of work and, more importantly, would increase the probability of Type 1 error. Fortunately, statisticians have developed a number of other tests for making multiple comparisons after finding a significant F ratio to pinpoint where the significant mean differences lie. We introduce **Tukey's HSD (Honestly Significant Difference)**, one of the most useful tests for investigating the multiple comparison of means. Tukey's HSD test is used only after a significant F ratio has been obtained. By Tukey's method, we compare the difference between any two mean scores against HSD. A mean difference is statistically significant only if it exceeds HSD. By formula,

TUKEY'S HSD (HONESTLY SIGNIFICANT DIFFERENCE)

A procedure for the multiple comparison of means after a significant F ratio has been obtained.

$$HSD = q\sqrt{\dfrac{MS_{within}}{N_{group}}}$$

where

q = table value (from Table E) at a given level of significance for the total number of group means being compared

MS_{within} = within-groups mean square (obtained from the analysis of variance)

N_{group} = number of subjects in each group (assumes the same number in each group)[1]

Unlike the t ratio, HSD takes into account that the likelihood of Type 1 error increases as the number of means being compared increases. The q value depends upon the number of group means, and the larger the number of group means, the more conservative HSD becomes with regard to rejecting the null hypothesis. As a result, fewer significant differences will be obtained with HSD than with the t ratio. Moreover, a mean difference is more likely to be significant in a multiple comparison of three means than in a multiple comparison of four or five means.

STEP-BY-STEP ILLUSTRATION

HSD for Analysis of Variance

To illustrate the use of HSD, let us return to the previous example in which fearfulness of high school students was found to differ by urban, suburban, or rural location of the school. More specifically, a significant F ratio was obtained for differences among the mean levels of fear for the three groups of students—urban, suburban, and rural—where

$$\overline{X}_1 = 6.2$$
$$\overline{X}_2 = 3.8$$
$$\overline{X}_3 = 3.2$$

---

[1]Although not an issue with the problems presented in this book, Tukey's method can be used for comparisons of groups of unequal size. In such cases, N_{group} is replaced by what is called the harmonic mean of the group sizes. The harmonic mean of the group sizes is the reciprocal of the mean of the reciprocal group sizes. That is, $N_{group} = \dfrac{k}{\frac{1}{N_1} + \frac{1}{N_2} + \ldots + \frac{1}{N_k}}$

where k is the number of groups being compared, and $N_1, N_2, \ldots N_k$ are the respective group sizes.

Step 1 Construct a table of differences between ordered means.

For the present data, the rank order of means (from smallest to largest) is 3.2, 3.8, and 6.2. These mean scores are arranged in table form so that the difference between each pair of means is shown in a matrix. Thus, the difference between $\overline{X}_1$ and $\overline{X}_2$ is .6; the difference between $\overline{X}_1$ and $\overline{X}_3$ is 3.0; and the difference between $\overline{X}_2$ and $\overline{X}_3$ is 2.4. The subscripts for the group means should not change when arranged in order. Thus, for example, $\overline{X}_2$ represents the mean of the group originally designated as number 2, not the second highest group mean.

	$\overline{X}_3 = 3.2$	$\overline{X}_2 = 3.8$	$\overline{X}_1 = 6.2$
$\overline{X}_3 = 3.2$	—	.6	3.0
$\overline{X}_2 = 3.8$	—	—	2.4
$\overline{X}_1 = 6.2$	—	—	—

Step 2 Find q in Table E in Appendix C.

To find q from Table E, we must have (1) the degrees of freedom (df) for MS_{within}, (2) the number of group means k, and (3) a significance level of either .01 or .05. We already know from the analysis of variance that $df_{within} = 12$. Therefore, we look down the left-hand column of Table E until we arrive at 12 degrees of freedom. Second, because we are comparing three mean scores, we move across Table E to a number of group means (k) equal to three. Assuming a .05 level of significance, we find that $q = 3.77$.

Step 3 Find HSD.

$$HSD = q\sqrt{\frac{MS_{within}}{N_{group}}}$$
$$= 3.77\sqrt{\frac{1.53}{5}}$$
$$= 3.77\sqrt{.306}$$
$$= (3.77)(.553)$$
$$= 2.08$$

Step 4 Compare HSD against the differences between means in the table above.

To be regarded as statistically significant, any obtained difference between means must exceed the HSD (2.08). Referring to the table of differences between means, we find that the feelings of safety difference of 3.0 between $\overline{X}_3$ (rural) and $\overline{X}_2$ (suburban) and feelings of safety difference of 2.4 between $\overline{X}_1$ (urban) and $\overline{X}_2$ (suburban) are greater than $HSD = 2.08$. As a result, we conclude that these differences between means are statistically significant at the .05 level. Finally, the difference in mean levels of feelings of safety of .6 between $\overline{X}_3$ (rural) and $\overline{X}_1$ (urban) is not significant because it is less than HSD.

REQUIREMENTS FOR USING THE F RATIO

The analysis of variance should be made only after the researcher has considered the following requirements:

1. *A comparison among three or more independent means.* The F ratio is usually employed to make comparisons among three or more means from independent samples. It is possible, moreover, to obtain an F ratio rather than a t ratio when a two-sample comparison is made. For the two-sample case, $F = t^2$, and identical results are obtained. However, a single sample arranged in a panel design (the same group studied at several points in time) cannot be tested in this way. Thus, for example, one may not study improvement in class performance across three examinations during the term using this approach.

2. *Interval data.* To conduct an analysis of variance, we assume that we have achieved the interval level of measurement. Categorized or ranked data should not be used.
3. *Random sampling.* We should have taken our samples at random from a given population of scores.
4. *A normal distribution.* We assume the sample characteristic we measure to be normally distributed in the underlying population.
5. *Equal variances.* The analysis of variance assumes that the population variances for the different groups are all equal. The sample variances, of course, may differ as a result of sampling. Moderate differences among the sample variances do not invalidate the results of the *F* test. When such differences are extreme (e.g., when one of the sample variances is many times larger than another), the *F* test presented here may not be appropriate.

Summary

The analysis of variance can be used to make comparisons among three or more sample means. Unlike the *t* ratio for comparing only two sample means, the analysis of variance yields an *F* ratio whose numerator represents variation between groups and whose denominator contains an estimate of variation within groups. The sum of squares represents the initial step for measuring variation. It is, however, greatly affected by sample size. To overcome this problem and control for differences in sample size, we divide our SS$_{between}$ and SS$_{within}$ by the appropriate degrees of freedom to obtain the mean square. The *F* ratio indicates the size of the between-groups mean square relative to the size of the within-groups mean square. The larger the *F* ratio (i.e., the larger the between-groups mean square

relative to its within-groups counterpart), the more likely we are to reject the null hypothesis and attribute our result to more than just sampling error. In the last chapter, we learned that in studying the difference between two sample means, we must compare our calculated *t* ratio against the table *t* (Table C). For the purpose of studying differences among three or more means, we now interpret our calculated *F* ratio by comparing it against an appropriate *F* ratio in Table D. On that basis, we decide whether or not we have a significant difference—whether to retain or reject the null hypothesis. Finally, after obtaining a significant *F*, we can determine exactly where the significant differences lie by applying Tukey's HSD method for the multiple comparison of means.

Questions and Problems

1. A *t* ratio compares two means and analysis of variance (ANOVA) compares more than two means. Why is ANOVA used rather than a series of *t* tests?
   a. It holds Type I error at a constant level
   b. It increases Type I error
   c. It is too much work to do a series of *t* tests
   d. Both methods provide the same information
2. To find a significant difference with an analysis of variance, you hope to maximize _____.
   a. group standard deviations
   b. the within-groups sum of squares
   c. variation between groups
   d. variation within groups
3. The *F* ratio is larger when the _____.
   a. the between-groups mean square is smaller
   b. the within-groups mean square is smaller
   c. the difference between means is negative
   d. the difference between means is smaller
4. Which of the following is *not* a requirement of analysis of variance?
   a. A comparison of three or more independent means
   b. Random sampling

   c. A normal distribution
   d. A before-after comparison
5. Tukey's Honestly Significant Difference (HSD) is used when the _____.
   a. *F* ratio is significant
   b. *F* ratio is not significant
   c. *t* ratio is significant
   d. *t* ratio is not significant
6. A researcher is interested in studying the effects of using a dress code in middle schools on students' feelings of safety. Three schools are identified as having roughly the same size, racial composition, income levels, and disciplinary problems. The researcher randomly assigns a type of dress code to each school and implements it for the beginning of the school year. In the first school (A), no formal dress code is required. In the second school (B), a limited dress code is used with restriction on the colors and styles of clothing. In the third school (C), school uniforms are required. Six months later, five students from each school are randomly selected and given a survey on fear of crime at school. The higher the score, the safer the student feels. Test the hypothesis that feelings of safety do not differ depending upon school dress codes.

School A	School B	School C
3	2	4
3	2	4
3	2	3
4	1	4
4	3	3

7. To learn exactly where the significant differences occur in Problem 6, conduct a multiple comparison of means using Tukey's method.

8. A criminal justice policy researcher is interested in monitoring public opinion about gun permits for handguns. One of the factors he examines is political affiliation. He randomly selects 10 people each from conservative, independent, and liberal political affiliations. Respondents are asked, "On a scale from 0 to 10, where 0 is not at all and 10 is completely, how important is it that gun permits should be required for people who wish to own a handgun?" Test the null hypothesis that public opinion about gun permits does not differ by political affiliation.

Conservative	Independent	Liberal
5	6	7
4	4	4
8	5	8
2	3	7
5	7	6
4	4	9
0	6	10
2	5	7
1	5	4
7	7	8
6	4	6
3	3	7
0	6	9
4	4	10
2	8	8

9. To learn exactly where the significant differences occur in Problem 8, conduct a multiple comparison of means using Tukey's method.

10. Punishment is one method to control children. Do social attitudes toward spanking differ by marital status? A researcher conducted a survey of people's attitudes toward spanking. Respondents were asked, "On a scale from 0 to 10 where 0 is not at all and 10 is completely, are you in favor of spanking as an effective method to discipline children?" Test the null hypothesis that attitudes toward spanking do not vary by marital status.

Married or Widowed	Divorced or Separated	Never Married
8	7	6
8	6	6
7	6	6
6	6	5
7	7	4
5	5	5
9	8	3
4	4	4
7	6	2
5	5	7

11. Conduct a multiple comparison of means by Tukey's method to determine exactly where the significant differences occur in Problem 10.

12. Consider an experiment to determine the effects of alcohol and marijuana on driving. Five randomly selected subjects are given alcohol to produce legal drunkenness and then are given a simulated driving test (scored from a top score of 10 to a bottom score of 0). Five randomly selected subjects are given marijuana and the same driving test. Finally a control group of five subjects is tested for driving while sober. Given the following means and standard deviations, test for the significance of differences among the means of the following groups:

	Alcohol	Drugs	Control
Mean	2.4	3.6	6.8
SD	1.3	1.8	1.3

13. Conduct a multiple comparison of means by Tukey's method to determine exactly where the significant differences occur in Problem 12.

Computer Exercises

1. From the General Social Survey, test whether the number of hours per day that people have to relax (HRSRELAX) varies by marital status (MARITAL). Hint: select ANALYZE, COMPARE MEANS, ONE-WAY ANOVA. Note also that the Tukey test is selected in the Post Hoc button and that means and standard deviations are selected in the Options button.

2. Based on the General Social Survey, test whether the number of self-reports of poor mental health during the past 30 days (MNTLHLTH) varies by marital status (MARITAL) using one-way ANOVA with the Tukey test and selecting means and standard deviations as an option.

3. Based on the General Social Survey, test whether the number of self-reports of poor mental health (MNTLHLTH) varies by age group (AGE recoded into a new variable AGEGRP) using one-way ANOVA with the Tukey test and selecting means and standard deviations as an option. Before doing yours analysis, recode age into a new variable (AGEGRP) using the following groups: 18 to 29; 30 to 44; 45 to 65; 65 or more.

4. Analyze two variables of your choice from the General Social Survey using one-way ANOVA. Remember the dependent variable needs to be an interval/ratio level variable and the independent variable needs to have three or more categories.

9

Nonparametric Tests of Significance

As indicated in Chapters 7 and 8, we must ask a good deal of the criminal justice researcher who employs a *t* ratio or an analysis of variance to make comparisons between his or her groups of respondents. Each of these tests of significance has a list of requirements that includes the assumption that the characteristic studied is normally distributed in a specified population (or a large sample size so that the sampling distribution is normal). In addition, each test asks for the interval level of measurement so that a score can be assigned to every case. When a test of significance, such as the *t* ratio or the analysis of variance, requires (1) normality in the population (or at least large samples so that the sampling distribution is normal) and (2) an interval-level measure, it is referred to as a **parametric test**.[1]

What about the researcher who cannot employ a parametric test, that is, who either cannot honestly assume normality, who does not work with large numbers of cases, or whose data are not measured at the interval level? Suppose, for example, that he or she is working with a skewed distribution or with data that have been categorized and counted (the nominal level) or ranked (the ordinal level). How does this researcher go about making comparisons between samples without violating the requirements of a particular test?

Fortunately, statisticians have developed a number of **nonparametric tests** of significance—tests whose list of requirements does not include normality or the interval level of measurement. To understand the important position of nonparametric tests in criminal justice research, we must also understand the concept of the **power of a test**, the probability of rejecting the null hypothesis when it is actually false and should be rejected.

Power varies from one test to another. The most powerful tests, those that are most likely to reject the null hypothesis when it is false, are tests that have the strongest or most difficult requirements to satisfy. Generally, these are parametric tests such as *t* or *F*, which assume that interval data are employed and that the characteristics being studied are normally distributed in their populations. By contrast, the nonparametric alternatives make less stringent demands but are less powerful tests of significance than their parametric counterparts. As a result, assuming that the null hypothesis is false (and holding constant such other factors as sample size), an investigator is more likely to reject the null hypothesis by the appropriate use of *t* or *F* than by a nonparametric alternative. In a statistical sense, you get what you pay for!

Understandably, researchers are eager to reject the null hypothesis when it is false. As a result, many of them would ideally prefer to employ parametric tests of significance and might

PARAMETRIC TEST

A statistical procedure that requires that the characteristic studied be normally distributed in the population and that the researcher have interval data.

NONPARAMETRIC TEST

A statistical procedure that makes no assumptions about the way the characteristic being studied is distributed in the population and requires only ordinal or nominal data.

POWER OF A TEST

The ability of a statistical test to reject the null hypothesis when it is actually false and should be rejected.

[1]This designation is based on the term *parameter,* which refers to any characteristic of a population.

even be willing to "stretch the truth" a little bit to meet the assumptions. For example, if ordinal data are fairly evenly spaced and therefore approximate an interval scale, and if the data are not normal but also not terribly skewed, one can "get away with" using a parametric test.

As previously noted, however, it is often not possible—without deceiving yourself to the limit—to come even close to satisfying the requirements of parametric tests. In the first place, much of the data of criminal justice research are nowhere near the interval level. Second, we may know that certain variables or characteristics under study are severely skewed in the population and may not have large enough samples to compensate.

When the requirements of a statistical test have been severely violated, it is not possible to know the power of the test. Therefore, the results of a parametric test whose requirements have been unsatisfied may lack any meaningful interpretation. Under such conditions, researchers wisely turn to nonparametric tests of significance. Some will simply accept the reduced power associated with the nonparametric alternative they decide to apply; others may seek alternative methods for overcoming the power deficiency and enhancing their ability accurately to reject the null hypothesis, for example, by increasing the size of their sample.

This chapter introduces some of the best-known nonparametric tests of significance for characteristics measured at the nominal or ordinal level: the chi-square test, the median test, the Mann-Whitney U Test, and the Kruskal-Wallis Test.

ONE-WAY CHI-SQUARE TEST

Have you ever tried to psych out your instructor while taking a multiple-choice test? You may have reasoned, "the last two answers were both B; he wouldn't possibly have three in a row." Or you may have thought, "there haven't been very many D answers; maybe I should change a few of the ones I wasn't sure of to D." You are assuming, of course, that your instructor attempts to distribute his correct answers evenly across all categories, A through E.

Suppose your instructor returns the exam and hands out the answer key. You construct a frequency distribution of the correct responses to the 50-item test as follows:

A	12
B	14
C	9
D	5
E	10

Thus, 12 of the 50 items had a correct answer of A, 14 had a correct answer of B, and so on. These are called the **observed frequencies** (f_o). Observed frequencies refer to the set of frequencies obtained in an actual frequency distribution, that is, when we actually do research or conduct a study.

OBSERVED FREQUENCIES

In a chi-square analysis, the results that are actually observed when conducting a study.

You can sense from this distribution that the instructor may favor putting the correct response near the top—that is, in the A and B positions. Conversely, he seems to shy away from the D response, for only five correct answers fell into that category.

Can we generalize about the tendencies of this professor observed from this one exam? Are the departures from an even distribution of correct responses large enough to indicate, for example, a real dislike for the category D? Or, could chance variations account for these results; that is, if we had more tests constructed by this instructor, could we perhaps see the pattern even out in the long run?

These are the kinds of questions we asked in Chapters 7 and 8 concerning sample means, but now we need a test for frequencies. **Chi-square** (pronounced "ki-square" and written χ^2) is the most commonly used nonparametric test; not only is it relatively easy to follow but it is also applicable to a wide variety of research problems.

CHI-SQUARE

A nonparametric test of significance whereby expected frequencies are compared against observed frequencies.

The *one-way chi-square* test can be used to determine whether the frequencies we observed previously differ significantly from an even distribution (or any other distribution we might hypothesize). In this example, our null and research hypotheses are as follows:

Null hypothesis: *The instructor shows no tendency to assign any particular correct response from A to E.*

Research hypothesis: *The instructor shows a tendency to assign particular correct responses from A to E.*

What should the frequency distribution of correct responses look like if the null hypothesis were true? Because there are five categories, 20% of the correct responses should fall in each category. With 50 questions, we should expect 10 correct responses for each category.

The **expected frequencies** (f_e) are those frequencies that are expected to occur under the terms of the null hypothesis. The expected frequencies for the hypothesized even distribution are as follows:

EXPECTED FREQUENCIES

The frequencies expected under the terms of the null hypothesis for chi-square.

A	10
B	10
C	10
D	10
E	10

Chi-square allows us to test the significance of the difference between a set of observed frequencies (f_o) and expected frequencies (f_e). We obtained 12 correct A answers, but we expected 10 under the null hypothesis; we obtained 14 correct B answers, but we expected 10 under the null hypothesis; and so on. Obviously, the greater the differences between the observed and the expected frequencies, the more likely we have a significant difference suggesting that the null hypothesis is unlikely to be true.

The chi-square statistic focuses directly on how close the observed frequencies are to what they are expected to be (represented by the expected frequencies) under the null hypothesis. On the basis of just the observed and expected frequencies, the formula for chi-square is

$$\chi^2 = \Sigma \frac{(f_o - f_e)^2}{f_e}$$

where f_o = observed frequency in any category
          f_e = expected frequency in any category

According to the formula, we must subtract each expected frequency from its corresponding observed frequency, square the difference, divide by the expected frequency, and then add up these quotients for all the categories to obtain the chi-square value.

Let's inspect how the chi-square statistic relates to the null hypothesis. If, in the extreme case, all the observed frequencies were equal to their respective expected frequencies (all $f_o = f_e$) as the null hypothesis suggests, chi-square would be zero. If all the observed frequencies were close to their expected frequencies, consistent with the null hypothesis except for sampling error, chi-square would be small. The more the set of observed frequencies deviates from the frequencies expected under the null hypothesis, the larger the chi-square value. At some point, the discrepancies of the observed frequencies from the expected frequencies become larger than could be attributed to sampling error alone. At that point, chi-square is so large that we are forced to reject the null hypothesis and accept the research hypothesis. Just how large chi-square must be before we reject the null hypothesis is something about which we will keep you in suspense, but only until we show you how chi-square is computed.

As stated earlier, we calculate our χ^2 value by computing the difference between the observed and expected frequency, square the difference, and divide by the expected frequency for each category. Setting it up in tabular form,

Category	f_o	f_e	$f_o - f_e$	$(f_o - f_e)^2$	$\dfrac{(f_o - f_e)^2}{f_e}$
A	12	10	2	4	.4
B	14	10	4	16	1.6
C	9	10	−1	1	.1
D	5	10	−5	25	2.5
E	10	10	0	0	0.0
					$\chi^2 = 4.6$

By summing the last column (containing the quotients) over all the categories, we obtain $\chi^2 = 4.6$. To interpret this chi-square value, we must determine the appropriate number of degrees of freedom.

$$df = k - 1$$

where k = number of categories in the observed frequency distribution

In our example, there are five categories, and thus

$$df = 5 - 1 = 4$$

Turning to Table F in Appendix C, we find a list of chi-square values that are significant at the .05 and .01 levels. For the .05 significance level, we see that the critical value for chi-square with 4 degrees of freedom is 9.488. This is the value that we must exceed before we can reject the null hypothesis. Because our calculated chi-square is only 4.6 and, therefore, smaller than the table value, we must retain the null hypothesis and reject the research hypothesis. The observed frequencies do not differ enough from the frequencies expected under the null hypothesis of an equal distribution of correct responses. Thus, although we did not observe a perfectly even distribution (10 for each category), the degree of unevenness was not sufficiently large to conclude that the instructor had any underlying preference in designing his answer key.

STEP-BY-STEP ILLUSTRATION

One-Way Chi-Square

To summarize the step-by-step procedure for calculating one-way chi-square, imagine that a researcher is interested in surveying perceptions of juvenile offenders concerning the aggressiveness of police officers. She questions a sample of 60 young offenders about whether they believe that police officers are becoming more aggressive, less aggressive, or staying the same in their law enforcement practices.

We might specify our hypotheses as follows:

Null hypothesis: *Juvenile offenders are equally divided in their perceptions of the aggressiveness of police officers.*

Research hypothesis: *Juvenile offenders are not equally divided in their perceptions of the aggressiveness of police officers.*

Let us say that of the 60 juveniles surveyed, 35 believe that the police have become more aggressive, 10 believe they have become less aggressive, and 15 believe they are about the same.

Step 1 Arrange the data in the form of a frequency distribution.

Category	Observed Frequency
More aggressive	35
Less aggressive	10
About the same	15
Total	60

Step 2 Obtain the expected frequency for each category.

The expected frequencies (f_e) are those frequencies expected to occur under the terms of the null hypothesis. Under the null hypothesis, we would expect the opinions to divide themselves equally across the three categories. Therefore, with three categories ($k = 3$) and $N = 60$,

$$f_e = \frac{60}{3} = 20$$

Category	Observed Frequency (f_o)	Expected Frequency (f_e)
More aggressive	35	20
Less aggressive	10	20
About the same	15	20
Total	60	60

Step 3 Set up a summary table to calculate the chi-square value.

Category	f_o	f_e	$f_o - f_e$	$(f_o - f_e)^2$	$\dfrac{(f_o - f_e)^2}{f_e}$
More aggressive	35	20	15	225	11.25
Less aggressive	10	20	−10	100	5.00
About the same	15	20	−5	25	1.25
					$\chi^2 = 17.50$

Step 4 Find the degrees of freedom.

$$df = k - 1 = 3 - 1 = 2$$

Step 5 Compare the calculated chi-square value with the appropriate chi-square value from Table F.

Turning to Table F in Appendix C, we look up the chi-square value required for significance at the .05 level for 2 degrees of freedom, and find that this critical value is 5.99. Because the calculated chi-square ($\chi^2 = 17.50$) is larger than the table value, we reject the null hypothesis. These findings suggest, therefore, that juvenile offenders are not equally divided about their views concerning the changing aggressiveness of police officers. In fact, the majority (35 out of 60) believed they are becoming more aggressive. More to the point, these findings cannot be passed off as merely the result of sampling error or chance.

STEP-BY-STEP ILLUSTRATION

One-Way Chi-Square with Unequal Expected Frequencies

In some cases the expected frequencies are derived from some external benchmark and may not be the same for all categories. Imagine that a criminologist is interested in studying racial profiling in traffic stops by police. Specifically, she decides to compare the race/ethnicity distribution of drivers (White/Black/Latino) within a random sample of 250 traffic stops to the race/ethnicity distribution of the state's population of licensed drivers. Department of Motor Vehicle records show the population of licensed drivers to be 70% white, 20% black, and 10% Latino.

We can specify our hypotheses as follows:

Null hypothesis: *The race/ethnicity distribution of drivers in traffic stops equals that of the population of licensed drivers*

Research hypothesis: *The race/ethnicity distribution of drivers in traffic stops does not equal that of the population of licensed drivers*

Step 1   Arrange the data in the form of a frequency distribution.

The race/ethnicity of the drivers within the random sample of 250 traffic stops were as follows:

Category	f	%
White	154	61.6
Black	64	25.6
Latino	32	12.8
Total	250	100.0

Step 2   Obtain the expected frequency for each category.

The expected frequencies (f_e) are the frequencies to be expected to occur under the terms of the null hypothesis. If the null hypothesis is true that the race/ethnicity distribution of traffic stops matched the driver licenses records, then 70% of the traffic stops should be of white drivers, 20% of black drivers, and 10% of Latino drivers. We can then multiply these expected percentages (70%, 20%, and 10%) by the sample size ($N = 250$) to obtain the expected frequencies given in the far right column below:

Category	f_o	f_e
White	154	175
Black	64	50
Latino	32	25
Total	250	250

Step 3   Set up a summary table to calculate the chi-square value.

Category	f_o	f_e	$f_o - f_e$	$(f_o - f_e)^2$	$\dfrac{(f_e - f_o)^2}{f_e}$
White	154	175	−21	441	2.52
Black	64	50	14	196	3.92
Latino	32	25	7	49	1.96
Total	250	250			$\chi^2 = 8.4$

Step 4   Find the degrees of freedom.

$$df = k - 1$$
$$= 3 - 1$$
$$= 2$$

Step 5   Compare the calculated chi-square value with the appropriate chi-square value from Table F.

Turning to Table F in Appendix C, we look up the chi-square value required for significance at the .05 level for 2 degrees of freedom and find that this critical value is 5.99. Because the calculated chi-square ($\chi^2 = 8.4$) is larger than the table value, we reject the null hypothesis. These findings suggest, therefore, that the race/ethnicity distribution of drivers in traffic stops does not match that of the population of licensed drivers. Although there are several alternative explanations for this discrepancy, the results would appear to suggest the presence of racial profiling.

TWO-WAY CHI-SQUARE TEST

As we saw in Chapter 2, nominal and ordinal variables are often presented in the form of a cross-tabulation. Specifically, cross-tabulations are used to compare the distribution of one variable, often called the dependent variable, across categories of some other variable, the independent variable. In a cross-tabulation, the focus is on the differences between groups, such as between males and females, in terms of some dependent variable, for example, their use of seat belts. We are now prepared to consider whether differences in a cross-tabulation, such as gender differences in seat belt usage, are statistically significant.

As in the case of the t ratio and analysis of variance, there is a sampling distribution for chi-square that can be used to estimate the probability of obtaining a significant chi-square value by chance alone rather than by actual population differences. Unlike these earlier tests of significance, however, chi-square is employed to make comparisons between frequencies rather than between mean scores. As a result, the null hypothesis for the chi-square test states that the populations do not differ with respect to the frequency of occurrence of a given characteristic, whereas the research hypothesis says that sample differences reflect actual population differences regarding the relative frequency of a given characteristic.

To illustrate the use of the chi-square for cross-tabulated frequency data (or for proportions that can be reduced to frequencies), imagine that we have been asked to investigate the effect of political orientation on leniency in sentencing. We might categorize our sample members on a strictly either-or basis; that is, we might decide that they are either lenient or punitive. Therefore,

Null hypothesis: *The relative frequency or percentage of liberals who are lenient is the same as the relative frequency of conservatives who are lenient.*

Research hypothesis: *The relative frequency or percentage of liberals who are lenient is not the same as the relative frequency of conservatives who are lenient.*

The two-way chi-square test of significance is, like the one-way chi-square test, concerned with the distinction between *expected frequencies* and *observed frequencies*. Once again, the expected frequencies (f_e) refer to the terms of the null hypothesis, according to which the relative frequency (or proportion) is expected to be the same from one group to another. For example, if a certain percentage of the liberals is expected to be lenient, then we expect the same percentage of the conservatives to be lenient. By contrast, observed frequencies (f_o) refer to the results that we actually obtain when conducting a study and, therefore, may or may not vary from one group to another. Only if the difference between expected and observed frequencies is large enough do we reject the null hypothesis and decide that a true population difference exists.

Let's consider the simplest possible case in which we have equal numbers of liberals and conservatives as well as equal numbers of lenient and punitive respondents. Assuming 40 respondents took part in the survey, the cross-tabulation showing the observed frequencies for each cell (f_o) might be as follows:

Attitude toward Punishment	Political Orientation		Total
	Liberal	*Conservative*	
Lenient	13	7	20
Punitive	7	13	20
Total	20	20	$N = 40$

In this cross-tabulation, there are four cells and 40 respondents. Therefore, to calculate the expected frequencies (f_e), we might expect 10 cases per cell, as shown in the following:

Attitude toward Punishment	Political Orientation		Total
	Liberal	*Conservative*	
Lenient	10	10	20
Punitive	10	10	20
Total	20	20	$N = 40$

This straightforward method of calculating expected frequencies works in this cross-tabulation, but *only* because the marginals, both row and column, are identical (they are all 20). Unfortunately, most research situations will not yield cross-tabulations in which both the row and column marginals are evenly split. By sampling technique, it may be possible to control the distribution of the independent variable, for example, to get exactly the same number of liberals and conservatives. But you cannot control the distribution of the dependent variable, for example, the number of lenient and punitive respondents. Thus, we must consider a more general approach to calculating expected frequencies— one that can be used when either or both the row and column marginals are not evenly distributed.

Continuing with the present example in which we drew samples of 20 liberals and 20 conservatives, suppose that we observed more lenient respondents than punitive respondents. Therefore, as shown in Table 9.1, the row marginals would not be equal.

The data in Table 9.1 indicate that 15 out of 20 liberals and 10 out of 20 conservatives were lenient. To determine if these frequencies depart from what one would expect by chance alone, we need to determine the expected frequencies under the null hypothesis of no difference.

The observed and expected frequencies for each cell are displayed together in Table 9.2. The expected frequencies are derived purposely to be in line with the null hypothesis, that is,

TABLE 9.1 Frequencies Observed in a Cross-Tabulation of Attitude toward Punishment by Political Orientation

Attitude toward Punishment	Political Orientation		Total
	Liberal	*Conservative*	
Lenient	15	10	25
Punitive	5	10	15
Total	20	20	$N = 40$

TABLE 9.2 Frequencies Observed and Expected in a Cross-Tabulation of Attitude toward Punishment by Political Orientation

Observed frequency   *Expected frequency*

Attitude toward Punishment	Political Orientation		Total
	Liberal	*Conservative*	
Lenient	15(12.5)	10(12.5)	25
Punitive	5 (7.5)	10(7.5)	15
Total	20	20	$N = 40$

Column marginal total   Row marginal total

they represent the frequencies that one would expect to see if the null hypothesis of no difference were true. Thus, 25 out of 40 of the respondents overall, or 62.5%, are lenient in their approach to sentencing. For there to be no difference between the liberals and the conservatives in this regard, as dictated by the null hypothesis, 62.5% of the liberals and 62.5% of the conservatives should be lenient. Translating into expected frequencies the fact that both groups should have the same percentage (or relative frequency) of lenient respondents, we expect 12.5 liberals (62.5% of 20, or $.625 \times 20 = 12.5$) to be lenient and 12.5 conservatives (62.5% of 20, or $.625 \times 20 = 12.5$) to be lenient if the null hypothesis were true. Of course, the expected frequencies of respondents who are punitive are 7.5 for both liberals and conservatives, because the expected frequencies must sum to the marginal totals (in this case, $12.5 + 7.5 = 20$). Finally, it is important to note that the expected frequencies (which we will learn how to calculate using a formula presented in the next section) do not have to be whole numbers.

As discussed earlier, chi-square focuses on how close the observed frequencies are to those expected under the null hypothesis. On the basis of the observed and expected frequencies, the chi-square formula is as follows:

$$\chi^2 = \sum \frac{(f_o - f_e)^2}{f_e}$$

where f_o = observed frequency in any cell

f_e = expected frequency in any cell

We subtract each expected frequency from its corresponding observed frequency, square the difference, divide by the expected frequency, and then add up these quotients for all the cells to obtain the chi-square value.

By applying the chi-square formula to the case at hand,

Cell	f_o	f_e	$f_o - f_e$	$(f_o - f_e)^2$	$\dfrac{(f_o - f_e)^2}{f_e}$
Upper-left	15	12.5	2.5	6.25	.50
Upper-right	10	12.5	−2.5	6.25	.50
Lower-left	5	7.5	−2.5	6.25	.83
Lower-right	10	7.5	2.5	6.25	.83
					$\chi^2 = 2.66$

Thus, we learn that $\chi^2 = 2.66$. To interpret this chi-square value, we must still determine the appropriate number of degrees of freedom. This can be done for tables that have any number of rows and columns by employing the formula

$$df = (r - 1)(c - 1)$$

where r = number of rows in the table of observed frequencies

c = number of columns in the table of observed frequencies

Because the observed frequencies in Table 9.2 form two rows and two columns (2×2):

$$df = (2 - 1)(2 - 1)$$
$$= (1)(1)$$
$$= (1)$$

Turning to Table F in Appendix C, we find a list of chi-square values that are significant at the .05 and .01 levels. For the .05 significance level, we see that the critical value for chi-square with 1 degree of freedom is 3.84. This is the value that must be exceeded before we can reject the null hypothesis. Because our calculated χ^2 is only 2.66 and therefore *smaller* than the table value, we must retain the null hypothesis and reject the research hypothesis. The observed frequencies do not differ enough from the frequencies expected by chance to indicate that actual population differences exist.

Finding the Expected Frequencies

The expected frequencies for each cell must reflect the operation of chance under the terms of the null hypothesis. If the expected frequencies are to indicate sameness across all samples, they must be proportional to their marginal totals, both for rows and columns.

To obtain the expected frequency for any cell, we multiply the column and row marginal totals for a particular cell and divide the product by N. Therefore,

$$\boxed{f_e = \frac{(\text{row marginal total})(\text{column marginal total})}{N}}$$

For the upper-left cell in Table 9.2 (lenient liberals),

$$f_e = \frac{(25)(20)}{40}$$
$$= \frac{500}{40}$$
$$= 12.5$$

Likewise, for the upper-right cell in Table 9.2 (lenient conservatives),

$$f_e = \frac{(25)(20)}{40}$$
$$= \frac{500}{40}$$
$$= 12.5$$

For the lower-left cell in Table 9.2 (punitive liberals),

$$f_e = \frac{(15)(20)}{40}$$
$$= \frac{300}{40}$$
$$= 7.5$$

For the lower-right cell in Table 9.2 (punitive conservatives),

$$f_e = \frac{(15)(20)}{40}$$
$$= \frac{300}{40}$$
$$= 7.5$$

These calculated expected frequencies are shown in parentheses next to the observed frequencies in Table 9.2. As we will see, the foregoing method for determining f_e can be applied to any chi-square problem for which the expected frequencies must be obtained.

STEP-BY-STEP ILLUSTRATION

Chi-Square Test of Significance

To summarize the step-by-step procedure for obtaining chi-square for a cross-tabulation, let us consider a study in which the effectiveness of hypnosis as a means of improving the memory of eyewitnesses to a crime is examined. The hypotheses might be specified as follows:

Null hypothesis: *Hypnosis does not affect the recognition memory of eyewitnesses to a crime.*

Research hypothesis: *Hypnosis does affect the recognition memory of eyewitnesses to a crime.*

To test the null hypothesis at the $\alpha = .05$ level of significance, all subjects first view a videotape of a pickpocket plying his trade. One week later, subjects are randomly assigned to one of two conditions. The subjects in the experimental group are hypnotized and then asked to pick the thief out of a lineup. Subjects in the control group are not hypnotized and attempt the same lineup identification. Suppose that the results are as shown in Table 9.3. We can see from the results that the hypnotized group actually did worse in attempting to identify the culprit. Only 7 of the 40 subjects in the experimental group were correct, whereas 17 of the 40 control subjects made the right choice. This difference may suggest that hypnosis does have an effect (although not the kind of effect that one might desire), but is the difference significant?

TABLE 9.3 Hypnosis and Accuracy of Eyewitness Identification		
	Hypnotized	**Control**
Correct identification	7	17
Incorrect identification	33	23
Total	40	40

Step 1 Rearrange the data in the form of a 2 × 2 table containing the observed frequencies for each cell.

	Hypnotized	**Control**	
Correct Identification	7	17	24
Incorrect Identification	33	23	56
	40	40	$N = 80$

Step 2 Obtain the expected frequency for each cell.

	Hypnotized	**Control**	
Correct Identification	7(12)	17(12)	24
Incorrect Identification	33(28)	23(28)	56
	40	40	$N = 80$

Upper left:
$$f_e = \frac{(24)(40)}{80}$$

$$= \frac{960}{80}$$

$$= 12$$

Upper right:
$$f_e = \frac{(24)(40)}{80}$$

$$= \frac{960}{80}$$

$$= 12$$

Lower left:
$$f_e = \frac{(56)(40)}{80}$$

$$= \frac{2.240}{80}$$

$$= 28$$

Lower right:
$$f_e = \frac{(56)(40)}{80}$$

$$= \frac{2.240}{80}$$

$$= 28$$

Step 3 Construct a summary table in which, for each cell, you report the observed and expected frequencies, subtract the expected from the observed frequency, square this difference, divide by the expected frequency, and sum these quotients to obtain the chi-square value.

Cell	f_o	f_e	$f_o - f_e$	$(f_o - f_e)^2$	$\dfrac{(f_o - f_e)^2}{f_e}$
Upper-left	7	12	−5	25	2.08
Upper-right	17	12	5	25	2.08
Lower-left	33	28	5	25	.89
Lower-right	23	28	−5	25	.89
					$\chi^2 = 5.94$

Step 4 Find the degrees of freedom.

$$df = (r - 1)(c - 1)$$

$$= (2 - 1)(2 - 1)$$

$$= (1)(1)$$

$$= 1$$

Step 5   Compare the obtained chi-square with the appropriate value in Table F .

$$\text{Obtained } \chi^2 = 5.94$$
$$\text{Table } \chi^2 = 3.84$$
$$df = 1$$
$$\alpha = .05$$

Because the calculated chi-square exceeds the table value, we reject the null hypothesis and conclude that hypnosis does affect the recognition memory of eyewitnesses.

Comparing Several Groups

Until now we have limited our illustrations of two-way chi-square to the widely employed 2 × 2 problem. It should be emphasized, however, that the chi-square test is frequently calculated for tables that are larger than 2 rows by 2 columns in which several groups or categories are to be compared. The step-by-step procedure for comparing several groups is essentially the same as its 2 × 2 counterpart.

Let us now illustrate with a 3 × 3 problem (3 rows by 3 columns), although any number of rows and columns could be used, and the number of rows and columns need not be the same. Recall the earlier step-by-step illustration comparing the race/ethnicity of drivers in a sample of 250 traffic stops to a benchmark based on the race/ethnicity distribution of licensed drivers. Suppose we go further by examining differences in the distribution of driver race/ethnicity linked to the race/ethnicity of the police officer making the traffic stop. We can use the two-way chi-square test to explore differences in driver race/ethnicity of traffic stops made by varying race/ethnicity groups of police officers.

The cross-tabulation in Table 9.4 expands the earlier distribution of driver race/ethnicity according to the race/ethnicity of the police officers making the traffic stop. Note that the independent variable is the officer's race/ethnicity (since the decision making is in the hands of the officer, not the driver). With the independent variable arranged on the columns, we focus on column percentages.

The cross-tabulation does suggest differences based on the race/ethnicity of the officer. For example, 30.0% of the stops executed by white officers involve black drivers, compared to only 14.0% of the stops made by black officers and 22.5% of those made by Latino officers. Also, minority officers are more inclined than white officers to stop white drivers: 66.0% among black officers and 62.5% among Latino officers, compared to 60% among white officers). Although we see differences in the race/ethnicity of drivers linked to the race/ethnicity of the officers within

TABLE 9.4	Cross-Tabulation of Race/Ethnicity of Drivers and of Police Officers in a Sample of Traffic Stops			
		Officer		
Driver	*White*	*Black*	*Latino*	**Total**
White	96 60.0%	33 66.0%	25 62.5%	154 61.6%
Black	48 30.0%	7 14.0%	9 22.5%	64 25.6%
Latino	16 10.0%	10 20.0%	6 15.0%	32 12.8%
Total	160 100.0%	50 100.0%	40 100.0%	250 100.0%

this random sample of 250 traffic stops, are the differences large enough to generalize to the population of traffic stops? To answer this question, we establish these hypotheses:

Null hypothesis: *The race/ethnicity distribution of drivers in traffic stops does not differ based on the race/ethnicity of the police officers.*

Research hypothesis: *The race/ethnicity distribution of drivers in traffic stops differs based on the race/ethnicity of the police officers.*

To determine whether there are significant differences in the race/ethnicity distribution of drivers among the race/ethnicity groups of officers, we must apply the original chi-square formula introduced earlier in the chapter to the data in Table 9.4:

$$\chi^2 = \sum \frac{(f_o - f_e)^2}{f_e}$$

STEP-BY-STEP ILLUSTRATION

Chi-Square Test for Several Groups

The chi-square formula can be applied to this 3×3 cross-tabulation using the following step-by-step procedure:

Step 1   Arrange the sample data in the form of a 3×3 cross-tabulation of observed frequencies.

f_o	Officer			
Driver	**White**	**Black**	**Latino**	**Total**
White	96	33	25	154
Black	48	7	9	64
Latino	16	10	6	32
Total	160	50	40	250

Step 2   Obtain the expected frequency for each cell.

Using W, B, and L to indicate race/ethnicity and Dr and Off to indicate the driver or the officer, the expected frequencies for the nine cells in the cross-tabulation can be calculated based on the row marginal total, the column marginal total, and the sample size:

$$f_e = \frac{(\text{row marginal total})(\text{column marginal total})}{N}$$

WDr-WOff: $f_e = \dfrac{(154)(160)}{250} = 98.56$

BDr-WOff: $f_e = \dfrac{(64)(160)}{250} = 40.96$

LDr-WOff: $f_e = \dfrac{(32)(160)}{250} = 20.48$

WDr-BOff: $f_e = \dfrac{(154)(50)}{250} = 30.80$

BDr-BOff: $f_e = \dfrac{(64)(50)}{250} = 12.80$

LDr-BOff: $f_e = \dfrac{(32)(50)}{250} = 6.40$

WDr-LOff: $f_e = \dfrac{(154)(40)}{250} = 24.64$

BDr-LOff: $$f_e = \frac{(64)(40)}{250} = 10.24$$

LDr-LOff: $$f_e = \frac{(32)(40)}{250} = 5.12$$

Step 3 Construct a summary table in which, for each cell, you report the observed and expected frequencies, subtract the expected frequency from the observed frequency, square this difference, divide by the expected frequency, and sum these quotients to obtain the chi-square value.

Cell	f_o	f_e	$f_o - f_e$	$(f_o - f_e)^2$	$\dfrac{(f_e - f_o)^2}{f_e}$
WDr-WOff	96	98.56	−2.56	6.554	0.066
BDr-WOff	48	40.96	7.04	49.562	1.210
LDr-WOff	16	20.48	−4.48	20.070	0.980
WDr-BOff	33	30.80	2.20	4.840	0.157
BDr-BOff	7	12.80	−5.80	33.640	2.628
LDr-BOff	10	6.40	3.60	12.960	2.025
WDr-LOff	25	24.64	0.36	0.130	0.005
BDr-LOff	9	10.24	−1.24	1.538	0.150
LWDr-LOff	6	5.12	0.88	0.774	0.151
					$\chi^2 = 7.373$

Step 4 Determine the number of degrees of freedom.

$$df = (c - 1)(r - 1)$$
$$= (3 - 1)(3 - 1)$$
$$= 4$$

Step 5 Compare the obtained chi-square value with the appropriate chi-square value in Table F in Appendix C.

$$df = 4$$
$$\alpha = .05$$
$$\text{Table } \chi^2 = 9.49$$
$$\text{Obtained } \chi^2 = 7.373$$

Therefore, we need a chi-square value above the tabled critical value of 9.49 to reject the null hypothesis. Because our obtained chi-square is only 7.373, we must retain the null hypothesis and attribute the observed sample differences to the operation of chance alone. We have not found statistically significant evidence that the distribution of driver race/ethnicity in traffic stops differs according to the race/ethnicity of the police officer executing the stop.

Correcting for Small Expected Frequencies

One of the primary reasons why the chi-square test is so popular among researchers is that it makes very few demands on the data. That is, the numerous assumptions associated with the t ratio and the analysis of variance are absent from the chi-square alternative. Despite this relative freedom from assumptions, however, chi-square cannot be used indiscriminately. In particular, chi-square does impose some rather modest requirements on sample size. Although chi-square does not require the same large samples as some of the parametric tests, an extremely small sample can sometimes yield misleading results, as we will see in what follows.

Generally, chi-square should be used with great care whenever some of the expected frequencies are below 5. There is no hard-and-fast rule concerning just how many expected frequencies below 5 will render an erroneous result. Some researchers contend that all expected frequencies should be at least 5, and others relax this restriction somewhat and insist that only most of the expected frequencies be at least 5. The decision concerning whether to proceed with the test depends on what impact the cells with the small expected frequencies have on the value of chi-square.

Consider, for example, the cross-tabulation in Table 9.5 of murder weapon and gender of offender for 200 homicide cases. The "female/other-weapon" cell has an expected frequency of only 2. For this cell, the observed frequency is 6 (females tend to use poison far more than men), and so its contribution to the chi-square statistic is

$$\frac{(f_o - f_e)^2}{f_e} = \frac{(6-2)^2}{2} = 8$$

No matter what happens with the seven other cells, this value of 8 for the female/other cell will cause the null hypothesis to be rejected. That is, for a 4×2 table ($df = 3$) the critical chi-square value from Table F is 7.815, which is already surpassed because of this one cell alone. One should feel uncomfortable indeed about rejecting the null hypothesis just because there were four more women than expected who used an "other" weapon, such as poison. The problem here is that the expected frequency of 2 in the denominator causes the fraction to be unstable. With even a modest difference between observed and expected frequencies in the numerator, the quotient explodes because of the small divisor. For this reason, small expected frequencies are a concern.

In instances like this in which expected frequencies of less than 5 create such problems, you should collapse or merge together some categories, but only if it is logical to do so. One would not want to merge together categories that are substantively very different. But in this instance, we can reasonably combine the "blunt object" and "other" categories into a new category that we can still label "other." The revised cross-tabulation is shown in Table 9.6. Note that now none of the cells has problematically low expected frequencies.

In 2×2 tables, the requirement for having all expected frequencies at least equal to 5 is particularly important. In addition, for 2×2 tables, distortions can also occur if expected frequencies are under 10. Fortunately, however, there is a simple solution for 2×2 tables with any expected frequency less than 10 but greater than 5, known as **Yates's correction**.[2] By using Yates's correction, the difference between observed and expected frequencies is reduced by .5. Since chi-square

YATES'S CORRECTION
In the chi-square analysis, a factor for small expected frequencies that reduces the overestimate of the chi-square value and yields a more conservative result (only for 2 × 2 tables).

TABLE 9.5	Cross-Tabulation of Murder Weapon and Gender of Offender (Expected Frequencies in Parentheses)		
	Male	Female	Total
Gun	100	20	120
	(90)	(30)	
Knife	39	21	60
	(45)	(15)	
Blunt object	9	3	12
	(9)	(3)	
Other	2	6	8
	(6)	(2)	
Total	150	50	N = 200

[2]Some researchers recommend that Yates's correction be used for all 2 × 2 tables, not just those with deficient expected frequencies. Although technically correct, it makes little practical difference when all the expected frequencies are fairly large. That is, the corrected and uncorrected chi-square are very similar with large expected frequencies.

TABLE 9.6	Revised Cross-Tabulation of Murder Weapon and Gender of Offender (Expected Frequencies in Parentheses)		
	Male	**Female**	**Total**
Gun	100 (90)	20 (30)	120
Knife	39 (45)	21 (15)	60
Other	11 (15)	9 (5)	20
Total	150	50	$N = 200$

depends on the size of that difference, we also reduce the size of our calculated chi-square value. The following is the chi-square formula for small expected frequencies, using Yates's correction:

$$\chi^2 = \sum \frac{(|f_o - f_e| - .5)^2}{f_e}$$

In the corrected chi-square formula, the vertical lines surrounding $f_o - f_e$ indicate that we must reduce the absolute value (ignoring minus signs) of each $f_o - f_e$ by .5.

To illustrate, suppose that an instructor at a U.S. university close to the Canadian border suspects that his Canadian students are more likely to be cigarette smokers than his U.S. students. To test his hypothesis, he questions the 36 students in one of his classes about their smoking status and nationality. The results are shown in Table 9.7.

If we were to use the original chi-square formula for a 2×2 problem ($\chi^2 = 5.13$), we would conclude that the difference between U.S. and Canadian students is significant. Before we make much of this result, however, we must be concerned about the potential effects of small expected frequencies and compute Yates's corrected formula.

The procedure for applying the corrected 2×2 chi-square formula can be summarized in tabular form:

f_o	f_e	$|f_o - f_e|$	$|f_o - f_e| - .5$	$(|f_o - f_e| - .5)^2$	$\dfrac{(|f_o - f_e| - .5)^2}{f_e}$
15	11.67	3.33	2.83	8.01	.69
5	8.33	3.33	2.83	8.01	.96
6	9.33	3.33	2.83	8.01	.86
10	6.67	3.33	2.83	8.01	1.20
					$\chi^2 = 3.71$

TABLE 9.7	Cross-Tabulation of Smoking Status and Nationality	
	Nationality	
Smoking Status	*American*	*Canadian*
Nonsmoker	15	5
Smoker	6	10
Total	21	15

As shown, Yates's correction yields a smaller chi-square value ($\chi^2 = 3.71$) than was obtained by means of the uncorrected formula ($\chi^2 = 5.13$). In the present example, our decision regarding the null hypothesis would depend on whether we had used Yates's correction. With the corrected formula, we retain the null hypothesis; without it, we reject the null hypothesis. Given these very different results, one should go with the more conservative formula that uses Yates's correction.

Requirements for the Use of Two-Way Chi-Square

The chi-square test of significance has few requirements for its use, which might explain in part why it is applied so frequently. Unlike the t ratio, for example, it does not assume a normal distribution in the population nor interval-level data. However, the following requirements still need to be considered before using chi-square:

1. *A comparison between two or more samples.* As illustrated and described in the present chapter, the chi-square test is employed to make comparisons between two or more *independent* samples. This requires that we have at least a 2 × 2 table (at least 2 rows and at least 2 columns). The assumption of independence indicates that chi-square cannot be applied to a single sample that has been studied in a before-after panel design. At least two samples of respondents must be obtained.
2. *Nominal data.* Chi-square does not require data that are ranked or scored. Only frequencies are required.
3. *Random sampling.* We should have drawn our samples at random from a particular population.
4. *The expected cell frequencies should not be too small.* Exactly how large f_e must be depends on the nature of the problem. For a 2 × 2 problem, no expected frequency should be smaller than 5. In addition, Yates's corrected formula should be used for a 2 × 2 problem in which an expected cell frequency is smaller than 10. For a situation wherein several groups are being compared (say, a 3 × 3 or 4 × 5 problem), there is no hard-and-fast rule regarding minimum cell frequencies, although we should be careful to see that few cells contain less than five cases. In such instances, categories with small numbers of cases should be merged if at all possible.

THE MEDIAN TEST

For ordinal data, the **median test** is a simple nonparametric procedure for determining the likelihood that two or more random samples have been taken from populations with the same median. Essentially, the median test involves performing a chi-square test of significance on a cross-tabulation in which one of the dimensions is whether the scores fall above or below the median of the two groups combined. Just as before, Yates's correction is used for a 2 × 2 problem (comparing two samples) having small expected frequencies.

MEDIAN TEST

A nonparametric test of significance for determining the probability that two random samples have been drawn from populations with the same median.

STEP-BY-STEP ILLUSTRATION

Median Test

To illustrate the procedure for carrying out the median test, suppose a police chief wanted to study urban versus rural police officers' reactions to confrontational situations. Specifically, he wondered whether there is a difference in the readiness of officers to call for backup in potentially dangerous confrontations. To examine this, the research division of the police department showed a sample of 15 urban and 12 rural state police officers a videotape of an interaction between a police officer and a citizen who has been pulled over for suspicion of driving while intoxicated. In the videotape, as the officer approaches the car, an apparently inebriated man gets out and walks toward the officer, yelling in an angry and aggressive manner. At this point, the tape stops and the officers are asked to predict what they would do if they were the officer in the videotaped scenario. The officers are asked to rate on a 20-point scale the likelihood that they would call for backup in this situation. The following table presents the likelihood scores of each subject, with higher scores indicating greater likelihood:

Urban	Rural	Urban	Rural
15	12	11	9
18	7	10	11
15	15	8	14
17	16	14	9
17	6	9	
16	8	18	
10	10	16	
13	6		

Step 1 Find the median of the two samples combined.

$$\text{Position of median} = \frac{N + 1}{2}$$

$$= \frac{27 + 1}{2}$$

$$= 14\text{th}$$

The median is the 14th score counting from either end of the distribution arranged in order of size. To find the median, we arrange all the scores for police officer in consecutive order (without regard for what sample they have come from) and locate the combined median:

18 18 17 17 16 16 16 15 15 15 14 14 13 12 11 11 10 10 10 9 9 9 8 8 7 6 6

——— Median (the 14th score from either end)

Step 2 Count the number in each sample falling above the median and not above the median (Mdn = 12).

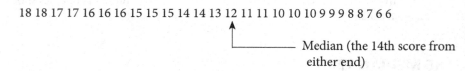

	Urban	Rural
Above median	10	3
Not above median	5	9
	N = 27	

As shown here, the numbers above and not above the median scores on the Likelihood of Calling for Backup Scale are presented in a 2 × 2 frequency table. In this table, we can see that 10 of the 15 urban officers but only 3 of the 12 rural officers gave ratings that were above the median rating for the group as a whole.

Step 3 Perform a chi-square test of significance.

If no urban-versus-rural differences exist with respect to likelihood of calling for backup, we would expect the same median split within each sample, so that half of the urban and half of the rural officers fall above the median. To find out whether the sample differences obtained are statistically significant or merely a product of sampling error, we conduct a chi-square test (using Yates's correction because there are expected frequencies less than 10). The following table shows the observed and expected frequencies:

	Urban	Rural
Above median	10 (7.22)	3 (5.78)
Not above median	5 (7.78)	9 (6.22)
		$N = 27$

$$\chi^2 = \Sigma \frac{(|f_o - f_e| - .5)^2}{f_e}$$

Setting up the calculations in tabular form:

f_o	f_e	$|f_o - f_e|$	$|f_o - f_e| - .5$	$(|f_o - f_e| - .5)^2$	$\frac{(|f_o - f_e| - .5)^2}{f_e}$
10	7.22	2.78	2.28	5.19	.72
3	5.78	2.78	2.28	5.19	.90
5	7.78	2.78	2.28	5.19	.67
9	6.22	2.78	2.28	5.19	.84
				$\chi^2 =$	3.13

Referring to Table F in Appendix C, we learn that chi-square must exceed 3.84 ($df = 1$) to be regarded as significant at the .05 level. Because our obtained $\chi^2 = 3.12$, we cannot reject the null hypothesis. There is insufficient evidence to conclude on the basis of our results that urban and rural police officers differ in their perceived likelihood of calling for backup in a specific potentially dangerous situation.

In this example, we were interested in comparing two groups on an ordinal level variable. This was accomplished by constructing a chi-square test on the 2 × 2 cross-tab of placement above versus not above the median by group membership (in this case, urban versus rural settings).

If we were instead interested in comparing three groups on an ordinal level variable, we would need to apply a chi-square for comparing several groups. That is, we would first compute the median for all three groups combined, then construct a 2 × 3 cross-tab of placement above versus not above the median by group membership, and finally calculate the chi-square test of significance.

Requirements for the Use of the Median Test

The following conditions must be satisfied to appropriately apply the median test to a research problem:

1. *A comparison between two or more medians.* The median test is employed to make comparisons between two or more medians from independent samples.
2. *Ordinal data.* To perform a median test, we assume at least the ordinal level of measurement. Nominal data cannot be used.
3. *Random sampling.* We should have drawn our samples on a random basis from a given population.

Mann-Whitney U Test

Although it can be used to test differences between two or more groups in terms of some ordinal measure, the median test suffers from one major drawback, limiting its power to reject the false null hypothesis of no difference. The median test makes inefficient use of the available data. It ignores the specific rank order of cases and concentrates only on the middle-most score, and whether cases fall above or below that divider.

Suppose that you were to rank-order a set of 12 cases, 6 from each of two groups denoted X_1 and X_2, according to size from high to low as follows:

High X_1 X_1 X_1 X_2 X_2 X_2 $|$ X_1 X_1 X_1 X_2 X_2 X_2 Low

Median

In this extreme example, half the cases from each group fall above the median and half from each fall below the median. Therefore, though the samples differ sharply in their rankings, the median test would yield a chi-square of zero, suggesting no difference whatsoever.

A much more efficient and, therefore, powerful nonparametric approach for comparing two samples is the **Mann-Whitney U test**. Like the median test, the Mann-Whitney U test is an appropriate substitute for the t ratio whenever ordinal data are involved. It is also an appropriate alternative for interval-level data when normality in the population distribution cannot be assumed and the samples are too small to assume a normal-shaped sampling distribution for the difference between sample means. As a great advantage over the median test, the Mann-Whitney U test examines the rank ordering of all cases. Specifically, it determines whether the ranked values for a variable are equally distributed throughout two samples.

The calculations for the Mann-Whitney U test actually involve two mirror-image equations:

$$U_a = N_1 N_2 + \frac{N_1(N_1 + 1)}{2} - \sum R_1$$

$$U_b = N_1 N_2 + \frac{N_2(N_2 + 1)}{2} - \sum R_2$$

where N_1 and N_2 are the number of cases in each of the two groups, and $\sum R_1$ and $\sum R_2$ are the sum of the ranks for the two groups, respectively. Following these calculations, the smaller value of U_a and U_b is used for testing the difference between groups. The null hypothesis of no difference is then rejected if U is *less than* the critical value found in Table G corresponding to samples sizes N_1 and N_2 as well as the level of significance α.

STEP BY STEP-BY-STEP ILLUSTRATION

Mann-Whitney U Test

In order to illustrate the use of the Mann-Whitney U test, consider the researcher who is studying gender differences in arrests made by rookie police officers. On a random basis, the researcher examines the arrest records of 9 female police officers and 9 male police officers in the same department during their first year on the job. The number of arrests by gender is given in the following table. Note that number of arrests represents interval data and therefore can be treated as a score, but the apparent skewness in the data (a few extremely large numbers of arrests) combined with small sample sizes should make us wary of using the t test for differences between means.

Female	Male
12	23
15	11
4	24
7	18
8	18
16	6
20	9
10	8
8	21

MANN-WHITNEY U TEST

A nonparametric to the t ratio that is employed to compare two independent samples but that requires only ordinal-level data.

Step 1 Rank-order the scores.

Rank-order all the scores in both groups combined, beginning with the smallest score. All scores should be ranked from lowest to highest (a rank of 1 should be assigned to the smallest score, 2 to the next smallest score, etc.). In the case of tied ranks, take an average of the tied positions; that is, add the tied positions and then divide by the number of cases involved in the tie. In the present example, three police officers were tied with an arrest record of 8 for positions 4, 5, and 6, and we assign each of the three the average rank of 5. There are two officers tied with 18 arrests, and so we assign them both a rank of 13.5, the average ranks 13 and 14.

Female		Male	
Score	Rank	Score	Rank
12	10	23	17
15	11	11	9
4	1	24	18
7	3	18	13.5
8	5	18	13.5
16	12	6	2
20	15	9	7
10	8	8	5
8	5	21	16

Step 2 Sum the ranks for each group.

$$\Sigma R_1 = 70 \quad \Sigma R_2 = 101$$

Step 3 Substitute in the formula to obtain U_a and U_b.

$$U_a = (9)(9) + \frac{9(9 + 1)}{2} - 70$$
$$= 81 + 45 - 70$$
$$= 56$$

$$U_a = (9)(9) + \frac{9(9 + 1)}{2} - 101$$
$$\doteq 81 + 45 - 101$$
$$= 25$$

Step 4 Compare the smaller of U_a and U_b with the table values of U.

Take the smaller value of U obtained in step 3 and compare it with the appropriate critical value of U in Table G in Appendix C corresponding to N_1, N_2, and the level of significance being used. To reject the null hypothesis at $\alpha = .05$, the obtained U (in this case $U = 25$) must be smaller than the table value (in this case, 18). We therefore retain the null hypothesis. We did not find conclusive evidence that gender makes a difference in the arrest record of rookie police officers in this particular department.

Notice that Table G applies only to situations in which both sample sizes are no greater than 20. When the size of samples exceeds the limits of Table G, it is safe to assume that the U statistic is normally distributed and to use a z ratio. After calculating U_a and U_b, the smaller U value is inserted into the following z formula, which then can be compared to the standard normal distribution:

$$z = \frac{U - \dfrac{N_1 N_2}{2}}{\sqrt{\dfrac{N_1 N_2 (N_1 + N_2 + 1)}{12}}}$$

Suppose that in a particular case, we obtain $U = 202$ with $N_1 = 20$ and $N_2 = 45$. The z score is calculated as

$$z = \frac{202 - \frac{(20)(45)}{2}}{\sqrt{\frac{(20)(45)(20 + 45 + 1)}{12}}}$$

To be significant at the $\alpha = .05$ level, the obtained z score must exceed the table critical value of ± 1.96. Thus, we reject the null hypothesis and conclude that the difference in ranks between the two groups is significant.

Requirements for the Use of the Mann-Whitney *U* Test

The following conditions must be satisfied to appropriately apply the Mann-Whitney test to a research problem:

1. A *comparison* between two independent samples.
2. *Ordinal data*. We assume at least the ordinal level of measurement. Nominal data cannot be used.
3. *Random sampling*. We should have drawn our samples on a random basis from a given population

Kruskal-Wallis Test

KRUSKAL-WALLIS TEST

A nonparametric alternative to the *F* ratio that is employed to compare several independent samples but that requires only ordinal-level data.

The **Kruskal-Wallis test**, a one-way analysis of variance by ranks, is a nonparametric alternative to the one-way analysis of variance (*F* ratio). It can be used to compare several independent samples but requires only ordinal-level data. The Kruskal-Wallis test can also be used for interval-level scores that are not normally distributed and too few in number to ensure that the group means would be normally distributed.

To apply the Kruskal-Wallis procedure, we find statistic H as follows:

$$H = \frac{12}{N(N + 1)} \sum \frac{(\sum R_i)^2}{n_i} - 3(N + 1))$$

where

$$N = \text{total number of cases}$$
$$n_i = \text{number of cases in a given sample}$$
$$\sum R_i = \text{sum of the ranks for a given sample}$$

STEP-BY-STEP ILLUSTRATION

Kruskal-Wallis Test

To illustrate the procedure for applying one-way analysis of variance by ranks, consider the effects of observational learning on aggressiveness. Nursery school children were randomly assigned to see one of three film sequences. In the first film, one child attacks another and then is shown enjoying himself (aggressive model rewarded). In a second film, the child engages in the same aggression, but the second child retaliates and overcomes the aggressor (aggressive model punished). The third film shows the two children engaged in vigorous but nonaggressive play (nonaggressive model control). The children were then observed in a free-play setting, and the number of aggressive acts that they initiated was recorded.

The researcher was sure that a greater number of aggressive acts represented greater aggressiveness, and so, the children could be ranked in terms of aggressiveness. He did not, however, think that the relative differences between aggressiveness scores reflected consistent gradations of aggressiveness, suggesting that the data were not interval but ordinal in nature. The following results were obtained:

Aggressive model rewarded	Aggressive model punished	Nonaggressive model
20	14	12
15	8	11
17	11	9
13	10	5
18	6	6
16	9	7

Step 1 Rank-order the total group of scores.

All scores should be ranked from lowest to highest. In the present illustration, the scores have been ranked from 1 (representing 5 acts of aggression) to 18 (representing 20 acts). In the case of tied ranks, the rank-splitting procedure presented in connection with the Mann-Whitney U test can be applied.

Group 1	R_1	Group 2	R_2	Group 3	R_3
20	18	14	13	12	11
15	12	8	5	11	9.5
17	14	11	9.5	9	6.5
13	11	10	8	5	1
18	15	6	2.5	6	2.5
16	13	9	6.5	7	4

Step 2 Sum the ranks for each sample.

$$\Sigma R_1 = 92 \quad \Sigma R_2 = 44.5 \quad \Sigma R_3 = 34.5$$

Step 3 Substitute into the formula for H.

$$H = \frac{12}{N(N+1)} \Sigma \frac{(\Sigma R_i)^2}{n_i} - 3(N+1)$$

$$= \frac{12}{18(19)} \left(\frac{(92)^2}{6} + \frac{(44.5)^2}{6} + \frac{(34.5)^2}{6} \right) - 3(19)$$

$$= \frac{12}{342} \left(\frac{8,464}{6} + \frac{1,980.25}{6} + \frac{1,190.25}{6} \right) - 57 = 68.04 - 57$$

$$= 11.04$$

Step 4 Find the degrees of freedom as one less than the number of groups (k).

$$df = k - 1 = 2$$

Step 5 Compare H with the appropriate chi-square value in Table F.

With 2 df and $\alpha = .05$, the critical value of $\chi^2 = 5.991$. Because $H = 11.04$ exceeds 5.991, we reject the null hypothesis of no difference between groups in terms of ranks and accept the research hypothesis. Our results indicate that there are significant differences, depending on the condition of observational learning, in the aggressiveness of nursery school children.

Requirements for the Use of the Kruskal-Wallis Test

The following conditions must be satisfied to appropriately apply the Kruskal-Wallis test to a research problem:

1. A *comparison* between three or more independent samples.
2. *Ordinal data*. We assume at least the ordinal level of measurement. Nominal data cannot be used.
3. *Random sampling*. We should have drawn our samples on a random basis from a given population.

Summary

It is not always possible to meet the requirements of parametric tests of significance such as the *t* ratio or analysis of variance. Fortunately, statisticians have developed a number of nonparametric alternatives—tests of significance whose requirements do not include a normal distribution or the interval level of measurement. Although less powerful than their parametric counterparts *t* and *F*, nonparametric techniques can be applied to a wider range of research situations. These tests are useful when a researcher works with ordinal or nominal data or with a small number of cases representing a highly asymmetrical underlying distribution. The most popular nonparametric test of significance, the chi-square test, is widely used to make comparisons between frequencies rather than between mean scores. In a one-way chi-square, the frequencies observed among the categories of a variable are tested to determine whether they differ from a set of hypothetical frequencies. But chi-square can also be applied to cross-tabulations of two variables. In a two-way chi-square, when the differences between expected frequencies (expected under the terms of the null hypothesis) and observed frequencies (those we actually obtained when we do research) are large enough, we reject the null hypothesis and accept the validity of a true population difference. The chi-square test of significance assumes that the expected frequencies are at least equal to 5. When several groups are being compared, it may be possible to collapse or merge some categories when the expected frequencies are small. In 2 $\times$ 2 tables, Yates's correction for small expected frequencies should be used, especially if there are expected frequencies below 10. The chi-square test requires only nominal (frequency) data. The median test, which is based on the chi-square analysis, is used to determine whether there is a significant difference between the medians of two or more independent variables. Ordinal or interval data are required for the median test. Other alternative tests for comparing groups with ordinal or ranked data are Mann-Whitney for two independent groups and Kruskal-Wallis for three or more independent groups.

Questions and Problems

1. A nonparametric test of significance should be considered when the characteristic we are studying _____.
   a. consists of frequencies rather than scores
   b. is not normally distributed in the population
   c. is not measured at the interval/ratio level
   d. all of the above
2. As compared to parametric statistics, nonparametric tests _____.
   a. are less powerful
   b. are more powerful
   c. have about the same power
   d. have unknown levels of power
3. In a chi-square test, the expected frequencies _____.
   a. are expected to occur under the terms of the null hypothesis
   b. are expected to occur under the terms of the research hypothesis
   c. refer to those frequencies actually observed
   d. are never known by the researcher
4. In a chi-square test, the larger the difference between expected and observed frequencies, the more likely you are to _____.
   a. choose to use a *t* ratio or some other parametric test
   b. reject the null hypothesis
   c. retain the null hypothesis
   d. use the median test
5. Which of the following is *not* a requirement of the chi-square test?
   a. a comparison of two or more samples
   b. ordinal data
   c. random sampling
   d. the expected frequencies should not be too small

6. To use the median test, you must be able to _____.
   a. assume a normal distribution
   b. compare three or more independent samples
   c. rank-order a series of cases
   d. reject the null hypothesis
7. A newspaper reporter in Major City calls a criminal justice researcher to ask about the validity of a survey that found 212 people who were satisfied and 241 people who were dissatisfied with their local police department. The researcher says that the best way to find out is to compare these survey results to a recent national poll that found 612 people who were satisfied and 431 who were not satisfied with their local police. Use a one-way chi-square test to compare satisfaction with police in Major City to the national study. What do your results indicate? Why is this problem a one-way chi-square test?
8. A police department is interested in the amount of warnings, tickets, and arrests made after traffic stops. During the past week, a random sample of 50 stops shows that there were 32 warnings, 14 tickets, and 4 arrests. Use a one way chi-square test to compare the outcomes of the traffic stops. Are the outcomes equally distributed?
9. The Criminal Justice Training Institute of a particular state developed a "new and improved" training course for police officers who were learning safety issues in domestic violence incidents. Sixty trainees were randomly assigned to two groups: 30 took the customary course and 30 took the new course. At the end of the course, all 60 trainees were given the same exam to measure their skills. Applying chi-square, test the null hypothesis that the new course is no better or worse than (or the same as) the old course in teaching police officers about safety issues in domestic violence incidents.

Skills Learned	Customary Course	New Course
Excellent	7	13
Good	15	15
Unsatisfactory	8	2

10. The following is a 2 × 2 cross-tabulation of capital punishment opinion by gender of respondent. Applying Yates's correction, conduct a chi-square test of significance.

Opinion Regarding Capital Punishment	Gender	
	Male	Female
Approve	8	12
Disapprove	10	15

11. A correctional researcher is interest in whether male prisoners are more likely than female prisoners to be incarcerated for violent offenses. He takes a random sample of 20 males and 20 females. The data for the prisoners are presented in the following table. Because of small expected frequencies, use a chi-square test with the Yates's correction to test the null hypothesis that there is no difference between sex in the offense leading to incarceration.

Violent Offense	Sex	
	Male	Female
Yes	8	3
No	12	17

12. A county official interested in job satisfaction among juvenile court workers selected random samples from employees in child protective services and the truancy division. He measured how satisfied each person was with his or her job. In the following results, satisfaction is scored on a 1 to 10 scale (from 1 for very dissatisfied to 10 for very satisfied). Apply the median test to find out if there is a significant difference in job satisfaction comparing the child protective services division to the truancy division.

Child Protective		Truancy	
7	7	3	3
5	7	3	4
7	8	4	4
5	9	4	7
4	7	5	
8	7	2	
8		1	
6		5	

13. Do types of crimes reported on television newscasts differ by the age of the criminals? A researcher uses her TiVo to record the local television news for a 2-week period. She records the types of crimes and notes the age of the offender. Use chi-square to test the null hypothesis that televised offense type does not vary by age group of offender.

Offense Type	Age		
	Young Adult	Middle Aged	Older Adult
Violent	27	10	3
Property	14	12	11
Sex	7	9	5

14. In a statewide telephone survey, a researcher used two questions about the death penalty to find out if support for capital punishment would change when the alternative was a life sentence with no possibility of parole. Use chi-square to test the null hypothesis that support for the death penalty does not vary by whether or not respondents are given the life sentence alternative.

Support for Death Penalty?	Question Type	
	Death Penalty Only Specified	Alternative to Death Penalty Specified
Yes	145	95
No	58	108

15. Does self-reported illegal drug use vary by social class? To find out, a criminologist questioned a random sample of 80 state residents about their occupation, education, and income, which she then used to categorize the resident as members of the upper, middle, working, and lower classes. Her results are as follows:

Social Class

Drug Use	Upper	Middle	Working	Lower
No	14	9	8	6
Yes	10	9	11	13

Applying chi-square, test the null hypothesis that self-reported drug use does not vary by social class. What do your results indicate?

16. Is there a gender difference in red-light running? A researcher completes an exploratory study at a major intersection in Crash City, USA. Observations are made watching cars from the point when the light turns from green (Go) to yellow (Caution), and then yellow to red (Stop). Traffic violations and gender of the driver are recorded. Applying chi-square, test the null hypothesis that there is no difference in red-light running by gender.

Gender

Action	Male	Female
Runs red	21	10
Runs yellow	23	22
Slows and stops	55	76

17. Conduct chi-square tests of significance for the choice of murder weapon by gender of offender in Tables 9.5 and 9.6. What is the effect of collapsing categories to gun versus other?

18. A criminologist wants to know if the homicide rate is the same in death penalty states and non–death penalty states.

Because normality cannot be assumed of the data presented in the table located at the bottom of the page, perform a median test to see if death penalty states have the same median as non–death penalty states.

19. A major national magazine has ranked 200 American cities in terms of their safety. A researcher selects 10 large cities and 10 small cities at random and wishes to test whether there is a difference in safety based on city size. The magazine's rankings (among the full list) of the cities that were selected are given in the following table:

Small cities	Large cities
17	19
18	47
3	85
10	8
13	178
92	116
17	120
111	14
124	75
69	192

Applying the Mann-Whitney U test, determine whether there is a significant difference between large and small cities with respect to safety. Note that the magazine's rankings should be re-ranked from 1 (most safe) to 20 (least safe) to reflect the order within the sample (e.g., the sample's safest city at #3 should be ranked 1, and the sample's least safe at #192 should be ranked 20).

20. The same researcher as in problem 19 then focuses on differences in safety by region. Selecting eight cities from each region of the country at random, he obtains the following rankings based on the magazine's assessments.

Homicide rates in 2010 for death penalty and non-death penalty states

Death Penalty	Homicide Rate	Death Penalty	Homicide Rate	Non–Death Penalty	Homicide Rate
Alabama	5.7	Nebraska	3.0	Alaska	4.4
Arizona	6.4	Nevada	5.9	Connecticut	3.6
Arkansas	4.7	New Hampshire	1.0	Hawaii	1.8
California	4.9	North Carolina	5.0	Illinois	5.5
Colorado	2.4	Ohio	4.1	Iowa	1.3
Delaware	5.3	Oklahoma	5.2	Maine	1.8
Florida	5.2	Oregon	2.4	Massachusetts	3.2
Georgia	5.8	Pennsylvania	5.2	Michigan	5.7
Idaho	1.3	South Carolina	6.1	Minnesota	1.8
Indiana	4.5	South Dakota	2.8	New Jersey	4.2
Kansas	3.5	Tennessee	5.6	New Mexico	6.9
Kentucky	4.3	Texas	5.0	New York	4.5
Louisiana	11.2	Utah	1.9	North Dakota	1.5
Maryland	7.4	Virginia	4.6	Rhode Island	2.8
Mississippi	7.0	Washington	2.3	Vermont	1.1
Missouri	7.0	Wyoming	1.4	West Virginia	3.3
Montana	2.6			Wisconsin	2.7

Eastern cities	Midwestern cities	Southern cities	Western cities
17	11	27	22
193	64	5	177
101	150	183	9
92	18	185	55
31	81	51	111
164	119	117	125
12	25	99	73
144	126	107	116

Applying the Kruskal-Wallis test, determine whether there is a significant difference among the regions with respect to safety. Note that the magazine's rankings should be re-ranked from 1 (most safe) to 32 (least safe) to reflect the order within the sample (e.g., the sample's safest city at #5 should be ranked 1, and the sample's least safe at #193 should be ranked 32).

21. A college president decides to examine how graduates from different majors fare in the job market. She collects the following starting salary data for a random sample of students in the Business School and the School of Arts and Sciences.

Business Graduate	Arts and Sciences Graduate
$85,000	$24,500
$35,000	$31,000
$67,000	$27,000
$29,500	$36,000
$26,000	$29,000
$54,000	$41,500
$48,000	$46,000
$30,500	$33,500
$46,500	$30,500
$54,000	$53,000

Because the sample sizes are small and the data skewed, it may be best not to use a t ratio, which assumes normality in the sampling distribution. As an alternative, apply the Mann-Whitney U test to determine whether a significant difference exists in the starting salaries of Business and Arts and Sciences graduates.

22. The dean of the School of Arts and Sciences at the same university as in the previous problem then decides to examine how graduates from different majors within the social sciences fare in the job market.

Criminal Justice	History	Political Science	Sociology	Social Work
$84,000	$24,500	$54,000	$41,500	$39,500
$35,000	$31,500	$47,000	$46,000	$27,500
$67,500	$28,000	$31,500	$33,500	$25,000
$32,500	$36,000	$46,500	$30,500	$32,500
$36,000	$29,000	$54,500	$53,000	$30,000

Because the sample sizes are small and the data skewed, it may be best not to use a F ratio, which assumes normality in the sampling distribution. As an alternative, apply the Kruskal-Wallis test to determine whether a significant difference exists in the starting salaries of various majors.

Computer Exercises

1. Use the General Social Survey to calculate a chi-square statistic to test the null hypothesis that opinions about capital punishment (CAPPUN) do not differ by marital status (MARITAL). *Hint*: ANALYZE, DESCRIPTIVE STATISTICS, CROSSTABS, select row and column variables, choose column and row percentages in options, and select chi-square in statistics.

2. Analyze the General Social Survey using a chi-square statistic to test if reports of sexual harassment on the job in the past 12 months (WKHARSEX) differ by sex (SEX).

3. Analyze the General Social Survey using a chi-square statistic to test if reports of threats on the job in the last 12 months (WKHAROTH) differ by sex (SEX).

4. Analyze the General Social Survey using a chi-square statistic to test if gun ownership (OWNGUN) differs by sex (SEX).

5. The General Social Survey sometimes changes question wording to see if it influences responses. Two questions ask respondents whether the federal government is spending enough to "halt the rising crime rate" or to "support law enforcement." Calculate a chi-square statistic to test if opinions about spending to reduce the national crime rate (NATCRIME) are independent of respondent sex (SEX). Compare this result to a similar chi-square test involving support for law enforcement (NATCRIMY) and SEX.

6. Analyze the General Social Survey using a chi-square statistic to test if opinions about elders living with their children (AGED) will differ by sex (SEX). Next, recode age (AGE) into a new variable (AGEGRP1) with two groups (ages 18 to 64 versus 65 to 89) and then test to see if opinions about elders living with their children (AGED) differ by age group (AGEGRP1).

7. Use the General Social Survey to calculate a chi-square statistic to test the following hypothesis: Being in favor of gun permits (GUNLAW) will differ by whether you or your spouse hunts (HUNT).
8. Using the General Social Survey, calculate a chi-square statistic to test the null hypothesis that attitudes toward abortion for any reason (ABANY) do not vary by age (AGE).
   a. How large will the cross-tab be? ($r \times c$ = #cells) _____ × _____ = _____ (Remember that age goes from 18 through 89.)
   b. What percentage of cells have small expected frequencies? _____
   c. Is this acceptable? Yes/No Explain.
   d. What could be done to improve it? Explain.
9. Recode age into three groups (18 to 39 = 1)(40 to 59 = 2) (60 and older = 3) by using TRANSFORM then RECODE INTO DIFFERENT VARIABLES and naming the new

variable AGEGRP3 (for age grouped in 3 categories). Actually, the new name is up to you, but this name is fairly clear. Recalculate chi-square from the previous problem. What is the level of measurement for grouped age? Apply a chi-square statistic to test the null hypothesis that attitudes toward abortion for any reason (ABANY) do not vary by grouped age (AGEGRP3).
10. Using the General Social Survey, calculate a chi-square statistic to test the null hypothesis that views about nuclear energy (NUKEELEC) do not vary by political party affiliation (PARTY).
   a. How large will the cross-tab be? ($r \times c$ = #cells) _____ × _____ = _____
   b. What percentage of cells have small expected frequencies? _____
   c. Is this acceptable? Yes/No Explain.
   d. What could be done to improve it? Explain.

LOOKING AT THE LARGER PICTURE
Testing for Differences

Until this point, we have flirted with the idea that smoking and drinking might differ by sex. At the end of Part I, we examined bar charts for sex differences in the percentage distribution for smoking and drinking, and at the end of Part II, we constructed confidence intervals for the percentage who smoke and the mean daily use of cigarettes, overall but also separately for males and females. There seemed to be some differences between male and female students, but now we can determine whether they are statistically significant.

Our null hypothesis is that there are no differences between male and female urban public high school students in terms of smoking percentage and mean cigarette usage as well as mean drinking frequency. The following table summarizes the calculations needed for a z test of proportions (for the percentage who smoke) and the t test of means (for daily cigarettes among smokers and drinking occasions for all students).

We see quite clearly that the difference in the percentage of male and female smokers within the sample is large enough to reject the null hypothesis of no difference in population proportions. Thus, there is indeed a significant sex difference in terms of whether a student is a smoker. Turning to the daily consumption of cigarettes among the smokers, we can see that the difference between sample means for males and females is not large enough to reject the null hypothesis. Therefore, there is not enough evidence of a true sex difference in the population. The t test for differences between sample means for drinking frequency does, however, lead us to reject the null hypothesis of no difference in population means for males and females. Specifically, males and females were found significantly different in their alcohol consumption.

Tests of Differences between Groups

Variable	Statistic	Males	Females
If smoker			
	N	127	123
	%	52.8	71.5
		SE = 6.14	
		z = 3.06	
		(significant)	
Daily smoking			
	N	67	88
	Mean	15.9	17.7
		SE = 1.68	
		t = −1.08	
		(not significant)	
Occasions drinking			
	N	127	123
	Mean	1.80	1.36
		SE = 0.14	
		t = 3.09	
		(significant)	

Other background characteristics are divided into more than two groups. Suppose that we want to compare whites, blacks, Latinos, and others (with so few Asians in the sample, we should collapse this group into the "other" category). Using the analysis of variance, we determine that the race differences in smoking are not significant (although whites appeared to smoke more heavily); that is, we cannot quite reject the null hypothesis of no differences between population means for the various races. The differences in sample mean drinking frequency by race appear rather minimal and to be the result of sampling variability alone. With a tabled critical value of 2.68, the F test is not quite large enough to indicate significance for racial differences by alcohol consumption.

Testing Differences between Groups with Analysis of Variance

Variable	Statistic	White	Black	Latino	Other
Daily smoking					
	N	103	24	18	10
	Mean	18.5	13.8	14.2	13.0
			$df = 3$ and 151		
			$F = 2.38$ (not significant)		
Occasions drinking					
	N	156	44	32	18
	Mean	1.53	1.68	1.75	1.50
			$df = 3$ and 246		
			$F = 0.45$ (not significant)		

Note that we cannot assess race differences in the percentage of students who smoke using an analysis of variance, because the variable smoke/not-smoke is nominal. Instead, we can construct a cross-tabulation of smoking by race, and calculate a chi-square test. Although the sample percentages of students who smoke may differ among the races, these differences are relatively small and turn out not to be statistically significant.

Cross-Tabulation of Race and Smoking

	Smoke	Not Smoke
White	103 (66.0%)	53 (34.0%)
Black	24 (54.5%)	20 (45.5%)
Latino	18 (56.2%)	14 (43.8%)
Other	10 (55.6%)	8 (44.4%)

$\chi^2 = 2.88$, 3 df (not significant)

Finally, we might also examine a cross-tabulation comparing whether a student smokes to whether one or both parents smoke. Over three-quarters of the students with a smoker parent themselves smoke, whereas about 57% of those with nonsmoker parents smoke. Using the chi-square test, we determine that this difference is large enough to lead us to reject the null hypothesis.

Cross-Tabulation of Parental Smoking and Student Smoking

	Student Smokes	Student Does Not Smoke
Parent smokes	49 (75.4%)	16 (24.6%)
Parents do not smoke	106 (57.3%)	79 (42.7%)

$\chi^2 = 6.68$, 1 df (significant)

In Part IV of the book, we will look at the relationship between variables. We can determine the strength of association not only between parents and respondents smoking but also between age and smoking or drinking.

10

Correlation

Characteristics such as gender, intelligence, and criminal history *vary* from one person to another and, therefore, are referred to as *variables*. In earlier chapters, we have been concerned with establishing the presence or absence of a relationship between any two variables, which we will now label X and Y; for example, between gender (X) and type of offense for which one is convicted (Y), between social class (X) and support for drug legalization (Y), or between nationality (X) and sexual assault victimization (Y). Aided by the t ratio, analysis of variance, or nonparametric tests such as chi-square, we previously sought to discover whether a difference between two or more samples could be regarded as statistically significant—reflective of a true population difference—and not merely the product of sampling error.

STRENGTH OF CORRELATION

CORRELATION

The strength and direction of the relationship between two variables.

Finding that a relationship exists does not indicate much about the strength and direction of association, or **correlation**, between two variables. Many relationships are statistically significant; few express *perfect* correlation. To illustrate, we know that height and weight are associated, since the taller a person is, the more he or she tends to weigh. There are numerous exceptions to the rule, however. Some tall people weigh very little; some short people weigh a lot. In the same way, a relationship between nationality (American vs. Canadian) and sexual assault victimization does not preclude the possibility of finding many victims among Canadian students or many non-victims among American students.

Correlations actually vary with respect to their *strength*. We can visualize differences in the strength of correlation by means of a **scatter plot** or *scatter diagram*, a graph that shows the way scores on any two variables, X and Y, are scattered throughout the range of possible score values. In the conventional arrangement, a scatter plot is set up so that the X variable is located along the horizontal baseline, and the Y variable is measured on the vertical line.

Turning to Figure 10.1, we find two scatter plots, each representing the relationship between years of education (X) and income (Y) for a sample of security guards and supervisors in a private security firm. Figure 10.1(a) depicts this relationship for males, and Figure 10.1(b) represents the relationship for females. Note that each and every point in these scatter plots depicts *two*

SCATTER PLOT

A graph that shows the way scores on any two variables X and Y are scattered throughout the range of possible score values.

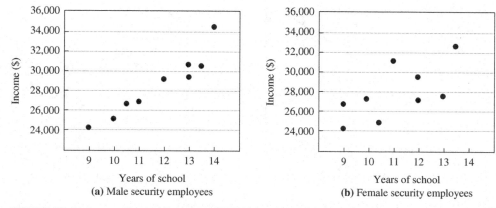

FIGURE 10.1 Scatter Plots Representing Differences in the Strength of the Relationship between Education and Income for Male and Female Employees of a Private Security Firm.

scores, education and income, obtained by *one* respondent. In Figure 10.1(a), for example, we see that a male having 9 years of education earned $24,000, whereas a male with 14 years of education made more than $34,000.

We can say that the strength of the correlation between X and Y increases as the points in a scatter plot more closely form an imaginary diagonal line across the center of the graph. Therefore, Figure 10.1(a) represents a stronger correlation than does Figure 10.1(b), although both scatter plots indicate that income tends to increase with greater education. Such data would indeed support the view that the income of women at this security firm (relative to that of men) is less related to the level of education they attain.

DIRECTION OF CORRELATION

Correlation can often be described with respect to direction as either positive or negative. A **positive correlation** indicates that respondents getting *high* scores on the X variable also tend to get *high* scores on the Y variable. Conversely, respondents who get *low* scores on X also tend to get *low* scores on Y. Positive correlation can be illustrated by the relationship between education and income. As we have previously seen, respondents completing many years of school tend to make large annual incomes, whereas those who complete only a few years of school tend to earn very little annually.

A **negative correlation** exists if respondents who obtain *high* scores on the X variable tend to obtain *low* scores on the Y variable. Conversely, respondents achieving *low* scores on X tend to achieve *high* scores on Y. The relationship between education and income would *not* represent a negative correlation, because respondents completing many years of school *do not* tend to make small annual incomes. A more likely example of negative correlation is the relationship between education and prejudice against minority groups. Prejudice tends to diminish as the level of education increases. Therefore, individuals having little formal education tend to hold strong prejudices, whereas individuals completing many years of education tend to be low with respect to prejudice.

A positive or negative correlation represents a type of **straight-line correlation**. Depicted graphically, the points in a scatter plot tend to form a straight line through the center of the graph. If a positive correlation exists, then the points in the scatter plot will cluster around the imaginary straight line indicated in Figure 10.2(a). In contrast, if a

POSITIVE CORRELATION

The direction of a relationship wherein individuals who score high on the *X* variable also score high on the *Y* variable; individuals who score low on the *X* variable also score low on the *Y* variable.

NEGATIVE CORRELATION

The direction of relationship wherein individuals who score high on the *X* variable score low on the *Y* variable; individuals who score low on the *X* variable score high on the *Y* variable.

STRAIGHT-LINE CORRELATION

Either a positive or negative correlation, so that the points in a scatter diagram tend to form a straight line through the center of the graph.

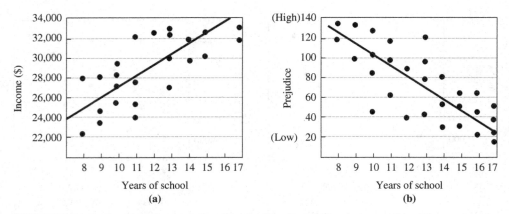

FIGURE 10.2   Scatter Plots Representing (a) a Positive Correlation between Education and Income and (b) a Negative Correlation between Education and Prejudice.

negative correlation is present, the points in the scatter plot will surround the imaginary straight line as shown in Figure 10.2(b).

CURVILINEAR CORRELATION

CURVILINEAR CORRELATION

A relationship between X and Y that begins as either positive or negative and then reverses direction.

For the most part, criminal justice researchers seek to establish straight-line correlation, whether positive or negative. It is important to note, however, that not all relationships between X and Y can be regarded as forming a straight line. There are many **curvilinear correlations**, indicating, for example, that one variable increases as the other variable increases until the relationship reverses itself, so that one variable finally decreases while the other continues to increase. That is, a relationship between X and Y that begins as positive becomes negative; a relationship that starts as negative becomes positive. To illustrate a curvilinear correlation, consider the relationship between age and fear of crime. As shown in Figure 10.3, the points in the scatter plot tend to form a U-shaped curve rather than a straight line. Thus, fear of crime tends to decrease with age until people reach their thirties after which fear tends to increase with age.

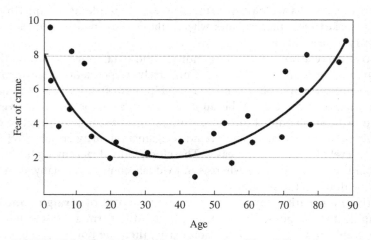

FIGURE 10.3   The Relationship between Age (X) and Fear of Crime (Y): A Curvilinear Correlation.

THE CORRELATION COEFFICIENT

The procedure for finding curvilinear correlation lies beyond the scope of this text. Instead, we turn our attention to **correlation coefficients**, which numerically express both the strength and direction of straight-line correlation. Such correlation coefficients generally range between −1.00 and +1.00 as follows:

CORRELATION COEFFICIENT

Generally ranging between −1.00 and +1.00, a number in which both the strength and direction of correlation are expressed.

−1.00 ← perfect negative correlation

−.60 ← strong negative correlation

−.30 ← moderate negative correlation

+.10 ← weak negative correlation

.00 ← no correlation

+.10 ← weak positive correlation

+.30 ← moderate positive correlation

+.60 ← strong positive correlation

+1.00 ← perfect positive correlation

We see, then, that negative numerical values such as −1.00, −.60, −.30, and −.10 signify negative correlation, whereas positive numerical values such as +1.00, +.60, +.30, and +.10 indicate positive correlation. Regarding the degree of association, the closer to 1.00 in either direction, the greater the strength of the correlation. Because the strength of a correlation is independent of its direction, we can say that −.10 and +.10 are equal in strength (both are weak); −.80 and +.80 have equal strength (both are very strong).

Pearson's Correlation Coefficient

With the aid of **Pearson's correlation coefficient** (r), we can determine the strength and the direction of the relationship between X and Y variables, both of which have been measured at the interval level. For example, we might be interested in examining the association between the length of a murder trial (in days) and the length of time (in hours) that the jury deliberates prior to reaching its verdict. Consider the following data involving a random sample of 10 trials:

PEARSON'S CORRELATION COEFFICIENT

A correlation coefficient for interval data.

Trial	Trial Length (days) X	Jury deliberation (hours) Y
A	3	6
B	1	3
C	6	11
D	5	9
E	4	10
F	7	6
G	5	12
H	2	2
I	3	3
J	4	8

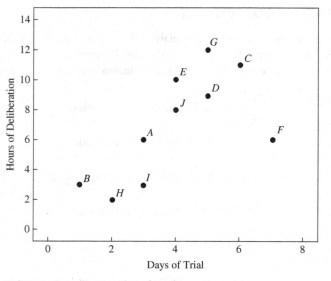

FIGURE 10.4 Scatter Plot of Trial Length and Jury Deliberation Time.

One would anticipate a positive association between trial length *(X)* and length of jury deliberation *(Y)*, as longer trials tend to involve a considerable amount of evidence for the jury to review in reaching a verdict. And the scatter plot shown in Figure 10.4 does indeed indicate a positive relationship. But note that there are some exceptions to the general rule that longer trials mean longer deliberation time. For example, Trial D took longer than trial E, but the jury in Trial D returned with its verdict sooner than the jury in Trial E. Similarly, the length of trial and deliberation for Trials F and J are opposite the general tendency.

These exceptions should not surprise us because the relationship between the length of trial and length of deliberation is not perfect. Overall, nonetheless, the observation that longer trials tend to involve longer jury deliberation times generally holds true: Trial G was much longer than Trial B, and the jury in Trial G deliberated much longer than the jury in Trial B; Trial I took a little longer than Trial H, and this resulted in a bit lengthier jury deliberation.

Pearson's *r* does more than just consider if trial length is associated with length of jury deliberation; it considers precisely how much the jury deliberation is extended with lengthier trials. The quantity that Pearson's *r* focuses on is the product of the *X* and *Y* deviations from their respective means. The deviation $(X - \overline{X})$ tells how much longer or shorter than average a particular trial is; the deviation $(Y - \overline{Y})$ tells how much longer or shorter than average a particular jury deliberation takes.

With Pearson's *r*, we add the products of the deviations to see if the positive products or negative products are more abundant and sizable. Remember, positive products indicate cases in which the variables go in the same direction (i.e., both longer than average trial and longer than average deliberation or both shorter than average trial and shorter than average deliberation); negative products indicate cases in which the variables go in opposite directions (i.e., longer than average trial but shorter than average deliberation or shorter than average trial but longer than average deliberation).

In Figure 10.5, dotted lines are added to the scatter plot of *X* and *Y* to indicate the location of the mean trial length ($\overline{X}$ = 4 days) and the mean length of jury deliberation ($\overline{Y}$ = 7 hours). Trial C took 2 days longer than average, and the jury required 4 hours longer than average to reach a verdict. These deviations from their respective mean, when multiplied, produce a product of +8. Trial D took only 1 day longer than average and its jury took only 2 hours longer than average; these deviations, when multiplied, produce a more modest product of +4. The greater influence that Trial C has over Trial D in producing the positive association, as indicated by the products of deviations, should be clear in the scatter plot. The more dramatically a trial

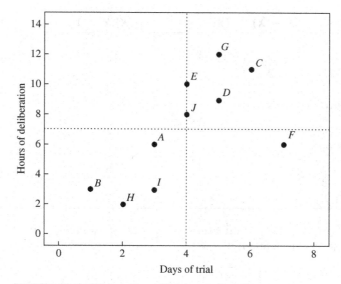

FIGURE 10.5 Scatter Plot of Trial Length and Jury Deliberation Time with Mean Axes.

demonstrates the tendency for longer trials to be associated with longer jury deliberation, the larger the product of the X and Y deviations.

On the lower end of the spectrum, Trial H was shorter in both trial length (by 2 days) and deliberation time (by 5 hours). These two negative deviations, when multiplied, produce a positive product of $+10$, which is consistent with a positive relationship between the two variables. Trial F, however, was 3 days longer than average but deliberation took 1 hour less than average; the $+3$ deviation from the mean of X and the -1 deviation from the mean of Y, when multiplied, yield a negative product of -3.

Calculating Pearson's r requires us to compute the sum of the products for all the cases. In the following table, columns two and three reproduce the trial lengths and jury deliberation times for the 10 trials in the sample. Columns four and five give the deviations from the means for the X and Y values. In column six, these deviations are multiplied and then summed.

Trial	X	Y	$(X - \bar{X})$	$(Y - \bar{Y})$	$(X - \bar{X})(Y - \bar{Y})$	
A	3	6	−1	−1	1	$N = 10$
B	1	3	−3	−4	12	$\bar{X} = 4$
C	6	11	2	4	8	$\bar{Y} = 7$
D	5	9	1	2	2	
E	4	10	0	3	0	
F	7	6	3	−1	−3	
G	5	12	1	5	5	
H	2	2	−2	−5	10	
I	3	3	−1	−4	4	
J	4	8	0	1	0	
					SP = 39	

The sum of the final column (denoted SP, for sum of products) is positive—indicating a positive association between X and Y. But, as we have learned, correlation coefficients are constrained to range from -1 to $+1$ to aid in their interpretation. The formula for r accomplishes this by dividing the SP value by the square root of the product of the sum of squares of both variables (SS_X and SS_Y). Thus, we need to add two more columns to our table in which we square and sum the deviations for X and for Y.

Trial	X	Y	$(X - \bar{X})$	$(Y - \bar{Y})$	$(X - \bar{X})(Y - \bar{Y})$	$(X - \bar{X})^2$	$(Y - \bar{Y})^2$
A	3	6	−1	−1	1	1	1
B	1	3	−3	−4	12	9	16
C	6	11	2	4	8	4	16
D	5	9	1	2	2	1	4
E	4	10	0	3	0	0	9
F	7	6	3	−1	−3	9	1
G	5	12	1	5	5	1	25
H	2	2	−2	−5	10	4	25
I	3	3	−1	−4	4	1	16
J	4	8	0	1	0	0	1
					SP = 39	SS_x = 30	SS_y = 114

With the sum of products (SP) and the sums of squares (SS_X and SS_Y), we have all that we need to calculate Pearson's correlation r:

$$r = \frac{SP}{\sqrt{SS_X SS_Y}}$$

$$= \frac{\Sigma(X - \bar{X})(Y - \bar{Y})}{\sqrt{\Sigma(X - \bar{X})^2 \Sigma(Y - \bar{Y})^2}}$$

$$= \frac{39}{\sqrt{(30)(114)}}$$

$$= \frac{39}{\sqrt{3420}}$$

$$= \frac{39}{58.48}$$

$$= +.667$$

Therefore, as suggested by the scatter plot, there is a fairly strong correlation between trial length and jury deliberation time.

A Computational Formula for Pearson's *r*

Computing Pearson's r from deviations helps relate the topic of correlation to our earlier discussions. However, the previous formula for Pearson's r requires lengthy and time-consuming calculations. Fortunately, there is an alternative formula for Pearson's r that works directly with raw scores, thereby eliminating the need to obtain deviations for the X and Y variables. Similar to the computational formulas for variance and standard deviation in Chapter 4, there are raw-score formulas for SP, SS_X, and SS_Y:

$$SP = \Sigma XY - N\bar{X}\bar{Y}$$
$$SS_X = \Sigma X^2 - N\bar{X}^2$$
$$SS_Y = \Sigma Y^2 - N\bar{Y}^2$$

Using these expressions in our formula for Pearson's correlation, we obtain the following computational formula for r:

$$r = \frac{\Sigma XY - N\bar{X}\bar{Y}}{\sqrt{\left(\Sigma X^2 - N\bar{X}^2\right)\left(\Sigma Y^2 - N\bar{Y}^2\right)}}$$

To illustrate the use of Pearson's r computational formula, consider the following data on the number of years of education (X) and the belief that drug treatment for offenders is an effective strategy for preventing crime (Y). Belief (Y) was measured on a 20-point scale, with higher scores indicating greater faith in the crime prevention effectiveness of drug treatment. To apply our formula, we must obtain the sums of X and Y (to calculate the means) and of X^2, Y^2, and XY:

X	Y	X²	Y²	XY	
12	12	144	144	144	$N = 8$
10	8	100	64	80	$\Sigma X = 84$
6	12	36	144	72	$\Sigma Y = 92$
16	11	256	121	176	$\bar{X} = \frac{\Sigma X}{N} = \frac{84}{8} = 10.5$
8	10	64	100	80	
9	8	81	64	72	$\bar{Y} = \frac{\Sigma Y}{N} = \frac{92}{8} = 11.5$
12	16	144	256	192	
11	15	121	225	165	$\Sigma X^2 = 946$
84	92	946	1,118	981	$\Sigma Y^2 = 1,118$
					$\Sigma XY = 981$

The Pearson's correlation is then equal to

$$r = \frac{\Sigma XY - N\bar{X}\bar{Y}}{\sqrt{\left(\Sigma X^2 - N\bar{X}^2\right)\left(\Sigma Y^2 - N\bar{Y}^2\right)}}$$

$$= \frac{981 - 8(10.5)(11.5)}{\sqrt{[946 - 8(10.5)^2][1118 - 8(11.5)^2]}}$$

$$= \frac{981 - 966}{\sqrt{(946 - 882)(1118 - 1058)}}$$

$$= \frac{15}{\sqrt{(64)(60)}}$$

$$= \frac{15}{\sqrt{3840}}$$

$$= \frac{15}{61.97}$$

$$= +.24$$

Thus, there is a modest positive correlation between education and belief in the efficacy of drug treatment.

Testing the Significance of Pearson's r

Pearson's r gives us a precise measure of the strength and direction of the correlation in the sample being studied. If we have taken a random sample from a specified population, we may still seek to determine whether the obtained association between X and Y exists in the *population* and is not due merely to sampling error.

To test the significance of a measure of correlation, we usually set up the null hypothesis that no correlation exists in the population. With respect to the Pearson correlation coefficient, the null hypothesis states that the population correlation ρ (rho) is zero. That is,

$$\rho = 0$$

whereas the research hypothesis says that

$$\rho \neq 0$$

As was the case in earlier chapters, we test the null hypothesis by selecting the alpha level of .05 or .01 and computing an appropriate test of significance. To test the significance of Pearson's r, we can compute a t ratio with the degrees of freedom equal to $N - 2$ (N equals the number of pairs of scores). For this purpose, the t ratio can be computed by the formula,

$$t = \frac{r\sqrt{N-2}}{\sqrt{1-r^2}}$$

where

$t = t$ ratio for testing the statistical significance of Pearson's r

$N =$ number of pairs of scores X and Y

$r =$ obtained Pearson's correlation coefficient

Returning to the previous example, we can test the significance of a correlation coefficient equal to +.24 between educational level (X) and the belief that offender drug treatment is an effective strategy for reducing crime (Y).

$$t = \frac{.24\sqrt{8-2}}{\sqrt{1-(.24)^2}}$$

$$= \frac{(.24)(2.45)}{\sqrt{1-.0576}}$$

$$= \frac{.59}{\sqrt{.9424}}$$

$$= \frac{.59}{.97}$$

$$= .61$$

When we turn to Table C in Appendix C, we find that the critical value of t with 6 degrees of freedom and $\alpha = .05$ is 2.447. Because our calculated t value does not even come close to exceeding this critical value, we cannot reject the null hypothesis $\rho = 0$. Although a correlation of +.24 is not weak, with a sample size of only 8, it is not nearly statistically significant. That is, given a small sample size of 8, it is very possible that the obtained r of +.24 is a result of sampling error. Thus, we are forced to retain the null hypothesis that the population correlation (ρ) is zero, at least until we have more data bearing on the relationship between education and belief in the crime prevention benefits of offender drug treatment.

A Simplified Method for Testing the Significance of r

Fortunately, the process of testing the significance of Pearson's r as previously illustrated has been simplified, so that it becomes unnecessary actually to compute a t ratio. Instead, we turn to Table H in Appendix C, where we find a list of significant values of Pearson's r for the .05 and .01 levels of significance with the number of degrees of freedom ranging from 1 to 90. Directly comparing our calculated value of r with the appropriate table value yields the same result as though we had actually computed a t ratio. If the calculated Pearson's correlation coefficient does not exceed the appropriate table value, we must retain the null hypothesis that $\rho = 0$; if, on the other hand, the calculated r is greater than the table critical value, we reject the null hypothesis and accept the research hypothesis that a correlation exists in the population.

For illustrative purposes, let us return to our previous example in which a correlation coefficient equal to +.24 was tested by means of a t ratio and found not to be statistically significant. Turning to Table H in Appendix C, we now find that the value of r must be at least .7067 to reject the null hypothesis at the .05 level of significance with 6 degrees of freedom. Hence, this simplified method leads us to the same conclusion as the longer procedure of computing a t ratio.

STEP BY STEP ILLUSTRATION

Pearson's Correlation Coefficient

A criminologist is conducting research on the relationship between juvenile delinquency and subsequent criminality during adulthood. She selects a sample of 12 offenders with juvenile arrest records and then collects information about their adult criminal history. Specifically, she is interested in the correlation between the age of first juvenile arrest and number of arrests between ages 18 and 30. Her overall research question is whether the extent of adult criminality is associated with how early in life one's criminal career begins.

The data on age at first arrest (X) and number of adult arrests (Y) are shown in the table that follows:

Age of First Juvenile Arrest (X)	Number of Adult Arrests (Y)
14	5
12	3
15	4
13	5
16	0
17	1
13	2
15	0
16	2
16	1
17	0
16	1

With these data, the criminologist establishes her null and research hypotheses as

$$\text{Null hypothesis:} \quad \rho = 0$$
$$\text{Research hypothesis:} \quad \rho \neq 0$$

Note that the hypotheses indicate a two-tailed test, permitting the null hypothesis to be rejected for either large positive or large negative correlations. Had the criminologist anticipated the direction (e.g., the earlier the start to a criminal career, the higher the rate of offending), a one-tailed test could have been employed.

To calculate and test the Pearson's correlation (r), we proceed through the following steps:

Step 1 Find the values of $\sum X$, $\sum Y$, $\sum X^2$, $\sum Y^2$, and $\sum XY$, as well as $\overline{X}$ and $\overline{Y}$.

X	Y	X^2	Y^2	XY	
14	5	196	25	70	$N = 12$
12	3	144	9	36	$\sum X = 180$
15	4	225	16	60	$\sum Y = 24$
13	5	169	25	65	
16	0	256	0	0	$\overline{X} = \dfrac{\sum X}{N} = \dfrac{180}{12} = 15$
17	1	289	1	17	
13	2	169	4	26	$\overline{Y} = \dfrac{\sum Y}{N} = \dfrac{24}{12} = 2$
15	0	225	0	0	
16	2	256	4	32	$\sum X^2 = 2730$
16	1	256	1	16	$\sum Y^2 = 86$
17	0	289	0	0	$\sum XY = 338$
16	1	256	1	16	
180	24	2,730	86	338	

Step 2 Insert the values from Step 1 into Pearson's correlation formula.

$$r = \frac{\sum XY - N\overline{X}\overline{Y}}{\sqrt{[\sum X^2 - N\overline{X}^2][\sum Y^2 - N\overline{Y}^2]}}$$

$$= \frac{338 - (12)(15)(2)}{\sqrt{[2730 - (12)(15)^2][86 - (12)(2)^2]}}$$

$$= \frac{338 - 360}{\sqrt{(2730 - 2700)(86 - 48)}}$$

$$= \frac{-22}{\sqrt{(30)(38)}}$$

$$= \frac{-22}{\sqrt{1140}}$$

$$= \frac{-22}{33.76}$$

$$= -.652$$

Our result indicates a rather strong negative correlation between age at first arrest and the subsequent number of adult arrests.

Step 3 Find the degrees of freedom.

$$df = N - 2$$
$$= 12 - 2$$
$$= 10$$

Step 4 Calculate the t ratio and compare it to the appropriate value in Table C in Appendix C.

$$t = \frac{r\sqrt{N - 2}}{\sqrt{1 - r^2}}$$

$$= \frac{-.652\sqrt{12 - 2}}{\sqrt{1 - (-.652)^2}}$$

$$= \frac{-.652(3.162)}{\sqrt{1 - .425}}$$

$$= \frac{-2.062}{.0758}$$

$$= -2.719$$

$$df = N - 2 = 10$$
$$\alpha = .05$$
$$\text{table } t = 2.226$$

Because the t ratio (-2.719) is larger in magnitude than the table value, the null hypothesis of no correlation in the population of all offenders can be rejected. The observed correlation between age of onset of juvenile delinquency and subsequent number of adult arrests by age 30 is statistically significant.

Requirements for the Use of Pearson's Correlation Coefficient

To employ Pearson's correlation coefficient correctly as a measure of association between X and Y variables, the following requirements must be taken into account:

1. *A straight-line relationship.* Pearson's r is only useful for detecting a straight-line correlation between X and Y.
2. *Interval data.* Both X and Y variables must be measured at the interval level, so that scores may be assigned to the respondents.
3. *Random sampling.* Sample members must have been drawn at random from a specified population to apply a test of significance.
4. *Normally distributed characteristics.* Testing the significance of Pearson's r requires both X and Y variables to be normally distributed in the population. In small samples, failure to meet the requirement of normally distributed characteristics may seriously impair the validity of the test. However, this requirement is of minor importance when the sample size equals or exceeds 30 cases.

THE IMPORTANCE OF SCATTER PLOTS

It seems instinctive to look for shortcuts and time-saving devices in our lives. For criminal justice researchers, the development of high-speed computers and simple statistical software has become what the advent of the automatic washer and liquid detergent was for the housekeeper. Unfortunately, these statistical programs have been used too often without sufficient concern for their appropriateness. This is particularly true in correlational analysis.

The correlation coefficient is a very powerful statistical measure. Moreover, for a data set containing several variables, with a computer, one can obtain a *correlation matrix* in just seconds, such as that in Table 10.1.

A correlation matrix displays in compact form the interrelationships of several variables simultaneously. Along the diagonal from the upper-left corner to the bottom-right corner is a series of 1.00s. These represent the correlation of each variable with itself, and so they are necessarily perfect and therefore equal to one. The off-diagonal entries are the intercorrelations. The entry in the second row, fourth column (.78) gives the correlation of $X2$ and $X4$ (offender's and spouse's education). The matrix is symmetrical—that is, the triangular portion above the diagonal is identical to that below the diagonal. Thus, the entry for the fourth row, second column is .78 as well.

The value of computer programs that produce results like this is that the researcher can quickly glance at the intercorrelations of a large number of variables—say 10—and quickly pick out the strong and interesting correlations. One immediate problem, as we discussed earlier in reference to analysis of variance, is that such a fishing expedition of a large number of correlations will tend to pick up correlations that are significant by chance. An even greater pitfall, however, is that correlations may gloss over some major violations of the assumptions of Pearson's r. That is, a correlation matrix provides only (linear) correlation coefficients; it does not tell if the relationships are linear in the first place or whether there are peculiarities in the data that are worth noting. To prevent falling victim to data peculiarities, one really should inspect scatter plots before jumping to conclusions about what is related to what.

It is a far more tedious task to look at scatter plots in conjunction with the correlation matrix, because they must be examined one pair at a time. For example, to inspect scatter plots for all pairs of 10 variables would require 45 plots and a great deal of time and effort. As a result, far too many students and researchers skip over this step, often with misleading or disastrous

TABLE 10.1 A Correlation Matrix				
	Offender's Age *X1*	Offender's Education *X2*	Family Income *X3*	Spouse's Education *X4*
X1	1.00	−.48	.35	−.30
X2	−.48	1.00	.67	.78
X3	.35	.67	1.00	.61
X4	−.30	.78	.61	1.00

results. Sometimes, as we shall see, what seems like a strong association on the basis of the correlation coefficient may be proven illusory after seeing the scatter plot. Conversely, truly important associations may be misrepresented by the single summary value of Pearson's *r*.

Consider, for example, the following data on homicide and suicide rates (per 100,000 population) for the six New England states:

State	Homicide Rate	Suicide Rate
Maine	3.2	14.3
New Hampshire	2.9	11.3
Vermont	4.3	17.8
Massachusetts	3.6	8.9
Rhode Island	4.2	12.3
Connecticut	5.4	8.6

Source: U.S. Bureau of the Census. *Statistical Abstract of the United States.* Washington, D.C., n.d.

The correlation coefficient is $-.17$, suggesting a weak to moderate negative relationship. This would seem to support the contention of some researchers that these two forms of violence (other-directed and self-directed) are trade-offs; when one rate is high, the other rate is low.

Before we get too excited about this result, however, let's inspect the scatter plot in Figure 10.6. Although the scatter plot appears to show a slight negative association, the lower-right-hand point deserves further consideration. This corresponds to Connecticut. There is some justification for suspecting that Connecticut is in fact systematically different from the rest of the New England states. Suppose, for the sake of argument, we exclude Connecticut and recalculate the correlation. By using only the five other states, $r = .44$. Indeed, Connecticut has both the lowest suicide rate and the highest homicide rate in New England, which seems to have distorted the initial correlation coefficient.

There are statistical procedures for determining if this or any other data point should be excluded; they are, however, beyond the scope of this book. Nevertheless, the importance of inspecting for these so-called *outliers* is a lesson well worth learning. It can be distressing to promote a particular correlation as substantively meaningful, only to find later that the exclusion of one or two observations radically alters the results and interpretation.

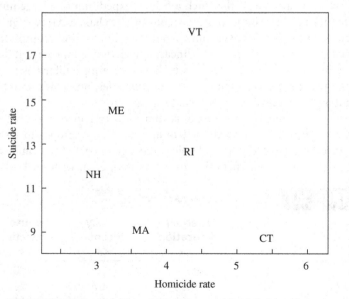

FIGURE 10.6 Scatter Plot of Homicide and Suicide Rates in New England.

PARTIAL CORRELATION

In this chapter, we have considered a powerful method for studying the association or relationship between two interval-level variables. It is important to consider if a correlation between two measures holds up when controlling for additional variables. That is, does our interpretation of the relationship between two variables change in any way when looking at the broader context of other related factors?

To see this most easily, we will focus again on scatter plots. A scatter plot visually displays all the information contained in a correlation coefficient—both its direction (by the trend underlying the points) and its strength (by the closeness of the points to a straight line). We can construct separate scatter plots for different subgroups of a sample to see if the correlation observed for the full sample holds when controlling for the subgroup or control variable. For example, there has been some research in recent years on the relationship between physical characteristics (such as attractiveness) and professional attainment (e.g., salary or goal fulfillment). Suppose that within the context of studying the relationship between personal attributes and salary, a criminal justice researcher stumbles upon a strong positive association between height and salary among parole officers, as shown in Figure 10.7. This would make sense to the researcher; he or she reasons that taller people tend to be more assertive and are afforded greater respect from others, which pays off in being successful in requests for raises.

But this researcher could be misled—in total or in part—if he or she fails to bring into the analysis other relevant factors that might alternatively account for the height–salary correlation. Gender is one such possible variable. Male officers tend to be taller than female offices, and, for a variety of reasons, tend to be paid more. Perhaps this could explain all or part of the strong correlation between height and salary. Figure 10.7 also provides scatter plots of height and salary separately for males and females in the sample. It is important to note, first, that if we superimposed these two scatter plots, they would produce the original plot.

Apparently, when we control for gender, the height–salary correlation weakens substantially—in fact, disappears. If any correlation remains in either of the two gender-specific subplots, it is nowhere near as strong as that which we saw at first in the uncontrolled scatter plot. Thus, had the researcher failed to consider the influence of gender, he or she would have been greatly misled.

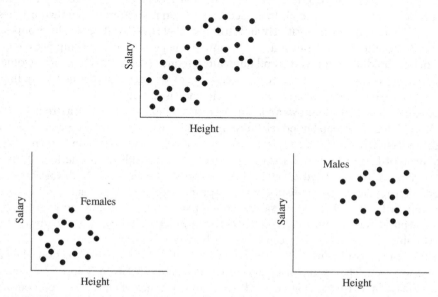

FIGURE 10.7 Scatter Plot of Salary and Height of Parole Officers Controlling for Gender.

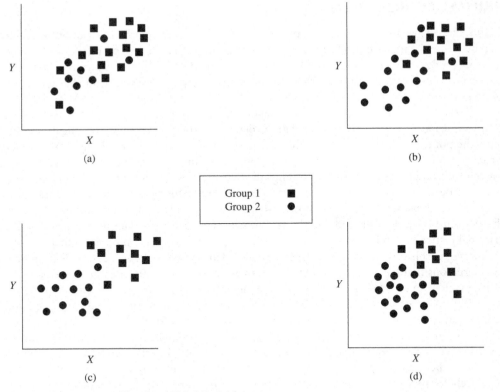

FIGURE 10.8   Controlling for a Third Variable.

Figure 10.8 illustrates additional possible outcomes when a control variable is introduced. Each scatter plot represents a positive correlation between X and Y. Observations in subgroup 1 are symbolized by squares and those in subgroup 2 by circles. This allows us to see the X–Y relationship within the two subgroups separately. Note that these are prototypes—in practice, one may not observe such clear-cut situations.

In scatter plot Figure 10.8(a), we see that the X–Y association observed overall holds for each subgroup as well. Group 1 tends to exceed Group 2 on both X and Y, and within these two groups, X and Y are still related positively and strongly. That is, controlling for the grouping variable does not alter the X–Y relationship. For example, the positive relationship between education and income holds both for whites and nonwhites. If one observes this kind of outcome when testing for a range of control variables (e.g., race, sex, age), one develops confidence in interpreting the association (e.g., between education and income) as causal.

Scatter plot Figure 10.8(b) shows a conditional relationship. Again, there is a strong relationship between X and Y for one group but no relationship for the other. If the grouping variable is ignored, the correlation between X and Y misrepresents the more accurate picture within the subgroups.

Scatter plot Figure 10.8(c) illustrates a spurious or misleading correlation. Within both subgroups, X and Y are unrelated. Overall, Group 1 tends to be higher on both variables. As a result, when ignoring the subgroup distinction, it appears as if X and Y are related. Our association noted previously between height and salary among parole officers is an example of a spurious correlation. Spurious correlations frequently occur in practice, and one should always be wary that two variables are related only because of their having a common cause.

Finally, scatter plot Figure 10.8(d) shows a relationship that changes direction when a third variable is controlled. That is, the original positive association between X and Y becomes negative within the two subgroups. That Group 1 was so much greater than Group 2 on both X and Y overshadowed the negative relationship within each subgroup. This type of situation occurs rarely in practice, but one still should be aware that an apparent finding could be just the opposite of what it should be.

All the comparisons we have considered thus far involve dichotomous (two-category) control variables. The same approach applies to control variables having three or more levels or categories. For example, one could investigate the influence of religion on the relationship between two variables by computing Pearson's r separately for Protestants, Catholics, and Jews.

How would one handle an interval-level control variable like age? There is a temptation to categorize age into a number of subgroups (e.g., under 18, 18–34, 35–49, 50 and older) and then to plot the X–Y association separately for each age category. This, however, would be both inefficient and a waste of information (e.g., the distinction between 18 and 34-year-olds is lost because these two ages are within the same category). Perhaps, then, we could use narrower age groups, but we still are being less precise than we could be. Fortunately, a simple method exists for adjusting a correlation between two variables for the influence of a third variable, when all three are interval level. That is, we do not have to categorize any variables artificially.

The **partial correlation coefficient** is the correlation between two variables, after removing (or partialing out) the common effects of a third variable. Like simple correlations, a partial correlation can range from −1 to +1 and is interpreted exactly the same way as a simple correlation. The formula for the partial correlation of X and Y controlling for Z is

PARTIAL CORRELATION COEFFICIENT

The correlation between two variables when one or more other variables are controlled.

$$r_{XY.Z} = \frac{r_{XY} - r_{XZ}r_{YZ}}{\sqrt{1 - r_{XZ}^2}\sqrt{1 - r_{YZ}^2}}$$

In the notation $r_{XY.Z}$ the variables before the period are those being correlated, and the variable after the period is the control variable. The partial correlation is computed exclusively on the basis of three quantities: the correlations between X and Y, X and Z, and Y and Z.

Suppose, for example, a consultant for a big city police department finds a −.44 correlation between performance on a physical fitness test (X) and salary (Y) for a sample of 50 police officers. At first glance, this might suggest that the police department pays a lower salary to its officers if they are in top physical shape. However, it makes sense that the number of years on the police force (Z) could be influencing both physical fitness and salary level.

	Physical Fitness (X)	Salary (Y)	Years on Force (Z)
Physical fitness (X)	1.00	−.44	−.68
Salary(Y)	−.44	1.00	.82
Years on force (Z)	−.68	.82	1.00

On the basis of these correlations, the partial correlation of physical fitness score (X) and salary (Y) holding constant years on the force (Z) can be calculated as follows:

$$r_{XY.Z} = \frac{r_{XY} - r_{XZ}r_{YZ}}{\sqrt{1 - r_{XZ}^2}\sqrt{1 - r_{YZ}^2}}$$

$$= \frac{(-.44) - (-.68)(.82)}{\sqrt{1 - (-.68)^2}\sqrt{1 - (.82)^2}}$$

$$= \frac{(-.44) - (-.56)}{\sqrt{1 - (-.46)}\sqrt{1 - (.67)}}$$

$$= \frac{.12}{\sqrt{1.46}\sqrt{.33}}$$

$$= \frac{.12}{(1.21)(.57)}$$

$$= \frac{.12}{.6897}$$

$$= +.17$$

Thus, the negative correlation between physical fitness score and salary becomes positive after controlling for the number of years on the police force.

The statistical significance of a partial correlation can be tested using a t ratio by using the same approach for Pearson's correlations, except that $N - 2$ is replaced by $N - 3$ in the t formula and for the degrees of freedom. The consultant obtained a partial correlation $r_{XY.Z} = .17$ with $N = 50$ cases. Thus,

$$\boxed{t = r_{XY.Z}\sqrt{\frac{N - 3}{1 - r_{XY.Z}^2}}}$$

$$= \frac{.17\sqrt{47}}{\sqrt{1 - (.17)^2}}$$

$$= \frac{.17(6.86)}{\sqrt{1 - .0289}}$$

$$= \frac{1.17}{.9854}$$

$$= 1.19$$

Because this t ratio does not exceed the value found in Table C in Appendix for $df = 47$ and $\alpha = .05$ (table $t = 2.021$), we conclude that the partial correlation of .17 with $N = 50$ cases is not statistically significant.

The partial correlation coefficient is a very useful statistic for finding spurious relationships, as is demonstrated in this classic case of a "vanishing" correlation.[1] The correlation between the rate of rape (per 100,000) in 1982 and the circulation of *Playboy* (per 100,000) in 1979 for 49 U.S. states (Alaska is an outlier on rape and is excluded) is $r = +40$. Because of this substantial correlation, many observers have asked: If *Playboy* has this kind of effect on sex crimes, imagine what harm may be caused by truly hardcore pornography?

This concern stems from the unjustified assumption that the correlation implies cause. Before making such a leap, however, we need to consider whether the two variables have a third variable as a common cause, thereby producing a spurious result.

As it turns out, both the rape and the *Playboy* subscription rates are related to the rate of homes without an adult female (per 1,000 households): For the rape rate (Y) and the rate of homes without an adult female (Z), $r_{YZ} = +.48$: for the rate of subscription to *Playboy* (X) and the rate of homes without an adult female (Z), $r_{YZ} = +.85$. Apparently both types of sexual outlet (one illegal and one legal) sometimes stem from the absence of adult females in the home.

To determine the correlation of *Playboy* (X) with rape (Y), controlling for homes without adult females (Z), we calculate the partial correlation:

$$r_{XY.Z} = \frac{r_{XY} - r_{XZ}r_{YZ}}{\sqrt{1 - r_{XZ}^2}\sqrt{1 - r_{YZ}^2}}$$

$$= \frac{.40 - (.85)(.48)}{\sqrt{1 - (.85)^2}\sqrt{1 - (.48)^2}}$$

[1]We thank Rodney Stark and Cognitive Development, Inc., for this fine illustration and for these data.

$$= \frac{.40 - .41}{\sqrt{1 - .7225}\sqrt{1 - .2304}}$$

$$= \frac{-.01}{\sqrt{.2775}\sqrt{.7696}}$$

$$= \frac{-.01}{(.53)(.88)}$$

$$= \frac{-.01}{.47}$$

$$= -.02$$

As a result, after controlling for one common variable, the original correlation disappears.

Summary

In this chapter, we went beyond the task of establishing the presence or absence of a relationship between two variables. In correlation, the criminal justice researcher is interested in the degree of association between the two variables. With the aid of the correlation coefficient known as Pearson's r, it is possible to obtain a precise measure of both the strength (from 0.0 to 1.0) and direction (positive vs. negative) of a relationship between two variables that have been measured at the interval level. Moreover, if a researcher has taken a random sample of scores, he or she may also compute a t ratio to determine whether the obtained relationship between X and Y exists in the population and is not due merely to sampling error. In addition, the partial correlation coefficient allows the researcher to control a two-variable relationship for the impact of a third variable.

Questions and Problems

1. When the points in a scatter plot cluster closely around a straight line, the correlation can be said to be _____.
   a. weak
   b. strong
   c. positive
   d. negative
2. A correlation coefficient expresses in a single number _____.
   a. the strength of a correlation
   b. the direction of a correlation
   c. both the strength and direction of a correlation
   d. the normality of a correlation
3. $r = -.73$ indicates a correlation that is fairly _____.
   a. strong and negative
   b. strong and positive
   c. weak and negative
   d. weak and positive
4. Which pair of correlations is strong?
   a. .73 and −.25
   b. −81 and .72
   c. .31 and .81
   d. .22 and −.11
5. Which of the following is not required by Pearson's r?
   a. a straight-line relationship
   b. nominal data
   c. random sample
   d. normally distributed characteristics
6. The following six students were questioned regarding (X), their attitudes toward the legalization of prostitution, and (Y), their attitudes toward the legalization of marijuana. Using the computational formula, compute a Pearson's r correlation coefficient for these data and determine whether the correlation is significant.

Student	X	Y
A	1	2
B	6	5
C	4	3
D	3	3
E	2	1
F	7	4

7. A criminologist wonders if there is a relationship between how often people watch television news (X) and their fear of crime (Y). The researcher conducts a survey asking how many days per week participants watch the local television news and how afraid they are to walk in their own neighborhood after dark. Degree of fear is measured on a scale from 0 to 10, where 0 is "none at all" and 10 is "completely." Using the computational formula, compute a Pearson's r correlation

coefficient for these data and determine whether the correlation is significant.

Watch TV News (Days/Week)	Fear (0–10)
1	2
2	7
2	2
3	5
3	3
6	5
6	5
6	5
7	3
7	3

8. A researcher interested in the consistency of school absenteeism over time studied a sample of eight high school students for whom complete school records were available. The researcher counted the number of days each student had missed school while in the 6th grade and then in the 10th grade. Using the computational formula, compute a Pearson's *r* correlation coefficient for these data and determine whether the correlation is significant.

Student	Days Missed (6th)	Days Missed (10th)
A	4	10
B	2	4
C	21	11
D	1	3
E	3	1
F	5	5
G	4	9
H	8	5

9. The following is a correlation matrix among unemployment rate (X), violent crime rate (Y), and divorce rate (Z) for a random sample of 50 cities.

	X	Y	Z
X	1.00	0.60	0.20
Y	0.60	1.00	0.30
Z	0.20	0.30	1.00

a. Which correlations are significant at the .05 level?
b. What is the partial correlation between unemployment rate and violent crime rate, holding the divorce rate constant? Discuss the difference between simple correlation r_{XY} and the partial correlation $r_{XY.Z}$.

10. A professor of criminal justice is studying the accuracy of eyewitness testimony and wonders whether particularly gruesome and horrible crimes are recalled accurately. To a sample of 10 adults, he shows videotapes of crimes that have been pretested and rated for the level of horror and disgust that witnesses experience (ranging from "0" for relatively benign crimes such as auto theft to a "7" for a brutal murder). The subjects view each one of the scenarios and are asked a series of questions about its details, such as the race and approximate age of the offender, the length of time the crime took to complete, and so on. The researcher's hypothesis was that witnesses would make more factual errors in their recollections of events of more shocking and horrible crimes.

Crime Scenario Rating (X)	Number of Errors (Y)
0	3
7	1
2	2
1	2
5	0
4	1
3	3
3	2
0	7
1	4

Determine the strength and direction of the correlation between the horror and disgust that witnesses experience and factual errors in the recollections of these crimes. Is the correlation significant at the .05 level?

11. A researcher is interested in the relationship between job experience and job stress. From a sample of 10 correctional officers, she collects data on the number of years of correctional work experience (X) and job stress (Y) measured on a scale ranging from 0 (none) to 10 (severe).

Years	Stress
0	10
1	9
1	8
2	8
2	7
3	6
3	5
4	4
4	5
4	3

Determine the strength and direction of the correlation between the length of correctional experience and job stress. Is the correlation significant at the .05 level?

12. A researcher was interested in determining the degree of association between unemployment rate (X) and the homicide rate per 100,000 (Y). She found data on both variables for the 14 largest cities in her region of the country. The results were as follows:

Unemployment Rate	Homicide Rate
6.5	1.2
7.1	4.7
6.0	4.5
5.2	4.0
7.9	2.1
8.2	3.4
5.5	6.2
6.2	1.6
5.2	5.3
7.2	4.1
7.7	1.5
5.9	1.1
6.3	2.3
7.5	1.3

a. Calculate Pearson's r.

b. Is the correlation between unemployment and the murder rate significant at the .01 level?

c. Is it significant at the .05 level?

d. Interpret the results. Be sure to discuss the importance of stating the null hypothesis.

13. A researcher is interested in studying the relationship between length of unemployment and job-seeking activity among offenders recently released from prison. He interviews a sample of 12 unemployed offenders recently released into the community, obtaining the number of weeks they have been unemployed (X), the number of job applications they have submitted during the past week (Y), and their age (Z). The results of his study follow:

X	Y	Z
2	8	30
7	3	42
5	4	36
12	2	47
1	5	29
10	2	56
8	1	52
6	5	40
5	4	27
2	6	31
3	7	36
4	1	33

a. Calculate Pearson's correlation coefficient and test the null hypothesis that there is no relationship between length of time unemployed and the number of job applications.

b. Determine the partial correlation of number of weeks unemployed and the number of job applications, holding the age of the offender constant.

Computer Exercises

1. Analyze the General Social Survey to generate a single correlation matrix that will allow you to test the following null hypotheses:

   Null hypothesis 1:   There is no relationship between days of poor mental health during the past 30 days (MNTLHLTH) and days of poor physical health during the past 30 days (PHYSHLTH).

   Null hypothesis 2:   There is no relationship between days of poor mental health during the past 30 days (MNTLHLTH) and age (AGE).

   Null hypothesis 3:   There is no relationship between days of poor physical health during the past 30 days (PHYSHLTH) and age (AGE).

   Create a correlation matrix of the three variables. Report the strength and direction of the Pearson's r correlation coefficients. *Hint:* ANALYZE, CORRELATE, BIVARIATE and choose the variables.

2. Generate a single correlation matrix that will allow you to test the null hypothesis of no relationship for all of the following pairs of variables from the General Social Survey:

   Job satisfaction (JOBSAT1) and income (REALRINC);
   Job satisfaction (JOBSAT1) and years of education (EDUC);
   Income (REALRINC) and education (EDUC); and
   Days of poor mental health during the past 30 days (MNTLHLTH) and job satisfaction (JOBSAT1).

   a. Create the correlation matrix.

   b. Report the strength and direction of the Pearson's r correlation coefficients for each pair of variables.

   c. What other pairs of variables could be tested using this same correlation matrix?

3. The subculture of violence theory is sometimes used to explain why some groups are more likely than others to use violence. The General Social Survey has five questions asking people if they would say that it is okay for police to use force in different situations (POLABUSE, POLATTAK, POLESCAP,

POLHITOK, and POLMURDR). The scale variable SUBCULT counts the number of "yes" responses about police use of force. It ranges from 0 to 5 with a higher number indicating a greater support for a subculture of violence. Use the General Social Survey to generate a single correlation matrix to test the null hypothesis of no relationship for all of the following pairs of variables:

> Subculture of violence (SUBCULT) and political views (POLVIEWS);
> Subculture of violence (SUBCULT) and individual income (RINCOM06);
> Individual income (RINCOM06) and political views (POLVIEWS); and
> Another variable of your choice to correlate with subculture of violence (SUBCULT).

a. Create the correlation matrix.
b. Report the strength and direction of the Pearson's *r* correlation coefficients for each pair of variables.

4. Using the General Social Survey, calculate Pearson's *r* to test the following null hypotheses:

Null hypothesis 1: Respondents' highest year of school completed (EDUC) is not related to their fathers' highest year of school completed (PAEDUC).

Null hypothesis 2: Respondent's highest year of school completed (EDUC) is not related to personal income (REALRINC).

a. Create the correlation matrix.
b. Report the strength and direction of the Pearson's *r* correlation coefficients for each pair of variables.

5. Choose two variables from the General Social Survey so that you may generate and interpret a Pearson's *r* correlation to test the null hypothesis of no correlation between the variables.

11

Regression Analysis

Certain concepts of statistics, such as percentages and means, are so commonplace that you may have understood them long before taking a statistics course. Other concepts are new, and in the process of learning statistics thoroughly, you'll begin to see the usefulness of measures that initially you may have learned to calculate by just "plugging into" a formula. It is analogous to becoming fluent in a foreign language: Initially one needs a dictionary to translate words, but later the context of the words also becomes meaningful.

In Chapter 4, we learned a new concept, that of variance. We also saw that in some instances, it was an even more important concept than the mean. But still you may not yet have a feel for what the variance signifies and its fundamental role in statistics. In the context of **regression analysis**, the important notion of variance should become clearer.

REGRESSION ANALYSIS

A technique employed in predicting values of one variable (Y) from knowledge of values of another variable (X).

Let's reconsider the problem in Chapter 4 concerning the length of sentences given to criminal defendants. Suppose that a criminologist collected data on sentences given to defendants convicted under a gun control law, which mandates a 1-year prison term for the illegal possession of a firearm. Obviously, the entire data set would consist of 12-month sentences. Although knowing how many people had been sentenced under the law might be mildly interesting, the mean sentence length of 12 would be of no analytic value: All sentences would be 12 months, and so the variance would be zero.

To learn something about sentencing patterns and the tendencies of judges in handing out their sentences, the criminologist would be far better off focusing on a crime for which the sentences vary. If nothing varies, there is nothing to explain. That is, the goal of research is to explain why variables vary. For example, why do certain defendants obtain short sentences and others long sentences? Can we identify characteristics of defendants or of the nature of their crimes that account for this variation in sentence length? Or, are sentence lengths to some degree random and thus unpredictable?

Suppose that a particular judge, known to be moody at times, has given these sentences (in months) to 10 defendants convicted of assault: 12, 13, 15, 19, 26, 27, 29, 31, 40, and 48. The immediate questions are, Why did certain defendants receive a term of or near 12 months? Why did one defendant receive as much as 48 months? Was it deserved? Is it because this defendant had a long criminal record or because the crime was particularly vicious? Or was it just a result of how the judge felt that day? Worse, could it have something to do with the defendant's race or the race of the victim?

The mean of these data is 26 months. There is nothing apparently unreasonable (not too harsh or too lenient) about the average sentence given by this judge. But our concern is with his

237

consistency in sentencing, that is, with how disparate his sentences seem. We find that the variance of these data is 125 (you should verify this yourself). This then is a measure of the amount of dissimilarity among the sentences. It may seem large, but, more to the point, is it justified? How much of this 125 value is a result of, say, the number of prior convictions that the defendants had?

Regression analysis is used to answer these questions. Each of us might have a theory about which factors encourage stiff prison sentences and which encourage leniency. But regression analysis gives us the ability to quantify precisely the relative importance of any proposed factor or variable. There is little question, therefore, why the regression technique is used more than any other in the social sciences.

THE REGRESSION MODEL

Regression is closely allied with correlation in that we are still interested in the strength of association between two variables, for example, the length of sentence and number of prior convictions. In regression, however, we are also concerned with specifying the nature of this relationship. We specify one variable as dependent and one as independent. That is, one variable is believed to influence the other. In our case, sentence length is dependent and number of prior convictions is independent.

In regression analysis, a mathematical equation is used to predict the value of the dependent variable (denoted Y) on the basis of the independent variable (denoted X):

$$Y = a + bX + e$$

Mathematically, this equation states that the sentence length (Y) received by a given defendant is the sum of three components: (1) a baseline amount given to all defendants (denoted a); (2) an additional amount given for each prior conviction (denoted b); and (3) a residual value (denoted e) that is unpredictable and unique to that individual's case.

The term a is called the **Y-intercept**. It refers to the expected level of Y when $X = 0$ (no priors). This is the baseline amount because it is what Y should be before we take the level of X into account.

The term b is called the **slope** (or the *regression coefficient*) for X. This represents the amount that Y changes (increases or decreases) for each change of one unit in X. Thus, for example, the difference in sentence length between a defendant with $X = 0$ (no priors) and $X = 1$ (one prior) is expected to be b; the difference in expected sentence length between an offender with $X = 0$ (no priors) and a defendant with $X = 2$ (two priors) is $b + b = 2b$.

Finally, e is called the **error term** or **disturbance term**. It represents the amount of the sentence that cannot be accounted for by a and bX. In other words, e represents the departure of a given defendant's sentence from that which would be expected on the basis of his number of priors (X).

Let's consider this model geometrically. Figure 11.1 gives the scatter plot of the sentence length and prior conviction data of Table 11.1 for the 10 defendants.

Clearly, there is a strong positive association between X and Y. Regression involves placing or fitting a line through the scatter of points: If the line is drawn accurately, the value of a (the Y-intercept) would be the location where the line crosses the Y axis. The value of b (the slope) would correspond to the incline or rise of the line for a unit increase in X. We learned in Chapter 10 that Pearson's correlation coefficient (r) measures the degree to which the points lie close to a straight line; the line to which we were referring is this **regression line**. It falls closest to all the points in a scatter plot.

Because regression is closely allied with correlation, it should not be surprising that the calculations are similar. In fact, almost all the computational steps for regression are the same as those for correlation.

Y-INTERCEPT

In regression, the point where the regression line crosses the *Y* axis. The Y-intercept is the predicted value of *Y* for an *X* value of zero.

SLOPE

In regression, the change in the regression line (i.e., the change in the *Y* variable) associated with a one-unit increase in the *X* variable

ERROR TERM (DISTURBANCE TERM)

The residual portion of a score that cannot be predicted by the independent variable. Also the distance of a point from the regression line.

REGRESSION LINE

A straight line drawn through the scatter plot that represents the best possible fit for making predictions of *Y* from *X*.

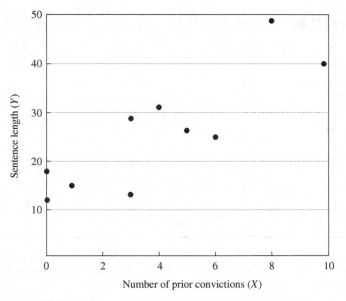

FIGURE 11.1 Scatter Plot of Sentencing Data in Table 11.1.

The values of a and b that most closely fit the data are given by

$$b = \frac{SP}{SS_X}$$

or

$$b = \frac{\sum (X - \overline{X})(Y - \overline{Y})}{\sum (X - \overline{X})^2} \quad \text{for deviations}$$

or

$$b = \frac{\sum XY - N\overline{X}\,\overline{Y}}{\sum X^2 - N\overline{X}^2} \quad \text{for raw scores}$$

and the intercept

$$a = \overline{Y} - b\overline{X}$$

The necessary calculations for the data given in Table 11.1 are shown in Table 11.2.

TABLE 11.1	Sentence Length and Prior Convictions for 10 Defendants	
Priors (X)	**Sentence (in Months) (Y)**
0	12
3	13
1	15
0	19
6	26
5	27
3	29
4	31
10	40
8	48

TABLE 11.2	Regression Calculations for the Data in Table 11.1						
X	Y	$X - \overline{X}$	$Y - \overline{Y}$	$(X - \overline{X})(Y - \overline{Y})$	$(X - \overline{X})^2$	$(Y - \overline{Y})^2$	
0	12	−4	−14	56	16	196	$\overline{X} = 4$
3	13	−1	−13	13	1	169	$\overline{Y} = 26$
1	15	−3	−11	33	9	121	SP = 300
0	19	−4	−7	28	16	49	$SS_X = 100$
6	26	2	0	0	4	0	$SS_Y = 1,250$
5	27	1	1	1	1	1	$r = +.85$
3	29	−1	3	−3	1	9	$b = 3$
4	31	0	5	0	0	25	$a = 14$
10	40	6	14	84	36	196	
8	48	4	22	88	16	484	
$\Sigma X = 40$	$\Sigma Y = 260$			SP = 300	$SS_x = 100$	$SS_y = 1,250$	

First, we compute the means of the two variables ($\overline{X}$ = mean number of priors; $\overline{Y}$ = mean sentence length in months):

$$\overline{X} = \frac{\Sigma X}{N}$$
$$= \frac{40}{10}$$
$$= 4$$
$$\overline{Y} = \frac{\Sigma Y}{N}$$
$$= \frac{260}{10}$$
$$= 26$$

Next we compute the sum of products and sum of squares:

$$SP = \Sigma(X - \overline{X})(Y - \overline{Y})$$
$$= 300$$
$$SS_X = \Sigma(X - \overline{X})^2$$
$$= 100$$
$$SS_Y = \Sigma(Y - \overline{Y})^2$$
$$= 1,250$$

Using these calculations, we now compute b and then a:

$$b = \frac{SP}{SS_X}$$
$$= \frac{300}{100}$$
$$= 3$$
$$a = \overline{Y} - b\overline{X}$$
$$= 26 - (3)(4)$$
$$= 26 - 12$$
$$= 14$$

The slope (*b*) and the *Y*-intercept (*a*) form the equation for the regression line. Because the regression line represents expected or predicted sentences, rather than the actual sentences, we use $\hat{Y}$ (the caret symbol ^ means *predicted*) on the left side to represent predicted sentence, as opposed to actual sentence (*Y*):

$$\hat{Y} = a + bX$$

$$\hat{Y} = 14 + 3X$$

The next step is to plot the regression line on the scatter plot. To do this, we need to find only two points on the line and then connect the points (two points uniquely determine a line).

The easiest point to plot is the *Y*-intercept. That is, the value of *a* is where the regression line crosses the *Y* axis. In other words, the regression line always passes through the point (*X* = 0, *Y* = *a*). The next easiest point to determine is the intersection of the two means. It makes intuitive sense that a case average on *X* can be predicted to be average on *Y*. In short, the regression line always passes through the point ($X = \bar{X}, Y = \bar{Y}$).

In our example, then, we know immediately that the regression line passes through the points (0,14) and (4, 26). And in Figure 11.2, we can connect these points to form this line.

At times, the two easiest points to plot—the *Y*-intercept and the intersection of the two means—are too close together to allow us to draw the regression line with accuracy. That is, if the points are too near, there is considerable room for error in setting down a ruler between them. In such cases, one needs to select a different point than the intersection of means. One should select a large value of *X* (so that the point is far from the *Y*-intercept) and plug it into the equation. In our example, we could select *X* = 10, and so

$$\begin{aligned}
\hat{Y} &= a + b(10) \\
&= 14 + (3)(10) \\
&= 14 + 30 \\
&= 44
\end{aligned}$$

Point (10,44) could be used with point (0,14) to plot the line. Besides the advantage of selecting points as far apart as possible to make the drawing simpler, it does not matter which points you choose—all the predicted points will lie on the same line.

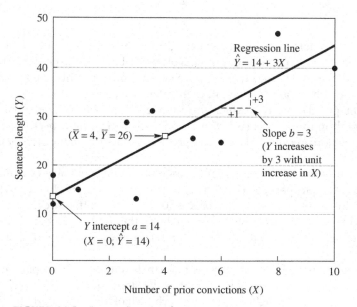

FIGURE 11.2 Regression Line for Sentencing Data.

Requirements for Regression

The assumptions underlying regression are the same as those for Pearson's *r*. In particular:

1. It is assumed that both variables are measured at the interval level.
2. Regression assumes a straight-line relationship. If this is not the case, there are various transformations (which are more advanced than this text) that can be used to make the relationship into a straight line. Also, if extremely deviant cases are observed in a scatter plot, these should be removed from the analysis.
3. Sample members must be chosen randomly to employ tests of significance.
4. To test the significance of the regression line, one must also assume normality for both variables or else have a large sample.

INTERPRETING THE REGRESSION LINE

Let's consider what the values of *a* and *b* mean in substantive terms. The *Y*-intercept corresponds to the expected or predicted value of *Y* when *X* is zero. In our case, then, we can expect that first offenders (i.e., those without prior convictions) will be sentenced to $a = 14$ months. Of course, not all first offenders will receive a 14-month sentence, and, in our sample, the two such defendants received 12- and 19-month prison terms, respectively. But in the long run, we estimate that the average sentence given to first offenders (those with $X = 0$) is 14 months.

The regression coefficient *b* refers to the increase or decrease in *Y* expected with each unit change in *X*. Here we can say that for each prior conviction, a defendant tends to get $b = 3$ additional months. As with the intercept, this rule will not hold in every case; however, 3 months is the long-run cost in terms of prison time for each prior conviction.

With this notion, we can also make predictions of a defendant's sentence on the basis of his number of prior convictions. If a defendant has five priors ($X = 5$), for example, we can expect or predict

$$\hat{Y} = a + b(5)$$
$$= 14 + (3)(5)$$
$$= 14 + 15$$
$$= 29$$

In other words, this defendant can be expected to receive the baseline of 14 months plus 3 additional months for each of his five priors. Note as well that this point (5, 29) also lies on the regression line drawn in Figure 11.2. Thus, we could simply use this line to make predictions of the sentence length for any defendant, even defendants outside this sample, as long as they are a part of the population from which this sample was drawn (i.e., defendants convicted of aggravated assault in the same jurisdiction). Although we cannot expect to predict sentences exactly, the regression line will make the best prediction possible on the basis of just the number of priors.

Unfortunately, the interpretation of the regression line is not always as direct and meaningful as in this example, particularly with regard to the *Y*-intercept. In our example, we could interpret the *Y*-intercept because a value of $X = 0$ was realistic. If, however, we were regressing weight on height (i.e., predicting weight from height), the *Y*-intercept would represent the predicted weight of an individual 0 ft tall. The interpretation would be as foolish as the thought of such a person.

Meaningful or not, the *Y*-intercept is nevertheless an important part of the regression equation, but never as substantively important as the slope. In the height–weight instance, the slope refers to the expected weight increase for each inch of height. Indeed, the old adage of 5 lb for every inch of growth is actually a regression slope.

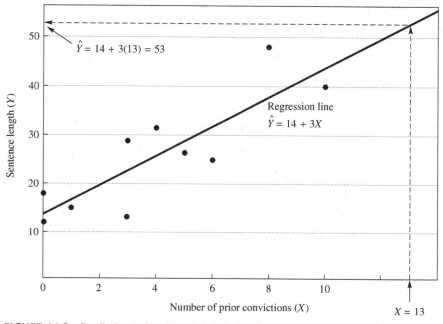

FIGURE 11.3 Prediction Using Sentencing Equation.

Regression equations are frequently used to project the impact of the independent variable (X) beyond its range in the sample. There were no defendants with more than 10 priors, but we could still predict the sentence given by the judge to a hypothetical defendant with 13 priors (see Figure 11.3):

$$\hat{Y} = a + b(13)$$
$$= 14 + (3)(13)$$
$$= 14 + 39$$
$$= 53$$

One has to be cautious, however, about making predictions that fall far afield from the sample of data points. It would be farfetched to use a height–weight regression to predict the weight of a 10-ft-tall man. Similarly, in our sentencing example, it would be mathematically possible to predict the sentence that would be awarded a defendant with 100 priors:

$$\hat{Y} = a + b(100)$$
$$= 14 + (3)(100)$$
$$= 14 + 300$$
$$= 314$$

A 314-month sentence (more than 26 years) for assault is absurd, but then so is the idea of a defendant with 100 prior convictions. Once you exceed the sample range of values too far, the ability to generalize the regression line breaks down. Because the largest value of X in the sample is 10, good sense would dictate against predicting sentences of defendants with more than, say, 15 priors. It would be quite unlikely that the mathematical rule of $b = 3$ months per prior would be applied to someone with as long a criminal record as this. Other considerations would surely intervene that would invalidate such a farfetched prediction.

PREDICTION ERRORS

In the special case in which the correlation is perfect ($r = +1$ or -1), all the points lie precisely on the regression line and all the Y values can be predicted perfectly on the basis of X. In the more usual case, the line only comes close to the actual points (the stronger the correlation, the closer the fit of the points to the line).

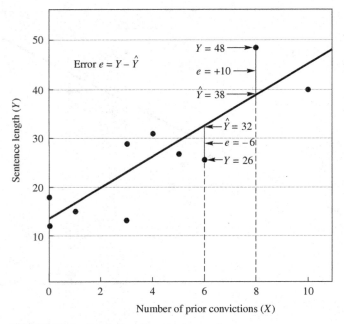

FIGURE 11.4 Prediction Error in Regression.

The difference between the points (observed data) and the regression line (the predicted values) is the error or disturbance term (e):

$$e = Y - \hat{Y}$$

The concept of a disturbance term is illustrated in Figure 11.4. A positive value of e means that the sentence given a defendant is greater than what you would expect on the basis of his prior record. For example, the defendant with eight priors has a predicted sentence length of

$$\hat{Y} = 14 + (3)(8) = 14 + 24 = 38$$

His actual sentence was as much as 48 months, however, yielding a prediction error of

$$e = Y - \hat{Y} = 48 - 38 = 10$$

Thus, on the basis of priors alone, this sentence is underpredicted by 10 months.

Negative prediction errors occur when the data points lie below the regression line. That is, on the basis of the X value, the Y value is overpredicted. For example, for the defendant with six priors, we would predict his sentence to be

$$\hat{Y} = 14 + (3)(6) = 14 + 18 = 32$$

In actuality, this defendant received only 26 months, producing a prediction error of

$$e = Y - \hat{Y} = 26 - 32 = -6$$

The predictive value of a regression line (e.g., for predicting sentences on the basis of priors) can be assessed by the magnitude of these error terms. The larger the error, the poorer is the regression line as a prediction device.

It would seem intuitively logical to add the error terms to obtain a measure of predictive ability. However, the negative and positive errors cancel out. That is, $\Sigma e = 0$. To prevent this, we can square the errors before we sum. The so-called *error sum of squares* (or *residual sum of squares*), denoted by SS_{error}, is

$$SS_{error} = \Sigma e^2 = \Sigma (Y - \hat{Y})^2$$

The usefulness of the error sum of squares lies in comparing it to the magnitude of error that would have resulted had one not used X in making predictions. Without knowing anything about a defendant, what would you guess his sentence to be? The best guess would be the average sentence, or $\overline{Y}$. If we guess or predict $\overline{Y}$ for every defendant, the errors would simply be the deviations from the mean:

$$\text{Error without knowing } X = Y - \overline{Y}$$

The sum of squared prediction errors or deviations without using X is called the *total sum of squares:*

$$SS_{total} = \Sigma(Y - \overline{Y})^2$$

The predictive value of the regression equation is in its ability to reduce prediction error—that is, the extent that SS_{error} is smaller than SS_{total}. The difference between the two is the sum of squares that X can explain, and this is called the *regression sum of squares* (or *explained sum of squares*). The regression sum of squares is then

$$SS_{reg} = SS_{total} - SS_{error}$$

To summarize:

	Not Knowing X	**Knowing X**
Actual value	Y	Y
Predicted value	$\overline{Y}$	$\hat{Y} = a + bX$
Prediction error	$Y - \overline{Y}$	$Y - \hat{Y}$
Sum of squares	$SS_{total} = \Sigma(Y - \overline{Y})^2$	$SS_{error} = \Sigma(Y - \hat{Y})^2$
Difference	$SS_{reg} = SS_{total} - SS_{error}$	

Let's now calculate these sums of squares for the sentencing data. We already have from Table 11.2 the total sum of squares (previously called SS_Y):

$$SS_{total} = \Sigma(Y - \overline{Y})^2 = 1{,}250$$

To calculate the error sum of squares, we need to obtain the predicted sentence length ($\hat{Y}$) for each defendant, subtract it from the actual sentence length (Y), square the difference, and then add:

X	Y	$\hat{Y} = a + bX$	$e = Y - \hat{Y}$	e^2
0	12	14	−2	4
3	13	23	−10	100
1	15	17	−2	4
0	19	14	5	25
6	26	32	−6	36
5	27	29	−2	4
3	29	23	6	36
4	31	26	5	25
10	40	44	−4	16
8	48	38	10	100
			$\Sigma e^2 =$	350

Thus,

$$SS_{error} = \Sigma e^2 = 350$$

and so

$$SS_{reg} = SS_{total} - SS_{error} = 1{,}250 - 350 = 900$$

The ability of a regression line to make predictions can be expressed in what is known as the proportionate reduction in error (PRE), that is, the proportion of the prediction error that can be reduced by knowing the independent variable. The proportionate reduction in error (PRE) due to X is

$$\text{PRE} = \frac{SS_{\text{total}} - SS_{\text{error}}}{SS_{\text{total}}}$$

$$= \frac{SS_{\text{reg}}}{SS_{\text{total}}}$$

$$= \frac{900}{1{,}250}$$

$$= .72$$

Thus, .72, or 72%, of the error in predicting sentence length is reduced by taking the number of priors into account. Put differently, 72% of the variance in sentence length is explained by the number of priors the defendant has on his record. This is precisely the information that we sought from the beginning.

THE LEAST SQUARES CRITERION

When first introducing the term, we characterized the regression line generally as that falling closest to all of the points in the scatter plot. It is important that we now be more specific about the meaning of "closest." The regression line is often referred to as the *least squares regression line.* This reflects the fact that the line of best fit is that which comes closest to the points in terms of minimizing the squared distances of the points to the line. That is, the criterion for best fit is the straight line, defined by the values of a and b, that minimizes the sum of squared error, $\sum e^2$.

In Chapter 4, we indicated that the best approach to summarizing the deviations from the mean of a set of scores is to square them before summing. By a similar logic, the best fitting line is that which minimizes the sum of squared deviations of points from the line rather than, what might seem intuitive, the line that minimizes the sum of the distances of points from the line regardless of direction.

Consider the example shown in the following figure. Clearly, the solid line appears to fit better than the dashed one, even though the dashed line actually fits two points perfectly and the solid line fits none perfectly. The objective is for the line to pass through all of the points as closely as possible, rather than to fall exactly on as many points as possible. The associated table of errors on p. 247 (distances from the line) shows, however, that Line 1 has a smaller sum of distances (error regardless of direction) than Line 2. However, Line 2 has the smaller (and actually as small as possible for any line) sum of squared distances of the points to the line. Known as the least squares regression line, Line 2 accomplishes the best fit by adjusting to all three points, not just the majority.

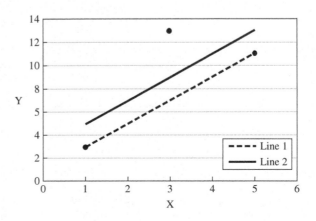

Data		Line 1			Line 2		
X	Y	$\hat{Y}$	e	e^2	$\hat{Y}$	e	e^2
1	3	3	0	0	5	2	4
3	13	7	6	36	9	4	16
5	11	11	0	0	13	2	4
			$\Sigma e = 6$	$\Sigma e^2 = 36$		$\Sigma e = 8$	$\Sigma e^2 = 24$

Note: Error terms are without the direction or sign.

REGRESSION AND PEARSON'S CORRELATION

We approached the problem of sentencing disparity by questioning why some defendants receive longer sentences than others. Using regression, we were able to determine that 72% of the variance in sentence length can be explained by the number of prior convictions. Obtaining the regression equation—the intercept and the slope—was fairly straightforward. It came directly from quantities (SP, SS_X, and SS_Y) derived in calculating the correlation (Pearson's r). However, the steps for computing SS_{error} and SS_{reg} were quite laborious, because they involved making a prediction for each person in the sample. Given the usefulness of determining the proportionate reduction in error (PRE), it would be helpful to employ a far simpler method.

If X and Y are uncorrelated (i.e., if Pearson's $r = 0$), SS_{total} and SS_{error} will be the same, because X will not help predict Y. The larger the value of r, the smaller the value of SS_{error} relative to SS_{total}. More precisely, the proportionate reduction in error (PRE) is the square of Pearson's r:

$$r^2 = \frac{SS_{total} - SS_{error}}{SS_{total}}$$

The squared correlation (r^2) is also called the **coefficient of determination**. That is, r^2 is the proportion of variance in Y determined or explained by X. The range of possible values for r^2 is from zero to one; r^2 is always positive, because even a negative correlation becomes positive when it is squared.

The complementary quantity $1 - r^2$ is called the **coefficient of nondetermination**. That is, the proportion of variance in Y that is not explained by X is $1 - r^2$:

$$1 - r^2 = \frac{SS_{error}}{SS_{total}}$$

For the sentencing data, using calculations from Table 11.2:

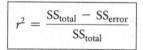

$$r = \frac{SP}{\sqrt{SS_X SS_Y}}$$

$$= \frac{300}{\sqrt{(100)(1,250)}}$$

$$= \frac{300}{\sqrt{125,000}}$$

$$= \frac{300}{353.55}$$

$$= .85$$

The coefficient of determination is then

$$r^2 = (.85)^2 = .72$$

COEFFICIENT OF DETERMINATION

Equal to the Pearson's correlation squared, the proportion of variance in the dependent variable that is explained by the independent variable.

COEFFICIENT OF NONDETERMINATION

Equal to one minus the Pearson's correlation squared, the proportion of variance in the dependent variable that is not explained by the independent variable.

Thus, 72% of the variance in sentence length is explained by the number of priors. This agrees with the results of the long method for calculating PRE from the last section.

The coefficient of nondetermination is

$$1 - r^2 = 1 - (.85)^2 = 1 - .72 = .28$$

Thus, 28% of the variance in sentence length is not explained by priors. This 28% residual could be a result of other factors concerning the defendant or his crime. Some portion of the 28% could even be random error—that is, error that cannot be attributed to any factor. We'll discuss this in more detail later in the chapter.

REGRESSION AND ANALYSIS OF VARIANCE

The focus on explained and unexplained variance may remind you of analysis of variance in Chapter 8. In that chapter, we decomposed the total sum of squares (SS_{total}) into sum of squares between groups ($SS_{between}$) and sum of squares within groups (SS_{within}). In regression, we decompose the total sum of squares into regression sum of squares (SS_{reg}) and error sum of squares (SS_{error}). In fact, there are very strong similarities between analysis of variance and regression analysis. In both, we attempt to account for one variable in terms of another. In analysis of variance, the independent variable is categorical or in groups (such as social class or religion), whereas in regression, the independent variable is measured at the interval level (such as number of prior convictions or height).

Fortunately, it is not necessary to calculate a predicted value for every respondent, as we did earlier, in order to decompose the total variation in the dependent variable into portions explained and not explained by the independent variable. Using the coefficients of determination and nondetermination as the proportions of explained and unexplained variation, we can quickly decompose the total sum of squares (SS_{total} or SS_Y) using the formulas:

$$\boxed{SS_{reg} = r^2 SS_{total}}$$

$$\boxed{SS_{error} = (1 - r^2)SS_{total}}$$

Just as in Chapter 8, an analysis of variance summary table is a convenient way of presenting the results of regression analysis. In Table 11.3, for example, we display under the heading "Source of Variation" the regression, error, and total sum of squares for our regression of sentence length on the number of priors. Next, the regression and error sums of squares are associated with degrees of freedom. The regression sum of squares has only 1 degree of freedom:

$$df_{reg} = 1$$

For the error sum of squares.

$$df_{error} = N - 2$$

where N is the sample size.

TABLE 11.3	Analysis of Variance Summary Table for Sentencing Data			
Source of Variation	**SS**	**df**	**MS**	**F**
Regression	900	1	900.00	20.57
Error	350	8	43.75	
Total	1,250	9		

As in Chapter 8, we can next calculate the *mean square regression* (MS_{reg}) and *mean square error* (MS_{error}) by dividing the sums of squares by their respective degrees of freedom:

$$MS_{reg} = \frac{SS_{reg}}{df_{reg}}$$

$$MS_{error} = \frac{SS_{error}}{df_{error}}$$

Finally, by dividing the mean square regression by the mean square error, we obtain an F ratio for testing the significance of the regression—that is, whether the regression explains a significant amount of variation:

$$F = \frac{MS_{reg}}{MS_{error}}$$

To determine if the calculated F ratio is significant, it must exceed the critical value in Table D for 1 and $N - 2$ degrees of freedom.

For our results in Table 11.3 for the sentencing data,

$$F = \frac{900.00}{43.75} = 20.57$$

In Table D, we find that for $\alpha = .05$ with 1 and 8 degrees of freedom, the critical F is 5.32. Thus, the number of prior convictions explains a significant portion of the variance in sentence length.[1]

STEP-BY-STEP ILLUSTRATION

Regression Analysis

To review the steps of regression analysis, let's reconsider the data on trial length and jury deliberation time presented in Chapter 10. In this illustration, we will use computational raw-score formulas for sums of squares to simplify the calculations. Days of trial (X) is the independent variable, and hours of jury deliberation (Y) is the dependent variable. Table 11.4 gives the values of X and Y for the sample of 10 trials along with the squares and products.

TABLE 11.4 Calculations for Trial Length and Jury Deliberation Time Data

X	Y	X²	Y²	XY
3	6	9	36	18
1	3	1	9	3
6	11	36	121	66
5	9	25	81	45
4	10	16	100	40
7	6	49	36	42
5	12	25	144	60
2	2	4	4	4
3	3	9	9	9
4	8	16	64	32
40	70	190	604	319

[1]This F test of the explained variance is equivalent to the test for the significance of the Pearson's correlation presented in Chapter 10. In fact, with one independent variable as we have here, $F = t^2$.

Step 1   Calculate the mean of X and the mean of Y.

$$\overline{X} = \frac{\sum X}{N} = \frac{40}{10} = 4$$

$$\overline{Y} = \frac{\sum Y}{N} = \frac{70}{10} = 7$$

Step 2   Calculate SS_X, SS_Y, and SP.

$$
\begin{aligned}
SS_X &= \sum X^2 - N\overline{X}^2 \\
&= 190 - 10(4)^2 \\
&= 190 - 160 \\
&= 30
\end{aligned}
$$

$$
\begin{aligned}
SS_Y &= \sum Y^2 - N\overline{Y}^2 \\
&= 604 - 10(7)^2 \\
&= 604 - 490 \\
&= 114
\end{aligned}
$$

$$
\begin{aligned}
SP &= \sum XY - N\overline{X}\,\overline{Y} \\
&= 319 - 10(4)(7) \\
&= 319 - 280 \\
&= 39
\end{aligned}
$$

Step 3   Determine the regression line.

$$
\begin{aligned}
b &= \frac{SP}{SS_X} \\
&= \frac{39}{30} \\
&= 1.3
\end{aligned}
$$

$$
\begin{aligned}
a &= \overline{Y} - b\overline{X} \\
&= 7 - 1.3(4) \\
&= 7 - 5.2 \\
&= 1.8
\end{aligned}
$$

$$
\begin{aligned}
\hat{Y} &= a + bX \\
&= 1.8 + 1.3X
\end{aligned}
$$

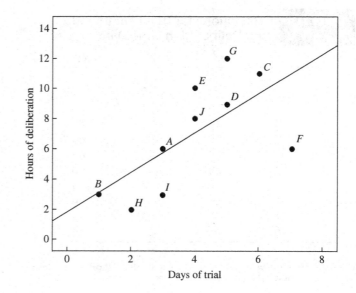

We can display the regression line on the scatter plot by taking any two values of X (say 0 and 8), and generate the respective predicted values. For $X = 0$, $\hat{Y} = 1.8 + 1.3(0) = 1.8$ (this is the Y-intercept); for $X = 8$, $\hat{Y} = 1.8 + 1.3(8) = 12.2$. We then can connect a line between the points (0, 1.8) and (8, 12.2).

We can interpret the regression line based on the Y-intercept ($a = 1.8$) and slope ($b = 1.3$). Jury deliberation time shows a baseline of 1.8 hours (for organization and procedural discussion) and then tends to increase by 1.3 hours for every day of trial.

Step 4 Determine correlation and coefficients of determination and nondetermination.

$$r = \frac{SP}{\sqrt{SS_X SS_Y}}$$

$$= \frac{39}{\sqrt{(30)(114)}}$$

$$= \frac{39}{\sqrt{3420}}$$

$$= 58.48$$

$$= .667$$

And thus,

$$r^2 = (.667)^2$$

$$= .448$$

$$= 44.8\%$$

$$1 - r^2 = 55.2\%$$

Thus, about 45% of the variance in jury deliberation time can be explained by trial length, while about 55% of the variance is unrelated to trial length.

Step 5 Calculate SS_{total}, SS_{reg}, and SS_{error}.

$$SS_{total} = SS_Y = 114$$
$$SS_{reg} = r^2 SS_Y = .448(114) = 50.7$$
$$SS_{error} = (1 - r^2)SS_Y = .552(114) = 63.3$$

Step 6 Calculate mean square regression and mean square error.

$$df_{reg} = 1$$

$$MS_{reg} = \frac{SS_{reg}}{df_{reg}} = \frac{50.7}{1} = 50.7$$

$$df_{reg} = N - 2 = 8$$

$$MS_{error} = \frac{SS_{error}}{df_{error}} = \frac{63.3}{8} = 7.913$$

Step 7 Calculate F and compare with the critical value from Table D.

$$F = \frac{MS_{reg}}{MS_{error}} = \frac{50.7}{7.913} = 6.408$$

$$df = 1 \text{ and } 8$$
$$\alpha = .05$$

Critical $F = 5.32$ (from Table D)

Because the calculated F is larger than the critical value, we conclude that trial length explains a significant amount of variance in jury deliberation time.

MULTIPLE REGRESSION[*]

We attempted earlier to account for variation in sentence length on the basis of the criminal history of the defendants—that is, to predict sentence length from the number of prior convictions. Overall, 72% of the variance was explained and 28% was not explained by criminal history. This approach is called *simple regression*—one dependent variable and one independent variable—just as Pearson's correlation is often called simple correlation.

Naturally, prior convictions is not the only factor relevant in analyzing sentencing data. It would be foolish to suggest that sentence length depends on just one factor, even though as much as 72% of the variance was explained. We might want to test sentencing models that include such variables as the age of the defendant and whether the defendant had pled guilty or not guilty to the charge. Perhaps in doing so, we can account for even more of the 28% of variance that sentence length could not.

Let's consider the case of two predictors: prior convictions and age. We add to our set of data another independent variable, the age of the defendant (Z).

Priors (X)	Age (Z)	Sentence (Y)
0	18	12
3	22	13
1	27	15
0	28	19
6	30	26
5	35	27
3	36	29
4	29	31
10	34	40
8	31	48

The means, variances, and standard deviations calculated for all three variables as well as their inter-correlations, are as follows:

	Mean	Variance	Standard Deviation	Correlation Matrix Priors (X)	Age (Z)	Sentence (Y)
Priors	4	10	3.16	1.00	.59	.85
Age	29	29	5.39	.59	1.00	.69
Sentence	26	125	11.18	.85	.69	1.00

One might be tempted also to use the simple regression approach for predicting sentence based on age, for example, and then combine the results with those from regressing sentence on priors performed earlier. Unfortunately, this would produce erroneous results. By squaring the correlations, priors explains $(.85)^2 = .72 = 72\%$ of the variance in sentence length, and age explains $(.69)^2 = .48 = 48\%$ of the variance in sentence length. If we tried to add together these percentages, it would exceed 100%, which is impossible.

The problem is that, to some extent, age and priors overlap in their abilities to explain sentence: Older defendants have accumulated more priors during their lifetimes. Therefore, because age and priors are themselves correlated ($r = .59$), part of the percentage of variance in sentences explained by priors is also explained by age, and vice versa. By adding the proportions that they each explain, a certain portion is double counted.

[*]The sections titled "Multiple Regression" through "Interaction Terms" and "Logistical Regression" through "Summary" are reproduced from Levin, Jack; Fox, James A.; and Forde, David R., Elementary Statistics in Social Research, 11th Edition, ©2010. Reprinted and electronically reproduced by permission of Pearson Education, Inc., Upper Saddle River, New Jersey. This content includes the text, Figures 11.5 and 11.6, and Tables 11.5, 11.6, 11.7, 11.8, and 11.9.

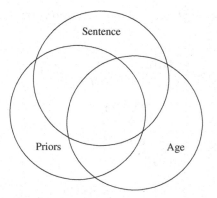

FIGURE 11.5 Overlap in explained variance.

The situation is illustrated in Figure 11.5, using overlapping circles to represent the three variables and their shared variance. Priors covers 72% of the sentence circle, reflecting the explained variance. Age covers 48% of the sentence circle, reflecting its explained variance. For these to be possible, however, priors and age must, to some extent, overlap. The objective in multiple regression is to determine what percentage of variance in sentence is explained by priors and age together—that is, what percentage of the sentence circle is eclipsed by priors, age, or both.

Multiple linear regression (or just **multiple regression**) is a generalization of simple regression when one uses two or more predictors. The regression model introduced at the start of this chapter for predicting Y from X extends to predicting Y from a linear combination of X and Z:

$$Y = b_0 + b_1X + b_2Z + e$$

where b_0 (rather than a) is used for the Y-intercept, b_1 and b_2 for the slopes of X and Z, respectively, and e for the residual or error term. Similar to the case of one predictor, the predicted values of the dependent variable are

$$\hat{Y} = b_0 + b_1X + b_2Z$$

The Y-intercept or constant term, b_0, is the expected value of Y when both X and Z are 0. The slope b_1 reflects the expected change in Y for every unit increase in X, holding constant Z. Similarly, the slope b_2 reflects the expected change in Y for every unit increase in Z, holding constant X.

The calculations for estimating the multiple regression coefficients are complex, especially when the number of predictors is more than just a few, and so computers are almost always needed. Moreover, it entails a number of issues and complications that are beyond the scope of this book. But just to whet your appetite for your next course in statistics, the case of two predictors can be worked out on a calculator yet includes all the concepts of more elaborate multiple regression analyses for which computers are essential.

The formulas for calculating regression coefficients with two predictor variables (such as priors and age) are a bit complex. The regression coefficient (or slope) for each predictor must be adjusted for whatever explanatory overlap exists with the other predictor. The adjustment is rather similar to the partial correlation calculation introduced in Chapter 10.

For the case of two predictor variables, the regression coefficients, including the Y-intercept, are given by:

$$b_1 = \frac{s_Y}{s_X}\left(\frac{r_{YX} - r_{YZ}r_{XZ}}{1 - r_{XZ}^2}\right)$$

$$b_2 = \frac{s_Y}{s_Z}\left(\frac{r_{YZ} - r_{XY}r_{XZ}}{1 - r_{XZ}^2}\right)$$

$$b_0 = \overline{Y} - b_1\overline{X} - b_2\overline{Z}$$

MULTIPLE REGRESSION

A technique employed in predicting values of one variable (Y) from knowledge of values of two or more variables.

Based on the means, standard deviations and correlations among sentence, priors, and age, we can calculate

$$b_1 = \frac{11.18}{3.16}\left(\frac{.85 - (.69)(.59)}{1 - (.59)^2}\right)$$

$$= 3.54\left(\frac{.4439}{.6519}\right)$$

$$= 3.54(.6794)$$

$$= 2.395$$

$$b_2 = \frac{11.18}{5.39}\left(\frac{.69 - .85(.59)}{1 - (.59)^2}\right)$$

$$= 2.07\left(\frac{.1885}{.6519}\right)$$

$$= .605$$

$$b_0 = 26 - 2.395(4) - .605(29)$$

$$= -1.132$$

With these results, the regression equation predicting sentence (Y) on the basis of priors (X) and age (Z) is as follows:

$$\hat{Y} = -1.132 + 2.395X + .605Z$$

Notice that each of the two predictors has its own regression coefficient or slope. Again, these slopes indicate the expected change in the dependent variable associated with a unit increase in a given predictor, holding constant the other predictor.

Based on these results, we can say that each additional prior (X) tends to carry a 2.395-month increase in sentence length (Y), holding constant defendant age (Z). For example, given two defendants of the same age, but where one has two more priors than the other, the first defendant can be expected to receive a sentence that is 2(2.395) or about 4.8 months longer than the other defendant.

Also, based on these results, we can say that each additional year of age (Z) tends to be associated with a .605-month increase in sentence length (Y), holding constant the number of priors (X). If two defendants have similar criminal records, but one is 5 years older, this defendant can be expected to receive a sentence length that is 5(.605) or about 3 months longer than the other defendant.

Finally, the Y-intercept represents the baseline, or expected sentence length, when both predictors are equal to zero. It shouldn't bother us in the least that the Y-intercept here is negative (-1.132 months); after all, how often do we encounter a newborn defendant with no priors?

An overall measure of fit of the actual Y values to those predicted by the regression line is given by the **multiple coefficient of determination** (also known as the *squared multiple correlation*). Symbolized by R^2 (in contrast to r^2 as in Pearson's coefficient for bivariate relationships), the multiple coefficient of determination is the proportion of variance in a dependent variable explained by a set of independent variables in combination. For two independent variables (X and Z),

MULTIPLE COEFFICIENT OF DETERMINATION

The proportion of variance in the dependent variable that is explained by a set of independent variables in combination.

$$R^2 = \frac{r_{YX}^2 + r_{YZ}^2 - 2r_{YX}r_{YZ}r_{XZ}}{1 - r_{XZ}^2}$$

Based on the correlations among sentence, priors, and age,

$$R^2 = \frac{(.85)^2 + (.69)^2 - 2(.85)(.69)(.59)}{1 - (.59)^2}$$

$$= \frac{.7225 + .4761 - .6921}{1 - .3481}$$

$$= \frac{.5065}{.6519}$$

$$= .78$$

Thus, age and number of prior convictions together explain 78% of the variance in sentence length. Apparently, the inclusion of age adds only a modest amount to the overall prediction of sentence length. Because the number of prior convictions by itself explains 72%, the inclusion of age as an additional variable increases the percentage of explained variance by only 6%.

Dummy Variables

All three variables used in the previous regression analysis are measured at the interval level, an assumption in regression analysis. As with other parametric techniques covered in this book, it is generally safe to use ordinal variables so long as the points along the continuum are approximately evenly spaced, as in a 7-point scale from strongly agree to strongly disagree. Nominal variables cannot be used as predictors, unless they are converted into a special kind of variable, called a *dummy variable*, having only two values and generally coded as 0 and 1.

To illustrate, suppose we wanted to include another variable, trial, coded as 1 if the defendant was convicted following a not-guilty plea and 0 if the defendant was sentenced after a guilty plea and no trial. If coded in this fashion, the coefficient of the dummy variable trial will represent the average difference in sentence for defendants convicted after a not-guilty plea and those pleading guilty, holding constant the other predictor variables.

Priors (X)	Age (Z)	Sentence (Y)	Trial (D)
0	18	12	1
3	22	13	0
1	27	15	0
0	28	19	1
6	30	26	0
5	35	27	1
3	36	29	1
4	29	31	0
10	34	40	0
8	31	48	1

With more than two predictors, the calculations for multiple regression are so elaborate that they are virtually impossible to accomplish without a computer and special statistical software (like SPSS). But the interpretation of the results is a direct extension of the two-predictor case.

Let's examine the most important portions of the output produced by SPSS for regressing (or predicting) sentence on priors, age, and trial. Table 11.5 reports regression coefficients, their respective standard errors, t values, and significance levels.

Shown in the first column, each of the regression coefficients (*b*) represents the expected change in Y corresponding to a unit increase in that predictor while holding constant all other predictors. The coefficient for priors, after controlling for age and trial, is 2.866. Thus, each additional prior offense tends to result in a 2.866-month increase in sentence length, controlling for

TABLE 11.5	Multiple Regression of Sentence Data				
	Unstandardized Coefficients		**Standardized Coefficients**		
	b	**Std. Error**	**Beta**	**t**	**Sig.**
Constant	.469	10.986		.043	.967
Priors	2.866	.781	.811	3.670	.010
Age	.379	.446	.183	.850	.428
Trial	6.130	4.023	.274	1.524	.178

age and whether the defendant went to trial. Suppose, for example, that hypothetical defendants A and B were the same age, and both had entered the same plea, but A had one more prior than B. Then one would expect A to receive a longer sentence than B by 2.866 months.

The other two coefficients would be interpreted in a similar fashion. Every year of age is expected to increase the sentence by .379 months, controlling for both priors and trial status. Finally, the coefficient for the dummy variable trial indicates that the sentence expected from a trial (if convicted) tends to be 6.061 months longer than that from a guilty plea, assuming the other two variables are held constant.

The t ratios are calculated by dividing the coefficient by its corresponding standard error. The t ratio (with $N - k - 1$ degrees of freedom, where k is the number of predictors) allows us to test if the regression coefficient is significantly different from 0 (the null hypothesis of no effect). We could compare each of the t values against the critical value of 2.447 found in Table C, in Appendix C for 6 degrees of freedom (here $N = 10$ and $k = 3$ predictors) and a .05 level of significance. In this case, only priors has a significant effect on sentence length. Alternatively, most regression software programs calculate the exact p value for each coefficient (denoted by "Sig."), representing the exact probability of obtaining a regression coefficient of at least this size if the null hypothesis of no effect were true. For priors, the exact probability ($p = .010$) is quite low and certainly below the .05 significance level. For the other two predictors, however, we fail to reject the null hypothesis of no effect.

It may seem a bit odd that the coefficient for priors (2.866) is significant while a much larger coefficient for trial (6.130) is not. This reflects the fact that an increase of one unit in trial (from guilty plea to conviction from a trial) is a major difference in criminal procedure, while an increase of one prior is not so dramatic. The reason why it is difficult to compare the numerical values of the two regression coefficients is that the underlying variables have rather different standard deviations (or scales).

The column headed by *standardized coefficient* (also called "beta") provides a measure of the impact of each predictor when placed on the same (standardized) scale. This makes substantive interpretation less meaningful. Each standardized coefficient represents the expected change in the dependent variable in terms of standard deviation units corresponding to a one-standard-deviation increase in the predictor while holding constant the other predictors. Although not particularly illuminating, at least the relative sizes of the standardized coefficients indicate their relative strengths in predicting the dependent variable. The .811 standardized coefficient for priors is much larger than those for the other two variables, clearly indicating the greater importance of this variable in predicting sentence lengths.

As in the case of regression with one predictor, we can divide the overall or total sum of squares in the dependent variable into two parts (the portions explained and unexplained by the group of predictor variables) and summarize and test the results using an analysis of variance table, as shown in Table 11.6.

Previously, when using only priors as a predictor, we were able to explain 900 of the total 1,250 sum of squares. With three predictors, this improves to 1,047.843, leaving 202.157 as error (or variation in sentence length unaccounted for by the three variables). As before, we obtain the

TABLE 11.6	Analysis of Variance Table for Regression of Sentence Data				
	Sum of Squares	df	Mean Square	F	Sig.
Regression	1,047.843	3	349.281	10.367	.009
Error	202.157	6	33.693		
Total	1,250.000	9			

mean square regression and mean square error by dividing the sums of squares by their corresponding degrees of freedom. Finally, the *F* ratio, found by dividing the mean square regression by the mean square error (or residual), can be compared to the critical value from Table D in Appendix C (4.76 for numerator *df* = 3, denominator *df* = 6, and a .05 level of significance). Alternatively, we can simply determine if the exact significance value (p = .009) provided by the software is less than our .05 significance level. Either way, F = 10.367 is statistically significant, allowing us to reject the null hypothesis of no predictability or effect within the entire regression equation.

Finally, the sums of squares can, as before, be used to calculate the multiple coefficient of determination or squared multiple correlation:

$$R^2 = \frac{SS_{total} - SS_{error}}{SS_{total}} = \frac{SS_{reg}}{SS_{total}}$$
$$= \frac{1,047.843}{1,250}$$
$$= .838$$

Thus, while priors alone explained 72% of the variance in sentence length, the group of three variables can explain 84%. And based on the *F* ratio from the analysis of variance table (F = 10.367), we can conclude that the proportion of variance explained by the model, this 84%, is statistically significant.

Interaction Terms

The regression coefficients for priors, age, and trial reflect the independent or separate effect of each variable holding constant the other two. These impacts are sometimes known as *main effects*. It is also possible for variables to have interaction effects—that is, for the size of the effect of one independent variable on the dependent variable to depend on the value of another independent variable.

To illustrate the distinction between main and interaction effects, consider a study that examines the benefits of diet and exercise on weight loss. Suppose that dieting alone produces an average weight loss of 2 pounds for the week and that an hour of daily exercise alone produces an average weight loss of 3 pounds for the week. What results would be expected if combining diet with exercise? Would it be the sum of the diet and exercise effects, that is 2 + 3 = 5 pounds? That would be true if there is no interaction. An interaction would exist if diet and exercise produced, say, an average weight loss of 6 pounds. In other words, the effect of dieting increases with exercise and the effect of exercise increases with diet.

Multiple regression can easily incorporate and test interaction effects by including the product of variables in the regression model. For example, we could create a new variable, priors × trial, by multiplying priors times trial. The revised regression results are as shown in Table 11.7. The interpretation would be that each prior offense increases the expected sentence by 2.490 years if there is no trial (when trial = 0, the interaction variable is zero and drops out of

TABLE 11.7	Multiple Regression of Sentence Data with Interaction				
	Unstandardized Coefficients		**Standardized Coefficients**		
	b	*Std. Error*	*Beta*	*t*	*Sig.*
Intercept	2.591	12.028		.215	.838
Priors	2.490	1.007	.704	2.472	.056
Age	.368	.463	.177	.795	.463
Trial	2.905	6.536	.130	.445	.675
Priors × Trial	.801	1.262	.193	.635	.554

the equation). For those defendants who go to trial, trial = 1 and, thus, priors × trial = priors), and the effect of each prior is 2.490 + 0.801 = 3.291. Thus, although the interaction effect is not statistically significant, particularly with such a small sample, going to trial increases the effect of each prior offense by .801 of a year, or about 9 months.

Multicollinearity

The great advantage of multiple regression is the ability to identify the impact on a dependent variable of each of several predictor variables over and above the effects of all others in the equation. Thus, the technique can be used to separate the effects of two (or more) predictor variables that themselves are correlated, as in distinguishing the effects of a defendant's age and priors on sentence length.

The capacity of multiple regression to disentangle the effects of correlated predictors has its limits, however. After all, it is a difficult task to distinguish between two predictors that are greatly overlapping and, therefore, fairly redundant. Suppose we were to attempt a regression of sentence length on prior convictions and prior arrests based on the following data:

Convictions	Arrests	Sentence
0	2	12
3	7	13
1	4	15
0	1	19
6	8	26
5	8	27
3	7	29
4	6	31
10	11	40
8	13	48

Not only are both Arrests and Convictions correlated with the dependent variable Sentence, but they are strongly correlated with each other ($r = .934$). Utilizing both as predictors forces regression analysis to attempt to disentangle the effects of two variables that are almost inseparable.

Following are three alternative regression models, using either Convictions or Arrests and then both Convictions and Arrests as predictors of Sentence. Either Convictions or Arrests by itself predicts Sentence rather well, with large R^2 values and significant regression coefficients. Including both in the same regression doesn't increase the proportion of explained variance (R^2)

very much because of the general redundancy between the two predictors. Particularly problematic, however, is that neither predictor has a significant regression coefficient when the other is included in the same regression.

Predictors	b	Std. Error	t	Sig.
Intercept	14.000	3.373	4.151	0.003
Convictions	3.000	0.661	4.536	0.002
$R^2 = 0.720$				

Predictors	b	Std. Error	t	Sig.
Intercept	8.238	4.670	1.764	0.116
Arrests	2.651	0.617	4.298	0.003
$R^2 = 0.699$				

Predictors	b	Std. Error	t	Sig.
Intercept	11.291	5.614	2.011	0.084
Convictions	1.891	1.921	0.984	0.358
Arrests	1.066	1.725	0.618	0.556
$R^2 = 0.735$				

This complication—when predictor variables in a regression are themselves strongly intercorrelated—is called **multicollinearity**. In the face of multicollinearity, the regression technique does its best to assess how much of, say, sentence length is due to prior convictions versus prior arrests, but the result will necessarily be a rough estimate subject to lots of error. This shows up in the two predictors sharing predictability and having inflated standard errors. Although the regression analysis determines what might be the best division of the effects of two overlapping variables, the extent of uncertainty in the split is high.

MULTICOLLINEARITY

The presence of strong intercorrelations among the predictor variables in a multiple regression that limits the ability to measure their separate impact on the dependent variable.

If the objective is only to predict the dependent variable, then multicollinearity is not problematic. Multicollinearity does not affect the overall fit of the regression equation as measured by R^2. Rather, it impacts only how much of the overall prediction depends on one variable or another. Thus, we may be able to determine the extent to which the variance in the dependent variable is explained by the set of independent variables as a group, but not be especially sure about the individual contributions of each of the overlapping variables. It is like easily recognizing the beautiful sound of a chorus but having difficulty being able to identify the voices of the individual members.

Logistic Regression

It should be fairly clear that multiple regression is an extremely useful tool for predicting a wide variety of characteristics, such as sentence lengths for convicted criminals, test scores for undergraduate majors, weight loss for dieters and exercisers—virtually any variable that is measured at the interval level. But what is the social researcher to do when predicting categorical variables—especially dichotomous ones—such as whether someone supports or opposes the legalization of gay marriage, which of two major party candidates will carry various states in a presidential election, or whether survey respondents report owning a handgun. While these types of variables can be used as dummy variable predictors, if that were the research objective, there would be problems in using them as dependent variables in linear regression.

Consider the following data for a randomly selected sample of applicants to a particular college, data that include sex (gender) coded as 0 for females and 1 for males, high school grade average (HSavg) measured on a typical 100-point scale, and admissions outcome (decision) coded as 0 for rejected and 1 for admitted.

Gender	HSavg	Decision
1	76	0
0	78	0
1	81	0
1	83	0
1	84	0
1	85	0
0	86	0
0	87	0
0	86	1
1	87	1
1	88	0
1	89	1
0	89	0
1	90	0
1	90	1
0	91	1
1	92	0
1	93	0
0	92	1
0	94	0
0	96	1
0	97	1
0	98	1
1	98	1
0	99	1

Let's focus first on the impact of HSavg on decision and the scatter plot in Figure 11.6. The scatter of points looks rather unusual—two horizontal strings of dots, the upper for admitted applicants and the lower for rejected applicants. It certainly appears that HSavg can, to some extent, predict decision. The HSavg scores for the admitted applicants (the upper string) tend to be further to the right (mean HSavg of 93.0) than those for the rejected applicants (mean HSavg of 86.1). Were we to apply traditional regression methods, the gray regression line (shown in Figure 11.6) would yield some curious results.

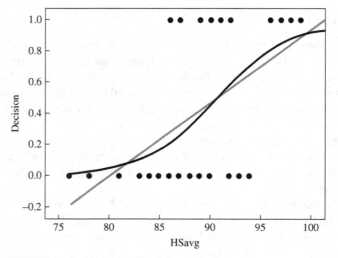

FIGURE 11.6 Linear and logistic regression.

The slope of the line, $b = 0.047$, would suggest that every point increase in HSavg would increase decision by 0.047. Because decision has only two values (0 for reject and 1 for accept), we could interpret the regression coefficient in terms of improving the probability of being admitted. Specifically, the chance of being admitted increases by 0.047 for every unit increase in HSavg. Continuing with this logic, there would be some applicants whose predicted probability of admission would fall below 0, as in fact happens for applicants with HSavg values less than 80. While they may have rather limited chances of being admitted, it certainly would be improper to say that they are less than none. At the other extreme, an applicant with a perfect HSavg of 100 would almost assuredly be admitted, but with straight-line regression, nothing prevents the predicted probability from exceeding 1.

A bit more subtle, it would also seem implausible that the benefit of increasing HSavg is the same at all levels. We might expect, for example, that the difference between 85 and 88 would boost the probability of admission more than the difference between 95 and 98. The extent of positive impact of HSavg on the likelihood of admission would likely diminish at a certain point.

The trouble is that linear regression is not suited for dependent variables constrained to be either 0 or 1. A more reasonable model would be one where below some HSavg level the chance of being admitted is virtually 0, then the chances increase for some mid-range levels of HSavg, and then approach a maximum of virtual certainty for especially high HSavg. The S-shaped curve shown in Figure 11.6, known as a *logistic curve*, captures this relationship between HSavg and decision. Logistic regression is the preferred approach for predicting dichotomous variables like decision.

Without getting bogged down in the mathematical details, some basic understanding of the concept of *odds* is needed to interpret **logistic regression** results. The odds of some event is defined as the probability that event will occur divided by the probability it will not occur:

LOGISTIC REGRESSION
a form of regression for predicting a dichotomous dependent variable.

$$Odds = \frac{P}{1 - P}$$

where P is the usual probability of occurrence. Odds are typically expressed against a benchmark of 1, as in "something-to-one." Thus, if an event has a $P = .75$ chance of occurring, its odds are 3-to-1 ($.75/.25 = 3$). Alternatively, an event with only a $P = .25$ probability, has odds of .33-to-1 ($.25/.75 = .33$). A 50/50 proposition, often called "even odds," has odds of 1-to-1 ($.50/.50 = 1$).

Unlike probability, such as the probability of admission, which varies from 0 to 1, the odds of an event has no ceiling or maximum. Odds can range from 0 (impossible) to infinity (a virtual certainty). Odds are typically used, moreover, to make comparisons between groups. For example, we might contrast the odds of being admitted between males and females based on the cross-tabulation in Table 11.8 of decision by gender. Of the 12 female applicants, $7/12 = 58.33\%$ were admitted, and $5/12 = 41.67\%$ were rejected, so that the odds of admission were $.5833/.4167 = 1.4$, or far more directly from dividing the number admitted by the number rejected, $7/5 = 1.4$. For the 13 male applicants, $4/13 = 30.77\%$ were admitted and $9/13 = 69.33\%$ were rejected. The odds for males are $.3077/.6933$ (or $4/9$) $= 0.44$.

TABLE 11.8 Cross-Tabulation of Decision by Gender

		Gender		
		0 = Female	1 = Male	Total
Decision	0 = Rejected	5	9	14
	1 = Admitted	7	4	11
	Total	12	13	25

The *odds ratio* is defined as the odds for one group divided by the odds for another group. Here, the odds of admission for females divided by the odds of admission for males is $1.4/0.44 = 3.15$. In other words, females have 3.15 *times* the odds of being admitted than do males. This, of course, begs the question of why females enjoy more than three times the odds of being admitted? Are admission decisions at this college unfair and discriminatory? Or perhaps does the greater odds for the female applicant reflect differences in their academic profiles and not just their gender?

This odds–ratio approach works fine for comparing one group to another, such as the odds of admission for females to that of males. However, when examining the impact of several variables simultaneously (including interval-level predictors) on the odds of some event (e.g., how gender and high school grade average impact the odds of being admitted), a regression approach is preferred.

Logistic regression accomplishes the same objectives with dichotomous dependent variables as multiple linear regression does for interval-level outcomes. The big difference is that logistic regression models the natural logarithm of the odds, thus the *log* in "logistic." The dependent variable is transformed into what is known as the log-odds, or *logit*, and is symbolized by *L*,

$$L = \log\left(\frac{P}{1 - P}\right)$$

The logit *L* has no bounds whatsoever. It ranges from minus infinity (for a virtual impossibility) to positive infinity (a virtual certainty). Moreover, negative values of *L* reflect less than even odds, an *L* of 0 reflects even odds, and positive values of *L* represent greater than even odds.

Fortunately, it is not necessary to work with logarithms in order to use this technique, except to know that logistic regression involves predicting the log-odds of a dependent variable, like decision, based on a linear combination of independent variables. The logistic regression equation for two predictor variables, for example, would be

$$L = b_0 + b_1 X_1 + b_2 X_2 + e$$

where b_0 is the constant (or *Y*-intercept in terms of the log-odds), b_1 and b_2 are the coefficients for predictor variables X_1 and X_2, and *e* is the residual or error term. Predicted log-odds would look the same but without the error term:

$$\hat{L} = b_0 + b_1 X_1 + b_2 X_2$$

Finally, the anti-log applied to each side gives us a prediction of the odds:

$$\text{Predicted Odds} = e^{b_0 + b_1 X_1 + b_2 X_2} = e^{b_0} e^{b_1 X_1} e^{b_2 X_2}$$

where $e = 2.718$ is the special constant known as Euler's number. Furthermore, the probability of admission can be predicted for any applicant given HSavg and gender by

$$\hat{P} = \frac{e^{b_0 + b_1 X_1 + b_2 X_2}}{1 + e^{b_0 + b_1 X_1 + b_2 X_2}}$$

This rather formidable-looking equation actually produces the S-shaped curve used to predict admission decisions.

It is not at all critical that one understand these algebraic manipulations involving logs and anti-logs. Moreover, the process of estimating the logistic regression coefficients b_0, b_1, and b_2 is quite complex, as is their interpretation. All that we really need to determine is whether or not they are statistically significant. However, the exponentiation of these coefficients (e^b) in the predicted odds equation provides a fairly straightforward approach to interpreting the effect of each predictor.

Table 11.9 provides the logistic regression estimates from predicting admission based on HSavg and gender. The coefficients (*b*) and their standard errors (S.E.) are used to determine the

TABLE 11.9	Logistic Regression Results for Predicting Admission					
Independent Variables	**b**	**S.E.**	**Wald**	**df**	**Sig.**	**Exp(b)**
Constant	−24.105	10.911	4.881	1	.027	.000
HSavg	.269	.120	5.019	1	.025	1.309
Gender	−.562	1.011	.309	1	.578	.570

statistical significance of the respective independent variables. The Wald statistic (W), used to determine statistical significance, is obtained from the square of a logistic regression coefficient divided by its standard error:

$$W = \left(\frac{b}{SE_b}\right)^2$$

W is treated like a chi-square value (with 1 degree of freedom) to assess when the null hypothesis of no effect in the population can be rejected. The significance value shown in the table is then the probability of obtaining a logistic regression coefficient at least as large as that estimated from the sample data by chance alone if the true effect in the population is zero. We see from the table that HSavg is a significant predictor at the .05 level ($p = .025$). However, the coefficient for gender is not statistically significant ($p = .578$) since the likelihood of obtaining a b value as large in magnitude as −.562 purely as a result of sampling error is quite high ($p = .578$). Thus, what initially appeared to be a decided advantage for females over males largely disappears once HSavg is entered into the logistic regression.

Significant or not, we still cannot easily interpret the estimated b coefficients because they represent changes in log-odds. However, the far-right column of the table–denoted Exp(b) representing e^b—gives the exponentiated coefficients which reflect a variable's effect on the odds of the dependent variable, like we did previously with the impact of gender alone on decision. Specifically, the e^b values indicate the multiplier by which each unit increase in the independent variable changes the predicted odds of the dependent variable, holding constant the other variables.

If $b > 0$, then $e^b > 1$, thereby magnifying the odds (multiplying by a factor greater than 1). On the other hand, if $b < 0$, then $e^b < 1$, thereby diminishing the odds (multiplying by a factor less than 1). Finally, if $b = 0$, then $e^b = 1$, thereby leaving the odds unchanged (multiplying by 1).

Consider the results contained in Table 11.9. For HSavg, $e^b = 1.309$, which indicates that every one-point increase in HSavg tends to magnify the odds of being admitted by a factor of 1.309, that is, about a 30% increase in the odds. Also, a two-point increase would predict a change of multiplying the odds twice by 1.301. A five-point increase, say from 85 to 90, would be associated with multiplying the odds by 1.301 five times, or by 3.73, thereby almost quadrupling the odds.

For gender, there are only two possible values, of course, 0 for female and 1 for male. The odds-multiplier, $e^b = .570$, suggests that the odds of admission for males is less than that for females, because the odds are reduced when multiplying by a number less than one. Specifically, a male applicant would tend to have 43% lower odds of being admitted as a female applicant with an identical grade average (multiplying a number by .57 reduces it by 43%). Though this finding could be disturbing for many potential applicants, remember that the estimated coefficient for gender was not statistically significant, leaving wide open the possibility that the apparent gender difference was a mere consequence of sampling error. Finally, this impact of gender holding constant HSavg, though in the same direction, is far less than we previously calculated for gender alone.

Finally, with mixed results in terms of statistical significance of the predictors, how well does the model as a whole predict decisions on admission? There is, unfortunately, no exact R^2 statistic, as in linear regression, to indicate what percentage of the variance in the dependent variable is explained by the independent variables in combination. However, logistic regression does have several options for assessing the overall fit, the most widely used of which is Nagelkerke's R^2, which varies from 0 for no fit to 1 for perfect fit. In our case, the SPSS results indicate that Nagelkerke's $R^2 = .442$, reflecting a fairly good fit, even with only two variables. Were we to include other predictors, such as SAT or ACT scores, the predictive fit would most likely improve.

Summary

In this chapter, we extended the concept of correlation to situations in which a social researcher is concerned with the effect of one variable (the independent variable) on another (the dependent variable). Whereas Pearson's r measures the strength and direction of correlation, the regression line, comprised of a slope and Y-intercept, specifies the exact nature of the impact of the independent variable on the dependent variable. In regression analysis, the value of the dependent variable (denoted Y) is predicted on the basis of the independent variable (denoted X). The proportion of variance in Y explained by X (known as the coefficient of determination) is separated from the proportion of variance in Y not explained by X (known as the coefficient of nondetermination). The procedure known as multiple regression goes beyond the simple regression technique introduced in this chapter to incorporate

not just one but two or more predictors simultaneously. In this case, the regression coefficients (slopes) indicate the effect of one independent variable on the dependent variable, holding constant the other predictor variables in the model. In addition, the multiple coefficient of determination assesses the proportion of variance in the dependent variable accounted for by the set of independent variables in combination. Although multiple regression is generally used with interval-level variables, dichotomous predictors—known as dummy variables—can be incorporated as well. In addition, interaction effects can be included by multiplying predictors. Finally, logistic regression provides a very useful extension to the case of predicting dichotomous dependent variables. Logistic regression focuses on the odds of an event, and the extent to which various predictor variables magnify or reduce the odds of one outcome over another.

Questions and Problems

1. An objective of regression analysis is to predict values of the _____.
   a. correlation variable
   b. dependent variable
   c. independent variable
   d. regression variable
2. Which of the following represents the slope or the regression coefficient for X?
   a. the Y-intercept
   b. the term a
   c. the error term
   d. the term b
3. The increase or decrease in Y with each unit change in X is known as _____.
   a. the Y-intercept, a
   b. the error term, e
   c. the regression coefficient, b
   d. alpha
4. The proportion of variance in Y explained by X is known as _____.
   a. alpha
   b. the coefficient of determination
   c. the coefficient of nondetermination
   d. the slope

5. Which of the following assumptions is true for regression?
   a. Both variables are measured at the interval level
   b. Regression assumes a straight-line relationship
   c. Samples are drawn randomly
   d. All of the above are true
6. A legal researcher wanted to measure the effect of the length of a criminal trial on the length of jury deliberation. He observed in a sample of 10 randomly selected courtroom trials the following data on length of trial (in days) and length of jury deliberation (in hours).

X (Days)	Y (Hours)
2	4
7	12
4	6
1	4
1	1
3	4
2	7
5	2
2	4
3	6

a. Draw a scatter plot of the data.
b. Using the formula for raw scores, calculate the regression slope and Y-intercept.
c. Draw the regression line on the scatter plot.
d. Predict the length of jury deliberation for a trial lasting 5 days.
e. Find the coefficients of determination and nondetermination. What do they mean?
f. What is the correlation between length of trial and length of jury deliberation? (*Hint:* The correlation coefficient is equal to one of the other statistics that is calculated in regression analysis using two variables.)

7. A researcher is interested in sentencing dispositions and their relationship with the severity of a crime. She asked a sample of 10 prospective jury members to rate the seriousness of a crime (X) on a 1 (not very serious) to 7 (extremely serious) scale along with the sentence (Y) in years that they would recommend.

X	Y
7	12
6	15
3	3
3	6
6	10
1	5
2	2
6	4
2	3
5	3

a. Draw a scatter plot of the data.
b. Using the formula for raw scores, calculate the regression slope and Y-intercept.
c. Draw the regression line on the scatter plot.
d. Predict the length of recommended sentence for a crime rated as a 5.
e. Find the coefficients of determination and nondetermination. What do they mean?

8. Neighborhoods in a downtown city have experienced an increase in robberies, particularly around bars. The police department decides to patrol bars around 11 neighborhoods varying in number from 0 patrols to 11 patrols. The police department would like to know if an increase in the number of patrols decreases the number of robberies. Conduct a regression analysis using the number of patrols as the independent variable and the number of robberies as the dependent variable.

# Patrols	# Robberies
0	7
1	6
2	7
3	5
4	5
5	4
6	6
7	4
8	2
9	0
10	1

a. What is the slope of the regression line?
b. What is the intercept of the regression line?
c. Are the results significant at the .05 level? How about the .01 level?
d. What would you predict the number of robberies to be if the police department made 11 patrols?

9. A criminologist was interested in the effects of unemployment and policing on murder. To conduct her study, she finds information on percentage unemployed, the number of police, and the number of murders in the 10 largest cities along with the population of each city. She uses this information to calculate homicide rates per 100,000 population and police officers per 1,000 population.

Homicide Rate	Unemployment Rate	Police Per 1,000
6.8	1.3	4.2
7.2	4.8	1.7
6.3	4.1	1.7
5.0	4.0	2.3
7.5	2.1	1.7
7.9	3.6	2.0
5.6	6.4	4.5
6.2	1.5	2.6
5.4	5.3	2.4
4.3	2.8	4.6

a. Conduct a multiple regression analysis of the homicide rate (Y) testing its relationship to unemployment (X) and police presence (Z).
b. What are the regression slopes and the intercept?
c. Which variables are significant at the .05 level?
d. What is the predicted homicide rate for a city with an unemployment rate of 5% and 2.5 police officers per 1,000 population?
e. What would be the predicted homicide rate in this city if the number of police officers per 1,000 population were increased from 2.5 to 5.0? Is doubling the number of police officers a reasonable request?
f. Find the coefficients of determination and nondetermination.

10. A researcher wishes to predict the graduation rates in a sample of 240 colleges and universities based on the percentage of first-year students who were in the top tier (10%) of their high school class and the percentage of classes that have fewer than 20 students. The correlation matrix of graduation rate (GRADRATE), percentage of first-year students in the top tier of their high school graduating class (TOPFRESH), and the percentage of classes at the college with fewer than 20 students (SMALLCLS) is shown as follows:

	GRADRATE	TOPFRESH	SMALLCLS
GRADRATE	1.000	.613	.544
TOPFRESH	.613	1.000	.404
SMALLCLS	.544	.404	1.000

a. What percentage of the variance in GRADRATE does each of the predictor variables explain individually?

b. What percentage of the variance in GRADRATE do the two predictors explain in combination?

c. Why doesn't the answer in (b) equal the sum of the two answers in (a)?

11. Following is a portion of an analysis of variance table from a multiple regression predicting students' quantitative SAT scores (QSAT) based on their high school grade average (HSAVG) and their gender (GENDER):

Source	SS	df	MS	F
Regression	127,510	2	?	?
Error	82,990	53	?	
Total	?			

a. Fill out the portions indicated with a question mark.

b. What is the sample size (N)?

c. What percentage of the variance in QSAT is explained by the two predictors combined?

d. Comment on the overall significance of the results.

12. Suppose that an emergency room doctor is interested in the relationships among gender, age, and sensitivity to pain among knife-assault victims. She collects from a sample of 57 hospital files information on patients' self-reported pain scores, ranging from 0 for no discomfort to 10 for the worst pain imaginable, along with the patients' ages in years and gender (1 for male and 0 for female). The results of her regression analysis predicting pain based on age and gender are shown in the following table:

Variable	b	SE	t	Sig.
Constant	1.321	0.239	5.527	0.000
Age	0.065	0.041	1.585	0.119
Gender	0.857	0.665	1.289	0.203

a. Interpret the constant (Y-intercept).

b. Interpret the regression coefficients for age and gender.

c. Indicate which, if either, of these two variables is a significant predictor of pain score.

13. The following table contains responses to a survey concerning support for allowing prison inmates to vote in statewide elections, comparing positions on the issue with political party affiliation of respondents.

Party Affiliation	Position toward Allowing Inmate Voting		Total
	Support	Oppose	
Democrat	45	64	109
Republican	21	72	93
Independent	24	60	84
Total	90	196	286

a. Calculate the odds of supporting inmate voting for each category of party affiliation.

b. Calculate the odds ratio for each pair of categories of party affiliation.

14. Referring back to problem 11, the same doctor then used the three variables—pain level (pain), age, and gender—to predict whether or not knife-assault victims were admitted to the hospital (admit = 1) by the ER or sent home (admit = 0). She performs a logistic regression that produces the following results:

Variable	b	SE	Wald	Sig.	e^b
Constant	−11.236	0.239	2210.2	0.000	0.000
Age	0.054	0.022	6.1342	0.013	1.056
Gender	−0.020	0.018	1.2597	0.262	0.980
Pain	0.263	0.043	37.447	0.000	1.301

a. Why did she use logistic regression rather than multiple regression?

b. Interpret the results for each of the three variables.

Computer Exercises

1. From the General Social Survey, is there a direct link between income and education? Test the null hypothesis that there is no relationship between a respondent's income (REALRINC) and his or her highest year of school completed (EDUC). *Hint:* ANALYZE, REGRESSION, LINEAR and then specify variables. Income is the dependent variable.

a. Find the ANOVA test of regression. Is it significant?

b. What is the regression slope and intercept?

c. Predict the amount of income in constant dollars (year 2000) for a person who has completed 12 years of education and 16 years of education.

d. Find the coefficient of determination. What does it mean?

2. Conduct a regression analysis to determine the relationship between the number of mental health days (MNTLHLTH) during the past 30 days and job satisfaction (SATJOB1).

a. Find the ANOVA test of regression. Is it significant?

b. What is the regression slope and intercept?

c. Predict the number of mental health days for a person who is not at all satisfied with his or her job. Run a frequency distribution on both variables to see the values on each scale.

d. Find the coefficient of determination. What does it mean?

3. Perform a regression analysis to predict how often people spend an evening at a bar (SOCBAR) on the basis of age (AGE) and highest year of education (EDUC).

a. Test the null hypothesis that the number of times that people go out to a bar is not related to age, holding years of education constant.

b. What are the regression slopes and the intercept?

c. Which variables are significant at the .05 level?

d. Find the multiple coefficient of determination (R^2). What does it mean? Did it improve over the amount explained in the two-variable regression models?

e. What is the predicted value for evenings out to the bar for a person who is 40 years old and has 14 years as his or her highest level of education? *Hint:* Remember to look for the values on each of the scales before doing your calculation.

4. Conduct a regression analysis to determine what predicts the number of mental health days (MNTLHLTH) during the past 30 days. Add age (AGE), physical health days (PHYSHLTH), job satisfaction (SAT1), and income (REALRINC) into the regression analysis as independent variables.

a. Find the ANOVA test of regression. Is it significant?

b. What are the regression slopes and intercept?

c. Which variables are significant at the .05 level?

d. Find the multiple coefficient of determination (R^2). What does it mean?

5. Use the General Social Survey to conduct a logistic regression analysis to test the null hypothesis that males and females do not differ in their fear of crime (SEX and FEAR). *Hint:* ANALYZE, REGRESSION, BINARY LOGISTIC, select variables, and specify whether independent variables are categorical.

a. What is the logistic regression slope and intercept?

b. Find the numerical value of e^b for SEX? What does it mean?

c. Find the Nagelkerke R-Square. What does this statistic mean?

6. Use the General Social Survey to conduct a logistic regression analysis to test the null hypothesis that males and females do not differ in their reports of sexual harassment at work (SEX and WKHARSEX). *Hint:* ANALYZE, REGRESSION, BINARY LOGISTIC, select variables, and specify whether independent variables are categorical.

a. What is the logistic regression slope and intercept?

b. Find the numerical value of e^b for SEX? What does it mean?

c. Find the Nagelkerke R-Square. What does this statistic mean?

Nonparametric Measures of Correlation

We saw previously that nonparametric alternatives to t and F were necessary for testing group differences with nominal and ordinal data. Similarly, we need nonparametric measures of correlation to use when the requirements of Pearson's r cannot be met. Specifically, these measures are applied if we have nominal or ordinal data or if we cannot assume normality in the population. This chapter introduces some of the best-known nonparametric measures of correlation: Spearman's rank–order correlation coefficient, Goodman's and Kruskal's gamma, phi coefficient, contingency coefficient, and Cramér's V.

SPEARMAN'S RANK–ORDER CORRELATION COEFFICIENT

We turn now to the problem of finding the degree of association for ordinal data—data that have been ranked or ordered with respect to the presence of a given characteristic.

To take an example from criminal justice, consider the relationship between socioeconomic status and the amount of money spent on automobile antitheft devices. Although the amount spent on auto security could be clearly measured at the interval level, socioeconomic status is considered ordinal, and thus a correlation coefficient for ordinal or ranked data is required. Imagine that a sample of eight respondents could be ranked as in Table 12.1.

As shown in the table, Don ranked first (highest) with respect to socioeconomic status, but second in the amount of money spent on automobile security; Flora's socioeconomic status rank was second, but first in the amount spent on automobile security devices, and so on.

To determine the degree of association between socioeconomic status and amount spent on automobile security, we apply **Spearman's rank–order correlation coefficient** (r_s). By formula,

SPEARMAN'S RANK–ORDER CORRELATION COEFFICIENT

A correlation coefficient for data that have been ranked or ordered with respect to the presence of a given characteristic.

$$r_s = 1 - \frac{6\sum D^2}{N(N^2 - 1)}$$

where

r_s = rank–order correlation coefficient

D = difference in rank between X and Y variables

N = total number of cases

TABLE 12.1	Sample Ranked by Socioeconomic Status and Amount Spent on Auto Security

Respondent	Socioeconomic Status (X) Rank		Amount Spent on Auto Security (Y) Rank	
Don	1		2	
Flora	2	Highest in socioeconomic status	1	Most spent on auto security
Tong	3		3	
Min	4		5	
Juanita	5		4	
Lisa	6		8	
Emma	7		6	
Jason	8		7	

We set up the present example as shown in Table 12.2. By applying the rank–order correlation coefficient formula to the data in this table,

$$r_s = 1 - \frac{(6)(10)}{(8)(64 - 1)}$$

$$= 1 - \frac{60}{(8)(63)}$$

$$= 1 - \frac{60}{504}$$

$$= 1 - .12$$

$$= +.88$$

Therefore, we find a strong positive correlation ($r_s = +.88$) between socioeconomic status and the amount of money spent on automobile security devices: Respondents having high socioeconomic status tend to spend a good deal on auto security; respondents with low socioeconomic status tend to spend little on such devices.

TABLE 12.2	The Relationship between Socioeconomic Status and Amount Spent on Auto Security

Respondent	Socioeconomic Status (X)	Amount Spent on Auto Security (Y)	D = X − Y	D²
1	1	2	−1	1
2	2	1	1	1
3	3	3	0	0
4	4	5	−1	1
5	5	4	1	1
6	6	8	−2	4
7	7	6	1	1
8	8	7	1	1
				$\Sigma D^2 = 10$

Dealing with Tied Ranks

In actual practice, it is not always possible to rank or order our respondents, avoiding ties at each position. We might find, for instance, that two or more respondents spend exactly the same amount of money on automobile security, that the academic achievement of two or more criminal justice students is indistinguishable, or that several respondents have the same IQ score.

To illustrate the procedure for obtaining a rank–order correlation coefficient in the case of tied ranks, let us say we are interested in determining the degree of association between position in a graduating class and number of after-school detentions during the senior year. Suppose we are able to rank a sample of 10 students with respect to their class position and to obtain the number of detentions they have earned as follows:

Respondent	Class Rank (X)	Number of After-School Detentions (Y)
Jim	10 ← (last)	5
Tracy	9	10
Leroy	8	7
Mike	7	8
Mario	6	5
Kenny	5	5
Mitchell	4	1
Minny	3	3
Cori	2	0
Kumiko	1 ← (first)	0

Before following the standard procedure for obtaining a rank–order correlation coefficient, let us first rank the number of detentions of our 10 graduating seniors:

Respondent	Detentions	Rank
Jim	5	4
Tracy	10	1
Leroy	7	3
Mike	8	2
Mario	5	5
Kenny	5	6
Mitchell	1	8
Minny	3	7
Cori	0	9
Kumiko	0	10

Positions 4, 5, and 6 are tied

Positions 9 and 10 are tied

The table shows that Cori and Kumiko received absolutely no after-school detentions and are, therefore, tied for the ninth and tenth positions. Likewise, Kenny, Mario, and Jim all received five detentions, which places them in a three-way tie for the fourth, fifth, and sixth positions.

To determine the exact position in the case of ties, we must *add the tied ranks and divide by the number of ties.* Therefore, the position of zero detentions, which has been ranked as 9 and 10, would be the average rank:

$$\frac{9 + 10}{2} = 9.5$$

TABLE 12.3	The Relationship between Class Standing and Number of Detentions			
Student	**Class Standing (X)**	**Detentions Ranked (Y)**	**D = X − Y**	**D²**
Jim	10	5	5	25
Tracy	9	1	8	64
Leroy	8	3	5	25
Mike	7	2	5	25
Mario	6	5	1	1
Kenny	5	5	0	0
Mitchell	4	8	−4	16
Minny	3	7	−4	16
Cori	2	9.5	−7.5	56.25
Kumiko	1	9.5	−8.5	72.25
				$\Sigma D^2 = 300.5$

In the same way, we find that the position of five detentions is

$$\frac{4 + 5 + 6}{3} = 5.0$$

Each person in a tie is then assigned the average ranking. For example, Cori and Kumiko each receive a ranking of 9.5, and Kenny, Mario, and Jim each receive a ranking of 5. Having found the ranked position of each student's number of detentions, we can proceed to set up the problem at hand, as shown in Table 12.3.

We obtain the rank–order correlation coefficient for the problem in Table 12.3 as follows:

$$r_s = 1 - \frac{(6)(300.5)}{(10)(100 - 1)}$$

$$= 1 - \frac{1803}{990}$$

$$= 1 - 1.82$$

$$= -.82$$

The resultant rank–order correlation coefficient indicates a rather strong negative correlation between class standing and number of detentions. That is, students having *few* after-school detentions tend to rank *high* in their class; students who rank *low* in number of detentions tend to rank *high* in their class.

Testing the Significance of the Rank–Order Correlation Coefficient

How do we go about testing the significance of a rank–order correlation coefficient? For example, how can we determine whether the obtained correlation of −.82 between class standing and number of detentions can be generalized to a larger population? To test the significance of a computed rank–order correlation coefficient, we turn to Table I in Appendix C, where we find the critical values of the rank–order coefficient of correlation for the .05 and .01 significance levels. Notice that we refer directly to the number of pairs of scores (N) rather than to a particular number of degrees of freedom. In the present case, N = 10 and we find that the rank–order correlation coefficient must exceed .648 to be significant at the .05 level of significance. We therefore reject the null hypothesis that population correlation $\rho_s = 0$ and accept the research hypothesis that class standing and detentions are actually related in the population from which our sample was drawn.

STEP-BY-STEP ILLUSTRATION

Spearman's Rank–Order Correlation Coefficient

We can summarize the step-by-step procedure for obtaining the rank–order correlation coefficient with reference to the relationship between the degree of participation in criminal justice professional organizations and number of close friends. This relationship is indicated in the following sample of six respondents working in the field of criminal justice:

Respondent	Criminal Justice Organization Participation (X) Rank		Number of Friends (Y)
A	1	◄——Participates	6
B	2	most	4
C	3		6
D	4		2
E	5	Participates	2
F	6	◄——least	3

To determine the degree of association between voluntary association participation and number of friends, we carry through the following steps:

Step 1 Rank respondents on the *X* and *Y* variables.

As the previous table shows, we rank respondents with respect to *X*, participation in professional organization, assigning the rank of 1 to the respondent who participates most and the rank of 6 to the respondent who participates least.

We must also rank the respondents in terms of *Y*, the number of their friends. In the present example, we have instances of tied ranks, as shown in the following:

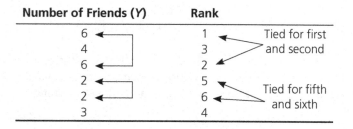

To convert tied ranks, we take an average of the tied positions:
For first and second positions:

$$\frac{1 + 2}{2} = 1.5$$

For fifth and sixth positions:

$$\frac{5 + 6}{2} = 5.5$$

Therefore, in terms of ranks, where X_R and Y_R denote the ranks on X and Y, respectively,

X_R	Y_R
1	1.5
2	3.0
3	1.5
4	5.5
5	5.5
6	4.0

Step 2 To find $\sum D^2$, we must find the difference between X and Y ranks (D), square each difference (D^2), and sum these squares ($\sum D^2$):

X_R	Y_R	D	D^2
1	1.5	−.5	.25
2	3.0	−1.0	1.00
3	1.5	1.5	2.25
4	5.5	−1.5	2.25
5	5.5	−.5	.25
6	4.0	2.0	4.00
			$\sum D^2 = 10.00$

Step 3 Plug the result of step 2 into the formula for the rank–order correlation coefficient.

$$r_s = 1 - \frac{6\sum D^2}{N(N^2 - 1)}$$

$$= 1 - \frac{(6)(10)}{(6)(36 - 1)}$$

$$= 1 - \frac{60}{210}$$

$$= 1 - .29$$

$$= +.71$$

Step 4 Compare the obtained rank–order correlation coefficient with the critical value of r_s in Table I.

$$\text{Obtained } r_s = .71$$

$$\text{Table } r_s = .886$$

$$N = 6$$

$$\alpha = .05$$

Turning to Table I in Appendix C, we learn that a correlation coefficient of .886 is necessary to reject the null hypothesis at the .05 level of significance with a sample size of 6. Therefore, although we have uncovered a strong positive correlation between professional organization participation and number of friends, we must still retain the null hypothesis that population correlation $\rho_s = 0$. Our result cannot be generalized to the population from which our sample was taken.

Table I applies only for samples of up to 30 cases. What then should we do if N exceeds this number? Consider an example having a somewhat larger number of observations. Table 12.4 provides rankings of the states according to correctional expenditures per capita (X) and the rate of violent crime per 100,000 residents (Y) for the year 2004, after resolving ties by the averaging approach presented earlier.

On the basis of these figures,

$$r_s = 1 - \frac{6\sum D^2}{N(N^2 - 1)}$$

$$= 1 - \frac{6(11,616)}{50(2,500 - 1)}$$

$$= 1 - \frac{69.696}{124,950}$$

$$= 1 - .558$$

$$= +.442$$

The positive correlation suggests that the higher the violent crime rate, the greater the per capital expenditure on state-operated corrections. While this result is quite reasonable, is the value of Spearman's rank–order correlation large enough to be considered statistically significant? Table I, of course, provides r_s crucial values only for N up to 30.

TABLE 12.4 State Rankings of Correctional Expenditures and Violent Crime Rate, 2004

State	X	Y	X_r	Y_r	D	D^2	State	X	Y	X_r	Y_r	D	D^2
Alabama	131	426.6	42	22	20	400.00	Montana	157	293.8	30	33	−3	9.00
Alaska	271	634.5	1	7	−6	36.00	Nebraska	169	308.7	22.5	30	−7.5	56.25
Arizona	205	504.1	15	9.5	2	4.00	Nevada	234	615.9	7	8	−1	1.00
Arkansas	167	499.1	24.5	15	9.5	90.25	New Hampshire	100	167.0	49	47	2	4.00
California	265	551.8	2	11	−9	81.00	New Jersey	209	355.7	11	26	−15	225.00
Colorado	181	373.5	20	25	−5	25.00	New Mexico	221	687.3	8	5	3	9.00
Connecticut	159	286.3	28.5	34	−5.5	30.25	New York	248	441.6	4	21	−17	289.00
Delaware	244	568.4	5	9	−4	16.00	North Carolina	155	447.8	31	20	11	121.00
Florida	204	711.3	16	2	14	196.00	North Dakota	93	79.4	50	50	0	0.00
Georgia	207	455.5	13	19	−6	36.00	Ohio	161	341.8	27	28	−1	1.00
Hawaii	125	254.4	43	39	4	16.00	Oklahoma	166	500.5	26	14	12	144.00
Idaho	167	244.9	24.5	41.5	−17	289.00	Oregon	212	298.3	9	31	−22	484.00
Illinois	144	542.9	37	12	25	625.00	Pennsylvania	207	411.1	13	23	−10	100.00
Indiana	147	325.4	36	29	7	49.00	Rhode Island	150	247.4	32.5	40	−7.5	56.25
Iowa	110	270.9	47	37	10	100.00	South Carolina	137	784.2	39	1	38	1444.00
Kansas	148	374.5	35	24	11	121.00	South Dakota	105	171.5	48	46	2	4.00
Kentucky	149	244.9	34	41.5	−7.5	56.25	Tennessee	135	695.2	41	4	37	1369.00
Louisiana	189	638.7	19	6	13	169.00	Texas	180	553.1	21	10	11	121.00
Maine	123	103.5	45	49	−4	16.00	Utah	169	236.0	22.5	43	−20.5	420.25
Maryland	236	700.5	6	3	3	9.00	Vermont	150	112.0	32.5	48	15.5	240.25
Massachusetts	159	458.8	28.5	18	10.5	110.25	Virginia	190	275.6	18	35	−17	289.00
Michigan	207	490.2	13	17	−4	16.00	Washington	201	343.8	17	27	−10	100.00
Minnesota	136	269.6	40	38	2	4.00	West Virginia	118	271.2	46	36	10	100.00
Mississippi	124	295.1	44	32	12	144.00	Wisconsin	210	209.6	10	45	−35	1225.00
Missouri	143	490.5	38	16	22	484.00	Wyoming	260	229.6	3	44	−11	1681.00
					97	3,123.00						−97	8,493.00

For large samples (for $N > 30$), the following expression tends to have a normal distribution and can be compared with critical values of z.

$$z = r_s \sqrt{N - 1}$$

For our example,

$$z = .442 \sqrt{50 - 1}$$
$$= .442(7)$$
$$= 3.095$$

Here z well exceeds the 1.96 critical value of z at the .05 level of significance. Therefore, we reject the null hypothesis of no relationship in the population between state correctional expenditures and the violent crime rate.

Requirements for Using the Rank–Order Correlation Coefficient

The rank–order correlation coefficient should be employed when the following conditions can be satisfied:

1. *A straight-line correlation.* The rank–order correlation coefficient detects straight-line relationships between X and Y.
2. *Ordinal data.* Both X and Y variables must be ranked or ordered.
3. *Random sampling.* Sample members must have been taken at random from a larger population to apply a test of significance.

GOODMAN'S AND KRUSKAL'S GAMMA

As we saw in connection with the rank–order correlation coefficient, it is not always possible to avoid tied ranks at the ordinal level of measurement. In fact, criminal justice researchers frequently work with crude ordinal measures that produce large numbers of tied ranks. Typically, this occurs with ordinal variables that are ranked in categories, such as high, medium, and low. When two such ordinal variables are cross-tabulated, **Goodman's and Kruskal's gamma** (G) is a particularly useful measure of association.

The basic formula for gamma is

$$G = \frac{N_a - N_i}{N_a + N_i}$$

where N_a = number of agreements
N_i = number of inversions

GOODMAN'S AND KRUSKAL'S GAMMA

An alternative to the rank–order correlation coefficient for measuring the degree of association between ordinal-level variables.

Agreements and inversions can be understood as expressing the direction of correlation between X and Y variables. Perfect agreement indicates a perfect positive correlation ($+1.00$): All individuals being studied have been ranked in exactly the same order on both variables.

By contrast, perfect inversion indicates a perfect negative correlation (-1.00), so that the individuals being studied are ranked in exactly reverse order on both variables.

The logic of agreements, inversions, and tied pairs can be illustrated by examining the following simple cross-tabulation in which the frequencies are supplemented by the 10 respondents' names:

		High	**Medium**	**Low**
			X	
Y	**High**	$f = 2$ Sam Mary	$f = 1$ Ann	$f = 0$
	Low	$f = 2$ Alex Jack	$f = 3$ Paul John Lisa	$f = 2$ Sue Bob

Mary and John are in agreement because she is higher than he is on both variables. Similarly, the pair Sam and Sue are in agreement because Sam is at a higher level than Sue on both variables. In all, there are 12 agreements ($N_a = 12$). Can you find all 12?

In contrast, the pair Alex and Ann is an inversion because Alex exceeds Ann on X but falls below her on Y. Overall, there are two inversions ($N_i = 2$). Can you find both pairs?

Finally, any pair that is at the same level on one or both variables represents a tie. For example, Alex and Jack are tied on both variables (i.e., they are in the same cell). Furthermore, although Alex surpasses Sue on X, they are at the same level on Y (i.e., they are in the same row), and thus they are counted as a tied pair. Fortunately, you can ignore ties in calculating gamma, because they do not enter into its formula.

STEP-BY-STEP ILLUSTRATION

Goodman's and Kruskal's Gamma

Using a larger example, let us now illustrate the procedure for obtaining a gamma coefficient for cross-tabulated ordinal variables. Suppose that a researcher wanting to examine the relationship between social class (X) and faith in the fairness of local police (Y) obtained the following data from a questionnaire study of 80 city residents: Among 29 upper-class respondents, 15 were high, 10 were medium, and 4 were low with respect to faith in the police; among 25 respondents who were middle class, 8 were high, 10 were medium, and 7 were low with respect to faith in the police; and among 26 lower-class respondents, 7 were high, 8 were medium, and 11 were low with respect to faith in the fairness of local police. Notice that tied ranks occur at every position. For instance, there were 29 respondents who tied at the rank of upper social class, the highest rank on the X variable.

Step 1 Rearrange the data in the form of a cross-tabulation.

Faith in Fairness of Local Police (Y)	Social Class (X)		
	Upper	**Middle**	**Lower**
High	15	8	7
Medium	10	10	8
Low	4	7	11
Total	29	25	26
		$N = 80$	

Notice that the preceding table is a 3×3 cross-tabulation containing nine cells (3 rows $\times$ 3 columns = 9). To ensure that the sign of the gamma coefficient is accurately depicted as either positive or negative, the X variable in the columns must always be arranged in decreasing order from left to right. In the table, for example, social class decreases—upper, middle, lower—from left to right columns. Similarly, the Y variable in the rows must decrease from top to bottom. In the preceding table, faith in the fairness of local police decreases—high, medium, low—from top to bottom rows.

Step 2 Obtain N_a.

To find N_a, begin with the cell ($f = 15$) in the upper left-hand corner. Multiply this number by the sum of all numbers that fall *below and to the right of it* (excluding the marginal totals). Reading from left to right, we see that all frequencies below *and* to the right of 15 are 10, 8, 7, and 11. Now repeat this procedure for all cell frequencies that have cells below and to the right of them. By working from left to right in the table,

Upper class/high faith in police	$(15)(10 + 8 + 7 + 11) = (15)(36) = 540$
Middle class/high faith in police	$(8)(8 + 11) = (8)(19) = 152$
Upper class/medium faith in police	$(10)(7 + 11) = (10)(18) = 180$
Middle class/medium faith in police	$(10)(11) = 110$

(Note that none of the other cell frequencies in the table—7 in the top row, 8 in the second row, and 4, 7, and 11 in the bottom row—has cells below *and* to the right.)

N_a is the sum of the products obtained in the previous table.

$$N_a = 540 + 152 + 180 + 110$$
$$= 982$$

Step 3 Obtain N_i.

To obtain N_i, reverse the procedure for finding agreements and begin in the upper-right corner of the table. This time, each number is multiplied by the sum of all numbers that fall *below and to the left of it*. Reading from right to left, we see that frequencies below *and* to the left of 7 are 10, 10, 7, and 4. As before, repeat this procedure for all frequencies having cells below and to the left of them.

Working from right to left,

Lower class/high faith in police	$(7)(10 + 10 + 7 + 4) = (7)(31) = 217$
Middle class/high faith in police	$(8)(10 + 4) = (8)(14) = 112$
Lower class/medium faith in police	$(8)(7 + 4) = (8)(11) = 88$
Middle class/medium faith in police	$(10)(4) = 40$

(Note that none of the other cell frequencies in the table—15 in the top row, 10 in the middle row, 11, 7, and 4 in the bottom row—has cells below *and* to the left.)

N_i, is the sum of the products computed in the previous table. Therefore,

$$N_i = 217 + 112 + 88 + 40$$
$$= 457$$

Step 4 Plug the results of Steps 2 and 3 into the formula for gamma.

$$G = \frac{N_a - N_i}{N_a + N_i}$$
$$= \frac{982 - 457}{982 + 457}$$
$$= \frac{525}{1439}$$
$$= +.36$$

A gamma coefficient of +.36 indicates a moderate positive correlation between social class and faith in local police. Our result suggests a correlation based on a dominance of agreements. (Note that a gamma coefficient of −.36 would have indicated instead a moderate *negative* correlation based on a dominance of *inversions*.)

Before continuing, let's take another look at how gamma functions in the context of cross-tabulations. Consider, for example, the center ("middle-medium") cell in the cross-tabulation of social class and faith in the fairness of local police. Cases that are below and to the right are agreements because they are lower on both variables. Cases that are below and to the left are inversions because they are lower on Y but greater on X. Why not count the 15 "upper-high" cases as agreements, too, with respect to our "middle-medium" reference cell? Although these are agreements, they would have already been counted: The 15 "middle-medium" cases are counted as agreements when "upper-high" is the reference cell. Counting agreements and inversions only toward the bottom of the table avoids any mistake of double counting.

Testing the Significance of Gamma

To test the null hypothesis that X and Y are not associated in the population—that $\gamma = 0$—we convert our calculated G to a z score by the following formula:

$$z = G\sqrt{\frac{N_a + N_i}{N(1 - G^2)}}$$

where G = calculated gamma coefficient

N_a = number of agreements

N_i = number of inversions

N = sample size

In the foregoing illustration, we found that $G = .36$ for the correlation between social class and faith in the fairness of local police. To test the significance of our finding, we substitute in the formula as follows:

$$z = (.36)\sqrt{\frac{982 + 457}{(80)[1 - (.36)^2]}}$$

$$= (.36)\sqrt{\frac{1,439}{(80)(.87)}}$$

$$= (.36)\sqrt{\frac{1,439}{69.60}}$$

$$= (.36)\sqrt{20.68}$$

$$= (.36)(4.55)$$

$$= 1.64$$

Turning to Table A (or the bottom row of Table C) in Appendix C, we see that z must exceed 1.96 to reject the null hypothesis at the .05 level of significance. Because our calculated z (1.64) is smaller than the required table value, we must retain the null hypothesis that faith in police $\gamma = 0$ and reject the research hypothesis that $\gamma \neq 0$. Our obtained correlation cannot be generalized to the population from which our sample was drawn.

Requirements for Using Gamma

The following requirements must be taken into account to employ gamma as a measure of association for cross-tabulations.

1. *Ordinal data.* Both X and Y variables must be ranked or ordered.
2. *Random sampling.* To test the null hypothesis ($\gamma = 0$), sample members must have been taken on a random basis from some specified population.

CORRELATION COEFFICIENT FOR NOMINAL DATA ARRANGED IN A 2 × 2 TABLE

In Chapter 9, a test of significance for frequency data known as chi-square was introduced. By a simple extension of the chi-square test, the degree of association between variables at the nominal level of measurement can now be determined. Let us take another look at the null hypothesis that

the proportion of smokers among American college students is the same as the proportion of smokers among Canadian college students.

In Chapter 9, this null hypothesis was tested in a sample of 21 American students and a sample of 15 Canadian students attending the same university. It was determined that 15 out of the 21 American students, but only 5 out of the 15 Canadian students, were nonsmokers. Thus, we have the 2 × 2 problem shown in Table 12.5.

TABLE 12.5	Smoking among American and Canadian College Students: Data from Table 9.7		

Smoking Status	Nationality		Total
	American	*Canadian*	
Nonsmoker	15	5	20
Smoker	6	10	16
Total	21	15	$N = 36$

The relationship between nationality and smoking status among college students was tested in Chapter 9 by applying the 2×2 chi-square formula (with Yates's correction because of small expected frequencies) using a summary table as follows:

$$\chi^2 = \Sigma \frac{(|f_o - f_e| - .5)^2}{f_e}$$

f_o	f_e	$|f_o - f_e|$	$|f_o - f_e| - .5$	$(|f_o - f_e| - .5)^2$	$\dfrac{(|f_o - f_e| - .5)^2}{f_e}$
15	11.67	3.33	2.83	8.01	.69
5	8.33	3.33	2.83	8.01	.96
6	9.33	3.33	2.83	8.01	.86
10	6.67	3.33	2.83	8.01	1.20
					$\chi^2 = 3.71$

Having calculated a chi-square value of 3.71, we can now obtain the **phi coefficient**(ϕ), which is a measure of the degree of association for 2×2 tables. By formula,

$$\phi = \sqrt{\frac{\chi^2}{N}}$$

where ϕ = phi coefficient

χ^2 = calculated chi-square value

N = total number of cases

By applying the foregoing formula to the problem at hand,

$$\phi = \sqrt{\frac{3.71}{36}}$$
$$= \sqrt{.1031}$$
$$= .32$$

Our obtained phi coefficient of .32 indicates the presence of a moderate correlation between nationality and smoking.

Testing the Significance of Phi

Fortunately, the phi coefficient can be easily tested by means of chi-square, whose value has already been determined, and Table E in Appendix C:

Obtained $\chi^2 = 3.71$
Table $\chi^2 = 3.84$
$df = 1$
$\alpha = .05$

PHI COEFFICIENT

Based on chi-square, a measure of the degree of association for nominal data arranged in a 2×2 table.

Because our calculated chi-square value of 3.71 is less than the required table value, we retain the null hypothesis of no association and reject the research hypothesis that nationality and smoking are associated in the population.

Requirements for Using the Phi Coefficient

To employ the phi coefficient as a measure of association between X and Y variables, we must consider the following requirements:

1. *Nominal data.* Only frequency data are required.
2. *A 2 × 2 table.* The data must be capable of being cast in the form of a 2 × 2 table (2 rows by 2 columns). It is inappropriate to apply the phi coefficient to tables larger than 2 × 2, in which several groups or categories are being compared.
3. *Random sampling.* To test the significance of the phi coefficient, sample members must have been drawn on a random basis from a larger population.

CORRELATION COEFFICIENTS FOR NOMINAL DATA IN LARGER THAN 2 × 2 TABLES

Until this point, we have considered the correlation coefficient for nominal data arranged in a 2 × 2 table. As we have seen in Chapter 9, there are times when we have nominal data, but are comparing several groups or categories. To illustrate, consider the cross-tabulation of punishment attitude by political affiliation shown in Table 12.6.

The relationship between punishment attitude and political affiliation can be tested by applying the chi-square formula:

f_o	f_e	$f_o - f_e$	$(f_o - f_e)^2$	$\dfrac{(f_o - f_e)^2}{f_e}$
7	10.79	−3.79	14.36	1.33
9	10.11	−1.11	1.23	.12
14	9.10	4.90	24.01	2.64
10	10.07	−.07	.00	.00
10	9.44	.56	.31	.03
8	8.49	−.49	.24	.03
15	11.15	3.85	14.82	1.33
11	10.45	.55	.30	.03
5	9.40	−4.40	19.36	2.06
				$\chi^2 = 7.57$

In the present context, however, we seek to determine the correlation or degree of association between political affiliation (X) and criminal justice punishment attitudes (Y). In a table larger

TABLE 12.6 Criminal Justice Punishment Attitudes by Political Affiliation: Data from Table 9.4

	Republican	Independent	Democrat	
Lenient	7	9	14	30
Moderate	10	10	8	28
Punitive	15	11	5	31
Total	32	30	27	$N = 89$

than 2 × 2, this can be done by a simple extension of the chi-square test, which is referred to as the **contingency coefficient (C)**. The value of C can be found by the formula:

$$C = \sqrt{\frac{\chi^2}{N + \chi^2}}$$

CONTINGENCY COEFFICIENT

Based on chi-square, a measure of the degree of association for nominal data arranged in a square table larger than 2 × 2.

where
C = contingency coefficient
χ^2 = calculated chi-square value
N = total number of cases

In testing the degree of association between political affiliation and attitudes,

$$C = \sqrt{\frac{7.57}{89 + 7.57}}$$

$$= \sqrt{\frac{7.57}{96.57}}$$

$$= \sqrt{.0784}$$

$$= .28$$

Our obtained contingency coefficient of .28 indicates that the correlation between political affiliation and criminal justice punishment attitudes can be regarded as a rather weak one. Political affiliation and punishment attitudes are related, but many exceptions can be found.

Testing the Significance of the Contingency Coefficient

Just as in the case of the phi coefficient, whether the contingency coefficient is statistically significant can be easily determined from the size of the obtained chi-square value. In the present example, we find that the relationship between political affiliation and criminal justice punishment attitudes is nonsignificant and, therefore, confined to the members of our samples. This is true because the calculated chi-square of 7.57 is smaller than the required table value:

$$\text{Obtained } \chi^2 = 7.57$$
$$\text{Table } \chi^2 = 9.49$$
$$df = 4$$
$$\alpha = .05$$

Requirements for Using the Contingency Coefficient

To appropriately apply the contingency coefficient, we must be aware of the following requirements:

1. *Nominal data.* Only frequency data are required. These data may be cast in the form of a square table that is larger than 2 × 2.
2. *Random sampling.* To test the significance of the contingency coefficient, all sample members must have been taken at random from a larger population.

An Alternative to the Contingency Coefficient

Despite its great popularity among researchers, the contingency coefficient has an important disadvantage: The number of rows and columns in a chi-square table will influence the maximum size taken by C. That is, the value of the contingency coefficient will not always vary between 0 and 1.0 (although it will never exceed 1.0). Under certain conditions, the maximum value of C may be .94; at other times, the maximum value of C may be .89, and so on. This situation is particularly troublesome in non-square tables, that is, tables that contain different numbers of rows and columns (e.g., 2 × 3, 3 × 5).

CRAMÉR'S V

An alternative to the
contingency coefficient
that measures the degree
of association for nominal
data arranged in a table
larger than 2 × 2.

To avoid this disadvantage of C, we may decide to employ another correlation coefficient, which expresses the degree of association between nominal-level variables in a table larger than 2 × 2. Known as **Cramér's V**, this coefficient does not depend on the size of the χ^2 table and has the same requirements as the contingency coefficient. By formula,

$$V = \sqrt{\frac{\chi^2}{N(k-1)}}$$

where V = Cramér's V

N = total number of cases

k = number of rows *or* columns, whichever is smaller (if the number of rows equals the number of columns as in a 3 × 3, 4 × 4, or 5 × 5 table, either number can be used for k)

Let's return to the cross-tabulation of race/ethnicity of the police officer and race/ethnicity of the driver in a sample of 250 traffic stops.

		Officer		
Driver	*White*	*Black*	*Latino*	Total
White	96	33	25	154
Black	48	7	9	64
Latino	16	10	6	32
Total	160	50	40	250

In Chapter 9, we obtained a chi-square value of 7.373 for this 3 × 3 cross-tabulation. This chi-square value can then be used to calculate Cramér's V as follows:

$$V = \sqrt{\frac{7.373}{250(3-1)}}$$

$$= \sqrt{\frac{7.373}{250(2)}}$$

$$= \sqrt{\frac{7.373}{500}}$$

$$= \sqrt{.0147}$$

$$= .1214$$

We had determined in Chapter 9 that the chi-square value for this cross-tabulation was not statistically significant (i.e., no significant difference was found). We also now see, based on the small value of Cramér's V, that the relationship between the race/ethnicity of the police officer and the race/ethnicity of the driver in the sample of traffic stops is fairly weak.

ELABORATION   In Chapter 10, we saw in the discussion of partial correlation that the relationship between two variables can be dramatically altered when controlling for a third variable. Nonparametric correlation coefficients based on cross-tabulations can similarly be changed by the introduction of a third factor. Some wise person must have known this and said, "Things aren't always what they seem at first glance." This is a lesson recently learned by a fictitious criminologist who conducted a small study of TV crime-drama viewing.

During spring break, this professor got hooked on watching such shows as *Hawaii Five-O*, *Bluebloods*, *CSI*, and *Law and Order SVU*. While engrossed in their plots, however, he was still able

TABLE 12.7 Cross-Tabulation of Level of Fear by Crime Drama Viewing Status

| Level of Fear | Crime Drama Viewer | | Total |
	Yes	No	
High	38	62	100
	54%	48%	50%
Low	32	68	100
	46%	52%	50%
Total	70	130	200
	100%	100%	100%

to maintain his scholarly perspective. As he watched, he began noticing a definite fear-arousing undertone in the prime-time crime shows. Although the "good guys" did eventually solve crimes and apprehend villains, most of the programs portrayed the gruesome details of violent crimes such as murder and rape perpetrated against vulnerable victims. Forever a researcher at heart, this professor designed a study to test if viewing of crime dramas was associated with fear of crime.

Our fictitious criminologist conducted telephone interviews with 200 respondents whose numbers were dialed at random. Among other things, the respondents were asked whether or not they watched TV crime dramas fairly regularly and whether or not they were fearful of being victimized by criminals. Because the professor considered TV viewing as his independent variable, he used column percentages for his cross-tabulation (see Table 12.7).

The professor was not surprised by the results. Supporting his hypothesis that viewing crime dramas would lead to higher levels of fear, he found that proportionately more viewers were fearful (54%) than were nonviewers (48%). As you might expect, our story does not end here. The professor next wondered whether the relationship observed between viewing and fear of crime would be the same for both males and females. So he separated the males from the females in his cross-tabulation. Table 12.8 is called a three-way cross-tabulation, that is, a frequency table involving three variables at once. Specifically, it shows the relationship between crime-drama viewing ("Yes" vs. "No") and level of fear ("High" vs. "Low") holding gender constant. By this, we mean that gender does not vary within each of the two sub-tables. The left sub-table includes only women and the right only men. (These are called sub-tables because they are obtained by subdividing the full table according to gender.)

This process is called **elaboration**. It involves looking deeper into the relationship between the independent and dependent variables by controlling for or holding constant another variable (or variables) that may play a role. By separating the males from the females, we elaborate on the initial finding that ignored gender.

ELABORATION

The process of controlling a two-variable cross-tabulation for additional variables.

TABLE 12.8 Cross-tabulation of Level of Fear of Crime by Viewing Status Holding Gender Constant

| | Females | | | | Males | | |
| Level of Fear | Crime Drama Viewer | | Total | Level of Fear | Crime Drama Viewer | | Total |
	Yes	No			Yes	No	
High	30	30	60	High	8	32	40
	60%	60%	60%		40%	40%	40%
Low	20	20	40	Low	12	48	60
	40%	40%	40%		60%	60%	60%
Total	50	50	100	Total	20	80	100
	100%	100%	100%		100%	100%	100%

The results in Table 12.8, holding gender constant, are noticeably different from those in the previous table. Among males, there is no difference in the level of fear of the crime drama viewers and the nonviewers; 40% of each group has a high level of fear. Among females, there is also no difference between viewers and nonviewers; 60% of each group is fearful.

We have then a very curious result. Crime drama viewing and fear of crime are unrelated among both the female and the male respondents. However, when you combine the two groups (as in Table 12.7), the TV viewers appear to have a higher level of fear.

The relationship between crime drama viewing and level of fear, as seen in Table 12.7, is called a spurious relationship (not genuine). That is, viewing of crime dramas does not influence level of fear of crime, nor does fear of crime affect one's television habits. Instead, both variables are influenced by a common factor: gender of respondent.

First, women are more inclined toward crime drama viewing than are men: In the column marginals of the sub-tables in Table 12.8, we see that 50 out of the 100 women (50%) versus 20 out of the 100 men (20%) are viewers of crime shows. Second, women are more fearful of crime than are men: According to the row marginals, 60% of the women but 40% of the men have high levels of fear. Thus, it may seem like viewers tend to be more fearful than nonviewers, but it is only because viewers and fearful respondents both tend to be female, and nonviewers and those who have low levels of fear both tend to be male. In sum, the relationship between viewing and fear of crime is spurious due to the gender of the respondent, and this is exposed when we elaborate on the original two-variable relationship (of Table 12.7) by introducing gender as a control variable in Table 12.8.

Because the relationship between crime drama viewing and fear of crime vanishes when gender is controlled, you may have gotten the impression that we played a trick with the numbers—a sort of statistical hocus-pocus. If so, you're only half right. We admit that the numbers in Tables 12.7 and 12.8 were fashioned to illustrate a perfectly spurious relationship. However, one must always be aware of possible contaminating factors that might alter first impressions based on two-variable relationships. With real data, these relationships might not vanish so completely, but they certainly can change in dramatic ways.

Summary

As we saw in Chapter 9 in connection with tests of significance, there are nonparametric tests to employ instead of t and F. Similarly, when the requirements of Pearson's r cannot be met, nonparametric alternatives become attractive to a social researcher who seeks to measure the degree of association between two variables. To determine the correlation between variables at the ordinal level of measurement, a researcher can apply Spearman's rank–order correlation coefficient (r_s). To use this measure appropriately, both X and Y variables must be ranked or ordered. Interval data are not required, in contrast to Pearson's r. When ordinal data are arranged in a cross-tabulation, Goodman's and Kruskal's gamma coefficient (G) becomes a useful correlation coefficient. A researcher can determine the degree of association between variables at the nominal level of measurement by a simple extension of the chi-square test of significance. For a 2×2 problem, it is appropriate to employ the phi coefficient. For tables larger than 2×2, it is appropriate to use the contingency coefficient for square tables (such as 3×3 or 4×4) or Cramér's V for square tables or non-square tables (such as 3×4 or 5×7). Finally, we introduced the logic of elaboration in which we consider whether a two-variable cross-tabulation is altered when controlling for a third variable.

Questions and Problems

1. Which of the following statistics is not a nonparametric measure of correlation?
   a. Cramér's V
   b. Goodman's and Kruskal's gamma
   c. Pearson's r
   d. Spearman's rank–order correlation

2. A nonparametric measure of correlation is used when _____.

a. measures are nominal or ordinal
b. requirements for Pearson's *r* fail
c. the distribution of a variable is not normal
d. all of the above

3. We would decide to test the significance of a rank–order, gamma, or contingency correlation coefficient in order to _____.

a. measure its strength
b. measure its direction
c. see whether we can generalize to the population from the sample
d. see whether we have met the requirements for using the test

4. The phi and contingency coefficients are extensions of which test?
a. Chi-square
b. Goodman's and Kruskal's gamma
c. Pearson's *r*
d. Spearman's rank–order correlation

5. In deciding to use a nonparametric measure of correlation instead of Pearson's *r*, we _____.
a. are being less cautious in our assumptions about Pearson's *r*
b. are being more cautious in our assumptions about Pearson's *r*
c. want more precision
d. want to use a *t* ratio

6. A researcher wonders whether the safest cities are also those with the largest police departments. Ten cities are ranked from safest (1) to most dangerous (10). The researcher also collects information on the number of police officers per 1,000 citizens.

Safe City Ranking	Police per 1,000
1	4.3
2	1.8
3	1.7
4	2.6
5	1.3
6	2.2
7	4.7
8	2.6
9	2.0
10	4.1

a. Rank the rate of police per 1,000 from highest (1) to lowest (10).
b. Calculate a Spearman's rank–order correlation to test the null hypothesis that the number of police per 1,000 citizens is not related to the safe city ranking.
c. Using Table G in Appendix C, determine whether the correlation is significant at the .05 significance level.

7. The following 96 college students were ranked from high to low with respect to their consumption of alcoholic beverages and their daily use of marijuana.

Use of Marijuana	Consumption of Alcohol		
	High	Medium	Low
High	5	7	20
Medium	10	8	15
Low	15	6	10

a. For these data, compute a gamma coefficient to determine the degree of association between consumption of alcohol and use of marijuana.
b. Indicate whether it is a significant relationship.

8. To collect evidence pertaining to gender differences within the police hierarchy, a sample of police department employees was classified by rank and gender. For the following cross-tabulation, use the formula to calculate chi-square and Cramér's *V*.

	Gender	
	Male	Female
Captain or Inspector	6	2
Sergeant or Lieutenant	15	6
Patrolman or Detective	20	30

9. Domestic violence in America is a serious problem. One recommended form of intervention is to have mandatory counseling for offenders. Does counseling reduce this offending? A researcher studied the number of sessions that offenders attended and the length of time for them to re-offend (get arrested again). She then ranked these data to show when they dropped out of counseling sessions (*X*) (1, first out; 2, second out; etc.), and she ranked them on re-offending (*Y*) (1, first rearrested; 2, second; etc.) finding:

Counseling	Re-offending
1	3
2	7
3	2
4	1
5	4
6	5
7	10
8	8
9	6
10	12
11	11
12	9

a. Compute a Spearman rank–order correlation coefficient.
b. Using Table G in Appendix C, indicate whether there is a significant relationship between counseling and re-offending.

10. Secure Communities is a nationwide policy that allows the United States to deport illegal immigrants after their arrest. A researcher is interested in how people from different

socioeconomic backgrounds perceive the fairness of the Secure Communities policy. The research team asked a random sample of 350 adults from varying socioeconomic backgrounds about the fairness of the policy.

Fairness of Policy	Socioeconomic Status			
	Lower	Lower-Middle	Upper-Middle	Upper
Low	4	10	6	2
Medium	15	16	20	8
High	12	24	18	14

a. Calculate gamma.
b. What is the significance of gamma?

11. A criminologist is interested in testing the hypothesis that offending is related to victimization. In order to test the hypothesis, the researcher collects data from 100 young adults concerning whether they had ever committed a violent crime and whether they had been the victim of violent crime.

Offending	Victimization	
	No	Yes
No	58	12
Yes	10	20

a. Use a chi-square test to determine if there is more overlap between victims and offenders than would be expected under the null hypothesis of no association.
b. Use the phi-coefficient to determine the correlation between offending and victimization.

12. A criminologist compares the outcome of traffic stops based on the race/ethnicity of the driver. For the following cross-tabulation, calculate chi-square and the Contingency Coefficient C.

Race/Ethnicity of Driver	Outcome of Traffic Stop		
	Ticket	Written Warning	Verbal Warning
White	22	31	46
Black	12	13	15
Hispanic	10	15	14

13. A researcher collected data from 198 people about their political leaning and whether they would favor reinstating the assault weapons ban. For the following cross-tabulation, calculate chi-square and Cramér's V.

Political leaning	Reinstate Assault Weapons Ban	
	Favor	Oppose
Liberal	56	7
Moderate	33	28
Conservative	11	63

Computer Exercises

1. Using *SPSS*, analyze the General Social Survey to find out if respondents' attitudes toward assistance with health care costs for the sick (HELPSICK) are related to their attitudes about the assistance with health care costs for the poor (HELPPOOR). Test the null hypothesis using Spearman's rank–order correlation coefficient. *Hint:* To obtain a Spearman's rank–order correlation, click on ANALYZE, CORRELATE, BIVARIATE, and check the box for Spearman (to obtain less output, unclick Pearson).

2. A researcher wonders whether people will give similar answers to questions about suicide depending on the circumstances. In particular, she wants to know whether people will or will not differ when the issue is asking about suicide if a person has an incurable disease (SUICIDE1) or suicide if a person was tired of living (SUICIDE4). Using the General Social Survey, find the contingency coefficient to test the null hypothesis that there is no difference in how people assess questions about suicide under different circumstances. *Hint:* The contingency coefficient is available as an optional statistic in the Crosstabs procedure.

3. A researcher suspects that there may be a relationship between political views (POLVIEWS) and attitudes toward national support on issues related to foreign aid (NATAID);

military, armaments, and defense (NATARMS)' and assistance for child care (NATCHLD). Use the General Social Survey to find out whether she is right. Apply Gamma to test the null hypothesis that there is no relationship between political views and each of the other variables. *Hint:* Gamma is available as an optional statistic in the Crosstabs procedure.

4. The General Social Survey includes a variety of questions on activities that Americans may do at night. Apply Gamma to test the null hypothesis that there is no relationship between each of the different nighttime activities (SOCBAR, SOCCOMMUN, SOCFREND, SOCREL).

5. Are males more likely than females to have ever injected drugs? Find Phi for testing the null hypothesis that there is no relationship between ever injecting drugs (EVIDU) and sex (SEX). *Hint:* Phi is available as an optional statistic in the Crosstabs procedure.

6. Use the General Social Survey to find Cramér's V to test the null hypothesis that opinions about whether marijuana should be made legal (GRASS) do not differ by marital status (MARITAL). *Hint:* Phi and Cramér's V are found in the same place in *SPSS*. Compare your answer to this question to the answer for question 1 in Chapter 9.

LOOKING AT THE LARGER PICTURE
Measuring Association

In the last part of the text, we considered tests for differences between groups. Using the z test of proportions, for example, we tested differences by sex in the percentage of students who smoke. Using the t ratio and then analysis of variance, we assessed differences between sexes and then among races in terms of their mean levels of smoking and drinking. Using chi-square, we also tested for differences between groups (race and parents as smokers/nonsmokers) in terms of the percentage of respondents who were smokers. In this final portion of the text, we focused more on establishing the degree of association between variables, as opposed to focusing on differences between groups.

Let's look at the correlation between levels of smoking and drinking. Are these two forms of consumption connected in any way? We see in the scatter plot (Figure 12.1) that there is a tendency for the two variables to correlate. For those students who seldom drank, the dots tend to cluster at the low end of smoking; for those who drank more often, the dots spread over a wider range of smoking levels, especially the highest. The Pearson's correlation coefficient, $r = +.34$, indicates a fairly moderate and positive association. With $N = 155$ (only smokers included), the correlation is statistically significant ($t = 4.47$, 153 df). For the population, therefore, we can conclude that students who drink a lot also tend to smoke a lot.

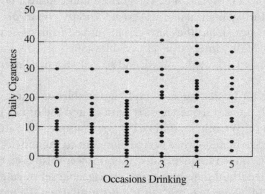

FIGURE 12.1 Scatterplot of Smoking and Drinking.

Next, we consider the relationship between age and drinking. By law, none of these students is supposed to drink, but clearly many of them report doing so. Is there a tendency for those who are closer to the legal drinking age to drink more often than younger students? As indicated by the correlation coefficient, $r = +.62$, older students do tend to drink more often. Since this correlation is significant, ($t = 12.44$, 248 df), we can conclude that age and smoking are correlated in the population of students.

Cross-Tabulation of Extent of Participation in Sports/Exercise and Smoking

	Smoke	Not Smoke
Very frequent	8	35
Often	48	39
Seldom	65	16
Never	34	5

$x^2 = 58.0$, 3 df (significant), Cramér's $V = .48$

Finally, we are interested in the association between athletic involvement and whether a student smokes. We can display these data in the form of a cross-tabulation and calculate Cramér's V, a measure of association designed for nonsquare tables. Unlike the age–drinking connection, however, it would be difficult to determine which is the independent variable and which is the dependent variable. Is it that athletic individuals are less likely to take up smoking or is it that smokers are less able to perform athletically? This is a question that these methods cannot resolve (although there are more advanced techniques and research designs that possibly could).

Applying Statistical Procedures
to Research Problems

It surely has been a long and sometimes difficult journey through the chapters of this book, from the early stages of statistical description through a set of some of the most commonly used techniques for statistically analyzing criminal justice data. In Chapter 1, we attempted to provide a roadmap of the major themes that you would encounter along this journey into statistics. At this final stop, it may be helpful to look back at the highlights of the trip and what you have learned en route.

Chapter 1 introduced some basic concepts concerning variables, the raw ingredients used in any statistical recipe. Most important, variables come in three types, depending on the precision and complexity of measurement. Nominal-level variables (such as whether last Saturday night's date was to "a movie," "a club," or "a party") can be categorized and counted. Ordinal-level variables (such as whether your Saturday night date was "great," "pretty good," or "never again") can likewise be categorized and counted, but they also can be ranked from one extreme to the other (e.g., from best to worst). Finally, interval-level variables (such as how long the Saturday night date lasted) can be categorized, counted, ranked, and scored on a fixed numerical scale (e.g., length in hours).

Chapter 2 then presented methods for tabulating and graphing variables as a first step in summarizing and describing their distributions. Frequency distributions and pie or bar graphs help us gain a clearer idea about our data. We might summarize, for example, the Saturday-night date experiences of a group of 40 classmates—what percentage went to the movies, what percentage were pleased with their date. Grouped frequency distributions were also used to help summarize interval-level variables like length of date into some manageable set of categories (e.g., "Under 2 hrs," "2 hrs up to 4 hrs," "4 hrs up to 6 hrs," and "6 hrs until dawn"). Frequency polygons were also used to explore the shape of a distribution, for example, whether date length tends to be symmetric or skewed among the 40 date-length scores.

Equipped with a basic summary of the distribution of a variable, Chapters 3 and 4 next introduced measures for describing in precise terms certain characteristics of a distribution. Specifically, three measures of central tendency provide different perspectives on "the average," depending on the research objective and level of measurement. For the date experiences of the 40 classmates, we might calculate the modal (most common) date type as "to a party." We might also determine the median (or middle-most) date quality as "pretty good," and the mean date length as 4.3 hrs.

There is more to a distribution of scores than the mode, median, and mean, of course. Measures of variability (range, variance, and standard deviation) were used to characterize how the data are dispersed around the center of a distribution. To say that the 40 classmates had a mean date length of 4.3 hrs is only half the story. Learning that their dates ranged from 1.5 to 12.0 hrs raises all sorts of interesting questions about how they got along and what they did while together.

Chapter 5 focused on the normal curve, a particular distributional form (symmetric and bell-shaped) having most cases falling near the middle and a few falling in either the high or low extremes or tails. Despite its familiarity to anyone who has been graded "on a curve," there are actually rather few variables (measures like IQ, SAT scores, height, and weight) that possess this kind of normal distribution. Still, the normal curve plays a very critical role in helping us make inferences from samples to populations.

Chapter 6 provided the theoretical foundation for understanding how we can generalize from modest size samples to large populations, for example, how we might generalize the average date length of a sample of 40 classmates to the population of the entire student body, if not to all college-age students across the country. It is perhaps the most important statistical "fact of life" that the sample mean (if based on a reasonably large number of cases) is normally distributed, no matter what the distribution of the raw scores on which the mean is based.

The sample of 40 classmates may have yielded a mean date length of 4.3 hrs, yet another similarly drawn sample of 40 students might have produced a shorter average (e.g., 4.1 hrs) if there were no "all-nighters" in the group. Or another sample could perhaps have produced a mean of 4.8 hrs. The actual sample mean obtained depends to some extent on the luck of the draw.

In practice, we only draw one sample of cases (e.g., $N = 40$ cases), yet we use the theory about the sampling distribution of all possible sample means of the date length of 40 students (which is normal in shape) to generalize to what the population mean date length would likely be. In practice, we use the sample mean and its standard error to construct an interval representing the range spanning 95% of all possible sample means. That is, we can conclude with 95% confidence that the true population mean is within a certain margin of error from our sample mean date length, for example, from 4.15 to 4.45 hrs. Chapter 6 also presented a method for estimating the population proportion based on a sample, for example, the percentage of all Saturday night dates in the population that involved a movie.

Chapter 7 introduced the logic of hypothesis testing in the context of making comparisons between two groups. For example, do residential students or commuters stay out longer on a Saturday night date? We might test the null hypothesis of no difference in mean date length for the populations of residential and commuter students at the .05 level of significance. The t ratio offers a method for determining whether a difference in mean date length between independently drawn samples of 65 dormitory residents and 48 commuters is large enough to allow us to reject the null hypothesis. We may obtain a mean of 4.39 for residential students and 4.13 for commuters; the t ratio helps us assess whether the difference between sample means ($4.39 - 4.13 = .26$ hrs) could just be the result of sampling error.

Chapter 7 also presented an approach for testing differences between means for the same sample measured twice. For example, we might compare the mean date length of the first and second dates for a sample of 20 students to see whether the dates tend to grow longer the second time around. Chapter 7 also presented a method for testing differences between groups in terms of proportions. For example, we might compare samples of residential and commuter students in terms of the percentage of dates involving clubbing to test the null hypothesis of no population difference between residential students and commuters in their likelihood of going to a club on Saturday night dates.

Chapter 8 extended the comparison of means approach to several groups, that is, samples from three or more populations. Through the analysis of variance, we can test whether the population mean date lengths for business majors, science majors, humanities majors, and social science majors are equal. We might obtain sample means of 4.4, 4.1, 4.3, and 4.8, respectively. We then examine whether the variability among these four group means is larger than what we could expect by chance if the population means were equal.

Chapter 9 introduced nonparametric techniques. Whereas the t ratio and analysis of variance make strong assumptions about the nature of the data, specifically interval-level scores (as with date length in hours), nonparametric approaches focus on counts or frequencies as well as percentages—basic characteristics of all types of variables. Thus, nonparametric tests are more widely applicable, but they also are less powerful, meaning that they are less able to reject the null hypothesis when it is false.

The chi-square test was presented for analyzing cross-tabulated data. In essence, the focus of chi-square is on whether the frequency distribution of some variable differs significantly between groups defined by some other variable. For example, we might examine whether type of date (movie, club, or party) differs by type of major. The chi-square test assesses whether the frequencies observed in a cross-tabulation diverge from the frequencies one would expect under the null hypothesis of no difference between groups (type of major) in terms of the distribution of date type. The Mann-Whitney and Kruskal-Wallis tests were also presented for comparing group differences when using ordinal data (or for highly skewed interval data where normality cannot be assumed).

Chapter 10 moved the focus to measuring the correlation between variables. Whereas Chapters 7 through 9 had focused on differences in the mean or proportion of some variable between groups defined by another variable, the measures of association presented in Chapters 10 through 12 consider the degree to which two variables are associated with each other.

Introduced in Chapter 10, Pearson's correlation coefficient measures the linear correlation between two interval-level variables. Pearson's r examines the extent to which two variables move in the same or opposite direction, whether changes in one variable tend to be linked statistically to changes in the other. We might correlate student age with date length, for example, to determine if older or younger students stay out longer on a Saturday night date. Furthermore, regression, described in Chapter 11, allows us to measure the impact of age (the independent variable) on date length (the dependent variable). A slope of .40 would suggest that among college-age students, dates tend to increase by .4 hrs (or 24 min) with each year of age.

Finally, Chapter 12 extended the correlational approach to variables that are measured at less than the interval level. Spearman's correlation is specifically designed to compare ranks on two ordinal-level variables. For example, you might rank your classmates in terms of both popularity and date length and use Spearman's correlation to test their association. Do more popular students stay out longer on dates than their less popular classmates? In addition, Gamma (for ordinal measures) and phi, contingency coefficient, and Cramér's V (for nominal measures) can be used to assess the strength of association for data presented in the form of a cross-tabulation.

As noted throughout the text, each statistical procedure has a set of assumptions for its appropriate application. In selecting among procedures, any researcher must therefore consider a number of factors such as the following:

1. Whether the researcher seeks to test for statistically significant differences, degree of association, or both
2. Whether the researcher has achieved the nominal, ordinal, or interval level of measurement of the variables being studied
3. Whether or not the variables being studied are normally distributed in the population from which they were drawn (and, if not, whether the sample size is large enough to relax this requirement)

This chapter provides a number of hypothetical research situations in which the foregoing criteria are specified. The reader is asked to choose the most appropriate statistical procedure for each research situation from among the following tests that have been covered in Parts III and IV of the text:

1. t ratio
2. Analysis of variance
3. Chi-square test
4. Median test

  5. Mann-Whitney U test
  6. Kruskal-Wallis test
  7. Pearson's r correlation coefficient and regression
  8. Spearman's rank–order correlation coefficient
  9. Goodman's and Kruskal's gamma
 10. Phi coefficient
 11. Contingency coefficient
 12. Cramér's V

Table 13.1 locates each statistical procedure with respect to some of the important assumptions that must be considered for its appropriate application. Looking at the columns of the table, we face the first major decision related to the selection of a statistical procedure: Do we wish to determine whether a relationship exists? The tests of significance discussed in Chapters 7 through 9 are designed to determine whether an obtained sample difference reflects a true population difference. Or do we seek instead to establish the strength and direction of the association between two variables? This is a question of correlation that can be addressed by means of the statistical procedures introduced in Chapters 10 through 12.

The rows of Table 13.1 direct our attention to the level at which our variables are measured. If we have achieved the interval level of measurement, we may well consider employing a parametric procedure such as t, F, or r. If, however, we have achieved either the nominal or ordinal level of measurement, the choice is limited to several nonparametric alternatives. Finally, for correlation problems involving variables of different levels of measurement, a correlation measure appropriate for the lower level of the two is used. For example, Spearman's rank–order coefficient can be used to measure the correlation between an interval and ordinal variable; Cramér's V can be used to measure the association between an ordinal and nominal variable.

The solutions to the following research situations can be found at the end of the chapter.

TABLE 13.1 Choosing an Appropriate Statistical Technique		
Level of Measurement	**Test of Difference (Chapters 7–9)**	**Measure of Correlation (Chapters 10–12)**
Nominal	**Chi-square test** (a nonparametric test for comparing the frequency distributions of two or more samples)	**Phi coefficient** (a nonparametric measure for 2 × 2 tables)
		Contingency coefficient and **Cramér's V** (nonparametric measures for larger than 2 × 2 tables)
Ordinal	**Median test** (a nonparametric test for comparing the medians of two or more samples)	**Spearman's rank–order correlation** (a nonparametric measure for ranked data)
	Mann-Whitney U test (a nonparametric test for comparing the ranks of two samples)	**Goodman's and Kruskal's gamma** (a nonparametric measure for ordinal data in a cross-tabulation)
	Kruskal-Wallis test (a nonparametric test for comparing the ranks of three or more samples)	
Interval/Ratio	**t ratio** (a parametric test for comparing the means of two samples)	**Pearson's r correlation coefficient** and **regression analysis** (parametric measures for interval/ratio level scores)
	Analysis of variance (a parametric test for comparing the means of three or more samples)	

RESEARCH SITUATIONS

Research Situation 1

A researcher conducted an experiment to determine the effect of a convicted criminal's race on potential juror's judgments of appropriate prison sentence length. In a mock jury experiment, 20 white registered voters were presented with information about a hypothetical case of assault with attempt to commit murder. Details about the nature of the offense, the victim, and the offender were presented in a manner like a criminal trial, and a judge handed down a guilty verdict. All of the information presented to the "jurors" was identical except that half of the jurors were told the offender was white, and the other half were told the offender was African American. The 20 experimental subjects in the role of jurors were asked to indicate what they believe would be the appropriate prison sentence length (in years). The following results were obtained:

Prison Sentence Length Judged Appropriate for White Offenders X_1	Prison Sentence Length Judged Appropriate for African American Offenders X_2
8	10
12	7
10	15
20	25
7	20
25	15
10	10
15	12
6	20
10	15

Which statistical procedure would you apply to determine whether there is a significant difference between these groups of jurors in terms of appropriate length of sentence?

Research Situation 2

A researcher wanted to determine if male and female associates in a large law firm are paid comparable salaries. She randomly selected 15 male and 15 female partners, obtaining the following data:

Males (in $)	Females (in $)
120,300	111,100
175,000	102,500
120,000	134,500
98,000	90,900
144,500	95,000
121,000	176,400
190,000	145,600
178,000	141,200
198,100	103,200
124,200	105,300
232,800	111,300

(Continued)

Males (in $)	Females (in $)
139,900	189,700
140,100	109,700
148,800	98,900
218,300	131,500

Recognizing the skewed nature of the income distribution, which statistical procedure would you apply to determine whether there is a significant difference in the salaries paid to male and female associates?

Research Situation 3

A correctional researcher is evaluating the effectiveness of an offender rehabilitation program, one component of which is remedial education. Part of this evaluation is an attempt to determine whether education skills are being effectively taught. To assess this, the researchers administered a reading examination to a sample of 20 offenders randomly selected from a large population of program participants. She also recorded the number of weeks each of these offenders had been in the program. The following results were obtained (higher reading scores indicated greater skill):

Offender	X (Weeks in Program)	Y (Reading Score)
A	2	56
B	9	81
C	5	75
D	8	72
E	3	50
F	3	45
G	1	39
H	6	87
I	3	59
J	5	56
K	3	69
L	8	78
M	3	69
N	1	57
O	2	35
P	2	47
Q	5	73
R	12	76
S	6	63
T	8	79

Which statistical procedure would you apply to determine the degree of association between reading scores and number of weeks in the program?

Research Situation 4

To investigate the validity of the reading test administered to the offenders in Research Situation 3, the researcher gave the reading test to 20 program participants whose reading skills had been previously ranked by their instructor. The test score and instructor's rank for each offender are listed in the following table:

Offender	X (Reading Score)	Y (Instructor's Rank)
A	28	18
B	50	17
C	92	1
D	85	6
E	76	5
F	69	10
G	42	11
H	53	12
I	80	3
J	91	2
K	73	4
L	74	9
M	14	20
N	29	19
O	86	7
P	73	8
Q	39	16
R	80	13
S	91	15
T	72	14

Which statistical procedure would you apply to determine the degree of association between reading scores and instructor's ranking?

Research Situation 5

To investigate regional differences in willingness of victims of minor property crimes (involving financial losses of less than $500) to report the offense to police, a team of researchers interviewed 400 victims of such crimes from the Northeastern, Southern, Midwestern, and Western regions of the United States. The victims were identified during the course of a large national crime victimization survey. In the interviews, the victims were asked whether they had reported the crime to the police. The following results were obtained:

	Region			
	Northeast	South	Midwest	West
Reported	55	69	82	61
Not reported	45	31	18	39
	100	100	100	100

Which statistical procedure would you apply to determine whether these regional differences are statistically significant?

Research Situation 6

A researcher is interested in determining the degree of association between political party and attitude toward gun control. He interviews a random sample of Democrats and Republicans and asks them whether they favor or oppose gun control. He finds that among 500 Democrats, 353 favor gun control and 147 oppose it. Among 450 Republicans, 125 favor gun control and 325 oppose it.

Which statistical procedure would you apply to determine the degree of association between political party and attitude toward gun control?

Research Situation 7

To investigate the relationship between family size and crime severity for female offenders, a researcher interviews a random sample of female inmates and collects information about the size of their family growing up (small, medium, or large). From their records, she also obtains information about the severity of the crimes the women committed (high, medium, or low). She obtains the following data:

	Family Size		
Crime Severity	Large	Medium	Small
High	6	16	12
Medium	11	23	9
Low	9	14	10
	26	53	31

Which statistical procedure would you apply to determine the degree of association between family size and crime severity?

Research Situation 8

A researcher was interested in the effect of boot camp on prisoners' self-esteem. To find out, she administered a self-esteem inventory to 10 boot camp inmates during their first week in a program, and again during their last week. Scores on the self-esteem scale range from 1 to 20, with higher scores indicating greater self-esteem. The following results were obtained:

Boot Camp Inmate	X_1 (Self-Esteem Scores at Beginning of Boot Camp)	X_2 (Self-Esteem Scores at End of Boot Camp)
A	16	12
B	12	10
C	15	14
D	12	9
E	11	11
F	14	8
G	17	13
H	8	5
I	13	12
J	15	10

Which statistical procedure would you apply to determine whether there is a significant difference in self-esteem scores between the beginning and end of the boot camp program?

Research Situation 9

To find out if type of delinquency is associated with socioeconomic status, a sample of juvenile offenders was classified by socioeconomic status (high, medium, or low) and whether the offense for which they had been arrested was a violent crime, a property crime, or a drug crime (juveniles who had committed other types of offenses, such as disturbing the peace, were excluded from the study). The following data were obtained:

Type of Delinquency	Socioeconomic Status		
	High	Medium	Low
Violent	19	13	23
Property	23	21	26
Drug	32	27	31

Which statistical procedure would you apply to determine the degree of association between socioeconomic status and type of delinquency?

Research Situation 10

To investigate the influence of education on the starting salary of people in criminal justice fields, researchers interviewed 21 individuals recently hired at their first jobs in criminal justice. The most recent college degree and starting salary of these criminal justice professionals are as follows:

Starting Salary (in $)		
Bachelor's in Criminal Justice	Master's in Criminal Justice	Law Degree
19,500	21,000	28,500
28,500	18,500	34,000
14,000	36,000	48,500
22,000	28,000	29,000
26,000	32,000	38,500
19,500	24,500	44,000
16,000	19,500	54,500

Which statistical procedure would you apply to determine whether there is a significant difference between these groups of respondents with respect to their starting salaries?

Research Situation 11

A researcher wanted to examine differences in prison sentence lengths received by offenders convicted of "white-collar crime" vs. "street crime." In particular, she was interested in whether criminals who stole money by means of embezzlement or fraud received shorter prison sentences than those who stole money by means of burglary and larceny. The researcher examined court records and selected 7 cases of white-collar theft of between $1,000 and $10,000, and 12 cases of burglary or larceny involving dollar amounts in the same range. The data obtained on these offenders are presented here:

Prison Sentence Length (in Months)	
White-Collar Theft of between $1,000 and $10,000	**Street Theft of between $1,000 and $10,000**
6	12
12	48
0	6
1	1
30	3
0	0
2	12
	18
	2
	36
	60
	8

Which statistical procedure would you apply to determine whether there is a significant difference in prison sentences for white-collar crime vs. street crime involving similar financial losses?

Research Situation 12

To find out if juvenile offenders from different socioeconomic backgrounds tend to commit different types of delinquencies, a researcher collected a sample of juvenile offenders and determined their socioeconomic status (high, medium, or low) and whether the offense for which they had been arrested was a violent crime or a property crime. Among 25 high-socioeconomic-status offenders, 17 had committed property crimes and 8 had committed violent crimes. Among 32 medium-socioeconomic-status offenders, 14 had committed property crimes and 18 had committed violent crimes. Among 35 low-socioeconomic-status offenders, 16 had committed property crimes and 19 had committed violent crimes.

Which statistical procedure would you apply to determine whether there is a significant difference in the types of delinquency committed by juvenile offenders from different socioeconomic backgrounds?

Research Situation 13

A researcher seized upon an interesting opportunity to study the impact of television on fear of crime. A small, isolated town of 600 residents in a remote part of the Pacific Northwest was beyond the reach of any television broadcast signals, and few households owned satellite dishes. Upon news that a cable television business would soon begin operation in the town, the researcher administered a fear of crime scale to one member of each of 15 randomly selected households. One year after the households received cable television, the 15 individuals were administered the same fear of crime scale. The following results were obtained (higher scores indicate greater fear of crime):

Respondent	X_1 (Fear of Crime Score before Cable TV)	X_2 (Fear of Crime Score after Cable TV)
A	4	5
B	2	9
C	2	8
D	0	4
E	4	7
F	1	6
G	1	4
H	2	7
I	1	8
J	1	6
K	3	10
L	7	9
M	1	7
N	2	4
O	1	5

Which statistical procedure would you apply to determine whether there is a statistically significant difference in fear of crime before and after the broad availability of television programs?

Research Situation 14

To investigate the relationship between socioeconomic status and fear of crime, a researcher questioned 500 residents randomly selected from adult population of a certain city. The respondents were asked questions about their education, occupation, and income, which the researcher used to classify the residents as belonging to the high, medium, or low socioeconomic status. They were also asked a series of questions about their fear of becoming the victim of several kinds of crime, which the researcher used to classify the respondents as having a high, medium, or low level of fear. Among the 150 respondents classified as having high socioeconomic status, 40 were high, 80 were medium, and 30 were low in their measured level of fear of crime. Among the 185 respondents of medium socioeconomic status, 55 were high, 110 were medium, and 20 were low in their level of fear of crime. Among those who were classified as having low socioeconomic status, 70 were high, 80 were medium, and 15 were low in their rated level of fear of crime.

Which statistical procedure would you apply to determine the degree of association between socioeconomic status and fear of crime?

Research Situation 15

A great deal of research over the past 20 years indicates that some people tend to hold the victims of sexual assault in dating situations at least partially responsible for their assault. A researcher interested in this subject conducted a study examining how the relationship between men and women before an episode of date rape affects the level of blame attributed to the victim. A sample of 40 randomly selected college students were given written descriptions of dating scenarios, each describing a date between a young man and woman leading up to a point where the man attempts to have sex with the woman, she resists (both verbally and physically), and he forces her to have intercourse. All of the scenarios meet a legal definition of rape. All of the respondents received date rape scenarios identical in all respects except for the earlier relationship between the man and woman. The 40 scenarios presented were evenly divided into those containing each of the following four relationship descriptions: (1) did not know each other, on a blind date set up by friends; (2) acquaintances on a first date; (3) had dated for a month and had not had sex with each other before; (4) had dated for a month and had had sex with each other before. After reading the scenarios, the respondents were asked to rate the level of victim blame on a 10-point scale, with higher scores indicating higher levels of blame attributed to the rape victim. The following data were obtained:

Victim Blame Scores

X_1 (No Prior Relationship; Blind Date)	X_2 (Acquaintances on First Date)	X_3 (Dating One Month, No Prior Sex)	X_4 (Dating One Month, Prior Sex)
2	1	2	1
1	3	6	8
9	2	4	4
3	6	5	7
1	3	1	3
1	1	3	10
6	4	8	4
2	1	4	5
1	3	2	1
1	2	5	4

Which statistical procedure would you apply to determine whether there is a significant difference in victim blame scores across date rape scenarios with different descriptions of the relationship between the victim and offender?

Research Situation 16

The researcher in Research Situation 15 was also interested in how the relationship between heterosexual dating partners affects men's perceptions of whether the victim would report to the police that she had been raped. He randomly selected 40 male college students, presenting them with date rape scenarios just as he had in Research Situation 15, but instead of asking them their level of victim blame, he asked them whether the woman would report to the police that she had been raped. Respondents were instructed to circle "yes" if they believed that she would report her rape to the police, and "no" if they believed she wouldn't. The following data were obtained:

Report to Police	X_1 (Strangers on Blind Date)	X_2 (Acquaintances on First Date)	X_3 (Dating One Month, No Prior Sex)	X_4 (Dating One Month, Prior Sex)
Yes	7	5	3	2
No	3	5	7	8

Which statistical procedure would you use to examine whether there is a significant association between the offender–victim relationship and men's judgments of whether the victim would report her rape to the police?

Research Situation 17

The researcher in Situations 15 and 16 wonders whether the number of years of college education affects judgments of appropriate prison sentence lengths for offenders convicted of date rape. He randomly selects 20 college students and presents each with identical scenarios describing a date between a man and a woman during which he forces her to have intercourse, she reports it to the police, and he is arrested and convicted. At this point, the respondents are asked to indicate their beliefs about the appropriate length of prison sentence (in years) that the convicted rapist should receive. He also asks respondents to report how many years of college they have completed. The following data were obtained:

Years of College Completed	Appropriate Prison Sentence Length in Years
1	0
3	5
1	3
1	1
4	3
3	7
2	3
3	10
1	2
1	4
4	8
2	3
1	0
2	0
2	4
3	15
3	6
1	2
2	6
2	1

Which statistical procedure would you apply to examine the degree of association between years of college education and perceived appropriate prison sentence length?

Research Situation 18

Suppose that the researcher wanted to determine whether gender affects beliefs about appropriate length of prison sentences for men convicted of date rape. If in Research Situation 17, the researcher had asked respondents their gender instead of their years of college education, which statistical procedure would be effective in determining whether males and females differ in their judgments of appropriate sentence length for the offenders described in the date rape scenarios? The following data were obtained:

Appropriate Sentence Length in Years	
Males	*Females*
0	5
1	3
3	7
3	10
2	4
0	8
0	3
4	15
2	6
6	1

Research Situation 19

It has been asserted that trying to integrate large numbers of new residents into communities creates conditions favorable for juvenile delinquency (e.g., in many communities, new residents take time to find employment, moving is a stressful life event for families, and children have difficulty adjusting to new schools). To assess the relationship between new residency and delinquency, data on seven metropolitan areas were obtained:

Metropolitan Area	X (Percentage of the Population Who Moved There within the Past Year)	Y (Rank with Respect to Delinquency Rates)
A	10	1
B	4	6
C	2	3
D	1	7
E	6	4
F	5	2
G	8	5

Which statistical procedure would you apply to determine the degree of association between the percentage of population who had recently moved and the ranked delinquency rate?

Research Situation 20

A city's police department wanted to determine the most effective method of responding to complaints of domestic violence. The department decided to perform an experiment in which police officers responding to domestic violence calls were to randomly select one of three responses: (1) arrest the alleged abuser, (2) attempt to mediate the dispute, or (3) separate the parties for at least 15 min to allow them to calm down and then carefully reunite them. The effectiveness of the interventions would be measured as the presence or absence of evidence that additional abuse occurred at any time after the intervention (indicators of abuse would be any of the following: reports to the police, one party seeking a restraining order on the other, and/or future arrests for abuse or violating a restraining order). During the first year of this field experiment, evidence of subsequent abuse was found in 35 of the 138 situations in which the police response was arrest. There was evidence of subsequent abuse in 46 of the 140 situations in which the police mediated, and in 43 of the 139 instances in which police separated the alleged abuser and victim.

Which statistical procedure would you apply to determine whether there is a significant difference by the method of police response in terms of subsequent domestic abuse?

Research Situation 21

A researcher is interested in whether there is a relationship between racial/ethnic category and the kinds of offenses for which people are arrested. To examine this, she draws a sample of the 475 most recent arrests in her city and examines the offense categories (violent, property, drug, and sex offenses) of the three largest racial/ethnic groups (Caucasian, Latino, African American). She finds that 65 of the 209 Caucasians were arrested for violent offenses, 50 for drug offenses, 32 for sex offenses, and 62 were arrested for property crimes. Of the 156 Latinos, 38 were arrested for violent offenses, 52 for drug offenses, 18 for sex offenses, and 48 for property offenses. Of the 110 African Americans, 24 were arrested for violent offenses, 39 for drug offenses, 17 for sex offenses, and 30 for property offenses.

Which statistical procedure would you apply to determine the degree of association between the race/ethnicity of a criminal defendant and the type of offense for which he or she has been arrested?

Research Situation 22

Some researchers believe that a major factor related to running away is the quality of a youth's relationship with his or her parents. On the basis of a small sample of adolescents, the following data were collected regarding the number of hours of quality time they spend with their parents each week and the number of times in the past 6 months they have considered running away from home:

Adolescent	Hours of Quality Time with Parents	Number of Times Considered Running Away
A	1	10
B	10	2
C	5	7
D	7	1
E	20	0
F	12	2
G	5	1

Which statistical procedure would you use to predict the number of times a child who spends 15 hrs of quality time with his or her parents each week would have considered running away from home in the past 6 months?

Research Situation 23

A criminal justice researcher wanted to examine whether male or female judges are more likely to give harsh prison sentences for females convicted of child abuse. To do so, he obtains from court records the prison sentences of the most recently convicted female child abusers sentenced by male and female judges. He randomly selects 10 sentences for such cases handed down by female judges, and 10 sentences meted out by male judges. The results are as follows:

Prison Sentence Length (in years)	
Male Judges	*Female Judges*
4	10
1	5
20	20
12	7
7	4
10	1
1	15
5	5
2	2
10	8

Which statistical procedure would you apply to determine whether there is a significant difference in the sentence lengths handed down by male and female judges in cases where women are convicted of child abuse?

Research Situation 24

A criminologist was interested in the effects of anomie—normlessness, or the breakdown of rules in a social setting—on suicide. On the basis of a variety of social and economic factors, she divided 15 cities into three groups of 5: high anomie, moderate anomie, and low anomie. She then obtained the following suicide rates (the number of suicides per 100,000 population):

Anomie		
High	*Moderate*	*Low*
19.2	15.6	8.2
17.7	20.1	10.9
22.6	11.5	11.8
18.3	13.4	7.7
25.2	14.9	8.3

Which statistical procedure would you apply to determine whether there is a significant difference by level of anomie in suicide rates?

Research Situation 25

A criminal justice graduate student wondered whether people who have previously been victimized tend to be more or less fearful of crime than people who have never been victimized. She collected information from a random sample of undergraduate students and found that among 38 students who had previously been victimized, 11 had a low fear of crime and 27 had a high fear of crime. Among 132 students who had not been previously victimized, 104 had a low fear of crime and 28 had a high fear of crime.

Which statistical procedure would you apply to determine whether there is a significant difference in fear of crime by whether or not a person has been previously victimized?

Research Situation 26

A state legislature was concerned about the rising use of prison health care, and as part of a large audit of the prison health care system commissioned a study of the relationship between the mental and physical health of prison inmates. A random sample of 250 inmates was questioned regarding their symptoms of depression (e.g., insomnia, lack of concentration, suicidal thoughts) and given a physical examination to uncover any symptoms of physical illness (e.g., high blood pressure, erratic EKG, high cholesterol). Among the 100 inmates categorized as being in "excellent physical health," only 5 exhibited symptoms of depression; among the 110 inmates categorized in "good health," 14 exhibited symptoms of depression; and among the 40 inmates categorized in "poor health," 20 exhibited symptoms of depression.

Which statistical procedure would you apply to determine the degree of association between depression and physical illness among prison inmates?

Research Situation 27

Another component of the study described in Research Situation 26 examined the relationship between gender and physical health of state prison inmates. A random sample of 200 inmates—100 men and 100 women—was given a physical examination to uncover any symptoms of physical illness (e.g., high blood pressure, erratic EKG, high cholesterol). Among the 100 men, 37 were categorized as being in "excellent physical health," 43 were categorized in "good health," and 20 were categorized in "poor health." Among the 100 women, 52 were categorized as being in "excellent physical health," 35 were categorized in "good health," and 13 were categorized in "poor health."

Which statistical procedure would you apply to determine the degree of association between gender and physical illness among state prison inmates?

Research Situation 28

Shortly after the criminal trial of O.J. Simpson ended, black and white Americans were asked by pollsters whether they agreed with the jury's not-guilty verdict. In one of many such studies, a researcher questioned 150 respondents—75 blacks and 75 whites—as to Simpson's guilt or innocence. He determined that 50 blacks but only 24 whites in his sample agreed with the jury that O.J. Simpson was not guilty.

Which statistical procedure would you apply to determine whether black and white Americans differ significantly in their agreement with the jury's verdict?

Research Situation 29

To study the impact of hypnosis on crime witnesses' ability to accurately recall details of crimes, 20 adults were shown a videotape of an armed robbery. Half the subjects were then hypnotized for 15 min and subsequently asked to recall details of the crime (the height, weight, hair color, clothing, race of the offender, number of bystanders present, physical surroundings, etc.). The other 10 subjects simply waited for 15 min after viewing the videotape before they were asked to recall details of the crime. The number of recall errors made by each of the respondents is listed here:

Recall Errors	
Hypnotized	**Not Hypnotized**
6	8
2	4
4	9
9	4
2	5
1	0
7	3
0	8
6	2
8	1
3	6
6	9
3	6
7	5
1	3
4	7
5	1
0	6
6	3
8	0

Which statistical procedure would you apply to determine whether the accuracy of crime witness recall is affected by hypnosis?

RESEARCH SOLUTIONS

Solution to Research Situation 1

(*t* **RATIO**)   Research Situation 1 represents a comparison between the sentence lengths given to two independent samples of offenders. The *t* ratio (Chapter 7) is employed to make comparisons between two means when interval data have been obtained.

Solution to Research Situation 2

(**MEDIAN TEST OR MANN-WHITNEY *U* TEST**)   Research Situation 2 represents a comparison between salaries paid to male and female associates in a large law firm. Because the salary distribution is highly skewed, the median test or the Mann-Whitney *U* test (Chapter 9) is a preferred nonparametric alternative to the *t* ratio.

Solution to Research Situation 3

(**PEARSON'S CORRELATION COEFFICIENT**)   Research Situation 3 is a correlation problem, because it asks for the degree of association between X (weeks in program) and Y (reading score). Pearson's r (Chapter 10) can be employed to detect a straight-line correlation between X and Y variables when both of these variables have been measured at the interval level. If X (weeks in program) and Y (reading score) are not normally distributed in the population, we could consider applying a non-parametric alternative such as Spearman's rank–order correlation coefficient (Chapter 12).

Solution to Research Situation 4

(**SPEARMAN'S RANK–ORDER CORRELATION COEFFICIENT**)   Research Situation 4 is a correlation problem, asking for the degree of association between X (reading score) and Y (instructor's rankings of reading ability). Spearman's rank–order correlation coefficient (Chapter 12) can be employed to detect a relationship between X and Y variables when both of these variables have been ordered or ranked. Pearson's r cannot be employed, because it requires interval-level measurement of X and Y. In the present case, reading scores (X) must be ranked from 1 to 20 before rank order is applied.

Solution to Research Situation 5

(**CHI-SQUARE TEST**)   Research Situation 5 represents a comparison between the frequencies (crime reported vs. not reported to the police) found in four groups (Northeast, South, Midwest, and West). The chi-square test of significance (Chapter 9) is used to make comparisons between two or more samples. Only nominal data are required. Present results can be cast in the form of a 2 $\times$ 4 table, representing 2 rows and 4 columns. Notice that the degree of association between crime reporting rate (X) and region (Y) can be measured by means of Cramér's V (Chapter 12). Note that the contingency coefficient is not a preferred measure here because the contingency table is not square.

Solution to Research Situation 6

(**PHI COEFFICIENT**)   Research Situation 6 is a correlation problem that asks for the degree of association between X (political party) and Y (attitude toward gun control). The phi coefficient (Chapter 12) is a measure of association that can be employed when frequency or nominal data can be cast in the form of a 2 × 2 table (two rows by two columns). In the present problem, such a table would take the following form:

	Political Party	
Attitude toward Gun Control	*Democratic*	*Republican*
Favor	353	125
Oppose	147	325
$N = 950$		

Solution to Research Situation 7

(GOODMAN'S AND KRUSKAL'S GAMMA)   Research Situation 7 is a correlation problem that asks for the degree of association in a cross-tabulation of X (family size) and Y (crime severity). Goodman's and Kruskal's gamma coefficient (Chapter 12) is employed to detect a relationship between X and Y when both variables are ordinal and have been cast in the form of a cross-tabulation. In the present problem, family size has been ranked from large to small, and crime severity has been ranked from high to low. The contingency coefficient (C) or Cramér's V (Chapter 12) represents an alternative to gamma that assumes only nominal-level data. However, because these variables are ordinal, gamma is preferable.

Solution to Research Situation 8

(t TEST OF DIFFERENCE BETWEEN MEANS FOR DEPENDENT SAMPLES)   Research Situation 8 represents a before–after comparison of a single sample measured at two points in time. The t ratio for dependent samples (Chapter 7) can be employed to compare two means from a single sample arranged in a before–after panel design.

Solution to Research Situation 9

(CONTINGENCY COEFFICIENT)   Research Situation 9 is a nonparametric correlation problem (Chapter 12) that asks for the degree of association between two variables—one variable is measured at the nominal level (type of delinquency), and the other is measured at the ordinal level (socioeconomic status). When variables are measured at two levels, statistical tests for the lower level are usually appropriate to apply. Because one of the variables is nominal, it would be inappropriate to use Goodman's and Kruskal's gamma, which requires two ordinal variables. Instead, it is appropriate to use the contingency coefficient, which is a measure of association for comparing several groups or categories at the nominal level when they can be arranged in a square table (in this case, 3 × 3).

Solution to Research Situation 10

(ANALYSIS OF VARIANCE OR KRUSKAL-WALLIS TEST)   Research Situation 10 represents a comparison of the scores of three independent samples of respondents. The F ratio (Chapter 8) is used to make comparisons between three or more independent means when interval data have been obtained. The Kruskal-Wallis test (Chapter 9) is a nonparametric alternative that can be employed if the salaries are not normally distributed in the population and the sample sizes are not large.

Solution to Research Situation 11

(t RATIO OR MANN-WHITNEY U TEST)   Research Situation 11 represents a comparison between the scores of two independent samples of respondents. The t ratio (Chapter 7) is employed to compare two means when interval data have been obtained. The Mann-Whitney U test

(Chapter 9) is a nonparametric alternative that can be employed if the sentence lengths are not normally distributed in the population and the sample sizes are not large. Also, the median test can be used as a quick, but less powerful, nonparametric alternative.

Solution to Research Situation 12

(CHI-SQUARE TEST) Research Situation 12 represents a comparison of the frequencies (property crimes vs. violent crimes) among three groups of juvenile offenders (high, medium, and low socioeconomic status). The chi-square test of significance (Chapter 9) is used to make comparisons between two or more samples when either nominal or frequency data have been obtained. Present results can be cast in the form of the following 2×3 table, representing two rows and three columns:

Type of Delinquency	Socioeconomic Status		
	High	*Medium*	*Low*
Property	17	14	16
Violent	8	18	19
	25	32	35

Solution to Research Situation 13

(t TEST OF DIFFERENCE BETWEEN MEANS FOR DEPENDENT SAMPLES) Research Situation 13 represents a before–after comparison of a single sample measured at two different points in time. The t ratio for dependent samples (Chapter 7) can be employed to compare two means from a single sample arranged in a before–after panel design.

Solution to Research Situation 14

(GOODMAN'S AND KRUSKAL'S GAMMA) Research Situation 14 is a correlation problem that asks for the degree of association between X (socioeconomic status) and Y (fear of crime). Goodman's and Kruskal's gamma coefficient (Chapter 12) is applied to detect a relationship between X and Y, when both variables are ordinal and can be arranged in a cross-tabulation. In the present situation, both socioeconomic status and fear of crime have been ranked from high to low.

Socioeconomic Status (Y)	Fear of Crime (X)			
	Low	*Medium*	*High*	*Total*
Low	15	80	70	165
Medium	20	110	55	185
High	30	80	40	150

Solution to Research Situation 15

(ANALYSIS OF VARIANCE OR KRUSKAL-WALLIS TEST) Research Situation 15 represents a comparison of the scores of four independent samples of respondents. The F ratio (Chapter 8) is employed to make comparisons with three or more independent means when interval data have been achieved. The Kruskal-Wallis test (Chapter 9) is a nonparametric alternative that can be employed if the victim blame scores cannot be treated as interval level, are not normally distributed in the population, and the sample sizes are not large.

Solution to Research Situation 16

(CRAMÉR'S V) Research Situation 16 is a nonparametric correlation problem (Chapter 12) that asks for the degree of association between two variables—one variable is measured at the nominal level (whether or not date rape was reported to the police) and the other variable is measured at the ordinal level (the degree of relationship between the victim and the dating partner). Cramér's V is a measure of association for comparing several groups or categories at the nominal level. When variables are measured at two levels, statistical tests for the lower level are usually appropriate to apply. In this case, because there are several groups arranged in a non-square table (2×4), Cramér's V is the most appropriate test for association.

Solution to Research Situation 17

(PEARSON'S CORRELATION COEFFICIENT) Research Situation 17 is a correlation problem because it asks for the degree of statistical relationship between X (years of college) and Y (years of prison judged to be an appropriate prison sentence length). Pearson's r (Chapter 10) is employed to examine linear correlation between X and Y variables when both have been measured at the interval level. If the years in college and the perceived appropriate length of prison sentences are not normally distributed in the population, we might consider a nonparametric alternative such as Spearman's rank–order correlation coefficient (Chapter 12).

Solution to Research Situation 18

(t RATIO OR MANN-WHITNEY U TEST) The t ratio is used to compare two means when interval data have been obtained and would be an appropriate way to analyze the data in Research Situation 18. Appropriate prison sentence lengths were measured in years (interval data), and two means (for males and females) are compared. The Mann-Whitney U test (Chapter 9) is a nonparametric alternative that can be employed if the sentence lengths are not normally distributed in the population and the sample sizes are not large.

Solution to Research Situation 19

(SPEARMAN'S RANK–ORDER CORRELATION COEFFICIENT) Research Situation 19 is a correlation problem asking for the degree of association between X (percentage of new population) and Y (delinquency rates). Spearman's rank–order correlation coefficient (Chapter 12) can be applied to detect a relationship between X and Y variables when both have been ranked or ordered. Pearson's r cannot be employed because it requires interval data on X and Y. In the present case, percentage of new population must be ranked from 1 to 7 before rank–order correlation is applied.

Solution to Research Situation 20

(CHI-SQUARE TEST) Research Situation 20 is a comparison of the frequencies (evidence of subsequent abuse vs. no such evidence) of three samples of domestic violence cases (police response of arrest, mediation, or separation). The chi-square test of significance (Chapter 9) is employed to compare two or more samples when nominal or frequency data have been obtained. A 2×3 table would be created with the type of police response along one axis and evidence of subsequent abuse on the other:

Police Response to Domestic Abuse	Evidence of Subsequent Domestic Abuse	
	Yes	*No*
Arrest	35	105
Mediation	46	94
Separation	43	97

Solution to Research Situation 21

(CRAMÉR'S V)   Research Situation 21 is a nonparametric correlation problem (Chapter 12) that asks for the degree of association between two variables measured at the nominal level: racial/ ethnic category and offense type. Cramér's V is a measure of association for comparing several groups or categories at the nominal level, particularly when they are arranged in a non-square table. To obtain Cramér's V, the data must be arranged in the form of a cross-tabulation as follows:

Offense Type (Y)	Racial/Ethnic Category (X)		
	Caucasian	*Latino*	*African American*
Violent	65	38	24
Drug	50	52	39
Sex	32	18	17
Property	62	48	30

Solution to Research Situation 22

(REGRESSION)   Research Situation 22 is a regression problem (Chapter 11) that asks for the prediction of variable Y (in this case, how many times an adolescent has considered running away from home) on the basis of another variable X (in this case, how many hours of quality time the adolescent spends with his or her parents each week). By calculating the regression slope and Y-intercept, it is possible to determine the regression line and to make predictions about Y on the basis of different values of X. It is also possible to determine how much of the variance in Y is explained by X by calculating the coefficient of determination.

Solution to Research Situation 23

(t RATIO OR MANN-WHITNEY U TEST)   Research Situation 23 represents a comparison be- tween the prison sentence lengths of two independent samples of judges. The t ratio (Chapter 7) is used to compare two means when interval data have been obtained. The Mann-Whitney U test (Chapter 9) is a nonparametric alternative that can be employed if the sentence lengths are not normally distributed in the population and the sample sizes are not large.

Solution to Research Situation 24

(ANALYSIS OF VARIANCE OR KRUSKAL-WALLIS TEST)   Research Situation 24 represents a comparison of the suicide rates in cities representing three anomie levels—low, moderate, and high. The F ratio (Chapter 8) is employed to make comparisons with three or more independent means when interval data have been achieved. The Kruskal-Wallis test (Chapter 9) is a nonpara- metric alternative that can be employed if the rates are not normally distributed in the popula- tion and the sample sizes are not large.

Solution to Research Situation 25

(CHI-SQUARE TEST)   Research Situation 25 is a comparison of the frequencies (high vs. low fear of crime) of two independent samples (victims vs. non-victims). The chi-square test of significance (Chapter 9) is employed to compare two or more samples when nominal or frequency data have been obtained. A 2 × 2 table would be created with victimization status along one axis and fear of crime along the other:

Fear of Crime	Victimization Status	
	Victim	*Non-Victim*
Low	11	104
High	27	28

Solution to Research Situation 26

(GOODMAN'S AND KRUSKAL'S GAMMA)   Research Situation 26 is a correlation problem that asks for the degree of association between two variables, X and Y, measured at the ordinal level: physical health and depression (note that an underlying order exists, even though only two levels of depression are indicated). Gamma (Chapter 12) is especially applicable when both variables are ordinal and can be arranged in the form of a cross-tabulation as follows:

Depression	Physical Health		
	Excellent	*Good*	*Poor*
Depressed	5	14	20
Not depressed	95	96	20

Solution to Research Situation 27

(CRAMÉR'S *V*)   Research Situation 27 is a nonparametric correlation problem (Chapter 12) that asks for the degree of association between two variables, one measured at the nominal level (gender) and the other measured at the ordinal level (physical health). Cramér's V is a measure of association for comparing several groups or categories at the nominal level. When variables are measured at two levels, statistical tests for the lower level are usually appropriate to apply. For example, Spearman's rank–order correlation coefficient is employed when X is an interval measure and Y is an ordinal measure. In the same way, Cramér's V is appropriate when X is nominal and Y is ordinal. To calculate Cramér's V, the data must be arranged in the form of a frequency table as follows:

Gender	Physical Health		
	Excellent	*Good*	*Poor*
Male	37	43	20
Female	52	35	13

Solution to Research Situation 28

(CHI-SQUARE TEST)   Research Situation 28 represents a comparison of the frequencies (belief that O.J. Simpson was guilty vs. not guilty) in two groups of people—black and white Americans. The chi-square test of significance (Chapter 9) is used to make comparisons between two or more samples when nominal or frequency data have been obtained. Present results can be cast in the form of the following 2 × 2 table, representing two rows and two columns:

Belief that O.J. Simpson Was	Race of Respondent	
	Black	*White*
Guilty	25	51
Not guilty	50	24

Solution to Research Situation 29

(*t* **RATIO OR MANN-WHITNEY *U* TEST**)   The *t* ratio is used to compare two means when interval data have been obtained and would be an appropriate way to analyze the data in Research Situation 29. The number of recall errors was measured at the interval level, and two means (hypnotized vs. non-hypnotized subjects) are compared. The Mann-Whitney *U* test (Chapter 9) is a nonparametric alternative that can be employed if the sentence lengths are not normally distributed in the population and the sample sizes are not large. The median test is a simple, but less powerful, nonparametric alternative.

APPENDIX A

Using *SPSS* and the General Social Survey

Several of the questions at the end of each chapter of this textbook assume the use of the Statistical Program for the Social Sciences (SPSS®, Inc., an IBM® Company).* To assist in using these tools, this appendix includes:

- Instructions for obtaining a copy of the instructional *SPSS* data set from the companion website; and
- Basic computer commands for the IBM Statistical Package for the Social Sciences (IBM *SPSS 20.0*).

Additionally, these features require access to *SPSS* software. *SPSS* software is a popular program that many universities and colleges have site-licensed use of in their computer labs. Other students wishing to work on their own computers may purchase a short-term site license so that they may download the program for student home use. Additional details on how to obtain *SPSS* for student home use are described on the website for this book.

WEBSITE FOR DATA SETS

The instructional *SPSS* data sets are available online as a supplement to Fox, Levin, and Forde's textbook. You will need to have Internet access using a browser such as Internet Explorer or Mozilla Firefox:

- Get a flash drive (portable drive or memory stick).
- Go to the textbook website and click on the links to save each file to the device on which you want to store the data.

There is one *SPSS* data file to download. The *SPSS* file has a codebook prepared in pdf format (requiring Adobe Acrobat Reader): GSS 2010 for 4E.sav. This is a subset of variables from the 2010 General Social Survey.

INTRODUCTION TO *SPSS*

The Statistical Program for the Social Sciences (*SPSS*) is a commonly used statistical program because it is relatively user-friendly. The program enables calculation of a wide variety of elementary and complex statistics. This appendix presents a few basic steps in *SPSS* so that you can use its drop-down menus to

- Open an existing data set
- Enter your own data
- Open *SPSS* files
- Recode or collapse categories
- Analyze data
- Select cases
- Weight cases
- Make a graph or chart
- Save computer output

*SPSS screen captures reprinted courtesy of International Business Machines Corporation, © SPSS, Inc., an IBM Company. SPSS was acquired by IBM in October, 2009. IBM, the IBM logo, ibm.com <http://ibm.com/>, and SPSS are trademarks of International Business Machines Corp., registered in many jurisdictions worldwide. Other product and service names might be trademarks of IBM or other companies. A current list of IBM trademarks is available on the Web at "IBM Copyright and trademark information <http://www.ibm.com/legal/copytrade.shtml>" at www.ibm.com/legal/copytrade. shtml <http://www.ibm.com/legal/copytrade.shtml>.

Opening an Existing Data File

There are many ways to retrieve an *SPSS* data file. Let's assume that you've started the *SPSS* program on a computer with a Microsoft Windows platform. A dialog box, shown below, comes up when *SPSS* 20.0 is started. Versions 18, 19, and 20 are similar to one another. By default, you are asked if you wish to "Run the tutorial." You may want to do so at another time, but right now, "Open an existing data source." Click your mouse on this bullet and it will be shaded. Also, notice that you may see a list of names of files that can be accessed.

Reprint Courtesy of International Business Machines Corporation, © SPSS, Inc., an IBM Company

To open an existing data file, click on OK at the bottom of the screen. It will bring up the next dialog box. In the Open Data box, change the "Look in" location (at the top of the box) to the location where you have downloaded and stored the data set. In this case, the file is stored on a portable flash drive inside a folder called "Fox."

Reprint Courtesy of International Business Machines Corporation, © SPSS, Inc., an IBM Company

A list of *SPSS* data files inside the folder will show up on this screen. Notice on the bottom of the screen that you can change the type of file. By default, *SPSS* data files ending with ".sav" are shown on the screen. Double-click on the file that you want to open and it will enter this information into the "File name" box and open the file. If you do not see the *SPSS* data file listed in this window, check that your flash drive is inserted into the port or click on "My Computer" and navigate to the correct port. You must specify the correct location of the file. After you have successfully launched the *SPSS* data file, an output screen appears and the data window is available for analysis.

The instructional data set for this book has been prepared as an "SPSS Statistics (*.sav)" file. The GSS 2010 for 4E.sav file can be opened by double-clicking it.

Entering Your Own Data

A few exercises in this textbook require you to enter your own data into *SPSS*. A large data set would make this quite a tedious task. Nevertheless, it is important for you to understand that every data set you use had to be created by someone. Let's make up some hypothetical data for an example with six people answering a survey about their gender and fear of crime. We'll record whether the person is male (1), female (2), or unknown (0). We'll use a question on fear of crime that has been included on several National Crime Victim Surveys asking people, "How safe do you (or would you) feel when walking alone at night in your own neighborhood?" Possible responses are very safe (4), safe (3), unsafe (2), very unsafe (1), and no response (0).

The following are the six people for this exercise:

Male and safe	1, 3
Female and unsafe	2, 2
Female and safe	2, 3
Male and very safe	1, 4
Female and very unsafe	2, 1
Male and no response	1, 0

SPSS version 20.0 is used in this example. Versions 16 to 20 have similar windows. The screens in *SPSS* 20.0 may look somewhat different from versions 16 to 19, but the features are essentially the

Reprint Courtesy of International Business Machines Corporation, © SPSS, Inc., an IBM Company

same. In Windows, click on the Start button, next move up to Programs, and finally down to the *SPSS* for Windows 20.0 icon. A successful start will take you to the default pop-up window asking you "What would you like to do?" Click in the circle for "Type in data" and then click on "OK." A new or untitled *SPSS* data file will be created. The variable names and case numbers are blank.

In *SPSS* 20.0, there are "Data View" and "Variable View" tabs at the bottom of the data editor screen. We're going to create two variables and enter some data for each. We will need to define the variables, designate a format, and then label everything! To begin, click on the variable view tab and type "gender" into the top left cell of the "Variable View" dialog box.

Reprint Courtesy of International Business Machines Corporation, © SPSS, Inc., an IBM Company

Notice that we may need to set the options on all aspects of variables. Right now, gender is set to the default with no labels and a numeric size of 8 digits wide with 2 decimal places and no labels, no missing values, and so on. Let's change each option to something appropriate.

In Chapter 1, we looked at levels of measurement. Note that levels of measurement as shown in the variable view include scale (interval/ratio), ordinal, and nominal. A user may designate for *SPSS* procedures that are appropriate for the level of measurement of a variable. If you do this, *SPSS* will attempt to assist you in selecting appropriate statistics. Next, note the important settings in this dialog box: type, labels, and missing values.

There are many types of formats of variables. The most common format is numeric. The numeric form is defined using a code of $x.y$ with x being the number of digits and y being the number of decimal places. The default format for numeric data in *SPSS* is 8.2. Let's look at our example. How many possibilities are there for gender? That is, how wide can the variable be? The numbers 0–9 have a width of 1, 10–99 are 2 figures, 100–999 are 3, and so on. There are no decimal places needed for gender. We will simply be coding male as 1 and female as 2. Therefore, we'll want to change the TYPE to 1 digit wide with 0 decimal places. Throughout this appendix, *SPSS* commands are shown in uppercase to emphasize the command or word that you should look for in the drop-down boxes. Click on TYPE and change it to 1.0 now.

Labeling of variables and their attributes is an important part of data entry. Labels should be *descriptive,* and there should be a label for *every attribute,* including missing values. The only exception to this rule is that on scales, we may want to just label the minimum and maximum values (e.g., very satisfied [1] to very dissatisfied [7] with intermediate values blank [2–6]). Try to avoid the use of abbreviations and acronyms because you may forget what they stand for and they make reading your work difficult for other people. You will encounter some acronyms in the General Social Survey data set used with this textbook. These acronyms were selected long ago when the computer software limited the names to eight characters in length. In some cases, the use of acronyms is clear and in others it is difficult to interpret the computer output without going to the codebook. The major goal in using labels is to make the computer output readable for you and for others.

Two kinds of labels can be added to a variable: variable labels and value labels. Variable labels should provide a description of the basic content of the variable. Click in the LABEL box for gender and type "Gender of the respondent."

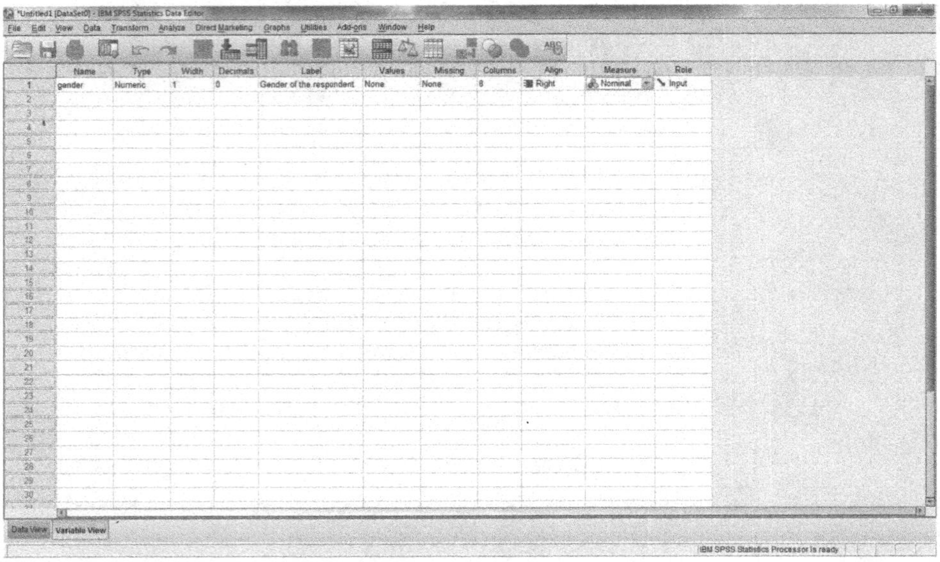

Reprint Courtesy of International Business Machines Corporation, © SPSS, Inc., an IBM Company

Next we need to add labels for each of the values/categories. Click on VALUES and three dots will appear on the right side of the box. Double-click on these dots to bring up the VALUE LABELS dialog box. These labels are entered one at a time by entering the value, the label, and then clicking on ADD. Every possible value of gender, including no response (0) should be labeled. Once everything has been entered, click on OK. These procedures are repeated for every variable.

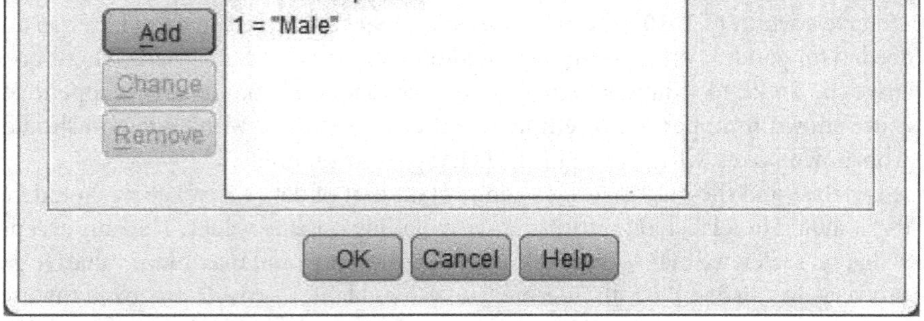

Reprint Courtesy of International Business Machines Corporation, © SPSS, Inc., an IBM Company

The third major feature in defining data is that values of variables may be set as *valid* or *missing*. Statistical analyses will count the number of *valid cases* for a variable. For example, people may refuse to answer a question, or they may not know, or a question may be not applicable. The researcher will want to know the average for people who answered the question and the number of missing cases in his or her statistical analysis. The statistical software must be instructed about the responses that are to be treated as *missing values*. This is done by clicking on the MISSING tab in the variable view. Missing values may be assigned as specific numbers or as a range of numbers. In this example, we want to set zero as a discrete missing value for gender. By setting a missing value, the software will distinguish valid cases (where information is known) from missing cases (where information is unknown). In this example, we want to exclude cases when the gender of the respondent is unknown (coded as 0).

Reprint Courtesy of International Business Machines Corporation, © SPSS, Inc., an IBM Company

Missing values are set by the researcher. You must look to see whether particular values are excluded or should be excluded from statistical analysis of data. Do not assume that these are set properly when you use a data set that has been put together by someone else. In fact, some researchers will turn all missing values off when they archive their data because different statistical packages may treat missing values in different ways. It is up to you as a researcher to ensure that these are set properly.

Now that the variable view is all set, switch to the data view at the bottom of your screen and enter these data. Your screen should look like the following box:

Reprint Courtesy of International Business Machines Corporation, © SPSS, Inc., an IBM Company

The real test to see how well you've entered the data and its associated information comes when you produce a frequency distribution. There should be *labels on everything* and *missing values should be set*. The basic steps to generate a frequency distribution are to click ANALYZE, DESCRIPTIVE STATISTICS, and FREQUENCIES from the pull-down menus and then select the variables. We'll go over the steps for analyzing data in much more detail shortly. The computer output is shown here:

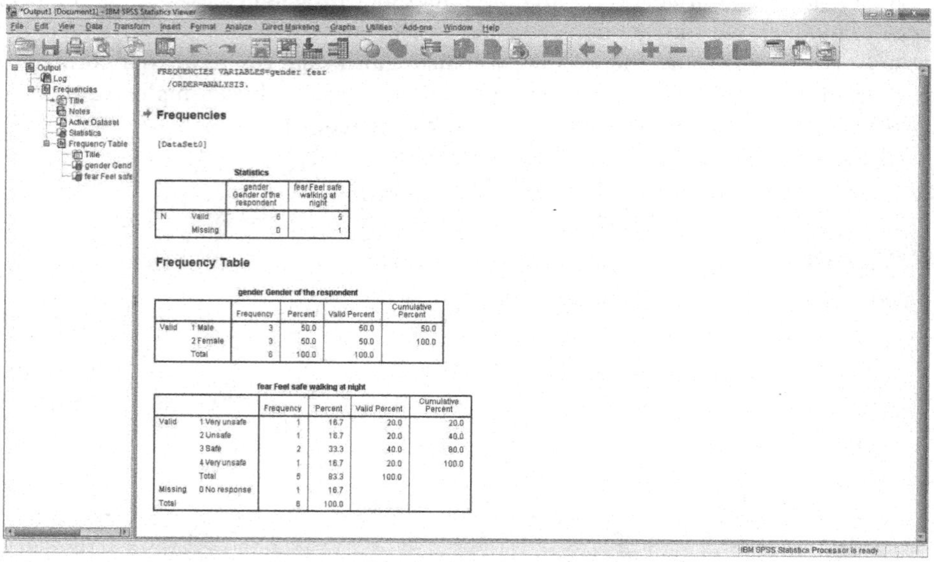

Reprint Courtesy of International Business Machines Corporation, © SPSS, Inc., an IBM Company

These frequency distributions are "clean" with labels on each of the variables and values. It is a normal part of data entry to examine computer output and to fix problems as they arise. Putting together a data set can be a lot of work. Thus, you may want to save your data file. This is done from the data editor window by clicking on "Untitled" data FILE, and then SAVE. You will need to click on the data file to save it. You can click on it at the bottom of the screen in most windows applications. You can also click on WINDOW in the top of the *SPSS* menu and then move to the desired window. If you wish to save the data, you must be in the data window. You can also save the computer output file.

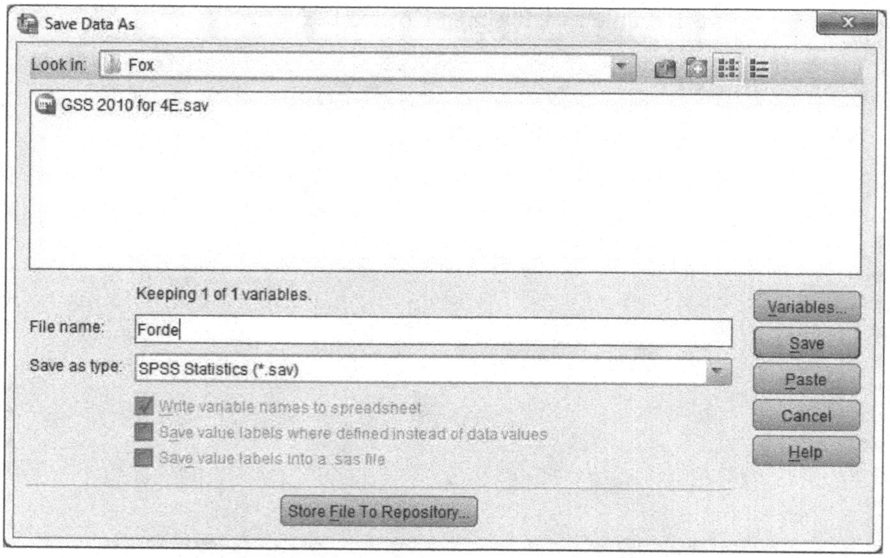

Reprint Courtesy of International Business Machines Corporation, © SPSS, Inc., an IBM Company

The default folder for *SPSS* is a folder called "SPSS." In most college computing labs, the default folder is the desktop of the computer. However, you may want to keep your file. As one of many possible solutions, I accomplish this by moving the location of the file to a folder on my jump drive that I created and called "Fox." The file may also be saved on a jump drive by changing the SAVE IN folder from *SPSS* to the jump drive (E:). The default type of file is an *SPSS* file (.sav). You'll need to name the file in order to save it. It is good practice to use descriptive names for files so that you can catalog them for later use. Here the file is named "Forde" for one of the authors of this book.

DATA FILES FROM ICPSR

Another important source of data files is the Inter-University Consortium for Political and Social Research (ICPSR). Many federally funded projects have a requirement that the data from the project be archived in a format that can be accessed by other people. ICPSR data librarians have taken investigators' data sets and saved them in formats that can be read by SPSS. Their hard work means that you have access to many data sets in the ICPSR data library. If you are considering a term paper, thesis, or advanced research project, you may want to access a data file from the ICPSR library.

Importantly, you now know that someone had to spend the time to enter these data, add variables and value labels, and set missing values. It is still quite a bit of work to prepare a data set from a data library, but it is a valuable resource potentially saving you the time that it took to collect the original data, and the cost is low (in fact free to most users).

The Inter-University Consortium for Political and Social Research is located at the University of Michigan in Ann Arbor. You can access it on the World Wide Web at http://icpsr.umich.edu. Its home page is shown here:

Inter-University Consortium for Political and Social Research

You may search the website for different types of data sets using key terms, investigators' names, and study numbers if you know them. Topical archives cover many areas including the census, crime, health, education, voting, and much more.

Notice that an ICPSR study description gives you a large amount of information about each study including who conducted it, which agency funded it, the methods used, and the access to files and their availability. In particular, we would like to know what the study is about, the format of the data files, whether there is an online codebook, and the structure of the data set(s).

The availability of data from some studies is restricted to ICPSR member institutions. If your college is a member of ICPSR, your college library should be able to tell you how to obtain permission to access these data files.

THE GENERAL SOCIAL SURVEY

The General Social Survey is one of the most important sources of information about social trends in the United States. Its home page is shown here.

National Option Research Center

To understand how variables were operationalized and to obtain the exact wording on questions on GSS surveys, it is useful to go to the GSS website where you may "Browse variables." The instructional data for this textbook is only a subset of variables from the 2010 General Social Survey. When you complete statistical analyses of questions at the end of each chapter in this book, you will most likely want to visit the GSS website to browse variables. The GSS data sets and information about them are free for public access.

Recoding Variables

You may wish to come back to this section on recoding variables when you are more familiar with data analysis. Whether you're working with a data file that someone else has created or with one of your own making, variables in a data file often need to be recoded—or changed—in some way, or values for new variables need to be calculated based on changes in the old variables. The following are some of the main reasons to recode variables:

- You may want to change the order of the categories so that the values go from what is intuitively the lowest to the highest.

- You may have two studies that have similar variables but different coding schemes. You might recode to make them as comparable as possible.
- You may want to recode so that you use a different statistic or procedure.
- You may wish to recode to collapse or group a large number of categories into a few categories.
- A recode and computation may allow you to look at combinations across several variables.

Let's look at an example from the General Social Survey that measured people's attitudes toward spanking to discipline a child as an ordinal variable with the following categories:

spanking FAVOR SPANKING TO DISCIPLINE CHILD

		Frequency	Percent	Valid Percent	Cumulative Percent
Valid	1 STRONGLY AGREE	334	16.3	23.6	23.6
	2 AGREE	642	31.4	45.4	68.9
	3 DISAGREE	333	16.3	23.5	92.5
	4 STRONGLY DISAGREE	107	5.2	7.5	100.0
	Total	1415	69.2	100.0	
Missing	0 IAP	613	30.0		
	8 DK	12	.6		
	9 NA	4	.2		
	Total	629	30.8		
Total		2044	100.0		

Suppose that we might want to recode the variable so that all people who said strongly agree or agree are combined and shown as Strongly agree or agree (1) and people who said disagree or strongly disagree are shown as Strongly disagree or disagree (2). To do this, we would recode 1,2 as 1 and 3,4 as 2.

To recode, click on TRANSFORM (located in the pull-down menu at the top of the screen) and then click on RECODE INTO DIFFERENT VARIABLES. It is a good idea to create a new variable rather than writing over the original variable because you may wish to keep the original variable for other analyses and to verify that the changes were correct.

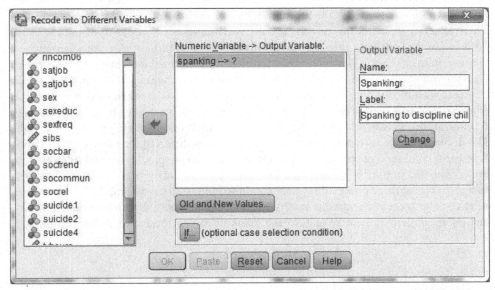

Reprint Courtesy of International Business Machines Corporation, © SPSS, Inc., an IBM Company

The original variable was Spanking and I named the new variable Spankingr using the "r" on the end to denote recoded. I also typed a label for it as Spanking to discipline child. Click on CHANGE to enter the name of the output variable.

Next, we need to enter the Old and New Values. Below, I've already added 1 and 2 to become 1. I'm working to recode 3 and 4 into a new value of 2. Look at the Range (on the left of the screen) with old values between 3 and 4 to become new value of 2. By clicking on ADD, this range will be added to the list of values to recode. Finally, click on CONTINUE and the recode is done.

Reprint Courtesy of International Business Machines Corporation, © SPSS, Inc., an IBM Company

The recode into a different variable process will create a new variable using categories that you've defined. You may also want to add variable and value labels to this new variable. The procedures to label variables were described earlier in this appendix.

The frequency distribution for the recoded variable shows that 68.9% of people in the United States say they strongly agree or agree with the statement that they favor spanking as a method to discipline a child. It is good practice to verify the combined information from strongly agree (23.6%) and agree (45.4%) in the original variable equals the recoded total (68.9%). The sum is correct within rounding error (69.0% versus 68.9%) as we have recoded spanking into a nominal variable with two categories. I have also relabeled each category by going to the data window, clicking on the variable view, and then adding labels and changing the variable width to 1 and 0 decimal places. Last, notice that there are 629 cases shown in the table as system missing. These cases combined people who were not asked the question, who refused to answer the question, or who did not know. All of these values were set in the original (or source) variable as "missing," and all of these other values were combined into system missing. For our purposes, what we've done to recode the variable into two groups will allow us compare people who gave valid answers about their agreement on favoring spanking as a method to discipline a child.

Spankingr Spanking to discipline child

		Frequency	Percent	Valid Percent	Cumulative Percent
Valid	1 Strongly agree or agree	976	47.7	68.9	68.9
	2 Strongly disagree or disagree	440	21.5	31.1	100.0
	Total	1415	69.2	100.0	
Missing	System	629	30.8		
Total		2044	100.0		

Recoding variables is often done to simplify complex variables so that we can use them appropriately in different statistical procedures. As social scientists, we will often want to recode variables into a smaller number of categories.

Data Analysis

The usual first step in every statistical analysis in *SPSS* is to click on ANALYZE at the top of the screen and then to choose your statistical analysis. For example, a frequency distribution in *SPSS* can be obtained by clicking on ANALYZE, then DESCRIPTIVE STATISTICS, and finally FREQUENCIES. The drop-down box on my computer is shown next. I have set the options so that variable names (rather than labels) are shown in the order that they appear in the data file. Other people may prefer labels, or alphabetical listings of acronyms, or the measurement level of variables.

Reprint Courtesy of International Business Machines Corporation, © SPSS, Inc., an IBM Company

You can change these settings (and you may really want to do so) by clicking on EDIT and OPTIONS. You'll need to do this each time you have a session on a computer in a public lab. You'll only need to do it once if it is on your own computer. I have also changed the output labels to "names and labels" and "values and labels." Make these changes and click APPLY (or close *SPSS* and restart it).

Reprint Courtesy of International Business Machines Corporation, © SPSS, Inc., an IBM Company

Changing the options will make it easier for you to read output and to locate variables within a data file. Try it and you'll see that it isn't too complicated. You can also proceed without making these changes.

Returning to the "frequencies" screen, move the variables from the list on the left to the right by selecting the variables and clicking the arrow to obtain a frequency distribution. The box that follows asks for a frequency distribution for a variable representing whether female respondents want an abortion for any reason (ABANY).

Reprint Courtesy of International Business Machines Corporation, © SPSS, Inc., an IBM Company

The frequencies procedure is "run" by clicking on "OK" at the bottom left of the box. But first, to obtain additional features for this variable, click on STATISTICS, which opens a box of choices from a wide variety of optional statistics, as shown below. Click on CONTINUE to exit from this box.

Reprint Courtesy of International Business Machines Corporation,
© SPSS, Inc., an IBM Company

There are too many statistical procedures to show all of them in a short appendix. The vast majority of tasks that you are asked to complete for this textbook will involve opening a data set, clicking on ANALYZE, and choosing the statistical procedure and its options. The frequencies procedure was ANALYZE, DESCRIPTIVE STATISTICS, and then FREQUENCIES. The problem sets will provide hints on where a statistical procedure is located in the drop-down menus.

SELECT CASES

A researcher may often wish to work with a portion of a data set. For example, you might want to examine just females for some statistical analysis. *SPSS* can "select cases" for statistical analysis. To do this, click on DATA at the top of the screen followed by SELECT CASES to open the following menu:

Reprint Courtesy of International Business Machines Corporation, © SPSS, Inc., an IBM Company

The SEX variable can be used to set the condition that only Females (Sex = 2) are selected. To do this, click on the "If" under IF CONDITION IS SATISFIED. I entered SEX = 2 and clicked CONTINUE. By clicking OK this filter is activated. It can be turned off by opening the menu again and clicking RESET.

The "Select cases" feature is very useful for doing repeated analyses on a subset of a larger data set. I could also save the selected cases as output from this window copied to a new data set. I named the data set "GSS Female," which generated a new data set of GSS respondents who were Female. You may do this kind of task if you want to limit your analysis to a subset. If you do so, be careful to keep a copy of your original data set.

WEIGHT CASES

Many complex data sets include a variable to weight cases. There are multiple weighting variables for the General Social Survey with one of them—WTSSALL—included as part of the instructional data set. Data may need to be weighted for various reasons. For example, the response rates for men may be lower in a survey so that there are fewer men in the sample than there actually are in the population. To correct for this sampling bias, a weighting variable can give more weight to a man's response and less weight to a woman's response so that the totals for the weighted response add up to the known total for the population. The GSS website has a detailed explanation on how its weighting variables are calculated.

Weights in *SPSS* are activated by clicking on DATA and WEIGHT CASES:

Reprint Courtesy of International Business Machines Corporation, © SPSS, Inc., an IBM Company

For the General Social Survey, I selected WTSSALL, which was provided with the original data set as the sampling variable for weighting. By clicking "OK," the current status will move to weighted by WTSSALL. Note that the bottom right corner of the data editor now shows as "Weight on."

GRAPHS AND CHARTS

Graphs provide a method to visually present information from a table to highlight an important statistic or trend. *SPSS* can generate many different types of graphs. Chapter 2 discussed the basics for pie charts, bar graphs, and line charts. As you build graphs in *SPSS*, remember that there often are multiple ways to transform tables into graphs and that you need to consider whether your choice is effective in providing appropriate titles, labels, and so on.

The interactive chart builder is a drop-down box accessed by clicking on GRAPHS at the top of the data dialog screen. We'll use it to make a bar chart for ATTEND to show how often people in the United States say that they attend religious services. The chart builder is quite easy to use, but it does assume that the level of measurement has been set for each of the variables. Click to the variable view in the data window. Notice that every variable in the data set is set by default to nominal. To make a graph for a variable, set the level of measurement to the appropriate level. I changed ATTEND to "ordinal" so that I could produce a bar chart.

To begin, I clicked on BAR CHART on the left side of the screen. Next, I dragged and dropped the simple bar chart into the chart preview area. To select ATTEND, I scrolled down the variable list shown on the left side of the screen, left-clicked on ATTEND, and dragged and dropped it into the box for the *x* axis.

Last, I changed the *y* axis from count to percentages using the statistics box for Element Properties of the chart. This box is shown as an option under STATISTICS on the far left of the screen when the chart builder opens.

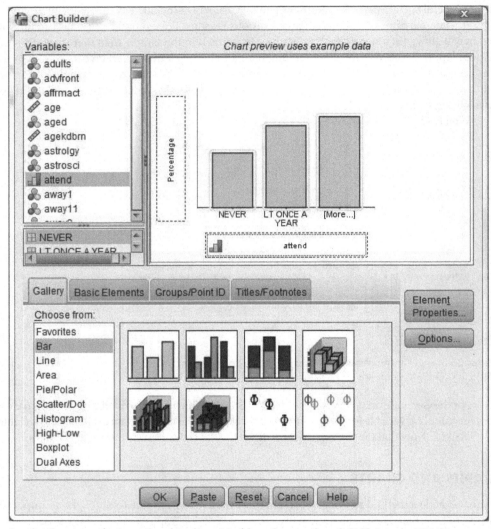

Reprint Courtesy of International Business Machines Corporation, © SPSS, Inc., an IBM Company

Element Properties

Edit Properties of:

Bar1
X-Axis1 (Bar1)
Y-Axis1 (Bar1)

Statistics
Variable:
Statistic:
Percentage ()

Set Parameters...

☐ Display error bars

Error Bars Represent
◉ Confidence intervals
    Level (%): 95
◉ Standard error
    Multiplier: 2
◉ Standard deviation
    Multiplier: 2

Bar Style:
▮ Bar

Apply   Close   Help

Reprint Courtesy of International Business Machines
Corporation, © SPSS, Inc., an IBM Company

Titles and footnotes can be added to the chart by clicking on their tab in the chart builder. Finally, click on OK and the chart will be generated. The *SPSS*-generated bar chart for ATTEND follows:

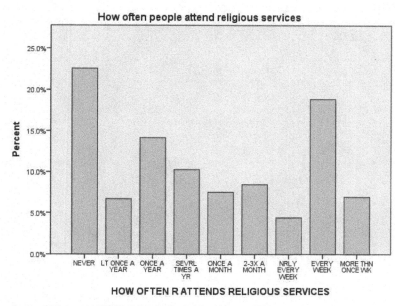

Source: Author computation based on the General Social Survey, 2010

To complete the chart using *SPSS*, double-click on it and the "Chart editor" will open. In this editor, you may click on FOOTNOTE (or click where the footnote should be) to edit it and click on each label to edit and change options, change the title, change fill patterns, and much more. You can save your chart onto a flash drive and make additional changes using *SPSS* similar to what you would to revise a regular word processing file. You may also copy the completed chart as a picture into a word processor such as Microsoft Word.

It is also possible to copy computer output from SPSS into other computer applications such as Microsoft Word. With some practice, you can dazzle your professor with reports including statistical output and graphs. This appendix has provided a very brief introduction to *SPSS*. For more information, see http://www-01.ibm.com/software/analytics/spss/. In the meantime, Happy Computing!

Computer Output

SPSS can be used to generate a large amount of computer output. You may save computer output for later use by clicking on FILE, SAVE AS, and then give it a name and location (on your computer or flash drive). You do not have to save computer output. You can delete any output by clicking on it and pressing delete. You can also delete the entire file simply by closing it. If you do this, *SPSS* will create a new output file the next time you analyze a variable.

StatCrunch
Data analysis on the Web
www.statcrunch.com

PEARSON

About This Study Card

StatCrunch is a Web-based statistical software package for analyzing data. To access StatCrunch, visit **http://www.statcrunch.com**. This study card is intended to serve as a brief introduction to the use of StatCrunch covering the procedures that most students will encounter in an introductory statistics course. Follow the help links at the statcrunch.com site for more extensive documentation.

Data > Load data > from file

1. Choose **My computer** to load a data file from the local system or **WWW** to load a data file from the Web.
2. Specify the location of a text file (.txt, .csv, etc.) or Microsoft Excel file.
3. If the first line in your file does not contain column names, deselect the **use first line as column names** option.
4. For text files (not Excel files), specify the delimiter for the data values. For example, the delimiter for a .csv file is a comma.
5. Click the **Load File** button to upload the data file.

About this data set: The data set contains information from a random sample of 30 four-bedroom homes listed for sale in the Bryan–College Station, Texas area in December 2008. For each home, the data set contains the list price in thousands of dollars (Price), square footage (Sqft), number of bathrooms (Baths), and location (Bryan, TX, or College Station, TX). It is currently being shared on the StatCrunch site at http://www.statcrunch.com/5.0/index.php?dataid=359673.

Example: Loading an Excel file from the local file system or from a Web address

Data > Compute Expression

1. Enter a mathematical or Boolean expression in the **Expression** input box.
2. Alternatively, use the menus for **Y, X, a, b,** and **Function** to construct the expression. Then, click **Set Expression**.
3. Click **Compute** and the results of the expression will be added as a new column to the StatCrunch data table.

Note: A Boolean (true/false) expression can be used as a **Where** statement in many StatCrunch procedures to exclude outliers or to focus an analysis on a subset of the data. Some of the following examples illustrate this feature.

Example: Computing the mathematical expression, 1000*(Price/Sqft)

ISBN-13: 978-0-321-62892-3
ISBN-10:   0-321-62892-6

90000

EAN

9 780321 628923

Graphics > Bar plot

1. Choose the **with data** option to use data consisting of individual outcomes in the data table.
    a. Select the column(s) to be displayed.
    b. Use an optional **Where** statement to specify the data included.
    c. Select an optional **Group by** column for a side-by-side bar plot.
    Choose the **with summary** option to use summary information consisting of categories and counts.
    a. Select the column containing the categories.
    b. Select the column containing the counts.
2. Click **Next** to set additional options such as **Type** (Frequency or Relative Frequency).
3. Click **Create Graph!** to construct the bar plot(s).

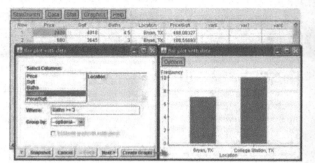

Example: A bar plot showing the number of homes in each location with three or more baths

Graphics > Histogram

1. Select the column(s) to be displayed.
2. Use an optional **Where** statement to specify the data included.
3. Select an optional **Group by** column to color code the bars.
4. Click **Next** to set additional options such as the starting value of the bins and the bin width.
5. Click **Next** again to specify an optional density to overlay on the histogram(s).
6. Click **Create Graph!** to construct the histogram(s).

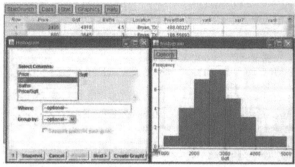

Example: A histogram of the Sqft column

Graphics > Boxplot

1. Select the column(s) to be displayed. By default, a boxplot for each column will be included on a single graph.
2. Use an optional **Where** statement to specify the data included.
3. Select an optional **Group by** column to compare boxplots across groups on a single graph.
4. Click **Next** to indicate whether or not to use fences for the boxplots. By default, the five-number summary is used.
5. Click **Create Graph!** to construct the boxplot(s).

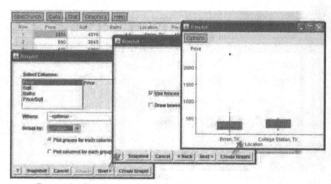

Example: Boxplots comparing price across locations

Graphics > Scatter Plot

1. Select the **X variable** and **Y variable** for the plot.
2. Use an optional **Where** statement to specify the data included.
3. Color code points with an optional **Group by** column.
4. Click **Create Graph!** to produce the plot.

Example: Scatter plot of Price vs. Sqft color coded by location

Graphics > QQ Plot

1. Select the column(s) to be displayed.
2. Use an optional **Where** statement to specify the data included.
3. Select an optional **Group by** column to produce separate plots for different groups.
4. Click **Create Graph!** to construct the plot(s).

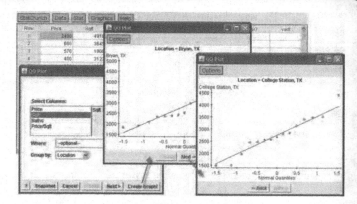

Example: QQ plot of the Sqft column grouped by Location

Interacting with Graphics

1. Click and drag the mouse around graph objects to highlight them.
2. The corresponding rows will be highlighted in the data table and in all other graphics.
3. Toggle highlighting on and off by clicking on the row number in the data table.
4. To clear all highlighted rows, click on the **Row** heading atop the first column in the data table.
5. To highlight rows based on categories or numeric ranges, use the **Data > Row selection > Interactive tools** option.

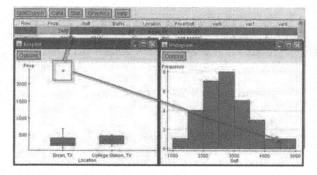

Example: Highlighting an outlier in a boxplot

Stat > Summary Stats > Columns

1. Select the column(s) for which summary statistics are to be computed.
2. Use an optional **Where** statement to specify the data included.
3. Compare statistics across groups using an optional **Group by** column.
4. Click **Next** for additional options such as the statistics to be computed.
5. Click **Calculate** to compute the summary statistics.

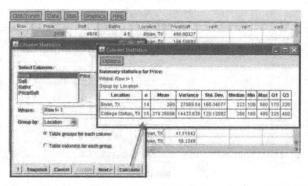

Example: Comparing prices of homes listed in Bryan to those listed in College Station with the potential outlier removed

Stat > Tables > Frequency

1. Select the column(s) for which a frequency table is to be computed.
2. Use an optional **Where** statement to specify the data included.
3. Click **Calculate** to compute the frequency table(s).

Example: A frequency table for the number of bathrooms

Stat > Proportions > One sample

1. Choose the **with data** option to use data from the data table.
   a. Select the column containing the sample values.
   b. Specify the outcome that denotes a **success**.
   c. Use an optional **Where** statement to specify the data included.
   Choose the **with summary** option to enter the **number of successes** and **number of observations**.
2. Click **Next** and select the **hypothesis test** or **confidence interval** option.
   a. For a hypothesis test, enter the **Null** proportion and choose $\neq$, $<$, or $>$ for **Alternative**.
   b. For a confidence interval, enter a value between 0 and 1 for **Level** (0.95 provides a 95% confidence interval). For **Method**, choose **Standard-Wald** or **Agresti-Coull**.
3. Click **Calculate** to view the results.

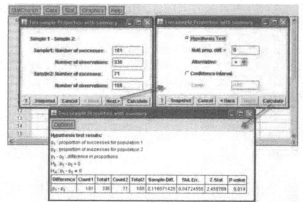

Example: For each of 998 North Carolina births, this data set indicates whether or not the birth was premature. A 95% confidence interval for the proportion of all North Carolina births that are *not* premature is shown above.

Stat > Proportions > Two sample

1. Choose the **with data** option to use sample data from the StatCrunch data table.
   a. Select the columns containing the first and second samples.
   b. Specify the sample outcomes that denote a success for both samples.
   c. Enter optional **Where** statements to specify the data rows to be included in both samples. If the two samples are in separate columns, this step is typically not required.
   Choose the **with summary** option to enter the **number of successes** and **number of observations** for both samples.
2. Click **Next** and select the **hypothesis test** or **confidence interval** option.
   a. For a hypothesis test, enter the **Null** proportion difference and choose $\neq$, $<$, or $>$ for **Alternative**.
   b. For a confidence interval, enter a value between 0 and 1 for **Level** (0.95 provides a 95% confidence interval).
3. Click **Calculate** to view the results.

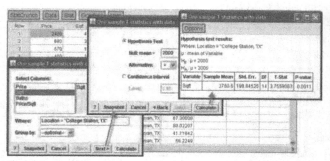

Example: In a survey, 181 of 336 people who attended church services at least once a week said the use of torture against suspected terrorists is "often" or "sometimes" justified. Only 71 of 168 people who "seldom or never" went to services agreed. Using this **summary** information, a two-sided hypothesis test is performed below to compare the proportion with this opinion for these two populations.

Stat > T statistics > One sample

1. Choose the **with data** option to use sample data from the StatCrunch data table.
   a. Select the column containing the sample data values.
   b. Use an optional **Where** statement to specify the data included.
   Choose the **with summary** option to enter the **sample mean**, **sample standard deviation**, and **sample size**.
2. Click **Next** and select the **hypothesis test** or **confidence interval** option.
   a. For a hypothesis test, enter the **Null** mean and choose $\neq$, $<$, or $>$ for **Alternative**.
   b. For a confidence interval, enter a value between 0 and 1 for **Level** (0.95 provides a 95% confidence interval).
3. Click **Calculate** to view the results.

Example: Testing to see if the average home listed in College Station, Texas, is larger than 2000 square feet.

Stat > T statistics > Two sample

1. Choose the **with data** option to use sample data from the data table.
   a. Select the columns containing the first and second samples.
   b. Enter optional **Where** statements to specify the data rows to be included in both samples. If the two samples are in separate columns, this step is typically not required.

   Choose the **with summary** option to enter the **sample mean**, **sample standard deviation**, and **sample size** for both samples.
2. Deselect the **Pool variance** option if desired.
3. Click **Next** and select the **hypothesis test** or **confidence interval** option.
   a. For a hypothesis test, enter the **Null** mean difference and choose $\neq$, $<$, or $>$ for **Alternative**.
   b. For a confidence interval, enter a value between 0 and 1 for **Level** (0.95 provides a 95% confidence interval).
4. Click **Calculate** to view the results.

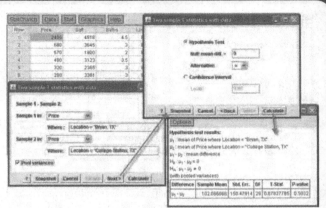

Example: Hypothesis test comparing the prices of homes listed in Bryan to those in College Station, with potential outliers included.

Stat > T statistics > Paired

1. Select the columns containing the first and second samples.
2. Use an optional **Where** statement to specify the data included.
3. Click **Next** and select the **hypothesis test** or **confidence interval** option.
   a. For a hypothesis test, enter the **Null** mean difference and choose $\neq$, $<$, or $>$ for **Alternative**.
   b. For a confidence interval, enter a value between 0 and 1 for **Level** (0.95 provides a 95% confidence interval).
4. Click **Calculate** to view the results.

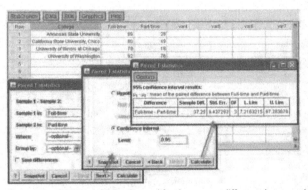

Example: A 95% confidence interval for the average difference between the graduation rate of full- and part-time students across all colleges based on a random sample of four colleges.

Stat > Regression > Simple Linear

1. Select the **X variable** (independent variable) and **Y variable** (dependent variable) for the regression.
2. Use an optional **Where** statement to specify the data included.
3. Compare results across groups by selecting an optional **Group by** column.
4. Click **Next** to specify optional X values for predictions and to indicate whether or not to save residuals/fitted values.
5. Click **Next** again to choose from a list of optional graphics for plotting the fitted line and examining residuals.
6. Click **Calculate** to view the results.

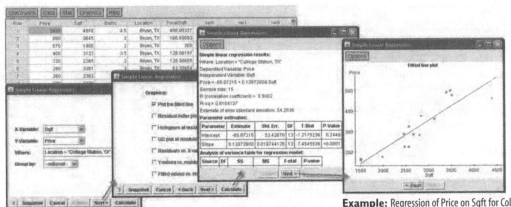

Example: Regression of Price on Sqft for College Station

Stat > ANOVA > One way

1. Select one of the following options:
   a. If the samples are in separate columns, select the **Compare selected columns** option and then select the columns containing the samples.
   b. If the samples are in a single column, select the **Compare values in a single column** option. Then specify the column containing the samples (**Responses In**) and the column containing the population labels (**Factors In**).
2. Use an optional **Where** statement to specify the data to be included.
3. Select the **Tukey HSD** option and specify a confidence level to perform a post hoc means analysis. The default value of 0.95 provides 95% confidence intervals for all pairwise mean differences.
4. Click **Calculate** to view the results.

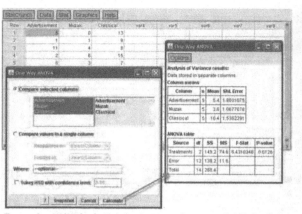

Example: ANOVA for the time, in minutes, a caller stays on hold before hanging up under three different treatments.

Stat > Tables > Contingency

1. Select one of the following options:
   a. Choose the **with data** option to cross tabulate two columns of raw data from the data table. Then,
      A. Select the column to be tabulated across the rows.
      B. Select the column to be tabulated across the columns.
      C. Use an optional **Where** statement to specify the data included.
      D. Select an optional **Group by** column to compute separate tables across groups.
   b. Choose the **with summary** option to use a two-way cross classification already entered in the data table. Then,
      A. Select the columns that contain the summary counts.
      B. Select the column that contains the row labels.
      C. Enter a name for the column variable.
2. Click **Next** to specify additional information to be displayed in each table cell.
3. Click **Calculate** to view the results.

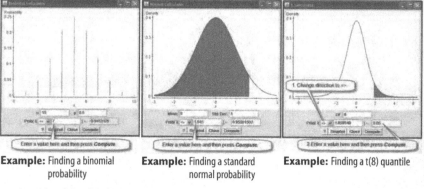

Example: Using **summary** counts cross tabulating gender and back problems, a test of independence between the two factors is shown below. Note that the back problems variable is represented by the second and third columns in the data table.

Stat > Calculators

1. Select the name of the desired distribution from the menu listing (e.g., Binomial, Normal, etc.).
2. In the first line below the plot in the calculator window, specify the distribution parameters. As examples, with the normal distribution, specify the mean and standard deviation or with the binomial distribution, specify n and p.
3. In the second line below the plot, specify the direction of the desired probability.

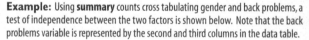

Example: Finding a binomial probability

Example: Finding a standard normal probability

Example: Finding a t(8) quantile

   a. To compute a probability, enter a value to the right of the direction selector and leave the remaining field empty (e.g., $P(X < 3) =$ ___).
   b. To determine the point that will provide a specified probability, enter the probability to the right of the direction selector and leave the other field empty (e.g., $P(X >$ ___ $) = 0.25$). This option is available only for continuous distributions.
4. Click **Compute** to fill in the empty fields and to update the graph of the distribution.

APPENDIX C

Tables

Percentage of Area under the Normal Curve

Column a gives z, the distance in standard deviation units from the mean. Column b represents the percentage of area between the mean and a given z. Column c represents the percentage at or beyond a given z.

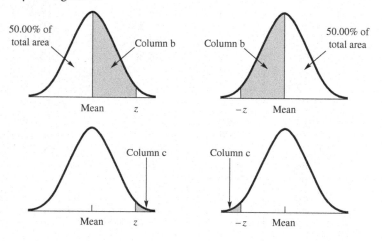

(a) z	(b) Area between Mean and z	(c) Area beyond z	(a) z	(b) Area between Mean and z	(c) Area beyond z
.00	.00	50.00	.22	8.71	41.29
.01	.40	49.60	.23	9.10	40.90
.02	.80	49.20	.24	9.48	40.52
.03	1.20	48.80	.25	9.87	40.13
.04	1.60	48.40	.26	10.26	39.74
.05	1.99	48.01	.27	10.64	39.36
.06	2.39	47.61	.28	11.03	38.97
.07	2.79	47.21	.29	11.41	38.59
.08	3.19	46.81	.30	11.79	38.21
.09	3.59	46.41	.31	12.17	37.83
.10	3.98	46.02	.32	12.55	37.45
.11	4.38	45.62	.33	12.93	37.07
.12	4.78	45.22	.34	13.31	36.69
.13	5.17	44.83	.35	13.68	36.32
.14	5.57	44.43	.36	14.06	35.94
.15	5.96	44.04	.37	14.43	35.57
.16	6.36	43.64	.38	14.80	35.20
.17	6.75	43.25	.39	15.17	34.83
.18	7.14	42.86	.40	15.54	34.46
.19	7.53	42.47	.41	15.91	34.09
.20	7.93	42.07	.42	16.28	33.72
.21	8.32	41.68	.43	16.64	33.36

(continued)

TABLE A	Continued

(a) z	(b) Area between Mean and z	(c) Area beyond z	(a) z	(b) Area between Mean and z	(c) Area beyond z
.44	17.00	33.00	.92	32.12	17.88
.45	17.36	32.64	.93	32.38	17.62
.46	17.72	32.28	.94	32.64	17.36
.47	18.08	31.92	.95	32.89	17.11
.48	18.44	31.56	.96	33.15	16.85
.49	18.79	31.21	.97	33.40	16.60
.50	19.15	30.85	.98	33.65	16.35
.51	19.50	30.50	.99	33.89	16.11
.52	19.85	30.15	1.00	34.13	15.87
.53	20.19	29.81	1.01	34.38	15.62
.54	20.54	29.46	1.02	34.61	15.39
.55	20.88	29.12	1.03	34.85	15.15
.56	21.23	28.77	1.04	35.08	14.92
.57	21.57	28.43	1.05	35.31	14.69
.58	21.90	28.10	1.06	35.54	14.46
.59	22.24	27.76	1.07	35.77	14.23
.60	22.57	27.43	1.08	35.99	14.01
.61	22.91	27.09	1.09	36.21	13.79
.62	23.24	26.76	1.10	36.43	13.57
.63	23.57	26.43	1.11	36.65	13.35
.64	23.89	26.11	1.12	36.86	13.14
.65	24.22	25.78	1.13	37.08	12.92
.66	24.54	25.46	1.14	37.29	12.71
.67	24.86	25.14	1.15	37.49	12.51
.68	25.17	24.83	1.16	37.70	12.30
.69	25.49	24.51	1.17	37.90	12.10
.70	25.80	24.20	1.18	38.10	11.90
.71	26.11	23.89	1.19	38.30	11.70
.72	26.42	23.58	1.20	38.49	11.51
.73	26.73	23.27	1.21	38.69	11.31
.74	27.04	22.96	1.22	38.88	11.12
.75	27.34	22.66	1.23	39.07	10.93
.76	27.64	22.36	1.24	39.25	10.75
.77	27.94	22.06	1.25	39.44	10.56
.78	28.23	21.77	1.26	39.62	10.38
.79	28.52	21.48	1.27	39.80	10.20
.80	28.81	21.19	1.28	39.97	10.03
.81	29.10	20.90	1.29	40.15	9.85
.82	29.39	20.61	1.30	40.32	9.68
.83	29.67	20.33	1.31	40.49	9.51
.84	29.95	20.05	1.32	40.66	9.34
.85	30.23	19.77	1.33	40.82	9.18
.86	30.51	19.49	1.34	40.99	9.01
.87	30.78	19.22	1.35	41.15	8.85
.88	31.06	18.94	1.36	41.31	8.69
.89	31.33	18.67	1.37	41.47	8.53
.90	31.59	18.41	1.38	41.62	8.38
.91	31.86	18.14	1.39	41.77	8.23

(a) z	(b) Area between Mean and z	(c) Area beyond z	(a) z	(b) Area between Mean and z	(c) Area beyond z
1.40	41.92	8.08	1.89	47.06	2.94
1.41	42.07	7.93	1.90	47.13	2.87
1.42	42.22	7.78	1.91	47.19	2.81
1.43	42.36	7.64	1.92	47.26	2.74
1.44	42.51	7.49	1.93	47.32	2.68
1.45	42.65	7.35	1.94	47.38	2.62
1.46	42.79	7.21	1.95	47.44	2.56
1.47	42.92	7.08	1.96	47.50	2.50
1.48	43.06	6.94	1.97	47.56	2.44
1.49	43.19	6.81	1.98	47.61	2.39
1.50	43.32	6.68	1.99	47.67	2.33
1.51	43.45	6.55	2.00	47.72	2.28
1.52	43.57	6.43	2.01	47.78	2.22
1.53	43.70	6.30	2.02	47.83	2.17
1.54	43.82	6.18	2.03	47.88	2.12
1.55	43.94	6.06	2.04	47.93	2.07
1.56	44.06	5.94	2.05	47.98	2.02
1.57	44.18	5.82	2.06	48.03	1.97
1.58	44.29	5.71	2.07	48.08	1.92
1.59	44.41	5.59	2.08	48.12	1.88
1.60	44.52	5.48	2.09	48.17	1.83
1.61	44.63	5.37	2.10	48.21	1.79
1.62	44.74	5.26	2.11	48.26	1.74
1.63	44.84	5.16	2.12	48.30	1.70
1.64	44.95	5.05	2.13	48.34	1.66
1.65	45.05	4.95	2.14	48.38	1.62
1.66	45.15	4.85	2.15	48.42	1.58
1.67	45.25	4.75	2.16	48.46	1.54
1.68	45.35	4.65	2.17	48.50	1.50
1.69	45.45	4.55	2.18	48.54	1.46
1.70	45.54	4.46	2.19	48.57	1.43
1.71	45.64	4.36	2.20	48.61	1.39
1.72	45.73	4.27	2.21	48.64	1.36
1.73	45.82	4.18	2.22	48.68	1.32
1.74	45.91	4.09	2.23	48.71	1.29
1.75	45.99	4.01	2.24	48.75	1.25
1.76	46.08	3.92	2.25	48.78	1.22
1.77	46.16	3.84	2.26	48.81	1.19
1.78	46.25	3.75	2.27	48.84	1.16
1.79	46.33	3.67	2.28	48.87	1.13
1.80	46.41	3.59	2.29	48.90	1.10
1.81	46.49	3.51	2.30	48.93	1.07
1.82	46.56	3.44	2.31	48.96	1.04
1.83	46.64	3.36	2.32	48.98	1.02
1.84	46.71	3.29	2.33	49.01	.99
1.85	46.78	3.22	2.34	49.04	.96
1.86	46.86	3.14	2.35	49.06	.94
1.87	46.93	3.07	2.36	49.09	.91
1.88	46.99	3.01	2.37	49.11	.89

(continued)

TABLE A	Continued				
(a)	**(b)**	**(c)**	**(a)**	**(b)**	**(c)**
	Area between	**Area**		**Area between**	**Area**
z	**Mean and z**	**beyond z**	**z**	**Mean and z**	**beyond z**
2.38	49.13	.87	2.87	49.79	.21
2.39	49.16	.84	2.88	49.80	.20
2.40	49.18	.82	2.89	49.81	.19
2.41	49.20	.80	2.90	49.81	.19
2.42	49.22	.78	2.91	49.82	.18
2.43	49.25	.75	2.92	49.82	.18
2.44	49.27	.73	2.93	49.83	.17
2.45	49.29	.71	2.94	49.84	.16
2.46	49.31	.69	2.95	49.84	.16
2.47	49.32	.68	2.96	49.85	.15
2.48	49.34	.66	2.97	49.85	.15
2.49	49.36	.64	2.98	49.86	.14
2.50	49.38	.62	2.99	49.86	.14
2.51	49.40	.60	3.00	49.87	.13
2.52	49.41	.59	3.01	49.87	.13
2.53	49.43	.57	3.02	49.87	.13
2.54	49.45	.55	3.03	49.88	.12
2.55	49.46	.54	3.04	49.88	.12
2.56	49.48	.52	3.05	49.89	.11
2.57	49.49	.51	3.06	49.89	.11
2.58	49.51	.49	3.07	49.89	.11
2.59	49.52	.48	3.08	49.90	.10
2.60	49.53	.47	3.09	49.90	.10
2.61	49.55	.45	3.10	49.90	.10
2.62	49.56	.44	3.11	49.91	.09
2.63	49.57	.43	3.12	49.91	.09
2.64	49.59	.41	3.13	49.91	.09
2.65	49.60	.40	3.14	49.92	.08
2.66	49.61	.39	3.15	49.92	.08
2.67	49.62	.38	3.16	49.92	.08
2.68	49.63	.37	3.17	49.92	.08
2.69	49.64	.36	3.18	49.93	.07
2.70	49.65	.35	3.19	49.93	.07
2.71	49.66	.34	3.20	49.93	.07
2.72	49.67	.33	3.21	49.93	.07
2.73	49.68	.32	3.22	49.94	.06
2.74	49.69	.31	3.23	49.94	.06
2.75	49.70	.30	3.24	49.94	.06
2.76	49.71	.29	3.25	49.94	.06
2.77	49.72	.28	3.30	49.95	.05
2.78	49.73	.27	3.35	49.96	.04
2.79	49.74	.26	3.40	49.97	.03
2.80	49.74	.26	3.45	49.97	.03
2.81	49.75	.25	3.50	49.98	.02
2.82	49.76	.24	3.60	49.98	.02
2.83	49.77	.23	3.70	49.99	.01
2.84	49.77	.23	3.80	49.99	.01
2.85	49.78	.22	3.90	49.995	.005
2.86	49.79	.21	4.00	49.997	.003

TABLE B   Random Numbers

Column Number

Row	1	2	3	4	5	6	7	8	9	10	11	12	13	14	15	16	17	18	19
1	0	6	9	0	6	2	8	5	3	6	9	6	4	3	3	2	8	1	2
2	4	9	6	8	5	5	3	0	7	8	9	2	9	2	2	1	0	1	1
3	9	4	6	2	2	3	8	6	7	8	4	0	1	1	1	7	0	3	7
4	9	5	0	4	6	2	2	4	6	4	0	9	6	7	4	8	0	0	7
5	2	0	3	2	7	6	6	2	3	9	7	5	1	4	8	8	7	9	7
6	7	1	4	1	1	1	7	6	3	7	0	2	8	8	9	9	7	5	2
7	1	3	7	0	9	3	3	0	0	2	5	7	3	2	9	0	7	6	6
8	5	9	6	2	2	3	3	3	4	7	4	5	3	7	8	9	1	3	1
9	3	6	5	9	1	6	2	0	7	3	3	2	8	5	0	1	2	3	5
10	3	4	4	3	6	8	5	5	1	5	2	1	1	2	6	6	7	3	1
11	2	1	7	1	4	3	3	7	8	2	2	7	4	6	7	5	6	2	3
12	8	3	7	9	5	9	0	6	5	9	9	8	2	3	7	5	6	6	9
13	8	8	2	3	4	8	6	8	4	0	1	1	7	7	4	4	8	8	5
14	0	4	4	7	5	3	2	9	8	4	9	6	5	8	9	9	1	1	6
15	3	4	3	4	4	8	3	0	8	2	0	1	6	5	2	2	5	8	3
16	6	9	7	1	0	6	6	2	5	7	2	3	3	9	9	1	0	0	9
17	0	5	7	9	7	9	2	5	3	0	9	3	7	1	3	7	2	8	7
18	3	6	6	8	0	0	9	4	9	1	7	1	9	4	1	0	3	9	8
19	7	1	2	2	2	7	2	6	8	7	9	3	1	5	5	3	6	9	4
20	3	4	4	1	0	3	6	4	0	2	4	8	4	1	3	3	7	8	9
21	4	1	8	9	3	9	9	7	6	6	5	9	6	2	0	9	0	5	3
22	8	9	2	7	0	6	5	2	8	0	2	3	6	6	1	6	4	3	3
23	3	5	2	6	3	7	2	3	1	6	5	9	6	4	2	1	5	7	9
24	5	4	8	5	4	9	7	0	7	5	4	6	5	1	8	5	1	6	1
25	7	4	5	4	9	2	1	5	5	0	1	5	6	0	3	9	2	7	2
26	5	0	2	6	7	7	8	4	0	8	6	9	2	4	1	8	2	4	5
27	3	6	4	3	0	9	1	9	4	0	8	7	2	6	3	5	7	7	2
28	8	2	3	7	4	6	9	9	9	1	9	3	1	4	0	2	7	3	0
29	7	9	2	1	7	5	6	0	3	1	0	2	1	5	8	5	6	7	0
30	9	0	6	5	1	2	1	1	5	8	3	5	8	0	1	4	9	2	9
31	8	8	0	2	3	0	1	1	1	9	7	4	8	7	1	3	9	5	0
32	4	4	0	9	2	6	5	6	5	9	7	4	7	7	6	5	4	7	6
33	5	1	6	6	6	6	1	4	1	2	6	3	6	8	1	6	7	4	4
34	2	5	6	7	4	8	3	5	2	6	3	6	9	9	0	1	5	9	9
35	6	0	0	4	3	1	8	7	2	6	3	5	0	0	0	9	3	0	9
36	8	9	7	7	0	8	5	0	3	7	6	9	8	2	1	2	5	0	5
37	2	9	7	6	9	4	3	8	5	8	9	7	4	3	6	7	9	1	0
38	0	5	0	7	3	8	2	4	1	6	9	0	3	4	0	4	5	2	9
39	8	9	9	4	4	6	8	9	3	1	7	9	2	8	0	1	2	7	4
40	8	6	0	2	0	9	4	2	9	6	4	9	0	1	8	3	4	1	8

(continued)

TABLE B Continued

									Column Number												
20	**21**	**22**	**23**	**24**	**25**	**26**	**27**	**28**	**29**	**30**	**31**	**32**	**33**	**34**	**35**	**36**	**37**	**38**	**39**	**40**	**Row**
0	1	3	8	9	9	9	7	9	9	2	8	5	4	1	5	3	9	8	2	3	1
0	2	3	0	9	3	4	8	5	2	0	6	3	2	6	0	4	5	0	0	1	2
0	0	2	5	2	8	4	8	0	1	0	5	2	8	5	0	5	0	3	0	6	3
4	5	3	2	1	5	8	1	9	3	3	0	5	9	2	3	7	6	1	7	3	4
5	7	9	5	2	4	5	4	2	2	4	4	3	1	0	1	7	4	4	8	9	5
2	7	2	3	0	2	5	3	4	9	8	7	6	3	8	4	3	1	2	4	9	6
9	2	9	0	9	0	6	0	0	0	3	8	7	5	8	4	4	6	4	4	5	7
7	7	1	5	6	4	1	4	9	4	5	8	1	2	6	7	1	6	1	2	7	8
3	3	6	5	3	2	9	6	1	8	9	2	4	3	8	9	1	1	9	1	8	9
6	5	9	6	7	4	3	6	5	8	3	3	5	5	4	7	3	1	1	8	9	10
8	2	4	0	4	4	3	1	8	8	9	8	2	3	6	1	4	7	9	4	4	11
0	4	7	1	6	6	4	6	4	7	0	7	3	0	7	2	8	1	9	9	9	12
2	4	0	8	8	9	4	5	7	1	6	0	5	8	1	3	5	6	4	9	4	13
9	9	3	4	1	6	5	0	3	4	8	4	7	7	5	9	5	3	3	8	3	14
5	9	3	8	9	5	2	5	1	6	8	7	4	4	8	8	9	0	8	8	5	15
5	5	5	9	2	3	1	6	1	7	4	7	9	7	6	7	4	7	7	0	2	16
5	9	8	2	6	2	0	2	6	5	0	9	0	0	0	1	6	8	7	0	4	17
6	8	0	1	0	9	4	4	5	3	2	0	8	3	0	7	6	8	0	1	9	18
6	0	4	6	0	2	9	1	4	3	2	1	5	5	4	3	3	2	0	6	6	19
5	6	6	5	2	4	4	8	1	7	7	3	0	2	7	1	3	8	0	1	8	20
8	4	0	2	1	7	9	4	5	8	2	1	7	5	3	2	3	7	5	9	8	21
7	8	3	2	0	7	5	0	7	8	8	5	0	5	7	5	7	5	1	0	9	22
7	4	3	8	8	3	1	6	4	1	7	0	5	1	2	0	0	5	3	4	4	23
5	7	0	3	4	1	9	5	8	6	9	3	6	3	8	2	1	2	5	6	7	24
5	8	1	6	6	9	7	4	8	1	9	2	3	1	7	4	1	6	4	5	5	25
9	9	0	3	3	1	2	4	3	2	7	9	1	0	4	9	2	0	5	4	8	26
4	9	0	1	1	2	9	2	1	7	9	0	7	4	5	4	7	4	9	2	7	27
4	1	4	9	2	3	9	9	6	4	6	1	3	0	2	5	0	4	3	1	2	28
0	1	0	4	5	7	1	0	8	0	5	4	5	0	0	1	4	8	9	1	3	29
6	6	0	4	6	9	3	0	8	4	8	1	9	3	6	6	5	0	3	0	9	30
0	0	9	3	5	1	2	1	0	0	6	0	9	8	8	6	5	6	4	4	0	31
4	9	0	9	5	2	6	1	3	0	5	4	3	2	2	8	3	2	2	1	5	32
6	2	1	1	1	8	3	0	4	3	5	8	4	8	8	2	2	8	3	6	7	33
4	8	2	4	9	4	2	5	5	7	2	3	1	9	8	1	7	3	5	9	6	34
9	4	8	8	5	8	3	7	0	4	7	1	1	6	0	7	3	5	7	3	5	35
3	6	6	8	9	0	3	2	8	7	0	7	7	2	3	5	8	4	0	6	7	36
0	3	2	6	6	3	3	8	8	8	1	6	4	0	3	9	7	5	5	8	8	37
1	1	7	9	8	1	0	0	5	7	0	8	3	9	4	2	6	2	5	9	2	38
4	7	0	6	3	6	2	4	7	9	2	9	6	6	3	3	2	8	0	5	4	39
9	6	6	6	0	7	8	1	7	2	5	9	8	9	9	6	5	7	2	6	3	40

TABLE C Critical Values of *t*

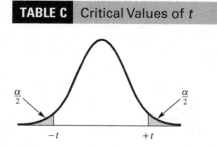

For any given *df*, the table shows the values of *t* corresponding to various levels of probability. Obtained *t* is significant at a given level if it is *larger than* the value shown in the table (ignoring the sign).

	Level of Significance for Two-Tailed Test (α)					
df	.20	.10	.05	.02	.01	.001
1	3.078	6.314	12.706	31.821	63.657	636.619
2	1.886	2.920	4.303	6.965	9.925	31.598
3	1.638	2.353	3.182	4.541	5.841	12.941
4	1.533	2.132	2.776	3.747	4.604	8.610
5	1.476	2.015	2.571	3.365	4.032	6.859
6	1.440	1.943	2.447	3.143	3.707	5.959
7	1.415	1.895	2.365	2.998	3.499	5.405
8	1.397	1.860	2.306	2.896	3.355	5.041
9	1.383	1.833	2.262	2.821	3.250	4.781
10	1.372	1.812	2.228	2.764	3.169	4.587
11	1.363	1.796	2.201	2.718	3.106	4.437
12	1.356	1.782	2.179	2.681	3.055	4.318
13	1.350	1.771	2.160	2.650	3.012	4.221
14	1.345	1.761	2.145	2.624	2.977	4.140
15	1.341	1.753	2.131	2.602	2.947	4.073
16	1.337	1.746	2.120	2.583	2.921	4.015
17	1.333	1.740	2.110	2.567	2.898	3.965
18	1.330	1.734	2.101	2.552	2.878	3.922
19	1.328	1.729	2.093	2.539	2.861	3.883
20	1.325	1.725	2.086	2.528	2.845	3.850
21	1.323	1.721	2.080	2.518	2.831	3.819
22	1.321	1.717	2.074	2.508	2.819	3.792
23	1.319	1.714	2.069	2.500	2.807	3.767
24	1.318	1.711	2.064	2.492	2.797	3.745
25	1.316	1.708	2.060	2.485	2.787	3.725
26	1.315	1.706	2.056	2.479	2.779	3.707
27	1.314	1.703	2.052	2.473	2.771	3.690
28	1.313	1.701	2.048	2.467	2.763	3.674
29	1.311	1.699	2.045	2.462	2.756	3.659
30	1.310	1.697	2.042	2.457	2.750	3.646
40	1.303	1.684	2.021	2.423	2.704	3.551
60	1.296	1.671	2.000	2.390	2.660	3.460
120	1.289	1.658	1.980	2.358	2.617	3.373
∞	1.282	1.645	1.960	2.326	2.576	3.291

Note: The bottom row ($df = \infty$) also equals critical values for z.

TABLE C   Continued

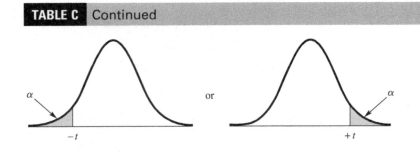

For any given *df*, the table shows the values of *t* corresponding to various levels of probability. Obtained *t* is significant at a given level if it is *larger than* the value shown in the table (ignoring the sign).

	Level of Significance for One-Tailed Test (α)					
df	.10	.05	.025	.01	.005	.0005
1	3.078	6.314	12.706	31.821	63.657	636.619
2	1.886	2.920	4.303	6.965	9.925	31.598
3	1.638	2.353	3.182	4.541	5.841	12.941
4	1.533	2.132	2.776	3.747	4.604	8.610
5	1.476	2.015	2.571	3.365	4.032	6.859
6	1.440	1.943	2.447	3.143	3.707	5.959
7	1.415	1.895	2.365	2.998	3.499	5.405
8	1.397	1.860	2.306	2.896	3.355	5.041
9	1.383	1.833	2.262	2.821	3.250	4.781
10	1.372	1.812	2.228	2.764	3.169	4.587
11	1.363	1.796	2.201	2.718	3.106	4.437
12	1.356	1.782	2.179	2.681	3.055	4.318
13	1.350	1.771	2.160	2.650	3.012	4.221
14	1.345	1.761	2.145	2.624	2.977	4.140
15	1.341	1.753	2.131	2.602	2.947	4.073
16	1.337	1.746	2.120	2.583	2.921	4.015
17	1.333	1.740	2.110	2.567	2.898	3.965
18	1.330	1.734	2.101	2.552	2.878	3.922
19	1.328	1.729	2.093	2.539	2.861	3.883
20	1.325	1.725	2.086	2.528	2.845	3.850
21	1.323	1.721	2.080	2.518	2.831	3.819
22	1.321	1.717	2.074	2.508	2.819	3.792
23	1.319	1.714	2.069	2.500	2.807	3.767
24	1.318	1.711	2.064	2.492	2.797	3.745
25	1.316	1.708	2.060	2.485	2.787	3.725
26	1.315	1.706	2.056	2.479	2.779	3.707
27	1.314	1.703	2.052	2.473	2.771	3.690
28	1.313	1.701	2.048	2.467	2.763	3.674
29	1.311	1.699	2.045	2.462	2.756	3.659
30	1.310	1.697	2.042	2.457	2.750	3.646
40	1.303	1.684	2.021	2.423	2.704	3.551
60	1.296	1.671	2.000	2.390	2.660	3.460
120	1.289	1.658	1.980	2.358	2.617	3.373
∞	1.282	1.645	1.960	2.326	2.576	3.291

Note: The bottom row ($df = \infty$) also equals critical values for *z*.

TABLE D   Critical Values of *F* at the .05 and .01 Significance Levels

df for the Denominator	df for the Numerator, $\alpha = .05$							
	1	2	3	4	5	6	8	12
1	161.4	199.5	215.7	224.6	230.2	234.0	238.9	243.9
2	18.51	19.00	19.16	19.25	19.30	19.33	19.37	19.41
3	10.13	9.55	9.28	9.12	9.01	8.94	8.84	8.74
4	7.71	6.94	6.59	6.39	6.26	6.16	6.04	5.91
5	6.61	5.79	5.41	5.19	5.05	4.95	4.82	4.68
6	5.99	5.14	4.76	4.53	4.39	4.28	4.15	4.00
7	5.59	4.74	4.35	4.12	3.97	3.87	3.73	3.57
8	5.32	4.46	4.07	3.84	3.69	3.58	3.44	3.28
9	5.12	4.26	3.86	3.63	3.48	3.37	3.23	3.07
10	4.96	4.10	3.71	3.48	3.33	3.22	3.07	2.91
11	4.84	3.98	3.59	3.36	3.20	3.09	2.95	2.79
12	4.75	3.88	3.49	3.26	3.11	3.00	2.85	2.69
13	4.67	3.80	3.41	3.18	3.02	2.92	2.77	2.60
14	4.60	3.74	3.34	3.11	2.96	2.85	2.70	2.53
15	4.54	3.68	3.29	3.06	2.90	2.79	2.64	2.48
16	4.49	3.63	3.24	3.01	2.85	2.74	2.59	2.42
17	4.45	3.59	3.20	2.96	2.81	2.70	2.55	2.38
18	4.41	3.55	3.16	2.93	2.77	2.66	2.51	2.34
19	4.38	3.52	3.13	2.90	2.74	2.63	2.48	2.31
20	4.35	3.49	3.10	2.87	2.71	2.60	2.45	2.28
21	4.32	3.47	3.07	2.84	2.68	2.57	2.42	2.25
22	4.30	3.44	3.05	2.82	2.66	2.55	2.40	2.23
23	4.28	3.42	3.03	2.80	2.64	2.53	2.38	2.20
24	4.26	3.40	3.01	2.78	2.62	2.51	2.36	2.18
25	4.24	3.38	2.99	2.76	2.60	2.49	2.34	2.16
26	4.22	3.37	2.98	2.74	2.59	2.47	2.32	2.15
27	4.21	3.35	2.96	2.73	2.57	2.46	2.30	2.13
28	4.20	3.34	2.95	2.71	2.56	2.44	2.29	2.12
29	4.18	3.33	2.93	2.70	2.54	2.43	2.28	2.10
30	4.17	3.32	2.92	2.69	2.53	2.42	2.27	2.09
40	4.08	3.23	2.84	2.61	2.45	2.34	2.18	2.00
60	4.00	3.15	2.76	2.52	2.37	2.25	2.10	1.92
120	3.92	3.07	2.68	2.45	2.29	2.17	2.02	1.83
∞	3.84	2.99	2.60	2.37	2.21	2.09	1.94	1.75

(continued)

TABLE D   Continued

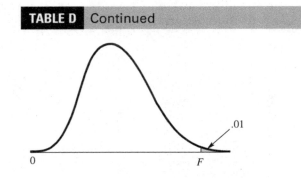

.01

0   F

df for the Denominator	*df* for the Numerator, α = .01							
	1	**2**	**3**	**4**	**5**	**6**	**8**	**12**
1	4052	4999	5403	5625	5764	5859	5981	6106
2	98.49	99.01	99.17	99.25	99.30	99.33	99.36	99.42
3	34.12	30.81	29.46	28.71	28.24	27.91	27.49	27.05
4	21.20	18.00	16.69	15.98	15.52	15.21	14.80	14.37
5	16.26	13.27	12.06	11.39	10.97	10.67	10.27	9.89
6	13.74	10.92	9.78	9.15	8.75	8.47	8.10	7.72
7	12.25	9.55	8.45	7.85	7.46	7.19	6.84	6.47
8	11.26	8.65	7.59	7.01	6.63	6.37	6.03	5.67
9	10.56	8.02	6.99	6.42	6.06	5.80	5.47	5.11
10	10.04	7.56	6.55	5.99	5.64	5.39	5.06	4.71
11	9.65	7.20	6.22	5.67	5.32	5.07	4.74	4.40
12	9.33	6.93	5.95	5.41	5.06	4.82	4.50	4.16
13	9.07	6.70	5.74	5.20	4.86	4.62	4.30	3.96
14	8.86	6.51	5.56	5.03	4.69	4.46	4.14	3.80
15	8.68	6.36	5.42	4.89	4.56	4.32	4.00	3.67
16	8.53	6.23	5.29	4.77	4.44	4.20	3.89	3.55
17	8.40	6.11	5.18	4.67	4.34	4.10	3.79	3.45
18	8.28	6.01	5.09	4.58	4.25	4.01	3.71	3.37
19	8.18	5.93	5.01	4.50	4.17	3.94	3.63	3.30
20	8.10	5.85	4.94	4.43	4.10	3.87	3.56	3.23
21	8.02	5.78	4.87	4.37	4.04	3.81	3.51	3.17
22	7.94	5.72	4.82	4.31	3.99	3.76	3.45	3.12
23	7.88	5.66	4.76	4.26	3.94	3.71	3.41	3.07
24	7.82	5.61	4.72	4.22	3.90	3.67	3.36	3.03
25	7.77	5.57	4.68	4.18	3.86	3.63	3.32	2.99
26	7.72	5.53	4.64	4.14	3.82	3.59	3.29	2.96
27	7.68	5.49	4.60	4.11	3.78	3.56	3.26	2.93
28	7.64	5.45	4.57	4.07	3.75	3.53	3.23	2.90
29	7.60	5.42	4.54	4.04	3.73	3.50	3.20	2.87
30	7.56	5.39	4.51	4.02	3.70	3.47	3.17	2.84
40	7.31	5.18	4.31	3.83	3.51	3.29	2.99	2.66
60	7.08	4.98	4.13	3.65	3.34	3.12	2.82	2.50
120	6.85	4.79	3.95	3.48	3.17	2.96	2.66	2.34
∞	6.64	4.60	3.78	3.32	3.02	2.80	2.51	2.18

TABLE E Percentage Points of the Studentized Range (q) for the .05 and .01 Levels of Significance (α)

df for MS_{within}	α	2	3	4	5	6	7	8	9	10	11
					k = Number of Means						
5	.05	3.64	4.60	5.22	5.67	6.03	6.33	6.58	6.80	6.99	7.17
	.01	5.70	6.98	7.80	8.42	8.91	9.32	9.67	9.97	10.24	10.48
6	.05	3.46	4.34	4.90	5.30	5.63	5.90	6.12	6.32	6.49	6.65
	.01	5.24	6.33	7.03	7.56	7.97	8.32	8.61	8.87	9.10	9.30
7	.05	3.34	4.16	4.68	5.06	5.36	5.61	5.82	6.00	6.16	6.30
	.01	4.95	5.92	6.54	7.01	7.37	7.68	7.94	8.17	8.37	8.55
8	.05	3.26	4.04	4.53	4.89	5.17	5.40	5.60	5.77	5.92	6.05
	.01	4.75	5.64	6.20	6.62	6.96	7.24	7.47	7.68	7.86	8.03
9	.05	3.20	3.95	4.41	4.76	5.02	5.24	5.43	5.59	5.74	5.87
	.01	4.60	5.43	5.96	6.35	6.66	6.91	7.13	7.33	7.49	7.65
10	.05	3.15	3.88	4.33	4.65	4.91	5.12	5.30	5.46	5.60	5.72
	.01	4.48	5.27	5.77	6.14	6.43	6.67	6.87	7.05	7.21	7.36
11	.05	3.11	3.82	4.26	4.57	4.82	5.03	5.20	5.35	5.49	5.61
	.01	4.39	5.15	5.62	5.97	6.25	6.48	6.67	6.84	6.99	7.13
12	.05	3.08	3.77	4.20	4.51	4.75	4.95	5.12	5.27	5.39	5.51
	.01	4.32	5.05	5.50	5.84	6.10	6.32	6.51	6.67	6.81	6.94
13	.05	3.06	3.73	4.15	4.45	4.69	4.88	5.05	5.19	5.32	5.43
	.01	4.26	4.96	5.40	5.73	5.98	6.19	6.37	6.53	6.67	6.79
14	.05	3.03	3.70	4.11	4.41	4.64	4.83	4.99	5.13	5.25	5.36
	.01	4.21	4.89	5.32	5.63	5.88	6.08	6.26	6.41	6.54	6.66
15	.05	3.01	3.67	4.08	4.37	4.59	4.78	4.94	5.08	5.20	5.31
	.01	4.17	4.84	5.25	5.56	5.80	5.99	6.16	6.31	6.44	6.55
16	.05	3.00	3.65	4.05	4.33	4.56	4.74	4.90	5.03	5.15	5.26
	.01	4.13	4.79	5.19	5.49	5.72	5.92	6.08	6.22	6.35	6.46
17	.05	2.98	3.63	4.02	4.30	4.52	4.70	4.86	4.99	5.11	5.21
	.01	4.10	4.74	5.14	5.43	5.66	5.85	6.01	6.15	6.27	6.38
18	.05	2.97	3.61	4.00	4.28	4.49	4.67	4.82	4.96	5.07	5.17
	.01	4.07	4.70	5.09	5.38	5.60	5.79	5.94	6.08	6.20	6.31
19	.05	2.96	3.59	3.98	4.25	4.47	4.65	4.79	4.92	5.04	5.14
	.01	4.05	4.67	5.05	5.33	5.55	5.73	5.89	6.02	6.14	6.25
20	.05	2.95	3.58	3.96	4.23	4.45	4.62	4.77	4.90	5.01	5.11
	.01	4.02	4.64	5.02	5.29	5.51	5.69	5.84	5.97	6.09	6.19
24	.05	2.92	3.53	3.90	4.17	4.37	4.54	4.68	4.81	4.92	5.01
	.01	3.96	4.55	4.91	5.17	5.37	5.54	5.69	5.81	5.92	6.02
30	.05	2.89	3.49	3.85	4.10	4.30	4.46	4.60	4.72	4.82	4.92
	.01	3.89	4.45	4.80	5.05	5.24	5.40	5.54	5.65	5.76	5.85
40	.05	2.86	3.44	3.79	4.04	4.23	4.39	4.52	4.63	4.73	4.82
	.01	3.82	4.37	4.70	4.33	5.11	5.26	5.39	5.50	5.60	5.69
60	.05	2.83	3.40	3.74	3.98	4.16	4.31	4.44	4.55	4.65	4.73
	.01	3.76	4.28	4.59	4.82	4.99	5.13	5.25	5.36	5.45	5.53
120	.05	2.80	3.36	3.68	3.92	4.10	4.24	4.36	4.47	4.56	4.64
	.01	3.70	4.20	4.50	4.71	4.87	5.01	5.12	5.21	5.30	5.37
∞	.05	2.77	3.31	3.63	3.86	4.03	4.17	4.29	4.39	4.47	4.55
	.01	3.64	4.12	4.40	4.60	4.76	4.88	4.99	5.08	5.16	5.23

TABLE F Critical Values of Chi-Square at the .05 and .01 Levels of Significance (α)

df	α		df	α	
	.05	.01		.05	.01
1	3.841	6.635	16	26.296	32.000
2	5.991	9.210	17	27.587	33.409
3	7.815	11.345	18	28.869	34.805
4	9.488	13.277	19	30.144	36.191
5	11.070	15.086	20	31.410	37.566
6	12.592	16.812	21	32.671	38.932
7	14.067	18.475	22	33.924	40.289
8	15.507	20.090	23	35.172	41.638
9	16.919	21.666	24	36.415	42.980
10	18.307	23.209	25	37.652	44.314
11	19.675	24.725	26	38.885	45.642
12	21.026	26.217	27	40.113	46.963
13	22.362	27.688	28	41.337	48.278
14	23.685	29.141	29	42.557	49.588
15	24.996	30.578	30	43.773	50.892

TABLE G Critical Values of the Mann-Whitney *U* Test

Larger N	α	4	5	6	7	8	9	10	11	12	13	14	15	16	17	18	19	20
4	.05	0																
	.01	---																
5	.05	1	2															
	.01	---	---															
6	.05	2	3	5														
	.01	0	1	2														
7	.05	3	5	6	8													
	.01	0	1	3	4													
8	.05	4	6	8	10	12												
	.01	1	2	4	6	8												
9	.05	4	7	10	12	15	17											
	.01	1	3	5	7	9	11											
10	.05	5	8	11	14	17	20	23										
	.01	2	4	6	8	11	13	16										
11	.05	6	9	13	16	19	23	26	30									
	.01	3	5	7	10	13	16	18	21									
12	.05	7	11	14	18	22	26	29	33	37								
	.01	3	6	9	11	15	18	21	24	28								
13	.05	8	12	16	20	24	28	33	37	41	45							
	.01	3	7	10	13	16	20	24	27	30	34							
14	.05	9	13	17	22	26	31	36	40	45	50	55						
	.01	4	7	11	14	19	22	26	30	34	38	42						
15	.05	10	14	19	24	29	34	39	44	49	54	59	65					
	.01	5	8	12	16	20	24	29	33	37	42	46	51					
16	.05	11	15	21	26	31	37	42	47	53	59	64	70	75				
	.01	5	9	13	18	22	27	31	36	40	45	50	55	60				
17	.05	11	17	22	28	34	39	45	51	57	63	69	75	81	87			
	.01	6	10	15	19	24	29	34	39	44	49	54	59	65	70			
18	.05	12	18	24	30	36	42	48	55	61	67	74	80	86	93	99		
	.01	6	11	16	21	26	31	36	42	47	53	58	64	70	75	81		
19	.05	13	19	25	32	38	45	52	58	65	72	78	85	92	99	106	113	
	.01	7	12	17	23	28	34	39	45	51	57	62	68	75	81	87	93	
20	.05	14	20	27	34	41	48	55	61	69	76	83	90	98	105	112	120	127
	.01	8	13	18	24	30	36	42	48	54	60	67	73	80	86	92	99	105

| TABLE H | Critical Values of r at the .05 and .01 Levels of Significance (α) |

	α				α	
df	.05	.01	df		.05	.01
1	.99692	.999877	16		.4683	.5897
2	.95000	.990000	17		.4555	.5751
3	.8783	.95873	18		.4438	.5614
4	.8114	.91720	19		.4329	.5487
5	.7545	.8745	20		.4227	.5368
6	.7067	.8343	25		.3809	.4869
7	.6664	.7977	30		.3494	.4487
8	.6319	.7646	35		.3246	.4182
9	.6021	.7348	40		.3044	.3932
10	.5760	.7079	45		.2875	.3721
11	.5529	.6835	50		.2732	.3541
12	.5324	.6614	60		.2500	.3248
13	.5139	.6411	70		.2319	.3017
14	.4973	.6226	80		.2172	.2830
15	.4821	.6055	90		.2050	.2673

| TABLE I | Critical Values of r_s at the .05 and .01 Levels of Significance (α) |

	α				α	
N	.05	.01	N		.05	.01
5	1.000	—	16		.506	.665
6	.886	1.000	18		.475	.625
7	.786	.929	20		.450	.591
8	.738	.881	22		.428	.562
9	.683	.833	24		.409	.537
10	.648	.794	26		.392	.515
12	.591	.777	28		.377	.496
14	.544	.714	30		.364	.478

APPENDIX D

A Review of Some Fundamentals of Mathematics

For students of statistics who need to review some of the fundamentals of algebra and arithmetic, this appendix covers the problems of working with decimals, negative numbers, and the summation sign.

WORKING WITH DECIMALS

When adding and subtracting decimals, be sure to place decimal points of the numbers directly below one another. For example, to add 3,210.76, 2.541, and 98.3,

$$
\begin{array}{r}
3{,}210.76 \\
2.541 \\
+98.3 \\
\hline
3{,}311.601
\end{array}
$$

To subtract 34.1 from 876.62,

$$
\begin{array}{r}
876.62 \\
-34.1 \\
\hline
842.52
\end{array}
$$

When multiplying decimals, be sure that your answer contains the same number of decimal places as both multiplicand and multiplier combined. For example,

Multiplicand →	63.41	2.6	.0003	.5
Multiplier →	× .05	× 1.4	× .03	× .5
Product →	3.1705	3.64	.000009	.25

Before dividing, always eliminate decimals from the divisor by moving the decimal point as many places to the right as needed to make the divisor a whole number. Make a corresponding change of the same number of places for decimals in the dividend (i.e., if you move the decimal two places in the divisor, then you must move it two places in the dividend). This procedure will indicate the number of decimal places in your answer.

$$\frac{2.44}{.02} = 122 \qquad\qquad \overset{122.}{\underset{.02\,\overline{)2.44}}{}}\; \leftarrow \text{quotient}$$

divisor $\longrightarrow$ .02$\overline{)2.44}$ $\longleftarrow$ dividend

$$\frac{.88}{.4} = 2.2 \qquad\qquad \overset{2.2}{.4\,\overline{)\,.88}}$$

$$\frac{10.10}{.10} = 101 \qquad\qquad \overset{1.01}{10\,\overline{)10.10}}$$

$$\frac{1010}{.10} = 10100 \qquad\qquad \overset{10100}{.10\,\overline{)1010.00}}$$

Arithmetic operations frequently yield answers in decimal form; for instance, 2.034, 24.7, and 86.001. The question arises as to how many decimal places we should have in our answers. A simple rule to follow is to carry every intermediate operation as fully as convenient and to round off the final answer to two more decimal places than found in the original set of numbers.

To illustrate, if data are derived from an original set of whole numbers (for instance, 12, 9, 49, or 15), we might carry out operations to three decimal places (to thousandths) but express our final answer to the nearest hundredth. For example,

$$3.889 = 3.89$$
$$1.224 = 1.22$$
$$7.761 = 7.76$$

Rounding to the nearest decimal place is generally carried out as follows: Drop the last digit if it is less than 5 (in the examples that follow, the last digit is the thousandth digit):

less than 5
$$26.234 = 26.23$$
$$14.891 = 14.89$$
$$1.012 = 1.01$$

Add 1 to the preceding digit if the last digit is 5 or more (in the examples that follow, the preceding digit is the hundredth digit):

5 or more
$$26.236 = 26.24$$
$$14.899 = 14.90$$
$$1.015 = 1.02$$

The following have been rounded to the nearest whole number:

$$3.1 = 3$$
$$3.5 = 4$$
$$4.5 = 5$$
$$4.8 = 5$$

The following have been rounded to the nearest tenth:

$$3.11 = 3.1$$
$$3.55 = 3.6$$
$$4.45 = 4.5$$
$$4.17 = 4.2$$

The following have been rounded to the nearest hundredth:

$$3.328 = 3.33$$
$$4.823 = 4.82$$
$$3.065 = 3.07$$
$$3.055 = 3.06$$

DEALING WITH NEGATIVE NUMBERS

When adding a series of negative numbers, make sure that you give a negative sign to the sum. For example,

$$
\begin{array}{rr}
-20 & -3 \\
-12 & -9 \\
\underline{-6} & \underline{-4} \\
-38 & -16
\end{array}
$$

To add a series containing both negative and positive numbers, first group all negatives and all positives separately; add each group and then subtract their sums (the remainder gets the sign of the larger number). For example,

$$
\begin{array}{cccc}
-6 & +4 & -6 & +6 \\
+4 & +2 & -1 & -10 \\
+2 & \overline{+6} & -3 & \overline{-4} \\
-1 & & \overline{-10} & \\
-3 & & & \\
\overline{-4} & & &
\end{array}
$$

To subtract a negative number, you must first give it a positive sign and then follow the procedure for addition. The remainder gets the sign of the larger number. For example,

$$
\begin{array}{r}
24 \\
-(-6) \\
\hline 30
\end{array}
$$
   −6 gets a positive sign and is therefore added to 24. Because the larger value is a positive number (24), the remainder (30) is a positive value.

$$
\begin{array}{r}
-6 \\
-(-24) \\
\hline 18
\end{array}
$$
   −24 gets a positive sign and is therefore added. Because the larger value is a positive number (remember that you have changed the sign of −24), the remainder (18) is a positive value.

$$
\begin{array}{r}
-24 \\
-(-6) \\
\hline -18
\end{array}
$$
   −6 gets a positive sign and is therefore added. Because the larger value is a negative number (−24), the remainder (−18) is a negative value.

When multiplying (or dividing) two numbers that have the same sign, always assign a positive sign to their product (or quotient). For example,

$$(+8) \times (+5) = +40$$

$$
+5\overline{)+40}^{\,+8} \qquad -5\overline{)-40}^{\,+8}
$$

$$(-8) \times (-5) = +40$$

In the case of two numbers having different signs, assign a negative sign to their product (or quotient). For example,

$$(-8) \times (+5) = -40 \qquad +5\overline{)-40}^{\,-8}$$

THE SUMMATION SIGN

The greek letter Σ (capital sigma) is used in statistics to symbolize the sum of a set of numbers. Thus, for example, if the variable X has the values

$$3 \quad 6 \quad 8 \quad 5 \quad 6$$

then

$$
\begin{aligned}
\Sigma X &= 3 + 6 + 8 + 5 + 6 \\
&= 28
\end{aligned}
$$

The summation sign Σ is a very convenient way to represent any kind of sum or total. However, there are a couple of basic rules that will enable you to use it properly in computing various statistics. In evaluating a complex formula having a summation sign, any operation involving an exponent (such as a square), multiplication, or division is performed before the summation, *unless* there are parentheses that dictate otherwise. (In math, parentheses always take precedence, meaning that you always perform the operation within them first.)

Applying these rules, the term $\sum X^2$ means: Square the X scores and then add. In contrast, the notation $(\sum X)^2$ dictates: Add the X scores and then square the total. Let's set the preceding X values and their squares in column form and calculate these two expressions.

X	X^2
3	9
6	36
8	64
5	25
6	36
$\sum X = 28$	$\sum X^2 = 170$

Thus, whereas $\sum X^2 = 170$, $(\sum X)^2 = (28)^2 = 784$. It is essential that you keep in mind this distinction through many of the calculations in this book.

To illustrate the same concept with multiplication rather than squares, let's add to our X values another variable Y:

$$8 \quad 2 \quad 1 \quad 0 \quad 3$$

We now form three columns: one for X, one for Y, and one for their product (XY).

X	Y	XY
3	8	24
6	2	12
8	1	8
5	0	0
6	3	18
$\sum X = 28$	$\sum Y = 14$	$\sum XY = 62$

Thus, similar to what we found with squares, the sum of products is very different from the product of sums. Whereas, $\sum XY = 62$, $(\sum X)(\sum Y) = (28)(14) = 392$.

APPENDIX E

List of Formulas

Name	Formula	Page
Proportion	$P = \dfrac{f}{N}$	25
Percentage	$\% = (100)\dfrac{f}{N}$	26
Rate of change	$\text{Rate of change} = (100)\left(\dfrac{\text{time } 2f - \text{time } 1f}{\text{time } 1f}\right)$	27
Midpoint	$m = \dfrac{\text{lowest score value} + \text{highest score value}}{2}$	30
Cumulative percentage	$c\% = (100)\dfrac{cf}{N}$	31
Total percentage	$\text{total } \% = (100)\dfrac{f}{N_{\text{total}}}$	37
Row percentage	$\text{row } \% = (100)\dfrac{f}{N_{\text{row}}}$	37
Column percentage	$\text{column } \% = (100)\dfrac{f}{N_{\text{column}}}$	38
Position of the median value	$\text{Position of median} = \dfrac{N + 1}{2}$	52
Sample mean	$\bar{X} = \dfrac{\Sigma X}{N}$	53
Deviation from the sample mean	$\text{Deviation} = X - \bar{X}$	54
Mean of a simple frequency distribution	$\bar{X} = \dfrac{\Sigma fX}{N}$	57
Range	$R = H - L$	65
Variance	$s^2 = \dfrac{\Sigma(X - \bar{X})^2}{N}$	66
Standard deviation	$s = \sqrt{\dfrac{\Sigma(X - \bar{X})^2}{N}}$	66
Raw-score formula for variance	$s^2 = \dfrac{\Sigma X^2}{N} - \bar{X}^2$	68

(continued)

Name	Formula	Page
Raw-score formula for standard deviation	$s = \sqrt{\dfrac{\sum X^2}{N} - \overline{X}^2}$	68
Variance of a simple frequency distribution	$s^2 = \dfrac{\sum fX^2}{N} - \overline{X}^2$	70
Standard deviation of a simple frequency distribution	$s = \sqrt{\dfrac{\sum fX^2}{N} - \overline{X}^2}$	70
Probability of an outcome or event	$P = \dfrac{\text{number of times an outcome can occur}}{\text{total number of times any outcome can occur}}$	82
z score	$z = \dfrac{X - \mu}{\sigma}$	95
Raw-score equivalent of a z score	$X = \mu + z\sigma$	100
z ratio of a sampling distribution	$z = \dfrac{\overline{X} - \mu}{\sigma_{\overline{X}}}$	113
Standard error of the mean	$\sigma_{\overline{X}} = \dfrac{\sigma}{\sqrt{N}}$	114
95% confidence interval	$95\% \text{ CI} = \overline{X} \pm 1.96\sigma_{\overline{X}}$	118
99% confidence interval	$99\% \text{ CI} = \overline{X} \pm 2.58\sigma_{\overline{X}}$	118
Standard error of the mean	$s_{\overline{X}} = \dfrac{s}{\sqrt{N - 1}}$	121
t ratio	$t = \dfrac{\overline{X} - \mu}{s_{\overline{X}}}$	121
Confidence interval	$\text{CI} = \overline{X} \pm ts_{\overline{X}}$	123
Standard error of the proportion	$s_p = \sqrt{\dfrac{P(1 - P)}{N}}$	127
95% confidence interval for a proportion	$95\% \text{ CI} = P \pm (1.96)s_p$	128
z test of difference between means of independent samples	$z = \dfrac{\overline{X}_1 - \overline{X}_2}{\sigma_{\overline{X}_1 - \overline{X}_2}}$	142
Standard error of the difference between means (pooled)	$s_{\overline{X}_1 - \overline{X}_2} = \sqrt{\left(\dfrac{N_1 s_1^2 + N_2 s_2^2}{N_1 + N_2 - 2}\right)\left(\dfrac{N_1 + N_2}{N_1 N_2}\right)}$	147
t test of difference between means of independent samples	$t = \dfrac{\overline{X}_1 - \overline{X}_2}{s_{\overline{X}_1 - \overline{X}_2}}$	148
Standard deviation of differences between related samples	$s_D = \sqrt{\dfrac{\sum D^2}{N} - (\overline{X}_1 - \overline{X}_2)^2}$	152

Name	Formula	Page
Standard error of the difference between means of related samples	$s_{\overline{D}} = \dfrac{s_D}{\sqrt{N-1}}$	152
t test of difference between means of related samples	$t = \dfrac{\overline{X}_1 - \overline{X}_2}{s_{\overline{D}}}$	155
z test of difference between sample proportions	$z = \dfrac{P_1 - P_2}{s_{P_1 - P_2}}$	156
Pooled sample proportion	$P* = \dfrac{N_1 P_1 + N_2 P_2}{N_1 + N_2}$	156
Standard error of the difference between sample proportions	$s_{P_1 - P_2} = \sqrt{P*(1 - P*)\left(\dfrac{N_1 + N_2}{N_1 N_2}\right)}$	156
Total sum of squares from deviations	$SS_{total} = \Sigma(X - \overline{X}_{total})^2$	172
Within-groups sum of squares from deviations	$SS_{within} = \Sigma(X - \overline{X}_{group})^2$	173
Between-groups sum of squares from deviations	$SS_{between} = \Sigma N_{group}(\overline{X}_{group} - \overline{X}_{total})^2$	174
Total sum of squares from raw scores	$SS_{total} = \Sigma X_{total}^2 - N_{total}\overline{X}_{total}^2$	174
Within-groups sum of squares from raw scores	$SS_{within} = \Sigma X_{total}^2 - \Sigma N_{group}\overline{X}_{group}^2$	174
Between-groups sum of squares from raw scores	$SS_{between} = \Sigma N_{group}\overline{X}_{group}^2 - N_{total}\overline{X}_{total}^2$	174
Between-groups mean square	$MS_{between} = \dfrac{SS_{between}}{df_{between}}$	176
Within-groups mean square	$MS_{within} = \dfrac{SS_{within}}{df_{within}}$	176
F ratio	$F = \dfrac{MS_{between}}{MS_{within}}$	177
Tukey's honestly significant difference	$HSD = q\sqrt{\dfrac{MS_{within}}{N_{group}}}$	182
Chi-square	$\chi^2 = \Sigma\dfrac{(f_o - f_e)^2}{f_e}$	188
Chi-square with Yates's correction	$\chi^2 = \Sigma\dfrac{(|f_o - f_e| - .5)^2}{f_e}$	202

(continued)

Name	Formula	Page
Mann-Whitney U	$U_a = N_1 N_2 + \dfrac{N_1(N_1 + 1)}{2} - \Sigma R_1$ $U_b = N_1 N_2 + \dfrac{N_2(N_2 + 1)}{2} - \Sigma R_2$	206
z-ratio for Mann-Whitney U test	$z = \dfrac{U - \dfrac{N_1 N_2}{2}}{\sqrt{\dfrac{N_1 N_2 (N_1 + N_2 + 1)}{12}}}$	207
Kruskal-Wallis test	$H = \dfrac{12}{N(N + 1)} \Sigma \dfrac{(\Sigma R_i)^2}{n_i} - 3(N + 1)$	208
Pearson's correlation	$r = \dfrac{SP}{\sqrt{SS_x SS_y}}$	222
Pearson's r from deviations	$r = \dfrac{\Sigma (X - \bar{X})(Y - \bar{Y})}{\sqrt{\Sigma (X - \bar{X})^2 \Sigma (Y - \bar{Y})^2}}$	222
Pearson's r from raw scores	$r = \dfrac{\Sigma XY - N\bar{X}\bar{Y}}{\sqrt{(\Sigma X^2 - N\bar{X}^2)(\Sigma Y^2 - N\bar{Y}^2)}}$	222
t ratio for testing the significance of r	$t = \dfrac{r\sqrt{N - 2}}{\sqrt{1 - r^2}}$	224
Partial correlation coefficient	$r_{XY.Z} = \dfrac{r_{XY} - r_{XZ}r_{YZ}}{\sqrt{1 - r_{XZ}^2}\sqrt{1 - r_{YZ}^2}}$	231
t ratio for partial correlation	$t = r_{XY.Z}\sqrt{\dfrac{N - 3}{1 - r_{XY.Z}^2}}$	232
Regression model	$Y = a + bX + e$	238
Regression coefficient	$b = \dfrac{SP}{SS_X}$	239
Regression coefficient from deviations	$b = \dfrac{\Sigma (X - \bar{X})(Y - \bar{Y})}{\Sigma (X - \bar{X})^2}$	239
Regression coefficient from raw scores	$b = \dfrac{\Sigma XY - N\bar{X}\bar{Y}}{\Sigma X^2 - N\bar{X}^2}$	239
Y-intercept	$a = \bar{Y} - b\bar{X}$	239
Regression line	$\hat{Y} = a + bX$	241
Error term	$e = Y - \hat{Y}$	244
Error sum of squares	$SS_{error} = \Sigma (Y - \hat{Y})^2$	244
Total sum of squares	$SS_{total} = \Sigma (Y - \bar{Y})^2$	245

Name	Formula	Page
Regression sum of squares	$SS_{reg} = SS_{total} - SS_{error}$	245
Coefficient of determination	$r^2 = \dfrac{SS_{total} - SS_{error}}{SS_{total}}$	247
Coefficient of nondetermination	$1 - r^2 = \dfrac{SS_{error}}{SS_{total}}$	247
Mean square regression	$MS_{reg} = \dfrac{SS_{reg}}{df_{reg}}$	249
Mean square error	$MS_{error} = \dfrac{SS_{error}}{df_{error}}$	249
F ratio for testing the significance of the regression	$F = \dfrac{MS_{reg}}{MS_{error}}$	249
Regression coefficients for two predictors	$b_1 = \dfrac{s_Y}{s_X}\left(\dfrac{r_{YX} - r_{YZ}r_{XZ}}{1 - r_{XZ}^2}\right); b_2 = \dfrac{s_Y}{s_Z}\left(\dfrac{r_{YZ} - r_{XY}r_{XZ}}{1 - r_{XZ}^2}\right)$	253
Y-intercept for two predictors	$b_0 = \bar{Y} - b_1\bar{X} - b_2\bar{Z}$	253
Multiple coefficient of determination	$R^2 = \dfrac{r_{YX}^2 + r_{YZ}^2 - 2r_{YX}r_{YZ}r_{XZ}}{1 - r_{XZ}^2}$	254
Odds	$\text{Odds} = \dfrac{P}{1 - P}$	261
Log-odds or *logit*	$L = \log\left(\dfrac{P}{1 - P}\right)$	262
Spearman's rank–order correlation	$r_s = 1 - \dfrac{6\sum D^2}{N(N^2 - 1)}$	268
z ratio to test the significance of Spearman's correlation	$z = r_s\sqrt{N - 1}$	275
Goodman's and Kruskal's gamma	$G = \dfrac{N_a - N_i}{N_a + N_i}$	275
z ratio for testing the significance of gamma	$z = G\sqrt{\dfrac{N_a + N_i}{N(1 - G^2)}}$	277
Phi coefficient	$\phi = \sqrt{\dfrac{\chi^2}{N}}$	279
Contingency coefficient	$C = \sqrt{\dfrac{\chi^2}{N + \chi^2}}$	281
Cramér's V	$V = \sqrt{\dfrac{\chi^2}{N(k - 1)}}$	282

GLOSSARY

95% confidence interval The range of mean values (proportions) within which there are 95 chances out of 100 that the true population mean (proportion) will fall. [p. 117]

99% confidence interval The range of mean values (proportions) within which there are 99 chances out of 100 that the true population mean (proportion) will fall. [p. 118]

addition rule The probability of obtaining any one of several outcomes equals the sum of their separate probabilities. [p. 82]

alpha The probability of committing a Type I error. [p. 145]

analysis of variance A statistical test that makes a single overall decision as to whether a significant difference is present among three or more sample means. [p. 170]

area under the normal curve That area which lies between the curve and the baseline containing 100% or all of the cases in any given normal distribution. [p. 90]

bar graph and histogram Graphic methods in which rectangular bars indicate the frequencies for the range of score values or categories. [p. 41]

between-groups sum of squares The sum of the squared deviations of every sample mean from the total mean. [p. 174]

bimodal distribution A frequency distribution containing two (or more) modes. [p. 52]

central tendency What is average or typical of a set of data; a value generally located toward the middle or center of a distribution. [p. 51]

chi-square A nonparametric test of significance whereby expected frequencies are compared against observed frequencies. [p. 187]

class interval A category in a group distribution containing more than one score value. [p. 29]

coefficient of determination Equal to the Pearson's correlation squared, the proportion of variance in the dependent variable that is explained by the independent variable. [p. 247]

coefficient of nondetermination Equal to one minus Pearson's correlation squared, the proportion of variance in the dependent variable that is not explained by the independent variable. [p. 247]

coefficient of variation (CV) A measure of variability that expresses the standard deviation as a percentage of the sample mean. [p. 72]

Cohen's *d* An estimate of effect size based on sample means and standard deviations. [p. 163]

column percent In a cross-tabulation, the result of dividing a cell frequency by the number of cases in the column. Column percents sum to 100% for each column of a cross-tabulation. [p. 38]

confidence interval The range of mean values (proportions) within which the true population mean (proportion) is likely to fall. [p. 116]

contingency coefficient Based on chi-square, a measure of the degree of association for nominal data arranged in a square table larger than 2 × 2. [p. 281]

converse rule The probability of an event not occurring equals one minus the probability that it does. [p. 82]

correlation The strength and direction of the relationship between two variables. [p. 216]

correlation coefficient Generally ranging between −1.00 and +1.00, a number in which both the strength and direction of correlation are expressed. [p. 219]

Cramér's *V* An alternative to the contingency coefficient that measures the degree of association for nominal data arranged in a table larger than 2 × 2. [p. 282]

critical region (rejection region) The area in the tail(s) of a sampling distribution that dictates that the null hypothesis be rejected. [p. 143]

cross-tabulation A frequency and percentage table of two or more variables taken together. [p. 35]

cumulative frequency The total number of cases having any given score or a score that is lower. [p. 31]

cumulative percentage The percentage of cases having any score or a score that is lower. [p. 31]

curvilinear correlation A relationship between *X* and *Y* that begins as either positive or negative and then reverses direction. [p. 218]

degrees of freedom In small-sample comparisons, a statistical compensation for the failure of the sampling distribution of differences to assume the shape of the normal curve. [p. 121]

deviation The distance and direction of any raw score from the mean. [p. 54]

effect size A measure of the size of the difference between two populations means. [p. 163]

elaboration The process of controlling a two-variable cross-tabulation for additional variables. [p. 283]

error term (disturbance term) The residual portion of a score that cannot be predicted by the independent variable. Also the distance of a point from the regression line. [p. 238]

expected frequencies The cell frequencies expected under the terms of the null hypothesis for chi-square. [p. 188]

F ratio The result of an analysis of variance, a statistical technique that indicates the size of the between-groups mean square relative to the size of the within-groups mean square. [p. 171]

five percent level (.05) of significance A level of probability at which the null hypothesis is rejected if an obtained sample difference occurs by chance only 5 times or less out of 100. [p. 143]

frequency distribution A table containing the categories, score values, or class intervals and their frequency of occurrence. [p. 24]

frequency polygon A graphic method in which frequencies are indicated by a series of points placed over the score values or midpoints of each class interval and connected with a straight line that is dropped to the baseline at either end. [p. 43]

Goodman's and Kruskal's gamma An alternative to the rank–order correlation coefficient for measuring the degree of association between ordinal-level variables. [p. 275]

grouped frequency distribution A table that indicates the frequency of occurrence of cases located within a series of class intervals. [p. 29]

hypothesis An idea about the nature of social reality that is testable through systematic research. [p. 2]

interval level of measurement The process of assigning a score to cases so that the magnitude of differences between them is known and meaningful. [p. 14]

Kruskal-Wallis test A nonparametric alternative to the F ratio that is employed to compare several independent samples but that requires only ordinal-level data. [p. 208]

kurtosis The peakedness of a distribution. [p. 44]

leptokurtic Characteristic of a distribution that is quite peaked or tall. [p. 44]

level of significance A level of probability at which the null hypothesis can be rejected and the research hypothesis can be accepted. [p. 143]

line chart A graph of the differences between groups or trends across time on some variable(s). [p. 45]

logistic regression a form of regression for predicting a dichotomous dependent variable. [p. 261]

Mann-Whitney U test A nonparametric alternative to the t ratio that is employed to compare two independent samples but that requires only ordinal-level data. [p. 206]

margin of error The extent of imprecision expected when estimating the population mean or proportion, obtained by multiplying the standard error by the table value of z or t. [p. 108]

marginal distribution In a cross-tabulation, the set of frequencies and percentages found in the margin that represents the distribution of one of the variables in the table. [p. 37]

mean The sum of a set of scores divided by the total number of scores in the set; a measure of central tendency. [p. 53]

mean square A measure of variation used in an F test obtained by dividing the between-groups sum of squares or within-groups sum of squares (in analysis of variance) or the regression sum of squares or error sum of squares (in regression analysis) by the appropriate degrees of freedom. [p. 176]

measurement The use of a series of numbers in the data-analysis stage of research. [p. 9]

median The middle-most point in a frequency distribution; a measure of central tendency. [p. 52]

median test A nonparametric test of significance for determining the probability that two random samples have been drawn from populations with the same median. [p. 203]

mesokurtic Characteristic of a distribution that is neither very peaked nor very flat. [p. 44]

midpoint The middle-most score value in a class interval. [p. 30]

mode The most frequent, typical, or common value in a distribution. [p. 51]

multicollinearity The presence of strong inter correlations among the predictor variables in a multiple regression that limits the ability to measure their separate impact on the dependent variable. [p. 259]

multiple coefficient of determination The proportion of variance in the dependent variable that is explained by the set of independent variables in combination. [p. 254]

multiple regression A technique employed in predicting values of one variable (Y) from knowledge of values of several variables. [p. 253]

multiplication rule The probability of obtaining a combination of independent outcomes equals the product of their separate probabilities. [p. 82]

multistage sampling A random sampling method whereby sample members are selected on a random basis from a number of well-delineated areas known as clusters (or primary sampling units). [p. 107]

mutually exclusive outcomes Two outcomes or events are mutually exclusive if the occurrence of one rules out the possibility that the other will occur. [p. 10]

negative correlation The direction of relationship wherein individuals who score high on the X variable score low on the Y variable; individuals who score low on the X variable score high on the Y variable. [p. 217]

negatively skewed distribution A distribution in which more respondents receive high than low scores, resulting in a longer tail on the left than on the right. [p. 44]

nominal level of measurement The process of placing cases into categories and counting their frequency of occurrence. [p. 10]

nonparametric test A statistical procedure that makes no assumptions about the way the characteristic being studied is distributed in the population and requires only ordinal or nominal data. [p. 186]

normal curve A smooth, symmetrical distribution that is bell-shaped and unimodal. [p. 44]

null hypothesis The hypothesis of equal population means. Any observed difference between samples is seen as a chance occurrence resulting from sampling error. [p. 136]

observed frequencies In a chi-square analysis, the results that are actually observed when conducting a study. [p. 187]

one percent (.01) level of significance A level of probability at which the null hypothesis is rejected if an obtained sample difference occurs by chance only 1 time or less out of 100. [p. 144]

one-tailed test A test in which the null hypothesis is rejected for large differences in only one direction. [p. 157]

ordinal level of measurement The process of ordering or ranking cases in terms of the degree to which they have any given characteristic. [p. 10]

parametric test A statistical procedure that requires that the characteristic studied be normally distributed in the population and that the researcher have interval data. [p. 186]

partial correlation coefficient The correlation between two variables when one or more other variables are controlled. [p. 231]

Pearson's correlation coefficient A correlation coefficient for interval data. [p. 219]

percentage A method of standardizing for size that indicates the frequency of occurrence of a category per 100 cases. [p. 26]

percentage distribution The relative frequency of occurrence of a set of scores or class intervals. [p. 30]

phi coefficient Based on chi-square, a measure of the degree of association for nominal data arranged in a 2×2 table. [p. 279]

pie chart A circular graph whose pieces add up to 100%. [p. 40]

platykurtic Characteristic of a distribution that is rather flat. [p. 44]

population (universe) Any set of individuals who share at least one characteristic. [p. 17]

positive correlation The direction of a relationship wherein individuals who score high on the X variable also score high on the Y variable; individuals who score low on the X variable also score low on the Y variable. [p. 217]

positively skewed distribution A distribution in which more respondents receive low rather than high scores, resulting in a longer tail on the right than on the left. [p. 44]

power of a test The ability of a statistical test to reject the null hypothesis when it is actually false and should be rejected. [p. 186]

primary sampling unit (cluster) In multistage sampling, a well-delineated area considered to include characteristics found in the entire population. [p. 107]

probability The relative frequency of occurrence of an event or outcome. The number of times any given event could occur out of 100. [p. 82]

proportion A method for standardizing for size that compares the number of cases in any given category with the total number of cases in the distribution. [p. 25]

random sampling A sampling method whereby each and every population member has an equal chance of being drawn into the sample. [p. 106]

range The difference between the highest and lowest scores in a distribution. A measure of variability. [p. 65]

rate A kind of ratio that indicates a comparison between the number of actual cases and the number of potential cases. [p. 26]

regression analysis A technique employed in predicting values of one variable (Y) from knowledge of values of another variable (X). [p. 237]

regression line A straight line drawn through the scatter plot that represents the best possible fit for making predictions of Y from X. [p. 238]

research hypothesis The hypothesis that regards any observed difference between samples as reflecting a true population difference and not just sampling error. [p. 137]

row percent In a cross-tabulation, the result of dividing a cell frequency by the number of cases in the row. Row percents sum to 100% for each row of a cross-tabulation. [p. 37]

sample A smaller number of individuals taken from some population (for the purpose of generalizing to the entire population from which it was taken). [p. 17]

sampling distribution of differences between means A frequency distribution of a large number of differences between random sample means that have been drawn from a given population. [p. 138]

sampling distribution of means A frequency distribution of a large number of random sample means that have been drawn from the same population. [p. 109]

sampling error The inevitable difference between a random sample and its population based on chance alone. [p. 108]

scatter plot A graph that shows the way scores on any two variables X and Y are scattered throughout the range of possible score values. [p. 216]

skewness Departure from symmetry. [p. 44]

slope In regression, the change in the regression line for a unit increase in X. The slope is interpreted as the change in the Y variable associated with a unit change in the X variable. [p. 238]

Spearman's rank–order correlation coefficient A correlation coefficient for data that have been ranked or ordered with respect to the presence of a given characteristic. [p. 268]

standard deviation The square root of the mean of the squared deviations from the mean of a distribution. A measure of variability that reflects the typical deviation from the mean. [p. 66]

standard error of the difference between means An estimate of the standard deviation of the sampling distribution of differences based on the standard deviations of two random samples. [p. 147]

standard error of the mean An estimate of the standard deviation of the sampling distribution of means based on the standard deviation of a single random sample. [p. 114]

standard error of the proportion An estimate of the standard deviation of the sampling distribution of proportions based on the proportion obtained in a single random sample. [p. 127]

statistically significant difference A sample difference that reflects a real population difference and not just sampling error. [p. 19]

straight-line correlation Either a positive or negative correlation, so that the points in a scatter diagram tend to form a straight line through the center of the graph. [p. 217]

stratified sampling A random sampling method whereby the population is first divided into homogenous subgroups from which simple random samples are then drawn. [p. 107]

sum of squares The sum of squared deviations from a mean. [p. 171]

systematic sampling A random sampling method whereby every nth member of a population is included in the sample. [p. 107]

t **ratio** A statistical technique that indicates the direction and degree that a sample mean difference falls from zero on a scale of standard error units. [p. 121]

total percent In a cross-tabulation, the result of dividing a cell frequency by the total number of cases in the sample. Total percents sum to 100% for the entire cross-tabulation. [p. 37]

total sum of squares The sum of the squared deviations of every raw score from the total mean of the study. [p. 172]

two-tailed test A test that is used when the null hypothesis is rejected for large differences in both directions. [p. 157]

Tukey's HSD (honestly significant difference) A procedure for the multiple comparison of means after a significant F ratio has been obtained. [p. 182]

Type I error The error of rejecting the null hypothesis when it is true. [p. 144]

Type II error The error of retaining the null hypothesis when it is false. [p. 145]

unimodal distribution A frequency distribution containing a single mode. [p. 52]

unit of observation The element that is being studied or observed. Individuals are most often the unit of observation, but sometimes collections or aggregates—such as families, census tracts, or states—are the unit of observation. [p. 2]

variability The manner in which the scores are scattered around the center of the distribution. Also known as dispersion or spread. [p. 65]

variable Any characteristic that varies from one individual to another. Hypotheses usually contain an independent variable (cause) and a dependent variable (effect). [p. 1]

variance The mean of the squared deviations from the mean of a distribution. A measure of variability in a distribution. [p. 66]

within-groups sum of squares The sum of the squared deviations of every raw score from its sample group mean. [p. 173]

Y-intercept In regression, the point where the regression line crosses the Y axis. The Y-intercept is the predicted value of Y for an X value of zero. [p. 238]

Yates's correction In the chi-square analysis, a factor for small expected frequencies that reduces the overestimate of the chi-square value and yields a more conservative result (only for 2×2 tables). [p. 201]

z score (standard score) A value that indicates the direction and degree that any given raw score deviates from the mean of a distribution on a scale of standard deviation units. [p. 95]

SOLUTIONS TO PROBLEMS

Chapter 1

1. b
2. c
3. a
4. b
5. d
6. (a) Content analysis, IV = time, DV = type of criminal offenses and level of resistance to arrest; (b) Experiment, IV = type of video game, DV = violent incidents; (c) Participant observation, IV = time of day, DV = number of panhandling incidents and rate of loud confrontations; (d) Survey, IV = income level, DV = attitude toward stiffer sentences; (e) Content analysis, IV = time period, DV = violent incidents
7. (a) Nominal; (b) Nominal; (c) Ordinal; (d) Nominal; (e) Nominal; (f) Interval/Ratio; (g) Interval/Ratio; (h) Ordinal; (i) Nominal; (j) Nominal
8. (a) Ordinal; (b) Interval/Ratio; (c) Nominal; (d) Nominal; (e) Ordinal; (f) Ordinal; (g) Interval/Ratio; (h) Interval/Ratio; (i) If the sample is small, choose "d" because there will be few responses in categories 1 to 4. If the sample is large, choose "e" the ordinal scale; (j) One example is none versus 1 or more tickets.
9. (a) Interval/ratio; (b) Ordinal; (c) Choose a table in the UCR.
10. (a) Experiment; (b) IV = program intervention; (c) Nominal; (d) DV = rearrest; (e) Interval/ratio

Chapter 2

1. b
2. b
3. c
4. b
5. c
6. a
7. c
8. (a) 70.1%; (b) 59.0%; (c) 0.299; (d) 0.410
9. (a) 12.5%; (b) 37.5%; (c) 0.875; (d) 0.625
10. 24.8
11. 83.6
12. −3.0%
13. −11.9%
14. 300%; instability when using small divisors

15.
Age	f	%
12	2	10
13	3	15
14	3	15
15	5	25
16	4	20
17	2	10
18	1	5
	20	100

16. (a) 10; (b) 5, 15, 25, 35; (c) 16.67%, 58.33%, 12.50%, 12.50%
17. (a) IV = victimization, gender, (b) 61.58%, 38.42%, 47.64%, 52.36% (c) males; (d) males more likely to be victimized than females
18. (a) Actual, prediction; (b) 85.71%, 14.29%, 19.32%, 80.68%; (c) 83.03%; (d) Risk assessment tool is a good predictor.
19. Draw a pie chart.
20. Draw a bar graph.
21. Draw a histogram.
22. Use a blank map to display the hate crimes.

Chapter 3

1. a
2. a
3. c
4. b
5. b
6. a
7. c
8. (a) Multiple modes: prerelease, minimum, and medium; (b) Minimum; (c) Because not interval/ratio level
9. Offense, mode, drugs; Sex, mode, male; Assigned drug testing, median, falls between daily and weekly; Months, mean, 2.6
10. (a) 0.5; (b) 1.6
11. (a) 3; (b) 4; (c) 12.0; (d) median
12. Mo = 0; Mdn = 1; $\overline{X}$ = 2.05
13. Mo = 3; Mdn = 4; $\overline{X}$ = 4.0
14. (a) Mo = 3, Mdn = 5.5, $\overline{X}$ = 5.5; (b) Mo = 8, Mdn = 5, $\overline{X}$ = 5.2; (c) Knowledge
15. Mo = 4, Mdn = 4, $\overline{X}$ = 3.84
16. Mo = 1, Mdn = 1, $\overline{X}$ = 1.6

Chapter 4

1. d
2. b
3. c
4. c
5. (a) Precinct A, 6.6 versus 5.8; (b) Precinct B, 0.75 versus 2.6
6. (a) 3; (b) 1.00; (c) 1.00
7. Below = 63, Above = 85
8. (a) 4; (b) 1.47; (c) 1.21
9. (a) 12; (b) 12.86; (c) 3.59
10. (a) 3; (b) 1.55; (c) 1.25
11. (a) 23, 7; (b) 43.20, 5.60; (c) 6.57, 2.37; Judge Allison
12. $s^2 = 2.978, s = 1.726$
13. $s^2 = 2.160, s = 1.470$

Chapter 5

1. b
2. c
3. b
4. b
5. (a) 0.2; (b) 0.6; (c) 0.8; (d) 0.9
6. (a) 34.13; (b) 34.13; (c) 47.72; (d) 95.44
7. (a) 1.273, promoted; (b) −0.909, not promoted
8. (a) 4.01; (b) 0.0401
9. (a) 0.1303; (b) 0.0674
10. (a) 34.13%; (b) 0.3413; (c) 68.26%; (d) 0.3413; (e) 0.1949
11. (a) 6.68%; (b) 0.0228; (c) 0.003%
12. (a) 21.19%; (b) 0.5517
13. (a) .20; (b) 198 month

Chapter 6

1. b
2. b
3. c
4. a
5. a
6. c
7. d
8. (a) 95% = 5.822; (b) 99% = 8.364
9. .478 to 12.122; −2.064 to 14.664
10. (a) 0.551 to 0.809; (b) 0.510 to 0.850
11. 20.79 to 46.21
12. 0.024 to 0.028
13. 6.624 to 10.042
14. 8.487 to 13.113
15. (a) 95% = 3.626 to 4.054; (b) 99% = 3.558 to 4.122
16. (a) Proportions; (b) 95%; (c) .025
17. (a) Proportions; (b) 95%; (c) .025; (d) 95% CI = .75 ± .025

Chapter 7

1. c
2. a
3. b
4. a
5. d
6. $t = -1.013, df = 18$, retain the null hypothesis at .05
7. (a) $t = 2.589, df = 16$, reject the null hypothesis at .05; (b) Yes, there appears to be racial disparity.
8. (a) $t = -2.9, df = 17$, reject the null hypothesis at .05; (b) $t = -2.9, df = 17$, retain the null hypothesis at .01
9. $t = 3.096, df = 18$, reject the null hypothesis at .05
10. (a) $t = -3.7, df = 9$, reject the null hypothesis at .05; (b) legal limit in your state
11. (a) $t = 3.372, df = 14$, reject the null hypothesis at .05
12. $t = -5.205, df = 14$, reject the null hypothesis at .05
13. $z = -2.86$, reject the null hypothesis at .05
14. $z = 4.18$, reject the null hypothesis at .05
15. $z = 4.81$, reject the null hypothesis at .05

Chapter 8

1. a
2. c
3. b
4. d
5. a
6. $F = 10.36$, reject null hypothesis at .05
7. HSD = 1.03, significant differences between Schools A and B and between Schools B and C
8. $F = 14.261$, reject null hypothesis at .05
9. HSD = 1.74, significant differences between liberals and conservatives, and between liberals and independents
10. $F = 4.050$, reject null hypothesis at .05
11. HSD = 1.61, significant difference between Married/ Widowed and Never Married only.
12. $F = 9.38$, reject null hypothesis at .05
13. HSD = 2.80, significant differences between alcohol and control, and between drugs and control

Chapter 9

1. d
2. a
3. a
4. b
5. b
6. c
7. $\chi^2 = 26.5$, $df = 1$, reject the null hypothesis at .05; one way because national poll gives expected frequencies in Major City as 265.9 and 187.1
8. $\chi^2 = 24.15$, $df = 1$, reject the null hypothesis at .05
9. $\chi^2 = 5.4$, $df = 2$, retain the null hypothesis at .05
10. $\chi^2 = 0.09$ (with Yates), $df = 1$, retain the null hypothesis at .05
11. $\chi^2 = 2.006$ (with Yates), $df = 1$, retain the null hypothesis at .05
12. Mdn = 5, $\chi^2 = 10.16$ (with Yates), $df = 1$, reject the null hypothesis at .05
13. $\chi^2 = 11.4$, $df = 4$, reject the null hypothesis at .05
14. $\chi^2 = 25.5$, $df = 1$, reject the null hypothesis at .05
15. $\chi^2 = 3.3$, $df = 3$, retain the null hypothesis at .05; no differences in drug use by social class
16. $\chi^2 = 6.9$, $df = 2$, reject the null hypothesis at .05
17. Table 9.5: $\chi^2 = 18.31$, $df = 3$, reject the null hypothesis at .05; Table 9.6: $\chi^2 = 11.91$, $df = 2$, reject the null hypothesis at .05; the χ^2 value decreases when the categories are collapsed.
18. Mdn = 4.35, $\chi^2 = 3.21$ (with Yates), $df = 1$, significant at .05, reject the null hypotheses
19. U = 32, retain the null hypothesis
20. H = .38, retain the null hypothesis
21. U = 28.5, retain the null hypothesis
22. H = 11.52, reject the null hypothesis

Chapter 10

1. b
2. c
3. a
4. b
5. b
6. $r = 0.86$, $df = 4$, reject the null hypothesis at .05
7. $r = 0.12$, $df = 8$, retain the null hypothesis at .05
8. $r = 0.61$, $df = 6$, retain the null hypothesis at .05
9. (a) r_{XY} and r_{YZ} are significant at the .05 level; (b) $r_{XY.Z} = .58$; the simple correlation r_{XY} just looks at the correlation between X and Y without considering other variables; the partial correlation $r_{XY.Z}$ looks at the correlation between X and Y while controlling for the influence of the third variable, Z.

10. $r = -0.73$, $df = 8$, reject the null hypothesis at .05
11. $r = -0.96$, $df = 8$, reject the null hypothesis at .05
12. (a) $r = -.40$, $df = 12$; (b) No; (c) No; (d) Unemployment rate and homicide rate do not show a correlation and are unrelated to each other.
13. (a) $r_{XY} = -0.69$ (b) $r_{XY.Z} = -0.42$

Chapter 11

1. b
2. d
3. c
4. b
5. d
6. (a) Draw a scatter plot; (b) $k = 1.03$, $a = 1.91$; (c) draw the regression line: $Y = 1.91 + 1.03X$; (d) $Y = 7.06$; (e) $r^2 = 0.41$, $1 - r^2 = 0.59$; (f) $r = .64$
7. (a) Draw a scatter plot; (b) $k = 1.39$, $a = 0.62$; (c) draw the regression line: $Y = 0.62 + 1.39X$; (d) $Y = 7.57$; (e) $r^2 = 0.44$, $1 - r^2 = 0.56$
8. (a) $b = -.64$; (b) $a = 7.45$; (c) Yes—both; (d) $Y = 7.45 + -.64(11)$, $Y = .41$
9. (a) Multiple regression; (b) $b_0 = 8.312$, $b_1 = -.174$, $b_2 = -5.29$; (c) None; (d) $\hat{Y} = 8.312 - .174(5.0) - .529(2.5) = 6.12$; (e) $\hat{Y} = 4.80$; (f) $R^2 = .35$, $1 - R^2 = .65$
10. (a) TOPFRESH alone explains 37.6%; SMALLCLS alone explains 29.6%; (b) TOPFRESH and SMALLCLS together explain 48.1%; (c) TOPFRESH and SMALLCLS overlap in their explained variance.
11. (a)

Source	SS	df	MS	F
Regression	127,510	2	63,755	40.72
Error	82,990	53	1,565.85	
Total	210,500			

(b) $N = 56$; (c) = 60.6%

12. (a) The baseline pain level when both variables are zero is $b_0 = 1.321$; (b) For each increase of one year of age, the expected pain level increases by $b_1 = .065$, holding constant gender. The expected level of pain for males is $b_2 = .857$ higher than for females, holding constant age. (c) Neither age nor gender has a significant effect on pain level.
13. (a) Odds: Democrat = .70, Republican = .29, Independent = .40; (b) Odds ratios: Dem vs. Rep = 2.41, Dem vs. Ind = 1.76, Rep vs. Ind = .73
14. (a) Because the dependent variable is a dichotomy (2 categories); (b) 1.056, .98, 1.201

Chapter 12

1. c
2. d
3. c
4. a
5. b
6. (a) Rank scores; (b) $r_s = .209, N = 10$; (c) Not significant at .05
7. (a) $G = 0.39$; (b) $z = -1.93$, not significant at .05
8. $\chi^2 = 7.75$, significant at .05; $V = .313$
9. (a) $r_s = .748, N = 12$; (b) Significant at .05
10. (a) $G = .108$; (b) not significant at .05
11. (a) $\chi^2 = 23.669$, significant at .05; (b) $\phi = .487$
12. $\chi^2 = 2.157, C = 0.109$
13. $\chi^2 = 75.049, V = 0.616$

INDEX